Customizing macOS Catalina

Fantastic Tricks, Tweaks, Hacks, Secret Commands & Hidden Features

Tom Magrini

Cover photo: Tom's MacBook Pro 13" by Tom Magrini

Created in the United States of America.
ISBN: 9781691847549

Terms & Conditions of Use

Some of the customizations contained in this book allow access to hidden preference settings not visible in macOS' System Preferences. These customizations do not add to or change any part of the macOS operating system. They are additional preference settings defined by Apple and built into macOS. All of the customizations are reversible and can be reset to the system default. The customizations were tested in public beta and released versions of macOS Catalina (10.15). There is always the possibility that future updates to macOS could cause some of the customizations to no longer work as expected.

While the author has taken every precaution in the preparation of this book, the author assumes no responsibility whatsoever for errors or omissions, or for damages resulting from the use of the information contained herein. The information contained in this book is used at your risk. Any use of the information contained in this book constitutes your agreement to be bound by these terms and conditions.

Table of Contents

1

macOS Catalina

Customizing macOS Catalina

Like previous macOS releases, macOS Catalina lets you completely customize your user experience until your Mac has a look and feel different from everyone else's. You can completely personalize your Mac, fine-tuning various aspects of the operating system to transform how you interact with it. Besides changing the look and feel, customizations allow you to be more productive and efficient by making macOS more closely match your personal computing style and the way you work.

Why customize macOS? Because you can. It's that simple.

The default macOS settings that come out of the box make your Mac incredibly easy and efficient to use. And for most people, the defaults are all they'll ever need. But if you are reading this book, then you are not like most people. You want to tinker and tweak macOS to personalize it to the way you use your Mac. Besides, who wants their Mac to look, feel, and operate just like every other Mac? And of course, its always cool to impress your friends when they notice your Mac does things theirs does not. This book will turn you into a macOS guru, showing you how to bend macOS to your every will.

You don't need to be an Apple genius to customize your user experience. Anyone with a little bit of familiarity with macOS can safely customize their user experience. Some customizations require a basic knowledge of how to use an application called Terminal. I'll teach you enough about Terminal in the next few pages to become truly dangerous (just kidding). My goal is not to turn you into a Terminal expert, but to give you a basic foundation so you can execute simple commands to customize your macOS user experience. Once you have learned the basics of Terminal, you will be able to configure all of the macOS customizations, hacks, and tweaks in this book to unlock macOS' hidden features.

Each chapter focuses on customizing a particular aspect of macOS. We'll start first with a short introduction to the basics of macOS customization in Chapter 1, where I introduce you to the System Preferences application and the command line interface of Terminal.

Next up are Gestures in Chapter 2. If you are new to Macs and macOS, I will make you an expert on gestures. Once we have covered the standard macOS gestures, I'll teach you how to create personal, custom trackpad and mouse gestures. Creating a unique set of gestures is guaranteed to increase your efficiency and productivity.

Once you've mastered these skills, we'll focus on the customization of each aspect of macOS starting first with the Desktop in Chapter 3. You'll learn how to customize the Desktop, personalize it, and make it more efficient and presentable.

In Chapter 4, we'll tweak Mission Control, which provides a view of everything on your Mac – windows, apps in Full-Screen and Split-View mode, and Desktop Spaces. You'll learn how to increase your Desktop real estate, declutter your Desktop, and efficiently manage window clutter.

We'll customize various options available in the Menu Bar, a component of the macOS Desktop in Chapter 5. I'll show you a few Menu Bar apps available in the Mac App Store to help squeeze a little more out of the Menu Bar.

Next up in Chapter 6 is the Dock, one of the most recognizable features of macOS, where I'll teach you how to fine-tune the default macOS Dock to make it your personal, highly productive Dock. You'll learn how to add shortcuts to the Dock.

Then we move on to Chapter 7, where you'll learn about Stacks, a cool feature of the Dock. You'll learn a dozen different tweaks guaranteed to increase your productivity, including how to create App Stacks.

Better searching is the topic of Chapter 8, where we'll customize Spotlight. I'll show you some tips and tricks for more accurate searches.

Next up is Siri, Apple's intelligent virtual assistant application, in Chapter 9.

Then we'll cover Notification Center in Chapter 10. I'll teach you how to fine-tune this one-stop-shop that consolidates alerts from a variety of sources. You'll learn how to customize Notification Center with Apple's and third-party widgets.

In Chapter 11, we'll explore some tweaks to Launchpad, a macOS feature that blurs the line between macOS, iOS, and iPadOS.

In Chapter 12, we'll focus on Finder, the macOS file manager application, which provides a user interface for managing files, disk drives, network drives, and to launch applications. We'll customize Finder to make it more useful and more efficient. And you'll learn about the seamless integration of iCloud, making online storage a part of the macOS operating system instead of an add-on app.

Window snapping is the focus of Chapter 13. I'll help those former Microsoft Windows users who miss Windows' window snapping feature. Everything is better on a Mac, including window snapping.

The keyboard is the topic of Chapter 14. I know what you are thinking. "Why a chapter on the keyboard?" "Everyone knows how to use a keyboard." I'll show you a few keyboard customization tricks. macOS lets you change the behavior of the keys and allows you to create custom keyboard shortcuts to boost your productivity.

In Chapter 15, we'll learn how to customize the Touch Bar, a dynamic input device with a strip of virtual keys that automatically change based on the running application and what you're doing. You'll learn how to create your own custom Touch Bars.

Next, we'll focus on customizing applications starting with Safari in Chapter 16 and Mail in Chapter 17. I'll show you how to customize these apps to make them perform more efficiently and add to your productivity.

The Internet can be a dangerous place. Security & Privacy is the focus of Chapter 18, where I'll show you some tweaks to make your Mac a little more secure and to keep your data safe.

Finally, Chapter 19 is a grab bag containing a line up of tricks, tweaks, and hacks to customize macOS.

How to Use This Book

There is no one way to use this book. If you want to impress your friends and make them think you are an Apple genius, read it cover to cover, trying out each of the tweaks, hacks, secret commands, and hidden features.

You could start by focusing on a specific chapter that interests you, say like the Dock, which by the way, was the first chapter I wrote. The Dock chapter was originally Chapter 2 when I wrote the draft of the first book in this series, *Taming the Pride: Customizing macOS Mountain Lion*, back in 2013.

Another option is to review the Table of Contents and go directly to a tweak, hack, secret command, or hidden feature that interests you. No matter how you use this book, I hope that the tweaks, hacks, secret commands, and hidden features help you become more efficient and productive while having fun.

Before we get started, let's review some of the conventions used in this book.

Keyboard Shortcuts

This book uses keyboard shortcuts extensively. A keyboard shortcut allows you to do actions that would normally require selecting a command from a menu or executing a gesture on a mouse or trackpad. Keyboard shortcuts require the use of one or more of the modifier keys listed below. These modifier keys are always bolded in the text.

fn	Function	**^**	Control	**⌥**	Option
⌘	Command	**⇧**	Shift	**F**	F key

Keyboard shortcuts are also listed in parenthesis. For example, **⇧⌘G** will be followed by (shift+command+G). To use a keyboard shortcut, you need to hold down the listed modifier key(s) while pressing the last key of the shortcut. For **⇧⌘G**, you will hold down the shift and command keys while pressing the letter "G."

Note that when I refer to an **F** key, I am not referring to the key for the letter "F." I am referring to the 12 function keys at the top of your keyboard that are labeled **F1** to **F12**. You should also note that Macs are a little different than Windows PCs. On a Mac, each of the function keys is pre-configured to execute a specific action, such as increasing or decreasing the volume, launching Mission Control, or pausing and playing your music. If you want to use a function key as a plain old **F** key, you need to hold down the **fn** (function) key to avoid executing the assigned key command. This is the opposite of how **F** keys work on a Windows PC.

Command Typeface

When a tweak, hack, secret command, or hidden feature requires you to type a command into the Terminal or Finder, I use a different typeface. When you see this typeface, these are commands that you will enter in the specified app.

```
defaults write com.apple.dock workspaces-edge-delay -float 0.5

killall Dock
```

By the way, don't let the "killall" command scare you. I'm not really asking you to kill your Dock. I wouldn't do that. I like the Dock. It is one of my favorite features of macOS. The "killall Dock" command simply restarts the Dock so the previous command can take effect.

When a button needs to be clicked, the button name is bolded, as in click the **Trackpad Options...** button.

Menus

Some commands in this book are executed using the **Apple Menu**. So when you see this symbol: I'm referring to the Apple Menu located on the Menu Bar in the upper left-hand corner of your Desktop. I bet you are wondering why "Apple Menu" is bolded in the first sentence of this paragraph. Whenever I introduce a new feature, I bold it, so you will know that I'm introducing a new concept.

Now back to menus, when I ask you to execute a command using a menu, it will look like this: ** > System Preferences… > Dock**. This is shorthand asking you to select the Apple Menu, then choose System Preferences… from the drop-down menu, and finally, to select the Dock preference pane from the next drop-down menu. Hint: whenever you see this symbol: **>** I'm asking you to make a selection from a menu.

In addition to the Apple Menu, I will ask you to make selections from other drop-down menus. In this example, **Finder > Preferences…**, I am asking you to select the Finder menu, then select Preferences. The Finder menu appears to the right of the Apple menu when Finder is the active application.

Graphical Controls

macOS uses graphical controls to enable, disable, tweak, and configure various features. These graphical controls are labeled in the Dock preference pane shown below.

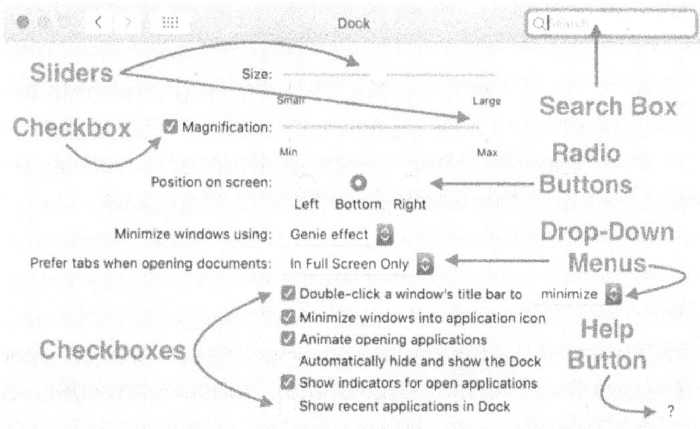

A slider allows you to choose any value between the pre-defined minimum and maximum values by dragging it anywhere within the range. Most sliders allow you to select any value within the range. However, some sliders are "stepped," meaning you can only select pre-defined values within the range.

A checkbox turns a feature on or off. I also use the terms enable and disable for on and off, respectively. Checking the checkbox enables or turns the feature on while unchecking disables, or turns it off. Sometimes a checkbox is combined with a slider. In the example above, you must first check the checkbox next to **Magnification:** to enable the dock magnification feature before you can move the slider. If this checkbox is not checked, magnification is disabled, and the slider is grayed out.

Drop-down menus are denoted by the white up and down arrows on a blue background (the default colors) at the right end of the drop-down menu. Clicking anywhere in the field drops down a menu of options from which to choose, thus the name "drop-down" menu.

Radio buttons are sometimes used instead of drop-down menus, particularly when the available options are few. Selecting one radio button deselects another as only one option can be selected.

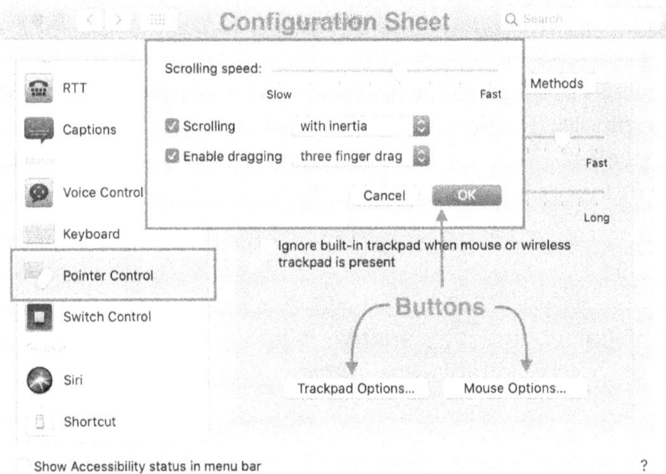

Finally, a configuration sheet appears to drop-down from underneath the title bar. It is typically used to select and configure additional options. The image above shows a configuration sheet that appears after selecting **Pointer Control** and clicking the **Trackpad Options...** button in the Accessibility preference pane.

System Preferences

We'll do a lot of customization work using preference panes available in the **System Preferences** application. macOS provides an extensive set of customization capabilities in System Preferences to modify system-wide settings and behavior. Most of these customization options are accomplished using the macOS graphical user interface (GUI) using sliders, checkboxes, drop-down menus, radio buttons, and configuration sheets accessible from various preference panes.

Throughout this book, I'll ask you to launch the **System Preferences** application to customize specific macOS parameters. In macOS, there are often multiple ways of doing the same thing, and there are several different ways to launch Systems Preferences. You can launch the System Preferences application by the following methods:

1. Click on the System Preferences icon in the **Dock**,
2. Launch System Preferences using **Launchpad**,
3. Select ** > System Preferences...** from the Apple menu,
4. Open **Spotlight**, search for System Preferences, and press the **return** key,
5. Launch **Finder**, open the **Applications** folder, and double-click on System Preferences, or
6. Launch Siri and ask it to "Launch System Preferences."

System Preferences displays a default set of 30 icons, called **Preference Panes**, organized into five rows. These preference panes contain a tremendous amount of customization power to tweak your macOS user experience safely. Your user name and picture will be displayed at the left in the top row.

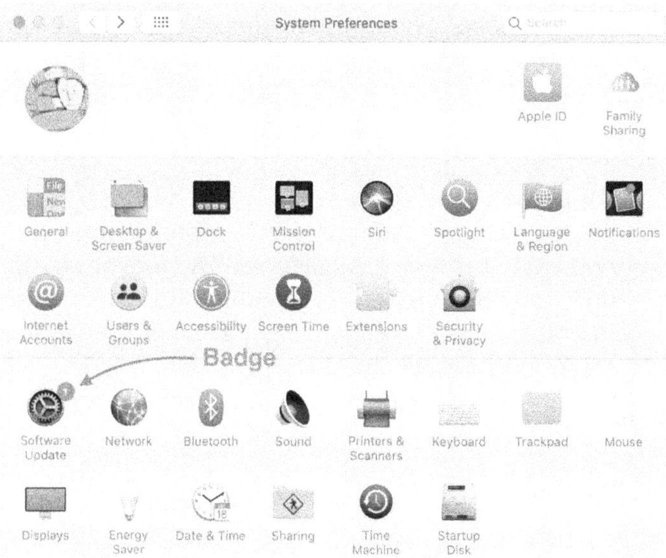

If you've upgraded from a previous version of macOS, the organization the Preference Panes will look very different. In versions of macOS prior to OS X Yosemite, Apple organized the Preference Panes into the rows by categories – Personal, Hardware, Internet & Wireless, System, and Other. Apple has since dropped these categories, instead organizing the preference panes into three general categories.

The two Preference Panes in the top row allow you to edit various parameters associated with your Apple ID such as your name, phone, email, password, two-factor authentication, payment, address, Family Sharing, and apps and devices associated with your Apple ID. The next set of preference panes configure software options within macOS itself. The bottom set of Preference Panes generally control hardware parameters.

Organize the Preference Panes Alphabetically

The organization of the preference panes in System Preferences is our very first customization. By default, the panes are organized into three categories. macOS lets you change the display to alphabetical. Select **View > Organize Alphabetically**.

The advantage of organizing the preference panes alphabetically is that you no longer have to know in which category or row a particular pane is located.

Select **View > Organize by Categories** to return to the default display.

The **View** menu also provides a drop-down list of all the preference panes in alphabetical order, allowing you to make a quick selection.

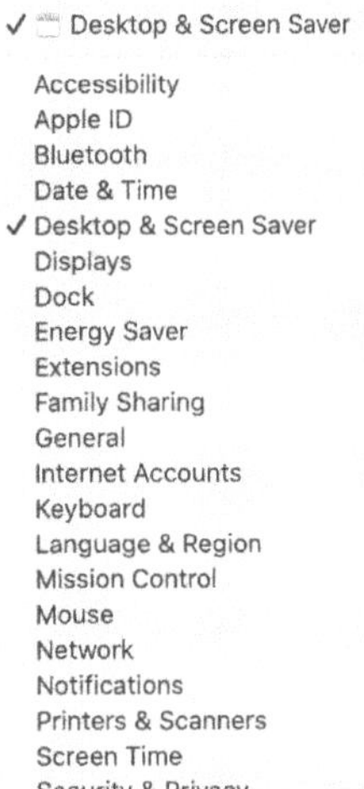

A secondary click on the **System Preferences** icon in the Dock displays a menu with the preference panes in alphabetical order. If you have a preference pane open, it is displayed at the top of the list with a checkmark next to its name in the alphabetical list.

At the very top of the System Preferences window is a toolbar with four controls: window controls, navigation buttons, a **Show All button**, and a **Search** field. The back navigation button is grayed out until you navigate to a preference pane since there is nothing to go back to until then. The forward button is grayed out until you have clicked on a preference pane and then returned to the main display. Essentially these navigation buttons serve the same purpose as they do in Safari, allowing you to navigate forward and backward through the preference panes.

Clicking and holding the **Show All** button, the button with a grid of 12 squares located to the right of the navigation buttons, displays an alphabetical list of the preference panes. If you know what preference pane you want, this option gets you there quickly. When viewing a preference pane, clicking the back button returns you to the main System Preferences display, as does clicking the Show All button.

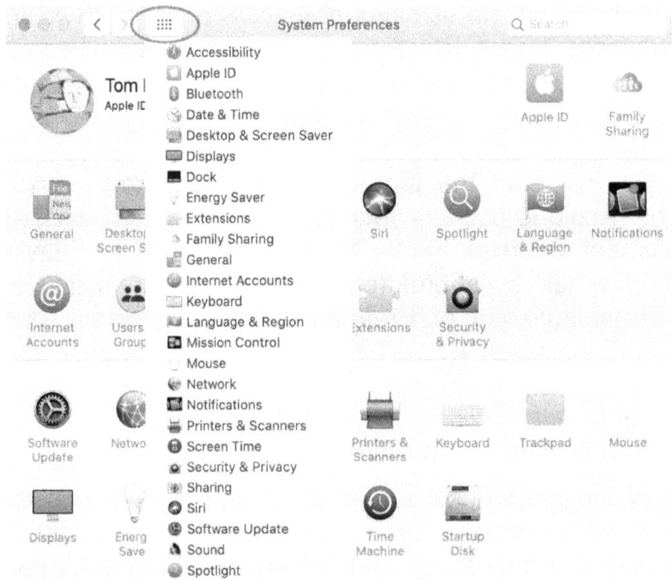

Search System Preferences

Sometimes finding the preference pane containing the specific setting you want to modify is not intuitive. The **Search field** comes in handy when you know which particular setting you want to modify, but don't know where to find it.

Click in the Search field or enter **⌘F** (command+F) to go directly to the Search Field. As you type, macOS highlights the preference panes that are most likely related to your search and displays a list of suggested items in the Spotlight menu below the search field. Eventually, macOS zeroes in on the applicable preference pane.

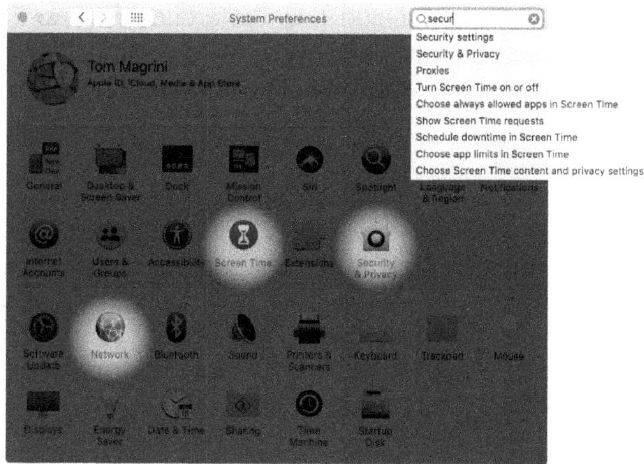

If you don't know exactly what the macOS setting is called, Spotlight offers suggestions to help you find the right preference pane. Click the highlighted preference pane or one of the items listed under the Search field to open the associated preference pane.

Find a Preference Pane Using Spotlight

Spotlight is the macOS search feature that allows you to search for items on your Mac and the Internet. To open **Spotlight**, click on the magnifying glass in the upper-right corner of the Menu Bar or press **⌘space** (command+space).

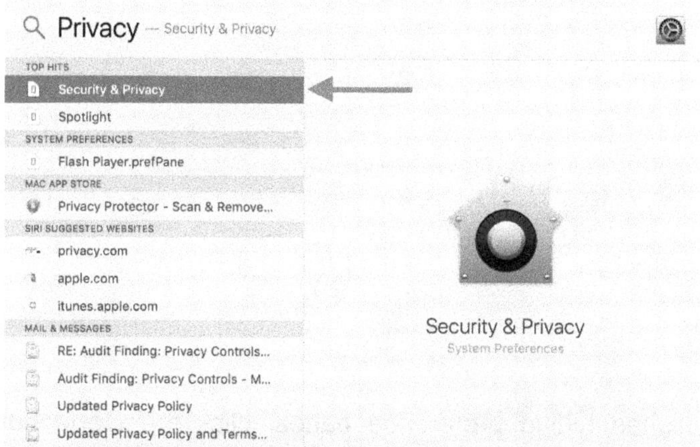

If you don't know which Preference Pane contains the specific setting you want to modify, open **Spotlight** and start typing in the **Spotlight Search** field. As you type, Spotlight offers results it thinks are likely matches, refining them as you type and organizing them into categories directly below the search field. Results are displayed in categories, with the **Top Hit**, the result Spotlight determined to be the most likely, highlighted at the top of the list. If you press **return**, macOS launches the **Top Hit**.

Spotlight organizes search results into categories. In the example above, when I searched for "Scrolling," Spotlight suggested two Preference Panes, Trackpad and Mouse, under the **System Preferences** category. To open the desired preference pane, highlight it, and press the **return** key or double-click on it.

Hide Preference Panes

Clicking and holding the **Show All** button reveals an alphabetical list of the preference panes and offers a **Customize...** option at the bottom of the list. Selecting **Customize...** puts little checkboxes in the lower-right of each preference pane icon. Unchecking the checkbox hides the associated preference pane. You can also access this feature from **View > Customize...** under the System Preferences View menu.

Why hide a preference pane? There are a few preference panes that you may never use, or you've made changes in one or more and have no desire to make additional changes. Hiding preference panes removes superfluous clutter that distracts you from the panes you actually need. For example, if you don't own a mouse, why do you need the Mouse preference pane?

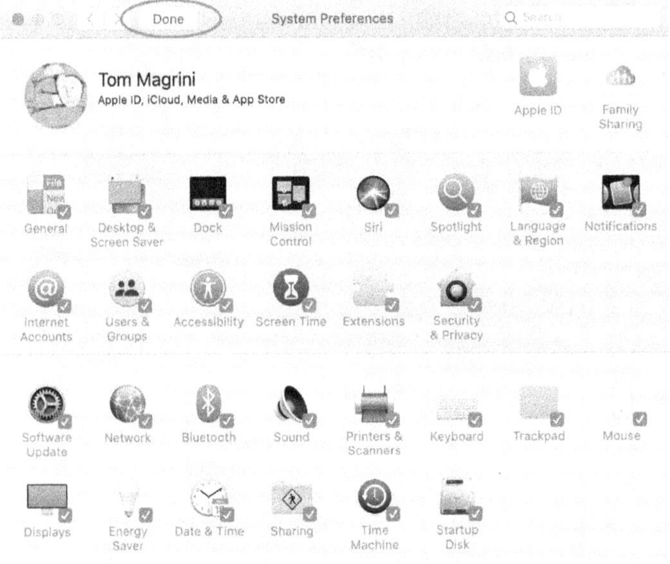

When you are finished hiding preference panes, click the **Done** button, which is located where the **Show All** button was. Note that unchecking a preference pane simply hides it from view. It does not delete it. And don't worry, a hidden preference pane can always be unhidden by selecting **Show All > Customize...** and checking its checkbox.

Delete Preference Panes

As you use your Mac, you'll likely install apps and uninstall them if they don't fit your needs. Sometimes third-party apps come with their own preference pane to modify various application preferences. Third-party preference panes are shown in the bottom row of System Preferences. If you want to delete a third-party preference pane you no longer use, secondary click on it to display the remove option.

macOS removes the preference pane icon from System Preferences and moves the preference pane to the Trash.

Note that macOS only allows you to remove third-party preference panes. macOS does not allow you to remove Apple preference panes as they are needed by macOS. If you don't want to see a specific preference pane, you should hide it as shown in the previous section.

System Preferences is extremely powerful, providing you the power to customize a multitude of system-wide settings. In each of the coming chapters, we'll focus on specific aspects of the macOS user experience, learning options available to tweak. Even if you find System Preferences a little intimidating, I'll show you just how easy it is to customize your macOS user experience. It's your Mac, so feel free to customize, hack, and tweak it.

Terminal

Apple offers customizations to change the behavior of macOS that are not accessible from the macOS GUI. There is nothing really secret about these features other than the fact they are not directly accessible using System Preferences. These hidden features require you to enter commands into an application called **Terminal**. Terminal provides a command line interface for you to interact with macOS directly, allowing you to take your macOS customization to an entirely new level not achievable using System Preferences.

If entering commands into a command line interface sounds intimidating, it isn't. First, I'll show you how to use the Terminal application. Once you have learned the basics of Terminal, you will be able to configure all of the macOS customizations, hacks, and tweaks in this book and unlock macOS's hidden features. I have tested each of the commands shown in this book on my own MacBook Pro. Many are my personal favorites.

The average Mac user may never know of the existence of the **Terminal** application, which is tucked away in the **Utilities** folder in **Applications**. Almost everything the average Mac user needs to do can be accomplished through the macOS GUI. Those who know of Terminal's existence may avoid it because they find its archaic command line interface strange and intimidating. The modern computer user sees Terminal as a throwback to the old days of computing before GUIs became the norm. Terminal reminds us of a time when geeky computer scientists with thick glasses sat hunched over their keyboards, pounding away in a strange language more familiar to a computer than a human. As you'll see in the next few pages, Terminal may seem archaic, but it certainly isn't very intimidating.

Why bother using Terminal in the first place? While Terminal appears at first glance to be a relic more appropriate for a museum then your modern, beautiful, and elegant macOS GUI, it is one of the most powerful, versatile, and useful applications in macOS. It has many uses beyond just customization of your macOS user experience. However, our focus in this book is customization and personalization of macOS, so I won't cover Terminal's other uses.

Terminal can be used by users of all skill levels, even a novice Mac user who is learning about Terminal for the first time. We'll take some baby steps to build your confidence and learn the basics, enough so that you are able to configure any of the macOS customizations, hacks, and tweaks in this book.

What is Terminal?

Terminal is Apple's implementation of a Unix command line interface, commonly called a shell or command line interpreter. The macOS operating system, as well as its precursor NeXTSTEP, are based on Unix, an operating system first developed by AT&T in the 1970s. Apple macOS represents the largest installed base of Unix.

Essentially, Terminal gives you text-based access to macOS, allowing you to enter Unix commands, which let you configure various attributes that are not presented via the GUI. Other than its function as a command line interpreter, Terminal acts like any other application on your Mac.

Before You Begin

Some of the customizations require you to use Terminal to change preference settings, which are not visible in the macOS System Preferences. These preference settings do not add or change any part of the macOS operating system. The preference settings described in this book are defined by Apple as part of macOS. All of the customizations are reversible.

While the Terminal commands in this book are safe to use and I have tested them on my MacBook Pro, you must enter the commands exactly as shown. In Terminal, every character is important, including the spaces. Since I cannot be there looking over your shoulder to correct you if you fat-finger a command, it is always good practice to have a current **Time Machine** backup in case you have to restore your Mac. To create a Time Machine backup, select **Back Up Now** from the **Time Machine** Menu Extra in the Menu Bar at the top of your Desktop to back up to an external disk drive.

Launching Terminal

Let's launch the **Terminal** application. Similar to System Preferences, there are multiple ways to launch the Terminal application. You can launch Terminal by any one of the following methods:

1. Launch Terminal using **Launchpad** by typing "Terminal" in the Launchpad search field,
2. Open **Spotlight**, search for Terminal, and press the **return** key,
3. Launch **Finder**, open the **Applications** folder, open the **Utilities** folder, and double-click on Terminal, or
4. Launch Siri and ask it to "Launch Terminal."

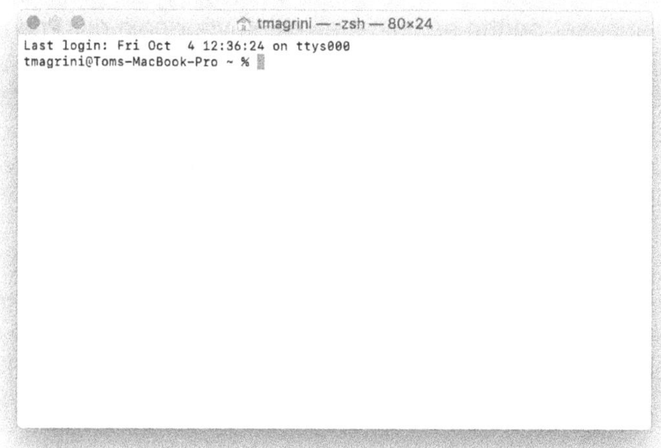

Terminal provides a text-based user interface showing your user name and the name of your computer, followed by a **%** sign. A gray rectangular pointer, called the **prompt**, waits patiently for your commands. The default view is shown in the picture below.

Note that the name of the current user, the type of shell (macOS Catalina uses a shell called zsh), and the size of the window (80 characters by 24 lines) is shown on the window's Title Bar.

Terminal Basics

The first thing you'll notice about Terminal is the **prompt**. The prompt is where we enter the commands shown in this book. When you open Terminal, the first two lines look something like this:

```
Last login: Fri Oct 4 12:36:24 on ttys000
```

```
tmagrini@Toms-MacBook-Pro: ~ % |
```

The first line tells you when you last logged in via the Terminal application. The second line contains the prompt. The cursor appears after the **%** sign. Depending on your selection in Terminal preference pane, which is accessed by entering **⌘,** (command+comma), the cursor may or may not blink and could appear as a block, an underline, or a vertical bar. The image on the next page shows the **Text** tab in the Terminal preference pane. The cursor options are at the bottom of the pane.

Commands are entered at the **prompt**. You do not have to use your mouse or trackpad as anything you type appears at the prompt. Once a command has been completely entered, you will press the **return** key to execute it.

A behavior first-time users often find odd is that Terminal provides no feedback when a command is entered correctly. Feedback is typically provided only when an invalid command is entered. And don't worry, macOS will not make any changes if the command is not valid. If a command is entered correctly, an error will be displayed, and a new prompt appears on the next line, awaiting your next command.

You will enter one command at a time into Terminal, pressing the **return** key after each to execute it. Note that commands shown in this book are case sensitive. Therefore, you must enter each one exactly as shown. Remember, every character is important in Terminal, including the spaces.

So far, it sounds pretty simple, doesn't it? The customizations that require the use of Terminal simply require you to type a few commands exactly as you see them in this book, pressing the **return** key after each command. Yes, it is that simple. Let's try a Dock customization to help you learn and gain more confidence using Terminal.

Your First Customization

Let's try a customization using the Terminal application.

macOS offers two standard animations when minimizing windows, the **Genie** and **Scale** effects, with the default being Genie. Unless you have changed the window minimization effect in the Dock preference pane in System Preferences, you are using the default, Genie. Let's launch the Terminal application and check. Once Terminal has launched, enter the following command.

```
defaults read com.apple.dock mineffect
```

The command you just entered is a **read** command, which you just used to find out the current setting of the **mineffect**, short for minimization effect. If the output looks like the following, telling you that com.apple.dock mineffect does not exist, that is okay. All it means is that you have never changed the minimization effect in System Preferences. Therefore, you are using the default effect called Genie.

```
Last login: Tue Oct  8 12:19:09 on ttys000
tmagrini@Toms-MacBook-Pro-13 ~ % defaults read com.apple.dock
mineffect
2019-10-08 12:22:47.706 defaults[43656:516687]
The domain/default pair of (com.apple.dock, mineffect) does not
exist
tmagrini@Toms-MacBook-Pro-13 ~ %
```

Now let's change the minimization effect using Terminal. First, minimize the Terminal window or an open window so you can view the animation. If you minimized the Terminal window, click on it in the Dock to reopen it. This time you will enter a **write** command, which is used to change a setting. Enter the following two commands and press the **return** key after you enter each command. Be sure to capitalize the **D** in **D**ock.

```
defaults write com.apple.dock mineffect -string scale
```

```
killall Dock
```

Now minimize the Terminal window and note the change to the minimization animation. It is no longer set to the default of Genie. You can check this by entering the following command.

```
defaults read com.apple.dock mineffect
```

The output should look like the following and indicates that the mineffect is now set to **scale** instead of the default of Genie.

```
tmagrini@Toms-MacBook-Pro-13 ~ % defaults read com.apple.dock
mineffect
scale
tmagrini@Toms-MacBook-Pro-13 ~ %
```

You can also check this setting using the System Preferences application. Launch System Preferences, then click on the **Dock** preference pane. Check out the setting next to **Minimize windows using**.

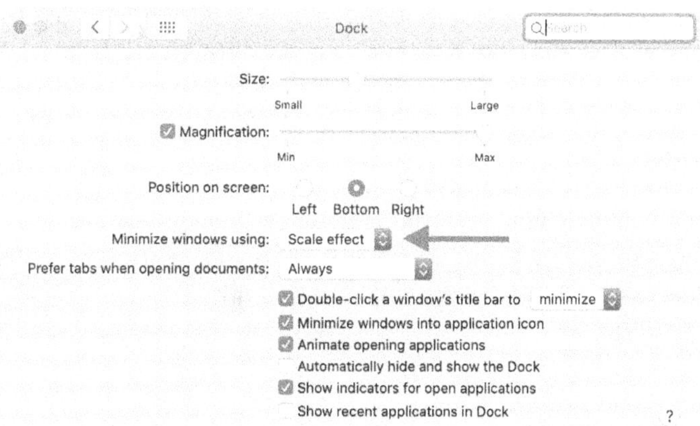

Wasn't that way cool? You just changed a macOS system parameter using the command line interface in Terminal.

If you want to change the window minimization effect back to Genie, you could simply select **Genie effect** from the drop-down menu next to **Minimize windows using:** in the Dock preference pane. But let's do it using Terminal instead. First, close the Dock preference pane then enter the following commands in the Terminal application.

```
defaults write com.apple.dock mineffect -string genie

killall Dock
```

Now try the read command again. This time the Terminal will return **genie**.

```
tmagrini@Toms-MacBook-Pro-13 ~ % defaults read com.apple.dock
mineffect
genie
```

Check the effect by minimizing the Terminal window or any other open window. You can also check the setting in the Dock preference pane in System Preferences. Note that if you didn't follow my directions (shame on you) and left the Dock preference pane open when changing back to the Genie effect, the change will not be reflected properly. Close the System Preferences app, launch it, and reopen the Dock preference pane to see the change.

You could have also reverted to the default Genie animation using a **delete** command, as shown below. When you delete a setting, macOS reverts to the system default, in this case, the Genie effect.

```
defaults delete com.apple.dock mineffect

killall Dock
```

Congratulations! You just completed your first customization using the Terminal command line, and reverted back to the macOS system default. I told you it was that easy!

Wait a minute. Why would you use Terminal to change the window minimization animation when it is so much easier to change it using System Preferences? That is because some settings are not available in System Preferences, like the third animation, the **suck** effect.

System Preferences allows you to switch between the Genie and Scale effects, but macOS has a third, hidden animation called **suck** that is not accessible in System Preferences. It can only be changed using a command in the Terminal app. I'll show you how to configure the suck effect in the chapter on the Dock.

History Command

Before we finish our basic lesson on Terminal, I'll show you a few commands that will come in handy. The first command provides a history of all the commands you have entered. **History** comes in handy when you want to see what you did, or you want to reuse a command. Copy and paste are supported in Terminal. Using the history command allows you to not only see the commands you entered but to copy a command you wish to reuse. Remember to copy only the command.

```
history
```

Now is probably a good time to remind you about the typeface. All Terminal commands are shown in the typeface shown above. When you see this typeface, it is your signal that these are commands you will enter into Terminal.

Up and Down Arrows

The **up** arrow key displays the last command you entered in Terminal. This lets you rerun the command by pressing the **return** key again or to backspace over part of the command to make changes. After you have entered a number of commands, pressing the **up** arrow lists each command in reverse order, essentially going back through your previously used commands. Terminal beeps to let you know when you have reached the end of your history.

Conversely, the **down** arrow moves you forward through your history of commands. The up and down arrows come in handy when you need to enter a previously used command again. Once you have found the command you want and it is displayed in Terminal, simply press the **return** key to execute it.

Clear

After entering many commands, the prompt will be at the bottom of the Terminal window, and the window will be full of commands. If you want to clear the window, enter this command. Don't forget to hit the **return** key.

```
clear
```

Note that using the clear command does not delete your command history. All the clear command does is clean up your interface.

Entering Long Commands

Some of the commands in this book are too long to fit on a single line in Terminal. A long command will flow onto the next line. A really long command can take two, three, or even four lines. Even though the command appears on multiple lines, it is still a single command and will not be executed until you press the **return** key. For example, note that the following command appears on one line in the book:

```
defaults write com.apple.screencapture disable-shadow -bool TRUE
```

However, when entered into Terminal, it appears on two lines, as shown in the image below. Remember, a command is executed when you press the **return** key, so do not press **return** until you have entered the entire command.

```
tom — -bash — 80×24
Last login: Mon Nov 12 08:29:24 on ttys000
Toms-MacBook-Pro:~ tom$ defaults write com.apple.screencapture disable-shadow -b
ool TRUE
```

Let's Start Customizing macOS

You can quit the Terminal application by selecting **Terminal > Quit Terminal** or by entering **⌘Q** (command+Q).

Now that you have learned the basics of the System Preferences and Terminal apps, you now have the basic knowledge necessary to configure any of the customizations in this book. I told you it was that easy!

Let's start with Gestures.

2

Gestures

In this chapter, I'll teach you how to create personal, custom trackpad, and mouse gestures. Creating a unique set of gestures is guaranteed to increase your efficiency and productivity, giving you precise and completely natural control over your Mac. First, we'll review the standard gestures for the trackpad and mouse as well as various attributes such as tracking speed, double-click speed, and Force Touch.

If you are an experienced Mac user, you may be thinking about skipping this chapter since you may already be familiar with gestures. If that's the case, I suggest you skim through this chapter as I introduce a few features that are not configured in either the Trackpad or Mouse preference panes.

Hands down, Apple has the best multi-touch trackpad and mouse in the industry. No other computer manufacturer comes close. A trackpad is standard on the MacBook, MacBook Air, and MacBook Pro series of laptops. If you have an iMac, Mac Mini, or Mac Pro Desktop computer, I highly recommend that you indulge yourself and spend $129 for an Apple Magic Trackpad 2 so you can take advantage of the full set of standard and custom gestures in macOS. It will look great next to your Apple Wireless Keyboard! If you are using an Apple Magic Mouse, you have access to a smaller number of gestures. macOS offers a total of 6 standard gestures for the Magic Mouse while the Magic Trackpad supports a total of 15. While creating custom gestures can help alleviate this limitation, I find that I am far more productive using a trackpad than I am using a mouse. Once you have mastered trackpad gestures, it's hard to go back to a mouse.

Those switching from a Windows PC typically find gestures to be strange and foreign. Where is the right mouse button? Never mind that, where is the left one? However, with just a little practice, macOS gestures become completely natural. In fact, macOS gestures will become so natural that eventually, you'll no longer need to think about which gesture does what. You'll rely on muscle memory, performing trackpad and mouse gestures without any conscious effort. Once you have mastered the built-in macOS gestures and have created a few custom ones, you'll never want to use a Windows PC again!

Trackpad Gestures

An Apple trackpad provides 15 standard gestures. However, Apple leaves a few disabled by default. I suggest you turn on all trackpad gestures and spend about a half an hour or so learning what each does. Learning a gesture is a snap because Apple provides handy videos that demonstrate each gesture in the Trackpad preference pane. After a little practice, you'll find the gestures will become completely natural, and you will no longer have to remember which gesture accomplishes what task.

Besides enabling and disabling gestures, the Trackpad preference pane allows you to customize 11 gestures. The Trackpad preference pane also allows you to adjust the pointer tracking speed and Force Touch options. If you are setting up a new Bluetooth trackpad, you'll do that in the Trackpad preference pane.

To open the **Trackpad** preference pane, launch System Preferences. You can also launch the Trackpad preference pane from the Apple menu by selecting ** > System Preferences... > Trackpad**. Another option is to enter **⌘space** (command+space) to activate **Spotlight**. Type "trackpad" in the Spotlight search window, and the Trackpad preference pane will be displayed under **Top Hits** by the time you type the "c" in "trackpad." Press **return** to launch it. Or give Siri a try. Hold down **⌘space** (command+space) and tell Siri to "Open the trackpad preference pane."

Set Up a New Bluetooth Trackpad

To set up a new Bluetooth trackpad, check to see if it's on. Then launch the **Trackpad** preference pane and click **Set Up Bluetooth Trackpad...** in the lower-right corner of the Trackpad preference pane. Your Mac will search for your new trackpad and discover it automatically.

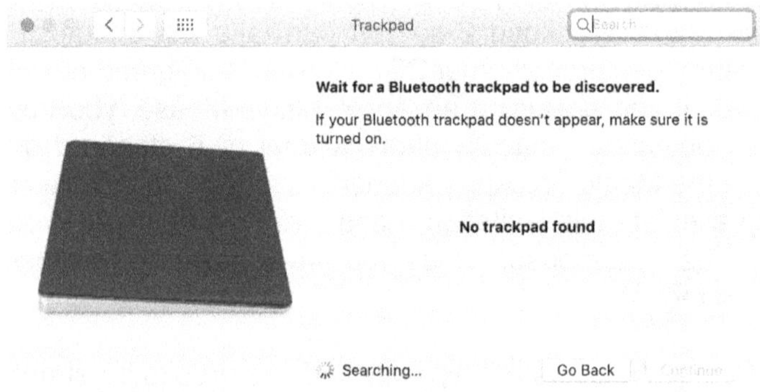

Bluetooth is enabled by default in macOS. If it is turned off, a **Turn On Bluetooth** button appears in the lower-right of the Trackpad discovery window. Once your trackpad is discovered, the Trackpad preference pane appears.

Configure Trackpad Gestures

The standard macOS trackpad gestures are enabled, disabled, and configured in the Trackpad preference pane. When you launch the Trackpad preference pane, you'll notice three tabs at the top for each of the gesture categories – **Point & Click**, **Scroll & Zoom**, and **More Gestures**. The currently selected tab is highlighted in blue.

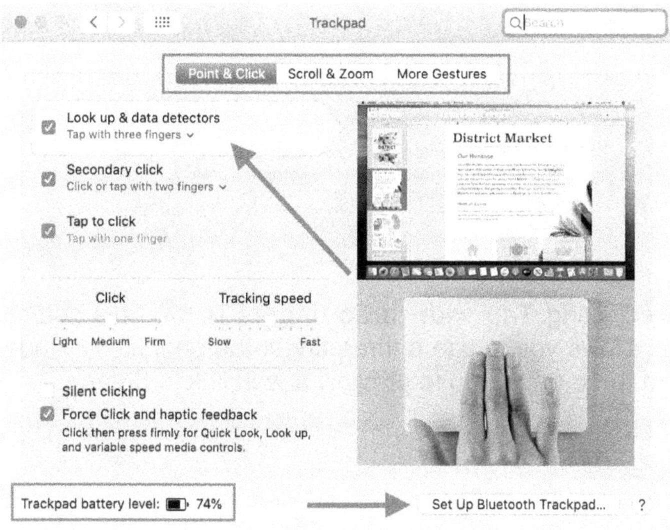

If you have an Apple Magic Trackpad or Magic Trackpad 2 connected via Bluetooth, you will see its battery level in the lower-left corner.

The left side of the Trackpad preference pane lists the available trackpad gestures with checkboxes next to each. To enable a gesture, check the checkbox. Unchecking the checkbox disables a gesture. A video on the right side of the pane demonstrates how to perform the selected gesture and what action the gesture does. Hover over any of the gestures with your pointer, and the video automatically changes to demonstrate the highlighted gesture and its associated action.

Look Up & Data Detectors

The **Look Up & Data Detectors** gesture gives you the option of using a three-finger tap or a one-finger Force Click. Using either gesture on a word or phrase and macOS will look it up in the dictionary, thesaurus, Wikipedia, or Siri. Depending on the word, you'll see other options such as apps, sports, TV, and movies. Note that you'll need a trackpad that supports Force Touch for the one-finger option to appear.

The Data Detector feature recognizes the type of data, such as dates and addresses. This is an extremely handy feature allowing you to quickly add a new event to Calendar or a contact to the Contacts app.

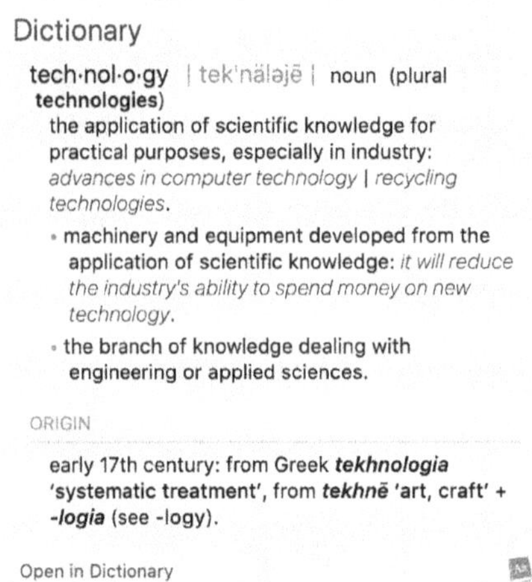

Dictionary
tech·nol·o·gy | tek'näləjē | noun (plural technologies)
the application of scientific knowledge for practical purposes, especially in industry: advances in computer technology | recycling technologies.
• machinery and equipment developed from the application of scientific knowledge: it will reduce the industry's ability to spend money on new technology.
• the branch of knowledge dealing with engineering or applied sciences.
ORIGIN
early 17th century: from Greek tekhnologia 'systematic treatment', from tekhnē 'art, craft' + -logia (see -logy).
Open in Dictionary

An advantage of selecting **Tap with three fingers** is that this setting also enables Quick Look, which allows you to use a three-finger tap on a file in Finder to preview it. You can also use a three-finger tap to preview a web link in Safari.

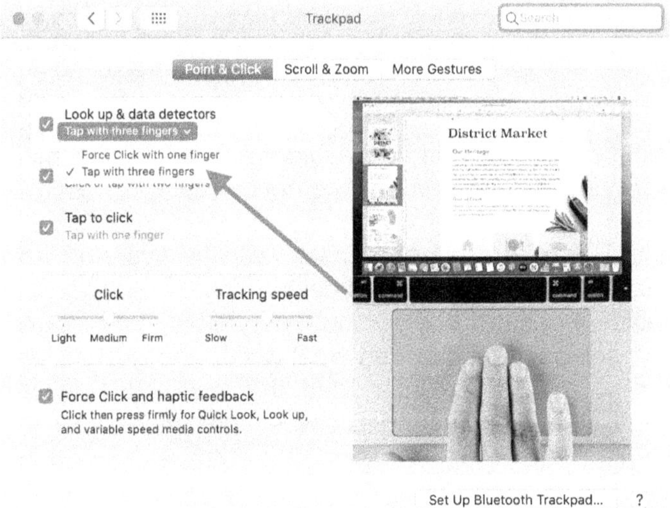

Configure the Dictionary

By default, macOS uses the language you chose when you first set up your Mac. If you would like to change or add additional languages to the dictionary, use the Look Up & Data Detectors gesture on a word in Safari, Mail, or another application. When the Look Up window appears, click on the tiny gear next to **Configure Dictionaries**. This reveals a preference pane where you can change or add languages, select a dictionary and thesaurus, and enable or disable Wikipedia.

The options are shown at the very bottom of the Look Up results window allow you to see other categories pertinent to the word you looked up. These could include the dictionary, thesaurus, Siri, sports scores, TV shows, movies, web videos, music, or results from the App Store.

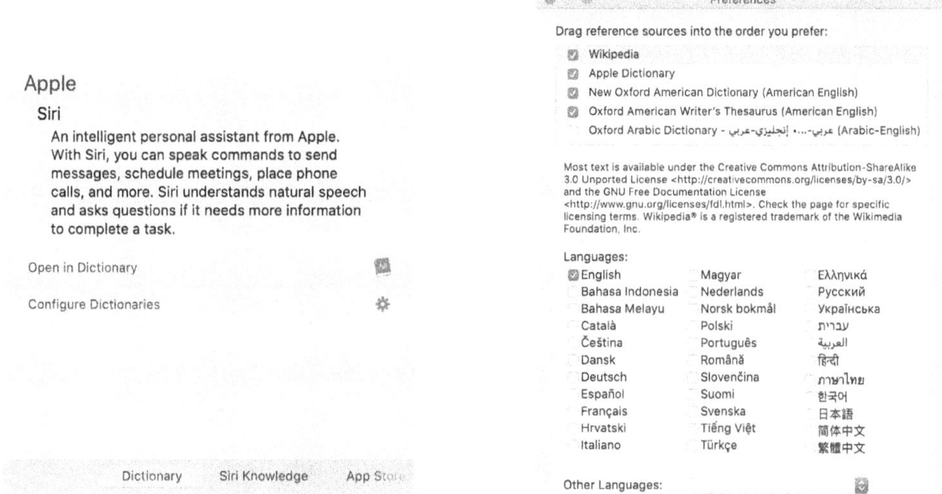

Configure Secondary Click

A secondary click is used to reveal context-sensitive menus, and for those of you familiar with Windows PCs, it is similar to a right button mouse click. Secondary click has three options – **Click or tap with two fingers**, **Click in the bottom right corner**, or **Click in the bottom left corner**.

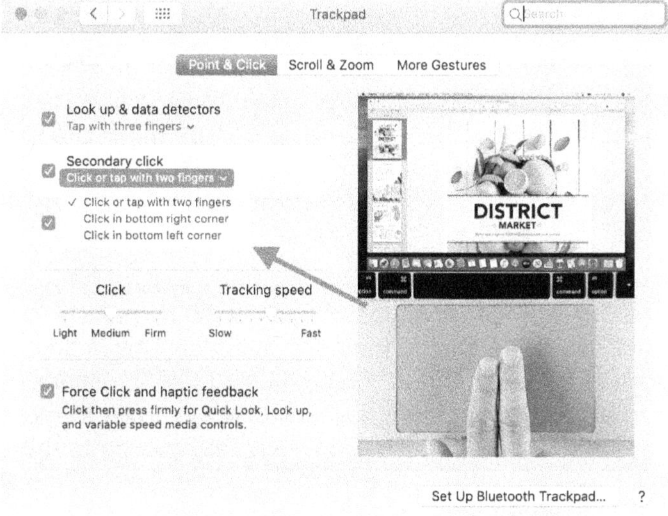

To tap with two fingers, you first have to enable the **Tap to click** gesture. Otherwise, you have to click to accomplish a secondary click. The difference between a click and tap is the amount of force you'll use to perform the gesture. A tap is a gentle tap on the trackpad while clicking requires you to press the trackpad. Enabling a **Tap to click** does not replace the click option as both are supported. You can also perform a secondary click by holding down the ⌘ (command) key while clicking or tapping.

Tap To Click

The **Tap to click** gesture is disabled by default, forcing you to press down on the trackpad to click. Enabling this option allows you to tap the trackpad to click. Tap to click does not replace pressing down on the trackpad to click, as both options are supported when tap to click is enabled. Enabling tap to click also adds the option to enable a two-finger tap for a secondary click.

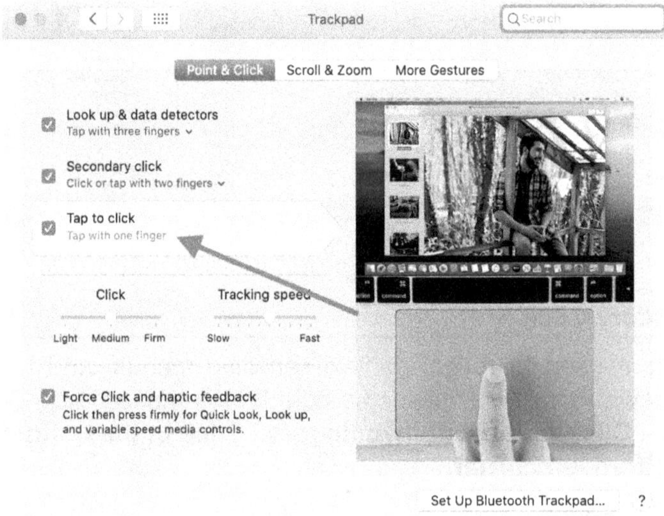

Pressing down on the trackpad is still required to perform a click and hold to drag, move, or lasso items, although you can accomplish these actions using three fingers when **three finger drag** is enabled. See "Enable Three Finger Dragging" later in this chapter.

Scroll Direction: Natural

For someone switching from a Windows PC to a Mac, natural scrolling is even stranger than the lack of the left and right mouse buttons. This is because the gesture is opposite how most of us learned how to scroll using the scrollbars. On a Windows PC, you scroll up to move your content down and scroll down to move your content up. Natural scrolling is exactly opposite – your content moves in the same direction as your fingers, which, by the way, is how scrolling works on an iPhone or iPad. So, in reality, you have been scrolling naturally for years without even realizing it.

With natural scrolling, you move your fingers in the direction you want to move your content with your content tracking your finger movement. If you want to move your content up, scroll up with two fingers. If you want to move your content down, scroll down with two fingers. If you want to disable natural scrolling, uncheck the checkbox next to **Scroll direction: Natural** in the Trackpad preference pane.

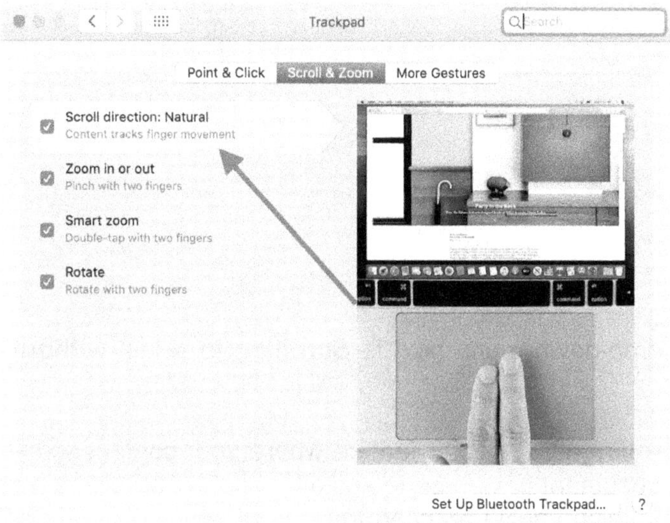

Another difference between macOS and Windows is that scrollbars only appear along the edges of a window when you are scrolling. This, of course, is customizable. I'll show you several scrollbar customizations in a later chapter.

Disable Scrolling Inertia

A neat macOS scrolling trick is to flick your fingers at the beginning or end of your scroll. This engages a feature called **Scrolling Inertia**, which is enabled by default. macOS mimics the scrolling experience of an iPhone or iPad, where a flick of your finger causes a window to scroll rapidly and gradually come to a stop. Scrolling inertia allows you to scroll past content rapidly to get to the content you want to see.

Start your scroll by moving two-fingers in the direction you want to scroll (i.e., up, down, left, or right) on and flick your fingers at the beginning of the scroll. The content scrolls rapidly and gradually slows to a stop. Flicking your fingers at the end of a scroll causes the content to accelerate, jumping past content until the scroll gradually stops. How fast the content scrolls by is proportional to how quickly you flick.

If you don't care for scrolling inertia, macOS allows you to disable it. Open the **Accessibility** preference pane in the System Preferences application. Next, select **Pointer Control** in the sidebar. Next, click **Trackpad Options....** <u>**Do not uncheck**</u> the box next to **Scrolling** as it disables scrolling. That's a very bad thing.

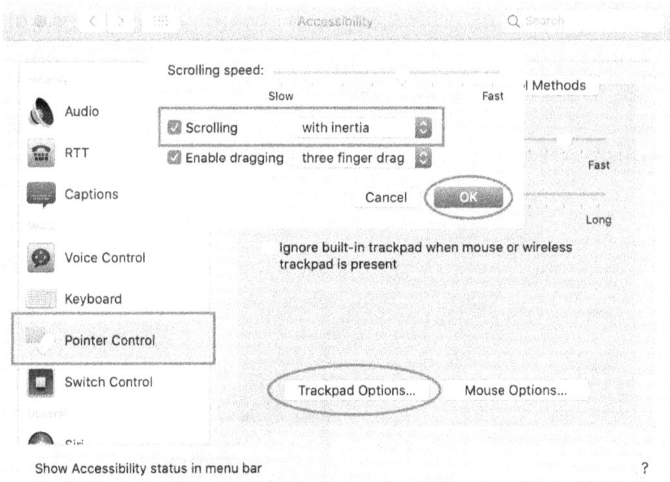

Instead, use the drop-down menu next to **Scrolling** to select **without inertia**. Click **OK** when finished.

Rubber band scrolling is a macOS feature where your content scrolls a little further past the end of a document or web page and then snaps back like a rubber band. This animation lets you know you've reached the end of your document and is the same animation used on the iPhone and iPad.

Adjust the Scrolling Speed

If you find the default scrolling speed too slow or too fast, you can adjust it until you get it just right. Open the **Accessibility** preference pane and select **Pointer Control** in the sidebar. Click **Trackpad Options...** to reveal a configuration sheet. Use the slider at the top to adjust the scrolling speed. Since changes take place immediately, I suggest you open a document and try out various speed settings. Click **OK** when done.

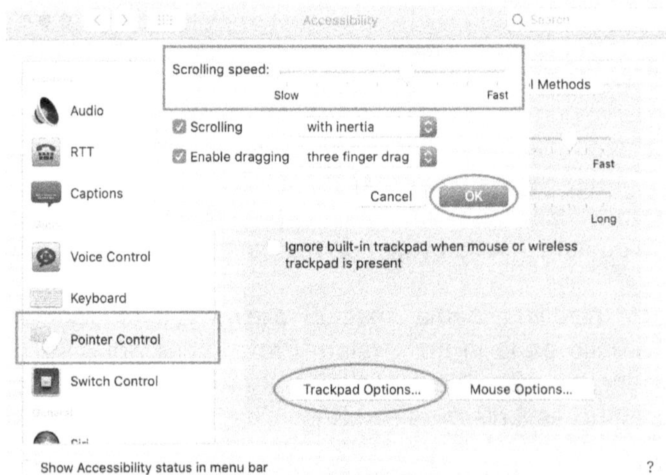

Zooming In or Out

macOS uses the same gestures to zoom in or out as an iPhone or iPad – spreading two fingers apart to zoom in and pinching two fingers together to zoom out.

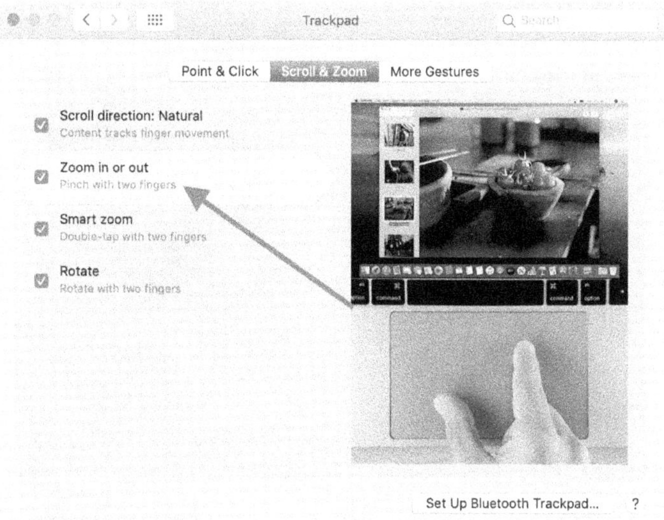

Place two fingers close together on your trackpad and spread them apart to zoom in. Be sure to maintain continuous contact with the trackpad while spreading your fingers apart. A rubber band animation lets you know when you have reached the maximum limit of a zoom. To zoom out, place two fingers apart on the trackpad and move them together in a pinching motion. A rubber band animation lets you know when you have fully zoomed out. To stop zooming in or out, stop moving your fingers and lift them off the trackpad.

When you have multiple tabs open in Safari, a two-finger pinch-zoom on a Safari tab executes the **Show All Tabs** command, displaying all web pages as a set of thumbnails. This is similar to entering ⇧⌘\ (shift+command+\). To take a tab back to full size, click on it or hover over it with the pointer and zoom by spreading two fingers apart on the trackpad.

Smart Zoom

Smart Zoom is a feature macOS borrows from the iPhone and iPad. When you want to zoom in, double-tap your trackpad with two fingers. Double-tap again to zoom out.

Rotate

Rotate is another handy feature I often use in the Photos application and when working with PDF documents. You can rotate a picture or a page in a PDF document by placing your thumb and forefinger on the trackpad and rotating in a clockwise or counterclockwise direction while maintaining continuous contact with the trackpad.

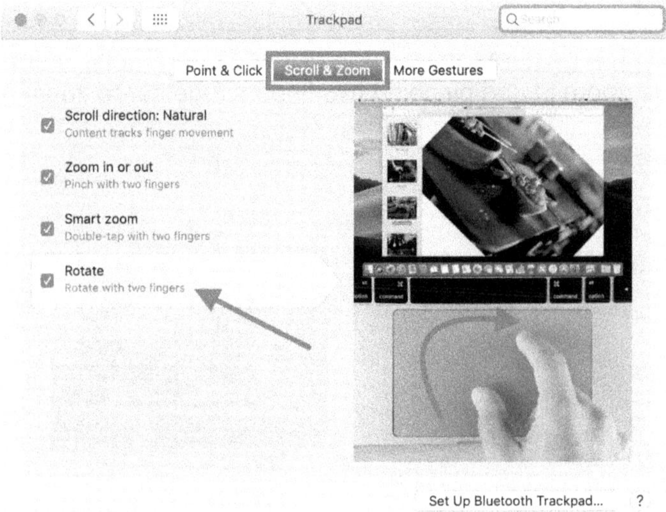

Swipe Between Pages

Swiping between pages is very much like thumbing through pages in a book. A common use for this gesture is to move forward and backward through web pages in Safari. There are three options available – **Scroll left or right with two fingers**, **Swipe with three fingers**, or an option to **Swipe with two or three fingers**.

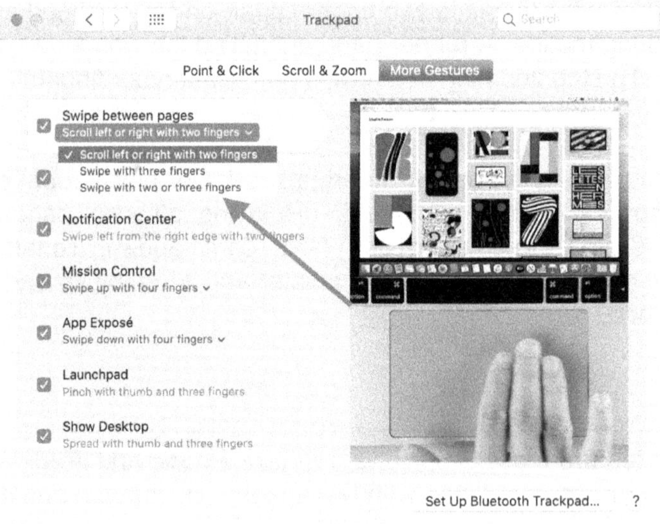

Swipe Between Full-screen Apps

If you use Full-screen apps or Desktop Spaces, both of which I cover in Chapter 4, this gesture lets you swipe between them by swiping left or right. This gesture can be configured to use either three or four fingers.

Swiping left moves the current Desktop Space left to reveal its neighboring Space or Full-screen app located to its right. Similarly, swiping right moves the current Desktop right, revealing its neighboring Space or Full-screen app located to its left. A rubber band animation signifies that you reached the last space or Full-screen app.

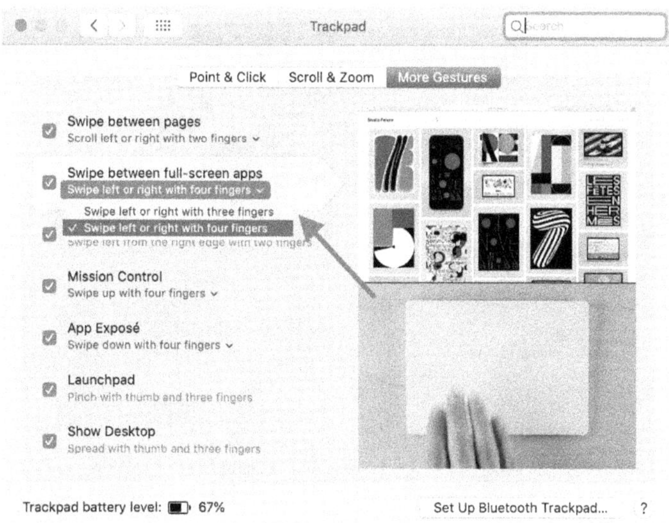

Notification Center

This gesture seems a little odd at first because you actually start off the right edge of your trackpad. Starting at the right edge, swipe left with two fingers to reveal **Notification Center**. Swipe in the opposite direction or click anywhere on the Desktop or an application window to hide it. We'll customize Notification Center in a later chapter.

Mission Control

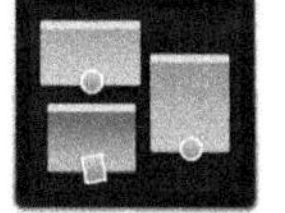

Mission Control is a handy feature that allows you to create, delete, manage, navigate, and rearrange Desktop Spaces and the application windows that reside on them. I cover Desktop Spaces in detail in Chapter 4. Mission Control provides a view of every window running in each Desktop Space as well as applications in Full-screen or Split View mode. Using Mission Control, you can quickly jump to another Desktop Space, Full-screen app, Split View app, or a window on another Desktop Space. Mission Control also allows you to drag windows from one Space to another.

You can configure the Mission Control gesture to swipe up using three or four fingers. You can also access Misson Control by pressing the **F3** key, **^up** (control+up arrow), or clicking the Mission Control icon in the Launchpad, Dock, or Applications folder.

To close Mission Control, swipe down with the same number of fingers as the swipe up gesture, press the **F3** key, enter **^up** (control+up arrow), click on one of the windows, Desktop Space, or tap its icon on the Touch Bar.

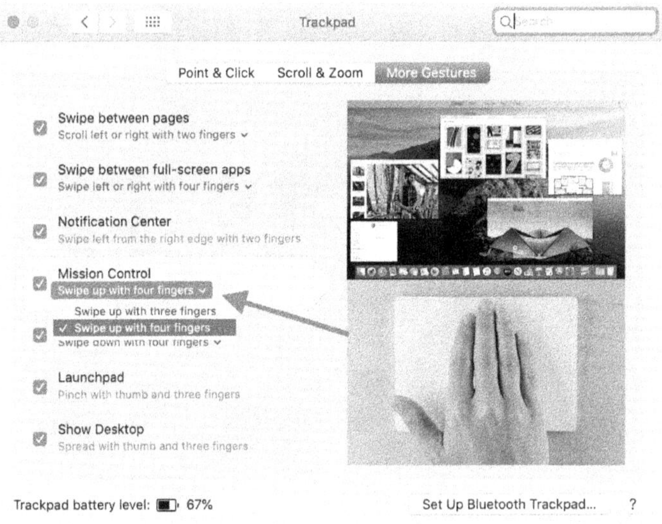

App Exposé

App Exposé lets you see all the windows of an app regardless of which Desktop Space the window resides. You can then jump quickly to a window by clicking on it.

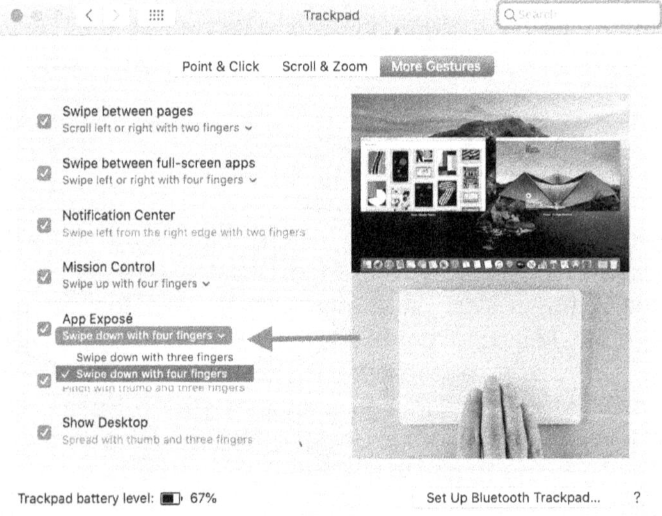

App Exposé differs from Mission Control. With App Exposé, you can see all the windows of an application regardless of which Desktop Space they reside. Mission Control shows you all windows on a Desktop Space even if they are from multiple applications. The App Exposé gesture can be configured to swipe down with three or four fingers.

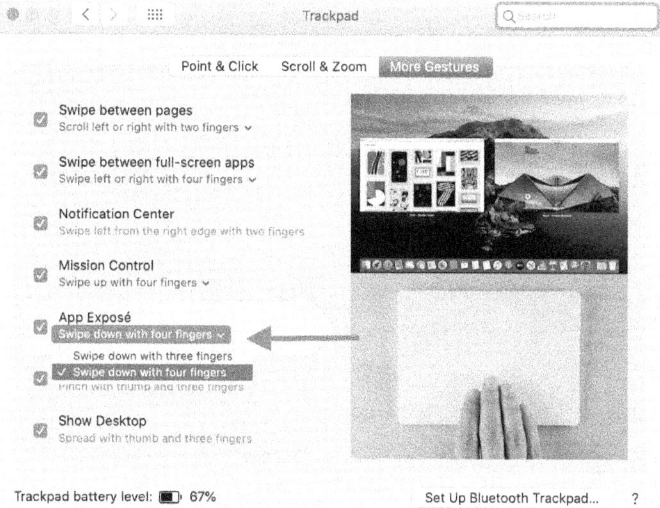

To close App Exposé, swipe up with the same number of fingers as the swipe down gesture or click one of the windows.

Launchpad

Launchpad is a feature macOS borrows from the iPhone and iPad. Launchpad allows you to see, organize, and launch the applications on your Mac. The Launchpad gesture is to pinch with your thumb and three fingers.

You can also access Launchpad by pressing the **F4** key, clicking the Launchpad icon in the Dock, or by launching it from the Applications folder. To exit Launchpad, press the **esc** key or use the **Show Desktop** gesture.

Show Desktop

Show Desktop is used to completely clear all windows from your Desktop. This gesture is the opposite of the Launchpad gesture. Starting with your thumb and three fingers placed close together on the trackpad, spread them apart. This gesture can also be used to exit Launchpad and return to the previous application.

You can also show the Desktop by using either of the following two keyboard shortcuts: **fn F11** (function+F11) or **⌘F3** (command+F3).

If **fn F11** does not work, it is because it has been disabled. To enable the **fn F11** keyboard shortcut, open the **Mission Control** preference pane from System Preferences, and select **F11** from the drop-down menu next to **Show Desktop**.

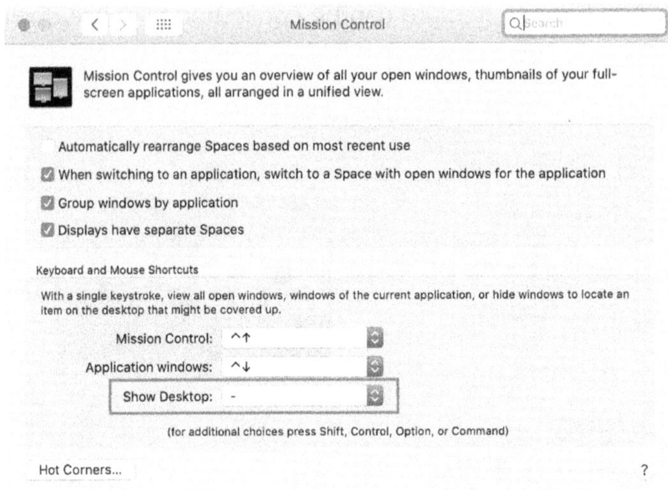

You also have the option of selecting any **F** key, the **fn** (function) key, or the right or left **Shift**, **Control**, **Option**, or **Command** keys. You can disable this feature by selecting **-**.

Enable Three-Finger Dragging

One of my favorite macOS gestures is not configured from the Trackpad preference pane – the three-finger drag. The three-finger drag gesture is extremely useful since it essentially accomplishes what a click, hold, and drag does in a single gesture. The three-finger drag gesture lets you drag, move, highlight, and lasso multiple items.

To enable three-finger dragging, open the **Accessibility** preference pane from System Preferences, and select **Pointer Control** from the sidebar at the left. Next, click the **Trackpad Options...** button to reveal a configuration sheet. Check **Enable dragging** if not already checked and select **three finger drag** from the drop-down menu. Click **OK** to finish.

To use a three-finger drag to move a window, position your pointer over the title bar, place three fingers on your trackpad, and move the window anywhere on the Desktop or to another Desktop Space. Lift your fingers off the trackpad to end the drag. This gesture can be used to move files in Finder by positioning your pointer over a file (or folder) and using a three-finger drag to move it to another folder or to the Trash. If you hold down the ⌥ (option) key, the file will be copied to the new location. A three-finger drag can also be used to lasso a group of files in Finder.

If you see an image on a web page that you want to download, position your pointer over the picture and use a three-finger drag to drag it to a Finder folder. The three-finger drag is also handy for selecting text. Position the pointer in your document and use the three-finger drag gesture to select text by dragging left or right. You can also use the gesture to lasso a group of emails in Mail.

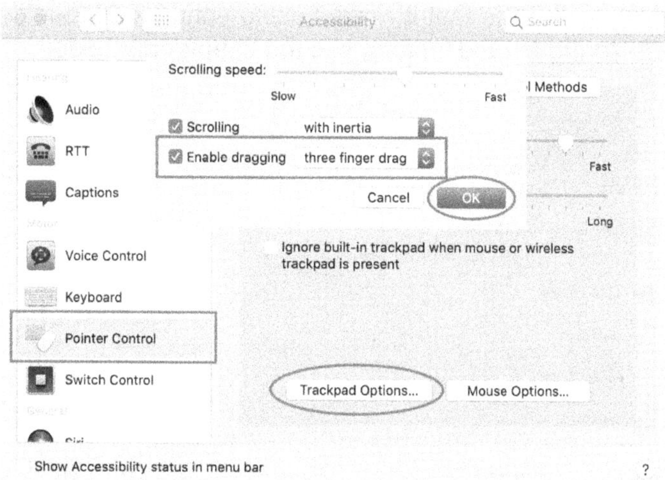

Coast with a Three-Finger Drag

Place your pointer on a window title bar and use a three-finger drag to move it. Leaving two adjacent fingers on the trackpad, flick your third finger left or right. The window will coast and slowly come to a stop. Coasting can also be used to select files, text, or items in a list, although this gesture does require some practice.

Double-Tap Dragging with Drag Lock

Another option to drag an item, a file to another folder, for example, is to double-tap the item without lifting your finger off the trackpad after the second tap. Keep your finger on the trackpad to drag the item to its new location. Exactly when the drag ends is configurable.

By default, dragging ends when you remove your finger(s) from the trackpad. By enabling the **Drag Lock** feature, you can change this behavior so that the drag ends when you tap the trackpad upon reaching the destination. This advantage of drag lock is that if you accidentally lift your finger off the trackpad, the drag will not prematurely end, nor will the item be mistakenly moved or copied into the wrong folder. Drag Lock comes in handy when you're dragging an item from one side of the screen to another as you often run out of trackpad space before completing your drag.

To enable Drag Lock, open the **Accessibility** preference pane from System Preferences. Next, scroll down and select **Pointer Control** in the list at the left. Click the **Trackpad Options...** button. Next, verify the checkbox next to **Enable dragging** is checked and then select **with Drag Lock** from the drop-down menu. Click **OK** to finish.

Similar to the three-finger drag, double-tap dragging with or without drag lock can be combined with the ⌥ (option) key to copy an item to its new location. An added benefit of enabling Drag Lock is that it makes using spring-loaded folders easier. For more information on spring-loaded folders, see the chapter on Finder.

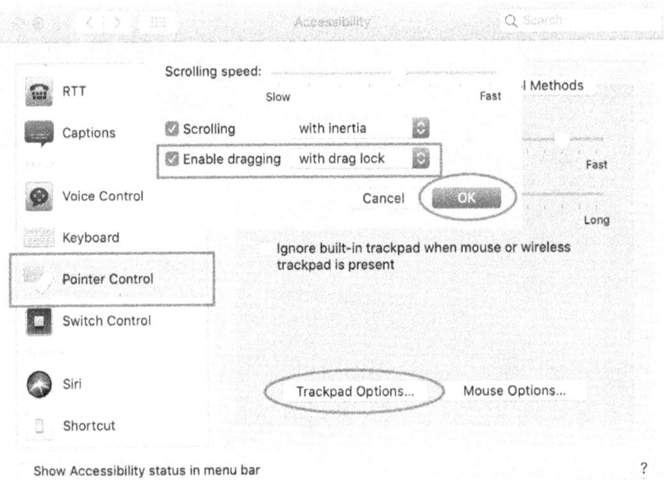

Adjust the Tracking Speed

If you are using your trackpad for the first time, you may notice that the pointer moves pretty slowly.

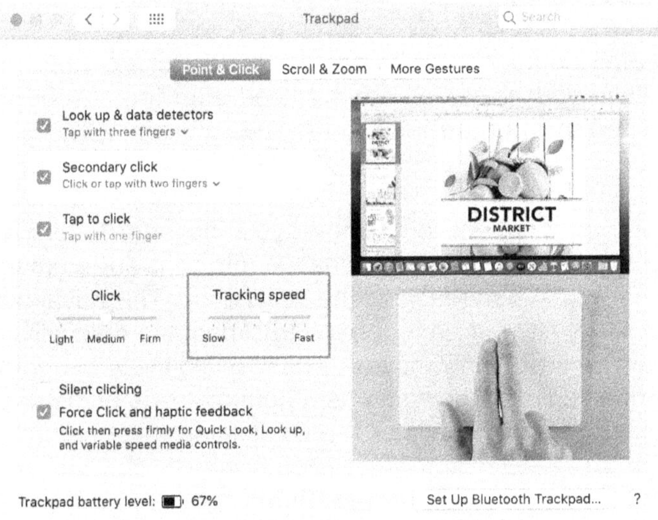

If you want the pointer to move more or less quickly, you can adjust the tracking speed from the **Point & Click** tab in the **Trackpad** preference pane. Move the Tracking speed slider to select your desired tracking speed. Changes take effect immediately so you can try out your new tracking speed and adjust if necessary.

Adjust the Double-Click Speed

To change the double-click speed, launch the **Accessibility** preference pane and select **Pointer Control** in the sidebar. Use the slider in the right-hand pane to adjust the **Double-click speed** from slow to fast.

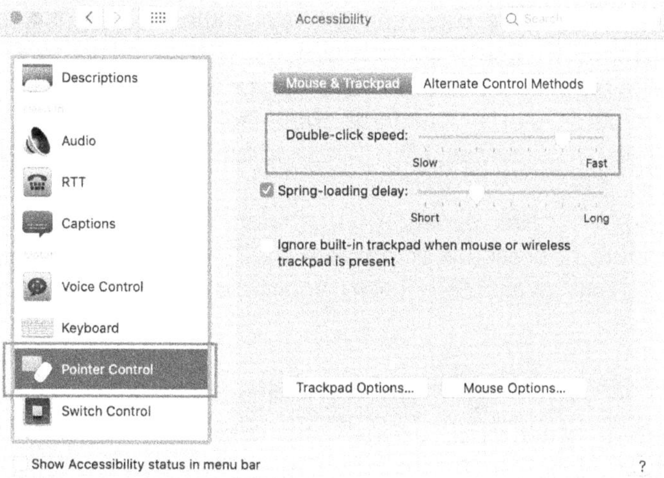

Ignore the Built-in Trackpad

I often use my external Bluetooth trackpad, and I find it annoying when I accidentally brush against the built-in trackpad of my MacBook Pro, and the pointer flies off into left field. There is a simple solution for this annoyance – configure macOS to ignore the built-in trackpad when a Bluetooth trackpad is connected.

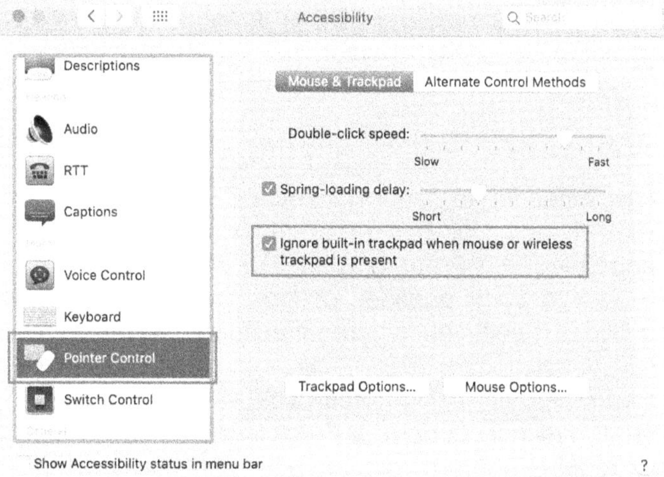

To ignore the built-in trackpad, open the **Accessibility** preference pane and scroll down to select **Pointer Control** in the left sidebar. Check the checkbox next to **Ignore**

built-in trackpad when mouse or wireless trackpad is present. Uncheck the checkbox to disable this feature.

Force Touch Gestures

Force Touch is a pressure-sensitive multi-touch technology developed by Apple that first became available in its MacBook and MacBook Pro laptops, starting with the 2015 models. Apple also released a new Force Touch version of its Bluetooth trackpad, the Magic Trackpad 2, to bring Force Touch technology to its iMac, Mac Mini, and Mac Pro series of Desktops.

Force Touch trackpads have sensors underneath the trackpad surface that can distinguish the amount of pressure being applied. This allows you to take advantage of additional functionality available in many applications and in the macOS operating system.

A trackpad with Force Touch technology can distinguish between a tap, a click, and a **Force Click** based on the amount of pressure applied to the trackpad surface. A Force Click is accomplished by applying more pressure to the trackpad than a standard click. To view a video demonstrating how to Force Click, launch the **Trackpad** preference pane and hover over the **Look up & data detectors** option on the **Point & Click** tab.

Here are some of the things you can do with a Force Click: Quick Look, App Exposé, rename a file, see Reminder details, see iMessage details, preview a web link, perform a lookup in the Dictionary, Thesaurus, or Wikipedia, add an event to Calendar, see event details, preview an address in Maps, empty the trash, access Dock preferences, drop a location pin in Maps, increase the fast forward rate in videos, track a package, and annotate a PDF or image in Mail. And with the custom gestures I show you at the end of this chapter, you can do even more.

Adjust Force Click Pressure

The amount of pressure needed to perform a Force Click is adjustable in the Trackpad preference pane. By default, this setting is set to **medium**. Launch the Trackpad preference pane and select the **Point & Click** tab at the top of the pane. A slider located just below Tap to Click provides options that let you adjust the pressure needed for a Force Click. Select your desired pressure from **Light**, **Medium**, or **Firm**.

If you are having a hard time engaging Force Click, set it to **Light**, which requires less pressure and makes it easier to perform a Force Click. If you adjust the pressure to **Firm**, a Force Click requires more muscle on your part but ensures that you will not accidentally trigger a Force Click when you wanted to do a standard click. Note that the sound associated with a Force Click changes as you change the pressure setting, becoming louder as you move the slider from **Light** to **Firm**.

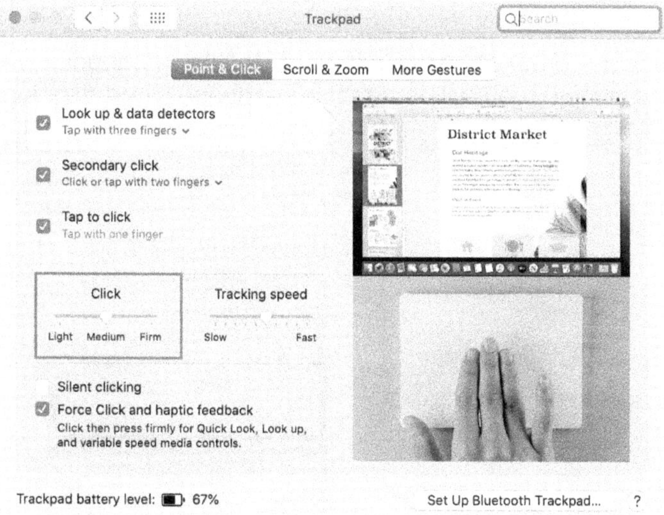

Silence Trackpad Clicking

Force Touch trackpads provide auditory feedback with clicking or Force Clicking. A standard trackpad click produces a single clicking sound while a Force Click produces two clicking sounds. If you prefer your trackpad to be silent, you can disable the trackpad clicking sounds in the **Trackpad** preference pane.

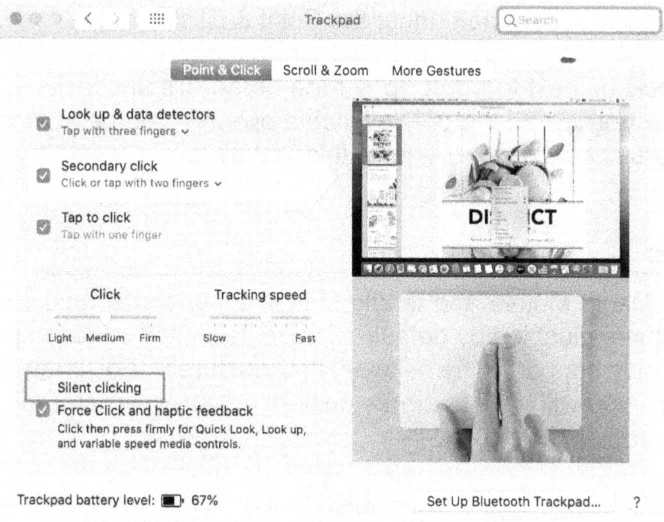

Launch the Trackpad preference pane and select the **Point & Click** tab. Check the checkbox next to **Silent clicking**. Note that this option does not completely disable the sound your trackpad makes when clicking or Force Clicking. However, your trackpad becomes much quieter when this option is enabled.

Disable Force Click

When Force Click is enabled, you will feel tactile feedback in certain Apple applications. For example, you will feel tactile feedback when aligning objects in the Preview app.

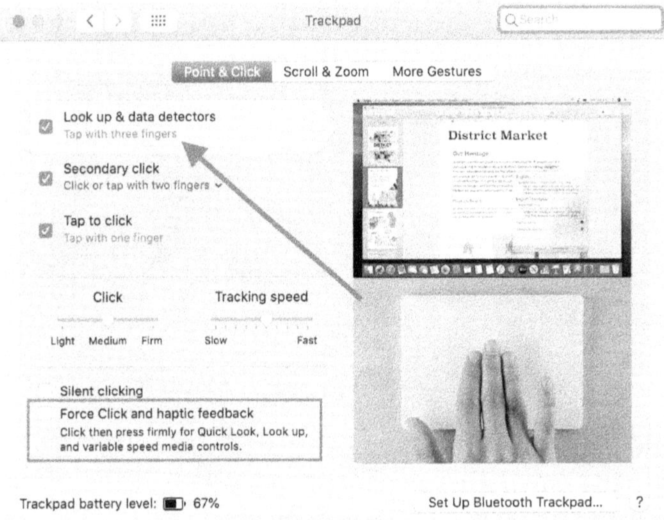

If you don't like or don't want to use Force Click, macOS gives you the option to disable it. Launch the Trackpad preference pane and uncheck the checkbox next to **Force Click and haptic feedback** under the Point & Click tab.

Note that the checkbox next to **Look up & data detectors** unchecks itself and reverts to **Tap with three fingers** as the only available option. You need to check the Look up & data detectors checkbox to re-enable this feature.

Mouse Gestures

Apple's Magic Mouse and Magic Mouse 2 support 6 gestures with three of the gestures disabled by default. Due to its limited surface space, the Magic Mouse only supports one or two-finger gestures. For three- and four-finger gestures, you will have to create custom gestures, which I will show you how to do later in this chapter.

All mouse gestures are enabled and disabled in the Mouse preference pane. Like the Trackpad preference pane, Apple provides handy videos demonstrating each of the gestures. I suggest you enable all of the mouse gestures and spend some time learning them. In no time at all, you'll learn all of the gestures and will wonder how you could have used a computer without them.

To open the **Mouse** preference pane, launch System Preferences. You can also launch the Mouse preference pane from the Apple menu by selecting ** > System Preferences… > Mouse**. Another option is to enter **⌘space** (command+space) to activate **Spotlight**. Type "mouse" in the Spotlight search window, and the Mouse preference pane will be displayed under **Top Hits** by the time you type the "u" in "mouse." Press **return** to launch it. Or give Siri a try. Hold down **⌘space** (command+space) and tell Siri to "Open the mouse preference pane."

Set Up a New Bluetooth Mouse

To set up a new Bluetooth mouse, first ensure your new mouse is turned on. Launch the **Mouse** preference pane and click **Set Up Bluetooth Mouse...** in the lower-right corner. Your Mac will search for your new mouse and discover it automatically.

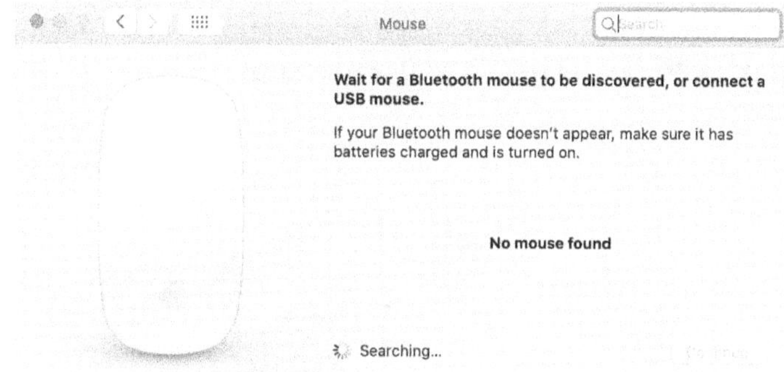

Bluetooth is enabled by default in macOS. If it is turned off, a **Turn On Bluetooth** button appears in the lower-right corner of the Mouse discovery window. Once your mouse is discovered, the Mouse preference pane appears.

Configure Mouse Gestures

The standard macOS mouse gestures are enabled, disabled, and configured in the **Mouse** preference pane. At the top of the Mouse preference pane are two tabs for each category of gestures – **Point & Click** and **More Gestures**. The current tab is highlighted in blue.

If you have an Apple Magic Mouse or Magic Mouse 2 connected via Bluetooth, you will see its battery level in the lower-left corner of the preference pane.

The left side of the pane lists the available mouse gestures with checkboxes next to each. To enable a gesture, check its associated checkbox. Unchecking a checkbox disables the gesture.

On the right side of the pane, a video demonstrates how to perform the highlighted gesture and what action the gesture does. Hover over any of the gestures with your pointer, and the video automatically changes to demonstrate the gesture and the action it performs.

Scroll Direction: Natural

For someone switching from a Windows PC to a Mac, natural scrolling is even stranger than the lack of the left and right mouse buttons. This is because this gesture is opposite how most of us learned how to scroll using the scrollbars on a Windows PC. On a Windows PC, you scroll up to move your content down and scroll down to move your content up. Natural scrolling is exactly opposite – your content moves in the same direction as your fingers, which, by the way, is exactly how scrolling works on an iPhone or iPad. So, in reality, you probably have been scrolling naturally for years without even realizing it.

With natural scrolling, you move your fingers in the direction you want to move your content with your content tracking your finger movement. If you want to move your content up, scroll up with one finger. If you want to move your content down, scroll down with one finger.

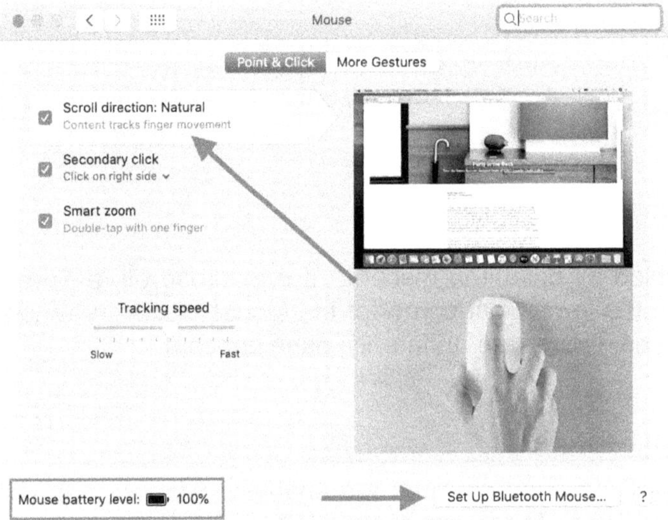

Another difference between macOS and Windows is that scrollbars only appear along the edges of a window when you are actually scrolling. This, of course, is customizable. I'll show you several scrollbar customizations in a later chapter.

If you want to disable natural scrolling, uncheck the checkbox next to **Scroll direction: Natural** in the Mouse preference pane.

Disable Scrolling Inertia

A neat macOS scrolling trick is to flick your fingers at the beginning or end of your scroll. This engages a feature called **Scrolling Inertia**, which is enabled by default. macOS mimics the scrolling experience of an iPhone or iPad, where a flick of your finger causes the window to scroll rapidly and gradually come to a stop. Scrolling inertia allows you to scroll past content rapidly to get to the content you want to see.

Scrolling is initiated by moving one-finger in the direction you want to scroll on your mouse. If you flick your fingers at the beginning of a scroll, the content scrolls rapidly and gradually slows to a stop. Flicking your fingers at the end of a scroll causes the content to accelerate, jumping past content until the scroll gradually stops. How fast the content scrolls by is proportional to how quickly you flick your finger.

If you don't care for scrolling inertia, macOS allows you to disable it. Open the **Accessibility** preference pane in the System Preferences application. Next, select **Pointer Control** in the sidebar. Next, click **Mouse Options....** **Do not uncheck** the box next to **Scrolling** as it disables scrolling. That's a very bad thing. Instead, use the drop-down menu next to **Scrolling** to select **without inertia**. Click **OK** when finished.

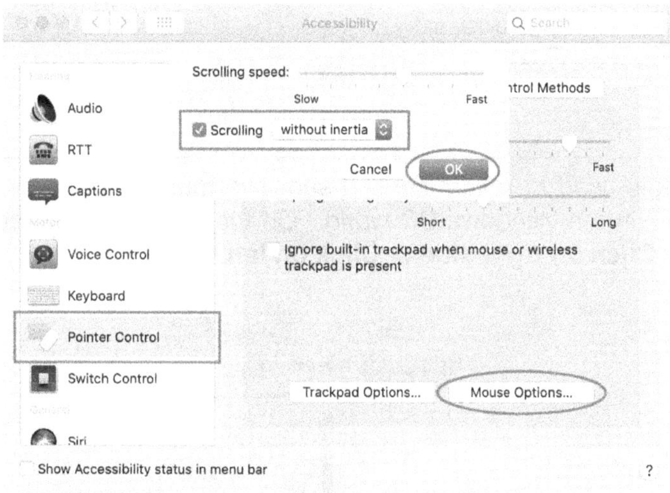

Rubber band scrolling is a macOS feature where your content scrolls a little further past the end of a document or web page and then snaps back like a rubber band. This animation lets you know you've reached the end of your document and is the same animation used on the iPhone and iPad.

Adjust the Scrolling Speed

If you find the default scrolling speed too slow or too fast, you can adjust it until you get it just right.

Open the **Accessibility** preference pane in the System Preferences application. Next, select **Pointer Control** in the left sidebar. Click **Mouse Options...** to reveal a configuration sheet. Use the slider at the top to adjust the scrolling speed.

Since changes take place immediately, I suggest you open a document and try out various speed settings. Click **OK** when done.

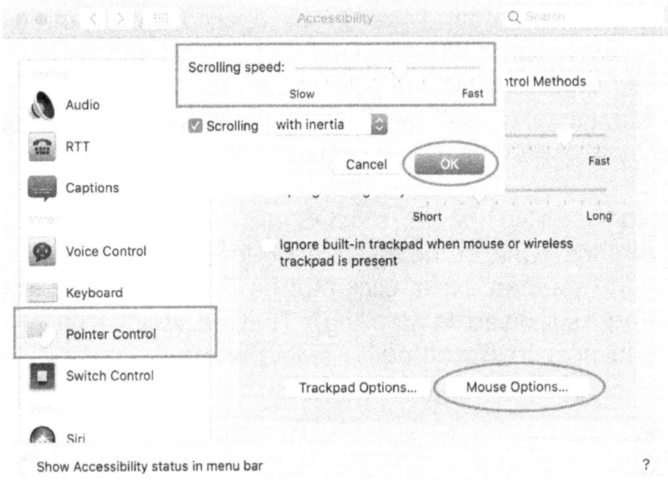

Secondary Click

A secondary click is used to reveal context-sensitive menus and is similar to a right button mouse click in the Windows PC world. On the Magic Mouse, secondary click has two options – **Click on right side** or **Click on left side**.

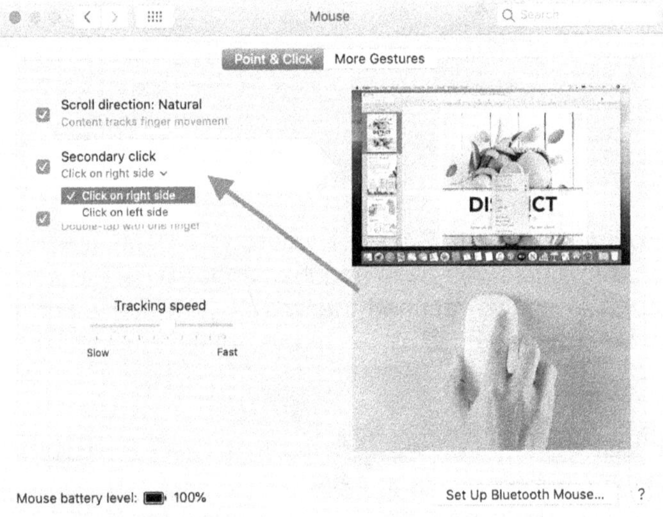

You can also accomplish a secondary click by holding down the ⌘ (command) key while clicking.

Smart Zoom

Smart Zoom is a feature macOS borrows from the iPhone and iPad. When you want to zoom in on a web page, double-tap your Magic Mouse with one finger and Safari zooms in. Double-tap again to zoom out.

Swipe Between Pages

Swiping between pages is very much like thumbing through pages in a book. You can use this gesture to move forward and backward through web pages in Safari by swiping right and left.

This gesture can often be used in other applications and can also be used to scroll horizontally in documents. There are three options – **Scroll left or right with one finger**, **Swipe left or right with two fingers** or an option to **Swipe with one or two fingers**.

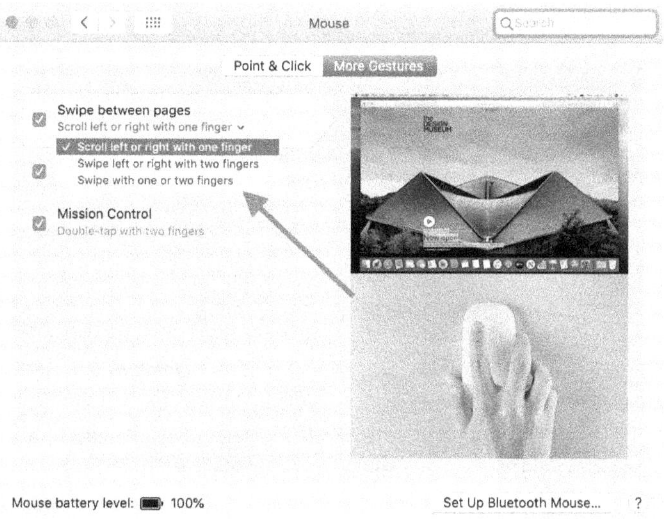

Note that if you configure swiping between pages to use either of the two-finger options, the swipe between Full-screen apps checkbox unchecks itself, and this feature is disabled. If you want to use both gestures, using one finger to swipe between pages is the only option that allows you to enable swiping between Full-screen apps.

Swipe Between Full-screen Apps

If you use Full-screen apps or Desktop Spaces, both of which I introduce in Chapter 4, this gesture lets you swipe between them.

Swiping left moves the current Desktop Space left to reveal its neighboring Space located to its right. Similarly, swiping right moves the current Desktop right, revealing its neighboring Space located to its left. A rubber band animation lets you know that you have reached the last space or Full-screen app.

Note that if you want to use the gestures to swipe between pages and between Full-screen apps, you must configure swipe between pages to use one finger. This is the only option that allows you to use both gestures.

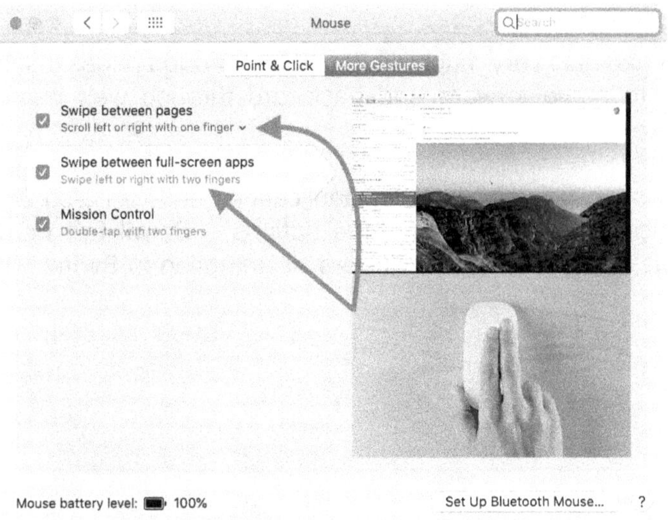

Mission Control

Mission Control is a handy feature that allows you to create, delete, manage, navigate, and rearrange Desktop Spaces and the application windows that reside on them. We'll cover Desktop Spaces in detail in Chapter 4. Mission Control also provides a view of every window running in each Desktop Space as well as applications in Full-screen or Split View mode. Using Mission Control, you can quickly jump to another Desktop Space, Full-screen app, Split View app, or a window on another Desktop Space. Mission Control also allows you to drag windows from one Space to another.

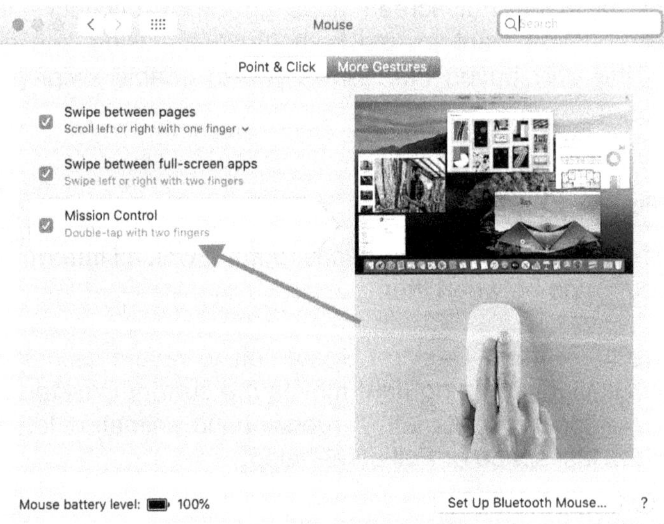

The Mission Control mouse gesture is a double-tap with two fingers and does the same thing as pressing the **F3** key or entering **^up** (control+up arrow).

To close Mission Control, double-tap again, press **F3**, enter **^up** (control+up arrow), or click on one of the windows or a Desktop Space.

Adjust the Mouse Tracking Speed

If you are using your mouse for the first time, you may notice that the pointer moves pretty slowly across the screen. If you want the pointer to move more or less quickly, you can adjust the tracking speed in the **Point & Click** tab of the Mouse preference pane. Move the Tracking speed slider to select your desired tracking speed.

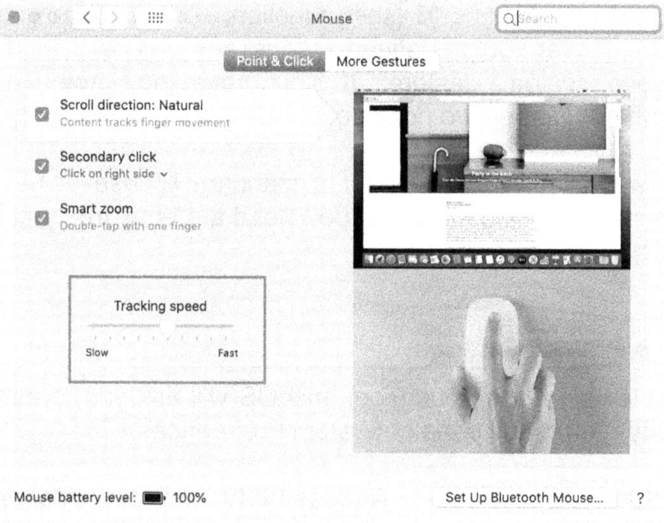

Adjust the Double-Click Speed

To change the double-click speed, launch the **Accessibility** preference pane, and select **Pointer Control** at the left. Use the slider in the right-hand pane to adjust the **Double-click speed**.

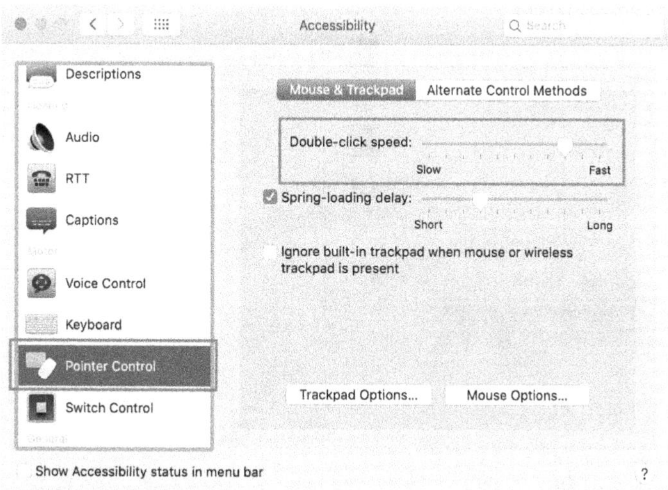

Create Custom Gestures

Now that you are familiar with the out-of-the-box macOS gestures let's learn how to create custom gestures. Creating gestures for common tasks helps you squeeze every drop of productivity from your trackpad or mouse and lets you truly personalize your Mac. There are a few utilities that allow you to create custom gestures, but my hands-down favorite is **BetterTouchTool** by Andreas Hegenberg.

BetterTouchTool lets you assign actions to gestures that use one, two, three, four, or five fingers combined with a tap, double-tap, tip-tap, swipe, or in combination with one or more modifier keys: ⇧ **fn** ^ ⌥ ⌘ (shift, function, control, option, and command). You can assign one of over 200 predefined actions, any keyboard shortcut, or a series of actions to your custom gesture. If you have a Force Touch trackpad, BetterTouchTool offers another two dozen gestures.

BetterTouchTool is available for $7.50 for a standard license or $21 for a lifetime license at the time of this writing. You can download a 45-day free trial of BetterTouch Tool from https://folivora.ai/.

Set the Security & Privacy Settings

The first time you launch BetterTouchTool, macOS will ask you to authorize it in the **Security & Privacy** preference pane of System Preferences.

Click on the **Privacy** tab and select **Accessibility** from the sidebar. If required, unlock the pane by clicking on the padlock in the lower-left corner and enter your password. Check the checkbox next to **BetterTouchTool** to authorize it.

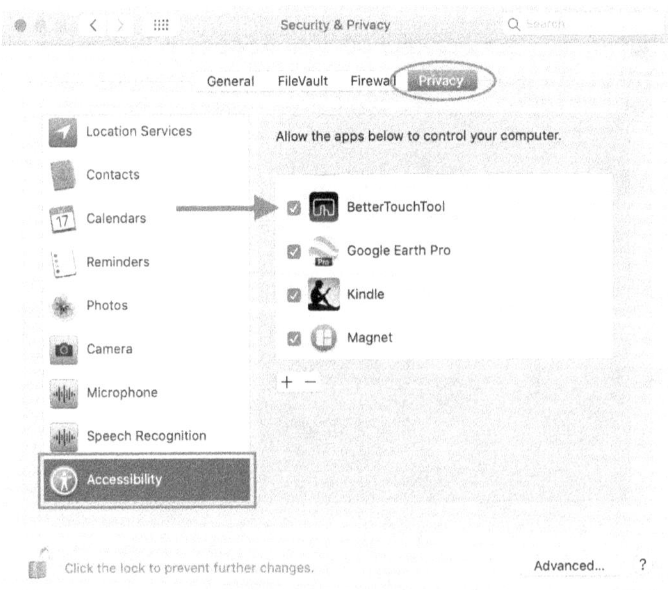

Configure Basic and User Interface Settings

After downloading and installing BetterTouchTool, you'll notice a new Menu Extra in your Menu Bar. Click this Menu Extra to reveal the drop-down menu and select **Configuration** to launch BetterTouchTool. To access BetterTouchTool's preferences, click on the gear in the upper-right corner of the BetterTouchTool window, enter **⌘,** (command+comma), or select **BetterTouchTool > Preferences**. Next, select **Basic** under **Standard Settings** in the left sidebar.

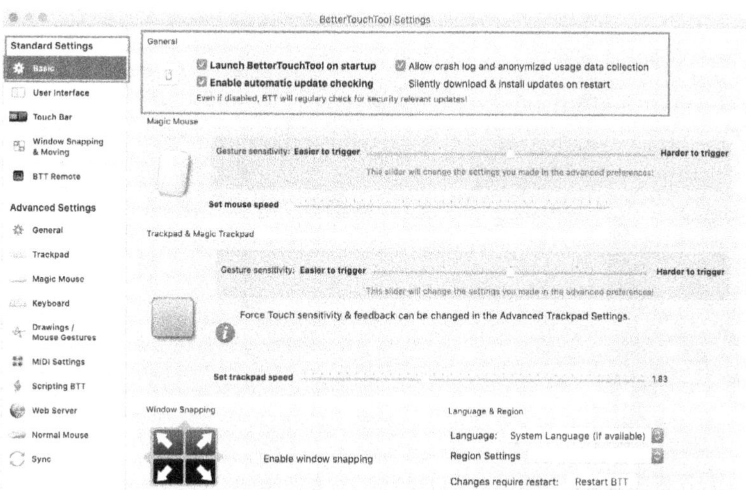

There are a couple of settings that you should validate before creating your first custom gesture. Ensure the following items are checked: **Launch BetterTouchTool on startup** and **Enable automatic update checking**. Launching BetterTouchTool on startup ensures it runs each time you restart your Mac. Enabling automatic updates allows the app to automatically check for updates and ensures that you always have the latest version. **Allow crash log and anonymized usage data collection** is checked by default. This option helps Andreas continually improve his app. I recommend you leave it checked.

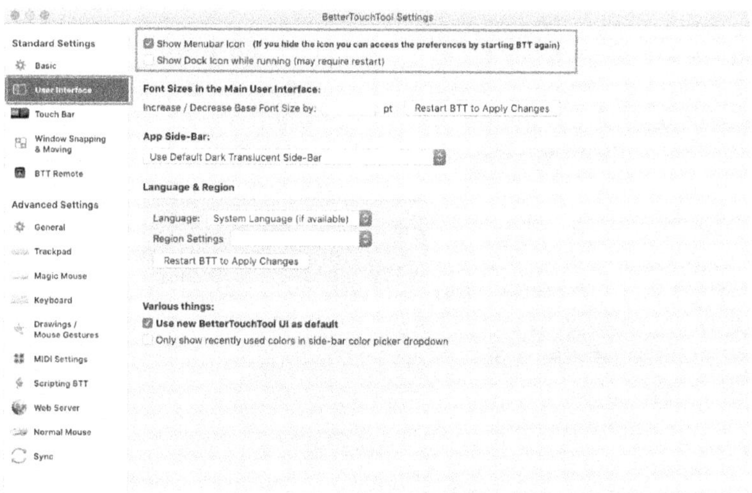

Next, select **User Interface** and validate that the checkbox next to **Show Menubar Icon** is checked. The Menu Bar icon is a convenient way to quickly configure BetterTouchTool, access documentation, or go to the BetterTouchTool Community Forum.

The BetterTouchTool icon does not appear in the Dock. If you want it in your Dock, check the checkbox next to **Show Dock Icon while running** and restart your Mac.

Create a Custom Gesture

Let's create your first custom gesture. First, select **Trackpad** or **Magic Mouse** from the drop-down menu in the toolbar at the top of the configuration pane.

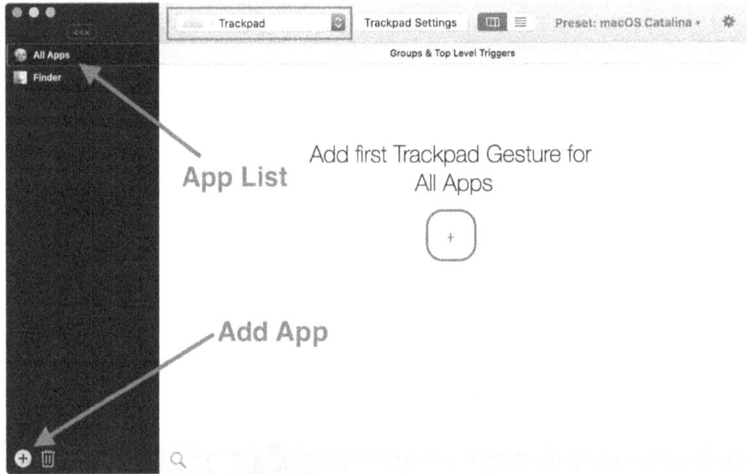

The black sidebar at the left of the BetterTouch Tool window contains the **App List**. Gestures can be created for a specific application or for **All Apps**. A gesture created for a specific application will only work when that application is active. A gesture created for **All Apps** works in all applications.

By default, you will see 2 items listed in the App List, **All Apps**, and **Finder**. You can add other applications by clicking the **+** button in the lower-left corner of the window to select an app from your Applications folder or one that is currently running. You can also drag an application from your Application folder into the App List.

To create a custom gesture, select All Apps or an application in the App List and click the large blue **+** button in the center of the BetterTouchTool window. This reveals the **Trigger List**, where you will select your gesture. You can choose from various 1-, 2-, 3-, 4-, or 5- finger gestures, Force Touch, or your own 4-finger gesture. In this example, I selected the 2-finger double-tap as my trigger.

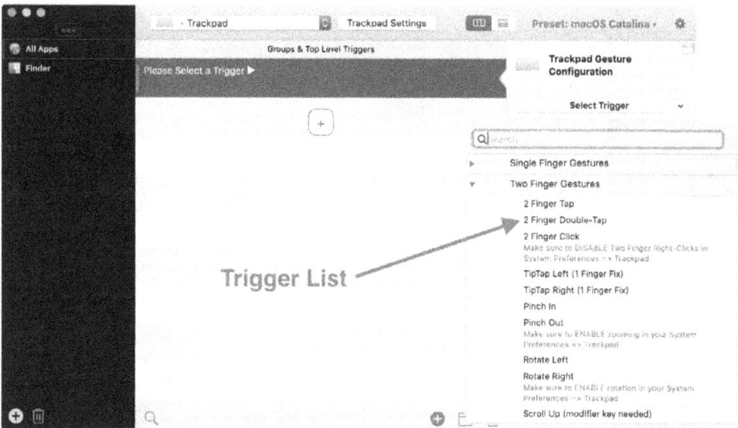

Once you have selected a trigger, the next step is to choose the action from the **Action List**. In this example, I chose **Empty Trash** under System Actions. You can also search for your desired action in the search field at the top of the Action List.

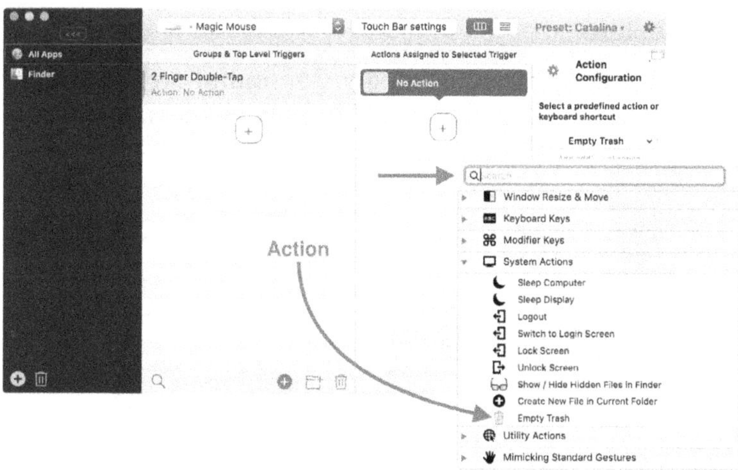

Did you notice the difference between the two images above? In the first image, I am configuring a Trackpad gesture while in the second image, I am creating the same gesture (a 2-finger double-tap) for a Magic Mouse. The important thing to note is that the interface is the same, whether you are creating custom gestures for your trackpad or mouse.

Create a Multiple Action Gesture

BetterTouchTool doesn't limit your gestures to a single action. In the example below, I have created an application-specific mouse gesture for Microsoft Word. A 3-Finger Tap combined with the ⇧ (shift) key saves and closes my currently active Word document, hides Microsoft Word, and opens Finder.

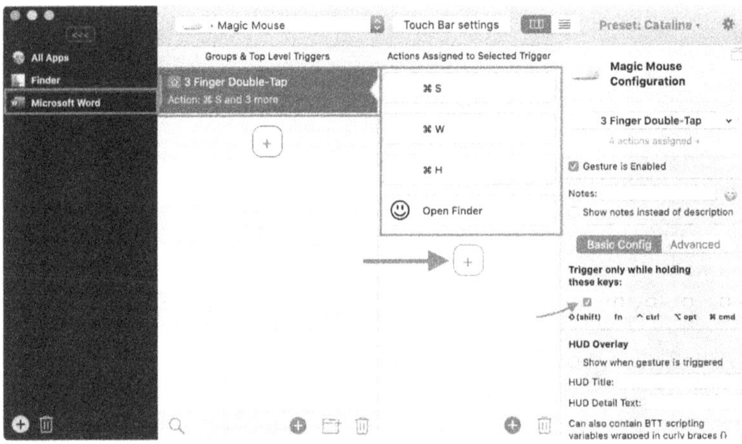

To create a multiple action gesture, click the **+** button in the Action List for each additional action you wish to add.

Modify a Custom Gesture

An existing gesture can be modified using the **Configuration Sidebar**. First, select the app from the App List and then click on the gesture in the Trigger List.

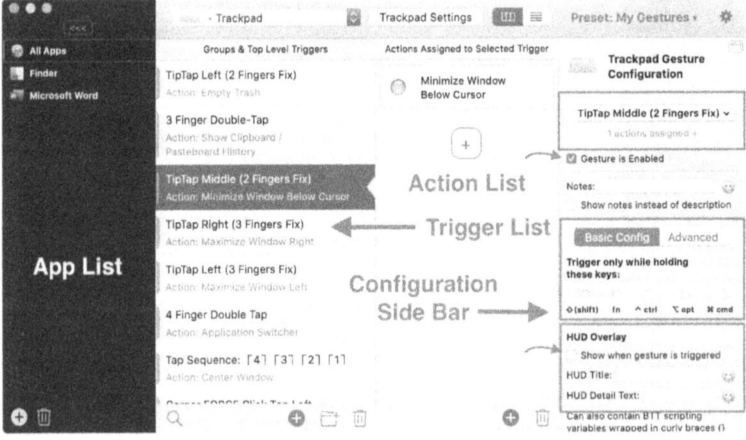

You can change the action associated with the gesture using the Action drop-down menu in the Configuration Sidebar or by double-clicking the action in the Action List. Both cause the Action List to appear where you can select the new action you want to associate with the trigger.

The Configuration Sidebar also allows you to configure an action to trigger only while holding down one or more modifier keys. By using modifier keys, you can use the same gesture to trigger different actions depending on the modifier key(s) held down. Check the checkbox above the ⇧ **fn** ^ ⌥ ⌘ (shift, function, control, option, and command) keys to configure one or more modify keys.

A Heads Up Display (HUD) Overlay can also be configured to display a title and text when a gesture is triggered. Check the checkbox next to **Show when gesture is triggered** and add a title and text in the **HUD Overlay** section of the Configuration Sidebar to enable.

Delete a Custom Trackpad Gesture

BetterTouchTool offers three deletion options. You can delete the action associated with a gesture, you can delete the gesture itself, or you can delete an application and all of its custom gestures.

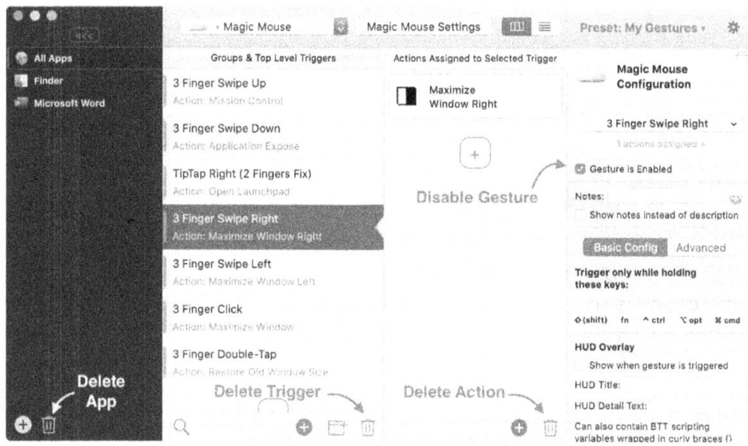

To delete an action associated with a gesture, highlight the gesture in the Trigger List and then click on the trash can icon in the Action List.

To delete an entire gesture, highlight the gesture you wish to delete and then click the trash can icon in the Trigger List.

If you want to delete an application and all of its associated gestures, highlight the application in the App List and click the trashcan. Note that BetterTouchTool will not let you delete **All Apps** and **Finder** from the App List.

Disable a Custom Gesture

If you prefer to disable a gesture rather than deleting it, you can do so by unchecking the checkbox next to **Gesture is Enabled** in the Configuration Sidebar.

Import and Export Gestures

If you want to share gestures with friends or want to create a backup of your custom gestures, you can export your BetterTouchTool gestures to a file. BetterTouchTool's **Preset** feature lets you import and export your gestures.

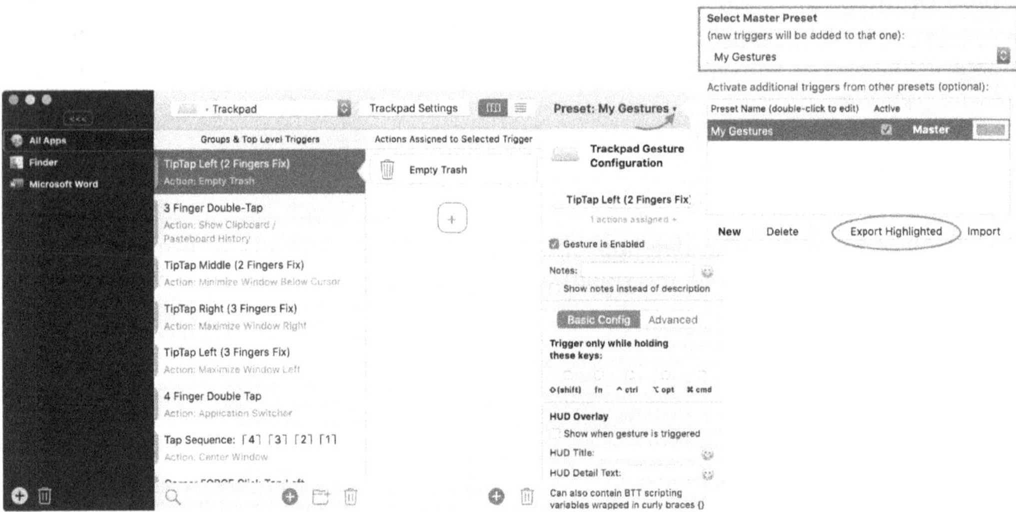

Click **Preset: My Gestures** in the upper-right corner of the BetterTouchTool configuration pane to reveal the Preset configuration sheet. Select the gestures from the list of presets and then click **Export Highlighted**. A save dialog opens. Choose to save **Only Tiggers** or **Triggers & Settings**. Name your file, choose the save location, and press **Save**.

To import a gesture file, click **Preset: My Gestures** and then click **Import** from the configuration sheet. Browse to the gesture file, select it, and click **Open**.

3

Desktop

The **Desktop** is the main component of macOS and provides the majority of your user experience. From the Desktop, you can launch and quit applications, tell your Mac to execute commands, manage files and folders, open, close, and move application windows, launch applets called Menu Extras, and restart, sleep, or shut down your Mac. All folders, files, and application windows appear on the Desktop. Even though you generally work within application windows, those windows are delivered to you via the Desktop.

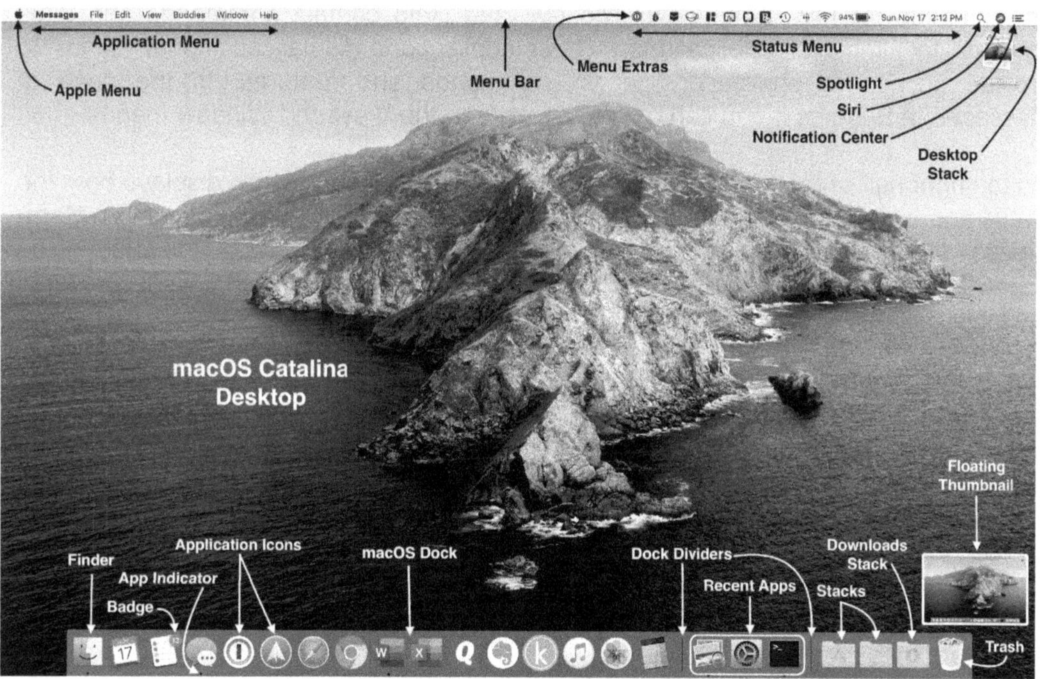

The Desktop consists of three major components – the **Menu Bar** along the top of your display, the **Dock** along the bottom, and the macOS Desktop itself. Both the Menu Bar and the Dock have sub-components that deliver specific features and functionality that we will discuss next.

The **Menu Bar**, located along the top of your Desktop, allows you to run system-wide commands, run commands within applications, check the status of your Mac, and execute applets that provide additional functionality. The Menu Bar consists of two halves. The left half is comprised of two elements, the Apple Menu in the upper-left corner of your display and the Application Menu, while the right half contains the Status Menu and icons to access Spotlight, Siri, and Notification Center.

The **Apple Menu**, denoted by the , is a drop-down menu where you can access system-wide commands to purchase and install applications from the Mac App Store, view hardware and software information, configure System Preferences, open recent applications and documents, force quit misbehaving apps, sleep, restart, or shut down your Mac, and log out.

To the immediate right of the menu is the **Application Menu**, a set of application-specific drop-down menus for the currently active application. Only one application is active at any given time, and the name of the currently active application is shown in bold text to the right of the menu. In the picture on the previous page, the active application is Messages. The Application Menu is named for the currently active application, and in this example, it is called the Messages Menu. You can always tell which application is active by looking at the Application Menu.

The Application Menu changes as you open or switch between applications. The drop-down menus for File, Edit, View, Window, and Help contain commands and tools common to almost all applications. Other applications display additional menus to provide access to application-specific commands and features. In the case of Messages, a Buddies menu can be found between the View and Window menus.

On the right half of the Menu Bar, you'll find the **Status Menu**, which displays both the status and provides quick access to various macOS features via applets called **Menu Extras**. Note that if you upgraded from a previous version of macOS and customized your Status Menu as I did, your Status Menu may look different than what is shown in the picture on the previous page.

I know they are hard to see, but the Menu Extras in the picture on the previous page are, from left to right, 1Password, Backblaze, Unclutter, Amphetamine, Magnet, BetterTouchTool, Deliveries, Bitdefender, Time Machine, Bluetooth, Wi-Fi, Battery Monitor, Date & Time, Spotlight, Siri, and Notification Center. We'll cover these applets in detail later.

Clicking the **Spotlight** icon launches Spotlight, where you can search for files, folders, applications, events, reminders, music, movie showtimes, nearby locations, Music, the App Store, messages, and the Internet.

Siri is Apple's intelligent virtual assistant application, familiar to anyone who owns an iPhone. If you use Siri on your iPhone, you'll find the macOS version to be quite similar. Siri on macOS features the same natural language interface that adapts to your language usage and search preferences.

In the upper-right-hand corner of the Menu Bar is the icon for **Notification Center**, a one-stop-shop that consolidates notifications from any Apple or third-party apps that support notifications including Mail, Messages, Reminders, Music, Calendar, Stocks, Evernote, Facebook, Twitter, LinkedIn, and many others. You can also configure Notification Center to provide notifications from websites that support Apple's push notification service.

And last but not least is the macOS **Desktop** itself, which is where windows appear when you launch an application. The Desktop is just like your desk at your home, school, or office. It's a place where all the fun happens, and occasionally, some work. You'll use the Desktop to move, organize, and close application windows. And just like a real desk, you can make it neat or leave it cluttered. You can personalize it, organize it, and keep the files you are currently working on handy.

I'll show you how to personalize your Desktop in this chapter. You'll learn techniques to manage the Desktop clutter that inevitably comes with using any computer. Once you've personalized your Desktop, I'll show you techniques to manage windows and how to increase your Desktop space. Then, I'll teach you how to customize the Menu Bar. The Dock is so customizable that I wrote a chapter specifically focusing on its customization. Because Stacks, which are a component of the Dock, are also extremely customizable, they deserved their chapter too. After the chapters on the Dock and Stacks, you'll learn about Spotlight and how to customize it and search more efficiently and accurately. Next up is Siri. We'll wrap up the Desktop topics by exploring Notification Center's features and personalization options. First, let's start with your first Desktop customization, changing the Desktop wallpaper.

Change the Desktop Wallpaper

Keeping with its tradition of naming macOS releases after iconic places in California, Apple named its latest macOS release after Santa Catalina Island, a rocky island off the coast of Southern California. The name of the island is often shortened to Catalina. Located in the Gulf of Santa Catalina 29 miles south-southwest of Long Beach, California, Catalina is one of the eight Channel Islands of California and is part of Los Angeles County. Eighty-five percent (85%) of the 76 square-mile island is Open Space Conservancy. The only incorporated city is Avalon, a seaport village located on the eastern side of the island with a permanent population of approximately 4,000. Catalina was developed into a tourist destination by chewing gum magnate William Wrigley, Jr. in the 1920s, and today over one million tourists visit Catalina annually.

Apple chose a spectacular image of the sun-baked, rocky northwestern point of Catalina, looking towards Silver Peak and Mount Orizaba, the highest point on the island, for the default Catalina Desktop wallpaper. Another default wallpaper features the same view at night. The nighttime wallpaper is perfect if you prefer the macOS Dark Mode while the daytime image can be used when in Light Mode. We'll cover Light and Dark Modes later in this chapter.

While the images of Catalina are stunning, you don't have to live with the wallpaper Apple chose for you. Apple included other images from which you can select, including backgrounds from previous releases of macOS. Or, if you wish, you can change your wallpaper to any picture or set of pictures you want.

There are often numerous ways to do the same thing in macOS. It is up to you to decide which method works best. To change your Desktop wallpaper, secondary click anywhere on the Desktop to display the Desktop contextual menu. Select **Change Desktop Background…** to open the **Desktop & Screen Saver** preference pane.

Another option is to open the **Desktop & Screen Saver** preference pane from the System Preferences application. Once the **Desktop & Screen Saver** preference pane opens, ensure the **Desktop** tab is selected. The current Desktop wallpaper is shown in the upper-left portion of the pane. In this case, I have selected the Catalina Day wallpaper. The sidebar allows you to select from images provided by Apple, colored backgrounds also provided by Apple, or images located in a folder on your of your choice. Thumbnails of the images are shown in the right pane.

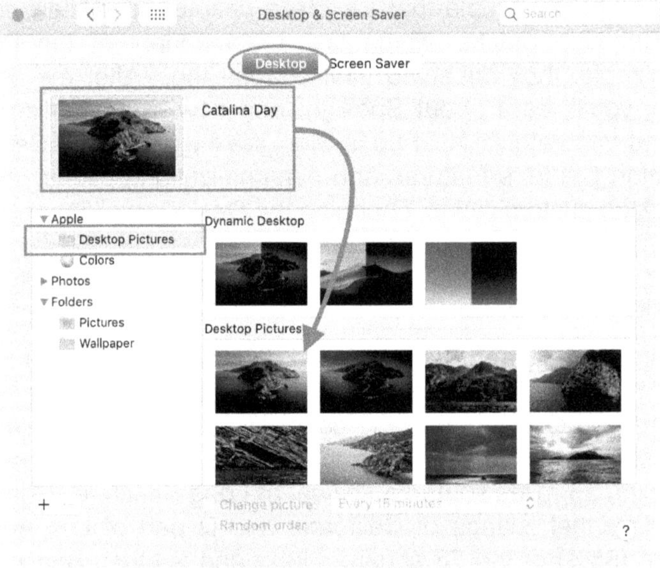

Apple provides a set of standard wallpaper images under **Apple > Desktop Pictures**. If you like one of the standard images, click to select it. Apple also offers a set of solid color wallpaper images under **Apple > Colors**.

You don't have to settle for one image. You can select any or all of the images, and macOS changes your Desktop wallpaper at an interval chosen by you. Check the checkbox next to **Change picture** and select how frequently you want macOS to change your Desktop wallpaper. You have a choice of refreshing your Desktop wallpaper image when logging in, when waking from sleep, every 5 seconds, 1 minute, 5 minutes, 15 minutes, 30 minutes, every hour, or every day.

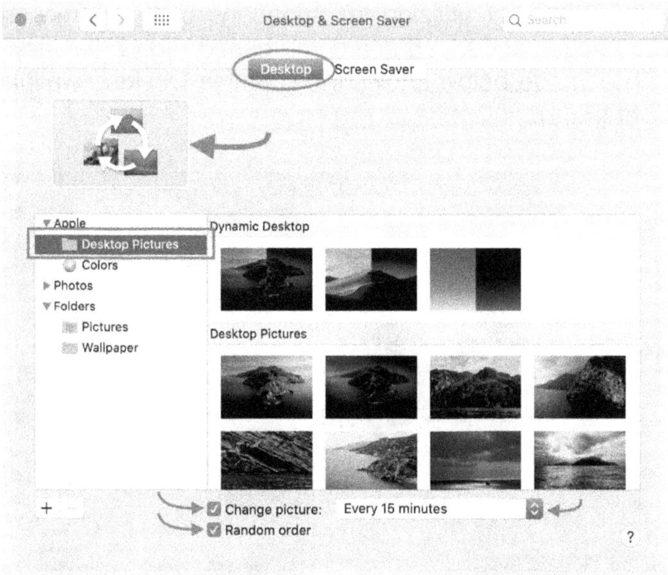

When you check **Change picture**, the picture in the upper-left of the **Desktop & Screen Saver** preference pane changes to show a set of circular arrows. Select how frequently you want macOS to change your wallpaper from the drop-down menu next to **Change picture**. By default, macOS cycles through the wallpaper sequentially from the first picture to the last. Check the checkbox next to **Random order**, and macOS selects images randomly.

Enable Dynamic Desktop

Dynamic Desktop changes the lighting conditions of the default Catalina wallpaper throughout the day based on the time in your location. As the sun moves across the sky, the lighting and shadows change until a nighttime version appears.

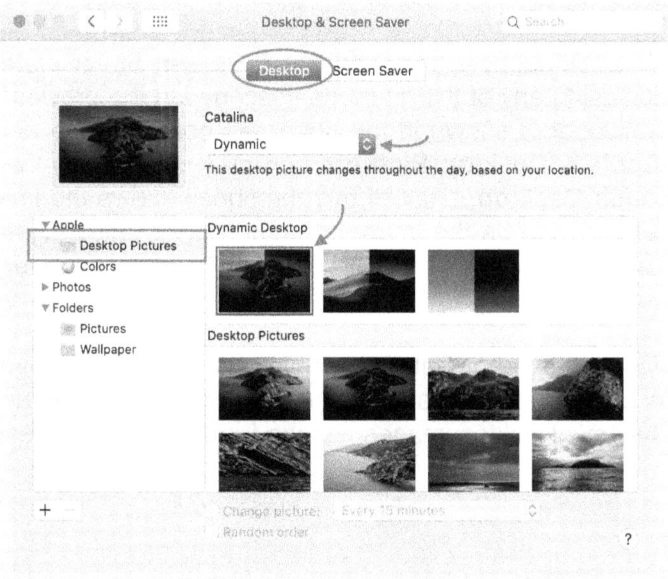

This effect is accomplished by utilizing 16 variations of the same image of Santa Catalina Island. The images are saved in a compressed High Efficiency Image Format (HEIF) container. The image below shows the Catalina Desktop wallpaper during the day (left) and at night (right).

HEIF is an image format that Apple began using on iPhones with the introduction of IOS 11 in 2017. The advantage of HEIF is that images saved in HEIF take up less storage space, support more colors, and are a higher quality compared to JPEG. HEIF uses a more complex, modern compression algorithm than JPEG, which has been around since 1992. A HEIF image can be a single image, like a JPEG, or a container for a series of images – think about Apple's Live Photos feature on iPhones.

To enable Dynamic Desktop, open the **Desktop & Screen Saver** preference pane in System Preferences using any of the methods described in the previous section. The current Desktop wallpaper is shown in the upper-left portion of the pane. In the left sidebar, choose **Apple > Desktop Pictures** and click on the thumbnail of Catalina Island under **Dynamic Desktop**. Half of this thumbnail shows the image during the day while the other half depicts the image at night. Next, select **Dynamic** from the drop-down menu under **Catalina**. That's it. Now enjoy watching your Desktop as it changes throughout the day.

If you don't care for the image of Catalina, Apple offers two other Dynamic Desktop images – the sand dunes of the Mojave Desert from macOS Mojave and an image of a blue sky. The Dynamic Desktop images change from day to night based on the time in your location.

Switch to Dark Mode

Catalina allows you to change the appearance of the buttons, menus, and windows displayed in macOS. You have three choices – **Light**, **Dark**, or **Auto**. Light was the default on all versions of macOS before macOS Mojave, which first introduced a true Dark Mode. Catalina goes one better with Auto, which automatically adjusts the appearance of your Mac from light to dark throughout the day based upon the time in your location.

To change the appearance of your Mac, open the **General** preference pane in System Preferences, and select your desired appearance from the three choices at the top of the preference pane.

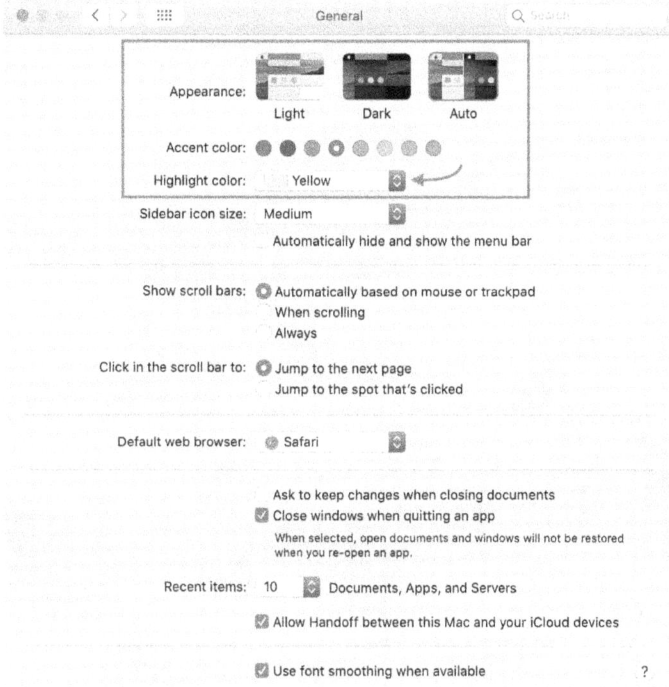

Change the Accent Color

The **Accent Color** is used for buttons, drop-down menus, and other macOS user interface controls. Blue is the default Accent Color in macOS. In addition to blue, Catalina offers purple, pink, red, orange, yellow, green, and graphite.

To change the Accent Color used by macOS, open the **General** preference pane in System Preferences, and select your desired Accent Color from the eight choices next to **Accent color**. Note that the **Highlight color** will change when you select your Accent color. You do not have to accept this and can change the Highlight Color using the drop-down menu next to **Highlight color**.

To switch back to the system defaults, open System Preferences, launch the **General** preference pane, and select **Light** in the **Appearance** section at the top of the pane. If you changed the **Accent Color** and **Highlight Color**, you can switch both back to the system default of **Blue**.

Use a Picture from Photos for your Desktop Wallpaper

Now that we know how to change the default Desktop wallpaper using the images provided by Apple let's leverage this knowledge to personalize your Desktop by using your images from the Photos application. You can use an image of your choice as your Desktop wallpaper, sharing it directly from the Photos application.

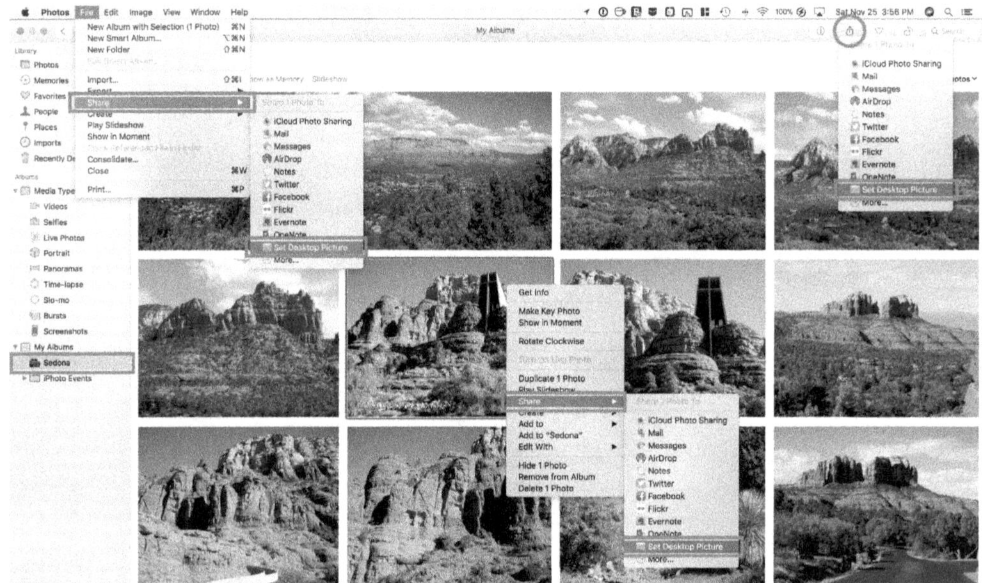

Launch the Photos application, find your desired picture, and click on it. A blue border appears around the photo. Click the **Share** button located in the upper-right of the Photos toolbar and select on **Set Desktop Picture** from the drop-down menu. You can also secondary click on your chosen image to reveal a contextual menu. Select **Share > Set Desktop Picture**. Alternatively, you can select **File > Share > Set Desktop Picture**. The picture above demonstrates all three available options.

If the size of your photo doesn't match the screen size of your Mac, open the **Desktop & Screen Saver** preference pane in the System Preferences application. Ensure the **Desktop** tab is selected. Use the drop-down menu to the right of the photo you selected. Choose the display option that works best – **Fill Screen**, **Fit to Screen**, **Stretch to Fill Screen**, **Center**, or **Tile**. The thumbnail will preview how your photo will look as you change the display option. A note of caution when using Stretch to Fill Screen, as this selection changes the aspect ratio of the photo and distorts the image.

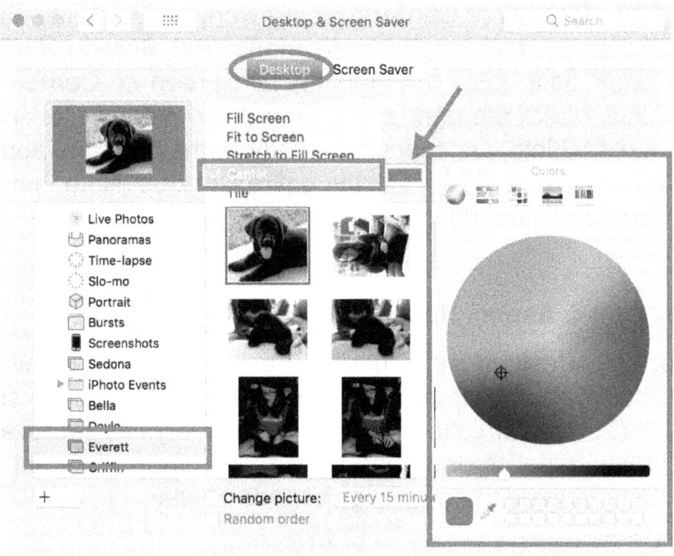

For photos in portrait mode, **Fit to Screen** and **Center** typically work best because the entire photo will be displayed. For photos in landscape mode, **Fill Screen**, **Fit to Screen**, or **Center** generally work best. For the **Fit to Screen** and **Center** options, you may notice a colored rectangle to the right of the drop-down menu. Clicking on the colored rectangle reveals a color wheel that lets you choose the color of the bars that appear on the left and right of your photo when the image doesn't fill the entire Desktop. This option will not appear if your image fills the entire Desktop.

Configure Multiple Pictures from Photos for your Desktop Wallpaper

You can choose multiple pictures in Photos and have macOS rotate through them. Open the **Desktop & Screen Saver** preference pane in System Preferences. Click on the gray triangle next to **Photos** in the sidebar at the left to open a list of available albums people, and shared photos. Click on one of the items in the list and select the photos you want as your wallpaper. Choose to display the photos sequentially or in random order. And don't forget to select how often you want macOS to change your picture.

If your photos are not in the same album, create a new album in Photos and add your pictures to it. You can create a new album in Photos by selecting **File > New Album…** or by entering **⌘N** (command+N). Once you have finished, open the **Desktop & Screen Saver** preference pane. In the sidebar at the left, expand Photos using the triangle, scroll to your new album, select it, and choose the display options. Be sure to configure how frequently your pictures change and whether macOS should display them in order or randomly.

If the size of your photo doesn't match the screen size of your Mac, use the drop-down menu to the right of the photos you selected and select the option that works best – **Fill Screen**, **Fit to Screen**, **Stretch to Fill Screen**, **Center**, or **Tile**. For photos in portrait mode, **Fit to Screen** or **Center** typically work best because the entire photo will be displayed. For photos in landscape mode, **Fill Screen**, **Fit to Screen** or **Center** generally work best. For both the **Fit to Screen** or **Center** options, you'll notice a colored rectangle to the right of the drop-down menu. Clicking on the color reveals a color wheel that lets you choose the color of the bars that appear on the left and right of your photo when it doesn't fill the entire Desktop. Note that this option will not appear if your image fills the entire Desktop.

Determine Resolution & Aspect Ratio

Another option for your Desktop wallpaper is to utilize a folder containing images. I like to collect Desktop wallpaper from the Internet, usually landscape scenes. I have hundreds of pictures in a folder called **Wallpaper** located in the **Pictures** folder of my **Home** directory. If you want to download wallpaper from the Internet, the first thing you need to do is to determine the resolution of your display.

When searching Google images (http://images.google.com) or any popular Desktop wallpaper site, you don't want just any image. You want images that match the native resolution of your display. An image with a resolution smaller than the native resolution will become pixelated, distorting the image when it is expanded to fit your higher resolution display.

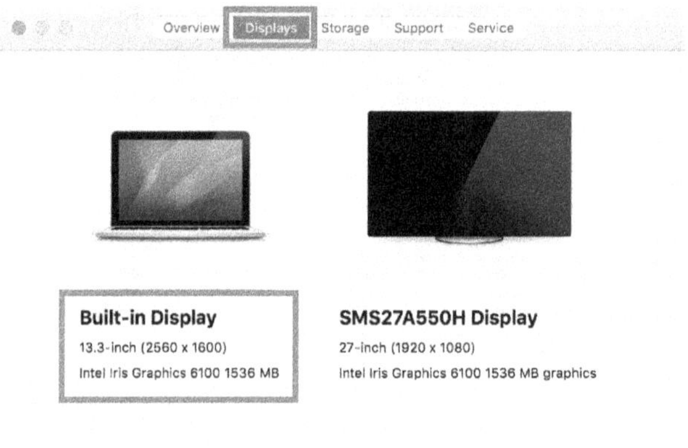

To find the resolution of your monitor, select > **About This Mac**. Click on the **Displays** tab to see your displays. The resolution of your monitor is listed under the name of the display. For example, the resolution of my 13-inch MacBook Pro's built-in monitor is 2560 x 1600. The numbers represent the width and height of the screen in pixels with the first number representing the width and the second, the height. The larger the number, the higher the resolution. I also have an older 27-inch external display, shown on the right in the picture below, with a resolution of 1920 x 1080.

Another important number is the aspect ratio, which is the proportional relationship between a display's width and its height. For my MacBook Pro's built-in display, the aspect ratio is calculated by dividing 2560 (its width in pixels) by 1600 (its height in pixels). The result is 1.6, which equates to an aspect ratio of 16:10. An image with an incorrect aspect ratio will not fit properly on the Desktop. When looking for wallpaper to fit my MacBook Pro, I look for images with a 16:10 aspect ratio and a minimum resolution of 2560 x 1600 pixels.

Use Images in a Folder as Desktop Wallpaper

To add an image folder, open the **Desktop & Screen Saver** preference pane in the System Preferences application. Click the **+** (plus) sign in the lower-left of the preference pane to open a **Finder** window so you can navigate to and select the folder containing your images.

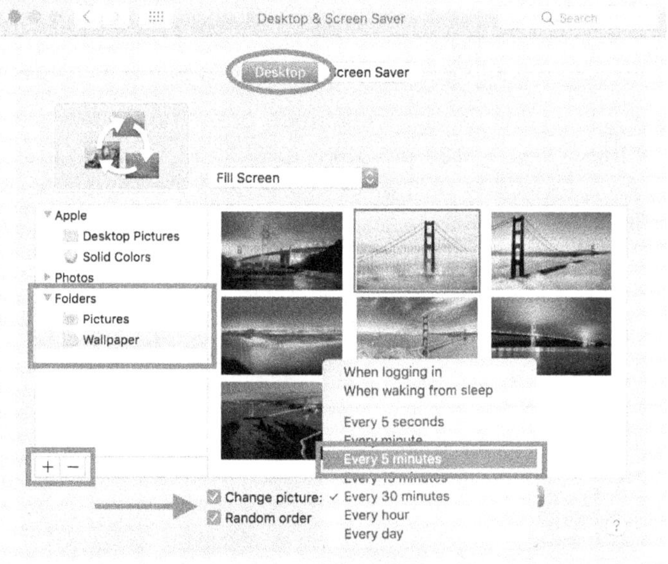

You can also drag a folder from a Finder window into the sidebar at the left of the Desktop & Screen Saver preference pane. To make the folder active, click on it and then choose display, frequency, and randomization options.

To remove a folder you no longer want to use, highlight it, and click the – (minus) button.

One of the advantages of using a folder as the source for your Desktop wallpaper is that macOS will automatically use any new images you add to this folder without any further configuration on your part. You can create multiple folders with themes (i.e., landscapes, animals, space, people) and use a different theme for each of your Desktop Spaces. We'll cover Desktop Spaces in the next chapter.

Access the Hidden Wallpaper Collections

Similar to previous versions of macOS, Apple bundled 40 beautiful high-resolution images in macOS Catalina that you can use as Desktop wallpaper. There are 7 gorgeous **Landscapes**, 8 images of the **Sierras**, 6 images of **Flowers**, 12 solid **Colors**, and 7 images of **Catalina**. Apple intended for you to use these images as screensavers; however, it only takes a couple of steps to add them to your wallpaper collection.

To use these hidden images as wallpaper, open **Finder**, and enter **⇧⌘G** (shift+command+G) to open the **Go to the folder** dialog box. Enter the following path and click **Go**.

```
/System/Library/Screen Savers/Default Collections/
```

Finder displays 5 folders, numbered from 1 to 5 and labeled **Landscapes**, **Sierras**, **Flowers**, **Colors**, and **Catalina**, respectively, each containing high-resolution images you can use as your Desktop wallpaper.

To use any of these collections as your wallpaper, open the **Desktop & Screen Saver** preference pane in the System Preferences application. Click on the **Desktop** tab at the top of the pane. Drag each of the folders or just the ones you want to the left sidebar under **Folders**.

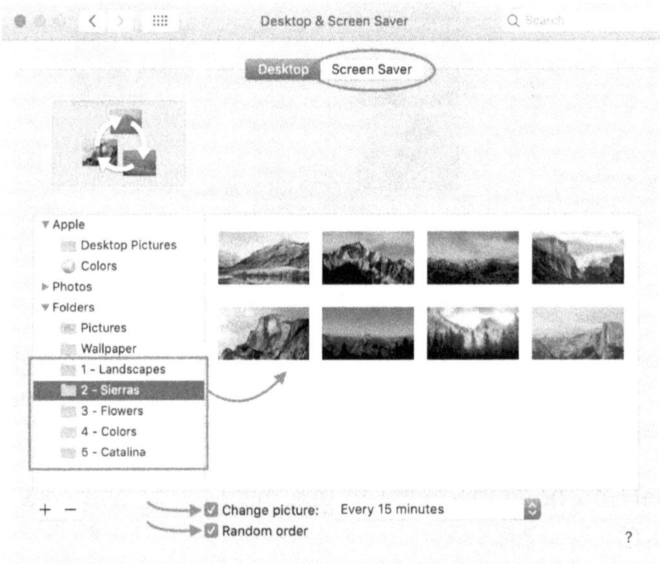

If you have a folder configured as the source for your Desktop wallpaper, you can copy the individual image files into your wallpaper folder. Open each of the collections by double-clicking its folder. Select the images you like, press the hold the ⌥ (option) key while dragging into your images folder to copy them.

Configure the Screensaver

Screen savers are a throwback to the days of cathode ray tube (CRT) monitors. If an image was displayed for too long on a CRT monitor, it would eventually burn a ghost image onto the screen. This is a phenomenon called phosphor burn-in. Screen savers were designed to prevent phosphor burn-in by filling the screen with moving images or patterns when the screen was not in use. Phosphor burn-in is no longer an issue with modern computers, which use Liquid Crystal Display (LCD) or Light Emitting Diode (LED) as these technologies are not susceptible to phosphor burn-in. Today screensavers are primarily used for entertainment purposes.

If you would like to configure a screen saver, open the **Desktop & Screen Saver** preference pane and click on the **Screen Saver** tab at the top of the pane. macOS Catalina offers 19 different screen saver options, which are shown in the list of screensavers in the sidebar of the **Desktop & Screen Saver** preference pane.

The screen saver option chosen in the sidebar can be previewed on the right side of the pane. Apple included 5 default collections: **Landscapes**, **Sierras**, **Flowers**, **Colors,** and **Catalina**, accessible under the drop-down list next to **Source**.

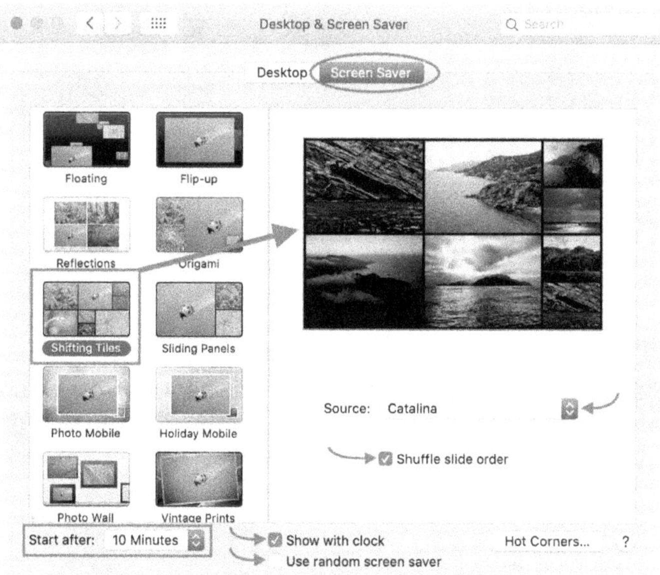

Checking the checkbox next to **Shuffle slide order** displays the images randomly.

Select an inactivity time from the drop-down menu next to **Start After**. You can start your screensaver after 1, 2, 5, 10, 20, 30, or 60 minutes of inactivity. You also can select **Never**, which effectively disables the screen saver.

If you want the screen saver to display the time, check the checkbox next to **Show with clock**. Check the checkbox next to **Use random screen saver** if you want macOS to select the screensaver randomly.

Use a Photos Library as your Screensaver

You can select a library from Photos for your screen saver. Select **Photo Library...** from the drop-down menu next to **Source** in the **Desktop & Screen Saver** preference pane. This populates the sidebar with **Albums**, **People**, and **Events** from your Photos app. Select your choice from the sidebar and click **Choose** to finish.

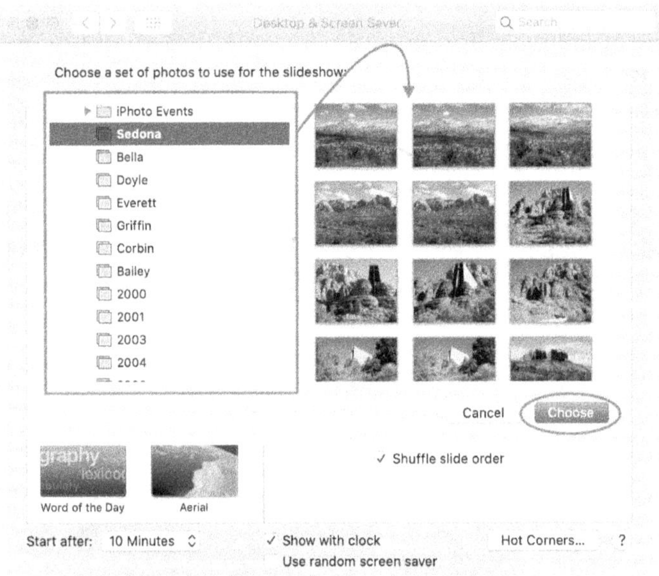

Display a Message as the Screensaver

macOS lets you display a message on your computer as your screen saver. From the **Desktop & Screen Saver** preference pane, click on the **Screen Saver** tab at the top of the preference pane.

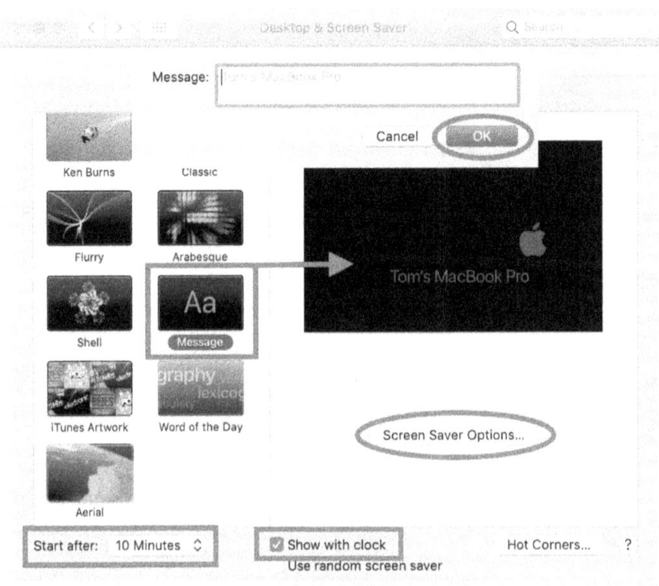

Scroll down to find the **Message** screen saver located towards the bottom of the sidebar. By default, macOS displays the name of your computer as the screen saver message. If you would like to display a custom message, click the **Screen Saver Options...** button. Enter your message in the drop-down configuration sheet and click **OK** when done.

Don't forget to set the inactivity timer from the drop-down menu under **Start after**. Check the box next to **Show with clock** if you would like to show the time along with your message.

Use an Images Folder for your Screensaver

You can also choose a folder by selecting **Choose folder...** from the drop-down menu next to **Source:** on the right side of the **Desktop & Screen Saver** preference pane. Doing so opens Finder, allowing you to navigate to a folder of images. Click the **Choose** button when you have selected your folder to finish.

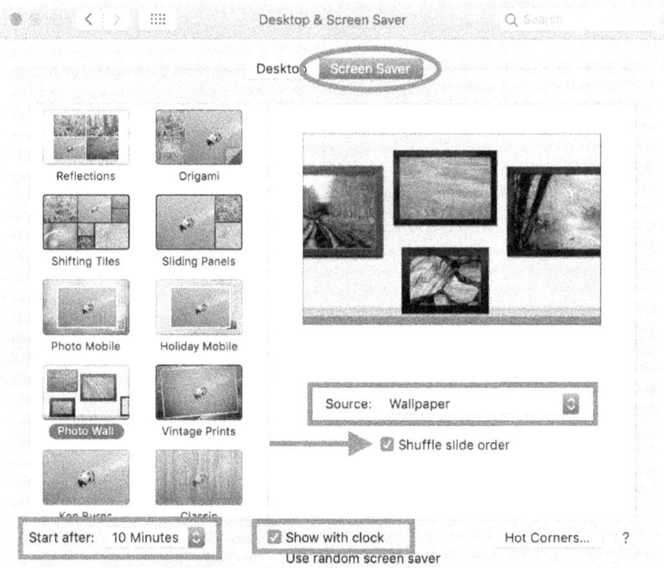

Don't forget to set the inactivity timer from the drop-down menu under **Start after**. Check the box next to **Show with clock** if you would like to show the time on your screen saver.

Use a Random Screensaver

Can't decide which Screen Saver to use? Apple makes it easy for you. Check the checkbox next to **Use random screen saver** and your Mac will randomly select a screensaver for you.

Configure Amazing AppleTV Aerial Screensavers

If you own an Apple TV, you've experienced its amazing, high-quality screensavers of daytime and nighttime flyover footage of China, Dubai, Greenland, Hawaii, Hong Kong, London, Los Angeles, New York City, San Francisco, and Earth. You can experience these gorgeous screensavers on your Mac by installing **Aerial** screensaver written by John Coates.

To add the AppleTV Aerial screensavers, download theAerial screensaver available at https://github.com/JohnCoates/Aerial. Once the file has downloaded, double-click Aerial.saver, which is saved in your **Downloads** folder.

If you have the default macOS security settings configured and will see a pop-up warning that Aerial.saver is from an unidentified developer. The security warning means that this application has not been registered with Apple. Click **OK** in the warning box and then launch the **Security & Privacy** preference pane from System Preferences. Click the **General** tab if it is not already highlighted. Under **Allow apps downloaded from** you will see the following warning. *"Aerial.saver" was blocked from opening because it is not from an identified developer.* Click **Open Anyway**.

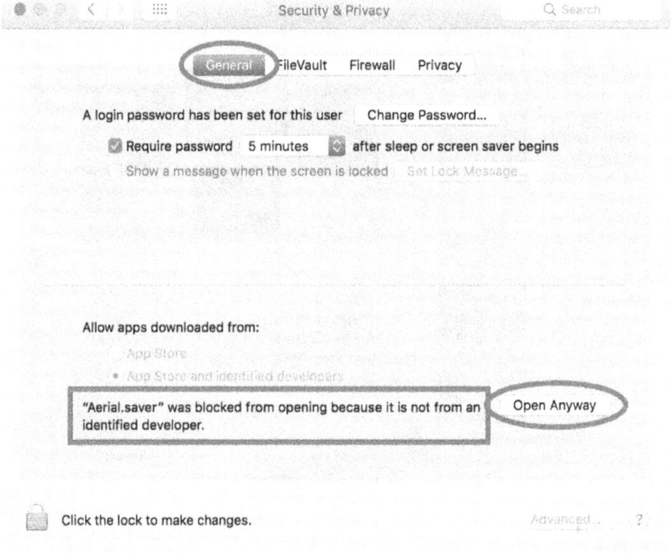

Next, select **Install for all users of this computer** from the configuration sheet and click **Install**. Once installed, launch the **Desktop & Screen Saver** preference pane and click on the Screen Saver tab. Scroll to the bottom of the list of screensavers in the left sidebar. Click on **Aerial** and then select **Screen Saver Options...** to customize Aerial screen saver.

Clicking **Screen Saver Options...** takes you to the configuration page, which allows you to configure Aerial's options, including the videos you want to play, video caching, and preferred video format. You can select all or a subset of the 88 screensavers. By default, all of the screensavers are enabled. Scrolling through the screensavers, you will see day and night scenes. Click on the screensavers to preview. By default, videos are cached as they are played. If you would like to cache the videos ahead of time, click the **Videos** tab, click the Settings button, the one that looks like a gear, and choose **Download Checked** or **Download All** from the drop-down menu.

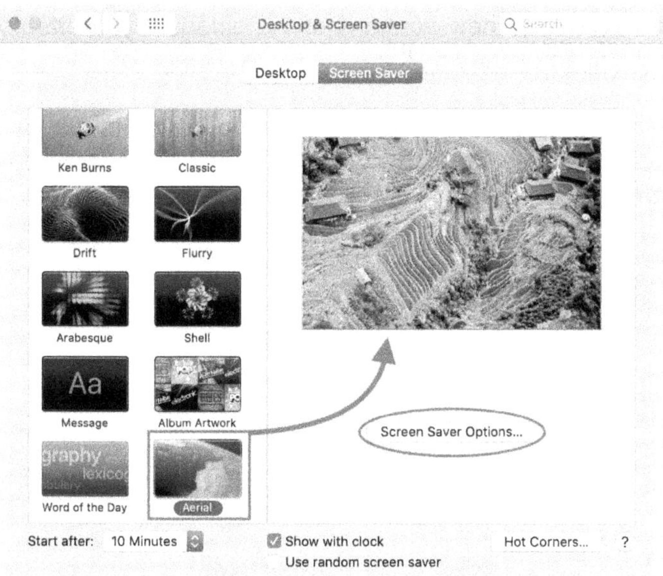

You can disable any of the screensavers by unchecking its checkbox. Be sure to set the inactivity timer from the drop-down menu under **Start after**. Check the box next to **Show with clock** if you would like to show the time when the screen saver plays. If you want to override the battery settings and play Aerial when your laptop is on battery power, check the checkbox next to **Override on battery** and choose a video format.

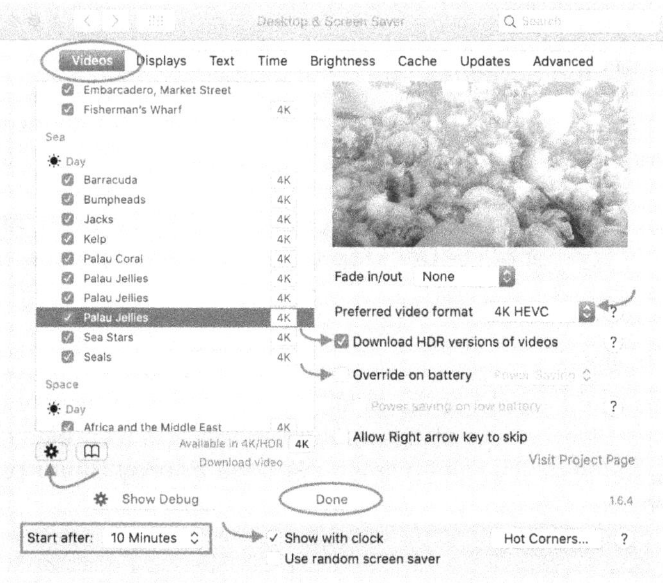

Set your **Preferred video format** from the drop-down menu. If your Mac is older than a 2017 model, you should choose 1080p H.264. Otherwise, you can choose 1080p HEVC or 4K HEVC. Note that videos are not available in every format with older videos not available in 4K and new videos not available in 1080 H.264. Aerial will play the best format available based on your preferred video format. With macOS Catalina, Aerial will download new versions of the videos if you enable HDR. These videos use Dolby Vision to display a Higher Dynamic Range of colors and lighting.

If you have multiple displays, Aerial screen saver allows you to play a different scene on each of your displays, which is really cool. Be sure the drop-down menus are configured, as shown in the image below. Click **Done** when finished.

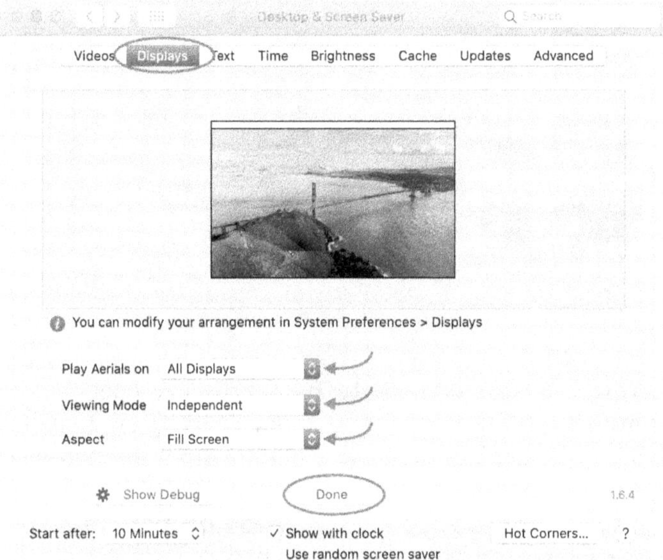

Permanently Disable the Screensaver

Since screensavers serve no useful purpose with modern computer displays, other than their entertainment value, you may wish to permanently disable the screen saver.

To disable the screen saver, select the **Never** option from the **Start After** drop-down menu in the lower-left corner of the **Desktop & Screen Saver** preference pane.

Put the Display to Sleep

If you don't want to use a screen saver at all, you can put your display to sleep after a period of inactivity. The benefit of this feature is that it saves electricity or battery power. To configure the display sleep timer, open the **Energy Saver** preference pane in System Preferences.

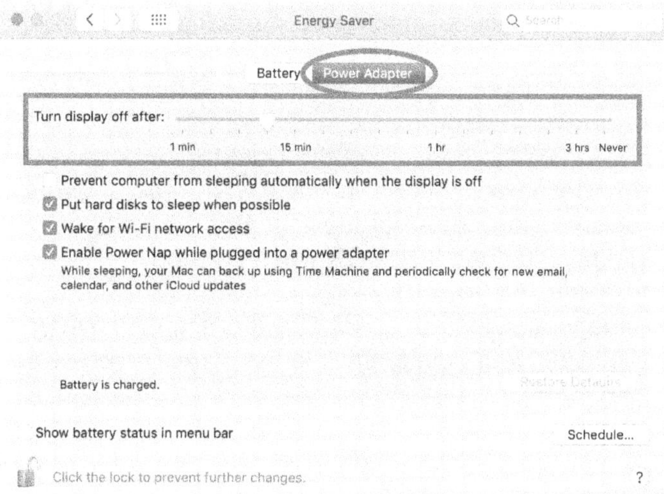

Note that the display sleep timer is configured separately for when your Mac is on battery or AC power. Select **Battery** or **Power Adapter** from the top of the **Energy Saver** preference pane. Next, configure the inactivity timer under **Display sleep** by dragging the slider to the left or right until the desired time has been selected. Be sure to configure inactivity timers for both **Battery** and **Power Adapter** if you own a MacBook, MacBook Air, or MacBook Pro laptop. When the inactivity timer expires, macOS turns off your display.

Configure Hot Corners

The macOS **Hot Corners** feature allows you to assign a specific action to any or all of the four corners of your Desktop. The associated command is executed by moving your pointer to the corner assigned the action you wish to perform.

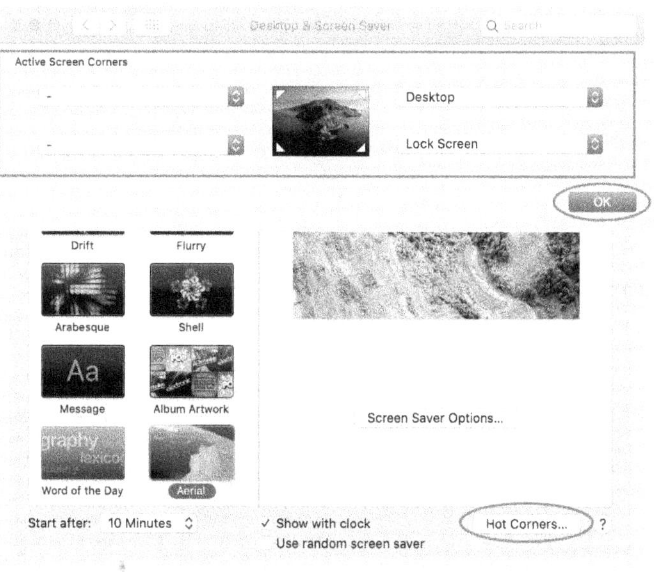

The supported commands include starting or disabling the screen saver, opening Mission Control, Application Windows (App Exposé), show the Desktop, Notification Center, or Launchpad, putting your display to sleep, and Lock Screen.

To assign commands to Hot Corners, open the **Desktop & Screen Saver** preference pane. Click the **Hot Corners...** button in the lower-right to reveal a configuration sheet. Assign an action to any or all of the four **Hot Corners** using the drop-down menu associated with each corner. Click **OK** when finished.

To execute the command assigned to a **Hot Corner**, simply move your pointer to the appropriate corner. Moving your pointer back to the corner reverses the command.

To turn off **Hot Corners**, open the **Desktop & Screen Saver** preference pane and select the **Screen Saver** tab. Next, click the **Hot Corners...** button in the lower-right corner of the pane. Select the – from the drop-down menu for each corner that you want to disable.

Hot corners can also be configured in the **Mission Control** preference pane. To set up Hot Corners, open the **Mission Control** preference pane in the System Preferences.

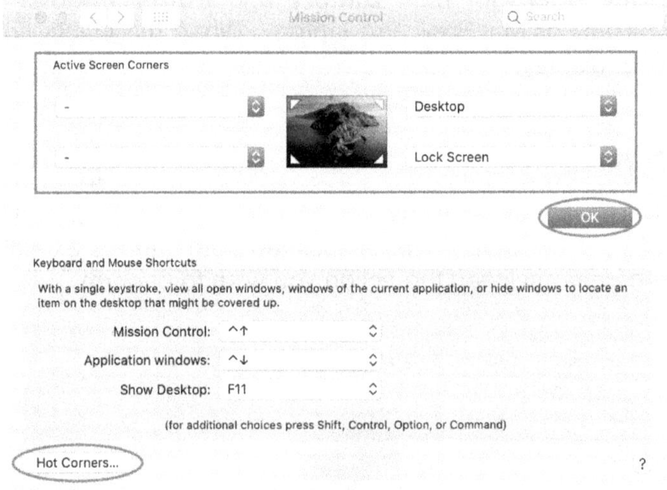

Next, click the **Hot Corners...** button in the lower-left of the pane to reveal the configuration sheet. You can assign a command to any or all of the corners. The supported commands are the same as those in the **Desktop & Screen Saver** preference pane.

To turn off Hot Corners, open the **Mission Control** preference pane and click the **Hot Corners...** button in the lower-left corner. Select the – from the drop-down menu for each corner that you want to turn off.

Avoid Accidentally Triggering a Hot Corner

The Hot Corners feature is very handy, but one problem is that by moving your pointer close to an Active Screen Corner, you can accidentally trigger the assigned command. Often simply moving the pointer to the menu accidentally triggers the command associated with the upper-left corner.

To avoid accidentally triggering an Active Screen Corner, you can configure Hot Corners to utilize a modifier key. For example, you can configure Hot Corners so that the ⌘ (command) key must be held down to execute the command when the pointer is moved to a Hot Corner. Using a modifier key eliminates the possibility of accidentally triggering a Hot Corner.

To configure Hot Corners to require a modifier key, open the **Desktop & Screen Saver** preference pane. Click on the **Screen Saver** tab at the top of the pane. Next, click the **Hot Corners...** button in the lower-right to display the Hot Corners configuration drop-down menu.

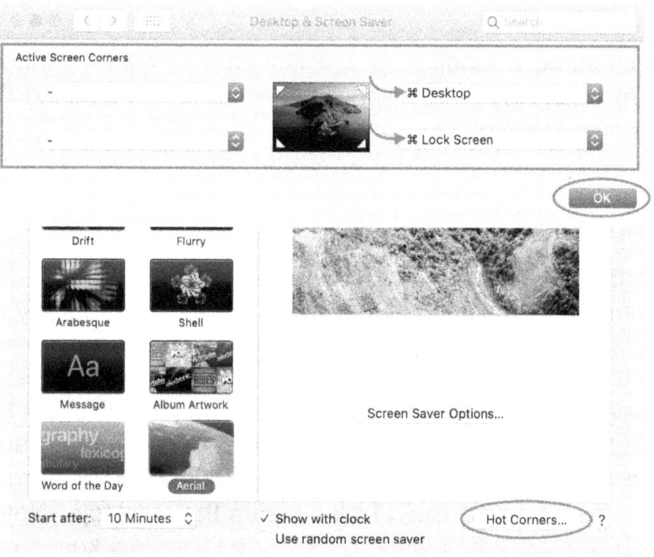

To add a modifier key, hold down the desired modifier key(s) when selecting an action from the drop-down menu. For example, I am holding down the ⌘ (command) key while selecting the **Desktop** and **Lock Screen** commands in the above image. Any of the following modifier keys are supported: ⇧ ⌘ ^ ⌥ (shift, command, control, or option). macOS even allows you to use any combination of two, three, or all four of the modifier keys.

You can also configure a Hot Corner modifier key in the **Mission Control** preference pane. Open the **Mission Control** preference pane and click the **Hot Corners...** button in the lower-left corner to reveal the drop-down configuration sheet. To add a modifier key, hold down the desired modifier key(s) when selecting an action from the drop-down menu. Any of the following modifier keys are supported: ⇧ ⌘ ^ ⌥ (shift, command, control, or option). macOS allows you to use any combination of two, three, or all four of the modifier keys.

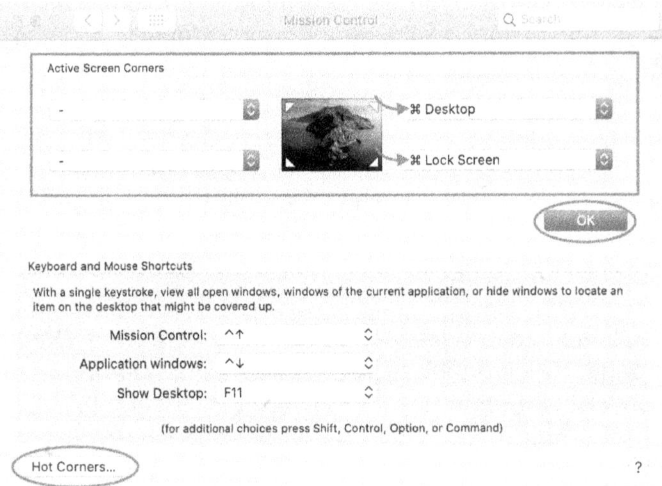

Once you have configured a modifier key, a Hot Corner will only trigger when you're holding down the modifier key(s) you specified – thereby eliminating the possibility of accidentally triggering a Hot Corner.

Show the Desktop

Have you ever wanted to look at a beautiful Desktop image only to find your Desktop is cluttered with windows? macOS offers several methods to quickly clear the clutter to view your Desktop wallpaper and put the clutter back when done.

If you configured the **Show Desktop** trackpad gesture, the quickest method to show the Desktop is by spreading your thumb and three fingers on your trackpad. All open windows will be pushed off the screen. Reverse the gesture to return the windows to their original locations. Pressing **fn F11** also clears the Desktop. Note that you have to hold down the **fn** (function) key while pressing **F11** as this key is normally used to lower the volume. Press **fn F11** to return the window clutter.

A couple of other options are to hold down the **⌘** (command) key while pressing **F3,** which is normally used to launch Mission Control. Enter **⌘F3** again to return the windows to their original locations on the Desktop.

You can also configure a Hot Corner to show the Desktop via the Desktop & Screen Saver or Mission Control preference panes.

Hide Applications to Clean Up Desktop Clutter

Having too many windows open on the Desktop can be distracting, especially if you are trying to concentrate on a particular window. Of course, you could always minimize or close all the windows or quit the applications entirely to clean up the clutter. But that takes time, and you may not want to quit all applications because you want to leave them open for later use. In that case, quitting or closing windows are not viable options. You could minimize each window; however, that could take a lot of time if you have lots of windows open. And minimized windows clutter the right side of the Dock, making each icon smaller and more difficult to differentiate as the Dock expands across the Desktop.

A handy feature is to hide all the other applications except for the one in which you are working. Hiding an application causes all of its windows to disappear without crowding the Dock. Because macOS remembers where the windows were located before you hid them, the windows will return to their original positions when unhidden. If you have lots of applications open and want to hide all but the application in which you are working, enter **⌥⌘H** (option+command+H). You can also choose to **Hide Others** from the Application Menu.

To hide the currently active application, enter **⌘H** (command+H), or select the **Hide** option from the Application Menu, the first menu to the right of the menu.

To unhide any application, simply click on its icon in the Dock, and macOS immediately restores the application's windows to their original locations. You can use **App Exposé** to see the windows of any application, whether hidden or not.

macOS also offers you the option of minimizing and hiding all windows using the keyboard shortcut **⌥⌘HM** (option+command+H+M). This keyboard shortcut minimizes the currently active application and hides all open windows.

How do you know which applications are hidden and which are not? By default, the macOS Dock does not differentiate between applications that are hidden and those that are not. A tweak I show you in the chapter on customizing the Dock will allow you to differentiate between hidden and unhidden applications.

Remove Devices from the Desktop

macOS displays icons of external hard drives or optical drives on the Desktop when you connect them to your Mac. These icons represent yet more Desktop clutter. There is no need to display external devices on the Desktop as they are available in the **Devices** list in the Finder Sidebar. macOS allows you to stop external devices from appearing on the Desktop. Additionally, turning off the display of external devices is particularly useful when you are using a Volumes Stack, which displays your internal and external drives and optical drives as a single stack in the Dock. See the chapter on Stacks to see how to create a Volumes Stack.

To disable the display of external devices on your Desktop open **Finder** and select **Preferences…** from the Finder menu or enter **⌘,** (command+comma). By default, macOS displays icons for hard drives, external drives, CDs, DVDs, iPods, and connected servers. To disable this feature, uncheck the checkboxes next to each of these items in the Finder preference pane. Changes take effect immediately, and any device icons on your Desktop will disappear. Don't worry. Your devices have not been removed. They have been hidden and can still be accessed from the Device list in Finder or through a Volumes Stack.

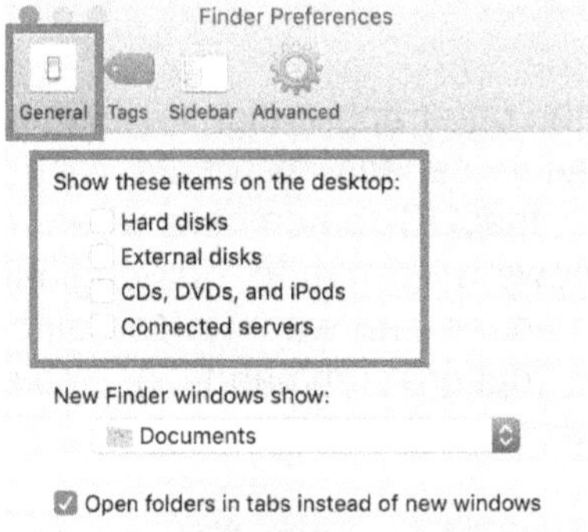

To return to the macOS default, open Finder and enter **⌘,** (command+comma) to open the Finder Preferences. Then check the checkboxes next to **Hard disks**, **External disks** and **CDs, DVDs, and iPods**, and **Connected servers**.

Enable Desktop Stacks

For many users, their Desktop quickly turns out to be the catch-all location for documents and other files they're working on. Screenshots are saved to the Desktop by default, and many applications save items there too. Desktop clutter can become overwhelming and detract from your ability to get work done. Not only does the mess make the Desktop look unsightly, it steals CPU and memory resources because each icon must be rendered and its contents previewed. If your Desktop has more icons than wallpaper, you have inadvertently made your Mac slower by forcing macOS to dedicate resources to render the clutter.

Items saved to the Desktop aren't saved to the Desktop. They are saved to the **Desktop** folder located in your **Home** directory. The Desktop folder is easily accessible from your Home directory, the Finder Sidebar, from a Desktop document stack in the Dock, or using the **Desktop Stacks** feature.

The Desktop Stacks feature is one of my favorite features of macOS. Desktop Stacks remove clutter by organizing and grouping the files on your Desktop into stacks. Desktop Stacks can instantly take a Desktop with a cluttered, unsightly, and disorganized mess of files and organize them by file type, date last opened, date added, date modified, date created, or by tags.

To enable Desktop Stacks, click on your Desktop to enable the Finder menu. Select **View > Use Stacks** or enter **^⌘0** keys (control+command+zero). Select **Group Stacks by** to group your files by **Kind**, **Date Last Opened**, **Date Added**, **Date Modified**, **Date Created**, or **Tags**. Choosing **None** disables Desktop Stacks.

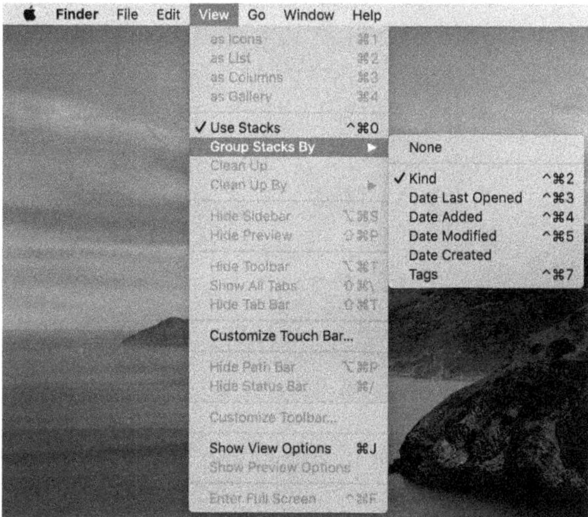

Desktop Stacks can instantly organize this unsightly mess of screenshots into an organized set of stacks based on your grouping choice. Click on a Desktop Stack to expand it to display its contents. Click on the Desktop Stack again to close the stack.

You can navigate through thumbnails of the files in a Desktop Stack by swiping left or right with your mouse or trackpad. Secondary click on the stack to reveal a contextual menu allows you to change the stack grouping.

Check out these before and after images to see how Desktop Stacks organized an unsightly mess of screenshots into a neat and tidy Desktop Stack.

You can also create a Desktop Stack in the Dock. See the chapter on customizing Stacks to learn how to create a Desktop Stack in the Dock.

Create a Pristine Desktop

If you want a super clean Desktop, this macOS tweak will give you a pristine Desktop, completely free of any clutter. Essentially this tweak turns off Desktop icons, preventing them from being displayed in the first place. This tweak also prevents you from dragging icons onto the Desktop. It also disables secondary clicking on the Desktop to create new folders, Get Info, or to change the Desktop wallpaper. However, each of these features is accessible via other means. This tweak also disables Desktop Stacks.

Launch **Terminal** and enter the following commands.

```
defaults write com.apple.finder CreateDesktop -bool FALSE
```

```
killall Finder
```

Any icons that normally would have appeared on your Desktop are safely tucked away in the Desktop folder in your Home directory, where they belong. This is a handy tweak if you are about to give an important presentation, and you are embarrassed by your lack of Desktop cleanliness.

To return to the default and risk a messy Desktop, enter the following commands.

```
defaults write com.apple.finder CreateDesktop -bool TRUE
```

```
killall Finder
```

Change the Desktop Icon and Text Size

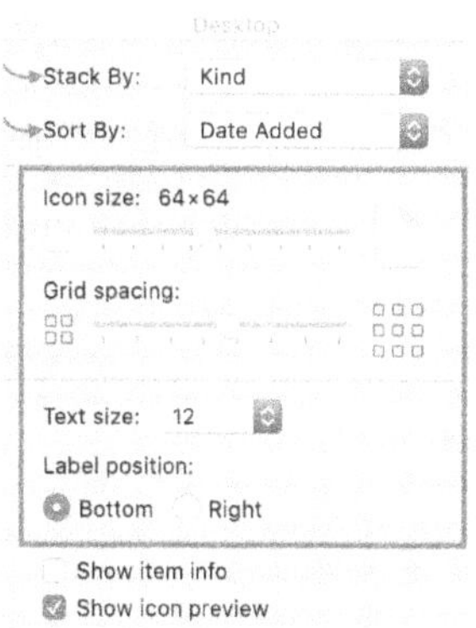

If you still want to see icons for devices and files on your Desktop, macOS gives you the option of changing the icon size.

To change the Desktop icon size, click anywhere on the Desktop and enter **⌘J** (command+J). This launches the **Desktop** view options panel. Note that the pristine Desktop hack must be disabled for **⌘J** to work. If it is enabled, open a Finder window and select **Desktop** under **Favorites** in the left sidebar and enter **⌘J** (command+J).

Use the **Icon size** slider to make the Desktop icons appear smaller by dragging the slider to the left. Or, if you want to make the icons appear bigger, drag the slider to the right. Changes take effect immediately. Note that the default size is 64 x 64.

The next slider controls the tightness of the grid separating the Desktop icons. For tighter spacing, drag the slider to the left. For more open spacing, drag the slider to the right.

The next section controls the size and location of the text label. macOS places the text label underneath the icon using a 12-point font. macOS lets you choose any text size between 10 and 16 points. The text label can be located at the bottom, which is the default, or to the right of the icon by selecting the appropriate radio button.

By default, **Show item info** is off. Checking this option adds the file size for files, the number of items in a folder, and the size and remaining space of disk drive to the text label.

By default, the **Show icon preview** checkbox is checked. Unchecking this box disables the macOS preview function. Only default icons indicating the application in which the file was created will be displayed instead of the file preview.

The top two options, pointed out by arrows, represent the current Desktop Stacks configuration. In the example shown above, items are stacked by **Kind** and Sorted by **Date Added**. The sort option is used to sort items within a Desktop Stack. Available sort options are by **Name**, **Kind**, **Date Last Opened**, **Date Added**, **Date Modified**, **Date Created**, **Size**, or **Tags**. Choosing **None** from the **Stack By** drop-down menu disables the Desktop Stacks feature. Choose any sort option to enable.

Adjust the Display Brightness

There are a couple of ways to adjust the display brightness of your Mac. First, you can use the **F1** and **F2** keys to adjust the brightness manually. Pressing **F1** makes your display darker, while **F2** makes it brighter.

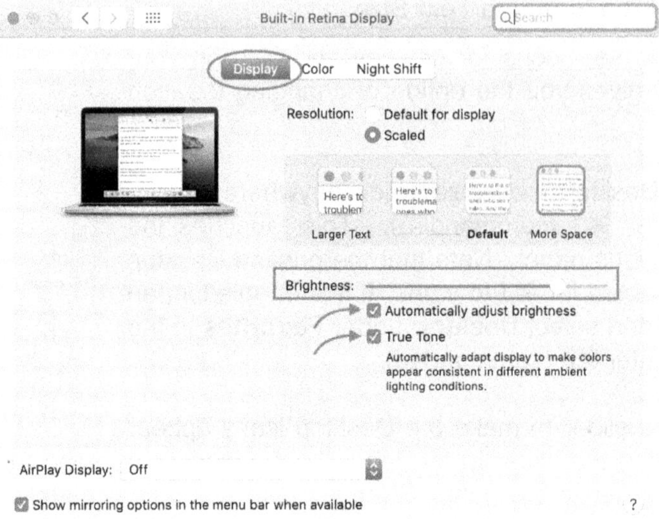

Another option is to adjust the display brightness in the **Displays** preference pane in System Preferences. Move the slider to the right to make the display brighter and to the left to make it darker.

Disable Automatic Brightness Adjustment

If your Mac has an ambient light sensor, it will adjust its display brightness automatically based on ambient light conditions. This feature is enabled by default in macOS. If you would like to disable it so that brightness can only be manually adjusted, launch the **Displays** preference pane and uncheck the checkbox next to **Automatically adjust brightness**.

If your Mac has a True Tone display, it will automatically adjust colors based on ambient lighting conditions. To disable this feature, uncheck the checkbox next to **True Tone** in the **Displays** preference pane.

Precisely Adjust the Display Brightness

Sometimes it seems you never can get the display brightness adjusted to your liking. One segment more is too much. One less is too little. Wouldn't it be awesome if you could adjust the display brightness in smaller increments? macOS has a solution!

Holding down the ⇧⌥ (shift+option) keys while pressing the **F1** or **F2** allows you to adjust the brightness in quarter-segment increments. This tweak also works if you have a MacBook Pro with a Touch Bar. Hold down the ⇧⌥ (shift+option) keys while tapping the display brightness control on the Touch Bar.

Sleep Better with Night Shift

The blue light emitted from your Mac's display mimics daylight, which can disrupt your body's sleep cycle. If you work on your Mac at night, your display's blue light tricks your brain into thinking it is daytime, causing your brain to not produce melatonin, making it harder for you to fall asleep.

Night Shift is a macOS feature that adjusts the color temperature of your display based on the time of day. Similar to the Night Shift feature on an iPhone and iPad, macOS will adjust your display's color temperature to provide warmer light during nighttime hours to help you sleep better.

To configure Night Shift, open the **Displays** preference pane in System Preferences. Select the **Night Shift** tab. Choose **Custom** or **Sunset to Sunrise** from the drop-down menu next to **Schedule**. If you select **Custom**, **From** and **to** fields appear for you to set the start and end times to enable and disable Night Shift. Choosing **Sunset to Sunrise** enables Night Shift based on when the sun sets and rises in your location. This is a handy feature if you travel with your Mac.

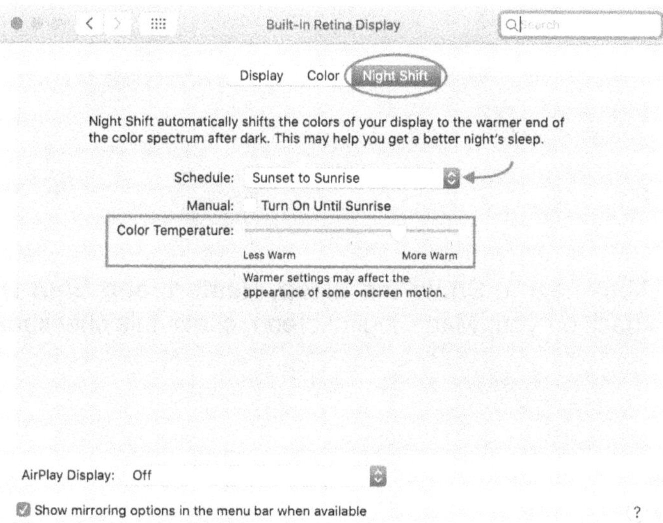

Use the slider next to **Color Temperature:** to select how warm you want your display when Night Shift is on. Move the slider to the right if you want more warmth and to the left, if you want less.

If you want to enable Night Shift immediately, check the checkbox next to **Turn On Until Sunrise**.

To disable Night Shift, launch the **Displays** preference pane, select the **Night Shift** tab, and choose **Off** from the drop-down menu next to **Schedule**.

Remove the Sleep, Restart, & Shutdown Buttons from the Login Screen

At the bottom of the login screen are three buttons – **Sleep**, **Restart**, and **Shut Down**. macOS lets you remove these buttons if you do not want them. Removing these buttons leaves you with only one option on the login screen – to log in.

To remove these buttons from the login screen, open the **Users & Groups** preference pane in the System Preferences application. Next, unlock the preference pane by clicking on the padlock in the lower-left corner, if locked. Enter your password when challenged. Select **Login Options** at the bottom left.

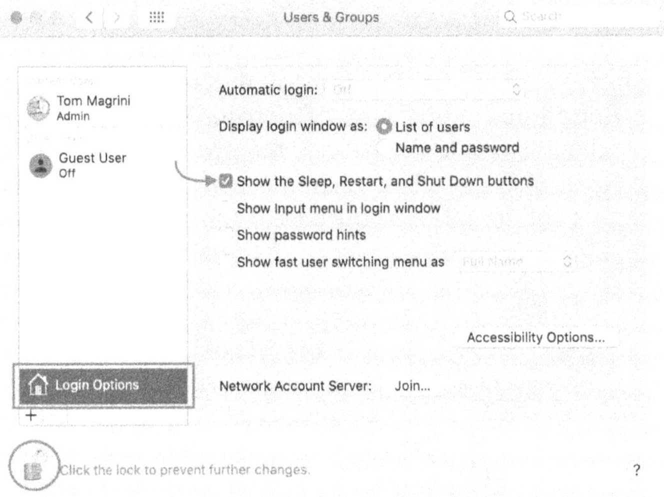

Uncheck the checkbox next to **Show the Sleep, Restart, and Shut Down buttons**. To put the buttons back on your Mac's login screen, check this checkbox.

4

Mission Control

Mission Control is the macOS feature that provides a view of everything on your Mac – windows, Full-screen apps, Split View apps, and Desktop Spaces. It allows you to jump to another Desktop, Full-screen app, apps running in Split View mode, or to an app running in another Space. Mission Control also allows you to move windows to other Desktops and create, rearrange, and delete Desktops.

To open **Mission Control**, use the trackpad gesture (swipe up with either 3 or 4 fingers), launch it from **Launchpad** or **Spotlight**, press the **F3** key, enter **^up** (control+up arrow), or tap its icon on the Touch Bar.

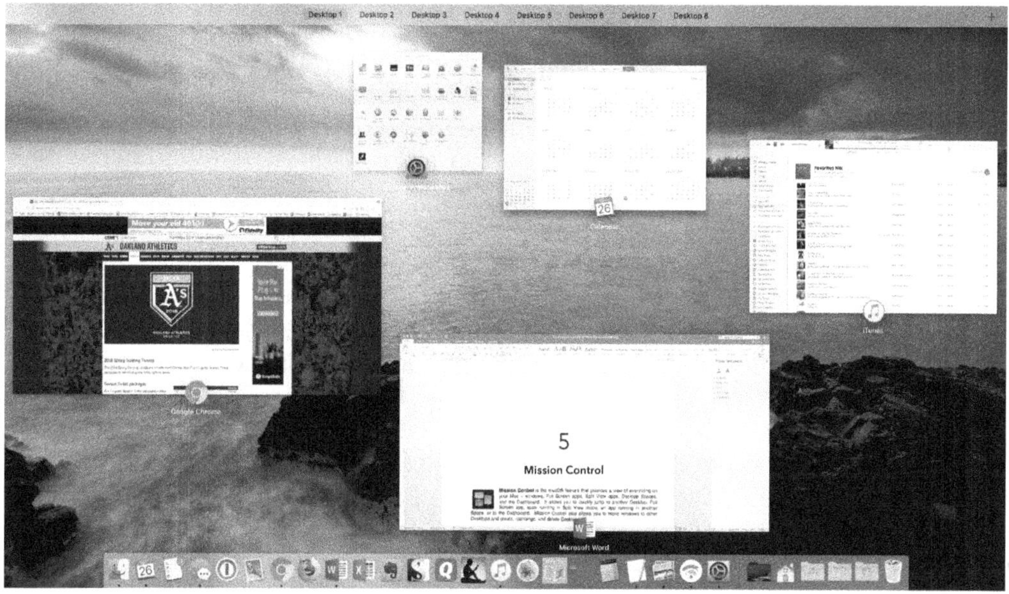

The ribbon at the top of Mission Control lists the Desktop Spaces. Moving your pointer into the ribbon expands the ribbon and the Desktop Spaces, Full-screen apps, and Split View apps into thumbnails, as shown in the image on the next page.

In the example above, Mission Control shows 8 Desktop Spaces, numbered Desktop 1 to 8 from left to right, and Music, located between Desktops 2 and 3, which I have expanded to a Full-screen application. Each Desktop Space is a virtual Desktop, created using the **Spaces** feature, and each one can have one or more windows assigned to it. The Spaces feature is a nifty way of increasing Desktop real estate to accommodate more windows. Spaces are covered in the next section.

You can rearrange the order of the Desktops by dragging and dropping them. Any Desktop, Full-screen application, or Split View app can be rearranged. macOS renumbers the Desktops accordingly as you rearrange them. Desktops are always numbered from left to right, starting from Desktop 1 at the left.

Navigating between the Desktops, Full-screen apps, and Split View apps is done by swiping either three or four fingers to the left or right on the trackpad. If you are using a Magic Mouse, swipe left or right with either one or two fingers. You can also hold down the ^ (control) key and press the left or right arrow to navigate. Clicking on any thumbnail in the Mission Control ribbon makes the Desktop Space active, bringing it, and the applications which are assigned to it, to the front.

The Dock appears at the bottom of Mission Control, letting you launch applications into the active Desktop Space, which is highlighted by a blue border in the ribbon at the top of Mission Control. If you try to launch an application while a Full-screen app is selected in Mission Control, the app opens in Desktop 1.

Add More Desktop Space

Desktop clutter can be a real productivity killer. If you have ever opened lots of applications and windows, you know how hard it is to sift through all of the windows looking for a particular one. If you only had more Desktop space, your Desktop would not be so cluttered, and life would be so much easier. macOS granted your wish. You can add more Desktop space with a macOS feature called **Spaces**.

Desktop Spaces is a feature of macOS that lets you create virtual Desktops. These virtual Desktops add real estate. Using Spaces, you can create additional Desktops, each containing a unique application or set of applications. Multiple Desktops remove clutter by allowing you to assign windows to separate Desktops instead of piling all the windows onto one Desktop. For example, let's say you were writing a book on customizing macOS using Microsoft Word, you can run Word on Desktop 1, and create separate Desktop Spaces for Music, Mail, and Safari – effectively quadrupling your Desktop real estate! Spaces are so flexible that windows from the same application can even be split between different Desktops.

Mission Control is the command center for Spaces, allowing you to create new Desktops, see and manage your Desktops, and see which windows are assigned to each. To create a new Desktop Space, first open Mission Control by using the trackpad gesture, launching it from Launchpad or Spotlight, pressing the **F3** key, entering **^up** (control+up arrow), or tapping its icon on the Touch Bar.

If you have never created a Desktop Space, the ribbon at the top of Mission Control will show a single Desktop, called **Desktop 1**. Creating a new Desktop Space is as simple as moving your pointer to the **+** sign at the far right edge of the Mission Control ribbon. When your pointer reaches the **+** sign, it expands to reveal a partial Desktop containing a **+** in a gray circle. Clicking this partial Desktop or the **+** creates a new Desktop Space.

macOS allows you to create up to 16 Desktop Spaces, numbered sequentially from left to right, starting with **Desktop 1**.

The picture above shows 4 Desktops in Mission Control, numbered 1 through 4. Microsoft Word and Chrome are running in Split View mode between Desktops 1 and 2. Music is running in Full-screen mode between Desktops 3 and 4. Did you notice anything about the Spaces in the image? Each one can have a different Desktop wallpaper.

Remove a Desktop Space

Removing a Desktop is done in **Mission Control**. Hover your pointer over the Desktop you want to remove at the top of Mission Control. An **X** appears in the upper-left corner of the Desktop thumbnail. Click the **X** to remove the Desktop. Any windows located in the deleted Desktop will be reassigned to the Desktop in the foreground. Any Desktop Space, Full-screen application, and Split View app can be removed in Mission Control.

You can use Mission Control to take an app out of Full-screen or Split View mode. Hover your pointer over a Full-screen or Split View app in Mission Control, and two arrows will appear in the upper-left corner. Click on the arrows, and the app exits Full-screen or Split View mode and moves to the next available Desktop to the left.

Another method to remove a Desktop is to move your pointer to the Mission Control ribbon and hold down the ⌥ (option) key. An **X** will appear in the upper left-hand corner of every Desktop. Remove Desktops by clicking on the **X** while keeping the ⌥ (option) key depressed. Full-screen and Split View apps display two arrows, allowing you to exit Full-screen or Split View mode. Release the ⌥ (option) key when finished.

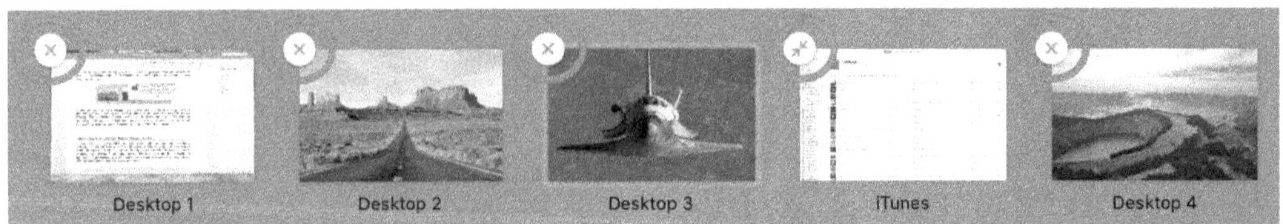

Take an App to Full-screen Mode in Mission Control

You can take any window to Full-screen mode by clicking the green control button in the upper-left corner of the window's Title Bar. Or you can take an app to Full-screen in Mission Control. Activate Mission Control and navigate to the Desktop with the app you want to take Full-screen. Drag the window onto the Mission Control ribbon between two Desktops or after the last Desktop in the ribbon. A new Desktop Space will appear with a **+** sign, as shown below. Drop the app onto this new Space to take it to Full-screen mode.

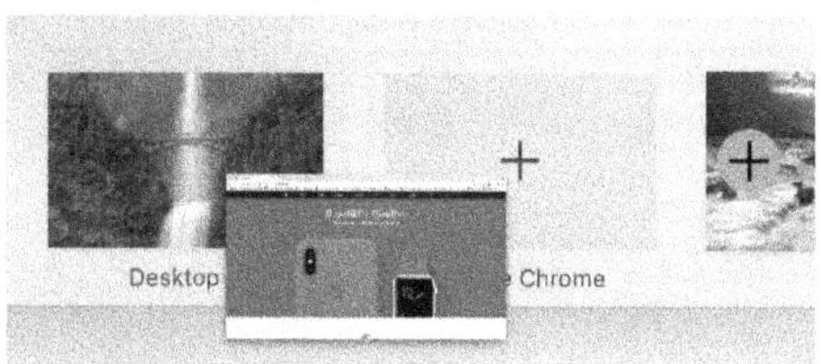

You can also put an app into Full-screen mode by clicking and holding the green control button in the application's Title Bar to reveal a drop-down menu. Choose **Enter Full-screen**.

Exit Full-screen Mode

You have a couple of options to exit Full-screen mode. You can hover your pointer over a Full-screen app in the Mission Control ribbon, and two arrows appear in the upper-left corner, as shown below. Click on the arrows, and the app exits Full-screen mode and its window moves to the next available Desktop.

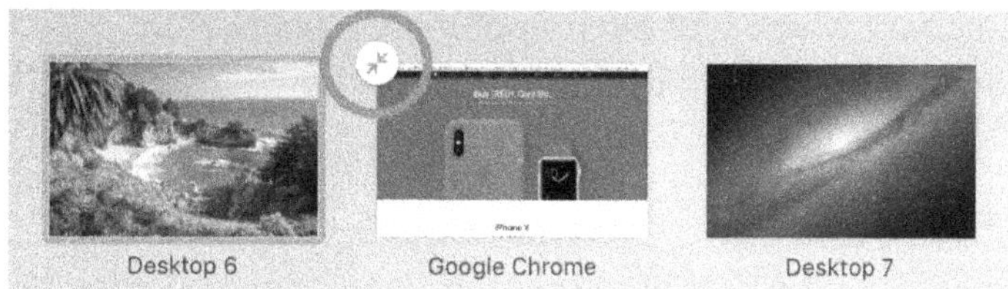

A second method is to make the app active and move your pointer to the top of your screen to reveal the Menu Bar and Title Bar controls. Click on the green control button in the upper-left corner of the Title Bar to exit Full-screen mode and restore the window to its original size. If you click on the red button, the window closes.

Use Split View to View 2 Apps Side by Side

Two applications can be placed side by side on the same Desktop using a Mission Control feature called **Split View**. Split View is a great feature when you need to compare two documents or need to move information from one document to the other. There are two different methods to put two apps into Split View.

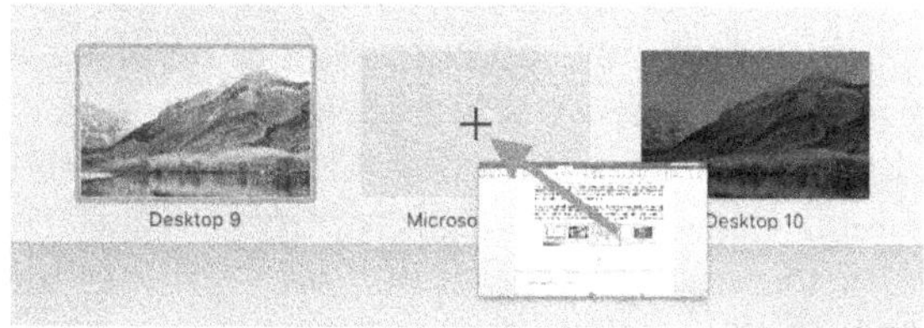

First, ensure that both application windows are in the same Desktop. Next, click and hold the green button in the first application's Title Bar to reveal a drop-down menu. Choose from **Tile window to left side of screen** or **Tile window to right side of screen**. Next, click on the thumbnail of the application that you want to occupy the other half of your Desktop. It immediately snaps into place.

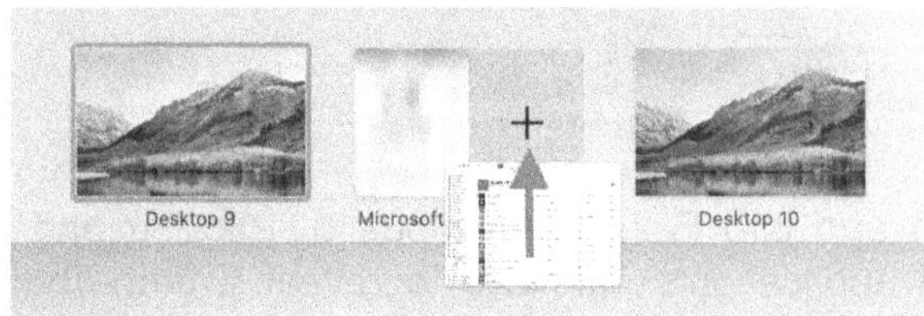

The second method is to use Mission Control. If neither application is running in Full-screen or Split View mode, open Mission Control and navigate to the Desktop with the first application window by swiping left or right with three or four fingers. Drag and drop the first window onto the Mission Control ribbon to put it into Full-screen mode. Next, navigate to the Desktop with the second application window and drag and drop it into the Mission Control ribbon onto the app in Full-screen. Note that the Full-screen app will blur and move to the left or right half of the Desktop, and the other half will have a **+** sign in it. Drop the app on the **+** sign to put the two apps in to Split View mode. You can control which half each application occupies by moving the second app to the left or right side of the Full-screen app before releasing your hold.

Resize Windows in Split View

Once your two apps are running side by side in Split View, you can adjust how much screen space each occupies. To resize an application window running in Split View mode, place your pointer on the vertical black separator between the two apps. A double-headed black arrow appears. Click and drag this arrow to the right or left to resize the windows.

Exit Split View

Similar to exiting Full-screen mode, there are several ways you can exit Split View mode and restore the application windows to their original sizes. You can hover your pointer over the Split View thumbnail in the Mission Control ribbon until two arrows appear in the upper-left corner. Click on the arrows, and the apps exit Split View mode and move to the active Desktop in the foreground (the one with the blue border).

Perhaps you don't want to restore both apps to their original sizes. You can restore the application window you no longer want in Split View mode to its original size while keeping the other window in Full-screen mode. Move your pointer to the top of your screen to reveal the Menu Bar and Title Bar controls. Click on the green control button on the Title Bar of the app you no longer want in Split View. The other app window will restore to Full-screen mode.

Turn Off Automatic Space Rearrangement

After working with Desktop Spaces for a while, you may notice something odd. Your Desktops seem to rearrange themselves automatically. No, your Mac is not haunted, and you're not losing your mind. macOS rearranges Desktops based on their most recent use. Therefore, Desktop 4 can work its way up to become Desktop 1 if the applications on Desktop 4 are used more recently than the applications on the other Desktops. If you find this behavior confusing, macOS allows you to disable it.

To disable automatic Desktop Space rearrangement, open the **Mission Control** preference pane in the System Preferences application. Uncheck the box next to **Automatically rearrange Spaces based on most recent use.**

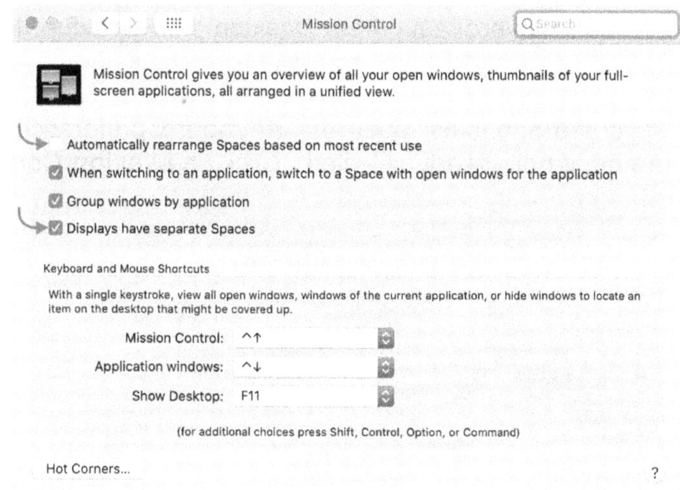

Configure Separate Spaces on other Displays

macOS allows you to have a separate, independent set of Desktop Spaces for each display in your system. In a dual-monitor setup, you can have up to 32 Desktops! An added benefit to this feature is that when enabled, each display has its own Menu Bar. Since the Menu Bar is available on all displays, you do not have to move your pointer back to the main display to access the Menu Bar. This provides a more independent treatment of each display rather than other displays being mere extensions of the main display.

If you wish to enable this feature, launch the Mission Control preference pane. Check the box next to **Displays have separate spaces**. You need to log out and log back in for the change to take effect.

Note that if you disable **Displays have separate spaces**, you will no longer enjoy the benefit of each display having its own Menu Bar. The Menu Bar will only appear on the main display. To learn how to move the Menu Bar to another display, see the next chapter.

Navigate Between Desktop Spaces

You don't have to be in Mission Control to navigate between Desktops. Swipe left or right with either three or four fingers on the trackpad. If you are using a Magic Mouse, swiping left or right with either one or two fingers navigates between your Desktops. You can also hold down the ^ (control) key and press the left or right arrow to move left or right through your Desktops, respectively.

Create Keyboard Shortcuts for Spaces

A handy method to quickly navigate between Desktops is to set up keyboard shortcuts for each Desktop Space to jump between Desktops without swiping or using Mission Control. Keyboard shortcuts are by far the quickest way to jump between Desktop Spaces because you can move directly from Desktop 1 to Desktop 4 with a single shortcut.

To enable these keyboard shortcuts, open the **Keyboard** preference pane. Next, select the **Shortcuts** tab if not already selected. Click on **Mission Control** in the left sidebar.

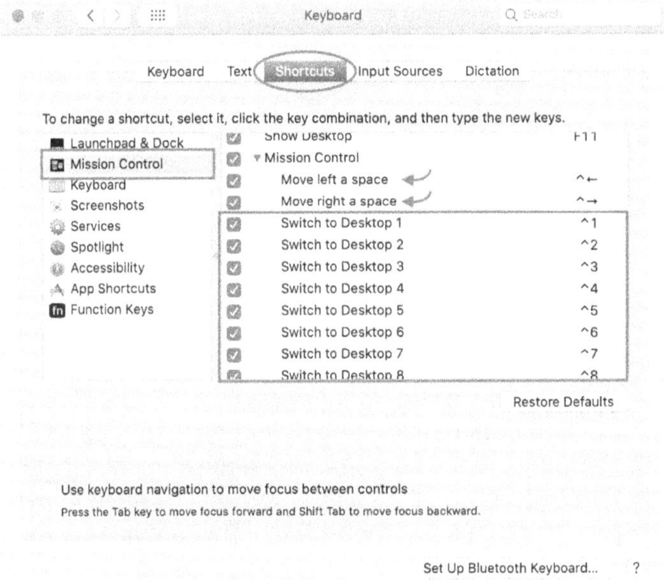

Scroll to the bottom of the right-hand pane to see the **Switch to Desktop** shortcuts. Two shortcuts are enabled by default, **^left** (control+left arrow) and **^right** (control+right arrow), which will move left or right a Desktop Space, respectively. The other **Switch to Desktop** shortcuts are disabled by default. Check the checkboxes next to each of your Desktop Space to enable the shortcuts. Once enabled, simply type the number of the Desktop space you want to go to while holding down the ^ (control) key. macOS immediately jumps to that space.

Note that if you add new Desktops, you will have to return to the Keyboard preference pane to enable the shortcuts for any newly created Desktops.

Switch Desktop Spaces with the Touch Bar

If you own a MacBook Pro with a Touch Bar, you can configure it to display buttons for your Desktop Spaces, allowing you to quickly jump between them with a tap. You can configure your Touch Bar to display your Desktops with or without the Control Strip. Another option is to configure your Touch Bar to show your Desktop Spaces when you hold down the **fn** (function) key. This second option allows you to display App Controls, the Expanded Control Strip, or **F** keys on the main Touch Bar.

To configure the Touch Bar to display your Desktop Spaces, open the **Keyboard** preference pane from System Preferences, and select **Keyboard**. Select **Spaces** from the drop-down menu next to **Touch Bar shows**. You can configure your Touch Bar to display buttons for your Desktop Spaces with or without the **Control Strip** by checking or unchecking, respectively, the checkbox next to **Show Control Strip.**

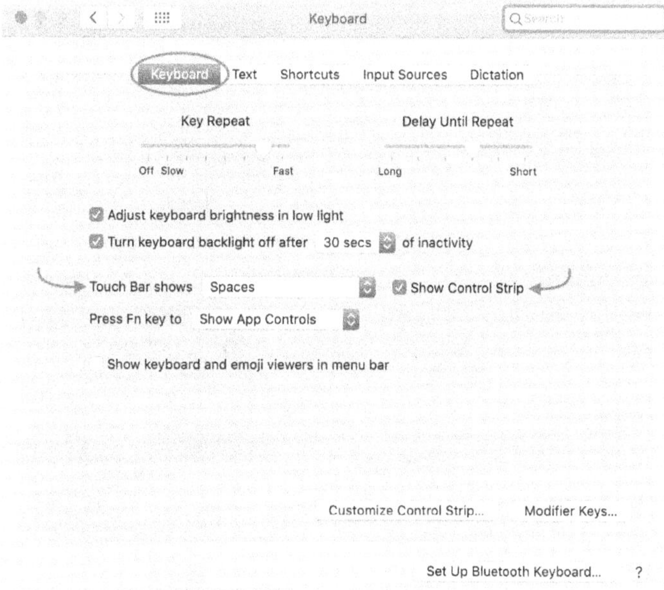

The following images show the Touch Bar configured for Spaces with and without the Control Strip. Note that the currently active Desktop is highlighted.

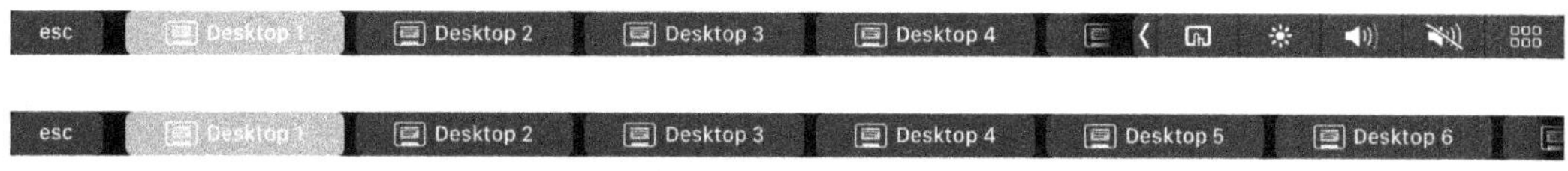

The Touch Bar can only display a maximum of 4 Desktop Spaces with the Control Strip enabled and 6 without the Control Strip. If you have more Spaces, slide your finger left or right along your Touch Bar to see them.

Alternatively, you can configure your Touch Bar to display the Desktop Spaces only when you are holding down the **fn** (function) key. From the **Keyboard** preference pane, select **Show Spaces** from the drop-down menu next to **Press Fn key to**.

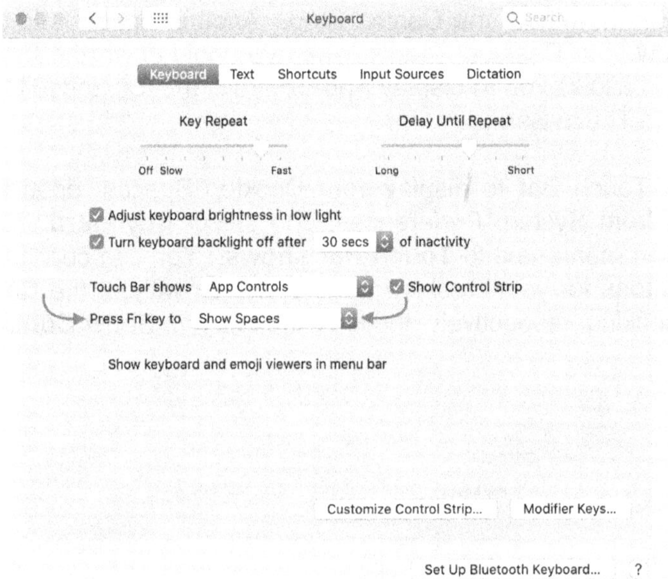

When this option is configured, the Touch Bar will show 6 of your Desktop Spaces when you hold down the **fn** (function) key. If you have more Spaces, slide your finger left or right along your Touch Bar while keeping the **fn** (function) key depressed to see them.

Move a Window to Another Desktop

A window can be moved from one Desktop Space to another in Mission Control by dragging the window from the active Desktop and dropping it onto your desired destination Desktop. Hover your pointer over an application window, and it will be highlighted by a blue border. Next, drag and drop the window to your desired destination in the Mission Control ribbon.

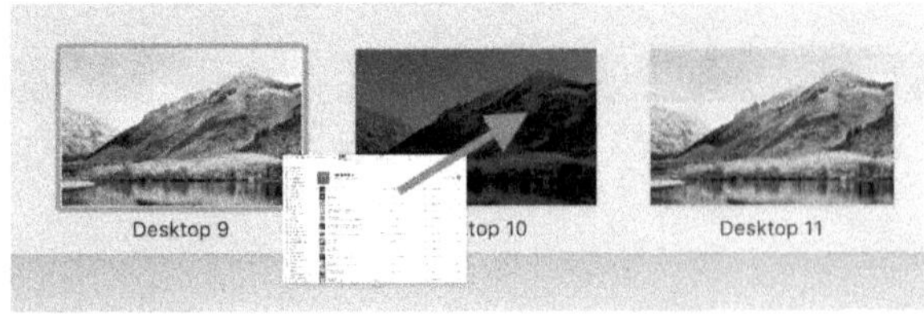

Windows from the same application can be split across multiple Desktops. This is quite handy when working with two or more documents from the same application. The only restriction is that you cannot assign an application window to a Full-screen application unless you want both apps to enter Split View mode.

Move All Windows of an Application to Another Desktop

Mission Control allows you to move individual windows to another Desktop. What if you have multiple application windows open and want to move all of them to another Desktop? macOS has a solution for you.

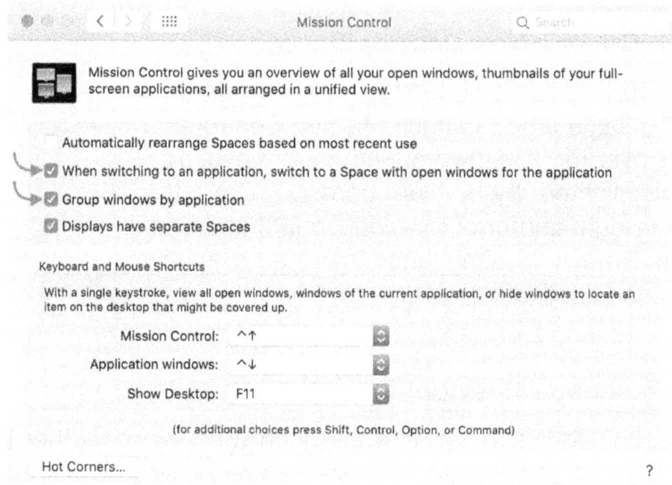

If you want to move all windows of an application to another Desktop space, first open the **Mission Control** preference pane in the System Preferences application. Ensure the checkbox next to **Group windows by application** is checked.

To move all of the windows of an application in Mission Control, drag and drop the application's icon, shown at the bottom of the top window, to the desired destination. All of the windows move as a group.

Another handy feature that is enabled in the Mission Control preference pane has the rather long name of **When switching to an application, switch to a Space with open windows for the application**. This feature is enabled by default and does what its name implies. For example, if you click on the Preview app in the Dock when the active Desktop Space does not contain any Preview windows, macOS will automatically switch to a Desktop Space that does.

Move a Window & Create a New Desktop Space

You can move an app window and create a new destination Desktop for it at the same time. Launch Mission Control and hover your pointer over the window you intend to move. The window will be highlighted by a blue border. Drag the window to the upper-right corner of Mission Control and onto the **Add Desktop Button** to simultaneously create a new Desktop and move the application window to it.

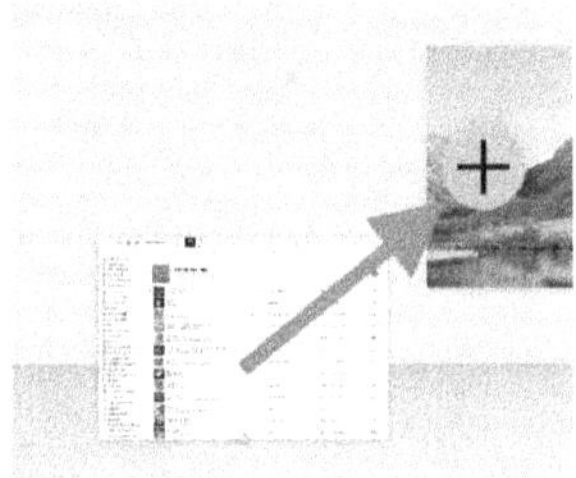

Drag a Window To Another Desktop

There are several methods to move an application window to another Desktop. You could use any of the methods described earlier to move a window in **Mission Control**. Another method is to simply drag the window over to the left or right edge of the Desktop until the pointer reaches the edge of the screen and can no longer move any further. macOS will move the window to the neighboring Desktop after a short delay.

Note that if you have multiple displays set up as an Extended Desktop, moving a window to the right or left edge of your Desktop moves the application window to the other display. Depending on how you arranged your displays in the **Display** preference pane determines whether your second display is to the left or right of your main display.

Remove the Drag Delay When Moving Windows between Desktops

If you move a window between Desktops by dragging it to the left or right edge, you will notice a slight delay before macOS moves the window to the neighboring Desktop. You can remove this delay by entering the following commands in Terminal.

```
defaults write com.apple.dock workspaces-edge-delay -float 0

killall Dock
```

Now you can move a window to the neighboring Desktop without a delay. However, I've found that without a delay, a window will fly across all the Desktops before I have a chance to drop it. So the delay we just eliminated was actually somewhat useful, albeit longer than necessary. The following commands configure a ½ second delay, just long enough to prevent a window from flying out of control but shorter and more responsive than the default.

```
defaults write com.apple.dock workspaces-edge-delay -float 0.5

killall Dock
```

Feel free to play with the decimal number after **-float** to adjust the delay to your personal preference.

To revert to the default macOS behavior, enter the following commands in **Terminal**.

```
defaults delete com.apple.dock workspaces-edge-delay

killall Dock
```

Create an Extended Desktop

If you have multiple displays, you can choose to set them up as an **Extended Desktop**. An Extended Desktop creates one large continuous Desktop across your displays, allowing you to drag a window from a Desktop on one display to a Desktop on another display.

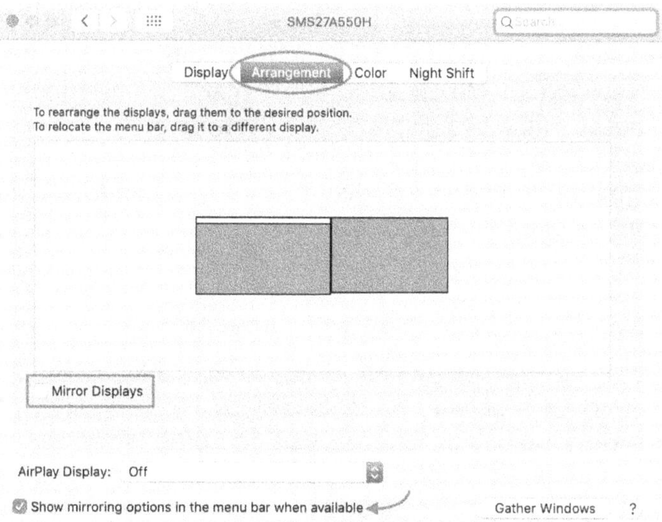

To create an Extended Desktop across your displays, launch the Displays preference pane and select the **Arrangement** tab. Uncheck the checkbox next to **Mirror Displays**. Choose which display will be on the left and the right by dragging the displays shown in the center of the preference pane to the positions you desire.

Mirror Displays

Another option for a multiple monitor setup is to mirror the displays. Mirroring displays your Mac's video output on both monitors simultaneously. This feature comes in handy when you need to project your display onto a screen or display during a meeting. You will be able to see what the audience is seeing without having to turn around and look at the projected image.

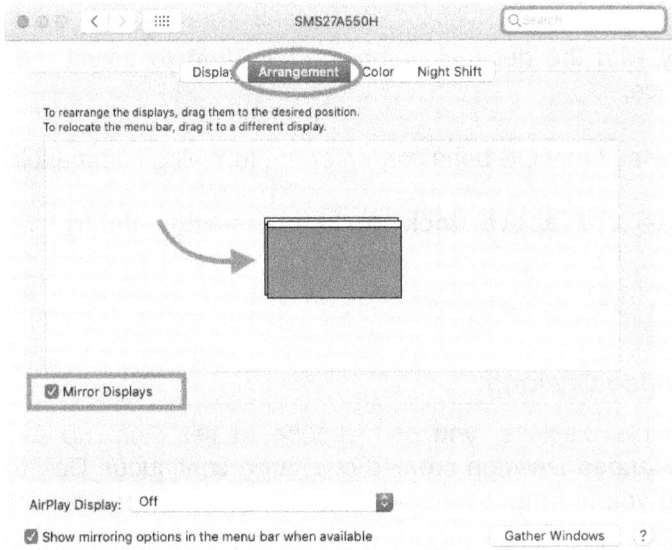

To mirror your displays, open the **Displays** preference pane in the System Preferences application. Select the **Arrangement** tab if not already highlighted. Check the checkbox next to **Mirror Displays**. macOS will attempt to match the closest resolution between the two displays when mirroring.

If you ever need to mirror your Mac's display quickly, you can toggle mirroring on and off with the keyboard shortcut **⌘F1** (command+F1).

Use your iPad as an External Display with Sidecar

Sidecar is a new feature introduced in macOS Catalina that lets you use your iPad as a second portable display by extending or mirroring your Mac's Desktop. With Sidecar, you can drag windows to your iPad and interact with them using your Mac's keyboard, trackpad, mouse, or your iPad's Apple Pencil. Unlike a traditional display, you don't have to attach your iPad to your Mac unless you want to charge your iPad at the same time as you are using it as a second display.

To use Sidecar, ensure that Wi-Fi and Bluetooth are enabled on both devices and that you are signed in to iCloud with the same Apple ID. Handoff must be enabled on both your iPad and Mac. On your iPad, select **Settings > General > Handoff** to enable Handoff. On your Mac, open the General preference pane from System Preferences and check the checkbox next to **Allow Handoff between this Mac and your iCould devices**.

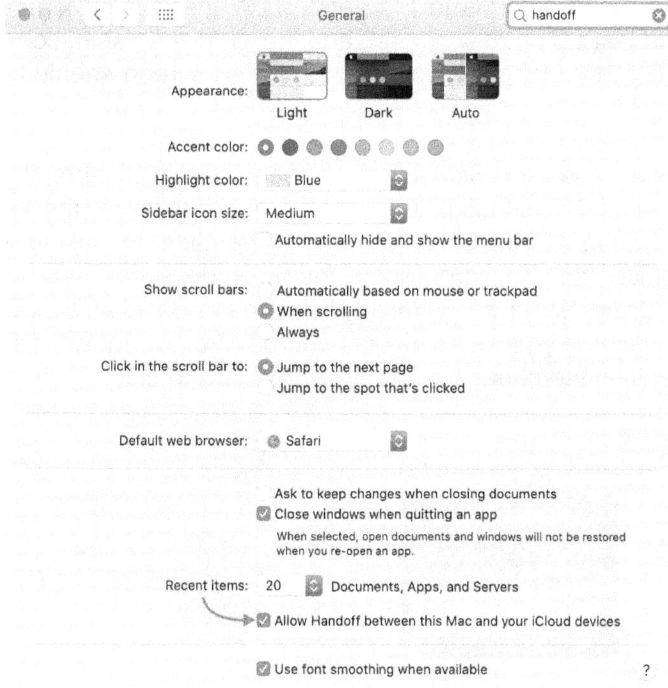

To use Sidecar, click the Airplay icon in the Menu Bar and select the option to connect to your iPad. Your iPad becomes an extension of your Desktop, allowing you to move windows to it like a regular display. When using Sidecar, note that the Airplay icon turns into a blue rectangle to indicate Sidecar is enabled.

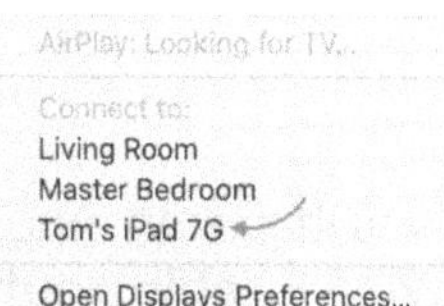

The image on the previous page shows Sidecar on my 7th Generation iPad. Note the black bar on the left side of the screen. This bar is called the Sidebar. The Sidebar contains commonly used controls to hide and show the Dock, Menu Bar, and iPad keyboard, undo the last action, disconnect, and the ⇧ ⌘ ^ ⌥ (shift, command, control, or option) keys. The bar along the bottom of the iPad screen should be familiar. It's the macOS Touch Bar.

To configure Sidecar, open the Sidecar preference pane in System Preferences. By default, the Sidebar and Touch Bar are enabled and shown on the left and bottom, respectively. You have the option of displaying the Sidebar on the left or right by selecting your choice from the drop-down menu or disabling it by unchecking the checkbox next to **Show Sidebar**. Similarly, the Touch Bar can be displayed on the bottom or top by selecting your desired location from the drop-down menu or it can be disabled by unchecking the checkbox next to **Show Touch Bar**.

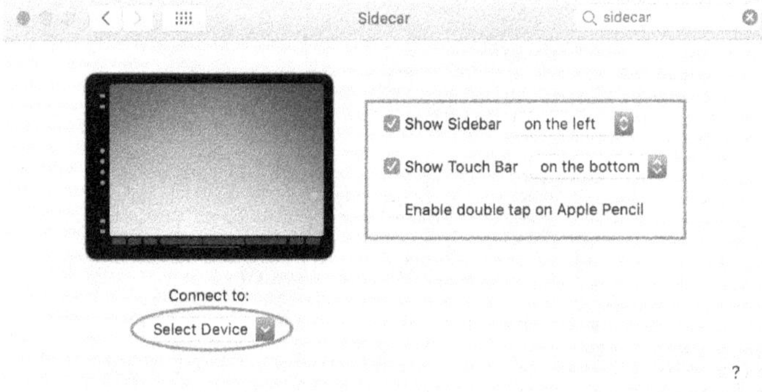

If you have an Apple Pencil, you can enable double-tap by checking the checkbox next to **Enable double tap on Apple Pencil.**

The Sidecar preference pane also allows you to connect to your iPad by selecting it from the drop-down menu under **Connect to**. When you are connected, the drop-down menu is replaced by the **Disconnect** button.

Sidecar is supported on the following Mac models and iPads running iPadOS 13.

Macs		iPads
2016 or later MacBook Pro	2016 or later MacBook	iPad Pro
2017 or later iMac	Late 2015 iMac Retina 5k	iPad (6th Gen or later)
2018 or later Mac mini	2019 or later Mac Pro	iPad mini (5th Gen)
2018 or later MacBook Air	iMac Pro	iPad Air (3rd Gen)

Assign an Application to a Desktop

If you value organization, macOS allows you to assign an application to a specific Desktop permanently. By assigning applications to Desktops, you ensure apps always open on the Desktop of your choice. You can use this feature to create a themed Desktop. For example, you can have one Desktop for all of your social media applications, another for your productivity apps, another for browsers, etc. How you organize your apps is up to you.

To assign an application to a specific Desktop, navigate to the Desktop to which you want to assign the application. If you need to create a new Desktop space, first launch Mission Control and click the **Add Desktop Button**. Find the application in the **Dock**. If the application is not in the Dock, launch the application using **Launchpad** to make it appear in the Dock. Secondary click on the application icon in the Dock to reveal the **Options** menu. By default, the **None** option is checked, which allows the application to be run on any Desktop. To assign the app to the current Desktop, select **This Desktop** from the menu.

If you have multiple displays, you can assign an app to a Desktop on a specific display. With two displays, the **Options** menu offers options for each display. Assigning an application to a Desktop does not prevent you from moving that application to another Desktop later. An app does not have to be added to the Dock for it to launch to its assigned Desktop. Once an application has been assigned to a Desktop, it always appears on its assigned Desktop regardless of how it was launched.

Assign an Application to Every Desktop

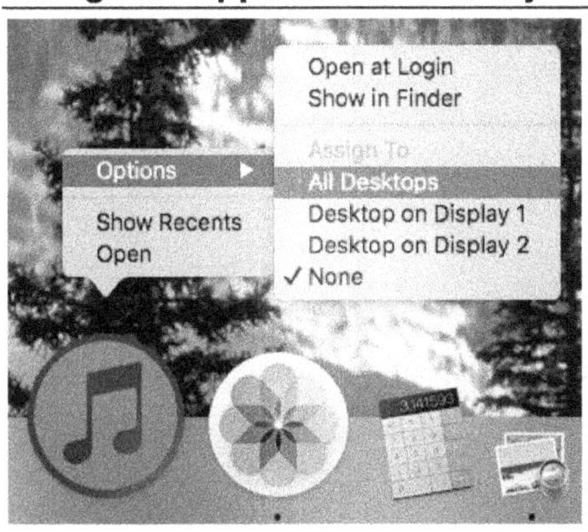

macOS offers an option to assign an application to every Desktop. This is a handy feature if you have an application you use frequently and desire quick access to it.

Find the application in the Dock. If the app is not in the Dock, launch it first. Secondary click on the application icon in the Dock to reveal the **Options** submenu. To assign the app to every Desktop, select **All Desktops**.

Toggle Mission Control On & Off

There are many ways to launch **Mission Control**. You can launch it using a trackpad gesture, open it from Launchpad, Spotlight or Siri, press the **F3** key, enter **^up** (control+up arrow), or tap Mission Control on the Touch Bar.

macOS offers one more alternative that allows you to toggle Mission Control on and off. Press and hold the **F3** key to toggle Mission Control. The moment you release the **F3** key, Mission Control will toggle off.

Quick Look

When windows are grouped in **Mission Control**, it is sometimes difficult to differentiate between them because they are grouped one on top of another. This is especially true if you have a lot of windows open on the same Desktop and are using a computer with a small screen. The solution is **Quick Look**.

To see the contents of any window in Mission Control, hover over it with the pointer, and when a blue border appears around the window, press the **spacebar**. Mission Control zooms in to the highlighted window. To toggle the zoom off, press the spacebar again, and the window shrinks back to its original size.

Quick Lock is especially useful when you have windows grouped by application enabled since this feature allows you to see the contents of windows underneath the top window.

Ungroup Windows in Mission Control

If you prefer that Mission Control not group windows from the same application, you can disable this feature in the Mission Control preference pane. Disabling app grouping makes it easier to discern a file's contents without having to use Quick Look.

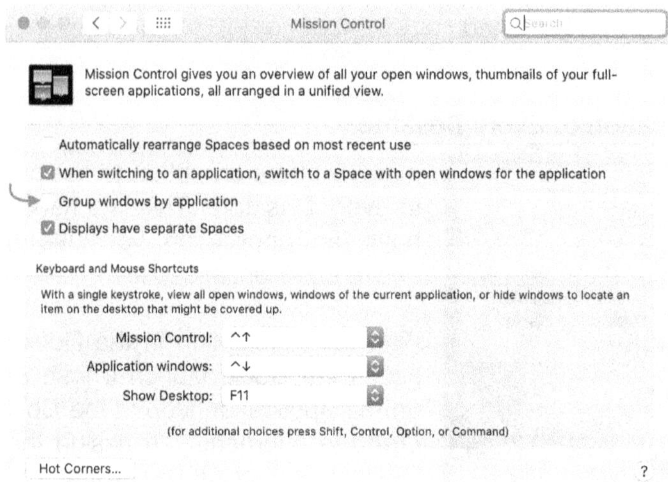

To disable the grouping of windows from the same application, launch the Mission Control preference pane. Uncheck the checkbox next to **Group windows by application**. With this option unchecked, windows from the same app are displayed separately, making it easier to distinguish their contents without using Quick Look.

Change the Mission Control Keyboard Shortcut

The default keyboard shortcut to launch **Mission Control** is ^**up** (control+up arrow). macOS allows you to change this shortcut to utilize any F key from **F1** to **F12**, the left or right ⇧ ^ ⌥ ⌘ (shift, control, option, or command) keys, or the **fn** (function) key.

To change the keyboard shortcut, open the Mission Control preference pane. Select your desired keyboard shortcut from the drop-down menu next to **Mission Control**. You can also use the following keys as modifiers: ⇧ ⌘ ^ ⌥ (shift, command, control, or option), alone or in any combination.

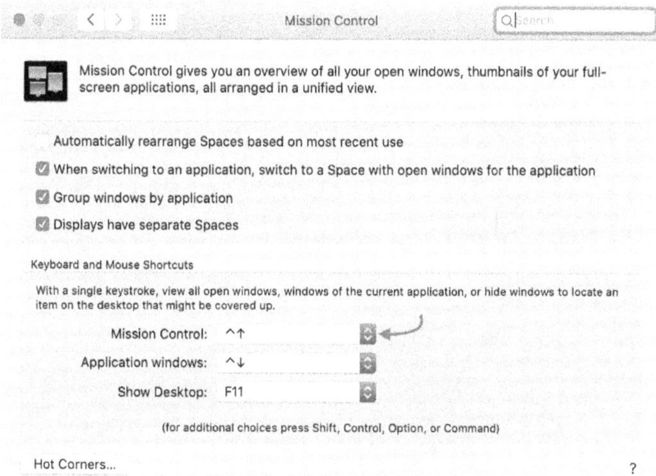

The Mission Control preference pane also lets you change the keyboard shortcuts for **Application windows** (App Exposé) and **Show Desktop**. Choose your desired shortcuts from the drop-down menus next to these options.

App Exposé removes Desktop clutter to reveal all the windows of a chosen application. To launch App Exposé, select an application with multiple windows open and enter ^**down** (control+down arrow). You can then select the desired window by clicking on it to make it active. App Exposé can also be executed with a trackpad gesture by swiping three or four fingers down, depending on how you configured the gesture in the Trackpad preference pane.

The **Show Desktop** command clears the Desktop of all open windows by pushing them off the edge of the screen.

To turn off any of the shortcuts, select the – option from the drop-down menus.

5

Menu Bar

macOS offers many customizations for the **Menu Bar**. Recall from Chapter 3 that there are two halves to the Menu Bar. The left half contains the **Apple** and **Application** menus, as shown in the image below.

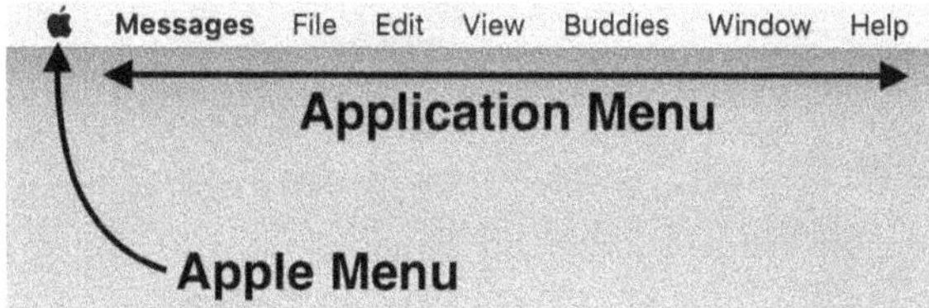

The right half, which is shown in the image below, contains the **Status Menu**. Note that if you upgraded from a previous version of macOS and customized your Status Menu (as I did), it will look different than what is shown below.

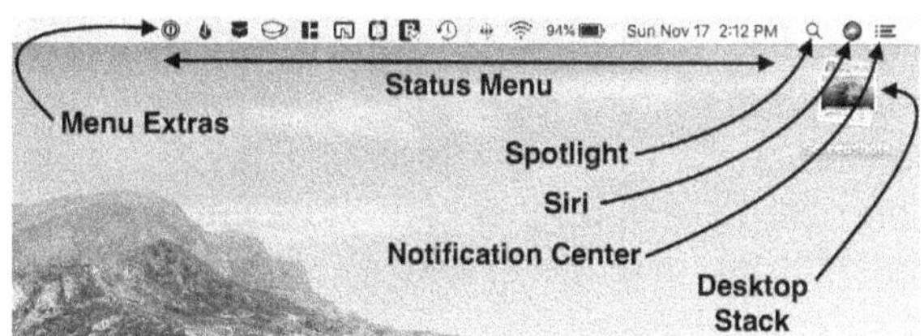

The **Status Menu** displays the status of and provides quick access to various macOS features and applications via small icons called **Menu Extras**. Menu Extras are also called menulets, menu items, or status items. **Menu Extras** are used to configure various macOS features and third-party applications.

At the far right of the Menu Extras are icons for **Spotlight**, **Siri**, and **Notification Center**. We will cover Spotlight, Siri, and Notification Center in later chapters.

Add a Menu Bar to Each Display

In a multiple display setup, you have a couple of options to configure the behavior of your displays. The first option is to treat each display independently, each with its own **Menu Bar**. Since the Menu Bar is available on all displays, you do not have to move the pointer back to your main display to access Menu Bar features. An added benefit of enabling this feature is that you can have a separate, independent set of Desktops for each monitor in your system. In a dual-monitor setup, you can have up to 32 Desktops!

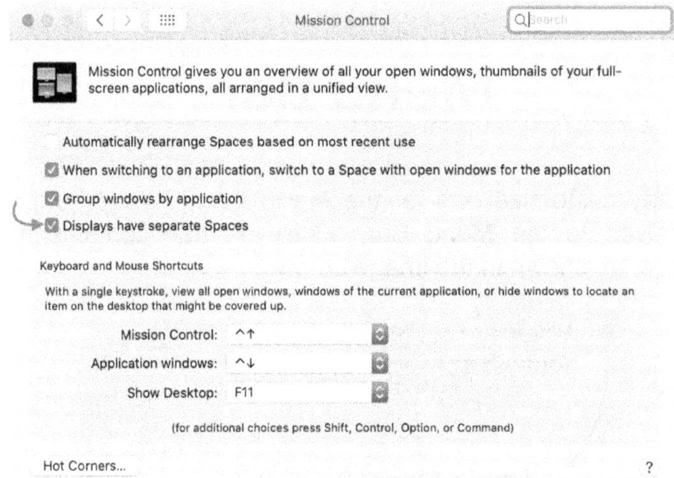

To add a Menu Bar to each display, open the **Mission Control** preference pane. Check the checkbox next to **Displays have separate Spaces**. You need to log out and log in for the change to take effect.

Relocate the Menu Bar to Another Display

Another option is to treat your second monitor as an extension of your main display. First, ensure that the checkbox next to **Displays have separate Spaces** in the **Mission Control** preference pane is unchecked. If you need to uncheck the box, you need to log out and log in for this change to take effect.

Next, configure on which display the Menu Bar will appear. To relocate the Menu Bar to another display, open the **Displays** preference pane in the System Preferences application. Select the **Arrangement** tab if not already highlighted. Drag the Menu Bar, which is represented by a white bar at the top of one of the displays, to the desired display.

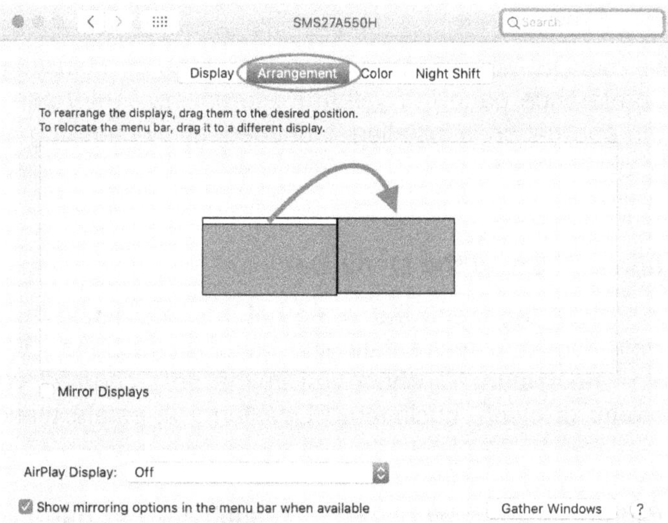

Rearrange the Menu Extras

The **Menu Extras** in the **Status Menu** are displayed generally in the order in which they started. If you launch a new third-party application that provides a Menu Extra, it will appear at the left end of the Status Menu. By default, native macOS Menu Extras are located on the right half of the Status Menu, while third-party Menu Extras appear on the left. However, macOS lets you rearrange your Menu Extras.

To move a Menu Extra, hold down the ⌘ (command) key while dragging it to a new location on the Status Bar. The Menu Extra will turn gray while you are dragging it, and other Menu Extras move out of the way to make room. Note that you can only reorder the Menu Extras within the Status Bar. You cannot relocate a Menu Extra to the left side of the Menu Bar as it is reserved for the Apple and Application Menus. If you try to move a Menu Extra to the Application Menu, it bounces back to the Status Bar. Except for Notification Center, you can rearrange any of the Menu Extras.

Take care not to drag a Menu Extra off the Menu Bar as you could accidentally remove it.

Remove a Menu Extra

If you don't need a particular **Menu Extra**, macOS allows you to remove it from the **Status Bar**. To remove a Menu Extra, hold down the ⌘ (command) key while dragging it off the Menu Bar. Release and poof, the Menu Extra disappears. Note that you cannot remove the Spotlight and Notification Center Menu Extras.

As for third-party application Menu Extras, generally, you cannot remove them using the ⌘ (command) key. However, some applications provide the ability to hide their Menu Extra in their preferences. For other third-party apps, removing their associated Menu Extra can only be accomplished by quitting the app.

Add Native macOS Menu Extras

You can add native macOS **Menu Extras** to the Menu Bar by checking the checkbox in the associated preference pane in System Preferences. Third-party Menu Extras are added when the application is installed, launched, or by checking an option in the application-specific preferences.

Automatically Hide and Show the Menu Bar

macOS allows you to hide the Menu Bar when not in use. Hiding the Menu Bar off-screen provides more Desktop real estate and fewer distractions. When combined with the Dock auto-hide feature I'll show you in the next chapter; you'll be simply amazed at the amount of clean, uncluttered Desktop real estate these two features provide.

Menu Bar auto-hiding is disabled by default. To enable Menu Bar auto-hiding, open the **General** preference pane. Check the checkbox next to **Automatically hide and show the menu bar**.

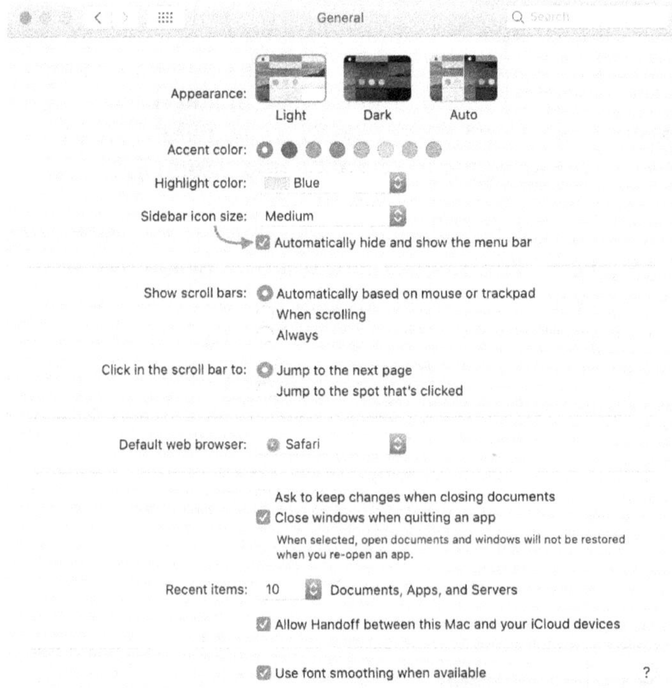

With this feature enabled, you can unhide the Menu Bar by moving your pointer to the top of the screen and leaving it there momentarily. The Menu Bar will automatically appear and disappear when no longer needed.

To return to the macOS default and disable Menu Bar auto-hiding, open the **General** preference pane and uncheck the checkbox next to **Automatically hide and show the menu bar**.

Customize the Date and Time

By default, the **Date & Time Menu Extra** displays the day of the week and the current time. Its drop-down menu lets you switch between an analog or digital clock. When the clock is configured as analog, a tiny clock is displayed in the Menu Bar. Clicking it reveals the drop-down menu, which displays the day of the week, date, and time in hours, minutes, and seconds. When the clock is configured as digital, the drop-down shows the day of the week and the date.

The Menu Extra provides direct access to the **Date & Time** preference pane in System Preferences, where the configuration options are located. Selecting **Open Date and Time Preferences...** takes you directly to the **Clock** tab in the **Date & Time** preference pane.

If you don't want to see the date and time in your Menu Bar, you can remove them entirely by unchecking the checkbox next to **Show date and time in the menu bar**. If you decide to keep the date and time, it does not have to look like the macOS standard clock. You have the option of configuring how the time and date are displayed.

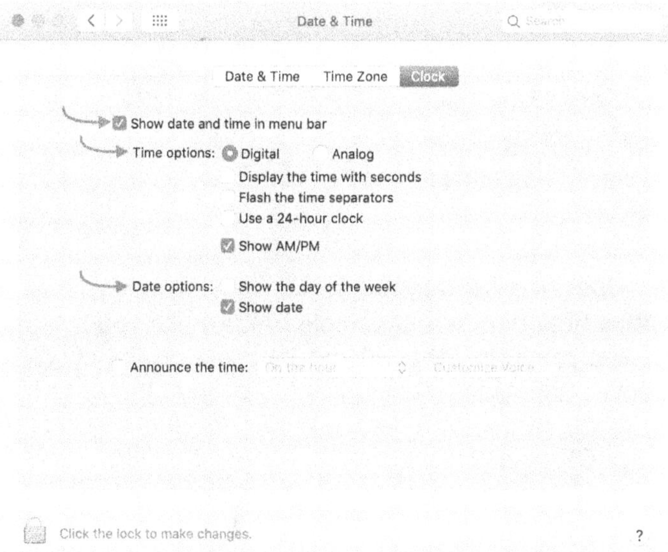

The time can be shown in either analog or digital format. If you select digital, you have 3 additional configuration options. The time can be displayed with or without seconds. The colons separating hours, minutes, and seconds can be set to flash on and off. And you have the option of displaying a 12-hour or 24-hour clock. If you select the 12-hour option, you can choose whether to show AM and PM.

Check the checkboxes next to the options you wish to configure. If you select the analog clock, you are prevented from configuring any additional options as they are all grayed out.

For the date, you have the option of showing the day of the week in addition to displaying the date.

You can also configure macOS to announce the time by checking the checkbox next to **Announce the time**. Choose how often you want the time announced from the drop-down menu. The default is **On the hour** with options for the quarter and half hour. Click **Customize Voice...** to access the voice configuration sheet. Select the voice you wish to use from the choices in the drop-down menu next to **Voice** or select **Customize...** at the bottom of the menu to download other voice options.

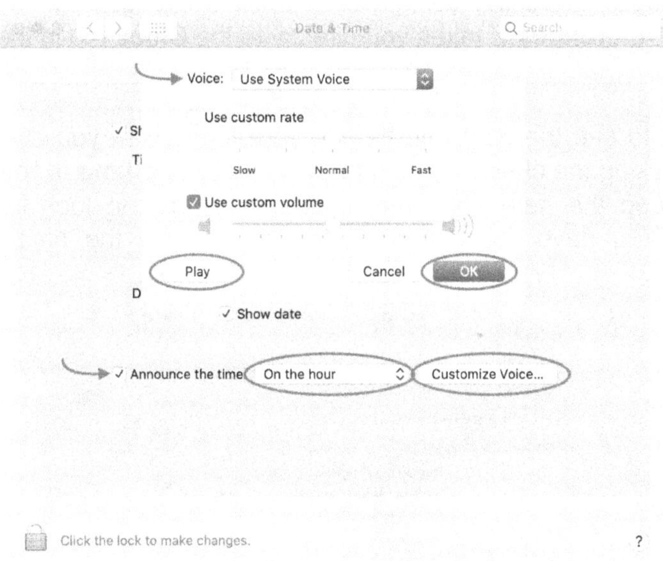

You can click the **Play** button to hear a sample of the voice you selected in the **Voice** drop-down menu. You can adjust the volume by checking the checkbox next to **Use custom volume** moving the slider. If you want to change the speed, either slowing it down or speeding it up, check the checkbox next to **Use custom rate** and adjust using the slider. Click **OK** when finished.

Connect to Wi-Fi

The **AirPort Menu Extra** allows you to turn Wi-Fi on and off, connect to a Wi-Fi network, create Wi-Fi networks, or open the Network preference pane. From the AirPort Menu Extra you can connect to any of the Wi-Fi networks listed, which are shown with their signal strengths. The more dark lines radiating outward, the stronger the Wi-Fi signal. If your smartphone has a Wi-Fi hotspot feature and it is enabled, you'll see it listed. If you own an iPhone, you'll be able to turn on the Personal Hotspot feature from your Mac.

A small padlock next to the network name indicates a password is needed to join the Wi-Fi network. The lack of this padlock denotes public Wi-Fi networks which are open for anyone to connect to. Note that public Wi-Fi networks transmit data without any encryption. Therefore, the data you transmit and receive can be seen by others running packet analyzer software. Never go online on a public Wi-Fi network. Check out the Security & Privacy chapter to learn about Virtual Private Network apps.

The bottom section of the drop-down menu allows you to join other Wi-Fi networks that are not listed. You can use the **Join Other Network...** option to connect to a network, which is hidden (i.e., not broadcasting its network name). A dialog box will appear where you can enter the network name and choose the security option. Once you have selected the security, the dialog box asks you to enter the network password. Checking the **Remember this network** checkbox tells macOS to remember this Wi-Fi network, allowing you to connect again without entering the password. Clicking the **Show Networks** button displays the available Wi-Fi networks to which you can connect. Click **Join** when finished.

You can open the **Network** preference pane in the System Preferences application by choosing **Open Network Preferences...** from the AirPort Menu Extra drop-down menu. This preference pane allows you to turn Wi-Fi on and off and connect to Wi-Fi.

Clicking the **Advanced** button allows you to see, reorder, and remove the Wi-Fi networks your Mac has previously joined. Drag the network name to rearrange your **Preferred Networks**. It is best to have the networks you join most frequently at the top of the list. To remove a Wi-Fi network, highlight it, and click the – button.

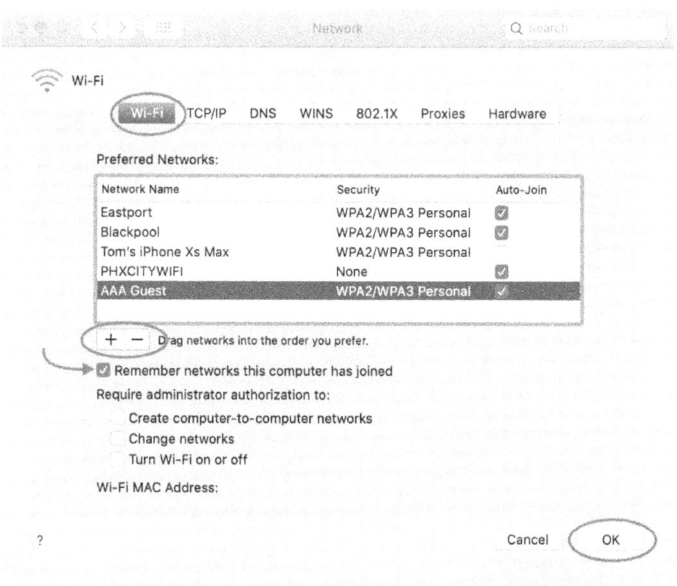

By default, macOS remembers the Wi-Fi networks your Mac has joined and adds them to the Preferred Networks list. Unchecking the checkbox next to **Remember networks this computer has joined** will disable this feature.

Hold Down the Option Key with the AirPort Menu Extra

Holding down the ⌥ (option) key while clicking on the **AirPort Menu Extra** provides additional Wi-Fi information that can be used to troubleshoot connectivity issues.

Three diagnostic options are available, which help when you are trying to troubleshoot Wi-Fi connectivity problems. **Enable Wi-Fi Logging** enables background logging, saving the log to a .log file. Be sure to disable logging when finished or when restarting as macOS will continue to log until you disable it. **Create Diagnostics Report On Desktop...** will do just that, create a diagnostics report in your Desktop folder for use by Apple technicians to troubleshoot Wi-Fi problems. **Open Wireless Diagnostics...** launches an application that detects common Wi-Fi problems.

Change How Battery Power is Displayed

If you're working on a MacBook, MacBook Air, or MacBook Pro, you'll want to keep the **Battery Menu Extra** in your Menu Bar to keep an eye on how much power is left in your battery. The information displayed by the Battery Menu Extra depends on whether your laptop is plugged into AC power or is running on battery. When plugged into AC power, the Battery Menu Extra tells you if the battery is charged, or if it is charging, how long it will take to charge fully. It also tells you which apps are using significant energy, allowing you to close them to save power.

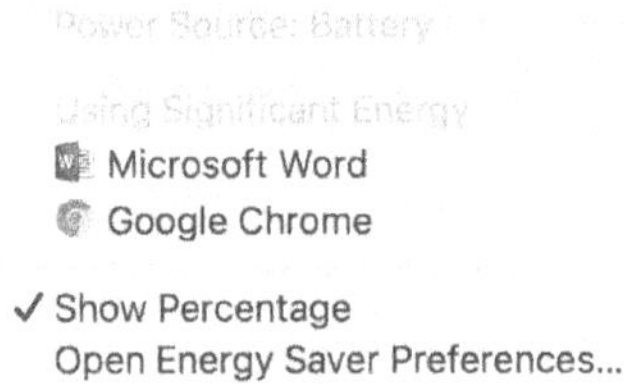

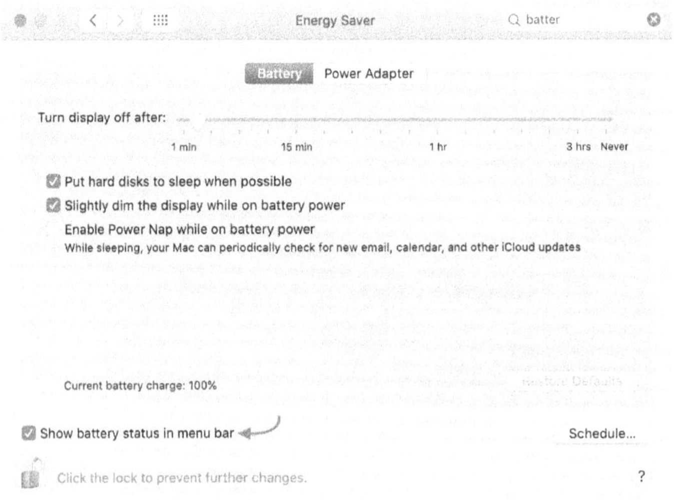

macOS shows a representation of a battery in the Menu Bar. If you want a more precise reading a battery power, select **Show Percentage** from the Battery Menu Extra drop-down menu.

If you're not interested in seeing how much power your battery has left, you can remove the Battery Menu Extra by holding down the ⌘ (command) key while dragging it off the Menu Bar. You can also remove it by selecting **Open Energy Saver Preferences...** from the Battery Menu Extra drop-down menu to open the **Energy Saver** preference pane. Uncheck the checkbox next to **Show battery status in menu bar**.

Set a Bedtime Schedule for your Mac

Another handy macOS feature is that you can put your Mac to sleep, shut it down, or restart it on a schedule. Whether you are trying to save electricity or want to ensure your Mac is ready when you are first thing in the morning, you can easily schedule regular shutdowns and startups.

To schedule start and shut down times, open the **Energy Saver** preference pane. Click **Schedule...** in the lower-right corner of the preference pane to reveal a configuration sheet. Check the checkbox next to **Sleep** and use the drop-down menu to select **Sleep**, **Restart**, **or Shutdown**, and then pick your desired days and time. You can choose **Everyday**, **Weekdays**, **Weekends**, or any day of the week.

If you choose to shut down or sleep, you may want to have your Mac automatically start or wake from sleep. Check the checkbox next to **Start up or wake** and select the days and time. Click **OK** when done.

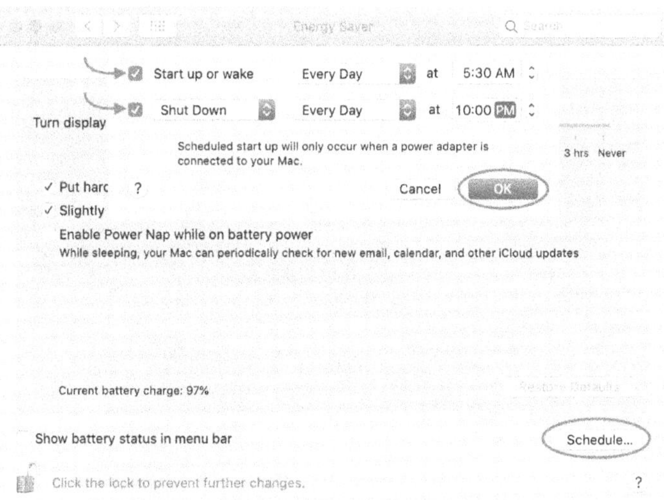

There are are few caveats. For your Mac to shut down automatically, it must be awake at the time you scheduled to shut it down. It also must remain awake for at least 10 minutes past your desired shut down time. If your Mac is asleep at your scheduled shut down time, it will continue to sleep instead of shutting down. Another caveat is that if your Mac is configured to go to sleep after less that 15 minutes of inactivity, it may go back to sleep before it can shut down. To avoid this possibility, check the checkbox next to **Start up or wake** and set it to start up or wake 5 minutes before your desired shut down time. Also, note that a scheduled start will only occur when your Mac is connected to a power adapter. Click **OK** when done.

Pair Bluetooth Devices

Bluetooth is a short-range wireless technology that lets you pair headsets, smartphones, printers, cameras, keyboards, mice, and trackpads to your Mac. The **Bluetooth Menu Extra**, lets you turn Bluetooth on and off, pair your Mac with a Bluetooth device, send or browse files on a paired device, and open the **Bluetooth** preference pane.

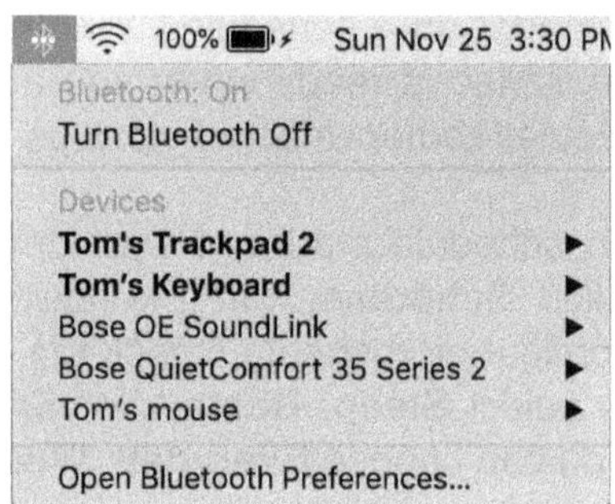

The Bluetooth Menu Extra also lists devices paired with your Mac. If the name of the device is bold, it indicates the device is currently connected. Hovering over any of the connected devices with your pointer reveals a contextual menu, allowing you to disconnect the device, see its battery level, or open its associated preference pane in System Preferences.

Selecting **Open Bluetooth Preferences...** opens the **Bluetooth** preference pane in System Preferences. From here, you can turn Bluetooth off and on, pair Bluetooth devices, and connect and disconnect paired devices. When the checkbox next to **Show Bluetooth in menu bar** is checked, the Bluetooth Menu Extra will appear in the Menu Bar.

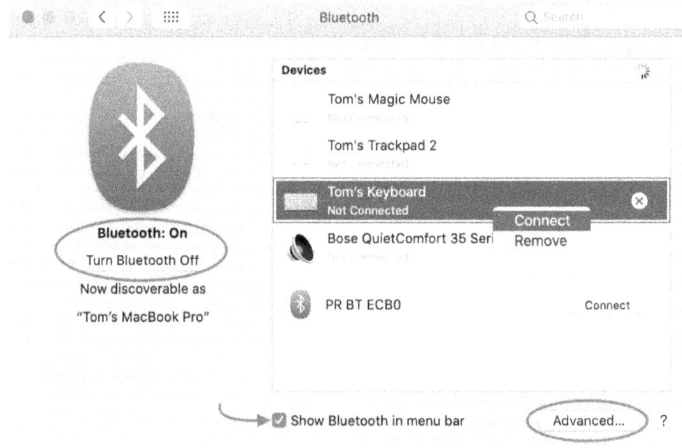

Clicking the **Advanced...** button in the lower-right corner of the preference pane displays a drop-down sheet with options to run the Bluetooth Setup Assistant if a keyboard, mouse, or trackpad is not detected and to allow Bluetooth devices to wake your Mac. These settings are enabled by default.

Tip: Bluetooth is an attack vector that hackers can use to break into your Mac. You should disable Bluetooth using the Bluetooth Menu Extra when you are using your MacBook, MacBook Air, or MacBook Pro laptop in a public place.

Hold Down the Option Key with the Bluetooth Menu Extra

Holding down the ⌥ (option) key while clicking on the **Bluetooth Menu Extra** provides additional information and options, including the version of Bluetooth, MAC address, and options to send files to or browse files on another device.

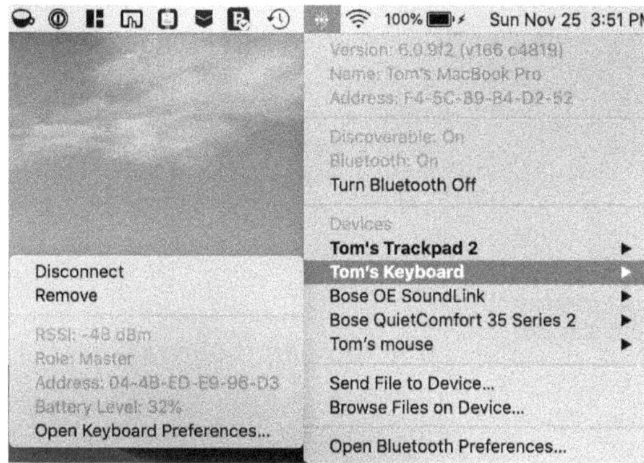

Moving your pointer to any of the paired devices while holding the ⌥ (option) key reveals a contextual menu with options to **Disconnect** or **Remove** the device, signal strength, MAC address, battery level, and to open the associated preference pane, if applicable.

Switch Users with the Fast User Switching Menu Extra

The **Fast User Switching Menu Extra** lets you quickly switch between users on your Mac. It also provides access to two other features – the **Login Window...** and the **Users & Groups** preference pane. If you have multiple users configured in the User & Groups preference pane, the users are listed in the drop-down menu with the current user grayed out.

Selecting **Login Window...** locks your Mac without logging you out. Selecting **Users & Groups Preferences...** takes you to the **Users & Groups** preference pane where you can add or remove users, change your password and profile picture, and choose login items.

The Fast User Switching Menu Extra can be enabled and disabled from the User & Groups preference pane. Select **Users & Groups Preferences...** from the Fast User Switching Menu Extra drop-down menu or open the **Users & Groups** preference pane from System Preferences. Next, unlock the preference pane by clicking on the padlock in the lower-left corner, if locked. Enter your password when challenged. Select **Login Options** at the bottom left.

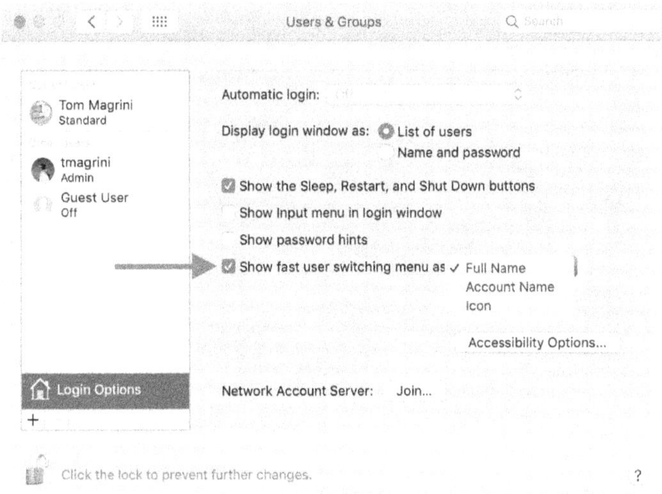

To enable the Fast User Switching Menu Extra, check the checkbox next to **Show fast user switching menu as**. macOS offers 3 display choices for this Menu Extra: **Full Name**, **Account Name**, or **Icon**.

To disable the Fast User Switching Menu Extra and remove it from the Menu Bar, uncheck the checkbox next to **Show fast user switching menu as**.

Adjust the Volume

You can view and switch between Bluetooth and AirPlay connected audio output devices directly from the **Volume Menu Extra**.

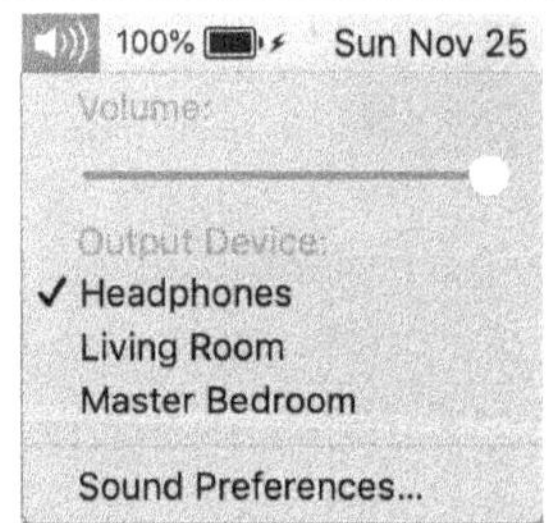

If you hold down the ⌥ (option) key when clicking the Volume Menu Extra, you can view and switch between your audio input devices.

To add the Volume Menu Extra to the Menu Bar, open the **Sound** preference pane in System Preferences. Check the checkbox next to **Show volume in menu bar** at the bottom of the Sound preference pane.

Mirror your Display to an AppleTV

If you own an Apple TV, the **AirPlay Menu Extra** lets you send video from your Mac to your Apple TV. **AirPlay** only works on Macs manufactured in 2011 or later. If your Mac does not support AirPlay, you will not see the AirPlay Menu Extra. The AirPlay Menu Extra also allows you to use a macOS Catalina feature called Sidecar, which turns your Sidecar-compatible iPad into an external display.

100% Sun Nov 25 4:02
Living Room
Master Bedroom
Open Displays Preferences...

To add the AirPlay Menu Extra to your Menu Bar, open the **Displays** preference pane in System Preferences. Check the checkbox next to **Show mirroring options in the menu bar when available** in the lower-left corner of the preference pane. You can then select an **Airplay Display** using the drop-down menu in the Menu Extra.

Configure Location Services

Location Services is an essential feature of macOS that allows you to get the local weather, restaurant recommendations, location-based reminders, and a host of other features that require knowledge of your current location. Many apps rely on your location to provide relevant information. Maps, Siri, Facebook, Weather, Calendar, Photos, and Reminders are a few examples.

When an application accesses your location, the Location Services icon shown in the image to the right will appear in your Menu Bar. The Location Services Menu Extra lists apps that are accessing your location and allows you to configure location services.

Open Privacy Preferences...

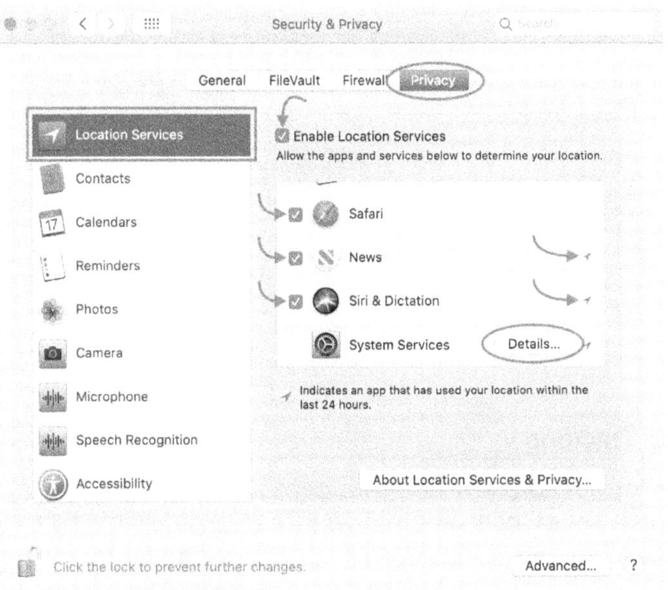

To control which apps can access your location, select **Open Privacy Preferences...** from the Location Services Menu Extra or open the **Security & Privacy** preference pane from System Preferences, and select the **Privacy** tab.

A small location services icon to the right of an application will identify that the app has accessed your location in the past 24 hours. Check the checkboxes next to the apps you will allow access to your location. Uncheck those which you do not want to know your location.

You should not disable **Location Services** by unchecking the box next to **Enable Location Services** unless you want to disable Location Services entirely. While this stops applications from accessing your location, it also prevents you from locating your Mac with the **Find My Mac** feature.

Scroll to the bottom of the list of apps and services to access **System Services**. Click the **Details...** button to reveal a configuration sheet. Here you can allow System Services to determine your location for various services, including location-based suggestions, time zone, location-based Apple ads, Find My Mac, HomeKit, Wi-Fi networking, Wi-Fi calling, and significant locations, which I'll discuss in more detail below. Check the checkbox next to **Show location icon in menu bar when System Services request your location** if you want the Location Services icon to appear in your Menu Bar when your location is requested. Click the **Done** button when finished.

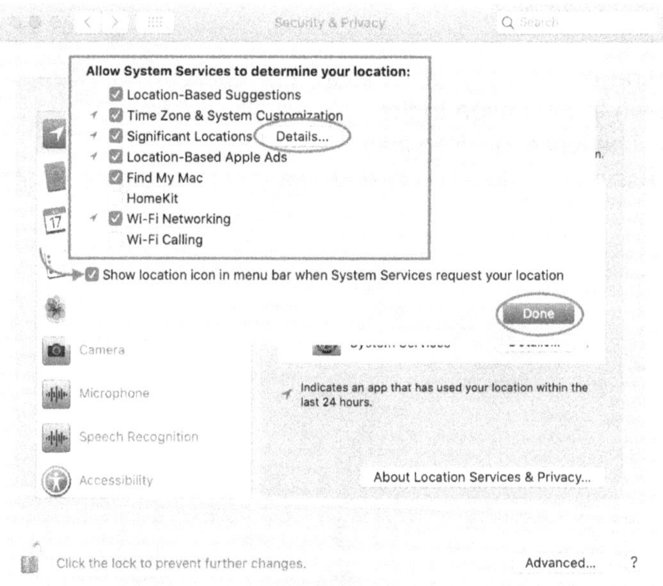

Disable Location Tracking

Clicking the **Details...** button next to **Significant Locations** will reveal a configuration sheet showing you a list of locations that your Mac has collected as you have hauled your laptop around town and on business and personal travel.

The location detail may surprise you. Apple states that location data is only used to provide *"...useful location-related information in Maps, Calendar, Photos, and more. Significant locations are encrypted and cannot be read by Apple."* You have to decide if the convenience of location data outweighs the potential privacy risk.

Click the triangle next to a city or town to see the locations your Mac considers significant. If the level of detail surprises you or if this invasion of privacy creeps you out, you can disable this feature. Click the **Clear History** button. Then click the **Done** button to go back to the previous configuration sheet and uncheck the checkbox next to **Significant Locations**.

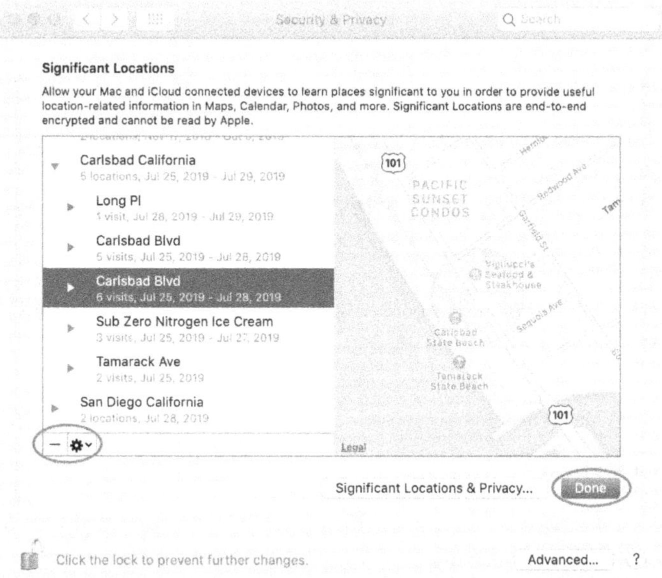

A single location can be removed by clicking on it to highlight it and then clicking the – button at the bottom of the Significant locations list. To clear the entire list, click on the settings (the gear) and choose **Clear History** from the drop-down menu.

Backup your Data or Restore Files

Time Machine is the macOS backup utility that automatically backs up your entire Mac to an external drive. Not only does it back up everything, but it also remembers how your Mac looked on any given day in the past, which is handy when you need to restore a file you accidentally deleted.

The **Time Machine Menu Extra** tells you when and to where Time Machine last backed up your Mac. By selecting **Back Up Now** you can immediately initiate a backup. To restore any lost files, select **Enter Time Machine**, find the files in the Time Machine Finder, select them, and click the **Restore** button.

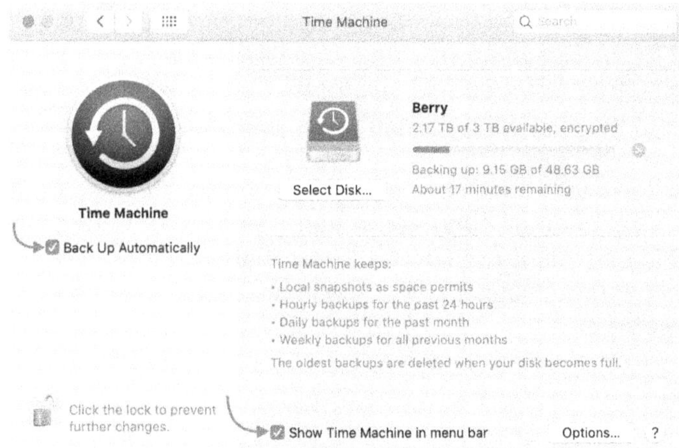

Selecting **Open Time Machine Preferences...** opens the **Time Machine** preference pane in System Preferences. This preference pane lets you turn **Time Machine** on and off, see the day and time of the last back up, and add or remove back up destinations.

At the bottom of the Time Machine preference pane is a checkbox next to **Show Time Machine in menu bar**. Checking this box places the Time Machine Menu Extra on your Menu Bar.

Third-party Menu Extras

Now that I have introduced you to the native macOS Menu Extras let's take a look at some handy third-party Menu Extras.

Track Your Packages

Deliveries is an efficient and straightforward Menu Extra that keeps track of your packages, so you'll always know when they will be delivered. The Deliveries app counts the days left until your package arrives, shows its current location on a map, and lets you view details at the carrier's website. Deliveries supports all major carriers as well as Amazon's Prime delivery service. The only exception seems to be OnTrac, which forces you to its website for information. With Deliveries, you will always know when your package is due to arrive.

Deliveries is available from the Mac App Store for $4.99 at the time of this writing at https://apps.apple.com/us/app/deliveries-a-package-tracker/id290986013.

Monitor Battery Status

If you have a MacBook, MacBook Air, or MacBook Pro, I recommend downloading **Battery Monitor**.

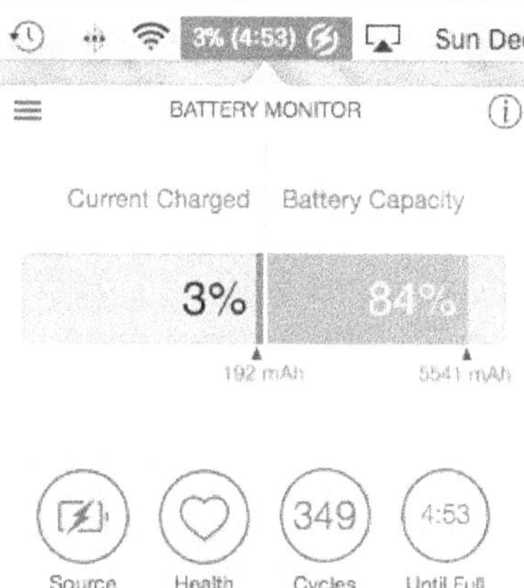

Battery Monitor provides more information than the native macOS Battery Menu Extra, displaying the current charge level, time remaining, the cycle count, health, battery capacity, and current charge in mAh. Battery Monitor is a simple app you can use to manage the health of your laptop's battery.

Battery Monitor is configured from its preference pane, which is accessible by clicking on the drop-down menu icon in the upper-left corner of the Battery Monitor information pane. The preference pane allows you to configure the behavior and the information Battery provides in its Menu Extra.

To ensure Battery Monitor is always running, make sure the checkbox next to **Open at Login** is checked. If you would like to see the Battery Monitor icon in the Dock, check the checkbox next to **Show in Dock**.

You can choose what information you want to be displayed on the Menu Extra and how you want it to appear in the next section. Checkboxes provide the option to **Show Percentage**, **Show Battery Time**, **Hide Icon** (the charge indicator icon in the Menu Bar), and **Show Charge Indicator,** which changes the charge indicator to the native macOS version.

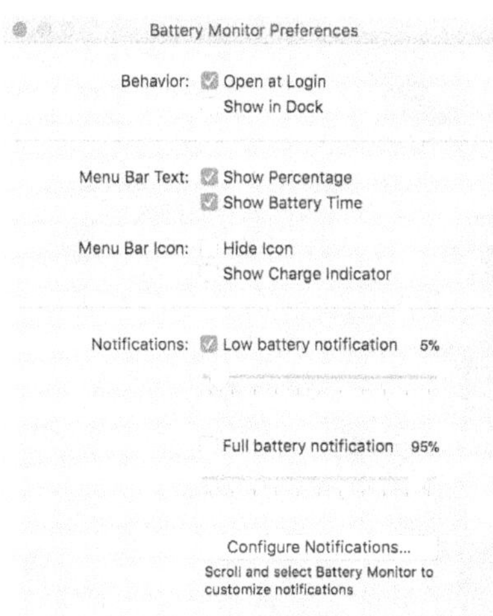

By default, Battery Monitor notifies you of a low battery condition when your battery charge is at 5%. You can change the percentage using the slider underneath **Low battery notification**.

Checking the checkbox next to **Full battery notification** enables a notification when your Mac laptop's battery reaches full charge. By default, this notification is disabled and set to 95%. Check the checkbox to enable and use the slider to change the percentage for the full charge notification.

Clicking the **Configure Notifications...** button opens the **Notifications** preference pane in System Preferences. Refer to the chapter on Notifications for details on how to customize macOS notifications.

Battery Monitor was available for free in the Mac App Store at the time of this writing at https://apps.apple.com/us/app/battery-monitor-health-status/id836505650?mt=12.

Unclutter Your Desktop

Despite the unsightly clutter, it is often very convenient to store files on the Desktop. For example, if you take a large number of screenshots, which are saved to the Desktop by default, having these files instantly available is not only convenient, but it also helps with productivity. It's too bad a Desktop cluttered with screenshots is unsightly. If you configured the Pristine Desktop tweak to keep your Desktop clear of clutter, it would be great if there was an app that could provide the convenience of storing files on the Desktop without the clutter.

This is where an app, appropriately named **Unclutter**, comes to the rescue. Written by Eugene Krupnov, Unclutter creates a handy place on your Desktop to store files, notes, and the clipboard history. Configuring the Pristine Desktop tweak and configuring Unclutter to use the Desktop folder gives you a completely clean Desktop while making the files in the Desktop folder instantly available from your Desktop.

To use Unclutter, move your pointer to the very top of your screen and scroll down with two fingers on your trackpad or mouse. The Unclutter window will drop from below the Menu Bar. The default configuration of Unclutter is in the image on the next page. Your clipboard history is shown at the left, files in the center, and notes on the right. Click anywhere outside Unclutter, on the Desktop or in a window, and the Unclutter window instantly disappears.

Files can be dragged into Unclutter's drop-zone located at the very top of your screen above the Menu Bar. Dragging a file into the drop-zone causes the Unclutter window to slide down from under the Menu Bar. Simply drop your file in the files area.

The clipboard history can store the last 10, 25, or 50 items that were cut or copied. You can scroll through them, selecting the one you need, and pasting it again. While I initially purchased Unclutter for quick access to files that would typically be on my Desktop, I find the clipboard history is one of its most useful features.

Let's customize Unclutter. Click on the Unclutter menu extra and select **Preferences...** or enter **⌘,** (command+comma) while the Unclutter window is displayed.

First, let's configure Unclutter's **General** preferences. Click the **General** tab. By default, Unclutter does not run when you start your Mac. Check the checkbox next to **Launch Unclutter at startup** to ensure Unclutter is always available when you start your Mac.

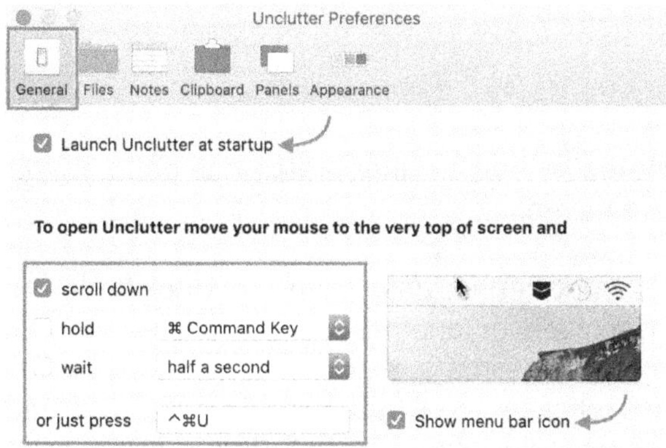

By default, the Unclutter window appears when you move your pointer to the very top of your screen and scroll down with two fingers. You have several options to activate Unclutter in addition to the two-finger scroll gesture. By checking the checkbox next to **hold**, you can configure Unclutter to use the ⇧, ^, ⌥, or ⌘ (shift, control, option, or command) keys. Hold down your chosen key and scroll up to the Menu Bar to activate Unclutter. Check the checkbox next to **wait** to configure Unclutter to activate when you move your pointer to the top of your Desktop and wait. You can configure the wait time to a half-second, 1 second, or 2 seconds. To configure a keyboard shortcut to reveal the Unclutter window, enter your desired shortcut in the box next to **or just press**. I've configured Unclutter to display its window when I enter **^⌘U** (control+command+U). To disable the two-finger scroll, uncheck the checkbox next to **scroll down**.

Unclutter puts a menu extra in the Menu Bar. If you do not want Unclutter's menu extra on your Menu Bar, uncheck the checkbox next to **Show menu bar icon**.

By default, Unclutter saves files to its own location. I find it very convenient to change the default location to the **Desktop** folder in my Home directory. This allows me to use the Pristine Desktop tweak for a completely clean Desktop, yet still have quick access to files saved in my Desktop folder. Additionally, Unclutter warns you that to enable Spotlight search for the files it has saved requires you to move files to a different location.

To change the default save location for files in Unclutter, click on the Unclutter menu extra and select **Preferences…** or enter **⌘,** (command+comma) while the Unclutter window is displayed. Click the **Files** tab. Select **Open…** from the drop-down menu next to **Store files in**. Navigate to your desired location (I use my Desktop folder) and click **Open**.

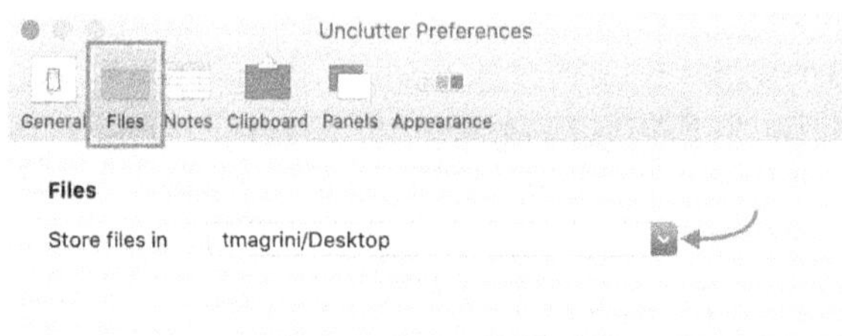

Similarly, clicking on **Notes** in the Unclutter preference pane allows you to change the location where notes are saved.

Sometimes you do not want certain data saved to Unclutter's clipboard history. For example, if you use Keychain or another password manager like 1Password, you probably don't want your passwords saved to the clipboard history. To exempt data from certain applications, click on the **Clipboard** tab in the Unclutter preference pane. Next, click the **+** at the lower-left and browse to the application you wish to exempt. Click on it and then click the **Open** button. Unclutter will not save or display data from an application in its **Sensitive Data** list.

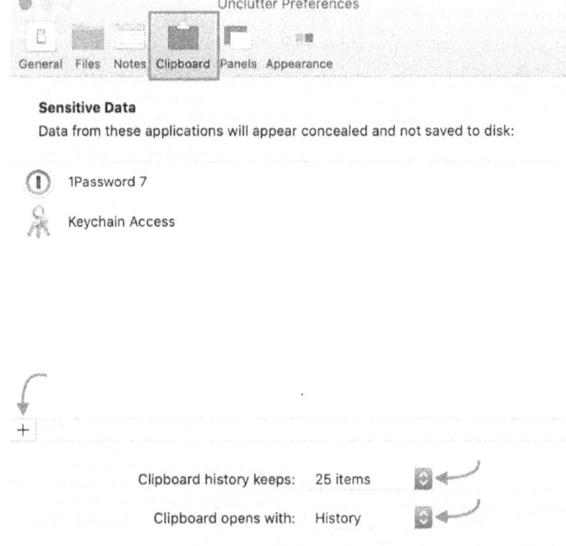

From the **Clipboard** tab, you can also configure the number of items Unclutter will save in the clipboard history. Use the drop-down menu next to **Clipboard history keeps** and select 10, 25, or 50 items.

By default, **Clipboard opens with** is set to **Last view**. The last view option displays the last clipboard item viewed. I have found it more convenient to configure this to **History**, which displays the clipboard history. You have a choice of **Item content**, **History**, **or Last view**.

The **Panels** tab in the Unclutter preference pane lets you disable any panels you do not want to use. By default, the checkboxes next to **Clipboard**, **Files**, and **Notes** are checked. If you do not wish to use a feature, uncheck the checkbox next to it.

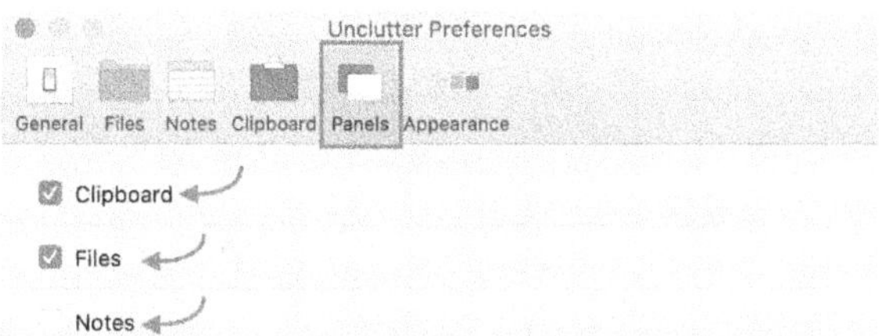

The last customizable item is the **Appearance** tab. By default, Unclutter is set to Auto **matches**, which automatically matches its theme to the current macOS Appearance. If you have configured macOS to use the Auto Appearance, leaving this setting at **Auto** is a good choice as it will match the current macOS Appearance as it changes throughout the day. If you prefer Unclutter's **Light** or **Dark** theme, you can select either from the drop-down menu next to **Theme**.

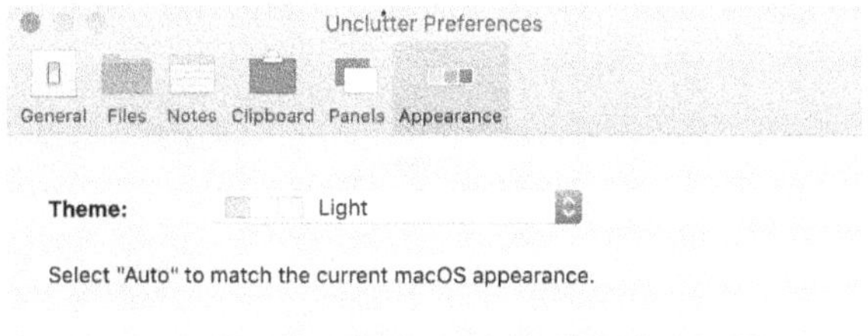

Unclutter is available from the Mac App Store for $19.99 at the time of this writing at https://apps.apple.com/us/app/unclutter/id577085396?mt=12

Focus with HazeOver

Having lots of open windows can be distracting, especially if you are trying to focus on one particular window. All those windows can kill your concentration, making you less productive as each window is another squirrel that demands your attention. Of course, you can always minimize or close windows and hide or quit applications, but all that window and application management is very distracting, drawing your attention from work at hand. A better solution is to use **HazeOver**, a distraction dimmer that highlights the active window while automatically dimming all background windows. Written by Maxim Ananov, HazeOver ensures you on task by letting all the background noise gently fade away. HazeOver lets you configure the amount background applications are dimmed, from a light, soft dim to a demandingly powerful black that guarantees to eliminate all distractions.

To configure HazeOver, click on its Menu Extra in the Menu Bar, and choose **Preferences...** from the drop-down menu.

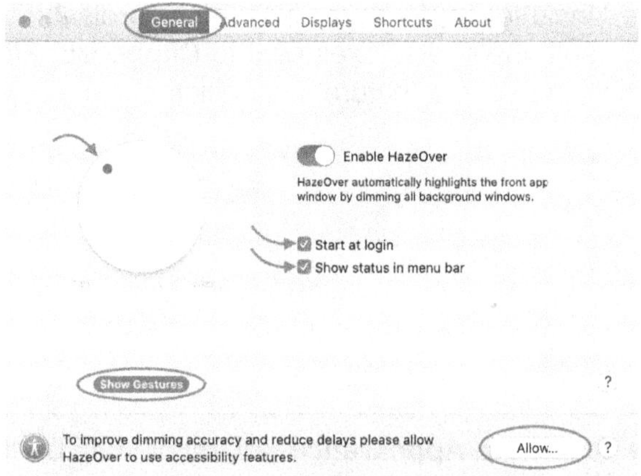

Select the **General** tab and ensure the switch next to **Enable HazeOver** is switched on. Next, configure the dimming percentage using the large wheel. You can move the wheel with a two-finger up or down scrolling motion or click and hold and drag with one finger. Click **Show Gestures** to view a video of the gestures. If you want HazeOver to start when you log in to your Mac, check the checkbox next to **Start at login**.

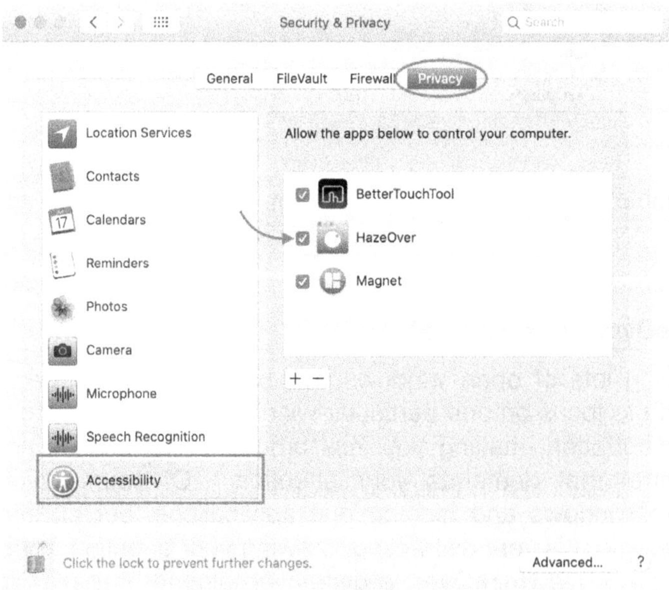

Be sure to click **Allow...** to allow HazeOver to use the macOS accessibility features to improve dimming accuracy. Click **Open System Preferences** when the security warning appears. The **Security & Privacy** preference pane opens with the **Privacy** tab highlighted. Check the checkbox next to **HazeOver**.

Now back to the HazeOver preference pane. Under the **Advanced** tab, You can select the background color (black is the default) and whether HazeOver highlights only one or all of the front windows of the active application. The animation speed can also be tweaked in the **Advanced** tab.

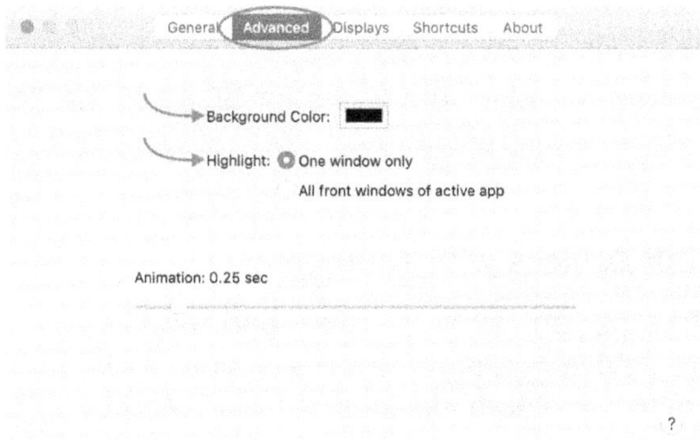

If you have multiple displays, you can configure how windows are dimmed across your displays in the **Displays** tab. You have two choices. The first is to **Dim all windows on displays without keyboard focus**. When selected, this option highlights only the active window on a single display, even if the active application has multiple windows open across your displays. Only the active window is highlighted while other windows are dimmed. The second option, **Highlight windows on displays without keyboard focus**, highlights the front windows of the active application on each of your displays.

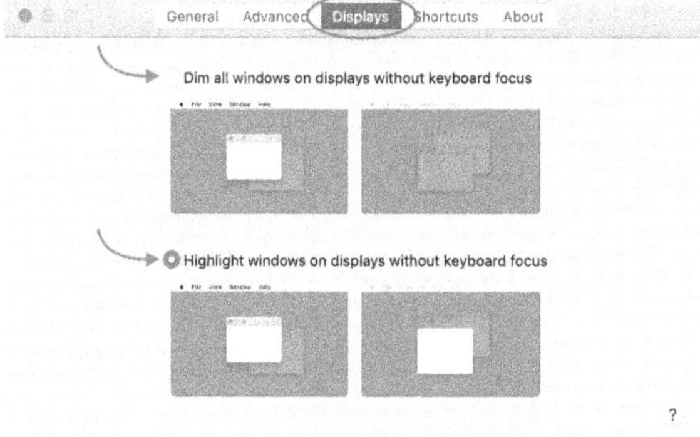

In the **Shortcuts** tab you can change the keyboard shortcut used to toggle HazeOver on and off. The default shortcut is **^⌥⌘H** (control+option+command+H). You can also record keyboard shortcuts to increase or decrease the dimming intensity in increments of +20% or -20%.

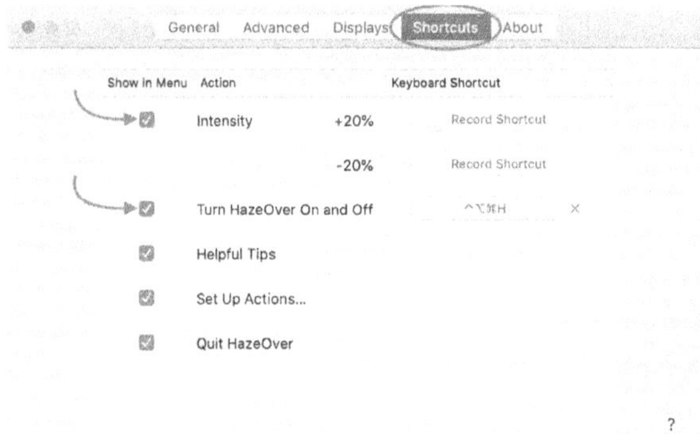

HazeOver is available from the Mac App Store for $5.99 at the time of this writing at https://apps.apple.com/us/app/distraction-dimmer-hazeover/id430798174?mt=12

Manage Your Bluetooth Devices with Toothpicks

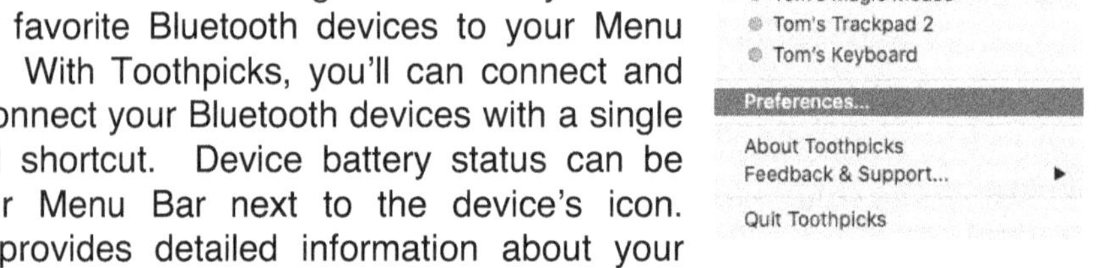

Toothpicks is an easy to use and handy Bluetooth device manager that lets you add your favorite Bluetooth devices to your Menu Bar. With Toothpicks, you'll can connect and disconnect your Bluetooth devices with a single click or keyboard shortcut. Device battery status can be displayed in your Menu Bar next to the device's icon. Toothpicks also provides detailed information about your connected devices when you hover over the device's icon in the Menu Bar.

To configure Toothpicks, select **Preferences...** from the Toothpicks drop-down menu and select the **General** tab. Check the checkbox next to **Launch at login** to ensure Toothpicks is running each time you log into your Mac. If you don't want to see the Toothpicks icon in the Dock, check the checkbox next to **Hide Dock icon**.

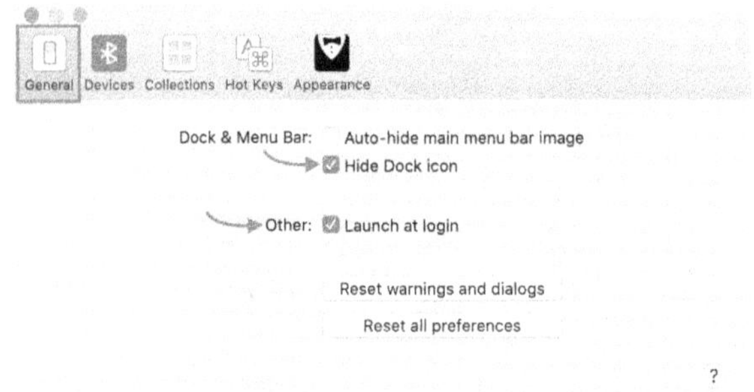

The **Devices** tab is where you can configure your Bluetooth devices. Select a device in the sidebar to highlight it. Record a keyboard shortcut to set a **Quick Connect/Disconnect Hot Key**. If you want the device to appear in your Menu Bar, check the checkbox next to **Include device in menu bar**. Use the drop-down menu next to **Show** to choose whether you want the device to **Always** appear or only when it is connected or disconnected. Choose an image from the **Image** drop-down menu. You can choose to have the **Battery Level Display** in **Numerical** or **Graphical** form or not at all by selecting **None**. Select left or right-click to connect and disconnect the device from the **Click Action** drop-down menu.

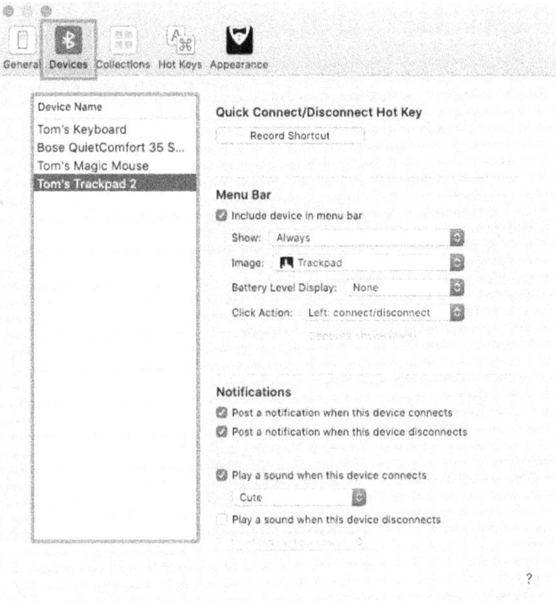

You can configure **Notifications** to occur when the highlighted device connects or disconnects by checking the appropriate checkbox. If you would like Toothpicks to play a sound when the highlighted device connects or disconnects, check the respective checkbox(es). Select a sound from the drop-down menu.

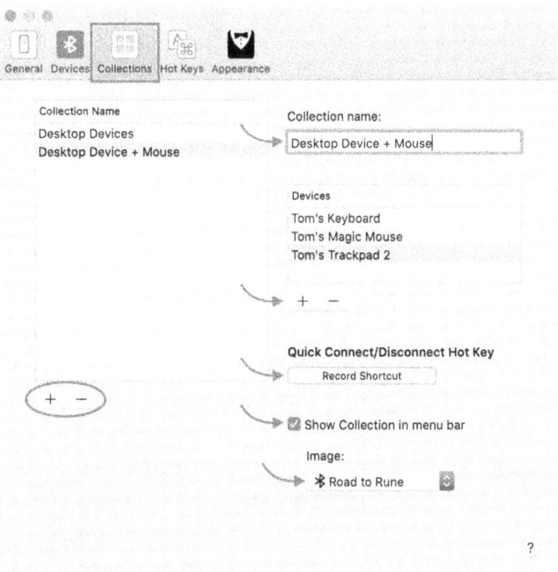

You can group your Bluetooth devices in the **Collections** tab. First, create a new collection by clicking the **+** button under the **Collection Name** section and give your new collection a name. Click the **+** button under **Devices** to add Bluetooth devices to your collection. Record a keyboard shortcut, if desired. If you want your collection to appear in the Menu Bar, check the checkbox next to **Show Collection in menu bar** and choose an **Image** from the drop-down menu.

Select **Hot Keys** tab to record keyboard shortcuts to **Show Main Menu**, **Connect All Devices**, and **Disconnect All Devices**.

The **Appearance** tab lets you change the Toothpicks **Main Menu Bar Image**, with the default being the **Holy Molar**. Choose your desired images from the drop-down menu. By default, green and red-colored dots are used the represent connected and disconnected device status, respectively. Uncheck the checkbox next to **Use color to represent device status** if you would rather see a checkmark and a dash for connected and disconnected status, respectively.

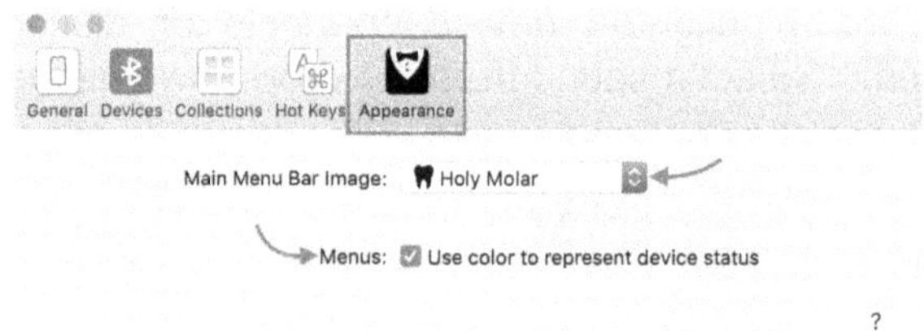

Toothpicks is available from the Mac App Store for $2.99 at the time of this writing at https://apps.apple.com/us/app/toothpicks/id998361254?mt=12.

Keep Your Mac Awake

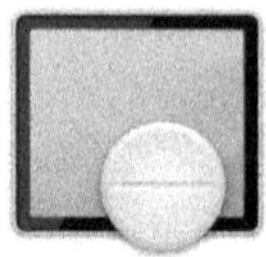

Sometimes you need to keep your Mac awake, overriding its energy-saving features. For example, you may need to keep your Mac awake if you subscribe to a cloud back up service. Typically, cloud back up services run more efficiently when you are not using your Mac. Depending on the size of your back up, you may need to run your cloud backup application for a couple of hours. Unfortunately, when you are not actively

Allow Display to Sleep
Start Screen Saver After 5 minutes
Enable Triggers
Enable Drive Alive
End Session if Battery is Below 10%
Show Session Time in Menu Bar

using your Mac, macOS will put it to sleep after the inactivity timer set in the Energy Savings preference pane expires.

If you want to leave your Mac unattended for a period of time but do not want it to go into sleep mode, you can override its energy saver settings and keep it awake using a free app called **Amphetamine**.

From Amphetamine's Menu Extra, you can choose one of the preset timers from 5 minutes to 24 hours listed under **Minutes** and **Hours**, keep your Mac awake indefinitely, until a specific time, or while an application is running or a file is downloading. A handy feature is the Quick Preferences menu, which allows you to enable or disable features from the Menu Extra.

To configure Amphetamine, select **Preferences...** from the Amphetamine Menu Extra drop-down menu. First, let's look at the **General** tab. **Launch Amphetamine at login** is enabled by default. Uncheck it if you prefer to launch Amphetamine each time you want to use it. The Amphetamine icon is displayed in the Dock when it is running. Check the checkbox next to **Hide Amphetamine in the Dock** to hide it.

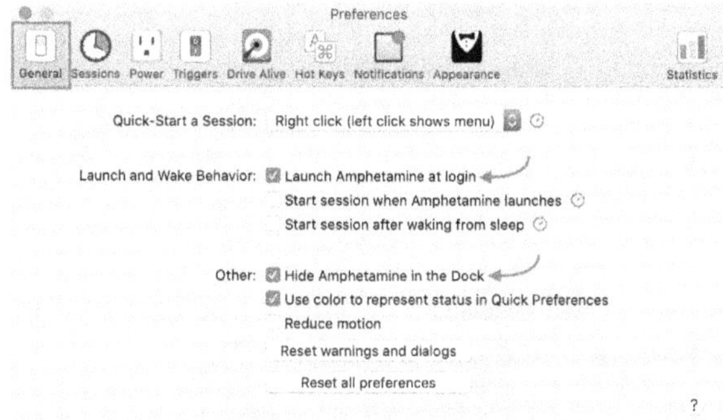

In the **Sessions** tab, you can configure a **Default Duration** for an Amphetamine session. The options in the drop-down menu mirror the session durations shown in the Menu Extra drop-down, from 5 minutes to 24 hours, indefinitely, or **Other Time...**, which allows you to configure your own duration.

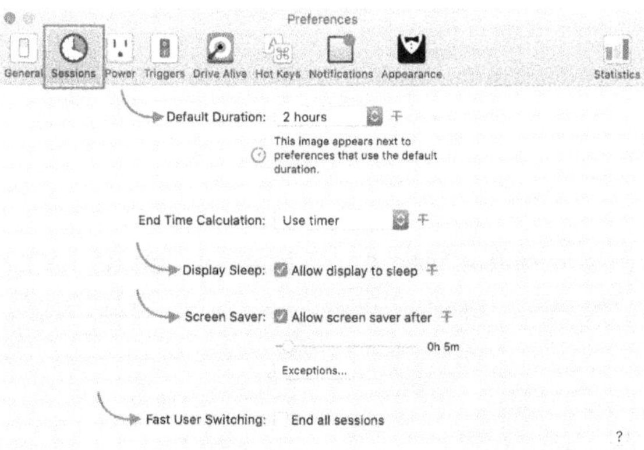

Check the checkbox next to **Allow display to sleep** to allow your display to sleep during a session. You can also enable the screen saver to start by checking the checkbox next to **Start screen saver after** and using the slider to configure the time. If you have Fast User Switching enabled, you can have Amphetamine **End all sessions** by checking the checkbox.

In the **Hot Keys** tab, you can record a single keyboard shortcut to start and end a session or separate shortcuts to start and end sessions. In the image below, I configured the keyboard shortcut ⌥⇧⌘A (option+shift+command+A) to start a new session with a duration of 2 hours. Use the drop-down menu to select a duration.

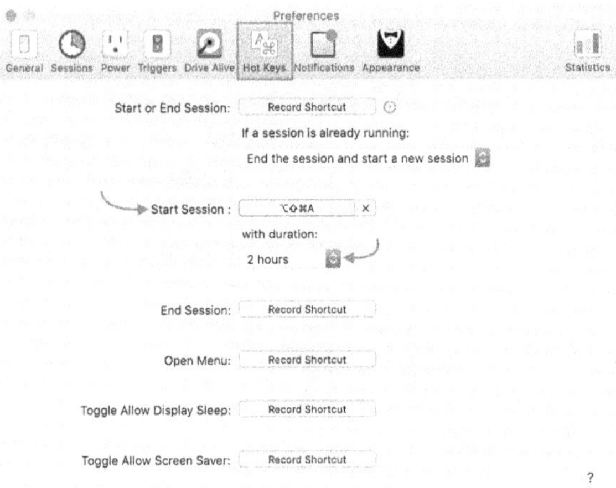

Use the **Notifications** tab to set session reminder notifications and to set the sound you want to play at the start and end of a session.

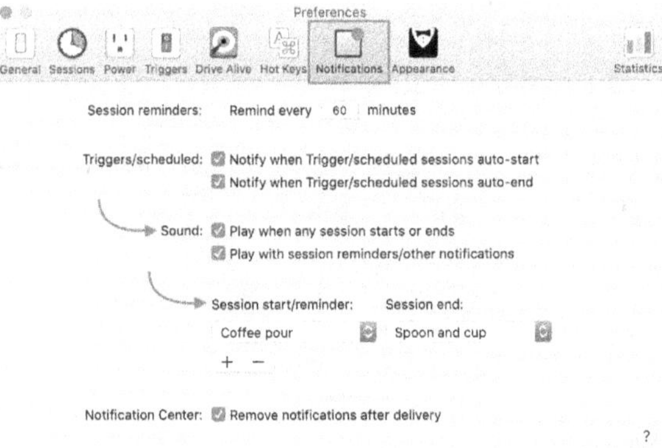

Amphetamine is available from the Mac App Store for free at the time of this writing at https://apps.apple.com/gb/app/amphetamine/id937984704?mt=12.

Caffeinate Your Mac

If you prefer to use **Terminal** to keep your Mac awake, you can use the following command to override the macOS inactivity timer.

```
caffeinate
```

If you want to keep your Mac awake for a set period of time, you can set a timer when issuing the caffeinate command. For example, the following command keeps your Mac awake for 12 hours. The time is measured in seconds; therefore, 12 hours equates to 43,200 seconds (12 hours x 60 minutes x 60 seconds).

```
caffeinate -t 43200
```

Once you issue the caffeinate command, your Mac will not sleep, dim its display, or play the screen saver until you end the command. You can terminate a caffeinate session by entering **^C** (control+C) with the Terminal app open.

Toggle Light & Dark Mode

NightOwl is a Menu Extra that allows you to toggle between Light and Dark modes quickly. With NightOwl, you can switch manually with a click or keyboard shortcut or automatically at a specific time or at sunrise and sunset.

You can toggle between Light and Dark Modes manually with a click from NightOwl's Menu Extra. If you want NightOwl to toggle between modes at sunrise and sunset, check the checkbox next to **Sunrise/Sunset** in the NightOwl Menu Extra. You can set a schedule by checking the checkbox next to **Scheduled** and setting times for Light and Dark Mode.

If you prefer to use Light Mode for specific applications, you can exempt them from Dark Mode by checking the checkbox(es) next to each application in the list under **Always stay light**. Position your pointer over this section and scroll to see the full list of applications.

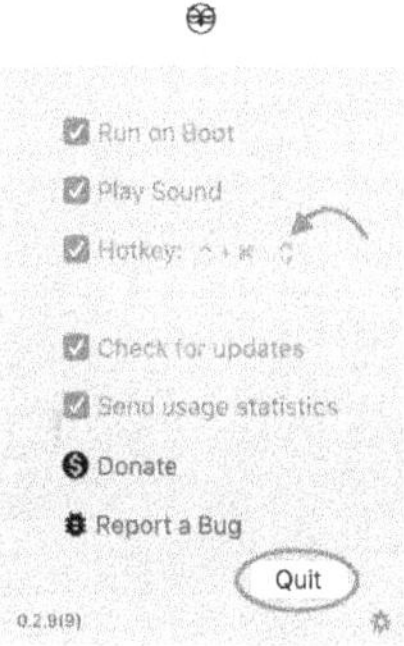

The small gear in the lower-right corner opens the NightOwl preference pane. To ensure that NightOwl runs each time you restart your Mac, verify that the checkbox next to **Run on Boot** is checked. By default, NightOwl plays an owl's hoot when switching modes. If you prefer no sound, uncheck the checkbox next to **Play Sound**. If you'd like to use a keyboard shortcut, check the checkbox next to **Hotkey**. The default keyboard shortcut is ^⌘ (control+command). You can choose from 2 other shortcuts, ⇧^⌥ (shift+control+option) or ^⌥⌘ (control+option+command) from the drop-down menu next to **HotKey**.

Check for updates and **Send usage statistics** are enabled by default. If you want to quit NightOwl, click the **Quit** button.

NightOwl is available for free, although the developer asks for a voluntary donation, at https://nightowl.kramser.xyz.

6

Dock

Whether you are starting your Mac for the first or the thousandth time, the most iconic and recognizable feature of the macOS Desktop is the **Dock**. The Dock is one of the most customizable features of macOS. The Dock appears as a strip of application and folder icons at the bottom of the Desktop and serves a twofold purpose, combining the functions of an application launcher to run applications and application switcher to jump between running applications. The Dock is an ingenious feature of macOS that provides a convenient and speedy method to launch applications, open documents and folders, or switch between applications with a single click of your trackpad or mouse.

The Dock is organized into three distinct sections by a pair of translucent vertical **Dock Dividers**. Applications are located on the left side of the Dock. The three most recent apps are located between the two Dock Dividers. Minimized windows, folders, stacks, and the trash can are located to the right of the right-most Dock Divider.

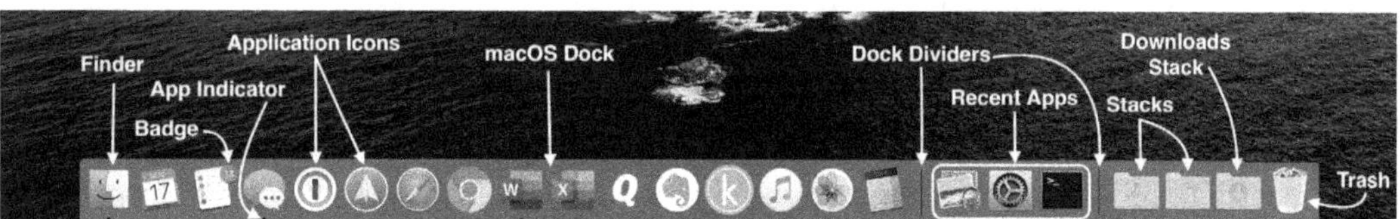

In the macOS Mojave release, Apple borrowed a feature from iPadOS and added a new section to the Dock for recently opened and running apps that are not already included in the application section of the Dock. This feature fundamentally changed how the Dock displays running applications. Previous versions of macOS would add running apps to the end of the application side of the Dock, to the left of the vertical Dock Divider. In macOS Catalina, running applications are shown in the Recent Apps section between the two vertical Dock Dividers. This section also shows the three most recently opened applications, even if they are not currently running. A tiny black dot denotes applications that are currently running beneath their icon.

Put Apps in Order

The first order of business in customizing the Dock is to put the application icons in the order in which you want to see them. This is easily accomplished by moving your pointer to the application icon you wish to move, clicking, holding, and dragging it horizontally, left or right, along the Dock to its new location. If you click and hold too long without moving the icon, a menu appears, and you won't be able to move the icon. In this case, click anywhere on the Desktop and try again. While you are moving the icon, other icons politely move out of the way. Once in its desired location, release your hold.

Remove Apps from the Dock

Once you have your application icons in the right order, the next step is to remove apps that you don't want in the Dock. Note that when you remove an application from the Dock, you are not removing it from your Mac. You only remove its alias from the Dock. The application remains safely tucked away in the **Applications** folder.

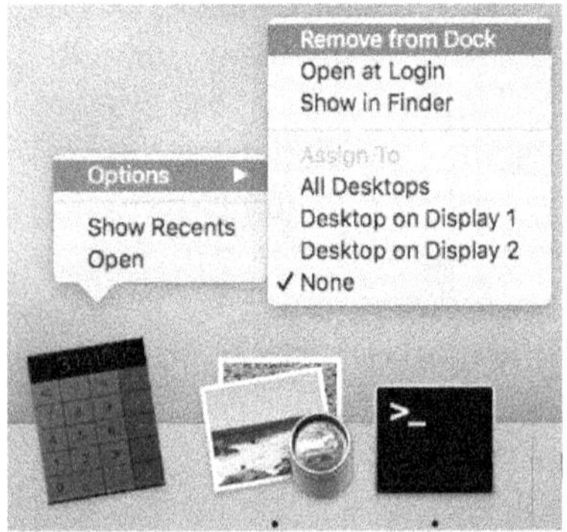

There are always multiple ways of doing things in macOS. It is your personal choice which method you prefer. You can always click and hold the icon you wish to remove until a contextual menu appears. You can also make this menu appear by using a secondary click, holding the control key down while clicking or by using the two-finger tap gesture. If a two-finger tap doesn't work, it means you haven't yet customized the trackpad. Select **Options > Remove from Dock**.

An application that is running behaves differently. You can click and hold the icon or use a secondary click to reveal the contextual menu. Select **Options**, and a submenu appears. Note the checkmark next to **Keep in Dock**. Select Keep in Dock to remove the checkmark. The menu disappears along with the checkmark. Since the application is running, its icon will not disappear until you quit the app.

By far, the fastest and easiest way to remove an app icon from the Dock is to drag it up past the middle of the Desktop. About halfway up the screen, **Remove** appears above the icon. Release the icon to remove it. If the app icon jumps back to the Dock, it means one of two things. Perhaps you didn't move it far enough away from the Dock. Be sure to move it far enough from the Dock until **Remove** appears above the app's icon. The other possibility is that the app is running. If the app is running, it won't disappear from the Dock until you quit it.

Oops! Everyone panics the first time they accidentally remove the wrong application icon from the Dock, and it disappears. Don't worry. There's an easy fix. Simply add the application back onto the Dock. We'll cover how to do that next.

Add Apps to the Dock

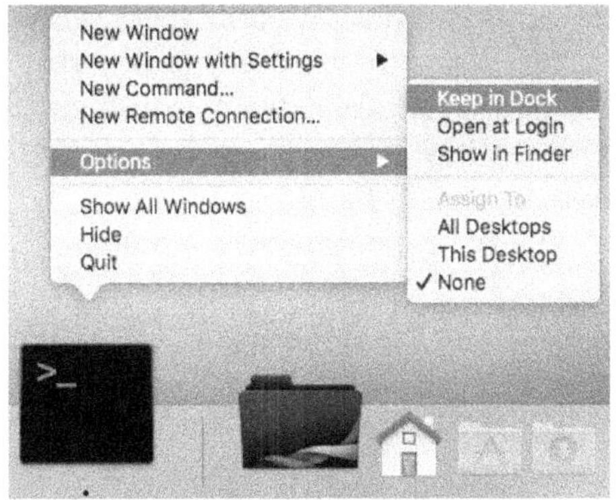

Adding an application to the **Dock** is even easier than removing one. Of course, there are multiple ways to do so. The simplest method is to launch the application, and once it appears in the Dock, drag it to the left to your desired location. The simple act of moving an app icon to the left along the Dock is a signal to macOS that you want to keep the app in the Dock. Another method is to secondary click to reveal the contextual menu. Select **Options > Keep in Dock**.

Another method to add an application to the Dock is to open the **Applications** folder in Finder, find the application icon, and drag it to the Dock. Note that you are not moving the app. You are creating an alias on the Dock. You can also add an application to the Dock using a keyboard shortcut. Find the app in the **Applications** folder, click on it to highlight it, and then enter the keyboard shortcut **⇧^⌘T** (shift+control+command+T).

Control Application Behavior

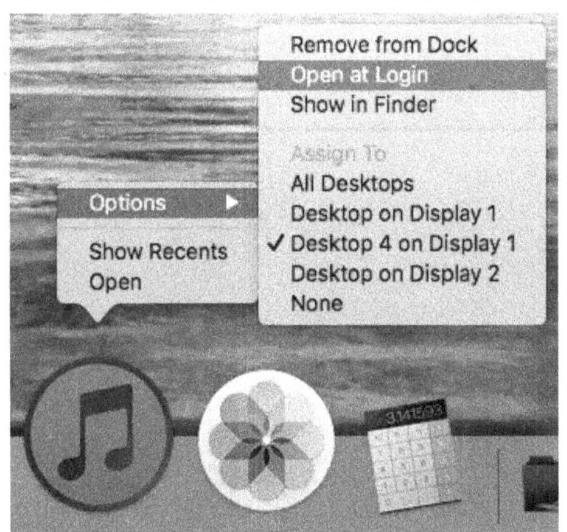

The **Options** contextual menu controls how an application behaves. Checking **Open at Login** opens the app immediately when you log in. This is handy if you have an app or set of apps you open every time you start your Mac. For example, if you always open Safari, Mail, and Music, setting these apps to open at login saves you from having to launch each one individually. Use a secondary click to make the **Options** menu appear and select **Open at Login**. A checkmark indicates the application launches when you log in or start your Mac. If you no longer want an application to open when you log in, select **Options > Open at Login** to remove the checkmark.

If you want to see the folder where the application is located in Finder, choose **Show in Finder**. This command immediately opens the Applications folder with the application highlighted. However, occasionally applications are mistakenly installed in other folders. This is handy if you need to navigate to the application's location to move or uninstall it.

The **Assign To** > **This Desktop** feature allows you to assign an application to appear on a specific Desktop. This feature is handy if you prefer certain applications to always appear on specific Desktops.

It is quite common to have more than one window open for the same application. As your Desktop becomes crowded with open windows from multiple applications, it becomes increasingly difficult to find a specific window. This is especially true if you moved a window or two to another Desktop. The **Show All Windows** command executes a feature called **App Exposé**, which removes the clutter to reveal all the windows of the chosen application. You can then select the desired window by pointing and clicking on it, making it active, and placing it on top of all other windows.

App Exposé can also be executed with a trackpad gesture. Click on any open window of the application you are interested in seeing and then swipe down with three or four fingers, depending on how you set up the gesture in the Trackpad preference pane.

Finally, macOS displays the recent items in a list above the **Options** menu. This is a handy feature if you need to reopen a document you recently closed.

Hide Recent Apps

If you don't like the way the Dock handles running and recent apps, macOS allows you to hide this section of the Dock. To hide the recent apps section, open the **Dock** preference pane from System Preferences and uncheck the checkbox next to **Show recent applications in Dock**.

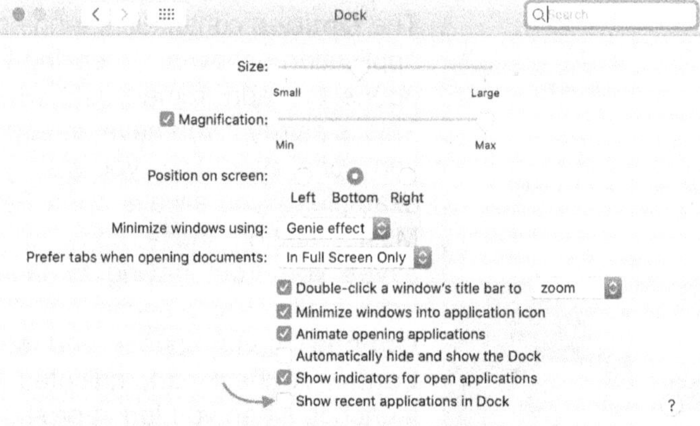

You can always see your recently opened apps by clicking **> Recent Items** or by creating a recent apps stack, which I show you in the next chapter.

The Other Side of the Divider

The Dock's translucent Divider separates applications from Stacks, minimized windows, documents, and the trash can. The icon at the end of the Dock that looks like a translucent white trash can is the **Trash**, a temporary holding area for files you want to delete. You can move files to the Trash by dragging them onto its icon. Another option is to utilize a secondary click on a file in Finder to display a contextual menu and select **Move to Trash**.

Once items are in the Trash, the icon changes to display a full trash can. If you secondary click on the Trash icon when there are items in it, you have the option to **Empty Trash** or display its contents with the **Open** command. The latter feature is handy if you accidentally drag a file into the trash and need to restore it. To restore a file you accidentally placed in the trash, click and drag the file back to its original location.

Select **Empty Trash** to empty the trash. A warning appears to confirm that you want to empty the trash.

Delete a File Immediately

You can delete files immediately when they are in the Trash without deleting any of the other files. To delete a file immediately from the Trash, first open the Trash folder by secondary clicking on its icon in the Dock and selecting **Open** from the contextual menu. The **Trash** Finder window opens. Secondary click on the file you want to delete and select **Delete Immediately…**. You also can hold down the ⌥ (option) key while selecting **File > Delete Immediately…** or enter the keyboard shortcut **⌥⌘delete** (option+command+delete). A dialog box appears to confirm the deletion and warn you that this action cannot be undone. Click the **Delete** button to delete the file immediately or click the **Cancel** button to cancel.

Note that the Delete Immediately option only appears in the **File** menu when you are holding down the ⌥ (option) key. When the ⌥ (option) key is held down, **Put Back** changes to **Delete Immediately**.

Automatically Hide and Show the Dock

Although the Dock is a handy feature of macOS, it takes up a significant amount of real estate. This can sometimes be problematic when moving your pointer to the bottom of a window as it sometimes inadvertently interacts with the Dock. macOS gives you the option of hiding the Dock when not in use and when combined with the Menu Bar auto-hide feature I showed you in the last chapter, you'll be amazed at the amount of clean, uncluttered Desktop real estate these two features provide. See the section "Automatically Hide and Show the Menu Bar" in the last chapter to learn how to hide the Menu Bar.

To enable Dock hiding, open the Dock preference pane from System Preferences. Check the box next to **Automatically hide and show the Dock**. The change takes effect immediately.

The Dock slips beneath the bottom of your Desktop when not in use. To make the Dock reappear, position your pointer at the bottom edge of the Desktop or enter **⌥⌘D** (option+command+D).

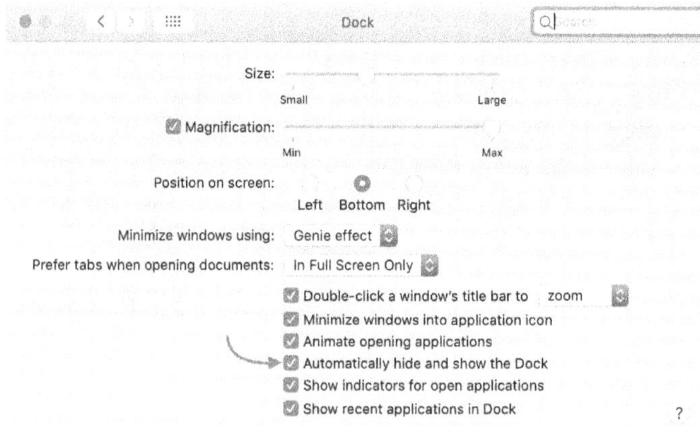

You can also enable the Dock Hiding feature from the Dock. Position your pointer over one of the Dock Dividers. When the pointer turns into a two-headed vertical white arrow, use a secondary click to open the Dock contextual menu. Select **Turn Hiding On**. To disable hiding, secondary click the Dock Divider and select **Turn Hiding Off**.

You can also use a keyboard shortcut to make the Dock disappear and reappear on demand by entering **⌥⌘D** (option+command+D).

Magnify the Dock Icons

Magnification is a handy feature that allows you to conserve Desktop real estate by keeping your Dock small and magnifying icons as you move your pointer over them. Magnification is particularly useful if you prefer a small Dock or your Dock is crowded with a large number of icons. As you add more icons to your Dock, it becomes smaller, adjusting its size to fit horizontally across the bottom or vertically along the left or right side of your Desktop, making it challenging to distinguish apps from each other. With magnification enabled, the icons in the Dock magnify as you move your pointer over them.

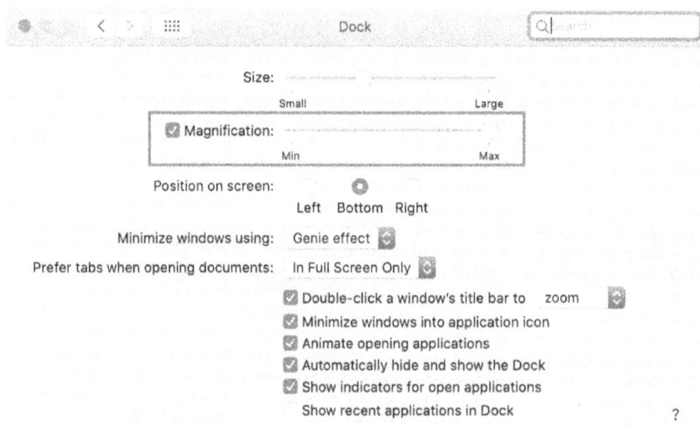

Magnification is enabled from the **Dock** preference pane in System Preferences. Check the box next to **Magnification** and use the slider to select your desired level of magnification from "Min," which is no magnification, to "Max," which is 128 pixels. The change takes effect immediately.

You can also enable the Dock magnification feature from the Dock. To enable Dock magnification, position your pointer over the Dock Divider. When the pointer turns into a two-headed vertical white arrow, use a secondary click to open the Dock contextual menu. Select **Turn Magnification On**.

To turn magnification off, secondary click the Dock Divider to open the Dock contextual menu and select **Turn Magnification Off** or uncheck the **Magnification** checkbox in the Dock preference pane.

Add More Magnification

If you want more magnification than what is configurable in the Dock preference pane, you can set magnification levels up to a ridiculously large 512 pixels. Open Terminal and enter the following commands. The 256 at the end of the first command doubles the default maximum magnification.

```
defaults write com.apple.dock largesize -float 256

killall Dock
```

Why not go all the way and double the magnification level again?

```
defaults write com.apple.dock largesize -float 512

killall Dock
```

Now that's ridiculously large! You can enter an integer between 1 and 512. Enter the following commands to revert to the default maximum magnification level.

```
defaults write com.apple.dock largesize -float 128

killall Dock
```

Toggle Dock Magnification On or Off

Holding down the ⇧^ keys (shift+control) while moving your pointer across the Dock toggles magnification on or off. If you have Dock magnification disabled, holding the ⇧^ (shift+control) keys while moving across the Dock temporarily enables magnification. Conversely, if you have Dock magnification enabled, holding the ⇧^ (shift+control) keys while moving across the Dock temporarily disables magnification.

Relocate the Dock

The default position of the Dock is at the bottom of the Desktop. macOS allows you to relocate the Dock to either the left or right edges of the Desktop. The following image shows what the Dock looks like when positioned at the left, bottom, or right edge of the Desktop.

To relocate the Dock, open the **Dock** preference pane in System Preferences. Select the **Left**, **Bottom**, or **Right** radio button next to **Position on screen**.

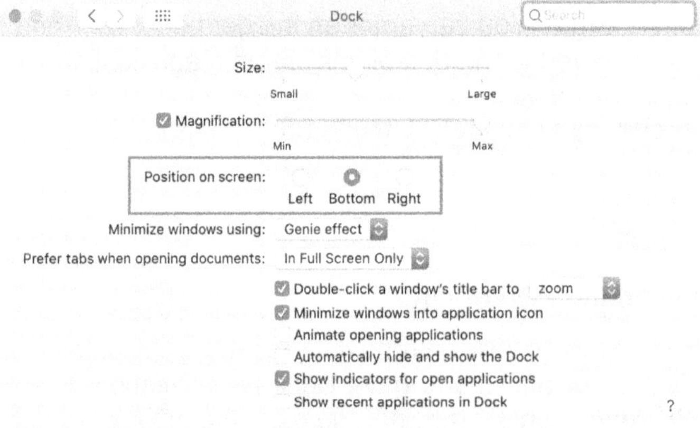

You can also relocate the Dock by positioning your pointer over the Dock Divider. When the pointer turns into a two-headed vertical white arrow, use a secondary click to open the Dock contextual menu. Select **Position on Screen** and select **Left**, **Bottom**, or **Right**. Your selection takes effect immediately.

Change How Windows Minimize

macOS features two standard animation effects when windows are minimized or maximized. The default is the **Genie effect**, in which windows minimize or maximize like a genie entering or exiting a magic lamp. The second option is the **Scale effect**, where a window scales smaller and smaller until it finally reaches the Dock. When maximizing, the window scales larger as it restores itself to its original size.

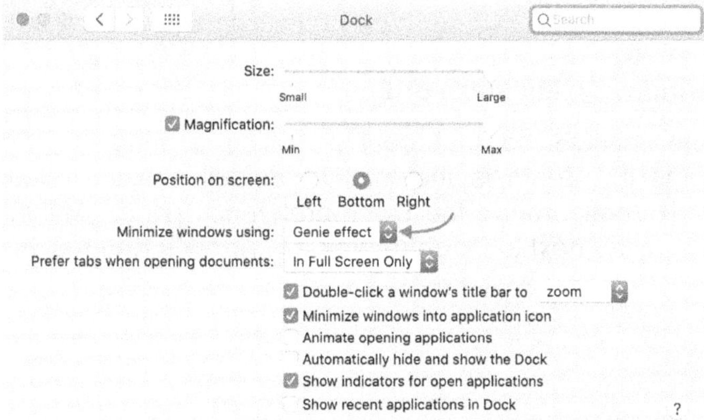

To change how windows minimize, open the **Dock** preference pane in the System Preferences application. Choose **Genie effect** or **Scale effect** from the drop-down menu next to **Minimize windows using**.

You can also change how windows are minimized from the Dock. Position your pointer over the Dock Divider. When the pointer turns into a two-headed vertical white arrow, use a secondary click to open the Dock contextual menu. Select **Minimize Using** and choose **Genie effect** or **Scale effect**.

Minimize Windows with the Hidden Suck Effect

macOS offers two standard animations when minimizing windows, the Genie and Scale effects, with the default being Genie. macOS offers one more animation, the **Suck** effect, which is not available from the Dock preference pane. As the name suggests, a minimized window appears as if it is being sucked into the Dock by a powerful vacuum cleaner. Maximizing reverses the effect with the window shooting back to its original position as it pushed by a powerful leaf blower.

To enable the suck effect, open Terminal, and enter the following commands. Be sure to press the **return** key after each line. The change takes place immediately. Minimize a window and check it out.

```
defaults write com.apple.dock mineffect -string suck

killall Dock
```

You could have also replaced **suck** with either **genie** or **scale** in the above write command to configure either window animation directly in Terminal.

To revert to the default Genie animation, enter the following commands in Terminal.

```
defaults delete com.apple.dock mineffect

killall Dock
```

Double-Click a Window to Minimize or Zoom

You can configure macOS so that double-clicking a window's Title Bar either minimizes or zooms it. Zoom is the macOS default setting. Double-clicking to minimize or zoom is configured in the **Dock** preference pane. Make your selection from the drop-down menu next to **Double-click a window's title bar to**.

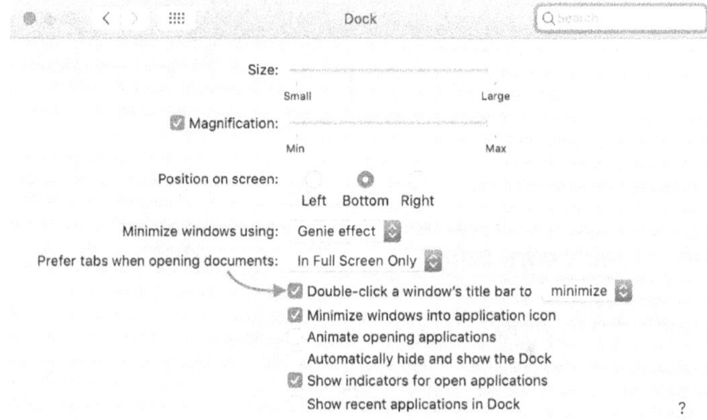

When set to minimize, double-clicking the Title Bar does the same thing as clicking a window's yellow control button. When set to zoom, double-clicking expands the window to cover all available Desktop space between the Menu Bar and the Dock. Double-clicking again returns the window to its previous size.

If you have chosen to hide both the Menu Bar and Dock when not in use, double-clicking to zoom expands the window to cover the entire Desktop. While this sounds like Full-screen mode, it is not. Mission Control does not recognize zoomed windows as Full-screen apps. You can still take an app to Full-screen mode when zoomed by clicking the green control button in its Title Bar.

Size the Dock

The Dock automatically resizes itself based on the number of icons docked. As you squeeze more icons into the Dock, it stretches across the bottom or the left or right edge of your Desktop. The size of the screen limits the Dock's maximum size.

macOS does not allow you to make the Dock so big that it won't fit on the screen, although the left- and right-most icons slide off the screen when magnified.

Once the Dock reaches the maximum size allowed by the screen, you can continue to add icons. However, each icon becomes smaller to allow all icons to fit. If your Dock has become overcrowded with app icons, check out the next chapter where I show you a nifty method to group apps into stacks and use them as application launchers.

Sizing the Dock is accomplished through the **Dock** preference pane. At the top of the pane is the **Size** slider, which controls the size of the Dock. When you make the Dock smaller, it takes up less space. Sometimes it seems that sliding the slider towards large does not affect the size of the Dock. This is because macOS scales the Dock to the maximum size horizontally (or vertically if positioned along the left or right edge) that will fit given the number of icons in the Dock.

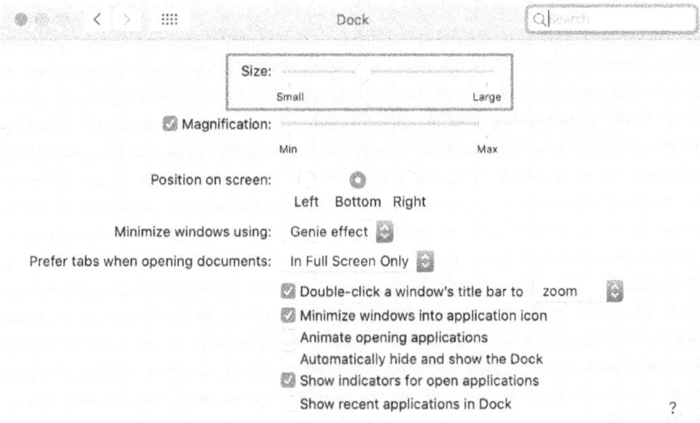

A second option is to change the size of the Dock from the Dock itself. Move your mouse pointer over the Divider. It turns into a double-headed vertical white arrow. Click, hold, and drag the white arrow up to make the Dock bigger and down to make it smaller. Remember, the maximum size is limited by the size of the screen. And while you can make the Dock very small, macOS limits you here too.

When you resize the Dock, you are changing the size of each of the icons displayed in the Dock. You can utilize Terminal to more precisely size the icons. Try out the following commands. They make your Dock small. Don't worry, you can resize it.

```
defaults write com.apple.dock tilesize -int 32
```

```
killall Dock
```

macOS allows you to replace the 32 in the first command with an integer from 1 to 256. The smaller the number, the smaller the Dock. Try using the integer 1.

```
defaults write com.apple.dock tilesize -int 1
```

```
killall Dock
```

Don't worry. Your Dock is still there. It's that tiny blob where your Dock used to be. A Dock this small is not useable even with magnification. Let's change the Dock to a more reasonable size.

```
defaults write com.apple.dock tilesize -int 64

killall Dock
```

There, that's better. You can try other integers between 1 and 256. If you were hoping for a super-sized Dock, you're out of luck. The size of the Dock is limited to the maximum size that fits on the screen.

Sometimes getting the Dock sized is like adjusting the driver's seat in your car. It's never quite right. If you want to return the Dock to its default size and start over, open Terminal and enter these commands.

```
defaults delete com.apple.dock tilesize

killall Dock
```

Change Minimize Window Behavior

By default, macOS minimizes windows to the right side of the Dock. This can become problematic if you minimize a large number of windows. As you minimize each window, the Dock expands. Once the Dock reaches its maximum size, each successive window minimization causes it to become smaller as macOS crowds more minimized window icons into the right side of the Dock. Eventually, overcrowding causes the icons in the Dock to become difficult to differentiate, especially the minimized windows.

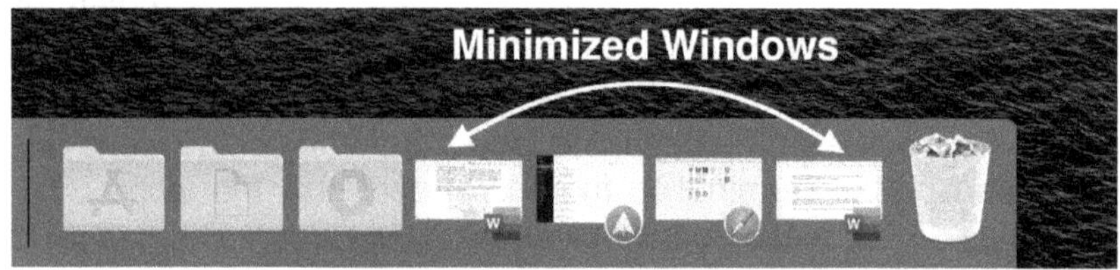

macOS has a solution available in the Dock preference pane. Instead of minimizing windows into the Dock, you can configure macOS to minimize windows into their respective application icon. This reduces the overcrowding and clutter on the right side of the Dock and avoids the Dock having to increase its size.

Open the Dock preference pane in the System Preferences application. Click the checkbox next to **Minimize windows into application icon**. When this option is checked, macOS minimizes windows into their application icon, saving a great deal of Dock real estate.

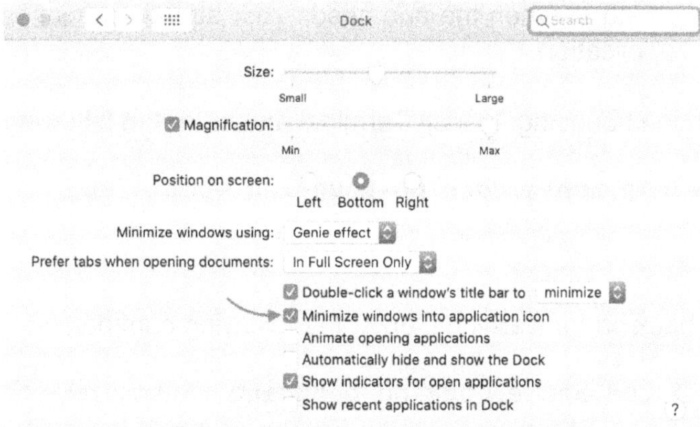

When you want to see all the windows of an application, use **App Exposé** on the associated application icon. **App Exposé** is activated by hovering the pointer over an application icon in the Dock and swiping down with either three or four fingers on the trackpad. Note that **App Exposé** has to be configured in the Trackpad preferences.

Stop Bouncing App Icons

Application icons in the Dock bounce when one of two events occur: upon launching the app or if the app needs your attention. The latter event typically occurs when a dialog box opens with a warning, needs your input, or the app wants to tell you a task has been completed.

Bouncing can be disabled in the **Dock** preference pane. **Animate opening apps** is enabled by default. Uncheck this checkbox if you do not like this animation. This will stop apps from bouncing when you open them from the Dock.

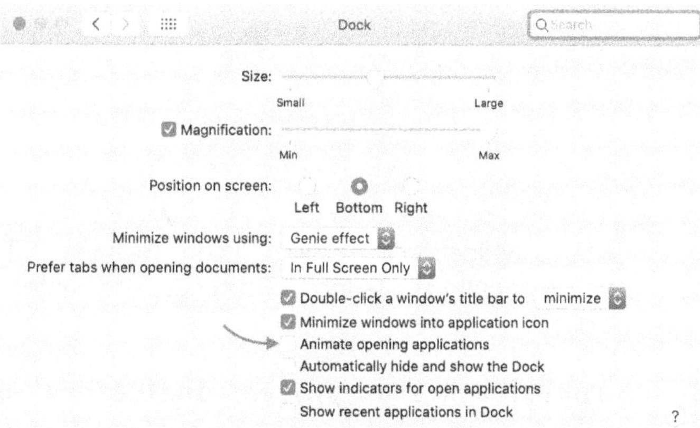

Some applications bounce their icon continuously until you respond by clicking the bouncing icon. The incessant bouncing can be irritating if you are busy doing something else and are not at a convenient breakpoint. Stopping icons from bouncing in response to a warning or when the app needs your attention requires configuration using the Terminal application.

To disable application bouncing, launch Terminal and enter the following commands.

```
defaults write com.apple.dock no-bouncing -bool TRUE

killall Dock
```

To turn bouncing back on for warnings, enter the following commands.

```
defaults delete com.apple.dock no-bouncing

killall Dock
```

Turn Off Open Application Indicators

By default, macOS puts a tiny black indicator dot underneath the Dock icon of open applications. If you move the Dock to the left or right edge of the Desktop, the indicator will be on the left or right, respectively. If you don't care to know which applications are open, you can disable this feature in the **Dock** preference pane. Uncheck the box next to **Show indicators for open applications**.

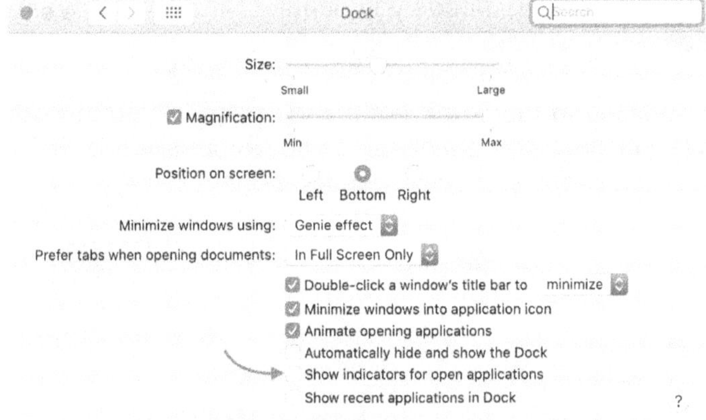

You can also turn off open application indicators using Terminal. To turn off the indicator lights for open applications, launch Terminal and enter the following commands.

```
defaults write com.apple.dock show-process-indicators -bool FALSE

killall Dock
```

If you open the Dock preference pane again, you will see that the checkbox next to **Show indicators for open applications** is now unchecked. If the Dock preference pane was open when you entered the commands in Terminal, it will not change. Close the preference pane and open it again to see the change.

Enter the following commands to turn the indicator lights back on.

```
defaults write com.apple.dock show-process-indicators -bool TRUE

killall Dock
```

Space Out Your Apps

Application icons are equally spaced next to each other in the Dock. Grouping icons together can help you better organize your apps. macOS allows you to add a blank space to the Dock, which can be used to separate application groups.

To add a blank space to your Dock, launch Terminal, and enter the following commands. The first two lines are a single command. **Do not** hit the **return** key until you have entered both lines.

```
defaults write com.apple.dock persistent-apps -array-add '{tile-
data={};tile-type="spacer-tile";}'

killall Dock
```

A blank space appears at the end of the app icons next to the Dock Divider. Drag the blank space to your desired location or move the other app icons to reposition the blank space. Repeat the Terminal commands if you want to add another space.

If you have the Dock configured to show recent apps, the blank space will appear to the left of the first Dock Divider, as shown in the image below.

Removing a blank space is rather interesting. You drag it off the Dock to remove it like any other icon. What makes this interesting is it appears as if you are dragging nothing because the blank space is invisible! If that is too weird for you, secondary click on the blank space to display the **Remove from Dock** option.

Space Out Your Trash Can

By default, the Trash is the very last icon in the Dock. This command adds a blank space to the left of the Trash to separate it from the other icons located on the right side of the Dock.

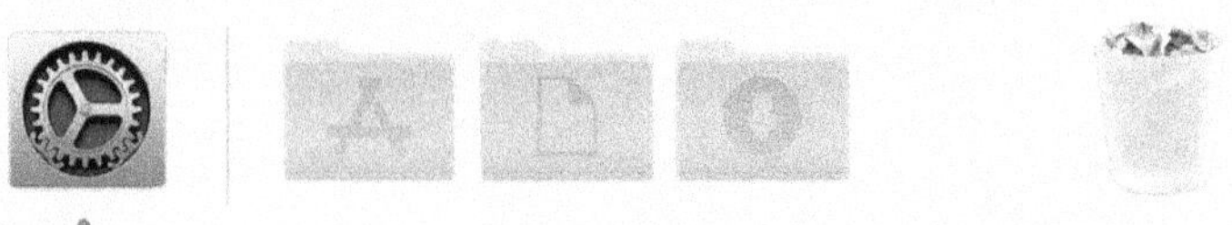

Open Terminal and enter the following commands. The first two lines are a single command. **Do not** hit the **return** key until you have entered both lines.

```
defaults write com.apple.dock persistent-others -array-add '{tile-
data={};tile-type="spacer-tile";}'

killall Dock
```

A blank space appears to the left of the Trash. Drag the space to your desired location. Repeat the commands if you want to add more spaces.

Remove the space by dragging it off the Dock past the middle of your Desktop and release. Remember, the blank space is invisible, so it appears that you are dragging nothing. If you prefer, you can secondary click on the blank space and select **Remove from Dock**.

Dim Hidden Apps

How do you know which applications are hidden? An indicator light under the icon denotes a running app, but the Dock provides no feedback to tell you which applications are hidden versus the ones that are not. You can customize the Dock to dim the icon of a hidden application, allowing you to spot the apps you have hidden at a glance.

Note the difference between the icons for Kindle Create, Photos, Calculator, Terminal, and System Preferences compared to Music, Nord VPN, and Preview, which are hidden and dimmed.

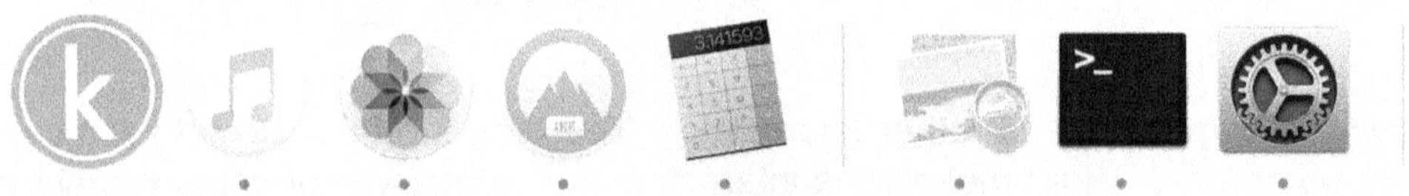

To enable this feature, open Terminal and enter the following commands.

```
defaults write com.apple.dock showhidden -bool TRUE
```

```
killall Dock
```

If you hid applications before entering the commands above, you'll notice no change to the icons. Click on the hidden apps and hide them again to dim.

Use the following commands to change the Dock back to its default behavior.

```
defaults write com.apple.dock showhidden -bool FALSE

killall Dock
```

Turn the Dock into a Taskbar

The Dock serves a twofold purpose, combining the functions of an application launcher and a taskbar to switch between open apps. macOS lets you change the behavior of the Dock so that it operates only as a taskbar, showing only the applications that are currently open.

Enter the following commands into Terminal to switch the Dock to taskbar mode.

```
defaults write com.apple.dock static-only -bool TRUE

killall Dock
```

Once the Dock is operating in taskbar mode, you may want to turn off the indicator lights for the running applications. Since the Dock now shows only running apps, the indicator lights are superfluous. You can disable indicator lights from the **Dock** preference pane by unchecking the box next to **Show indicators for open applications**.

With no applications open, your Dock displays only the Finder and Trash Can.

Running the Dock in taskbar mode is particularly useful if you don't want to use the Dock to launch applications. It is common to want to put all of the applications you routinely use in the Dock. The problem is the Dock's maximum size is limited, and once reached, each app icon becomes smaller and more difficult to differentiate from the others. macOS offers several alternative methods to launch applications. Launchpad offers a quick and easy method to launch your applications. Alternatively, if there is a particular set of applications you use regularly, you can set them to launch when you start your Mac. Another option is to enter **⌘space** (command+space) to activate **Spotlight** and use it as an application launcher. You can also hold down the **⌘space** (command+space) keys to activate **Siri** and use it to launch your applications.

To change the Dock back to its default behavior, enter the following commands.

```
defaults write com.apple.dock static-only -bool FALSE
```

```
killall Dock
```

Activate App Exposé with a Two-Finger Swipe

App Exposé can only be accessed using a trackpad, so you are out of luck if you use a Magic Mouse unless you activate this tweak (or install BetterTouchTool). This tweak allows you to open App Exposé using a swipe up gesture on an app icon in the Dock. Swipe up with one or two fingers on an Apple Magic Mouse or with two fingers on a trackpad. Swipe in the opposite direction with the same number of fingers to close App Exposé.

Open Terminal and enter the following commands to activate this feature.

```
defaults write com.apple.dock scroll-to-open -bool TRUE
```

```
killall Dock
```

If you configured your trackpad to launch App Exposé with a three- or four-finger swipe down, you may wonder why you should configure this tweak. The benefit is this tweak allows you to open and close a stack by swiping up or down, respectively.

Enter the following commands in Terminal to deactivate this feature.

```
defaults delete com.apple.dock scroll-to-open
```

```
killall Dock
```

Configure Single Application Mode

Hiding applications is a handy technique to keep your Desktop free of clutter and distractions to help you stay focused. A Dock shortcut allows you to accomplish two commands simultaneously – launching an application while hiding all other apps.

Hold down the ⌥⌘ (option+command) keys while clicking on an application icon in the Dock. The app launches and open windows from other running applications are instantly hidden. You can use this shortcut even if the application is already open.

If you like this behavior, you can make it permanent by configuring the Dock to operate in single application mode. Anytime you open a new application from the Dock or switch applications, all other apps are hidden. Note that this tweak does not affect applications launched from Launchpad, Spotlight, or the Applications folder.

Enter the following commands in Terminal to turn on single application mode.

```
defaults write com.apple.dock single-app -bool TRUE

killall Dock
```

To turn off single application mode and return the Dock to its default behavior, enter the following commands.

```
defaults delete com.apple.dock single-app

killall Dock
```

Change the Dock Animation Speed

If you like to keep your Dock hidden, you'll notice that macOS animates the Dock's disappearance and reappearance to and from underneath the Desktop. macOS allows you to eliminate this animation, making the Dock hide and unhide instantly.

Enter the following commands in Terminal to eliminate the Dock animation.

```
defaults write com.apple.dock autohide-time-modifier -float 0

killall Dock
```

macOS lets you increase the length of the animation. Setting the animation to a larger number slows the animation down. A smaller number speeds it up. The following commands set the animation to 2.5 seconds so you can watch the Dock animation in slow motion. You can even use decimals like 0.15 and 0.5 to tune the length of the animation to your exact specification.

```
defaults write com.apple.dock autohide-time-modifier -float 2.5

killall Dock
```

To restore the Dock to its default animation, enter the following commands.

```
defaults delete com.apple.dock autohide-time-modifier

killall Dock
```

Find an App's Location

A handy shortcut is to hold down the ⌘ (command) key while clicking on an app icon in the Dock. This shortcut takes you to the app's location in Finder and highlights it.

Add a Preference Pane to the Dock

If you find yourself frequently using a specific preference pane in the System Preferences application, you may find it convenient to add it to the Dock.

To add a preference pane to the Dock, open Finder. Enter **⇧⌘G** (shift+command+G) to open the **Go to the folder** dialog box. Enter the following and click **Go**.

```
/System/Library/PreferencePanes/
```

Locate the preference pane you want to add to the Dock and drag it to the right side of the Dock Divider. You are now able to access it directly from the Dock without having to launch System Preferences. In the image below, I added the Dock, Printers & Scanners, and Time Machine preference panes to my Dock.

To remove a preference pane from the Dock, drag it off like any other item you wish to remove.

Add iCloud Drive to the Dock

Like many features of macOS, there are several ways to access your **iCloud Drive**. I find that the most convenient and quickest way to open iCloud Drive is from the Dock, where it is immediately accessible without having to launch Finder.

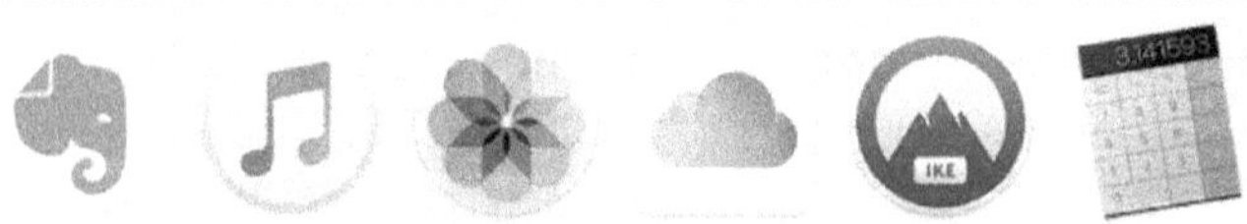

To add the iCloud Drive icon to the Dock, open Finder and enter **⇧⌘G** (shift+command+G) to open the **Go to the folder** dialog box. Enter the following and click **Go**.

```
/System/Library/CoreServices/Finder.app/Contents/Applications/
```

Locate **iCloud Drive** and drag and drop it into the Dock to the left of the Divider.

Lock Your Dock

You just spent a significant amount of time customizing the Dock to get it to look and perform exactly the way you like it. However, it is very easy to accidentally reorder or remove icons or resize or reposition the Dock. All it takes is one bad click from your trackpad or mouse to ruin your customization. It is easy to prevent this from happening by locking the Dock. macOS allows you to individually lock the Dock's contents as well as its size, position, magnification, and autohide settings. Be sure that the Dock preference pane is closed before executing any of the commands in the following sections.

Lock Your Dock Contents

To prevent unintentional changes to your Dock's contents, launch Terminal and enter the following commands. Hit the **return** key after each line.

```
defaults write com.apple.dock contents-immutable -bool TRUE

killall Dock
```

Lock Your Dock Size

The following commands prevent accidental changes to the size of your Dock. After running these commands, you'll notice the **Size** slider in the Dock Preference pane is grayed out. This command also disables the double-headed white arrow, which will no longer appear when you hover your pointer over one of the Dock Dividers.

```
defaults write com.apple.dock size-immutable -bool TRUE

killall Dock
```

Lock Your Dock Position

To lock your Dock's position on the Desktop, enter the following commands. After running these commands, you'll notice the **Position on screen** choices in the Dock Preference pane are grayed out.

```
defaults write com.apple.dock position-immutable -bool TRUE

killall Dock
```

Lock Dock Magnification

To prevent changes to your Dock's magnification setting, enter the following commands. After running these commands, you'll notice the **Magnification** slider in the Dock Preference pane is grayed out.

```
defaults write com.apple.dock magnify-immutable -bool TRUE

killall Dock
```

Lock Dock Autohide

To lock your Dock's autohide feature, enter the following commands. After running these commands, you'll notice the **Automatically hide and show dock** option in the Dock Preference pane is grayed out.

```
defaults write com.apple.dock autohide-immutable -bool TRUE

killall Dock
```

Although you have locked the Dock autohide feature, you can still use the **⌥⌘D** (option+command+D) keyboard shortcut to make the Dock disappear and reappear on demand.

Completely Lock the Dock

To completely lock all Dock features, enter the following commands in Terminal.

```
defaults write com.apple.dock contents-immutable -bool TRUE
defaults write com.apple.dock size-immutable -bool TRUE
defaults write com.apple.dock position-immutable -bool TRUE
defaults write com.apple.dock magnify-immutable -bool TRUE
defaults write com.apple.dock autohide-immutable -bool TRUE
killall Dock
```

Arrows highlight the disabled items in the image of the Dock preference pane when the Dock is completely locked.

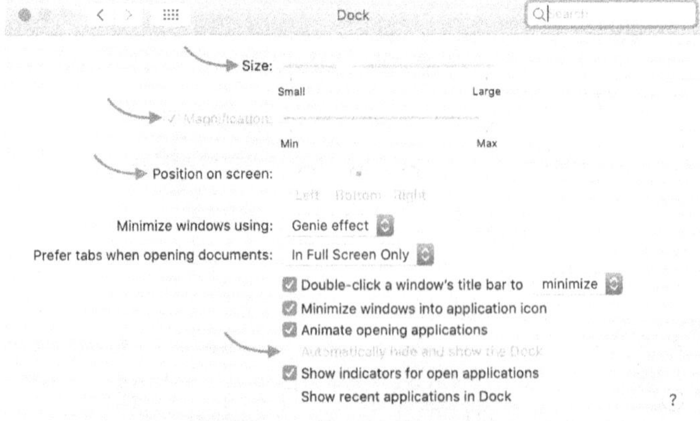

Unlock Your Dock

What happens if you want to make changes to a locked Dock? Well, unlock it, of course! Each of the locks for contents, size, position, magnification, and hiding can be unlocked individually.

Unlock Your Dock Contents

To unlock your Dock contents so you can make changes to its content or order, enter the following commands. Press the **return** key after each line.

```
defaults delete com.apple.dock contents-immutable

killall Dock
```

Unlock Your Dock Size

To unlock your Dock so you can change its size, enter the following commands.

```
defaults delete com.apple.dock size-immutable

killall Dock
```

Unlock Your Dock Position

To unlock your Dock's position on the Desktop, and enter the following commands.

```
defaults delete com.apple.dock position-immutable

killall Dock
```

Unlock Dock Magnification

To unlock Dock magnification to make changes, enter the following commands.

```
defaults delete com.apple.dock magnify-immutable

killall Dock
```

Unlock Dock Autohide

To unlock your Dock's autohide feature, enter the following commands.

```
defaults delete com.apple.dock autohide-immutable

killall Dock
```

Completely Unlock Your Dock

To completely unlock your Dock, enter the following commands in Terminal.

```
defaults delete com.apple.dock contents-immutable
defaults delete com.apple.dock size-immutable
defaults delete com.apple.dock position-immutable
defaults delete com.apple.dock magnify-immutable
defaults delete com.apple.dock autohide-immutable
killall Dock
```

Reset Your Dock

Do you need to start all over again? macOS lets your reset your Dock to the default by entering the following command in Terminal. Note that this command will delete your Mac's Dock preferences file.

```
defaults delete com.apple.dock

killall Dock
```

7

Stacks

Stacks are another cool feature of macOS, offering quick access to frequently used items directly from the Dock. Stacks are located to the right of the Dock Divider, the thin translucent vertical line separating applications and recent apps from the stacks, minimized windows, and the trash. Applications go to the left of the Dock Divider. Everything else goes on the right.

Unless you upgraded from a previous version of macOS where you customized the Dock, macOS gets you started with one stack, which is linked to the **Downloads** folder. The Downloads stack is the same Downloads folder you see under Favorites in the Finder Sidebar. Anything downloaded using Safari, Mail, Messages, or AirDrop is saved to this folder.

When you click on the **Downloads** stack, its contents spring from the Dock in a fan. Clicking on any item in a stack opens it. At the very top of the fan is a link to open the Downloads folder in **Finder**. Of course, you can change this behavior and view the contents as a **Fan**, **Grid**, or **List**. An **Automatic** option lets macOS select the most appropriate view depending on the number of items in the stack. Secondary click on the Downloads stack to access the contextual menu to configure how the stack is displayed and how its contents are viewed and sorted.

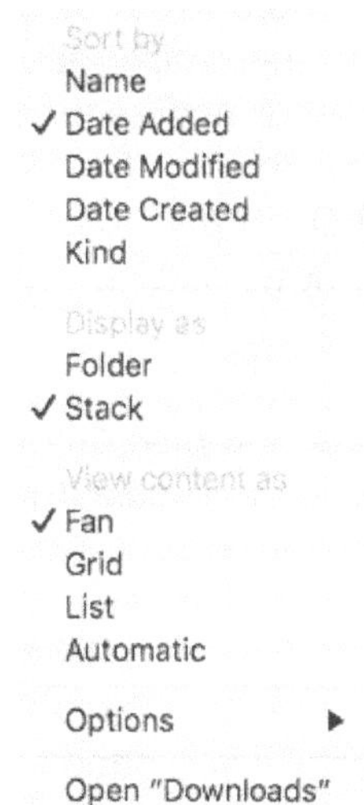

macOS offers four options to view stack contents. **Automatic** is the default, automatically switching between **Fan** and **Grid**, depending on the number of items in the stack. Choosing Fan always displays the contents as a fan; however, only the first ten items are shown. macOS shows you how many more items are available at the top of the fan. Clicking this circular icon opens a Finder window so you can see the remaining items.

As their names imply, **Grid** displays stack contents as a grid and **List** as a list. Both the Grid and List options behave differently than the Fan view. Clicking on a folder in a Fan stack opens the folder in Finder. Clicking on a folder in a Grid or List stack opens the sub-folder directly in the Grid or List view, allowing you to navigate through your folder hierarchy to your intended destination. If you don't want to navigate further in the grid or list, holding down the ⌘ (command) key while clicking a folder opens it in Finder. In addition to changing how you want the contents to display, the stack contextual menu allows you to change the stack icon to a folder.

macOS offers five sorting options. A stack's contents are sorted by **Name**, **Date Added**, **Date Modified**, **Date Created**, or **Kind**. The default is to sort by Name. In a Fan, the closest icon to the Dock is based on the sort type. For example, if a Fan is sorted by name, the closest item to the Dock is the first item alphabetically. Similarly, when the Fan is sorted by date added, the item with the most recent date appears closest to the Dock.

Add Stacks

You can customize the right side of the Dock by adding stacks for folders frequently accessed folders or devices. Adding a folder you frequently access to the Dock as a stack is more efficient than navigating to it in Finder. The image below shows stacks for my Microsoft Office Apps and my Home, Applications, Documents, and Downloads folders.

To add a folder stack to the Dock, locate the folder you wish to add in Finder and drag it to the Dock. It's that easy. Another method is to locate the folder in the Finder Sidebar and secondary click on it to open a contextual menu. Choose **Add to Dock**. Any item in the Finder Sidebar can be added to the Dock as a stack except for **AirDrop** and **iCloud Drive**. However, folders located in iCloud can be added to the Dock as stacks. macOS allows you to create as many stacks as you want or can fit on the Dock.

To add a disk drive, look under **Devices** in the Finder Sidebar. Secondary click the device and select **Add to Dock**. Note that the icon for a removable storage device turns into a question mark on top of a disk drive icon when the media is removed.

You can even drag individual documents into the Dock, although technically, a document is not a stack; it is an **alias**. Adding a document to the Dock is particularly useful if you need to access it frequently.

Once your stacks are in the Dock, you can arrange their order. Rearrange stacks by dragging them left or right. Remember, you cannot drag a stack to the left of the vertical Dock Divider as that side is reserved for applications.

Secondary click on a stack in the Dock to access options to **Remove from Dock** and **Show in Finder**.

You can drag and drop items contained in a stack to move them to another folder, stack, onto the Dock, to the Desktop, into the Trash, to an external disk drive, or any other location.

Remove Stacks

Removing a stack is done the same way as you would remove any item from the Dock. Drag it off the Dock until **Remove** appears above the icon. Release and the stack disappears. Stacks can also be removed by secondary clicking on the stack and selecting **Options > Remove from Dock**.

This Happens All the Time

You think you are dragging a file from the Downloads stack, but you accidentally dragged the entire Downloads stack off the Dock and poof, it's gone! Doh! Don't panic. You can put the Downloads folder back with one command.

Open Finder, navigate to the Downloads folder, and drag it back onto the Dock. If the Downloads folder is in the Finder Sidebar, secondary click on it and select **Add to Dock**. To avoid accidentally removing or rearranging items in the Dock, lock it. See "Lock the Dock" in the last chapter to learn how to lock and unlock the Dock.

Highlight Stack Items

macOS offers a feature that highlights an item in a Stack as you hover over it with the pointer. Highlighting is disabled by default.

To enable highlighting, open Terminal, and enter the following commands. Don't hit the **return** key until you have entered the first two lines.

```
defaults write com.apple.dock mouse-over-
hilite-stack -bool TRUE

killall Dock
```

To turn off highlighting and go back to the default, enter the following commands.

```
defaults delete com.apple.dock mouse-over-hilite-stack

killall Dock
```

Temporarily Highlight Stack Items

If you don't want to highlight stack items permanently, macOS lets you use highlighting as needed. If you want to highlight items temporarily, click and hold the Stack icon. Do not remove your finger from the trackpad or mouse as the Stack expands. With your finger still lightly pressing down on the trackpad or mouse, move up the Stack listing. The item your pointer is hovering over is highlighted. Continue to hold the trackpad or mouse until you hover over the item you want to open and then release. The highlighted item opens immediately.

Another option is to click and hold the stack icon, then immediately release after the stack expands. Now type the first few letters of the desired item's name. macOS highlights items as you type. Once the desired item is highlighted, press the **return** key to open it.

Create an App Stack

If your Dock is crowded with applications, making it difficult to find an app quickly, a solution to the overcrowding is to organize your apps into App Stacks. You can organize your apps by any method imaginable – by application types like productivity, social media, utilities, or browsers, or by how often you use them. This feature is particularly useful if you like a neat and tidy Dock or if you switched the Dock to taskbar mode, where it only shows the running applications.

Follow these steps to create an App Stack:

1. Open Finder and navigate to your Home directory.
2. Create a new folder using **⇧⌘N** or **File > New Folder** and name it "Stacks."
3. Open your new Stacks folder.
4. Create and name a new folder for your App Stack.
5. Open a new Finder Window using **⌘N** or **File > New Finder Window**. Click on the Applications folder in the Sidebar.
6. Select an application you wish to add to your App Stack from the Applications folder, hold down the ⌥⌘ (option+command) keys, and drag the app into your App Stack folder. Holding down ⌥⌘ (option+command) creates an **alias**.
7. Repeat step 6 for each application you want to add to your App Stack.
8. Drag and drop your App Stack folder onto the right side of the Dock.
9. Repeat starting at step 4 to create another App Stack, if desired.

Dragging a folder from the Stacks folder to the Dock creates the App Stack. By default, the contents of an App Stack are sorted by **Name**, displayed as a **Stack**, and content viewed as **Automatic**. Secondary click on the App Stack to set the sort, display, and view options.

The images on the next page show the contents of my Microsoft Office App Stack folder and how it appears in the Dock.

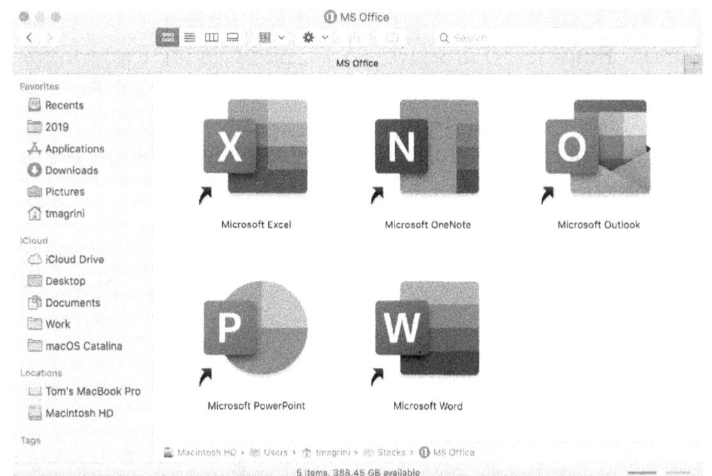

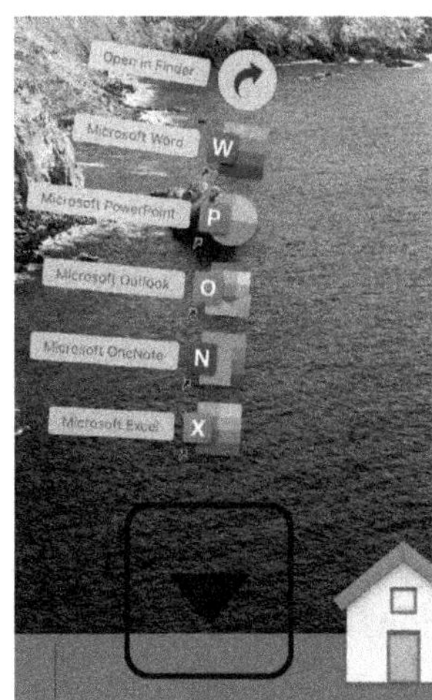

Adding a new application to an existing App Stack is easy. Open the Applications folder and drag the new app to your App Stack in the Dock.

Removing an app is just as easy. Open the App Stack in the Dock and drag the alias to the Trash. To remove an App Stack, drag it off the Dock. Release and the stack disappears.

Create a Document Stack

If you have a particular set of documents you access frequently, the quickest and easiest method to access them is to create a **Document Stack**. A Document Stack can be created for any folder in Finder, including your Home and Documents folders.

To create a Document Stack, locate the desired folder or create a new one in Finder, then drag it to the right side of the Dock. By default, the contents of a Document Stack are sorted by **Name**, displayed as a **Stack**, and content viewed as **Automatic**. Secondary click on the Document Stack to set the **Sort by**, **Display as**, and **View content as** options.

To remove a Document Stack, drag it off the Dock until **Remove** appears above the icon, release, and poof, the stack disappears.

Create a Desktop Stack

If you like a clean and clutter-free Desktop as I do, you probably configured the macOS tweak “Create a Pristine Desktop” from Chapter 3. However, a lot of items are saved to the Desktop by default. If they no longer appear on the Desktop, where do they go? In reality, macOS doesn't save these items to your Desktop. They are saved in a folder in your **Home** directory called **Desktop**. You can access this folder in Finder, but because so many items get saved to the Desktop folder by default, I suggest you add a Desktop Stack to your Dock for quick access to those items.

To create a Desktop Stack, open Finder. If the Desktop folder is in the Finder Sidebar, drag it to the right side of the Dock or secondary click on it and select **Add to Dock**. If the Desktop folder is not in the Finder Sidebar, find it in your Home directory. Drag it to the right side of the Dock. You may want to drag the Desktop Folder to the Finder Sidebar to provide another method to access it quickly.

By default, the contents of a Desktop Stack are sorted by **Name**, displayed as a **Stack**, and content viewed as **Automatic**. Secondary click on the Desktop Stack to set the sort, display, and options.

To remove a Desktop Stack, drag it off the Dock until **Remove** appears above the icon, release, and poof, the stack disappears.

Create a Volumes Stack

If you have multiple internal or external drives, wouldn't it be cool to see them all in one stack? While macOS allows you to drag each one individually from the **Devices** list in the **Finder** Sidebar, you have to use this tweak to see them all in a single stack.

If you like a clean, uncluttered Desktop, you probably wish macOS wouldn't show all of your disk drives on the Desktop. See Chapter 3 to learn how to disable this feature. Once macOS no longer displays your hard drives on your Desktop, a **Volumes Stack** makes accessing your internal or external hard drives a breeze.

Creating a Volumes Stack is a multi-step process.

1. Open Finder and enter **⇧⌘G** (shift+command+G) to open the **Go to the folder** dialog box.
2. Enter **/Volumes** in the dialog box and hit **return** to open the **Volumes** folder.
3. Click **Column** View in the Finder toolbar. The **Volumes** folder will be highlighted and grayed. This is because **Volumes** is a hidden folder.
4. Drag and drop the hidden **Volumes** folder to the right side of the Dock to create a Volumes Stack.

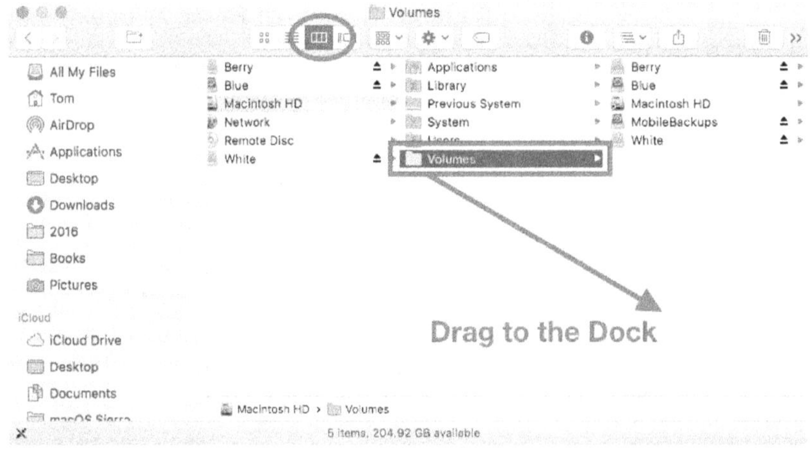

By default, the contents of a Volumes Stack are sorted by **Name**, displayed as a **Stack**, and content viewed as **Automatic**. Secondary click on the Volumes Stack to set the sort, display, and options.

To remove a Volumes Stack, drag it off the Dock until **Remove** appears above it. Release your hold to remove the stack.

Open Stacks with a Two-Finger Swipe

Typically a stack is opened using a single click or click and hold when using temporary highlighting. Another method is to scroll up with one finger on a mouse or to use two fingers on a trackpad.

To enable this feature, launch Terminal and enter the following commands.

```
defaults write com.apple.dock scroll-to-open -bool TRUE
```

```
killall Dock
```

Once enabled, you can open a stack by moving the pointer to the stack and scrolling up with a single finger on a mouse or with two fingers on a trackpad. Scroll down to close the stack. An additional benefit of this feature is that it also activates **App Exposé** when you use the scroll gesture on an application icon in the Dock.

Enter the following commands to disable this feature.

```
defaults delete com.apple.dock scroll-to-open
```

```
killall Dock
```

Quickly Open a Stack in a Finder Window

If you need to open a stack in Finder quickly, hold down the ⌥⌘ (option+command) keys while clicking on the stack. The folder linked to the stack opens immediately. Similarly, you can click on the Open in Finder control at the top of a fan stack or the bottom of a grid or list stack. This is a handy feature when you need to update the contents of a Stack.

Locate a Stack

Another handy Dock shortcut is to hold the ⌘ (command) key while clicking on a stack. This shortcut opens the stack's location in Finder with the item highlighted. This trick works for any stack except a Volumes Stack.

Spring Loaded Stacks

Try dragging a file onto a Stack, pause while hovering over the Stack, and suddenly, a Finder window opens, allowing you to move the file into the folder. If you hold down the ⌥ (option) key while dragging and hovering, you will copy the file instead of moving it. Holding down ⌥⌘ (option+command) will create an alias.

8

Spotlight

Spotlight retains its front and center look and feel in macOS Catalina as in previous versions of macOS. Spotlight is the macOS search utility that locates almost anything on your Mac. In addition to finding stuff on your Mac, Spotlight will make suggestions from the Internet, Music, the App Store, find movie showtimes, nearby locations, provide sports scores, weather forecasts, and find online videos.

Spotlight can search 20 different categories of data, which is configurable in the **Spotlight** preference pane. To make suggestions more relevant, Spotlight includes your location in its search request to Apple.

Spotlight is accessed by clicking on its icon, located in its usual spot in the upper-right corner of the Menu Bar next to Notification Center. Clicking on the Spotlight icon opens a large search window in the center of your Desktop. The default keyboard shortcut remains the same as in earlier versions, **⌘space** (command+space).

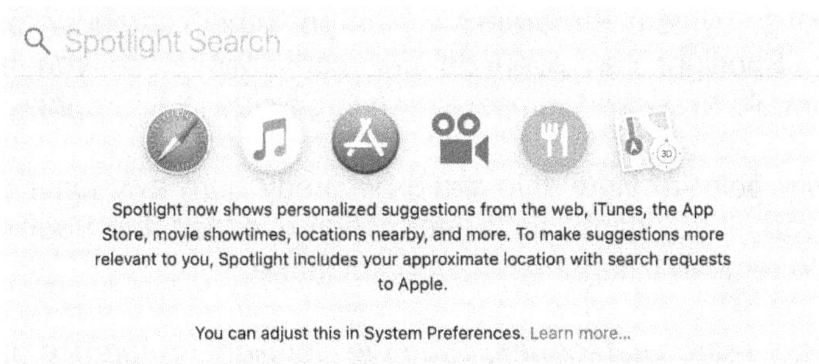

As you type in the Spotlight search field, Spotlight offers results it thinks are possible matches, refining them as you type and organizing them into categories directly below the search field. Results are displayed in categories, with the **Top Hit**, the result Spotlight determined to be the most likely, highlighted at the top of the list. If you press **return**, macOS immediately opens the Top Hit.

A large preview pane on the right allows you to preview results selected in the sidebar. Any item in the search results can be previewed by highlighting it. Clicking on an item in the Spotlight search results opens it. If an item is already highlighted because you were previewing it, pressing the **return** key opens it. To see the location of an item in the file system, hold down the **⌘** (command) key while clicking on the item. The file path is shown at the bottom of the preview pane.

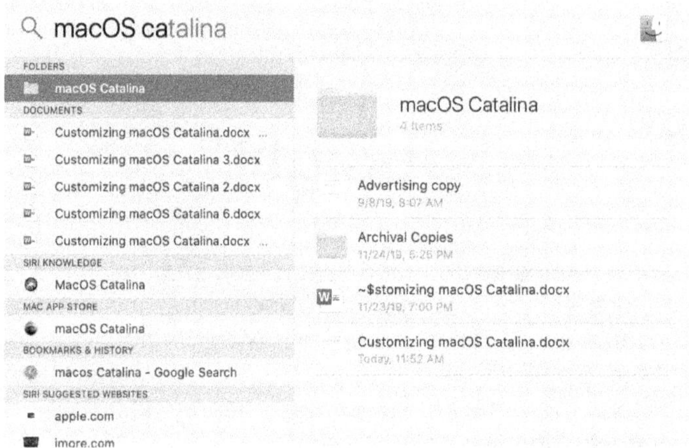

Spotlight displays search results from the categories listed in the Spotlight preference pane, skipping categories that lack a result.

Avoid Spotlight Information Overload

By default, **Spotlight** will search 20 different categories including files on your internal and external drives, the web, folders, music, movies, images, bookmarks, web browsing history, events, reminders, contacts, (take a deep breath), mail, messages, definitions, applications, system preferences, fonts, documents, presentations, spreadsheets, PDFs, System Preferences, plus an "other" category for those things not listed above. Spotlight can even do unit conversions, so you never have to remember that formula to convert temperatures in Celsius to Fahrenheit.

Depending on your point of view, this could be pretty darn awesome or just a lot of information overload. If you think this is information overload, the Spotlight preference pane allows you to remove categories that do not interest you.

To remove Spotlight search categories, open the Spotlight preference pane in System Preferences. Next, click **Search Results** at the top of the pane if it is not already highlighted. By default, all 20 categories are enabled. Uncheck the checkbox next to any category you do not want to include in your Spotlight results.

By default, Spotlight will include suggestions when you look up a word using the Look Up and Data Detectors feature. Depending on the word, you'll see other options such as apps, sports, TV, and movie suggestions. If you want to disable this feature, uncheck the checkbox next to **Allow Spotlight Suggestions in Look up**.

Usage data about your Look up and Spotlight Suggestions are sent to Apple. If you wish to disable this feature, uncheck the checkboxes next to **Allow Spotlight Suggestions in Look up** and **Spotlight Suggestions** in the categories list. When these checkboxes are unchecked, Spotlight only searches the contents of your Mac, and Look Up only searches the dictionaries installed on your Mac.

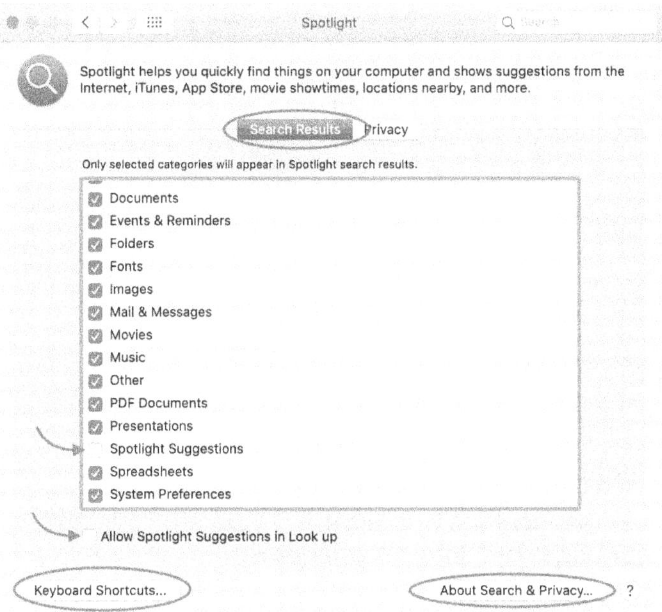

Click **About Search & Privacy...** to learn more about how Apple uses your data.

Clicking **Keyboard Shortcuts...** takes you to the Keyboard preference pane where you can change the shortcut for Spotlight.

Exclude Volumes or Folders from Spotlight

By default, **Spotlight** searches everything on your Mac. However, macOS lets you exclude specific volumes or folders from being searched.

To exclude a volume or folder, open the Spotlight preference pane in the System Preferences application. Click **Privacy** at the top of the pane if it is not already selected.

Click the **Add Button**, denoted by the **+** at the bottom left, to open a **Finder** window. Browse to the volume or folder you want to exclude. Click the **Choose** button. Your selection will be added to the exclusion list.

To remove a volume or folder previously excluded, highlight it in the list of excluded folders and click the – at the bottom left.

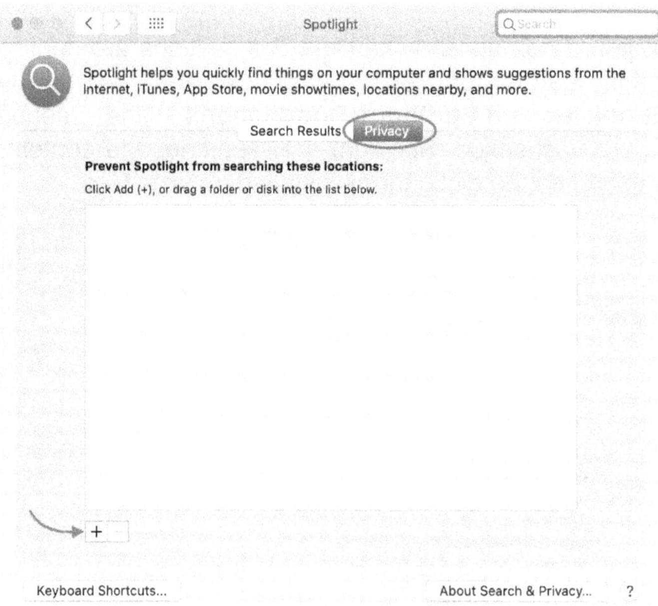

Change the Spotlight Keyboard Shortcut

The default keyboard shortcut for **Spotlight** is **⌘space** (command+space). macOS lets you configure any keyboard shortcut you desire.

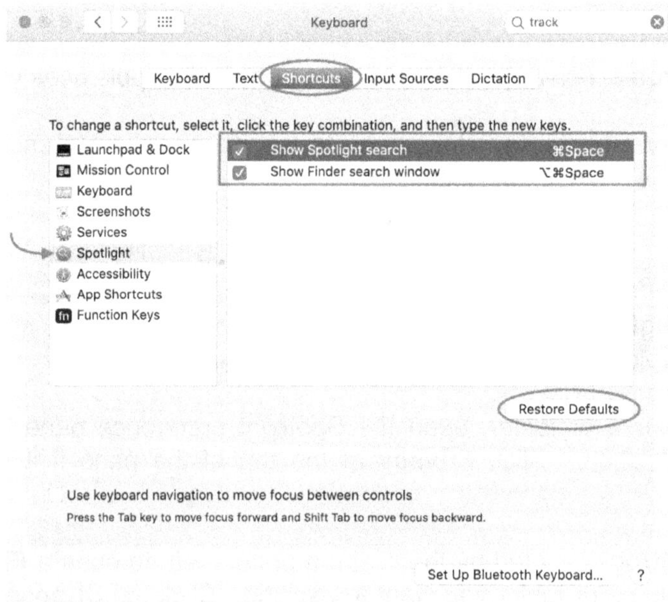

To change the keyboard shortcut for Spotlight, open the Spotlight preference pane in the System Preferences application. Click the **Keyboard Shortcuts...** button found in the lower-left-hand corner to open the **Keyboard** preference pane. This button is available on both the **Search Results** and **Privacy** tabs.

From the **Keyboard** preference pane, you can choose any combination of keys for Spotlight's shortcut. Click on the **Shortcuts** tab and select **Spotlight** in the left sidebar. **Show Spotlight search** is the first choice in the list of shortcuts in the right-hand pane. Click on **Show Spotlight search** to highlight it and click on **⌘space**. You can now enter your custom shortcut in the field provided. Be sure to select a shortcut that is not already in use. If you select a shortcut already in use, a yellow triangle warns you of the conflict. A yellow triangle also appears in the sidebar next to the category containing the conflict.

You can also change the keyboard shortcut for the Finder search window that is used to search for files in Finder. Click on **Show Finder search window** to highlight it and click on **⌥⌘space**. Enter your shortcut in the field provided.

To revert to the macOS defaults for both Spotlight and Finder Search Window, click the **Restore Defaults** button at the lower-right.

Improve Spotlight Search Results

Spotlight allows you to narrow your search to specific types of files using the search modifier **kind**. For example, if you are looking for a specific file type, such as a spreadsheet created in Excel, you can enter **kind:excel** followed by the name of the file. Spotlight limits the search results to only Excel files.

The following list of search modifiers can be used to improve your Spotlight searches. Enter the search term after the modifier. Entering a Spotlight search modifier alone without a search term returns all files of that type.

kind:alias	Returns results that are aliases.
kind:app	Used to locate applications.
kind:audio	Returns search results that are audio files.
kind:avi	Returns results that are AVI files.
kind:bookmark	Used to search Safari bookmarks.
kind:chat	Used to search the Messages logs.
kind:contact	Searches Contacts.
kind:developer	Returns results from the developer category.
kind:document	Used to search for document files.
kind:event	Searches Calendar events.
kind:folder	Finds folders.
kind:font	Used to search for fonts.
kind:gif	Returns images in GIF format.
kind:history	Searches your Safari history.
kind:image	Returns results that are image files.
kind:jpeg	Used to search for images in JPEG format.
kind:mail	Used to search Mail.
kind:message	Returns results from Messages.
kind:movie	Returns results that are movies.
kind:music	Used to search for music.

`kind:pdf`	Used to locate PDF files.
`kind:preferences`	Used to search for system preferences.
`kind:presentation`	Returns files that are presentations.
`kind:quicktime`	Used to locate QuickTime movies.
`kind:reminder`	Used to search for Reminders.
`kind:spreadsheet`	Returns files that are spreadsheets.
`kind:tiff`	Returns images in TIFF format.
`kind:web page`	Searches your Safari history.

Search by Specific Application

Spotlight can search for files created by specific applications. For example, to search for this book, which I wrote using Microsoft Word, I would enter **kind:word macOS** into the Spotlight search field.

The following list shows search modifiers that you can use to look for specific files produced by Apple's iWork suite and the Microsoft Office productivity suite.

`kind:pages`	**`kind:word`**
`kind:numbers`	**`kind:excel`**
`kind:keynote`	**`kind:powerpoint`**

Search Using Tag Color

If you use Finder tags, **Spotlight** allows you to search for files based on the color of their tag using the search modifier **tag**. For example, to find files with a red tag, you would enter **tag:red** into the Spotlight search field. Valid tag colors are red, orange, yellow, green, blue, purple, gray, and white.

Once you have begun to tag files, you may want to rename tags to something more descriptive. macOS allows you to search for tags based on their color or their name. Let's say you renamed the green tag to "vacation." Either of the following searches would return all of your files tagged with the green tag "vacation." For more information on using tags, see the chapter on Finder.

`tag:green`

`tag:vacation`

Search by Document Author

Spotlight allows you to use the search modifier **author** to search for documents written by a specific author. For example, to search for documents written by myself, I would enter the following into the Spotlight search field.

`author:Magrini`

Search by Date

Spotlight can search for files based on the date they were created or modified using the search modifier **date**. The date can be a specific date, a range, today, or yesterday. For example, entering **date:7/4/19** in the Spotlight search field will return files created or modified on July 4, 2019.

Spotlight also allows you to search for ranges. The following search would return all files created or modified in July 2019.

```
date:7/1/19-7/31/19
```

You can use greater than and greater than or equal to find files created or modified on or after a specific date. The following search would return all files created or modified after September 1, 2019.

```
date:>9/1/19
```

This search returns all files created or modified on and after September 1, 2019.

```
date:>=9/1/19
```

You can also look for files created or modified before a specific date. In this example, Spotlight returns all files created or modified before September 1, 2019.

```
date:<9/1/19
```

This search returns all files created or modified on and before September 1, 2019.

```
date:<=9/1/19
```

Spotlight also allows you to search for files created or modified yesterday or today.

```
date:yesterday
```

```
date:today
```

Spotlight understands yesterday and today. What about tomorrow? Yes, Spotlight does understand what tomorrow means. However, results are limited to Calendar events and Reminders since your Mac can't predict the files you will create or modify in the future.

```
date:tomorrow
```

In addition to the **date** search modifier, Spotlight understands **created** and **modified**.

```
created:<=10/1/19
```

```
modified:7/1/19
```

Use Multiple Search Modifiers

Any of the search modifiers can be used together to narrow your search. For example, the following Spotlight search would find all Microsoft Word documents I created or modified in September 2019.

```
kind:word date:9/1/19-9/30/19 author:Magrini
```

This search looks at Safari's history and returns any web pages about Catalina that I visited after August 1, 2019.

```
kind:history created:>8/1/19 Catalina
```

Handy Keyboard Shortcuts

Spotlight features some useful keyboard shortcuts. Use any of the following shortcuts after Spotlight displays search results.

⌘B	Opens **Safari** and searches the Internet for the terms listed in the Spotlight search field.
⌘D	Opens the **Dictionary** application and looks up the term in the Spotlight search field.
⌘K	Opens **Safari** and looks up the terms in Wikipedia.
⌘O	Opens the currently highlighted search result, the same as pressing **return**.
⌘R	Opens the containing folder of the currently highlighted result.
⌘T	Launches the **Top Hit**.
⌘down	Jumps down and highlights the first result in the next category of search results.
⌘up	Jumps up and highlights the first result in the category of search results above.

Show the File Path

Pressing the **⌘** (command) key while a Spotlight search result is highlighted displays the item's path at the lower-right of the window. Entering **⌘R** (command+R) or **⌘return** (command+return) opens the containing folder in Finder with the item highlighted.

Save a Spotlight Search

macOS allows you to save **Spotlight** searches for later reuse. To save a Spotlight search, highlight the **Show All in Finder** result at the bottom of the search results and then click on the large Finder icon in the right pane. This opens a Finder window displaying all of the results from the Spotlight search. Click the **Save** button at the upper-right of the Finder window to save the search.

A drop-down configuration sheet appears asking you to specify a name for the search and location to save it. macOS saves searches to the **Saved Searches** folder in your **Home** directory. A checkbox, which is checked by default, allows you to add the saved search to the Finder Sidebar. Click the **Save** button to save your search or **Cancel**. If you left the **Add To Sidebar** box checked, your search is saved in the Finder Sidebar.

What you have just created is a **Smart Folder**, a saved instance of a Spotlight search that dynamically updates its content based on your search criteria. Just click the Smart Folder under **Favorites** in the Sidebar to rerun the search. We'll cover Smart Folders in more detail in the chapter on Finder.

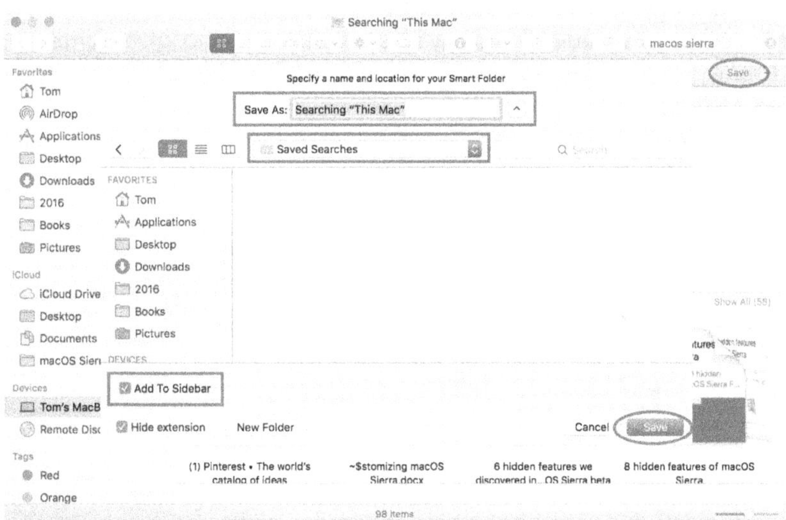

Use Spotlight as an Application Launcher

Spotlight is a pretty handy application launcher. This is an excellent feature if you're trying to launch an application that is not in the Dock or if you're running your Dock in taskbar mode where it only displays running applications. The best part is that your fingers never have to leave the keyboard to launch an app.

Start Spotlight by clicking on its icon in the Menu Bar, but that defeats the purpose of your fingers never leaving the keyboard; use **⌘space** (command+space) instead. Begin typing the name of the application into the search field. Spotlight zeroes in on the application after you enter a few letters of its name. The application appears as the **Top Hit**. You can launch the application by pressing **return**, entering **⌘T** (command+T), or clicking on the app within the search results. Spotlight learns which applications you launch the most and often finds your target application after you've typed just one letter.

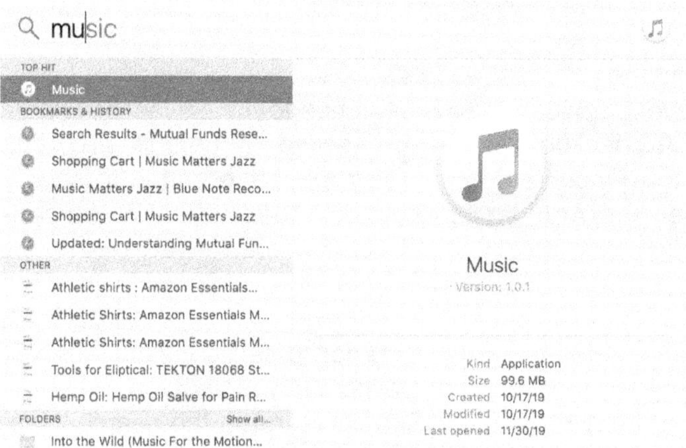

You can use an application's initials to find and launch it. For example, **Photos** can be launched by entering **ph**. QuickTime can be launched using **qt**. Similarly, you can use **ib** for **iBooks**, **mu** for **Music**, **wo** for **Word**, **ex** for **Excel**, **pa** for **Pages**, **ev** for **Evernote**, and so forth.

Search for Comments

Adding **Comments** to your files is a convenient way to organize related content without having to create folders in Finder. The Comments feature allows you to enter descriptive metadata into a file's **Get Info** window. This metadata facilitates searching.

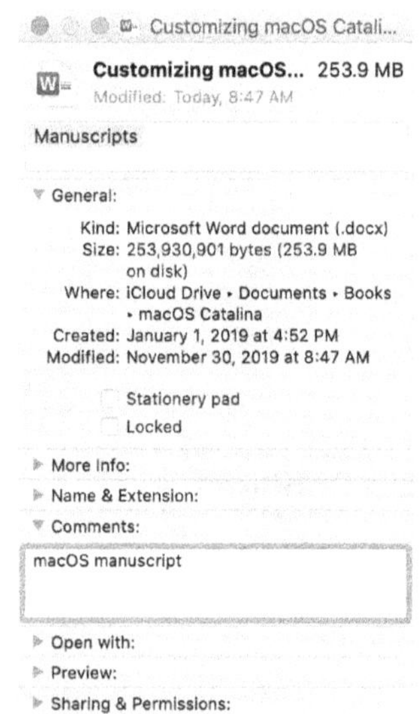

For example, if you are working on a large project, you may create many files from several applications. While all are related to your project, they may not be saved in the same location in Finder. Of course, you could create a folder in Finder and save or move your files to that folder.

To add comments to a file, locate the file in Finder. Next, highlight it, secondary click, and select **Get Info** or press **⌘i** (command+i). This opens the Get Info window. Expand the Comments section, if necessary, by clicking on the little triangular-shaped caret to the left of **Comments**. Enter your comments in the field provided. Enter multiple words by separating them with commas.

To do a Spotlight search using Comments, use the search modifier **comment:** followed by one of your comments.

```
comment:manuscript
```

To search for files tagged with multiple comments, type **comment:** into the Spotlight search field before each comment.

```
comment:macOS comment:manuscript
```

Comments are a great way to quickly find files while keeping them organized in their respective folders.

Use Spotlight as a Calculator

A neat feature of Spotlight is that it can also be used as a calculator. Type the formula in the Spotlight search field, and Spotlight calculates the answer. If you don't need this functionality, you can disable it in the Spotlight preference pane in System Preferences. Uncheck the checkbox next to **Calculator** in the Search Results tab.

Use Spotlight to Convert Currency

Another nice Spotlight feature is that you can use it as a currency converter. For example, if you want to know what 500 euros is in U.S. dollars, enter 500 euros in the Spotlight search field. Spotlight tells you that 500 euros equals $551.02 on the day I wrote this sentence. If you don't need this functionality, you can disable it in the Spotlight preference pane in System Preferences. Uncheck the checkbox next to **Conversion** in the Search Results tab. Note that by doing so, you will disable all conversions in addition to currency conversion.

Rebuild the Spotlight Index

Sometimes you'll swear that Spotlight cannot find a file you know is on your Mac or an external drive. You're not crazy. Sometimes the Spotlight index becomes corrupt, causing inaccurate searches. When this happens, it is time to rebuild the index.

To rebuild the Spotlight index, launch Terminal and enter the following command. The command erases the existing Spotlight index, forcing Spotlight to reindex the drive. Enter your password into Terminal when prompted.

```
sudo mdutil -E /
```

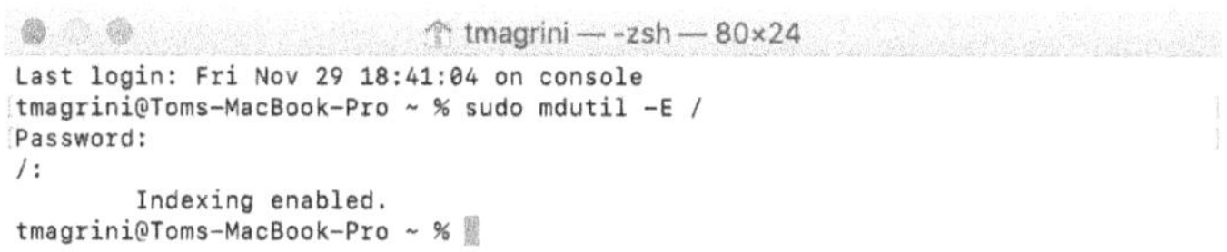

```
tmagrini — -zsh — 80×24
Last login: Fri Nov 29 18:41:04 on console
tmagrini@Toms-MacBook-Pro ~ % sudo mdutil -E /
Password:
/:
        Indexing enabled.
tmagrini@Toms-MacBook-Pro ~ %
```

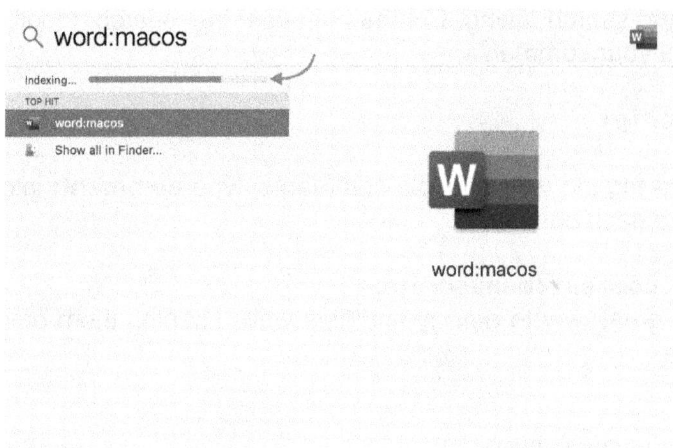

You can verify Spotlight is rebuilding its index by launching and looking for the indexing progress bar. The rebuilding process takes some time and is dependent upon the size and speed of your drive and the number of files it contains. Once the rebuilding process is complete, Spotlight will provide more accurate search results.

9

Siri

Siri is Apple's intelligent virtual assistant application, which is familiar to anyone who owns an iPhone or iPad. Siri works just like it does on your iPhone or iPad. Siri features the same natural language interface, which adapts to your language usage and search preferences.

Like many features in macOS, there are several ways to invoke Siri. You could click the Siri icon in the Dock, which macOS may have conveniently placed during its installation. If the Siri icon is not in your Dock, I'll show you how to add it later in this chapter. You can also click on the Siri Menu Extra, located between Spotlight and Notification Center in the Menu Bar.

If you prefer to use a keyboard shortcut, the default shortcut for Siri is **⌘space** (command+space). But wait, isn't **⌘space** (command+space) the keyboard shortcut for Spotlight? Yes, it is. To use Siri, you will need to hold down **⌘space** (command+space) until the Siri dialog box appears in the upper-right corner of your Desktop. That's where Siri will provide its text-based response. Siri also provides voice feedback and will speak its response as well. Dismiss the Siri window by clicking the **X** in the upper-left corner.

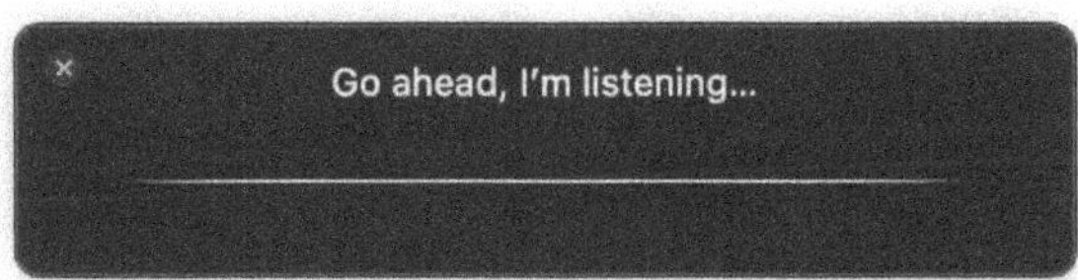

You don't have to hold the **⌘space** (command+space) key until you have finished speaking; however, I find doing so useful in case I pause. Releasing **⌘space** (command+space) lets Siri know you are finished speaking and that it should execute your command or search for your answer.

I find that Siri works best for routine everyday tasks like searching the web, finding the weather forecast, getting sports scores, launching applications, and looking for files on my Mac. Siri can modify a limited set of system preferences like adjusting the volume and brightness, enabling the Notification Center Do Not Disturb feature, or turning Bluetooth or Wi-Fi on and off.

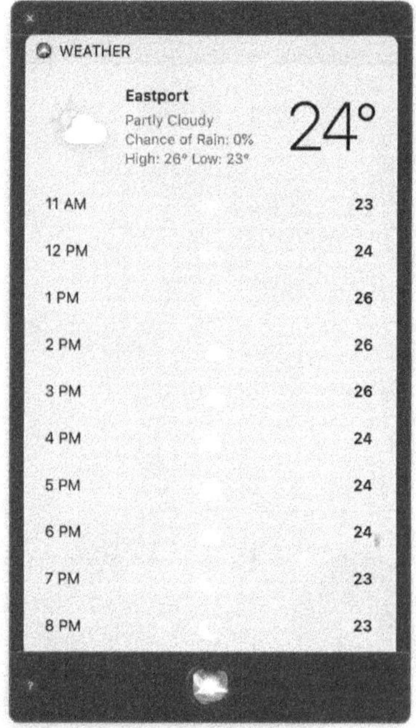

The easiest way to master Siri is to try a bunch of commands, starting with the mundane everyday stuff you do on a Mac such as launching applications, opening files, or searching the web. Ask Siri questions and request various information like movie showtimes, the weather forecast, or scores for your favorite sports teams.

Siri can give you a list of things you can ask it. Activate Siri from the Menu Bar, Dock, or by using the **⌘space** (command+space) shortcut and do not ask it a question. When you release **⌘space** (command+space), Siri will respond with a list of things you can ask it.

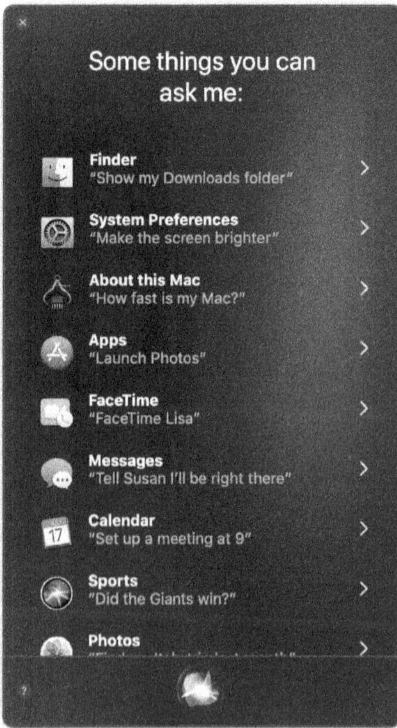

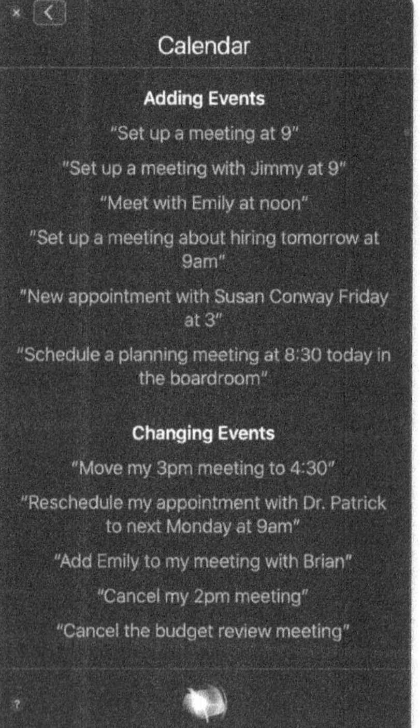

Scroll through the list and click on any of the items. Siri shows you sample questions and commands you can use.

Relocate the Siri Menu Extra

By default, macOS placed the Siri Menu Extra in the Menu Bar between Spotlight and Notification Center. If you don't find this location to be convenient, you can change the location of the Siri Menu Extra by holding down the ⌘ (command) key while dragging it to a new location anywhere along the right side of the Menu Bar.

Add Siri to the Dock

If you customized your Dock in a previous release of macOS, the upgrade to Catalina might not have installed the Siri icon in your Dock. Ask Siri to "open the applications folder in Finder." Siri will open your Applications folder in a Finder window. Find the Siri icon and drag it to your Dock. macOS will create an alias for Siri on the Dock.

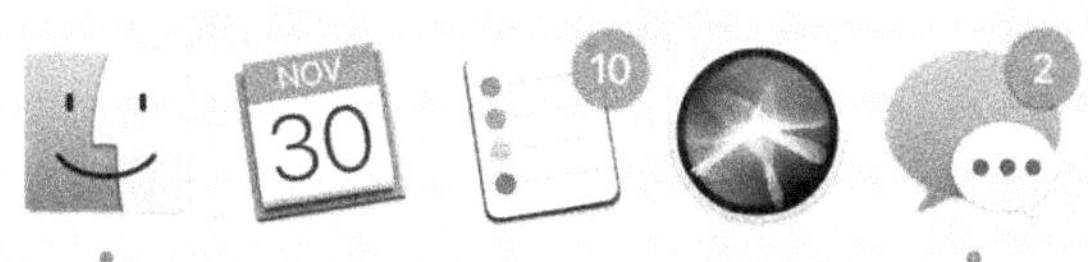

Remove the Siri Menu Extra

If you don't want the Siri Menu Extra in your Menu Bar, you can remove it from the Siri preference pane in System Preferences. Open the Siri preference pane and uncheck the checkbox next to **Show Siri in menu bar**.

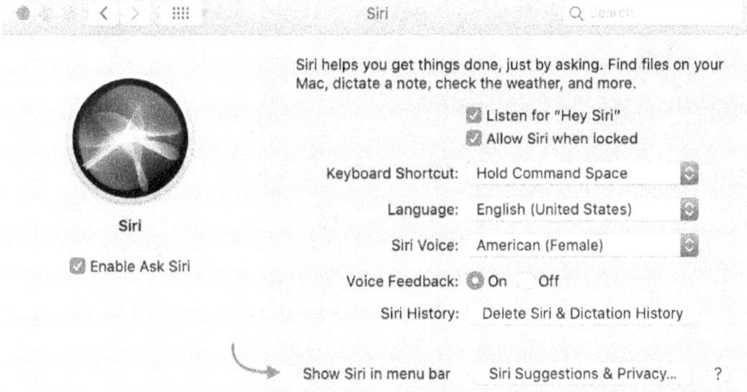

You can also remove the Siri Menu Extra from the Menu Bar by holding down the ⌘ (command) key while dragging it off the Menu Bar.

To revert to the macOS default, launch the Siri preference pane and check the checkbox next to **Show Siri in menu bar**.

Change Siri's Language

Siri supports over 40 different languages and dialects. To change Siri's language, launch the **Siri** preference pane from System Preferences. Select your desired language from the drop-down menu next to **Language**.

Change Siri's Voice

When set to American English, Siri's default voice is an American female. You have the option of changing Siri's voice to an American male. You also have the option of selecting from Australian, British, Irish, or South African female or male voices.

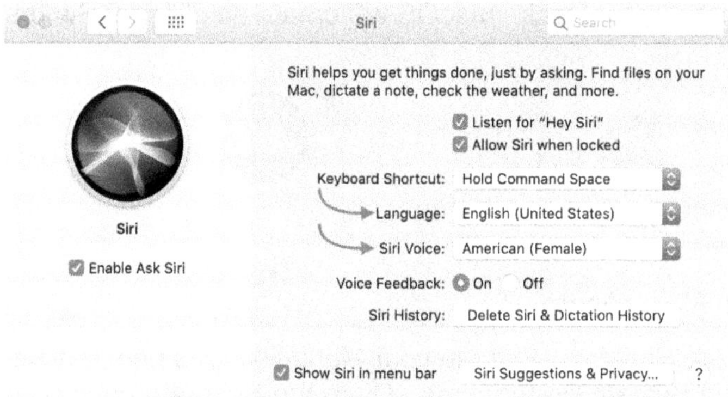

To change Siri's voice, launch the **Siri** preference pane from System Preferences. Select your desired voice from the drop-down list next to **Siri Voice**.

Disable Voice Feedback

If you prefer to read Siri's responses rather than having Siri speak to its responses, macOS allows you to disable **Voice Feedback** in the **Siri** preference pane. This feature comes in handy if you prefer that others do not overhear Siri's responses or if Siri's responses would be disruptive in a quiet office environment.

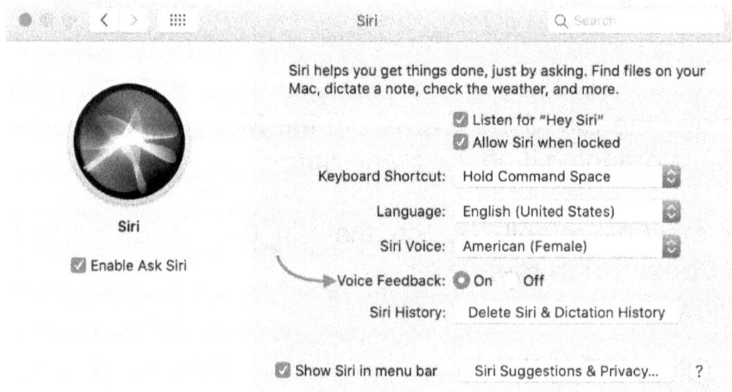

To disable voice feedback, launch the Siri preference pane and select the **Off** radio button to disable Voice Feedback. Siri will no longer speak when responding.

Change the Siri Keyboard Shortcut

By default, Siri's keyboard shortcut is to hold down **⌘space** (command+space) to activate Siri. If you want to change Siri's shortcut, launch the **Siri** preference pane in System Preferences.

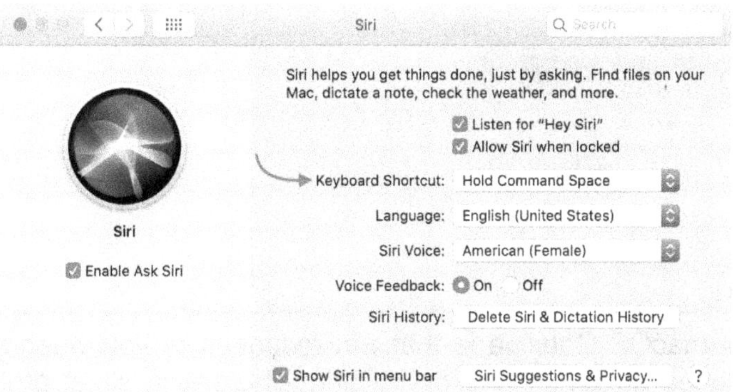

There are three pre-defined choices available: the default **⌘space** (command+space), **⌥space** (option+space), or **fn space** (function+space). You can create your Siri keyboard shortcut by selecting **Customize...** from the drop-down menu. To completely disable the Siri keyboard shortcut, select **Off**.

Type Siri Requests

You can also type your Siri requests instead of or in addition to speaking. This feature is useful if you don't want your Siri requests to be overheard by others when speaking to Siri in a quiet office environment would be disruptive, or if speaking is difficult. Another reason you may want to enable **Type to Siri** is when you are listening to music on your Mac and don't want Siri to interrupt your music.

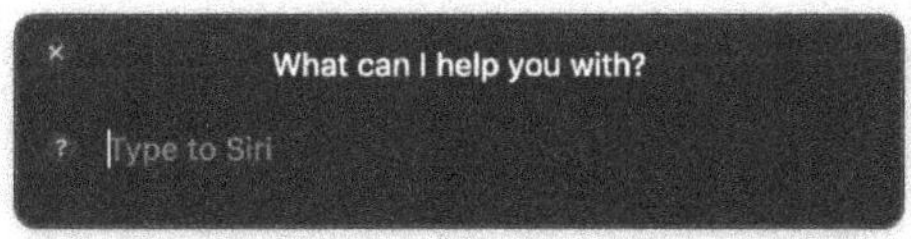

To enable **Type to Siri**, launch the **Accessibility** preference pane from System Preferences. Scroll down and select **Siri** in the sidebar. Then check the checkbox next to **Enable Type to Siri**. Uncheck the checkbox to disable this feature.

When type to Siri is enabled, you activate Siri with its keyboard shortcut. The Siri input dialog box appears in the upper-right corner of your Desktop and awaits your input. Type the question you want to ask Siri and press the **enter** key.

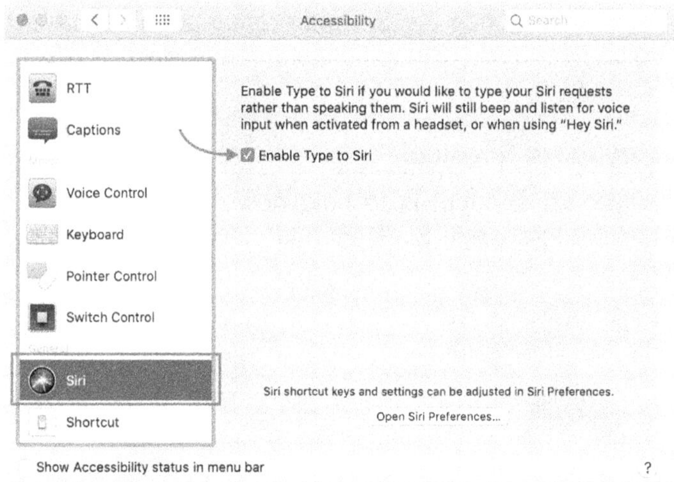

Disable Hey Siri

A new feature in macOS Catalina is that Siri responds to you when you say, "Hey Siri," just like it does on an iPhone and iPad. There is a slight problem with this feature. If you are wearing your Apple Watch and your iPhone and iPad are nearby, all four devices may respond when you say, "Hey Siri." This is especially problematic when you are sending a text as all four devices open Messages and send the same text message.

macOS lets you disable the Hey Siri feature by unchecking the checkbox next to **Listen for Hey Siri** in the Siri preference pane.

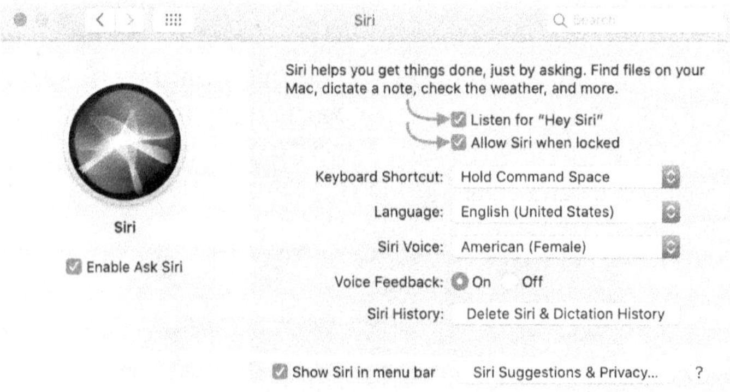

Disable Siri When Your Mac is Locked

By default, Siri responds when you say "Hey Siri" when your Mac is locked, which is another new feature in macOS Catalina. You can disable this feature by unchecking the checkbox next to **Allow Siri when locked** in the Siri preference pane.

Delete Your Siri History

Apple samples your Siri interactions to improve Siri. If you are concerned about the privacy of your Siri queries, you can delete them from Apple's servers.

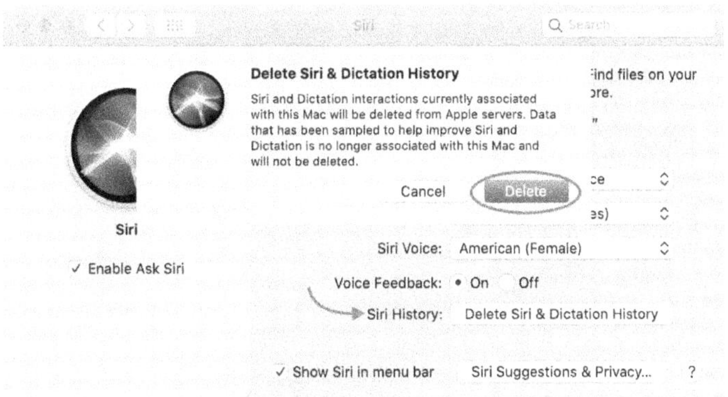

To disable your Siri history, open the Siri preference pane. Click **Delete Siri & Dictation History**. A configuration sheet appears. Click **Delete**. Note that deleting your Siri history also deletes your Dictation history.

Disable Siri

Don't like or don't want Siri? macOS allows you to disable it. To disable Siri, launch the **Siri** preference pane and uncheck the checkbox next to **Enable Ask Siri**. Click **Turn Off** in the warning dialog.

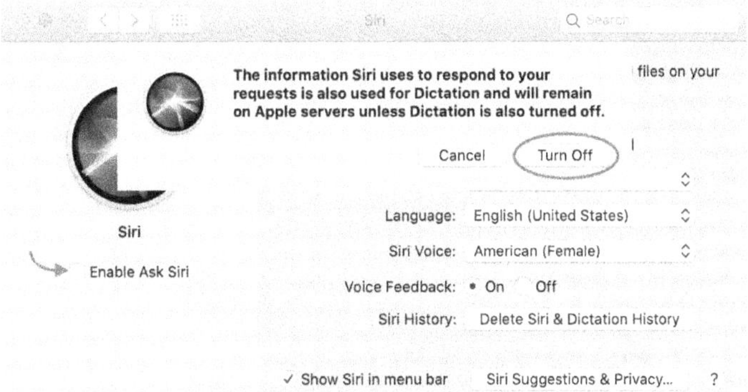

The Siri Menu Extra disappears from your Menu Bar, and the checkbox next to **Show Siri in menu bar** unchecks itself.

If you change your mind later, launch the Siri preference pane and check the checkbox next to **Enable Ask Siri**, then click **Enable** on the configuration sheet. Check the checkbox next to **Show Siri in menu bar** to add Siri to the Menu Bar.

If you added Siri to the Dock, its icon will remain there even though Siri is disabled. If you click on the Siri icon in the Dock, a dialog box asks if you want to enable Siri. Click **Cancel** unless you do want to enable Siri. In that case, Click **Enable**.

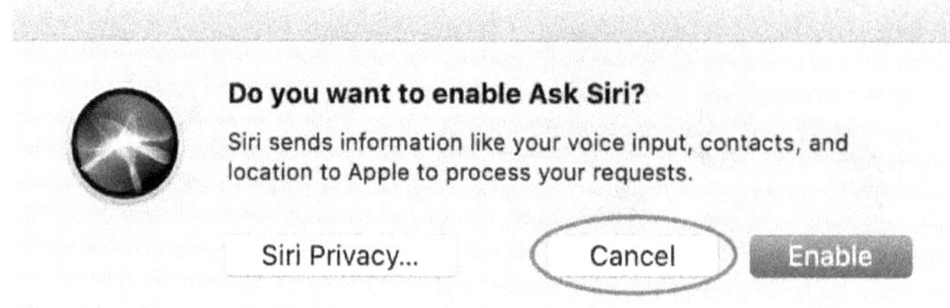

10

Notification Center

Notification Center is a hidden panel at the right edge of the Desktop that consists of two different views – **Today** and **Notifications**. The Today view features Apple and third-party widgets that provide quick access to information. The Notification view collects and displays notifications and alerts from various apps. You can choose which applications can save alerts to the Notification view.

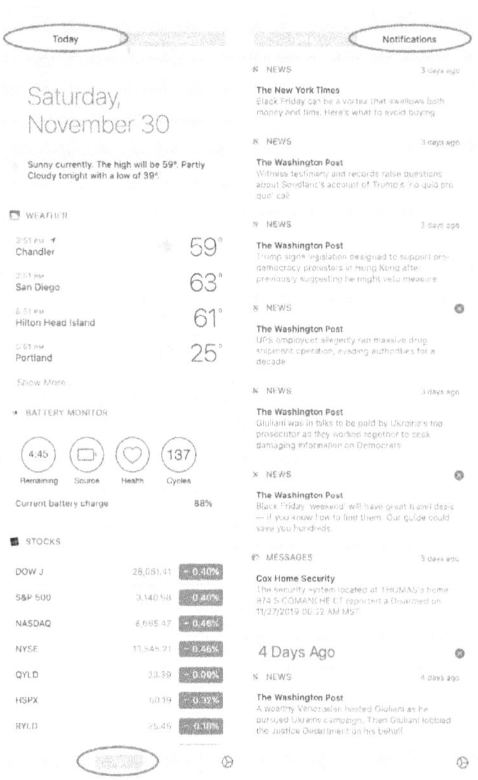

The gesture to display Notification Center seems a little odd at first because you start at the right edge of the trackpad and swipe left with two fingers to reveal the Notification Center panel. Swipe in the opposite direction or click anywhere outside the Notification Center panel to hide it. You can also access Notification Center by clicking on the Notification Center Menu Extra in the Menu Bar. Click the Menu Extra again or press the **esc** key, and Notification Center slides back under the right edge of your Desktop.

Customize Your Today View

macOS lets you customize your Today view, choosing the items you wish to display and their order. To edit the Today view, slide out the Notification Center panel and click on the Today tab at the top of the panel. Scroll down to the very bottom of the Today view and click the **Edit** button.

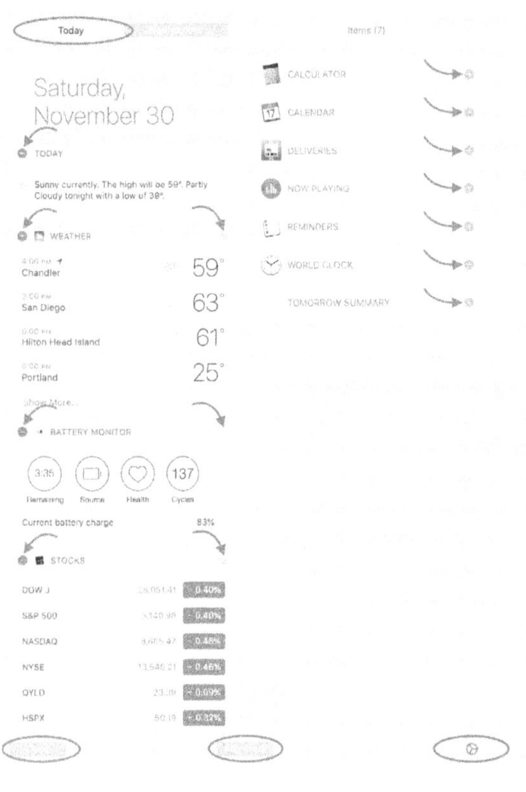

The panel expands to display a second column to the right, presenting a list of any available widgets that you can add to your Today view. To add a new widget, click on the green **+** button to the right of the widget's name.

To remove a widget from your Today view, click the red **–** button at the upper-left corner of the widget.

Widgets can be rearranged within your Today view by using the pancake handle to the right of the widget's name to drag the widget to your desired location.

Clicking the **App Store** button takes you to the **Notification Center Widgets** page in the Mac App Store, where you can discover and install new widgets.

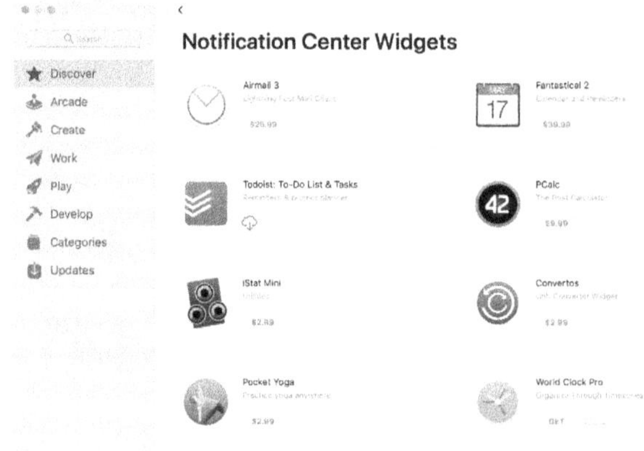

The control in the bottom right corner that looks like a gear launches the Notification Center preference pane in System Preferences.

Click the **Done** button in the lower-left corner when finished.

Select Widgets for Today View

You can also configure the widgets displayed in Notification Center's Today view by opening the **Extensions** preference pane in the System Preferences application.

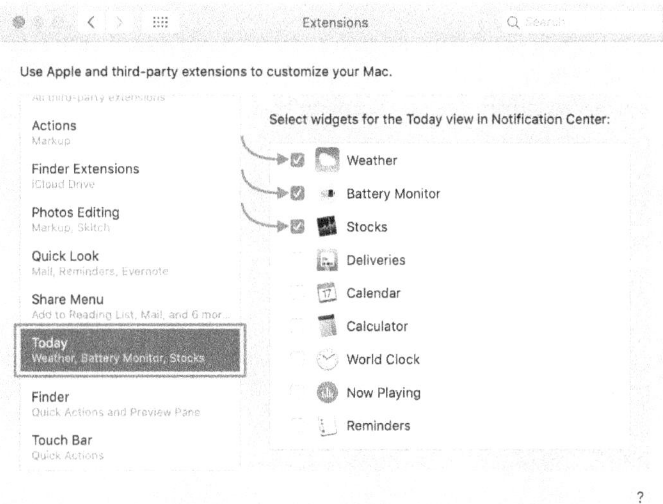

Select **Today** from the sidebar if not already highlighted. Use the checkboxes in the right side of the pane under **Select widgets for the Today view in Notification Center** to add or remove widgets

Customize Notifications

The Notifications view is a one-stop-shop consolidating notifications from a variety of Apple applications, including Messages, Mail, Calendar, Reminders, Music, Safari, FaceTime, Game Center, iMovie, and Maps. Notification Center supports notifications from social media applications like LinkedIn, Facebook, and Twitter, as well as from many third-party applications and websites.

Notifications are delivered to the upper-right-hand corner of your Desktop in the form of a **Banner** or **Alert**, depending on the style chosen in the Notifications preference pane. **Banners** appear and disappear automatically after a set period. A Music notification with the name and artist of the current song playing is an example of a Banner. **Alerts** stay on your Desktop until you dismiss them. Reminders are an example of an Alert, requiring you to take some action to dismiss the notification. All previous notifications, regardless of style, are stored in Notification Center.

To unhide Notification Center, start with two fingers on the right edge of your trackpad and swipe left. Select **Notifications** if not already highlighted. Alternatively, you can click on the Notification Center Menu Extra in the Menu Bar. Click the Menu Extra again to close Notification Center or press the **esc** key.

Clicking on a notification launches the application that created it. For example, clicking on a Mail notification takes you to the Mail application. Doing so marks the notification as read, and the notification is removed. Clicking the **X** at the top right of any application dismisses all notifications associated with that application.

Applications utilizing Apple's push notification service or local notifications can send notifications to Notification Center. macOS allows you to customize which applications are allowed to send notifications to the Desktop and Notification Center in the **Notifications** preference pane.

Disable Notifications

By default, all of the applications listed in the **Notifications** preference pane can display notifications in the upper-right-hand corner of your Desktop and deposit a notification in **Notification Center**. The number of applications configured in Notification Center could quickly inundate you with annoying and superfluous alerts. macOS allows you to turn off notifications from any of the apps listed in the Notifications preference pane.

To disable notifications, open the **Notifications** preference pane in System Preferences. The sidebar at the left lists the applications capable of sending notifications to your Desktop and to Notification Center.

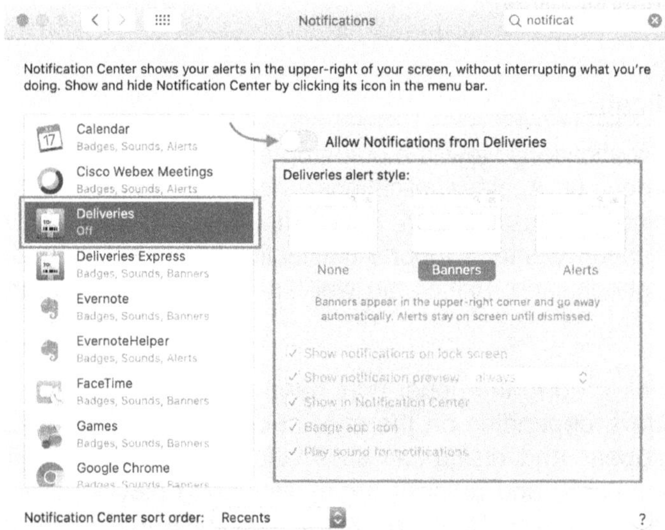

To stop an application from sending notifications, click to highlight the application in the sidebar. Next, turn off the switch next to **Allow Notifications from**. Turning the switch off stops an application from sending notifications and dims the alert style and other notification configuration options. In the example above, I've disabled notifications for the Deliveries app.

Choose Your Notification Style

You can customize the notification style used by each application when sending notifications to your Desktop. Notifications can be configured as a Banner or an Alert. There is a difference between a Banner and an Alert. A **Banner** is a notification that appears on your Desktop and disappears after a set amount of time. An **Alert** is a notification that stays on your Desktop until you respond or dismiss it.

Alert styles and options such as history, previews, badging, and sound are configured on a per-app basis in the Notifications preference pane. To choose a notification style, open the Notifications preference pane. Click on an application in the sidebar to highlight it. Once you have selected an application, the right-hand pane displays the current alert style, which is highlighted in blue, and available configuration options. Choose **Banners** or **Alerts** to change the alert style. If you choose **None**, the application's notifications will no longer appear on your Desktop, but are saved to Notification Center.

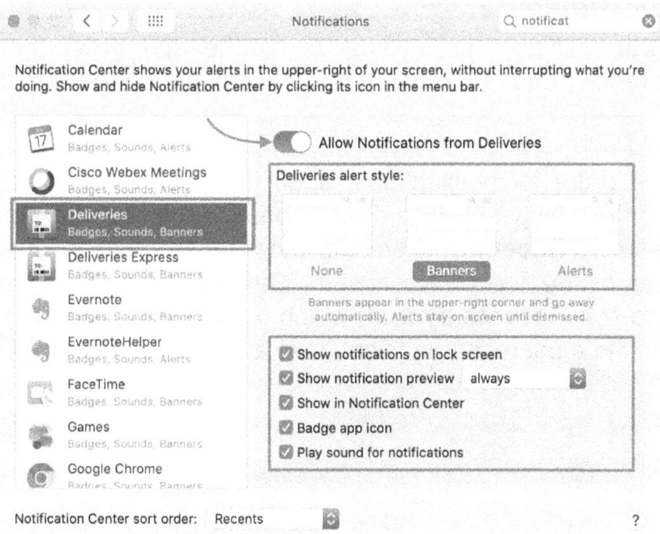

Once you have chosen your alert style, you can configure the various options shown below the alert style. The options are **Show notifications on lock screen**, **Show notification preview**, **Show in Notification Center**, **Badge app icon**, and **Play sound for notifications**. All of the checkboxes are checked by default.

Notifications received when your Mac was asleep will appear on the login window when you wake your Mac. This creates a potential privacy issue. If you want to disable this feature, uncheck the checkbox next to **Show notifications on lock screen.** When you disable this feature, the drop-down menu next to **Show notification preview** disappears.

If you decide to keep **Show notifications on lock screen** enabled, you can choose when to show notification previews from the drop-down menu next to **Show notification preview.** The default option is **always**, which displays notification previews on the login screen. The second option is **when unlocked**, which displays notification previews only when you are logged in to your Mac.

By default, the **Show in Notification Center** option is checked, which means the notification is saved in Notification Center. You have the option of disabling this feature by unchecking the checkbox. If you do so, you will only see messages on your Desktop and only if the alert style is set to **Banners** or **Alerts**.

The **Badge app icon** option displays the number of notifications in a red circular badge on the app's icon in the **Dock**. The app must be in the Dock for badges to appear. If you don't want the app icon badged, uncheck this checkbox.

Some notifications play a sound when they appear. If you prefer silent notifications, uncheck the checkbox next to **Play sound for notifications**.

Change the Notification Sort Order

Notification Center displays notifications using the sort order configured in the Notifications preference pane. By default, notifications are sorted with the most recent ones on top.

To change the sort order for notifications, open the **Notifications** preference pane. Change the sort order using the drop-down menu next to **Notification Center sort order**. You can sort by **Recents**, where the most recent notifications, regardless of application, appear at the top of Notification Center. This is the macOS default. Another option is to sort **Recents by app**, which organizes notifications by application where the app with the most recent notification is at the top of Notification Center.

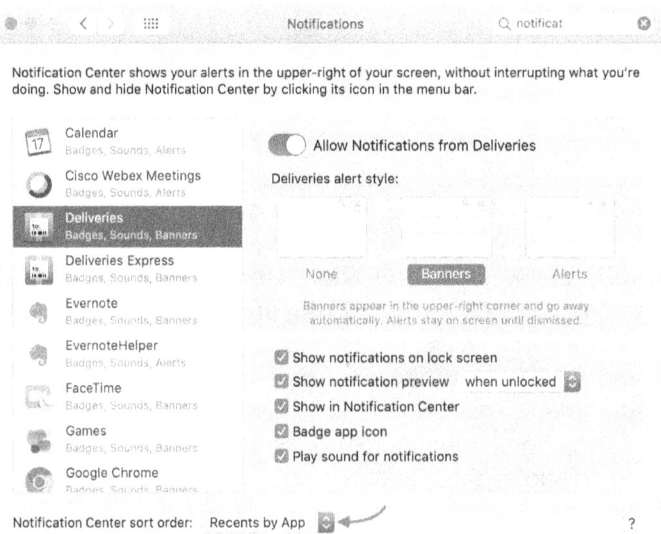

The final option, **Manually by app**, allows you to reorder the list of applications displayed in the sidebar of the Notifications preference pane. When selecting this option, you'll notice the list of applications in the sidebar rearranges itself to what Apple thinks is a logical sort order. Note the difference in the sidebar in the image above and the one below.

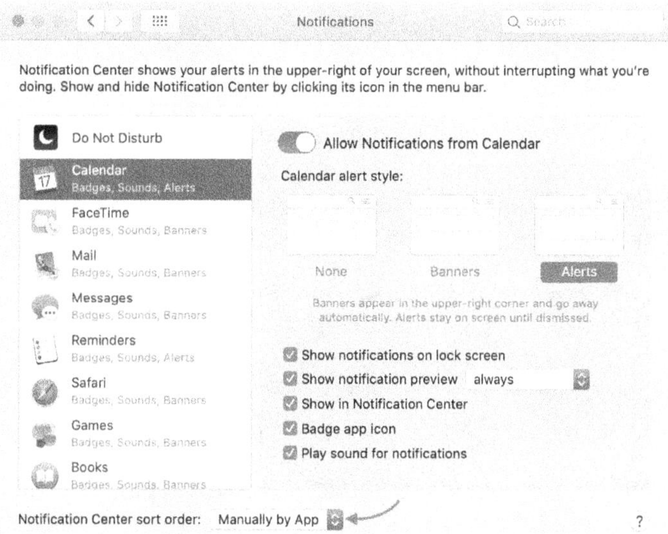

You don't have to accept Apple's suggestion. Drag and drop the applications in the sidebar into the order in which you want to see your notifications. Once finished, close the preference pane. The notifications will be displayed in your desired order. Any application without a notification is skipped.

Keep Banners Around Longer

Banners delivered to the upper-right-hand corner of your Desktop automatically disappear after 5 seconds. Often this is not enough time to read them. I find myself forced to check Notification Center to read the Banner I just missed. This tweak allows you to set the amount of time in seconds that Banners stay on your Desktop before disappearing.

To increase the Banner time, launch Terminal, and enter the following command. This command increases the Banner time to 20 seconds. You can change the 20 in the command below to any whole number you wish. You need to log out and log back in for the change to take effect.

```
defaults write com.apple.notificationcenterui bannerTime 20
```

If you want Banners to stick around until you dismiss them, enter the following command in Terminal. You need to log out and log back in for the change to take effect.

```
defaults write com.apple.notificationcenterui bannerTime 86400
```

To return to the macOS default of 5 seconds, enter the following command in Terminal. Log out and log back in for the change to take effect.

```
defaults delete com.apple.notificationcenterui bannerTime
```

Swipe to Dismiss a Notification

macOS allows you to dismiss any Desktop notification by swiping on the notification from left to right with two fingers on your trackpad. If you are using a Magic Mouse, swipe left to right with one finger. The notification fades away as it moves towards the right edge of the screen.

Some Desktop notifications include controls. For example, the Music notification allows you to skip a song. Hover your pointer over the Music notification, and a **Skip** button appears on the right. Click **Skip** to skip the current song.

Enable Night Shift

You can quickly enable **Night Shift** from Notification Center by switching the Night Shift switch to **On**. Night Shift is a macOS feature that adjusts the color temperature of your display based on the time of day. Similar to Night Shift on an iPhone or iPad, macOS adjusts the color temperature of your display to provide warmer light during nighttime hours to help you sleep better.

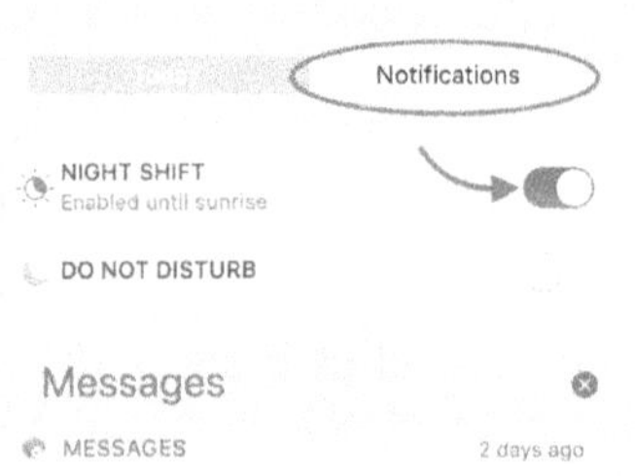

To enable Night Shift, open Notification Center and click on **Notifications** if not already selected. Turn the **Night Shift** switch on to enable this feature.

Enable Do Not Disturb

Do you find all those Desktop notifications a little distracting? The **Do Not Disturb** feature turns Notification Center off for the remainder of the day. To enable Do Not Disturb, open Notification Center and click on **Notifications**. Turn the **Do Not Disturb** switch on to enable this feature.

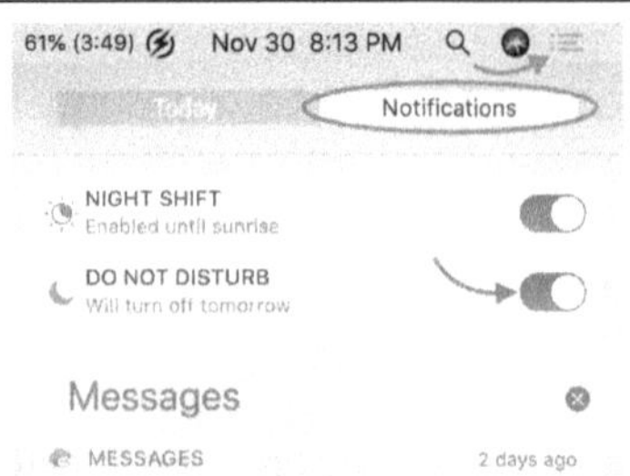

When Do Not Disturb is enabled, the Notification Center Menu Extra turns gray. Any notifications received while Do Not Disturb is enabled are available in Notification Center, but Banners and Alerts are not sent to your Desktop. macOS automatically turns Do Not Disturb off tomorrow. To disable Do Not Disturb, switch the Do Not Disturb switch off.

A quick way to enable the Do Not Disturb feature is to hold down the ⌥ (option) key while clicking the Notification Center Menu Extra. Click while holding the ⌥ (option) key again to disable Do Not Disturb.

Schedule Do Not Disturb

macOS allows you to schedule the **Do Not Disturb** feature to turn on and off automatically at a scheduled time each day. To schedule Do Not Disturb, open the **Notification** preference pane. Click on **Do Not Disturb** in the sidebar. Check the checkbox next to **From** and **to** and select your do not disturb time.

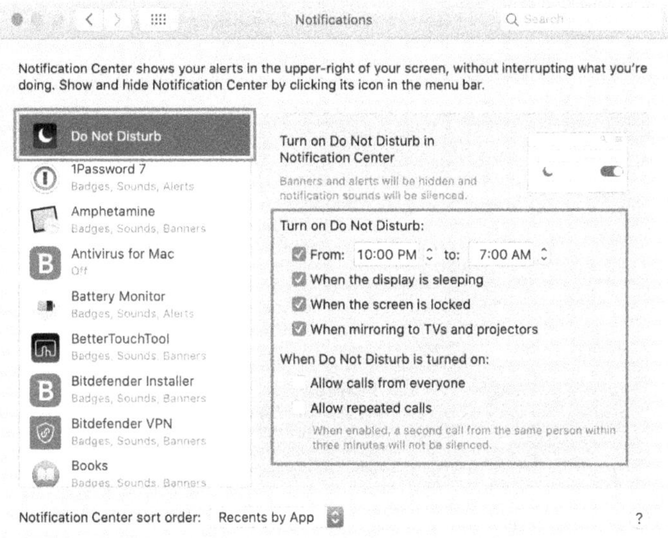

By default, macOS enables Do Not Disturb while your Mac is sleeping or mirroring its display to TVs and projectors. This is quite handy if you are streaming a video to your AppleTV or giving a presentation to a group of people and don't want notifications interrupting you. However, if you do want to receive Banners and Alerts when mirroring, you can disable this behavior by unchecking the checkbox next to **When mirroring to TVs and projectors**. Similarly, Do Not Disturb can be disabled when your Mac is sleeping or locked. Uncheck the checkboxes next to **When the display is sleeping** and **When the screen is locked**.

Your Mac will not disturb you if you receive a FaceTime call when Do Not Disturb is enabled. If you would like to accept all FaceTime calls, check the checkbox next to **Allow calls from everyone**. Another option is to only accept repeated calls by checking the **Allow repeated calls** checkbox. If a second call is received from the same person within 3 minutes, you will be notified. Both of these options are disabled by default.

Assign a Keyboard Shortcut for Notification Center

If you would like to assign a keyboard shortcut to open Notification Center, open the **Keyboard** preference pane from System Preferences. Click on the **Shortcuts** tab. Select **Mission Control** from the sidebar. By default, there is no keyboard shortcut for Notification Center in macOS Catalina. Previous versions of macOS used **⌥⌘left** (option+command+left arrow).

To assign a keyboard shortcut, ensure the checkbox next to **Show Notification Center** is checked and select a shortcut in the field provided. Be sure to select a key combination that is not used by another function. If you select a shortcut that is already assigned, a yellow triangle will appear to the right of the shortcut.

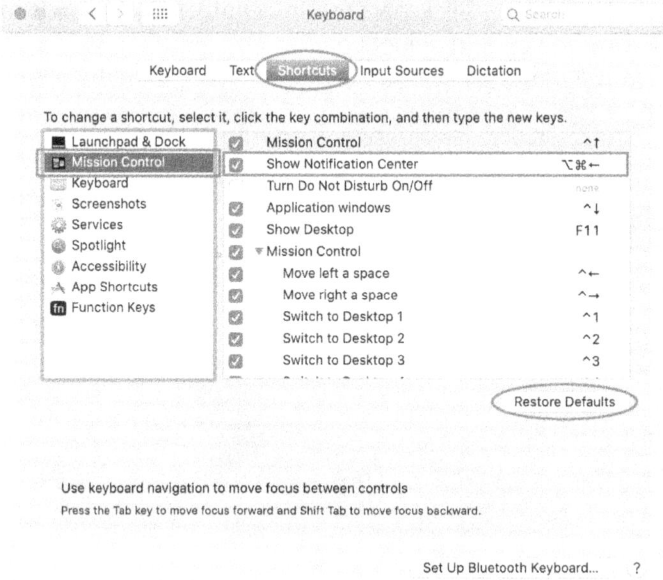

To disable, uncheck the checkbox next to **Show Notification Center**. If you want to restore all keyboard shortcuts to their macOS defaults, click the **Restore Defaults** button at the lower-right of the preference pane.

Assign a Keyboard Shortcut for Do Not Disturb

If you would like to assign a keyboard shortcut to turn on Do Not Disturb, open the **Keyboard** preference pane. Click on the **Shortcuts** tab. Select **Mission Control** from the sidebar. By default, there is no keyboard shortcut for Do Not Disturb in macOS Catalina. Previous versions of macOS used **⌥⌘right** keyboard shortcut (option+command+right arrow).

To assign a keyboard shortcut, ensure the checkbox next to **Turn Do Not Disturb On/Off** is checked and select a key combination. Once configured, this shortcut acts as a toggle to enable and disable Do Not Disturb. Remember that you can check the status of Do Not Disturb by looking at the Notification Center icon in the Menu Bar. If it is grayed out, Do Not Disturb is enabled. You can also check to see if the Do Not Disturb switch is turned on in Notification Center.

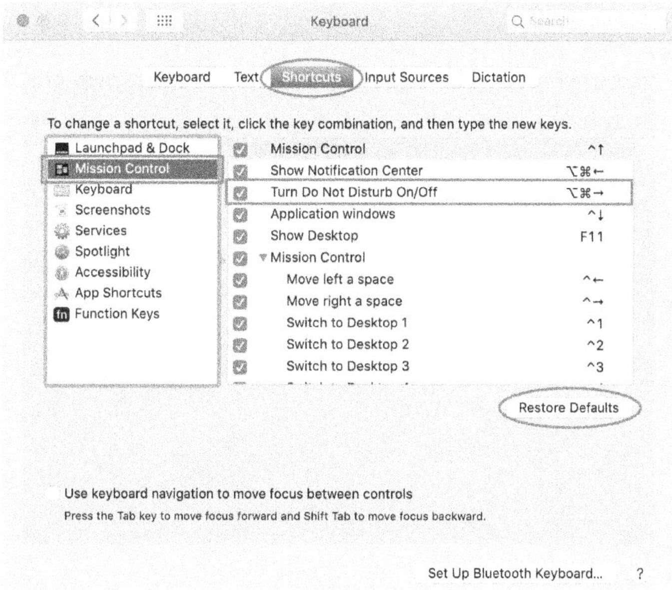

To disable, uncheck the checkbox next to **Turn Do Not Disturb On/Off**. If you want to restore all keyboard shortcuts to their macOS defaults, click the **Restore Defaults** button at the lower-right of the preference pane.

11

Launchpad

Launchpad is a macOS feature that blurs the line between iOS, iPadOS, and macOS. Like the home screen on iPhone and iPad, Launchpad allows you to see every application installed on your Mac on one or more pages. From Launchpad, you can search, launch, organize, and delete applications on your Mac.

To open Launchpad, click on its icon in the Dock, press the **F4** key, pinch your thumb and three fingers together on the trackpad or tap the Launchpad icon in your Touch Bar. When Launchpad opens, your Desktop background blurs, and windows disappear to reveal a grid of application icons similar to the home screen on an iPad or iPhone. The Dock, if hidden, reappears.

Launchpad provides a search field at the top center allowing you to quickly find applications, particularly ones that are hidden in a folder. Small dots at the bottom center represent pages. You can swipe left or right with one finger on a mouse or two fingers on a trackpad or hold down the ⌘ (command) key while pressing the left or right arrow keys to navigate between pages. You also can click on one of the dots to jump directly to that page. You can use the four arrow keys to move up, down, left, or right within the grid to highlight an application. Pressing the **return** key launches the highlighted application, as does clicking on its icon.

Folders are created the same way they are on an iPhone or iPad, by dragging one icon on top of another. Once a folder is created, it can be renamed, and other applications can be dragged into it. Folders are opened by clicking on them. Close an open folder by clicking anywhere outside it.

You can close Launchpad by clicking on the Desktop wallpaper, pressing the **F4** key again, pressing the **esc** key, using the Show Desktop gesture by spreading your thumb and three fingers apart on your Mac's trackpad, or by tapping the Launchpad icon on your Touch Bar.

Rearrange the App Icons

The application icons in **Launchpad** can be rearranged by dragging them into the order you desire. To move an icon between pages, drag it to the edge of the screen and hold it there until the page flips. Drop the icon on the desired destination page.

Delete an App Using Launchpad

Some applications can be deleted from your Mac using **Launchpad**. To delete an app, click and hold on an icon until all of the app icons begin shaking. An **X** appears in the upper-left corner of some of the app icons. Clicking the **X** deletes the app.

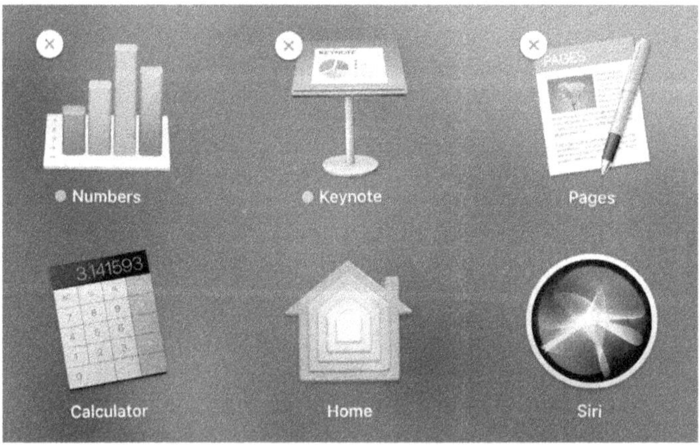

Add Finder to Launchpad

Open **Launchpad**. Now type **Finder** in the search field. No Results. Noticeably absent from Launchpad is one of the most critical apps in macOS, Finder.

To add Finder to Launchpad, open **Finder**. Enter **⇧⌘G** (shift+command+G) to open the **Go to the folder** dialog box. Enter the following into the field and click **Go**.

```
/System/Library/CoreServices/
```

Locate **Finder** in this folder and drag and drop it onto the **Launchpad** icon in the Dock. Now, check out Launchpad, and there's Finder.

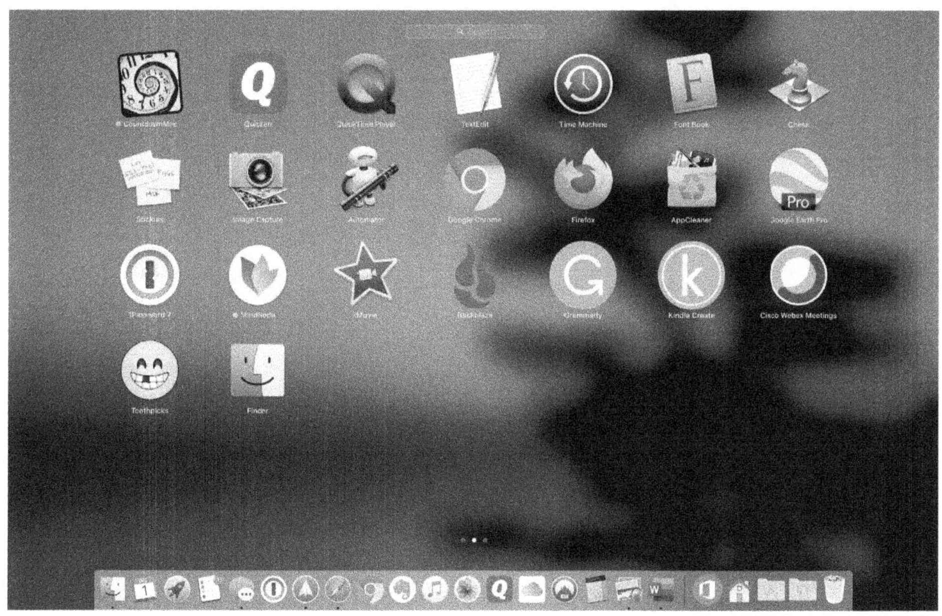

Change the Number of Apps per Page

On my 13-inch MacBook Pro display, macOS lays out a 7 column by 5 row grid in Launchpad, displaying 35 icons per page. If you want more application icons to appear on each Launchpad page, you do so by making the grid larger by adding more columns and rows.

For example, if you want Launchpad to display 60 application icons per page, you would need to resize the grid to 10 columns by 6 rows. To resize Launchpad, open Terminal and enter the following commands.

```
defaults write com.apple.dock springboard-columns -int 10

defaults write com.apple.dock springboard-rows -int 6

killall Dock
```

I suggest you experiment, trying different combinations of column and row sizes until you find the right combination. Replace the number after **–int** in each command with an integer to find your perfect size.

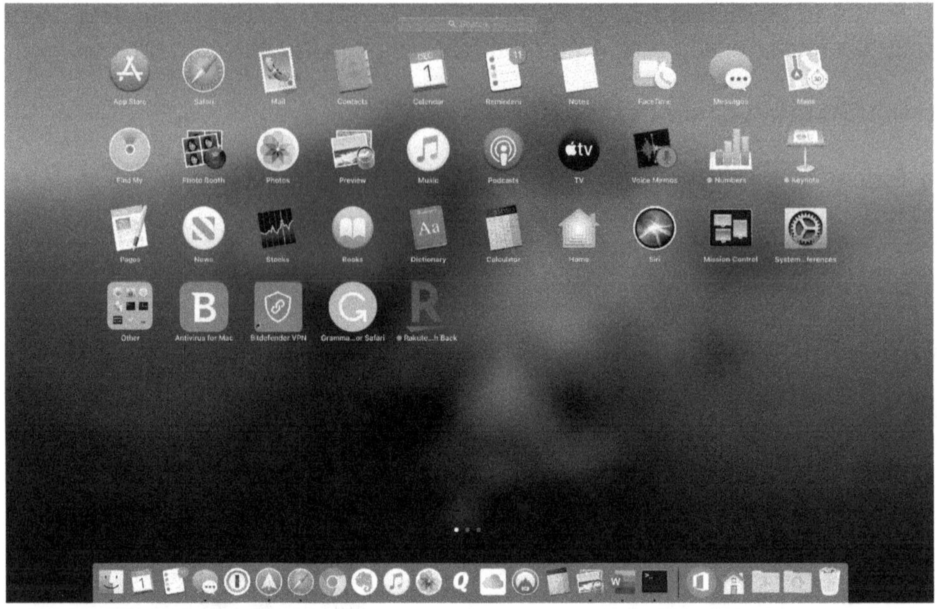

Increasing the size of the grid decreases the size of each icon. With Launchpad displaying more icons per page, it takes fewer pages to display your applications. In the image above, I configured Launchpad to display 60 icons in a 10-column by 6-row grid using the Terminal commands on the previous page. Why aren't there 60 icons on this page? macOS doesn't automatically rearrange the icon layout in Launchpad when you change the rows and columns. You have to do that manually.

Conversely, you can make the Launchpad grid smaller – i.e., fewer columns and rows – so that fewer application icons are on each page.

For example, if you want Launchpad to display 20 application icons per page, you would need to resize the grid to 5 columns by 4 rows. To resize Launchpad, enter the following commands in Terminal.

```
defaults write com.apple.dock springboard-columns -int 5

defaults write com.apple.dock springboard-rows -int 4

killall Dock
```

Decreasing the size of the grid increases the size of each icon. With Launchpad displaying fewer icons per page, it takes more pages to display all of your applications. In the example, it now takes 5 pages to display all of the application icons.

To revert to the macOS default of 7 columns by 5 rows, enter the following commands.

```
defaults delete com.apple.dock springboard-columns
```

```
defaults delete com.apple.dock springboard-rows

killall Dock
```

You probably noticed that as you changed the Launchpad grid size, your application icons spread out across multiple pages. Launchpad does not automatically rearrange the icons for you as you experiment with different grid sizes. Unfortunately, you have to rearrange the app icons manually.

Remove the Page Scrolling Delay

macOS introduces a delay when scrolling between pages in Launchpad. If you prefer pages appear immediately without delay, enter the following commands in Terminal.

```
defaults write com.apple.dock springboard-page-duration -int 0

killall Dock
```

To restore the default scroll animation between Launchpad pages, enter the following commands.

```
defaults delete com.apple.dock springboard-page-duration

killall Dock
```

Assign a Launchpad Keyboard Shortcut

If you would like to assign a keyboard shortcut to open Launchpad, open the **Keyboard** preference pane. Click on the **Shortcuts** tab and select **Launchpad & Dock** from the sidebar. By default, a keyboard shortcut is not assigned to Launchpad.

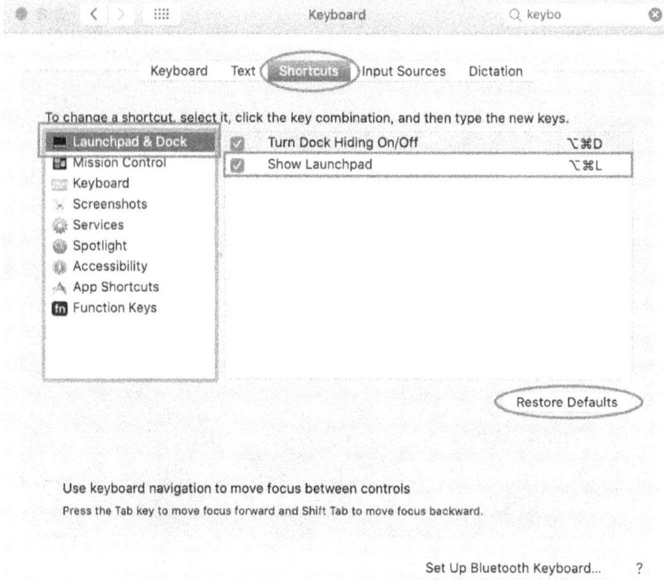

To assign a keyboard shortcut, ensure the checkbox next to **Show Launchpad** is checked and select a shortcut in the field provided. In the image above, I chose **⌥⌘L** (option+command+L). Be sure to select a key combination that is not used by another function. If you do, a yellow triangle warns you that your shortcut is already assigned to another command.

To remove the shortcut, uncheck the checkbox next to **Show Launchpad** or click the **Restore Defaults** button at the lower-right of the preference pane.

Add Launchpad to the Dock

If you have a new Mac that came with macOS Catalina pre-installed, the Launchpad icon should be in the Dock. If you upgraded from a previous version of macOS and the Launchpad icon is not in the Dock, adding it is simple.

Open the **Applications** folder in Finder and scroll down to the **Launchpad** application icon. Drag it to where you want it on the Dock.

To remove the Launchpad icon from the Dock, drag it off until **Remove** appears and then release.

Need to Start From Scratch?

If you need to revert to the macOS **Launchpad** defaults for any reason, enter the following commands in Terminal. This resets Launchpad to its out-of-the-box settings. Any tweaks, including folders you may have created, will be reset to their defaults.

```
defaults write com.apple.dock ResetLaunchPad -bool TRUE

killall Dock
```

12

Finder

Finder is the macOS file manager, providing a graphical user interface to manage files, disk drives, network drives, and to launch applications. A Finder window has three major components. At the very top of the Finder window is the **Toolbar**, which contains various tools to manipulate the window and its contents. The **Sidebar** is located on the left and is divided into four sections. **Favorites** lists shortcuts to favorite or frequently used items such as your Home, Desktop, Applications, Documents, Movies, Music, and Pictures folders. The Favorites category also allows access to AirDrop. Underneath Favorites is **iCloud**, which lists the contents of your iCloud Drive. Below iCloud is **Locations**, which lists the internal and external drives attached to your Mac and network shares connected to your Mac. The final section is the list of **Tags**, which are used to organize files. The contents of any folder selected in the Sidebar are displayed in the large pane on the right.

Clicking on the Finder icon in the Dock launches a Finder window showing the **All My Files** view, which displays files organized by file type and chronologically with the most recent at the top of the window. You can return to this view by clicking **All My Files** under **Favorites** in the Sidebar.

iCloud Desktop & Documents

macOS features seamless integration with **iCloud**, making online storage part of the operating system instead of an add-on app like Dropbox or Box. iCloud can be configured to automatically store your Desktop and Documents folders in Apple's cloud. A major benefit of storing your documents in iCloud in that they are available on all your Apple devices. iCloud also makes restoring your Mac or migrating to a new Mac a snap.

iCloud Desktop and Documents makes it easy, seamless, and effortless to synchronize and access your data across multiple devices since your data lives in iCloud. The advantage is that these folders and the files contained within them are accessible across all of your Apple devices (Mac, iPhone, iPad, AppleTV), through a browser, or even from Windows PCs. This feature is huge for those of us who work on multiple devices throughout the day. And since these folders are where a majority of files are saved, saving them to iCloud frees up storage space on your Mac's solid-state drive.

There are some caveats, of course. iCloud requires an Apple ID, which is a no-brainer. Apple gives you 5 GB of storage for free, which may or may not be sufficient depending on the size of your Documents folder. All files stored in that folder count against your iCloud storage allocation. You can, of course, purchase more storage from Apple. The table below shows the monthly cost of iCloud storage in the United States when this book went to press. Apple lets you share the 200 GB and 2 TB plans with your family. You can see how much iCloud storage costs in your country at Apple's iCloud Storage pricing page: https://support.apple.com/en-us/HT201238.

50 GB	99¢
200 GB	$2.99
2 TB	$9.99

Enable iCloud Desktop and Documents

iCloud saves your data automatically. There is no need to move or copy documents to iCloud. macOS keeps your documents synchronized. iCloud Drive safely stores all of your documents, allowing you to access them from any of your Apple devices, even Windows PCs.

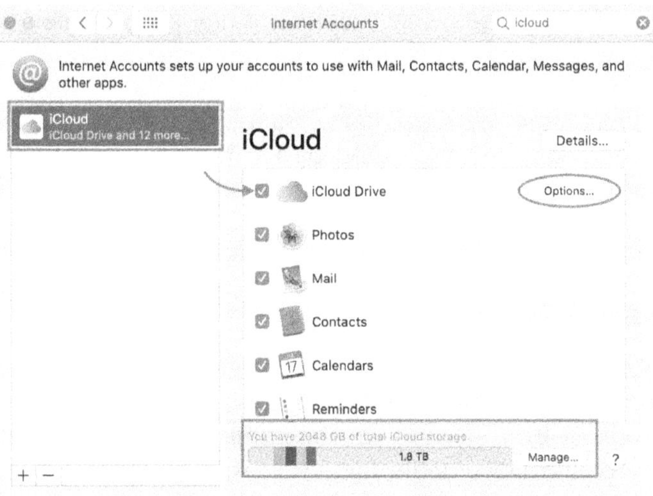

To enable iCloud Drive Desktop and Documents, launch the **Internet Accounts** preference pane in System Preferences. Check the checkbox next to **iCloud Drive**. Next, click the **Options** button and check the checkbox next to **Desktop & Documents Folders**. Click **Done** to finish.

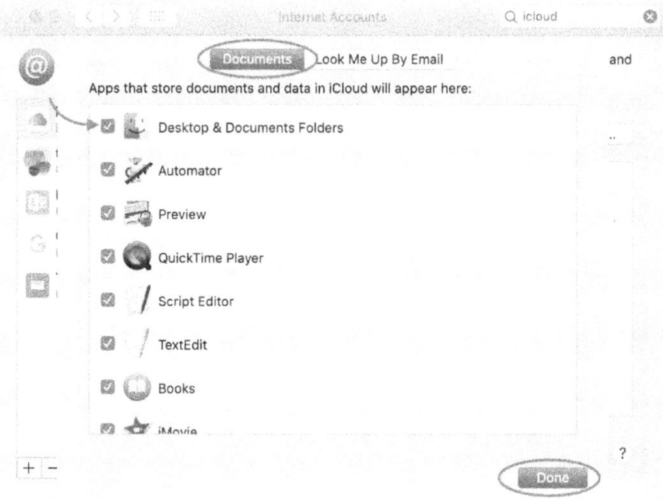

Your Desktop and Documents folders are now synchronized with iCloud. The time it takes to synchronize depends on the total size of your documents and the speed of your Internet connection. Note that your Desktop and Documents folders are now listed under the iCloud section in the Finder Sidebar.

Manage iCloud Storage

To manage the contents of your iCloud storage, click the **Manage...** button in the lower-right corner of the Internet Accounts preference pane.

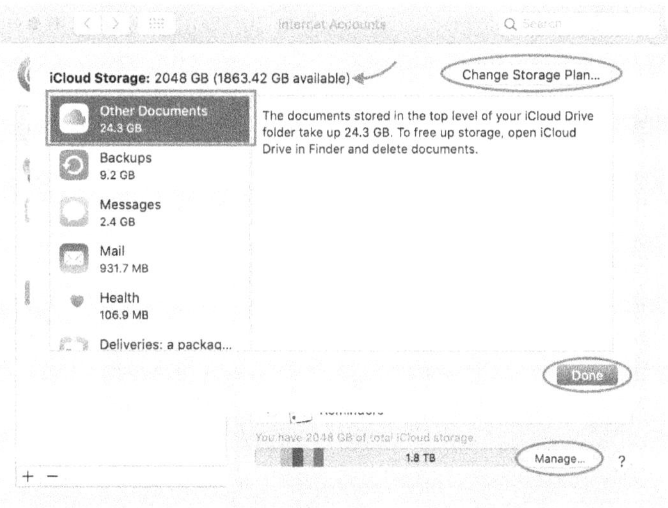

A configuration sheet appears, which lists the applications utilizing iCloud storage in the sidebar. Select an app to manage its data. For example, **Backups** often contain old backups of devices you no longer own. It is a good idea to delete old, unneeded backups to free iCloud storage space. Click **Done** when finished.

Change your iCloud Storage Plan

You can change your iCloud storage plan directly from the Internet Accounts preference pane. Click **Manage...** in the lower-right corner of the preference pane. Next, click the **Change Storage Plan...** button in the upper-right of the configuration sheet. A new panel appears with your storage options. Click **Next** to continue or **Cancel** to cancel the upgrade. Note that the credit card attached to your iTunes account is charged immediately for the cost of your new storage plan.

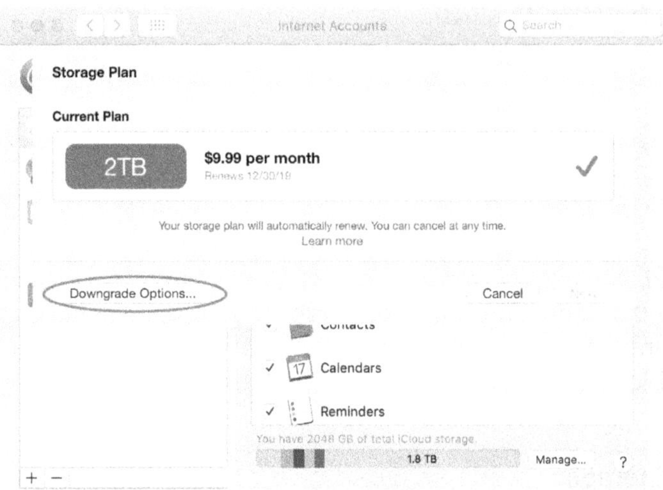

If you want to downgrade your current plan to one with less storage, click the **Downgrade Options**... button. Note that your new storage plan must be of sufficient size to accommodate the amount of data you are currently storing in iCloud.

Modify the Sidebar

The **Finder** Sidebar offers one-click access to items that you use the most, organized into four categories – **Favorites**, **iCloud**, **Locations**, and **Tags**.

The **Favorites** category provides quick, single-click access to folders and files that you access frequently. You can add any folder to Favorites by locating the folder in Finder and then dragging it into the Sidebar. You can change the order of the items listed under Favorites until they are arranged the way you want them. Any item in the Favorites list can be removed by dragging it off the Sidebar until a gray circle containing an **X** appears underneath its title. Release, and the item disappears.

Secondary clicking on an item in the **Favorites** list opens a submenu allowing you to **Open in New Tab**, **Show in Enclosing Folder**, **Get Info**, **Rename** the folder, **Remove from Sidebar**, or **Add to Dock**. Depending on the item, not all options may be available.

The iCloud section lists the contents of your iCloud Drive. Secondary clicking on an item in the **iCloud** list opens a submenu allowing you to **Open in New Tab**, **Show in Enclosing Folder**, **Get Info**, **Rename** the folder, **Remove from Sidebar**, or **Add to Dock**. Depending on the item, not all options may be available. Like the Favorites, you can rearrange items under iCloud by dragging them.

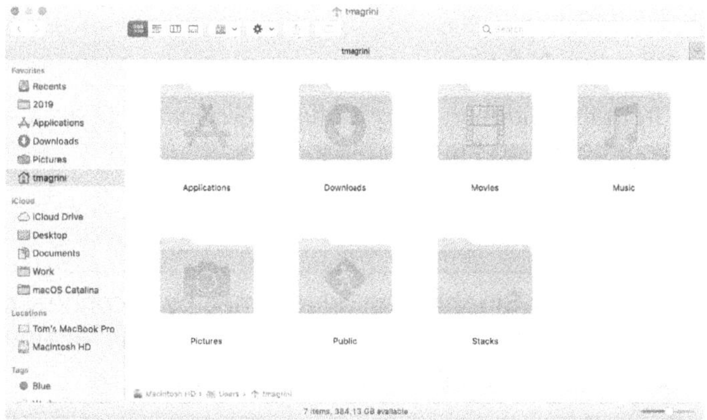

The **Locations** category includes internal drives, external drives, or other devices connected to your Mac. A secondary click on items in the list of **Devices** provides a different set of options allowing you to **Open in New Tab**, **Show in Enclosing Folder**, **Eject**, **Get Info**, **Manage Storage**, **Decrypt**, **Rename**, **Remove from Sidebar**, or **Add to Dock**. Depending on the item, not all options will be available.

The **Tags** category lists the Finder Tags. Clicking on a Tag populates the Finder window with all files tagged with the selected tag. Secondary clicking offers options to **Open in New Tab**, **Remove from Sidebar**, **Delete Tag**, or change its color.

Choose Which Items Appear in Sidebar

macOS lets you customize the Sidebar, choosing which items you want to display. To customize the Sidebar, select **Finder > Preferences...** or enter **⌘,** (command+comma).

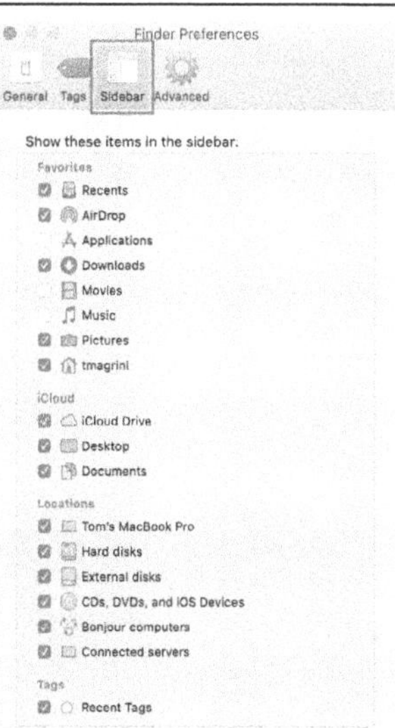

Once the preference pane appears, make sure **Sidebar** is selected from the set of four icons at the top of the pane. Using the checkboxes, check and uncheck items until you have configured the Sidebar to your liking.

Checked items are displayed in Sidebar, while unchecked items are hidden. Hidden items can be unhidden later by again accessing the Finder preferences and checking their associated checkbox(es).

Hiding Sidebar Lists

Hovering your mouse over any of the Sidebar categories reveals a **Hide/Show** toggle switch to the right of the category name. Clicking **Hide** collapses the category while clicking **Show** expands it.

Remove a Folder from the Sidebar

To remove a folder from the Sidebar, drag it off the Sidebar until an **X** appears below its name. Release your hold, and the item disappears.

Rename Sidebar Items

Any folder added to the Finder **Sidebar** can be renamed by secondary clicking on it to display a contextual menu. Renaming an item in the Sidebar renames the Sidebar shortcut and the original folder as well.

Change the Sidebar Icon Size

By default, macOS sets the size of the icons in the Sidebar to medium. If you have many items in the Sidebar, you may want to set the icons to a smaller size to avoid having to scroll. Conversely, you may want the Sidebar to display larger icons to make the items easier to read.

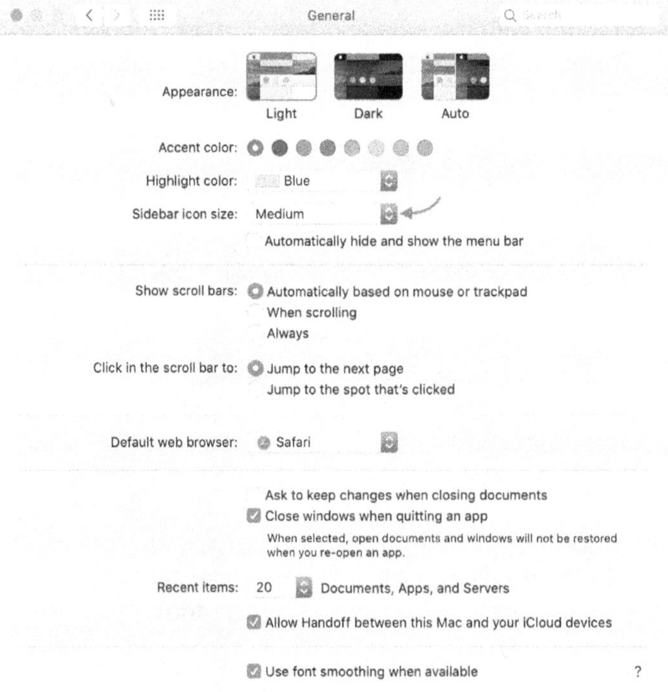

To change the icon size in Sidebar, open the **General** preference pane in the System Preferences application. Use the drop-down menu next to **Sidebar icons size** to choose **Small**, **Medium**, or **Large**. Changing the Sidebar icon size also changes the size of the text.

Hide the Sidebar

To hide the Sidebar, choose **View > Hide Sidebar** or enter **⌥⌘S** (option+command+S). The Sidebar can be toggled back on by selecting **View > Show Sidebar** or by entering **⌥⌘S** (option+command+S).

Another method is to hover over the dividing line between the Sidebar and the right-hand pane with your pointer. When the resizing pointer appears, slide it left or right to make the Sidebar smaller or larger, respectively. You can also hide the Sidebar by moving the resizing pointer to the left until the Sidebar disappears.

Show the Finder Bars

macOS offers many features in Finder that make navigating through the macOS file system more manageable or to provide additional information. These features consist of various bars that can be toggled on or off as needed. You can choose to show or hide the **Path Bar**, **Status Bar**, and **Tab Bar**, which are disabled by default. Let's enable them and see what they do.

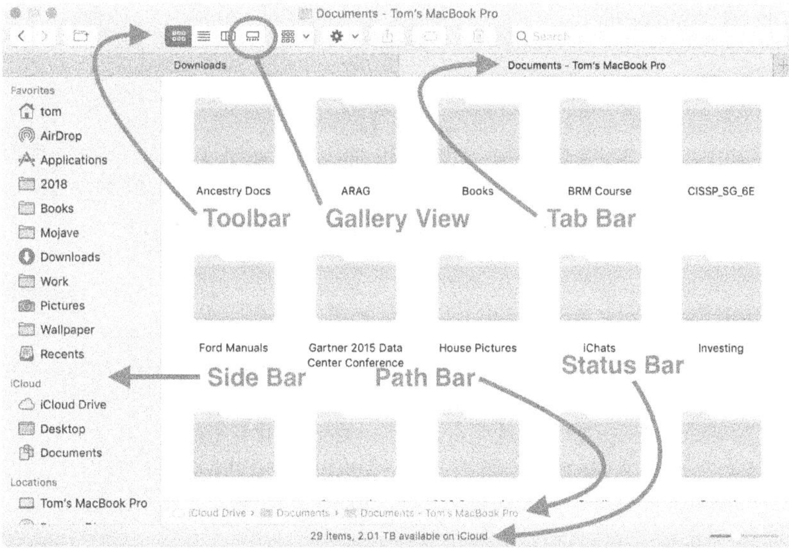

Show the Path Bar

To find the path to the currently displayed folder, could hold the **⌘** (command) key down while clicking on the folder name in Finder's Title Bar. Another way to see the path to a folder is to show the Finder **Path Bar**. The **Path Bar** displays the path taken to arrive at the folder currently displayed in Finder.

The **Path Bar** is located below the main Finder pane and displays the path from the folder shown to the top of your file system. To enable the Path Bar, select **View > Show Path Bar** or enter **⌥⌘P** (option+command+P). To turn the Finder Path Bar off, select **View > Hide Path Bar** or enter **⌥⌘P** (option+command+P). The Path Bar can be toggled on and off with the **⌥⌘P** (option+command+P) keyboard shortcut.

Path Bar Tips & Tricks

You can drag files into any folder listed in the **Path Bar** to move them. If you want to copy the file instead, hold down the ⌥ (option) key while dragging. To create an alias, hold down ⌥⌘ (option+command) keys while dragging. A folder can even be dragged within the Path Bar to move it to a new location. You can even drag between different Finder windows. While dragging, hover the pointer over the Path Bar of the inactive Finder window. It becomes active after a few moments.

If you change your mind while dragging, press the **esc** key to cancel. If you change your mind after completing the move, copy, or alias creation, select **Edit > Undo** or enter **⌘Z** (command+Z) to undo.

You can see the contents of any folder in the **Path Bar** by double-clicking on it. Its contents replace the items displayed in the current Finder window. If you hold down the ⌘ (command) key while double-clicking, the folder opens in a new tab. Holding down the ⌥ (option) key while double-clicking opens the folder in a new Finder window while simultaneously closing the source window or tab.

Sometimes a path is so long that it cannot fit in the Path Bar. In that case, macOS truncates the folder names. Hover your pointer over a truncated folder name to expand it so you can read its name.

Shorten the Path Bar

macOS lists the path from the root of the disk drive to the current directory, which, depending on the depth of your directory structure, can result in ridiculously long paths and truncated, challenging to read folder names in the path. If most of your file browsing is done in your **Home** directory, it would be better if the path was shortened to reflect your location as it relates to your Home directory.

To shorten the path shown in the **Path Bar**, open Terminal and enter the following commands. This change takes effect immediately.

```
defaults write com.apple.finder PathBarRootAtHome -bool TRUE

killall Finder
```

To revert to the macOS default and show the longer path, enter the following commands.

```
defaults delete com.apple.finder PathBarRootAtHome
```

```
killall Finder
```

Show the Path in the Title Bar

If you prefer not to use the Path Bar, macOS allows you to configure Finder's Title Bar to display the path. By default, the Title Bar shows the name of the current folder. If you would like to show the path instead, open Terminal and enter the following commands. This change takes effect immediately.

```
defaults write com.apple.finder _FXShowPosixPathInTitle -bool TRUE
```

```
killall Finder
```

To revert to the macOS default, enter the following commands.

```
defaults delete com.apple.finder _FXShowPosixPathInTitle
```

```
killall Finder
```

Show the Status Bar

The Finder **Status Bar** shows the number of items contained within a folder and the amount of free space left on the drive in which the folder is located.

To turn the Finder Status Bar on, select **View > Show Status Bar** or enter **⌘/** (command+/). When the Status Bar is enabled, every Finder window will display the Status Bar at the bottom, below the Path Bar.

Another handy feature of the Finder Status Bar is that it provides a slider in the lower-right corner that you can use to change the size of the icons displayed in the Finder window. Slide the slider left or right to make the icons smaller or larger, respectively.

To hide the Finder Status Bar, select **View > Hide Status Bar** or enter **⌘/** (command+/).

Show the Tab Bar

The **Tab Bar** appears just below the Finder Toolbar. Once multiple tabs are open, macOS automatically displays the Tab Bar. If you prefer to see the Tab Bar all the time, select **View > Show Tab Bar** or enter **⇧⌘T** (shift+command+T). When the Tab Bar is enabled, every Finder window will display the Tab Bar below the Finder Toolbar.

The Tab Bar will automatically unhide when a second tab is opened. To hide the Tab Bar, select **View > Hide Tab Bar** or enter **⇧⌘T** (shift+command+T). Note that you can only hide the Tab Bar when Finder is displaying a single tab. Whenever multiple Finder tabs are open, the Tab Bar will automatically appear, and the option to hide it will be grayed out in the **View** menu. Hiding the Tab Bar when you have a single tab open makes the Finder interface appear cleaner.

Switch to Gallery View

Gallery View is a Finder view that allows you to see a large preview of file content without having to use Quick Look. Gallery View replaced the old Cover Flow View in macOS releases prior to Mojave. Gallery View is accessed directly from the Finder Toolbar. I find Gallery View is perfect for viewing and working with image files.

Customize Gallery View

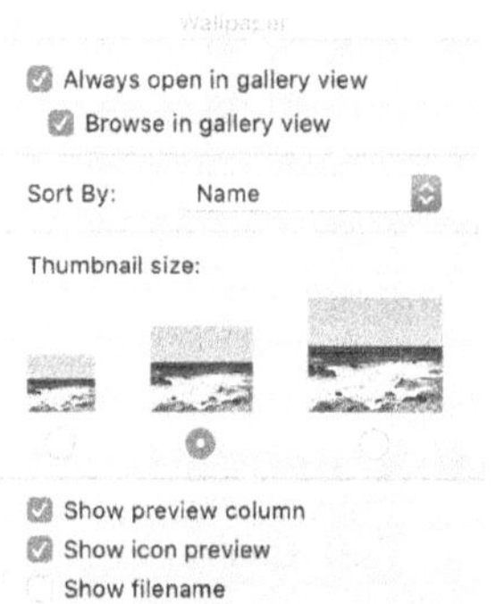

You can customize the Gallery View by entering **⌘J** (command+J) to reveal the Gallery View customization panel. Files in Gallery View can be sorted by name (the default), kind, date modified, date created, date last opened, date added, size, and tags. The **Thumbnail** size controls the size of the file thumbnails at the bottom of the window.

Check the checkbox next to **Show preview column** to add the Preview Column to Gallery View. The Preview Column allows you to see file metadata and access Quick Actions.

Show icon preview is enabled by default and displays the file content in the thumbnails along the bottom of the Gallery View. **Show filename** adds the filename to the thumbnails at the bottom of Gallery View. Click the **Use as Defaults** button to save your changes as the default when opening the folder you are viewing in Gallery View.

Show the Preview Panel

The **Preview Panel** displays a preview of file contents, file metadata such as the date it was created and last modified, tags, content, dimensions, resolution, and color space and profile. It also provides access to **Quick Actions**, shortcuts to various tools such as creating a PDF and rotating, trimming, and marking up a file. Quick Actions are accessed directly from the Preview Panel in any Finder View.

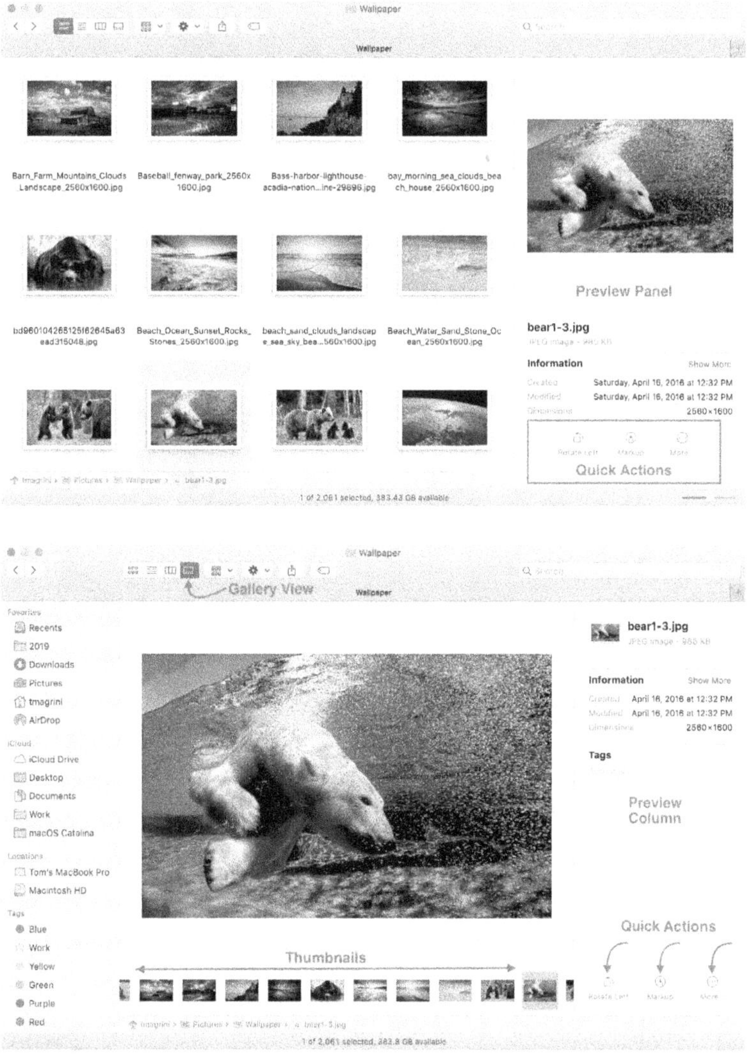

To show the Finder Preview Panel, select **View > Show Preview** or enter **⇧⌘P** (shift+command+P). Select any file to see it in the Preview Panel. Once you have enabled the Preview Panel, it is enabled for all new Finder windows. To hide the Preview Panel, select **View > Hide Preview** or enter **⇧⌘P** (shift+command+P).

The Preview Panel is called the Preview Column when in Gallery view. While it is organized slightly differently, it provides the same file metadata and access to Quick Actions.

Clicking on **More...** and then **Customize...** in the Preview Column opens the Extensions preference pane with Finder selected in the left sidebar. The Extension preference pane allows you to add or remove Quick Actions by checking or unchecking the checkboxes. Close the Extension preference pane when finished customizing.

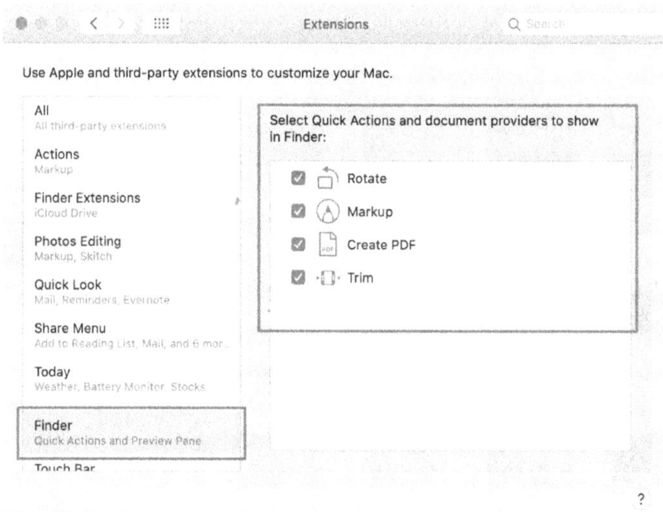

Customize the Toolbar

The Finder **Toolbar**, located at the top of the Finder window, provides tools to manipulate the contents of folders displayed in the Finder window's right-hand pane. From left to right, the Toolbar provides **Back/Forward** buttons to navigate through folders.

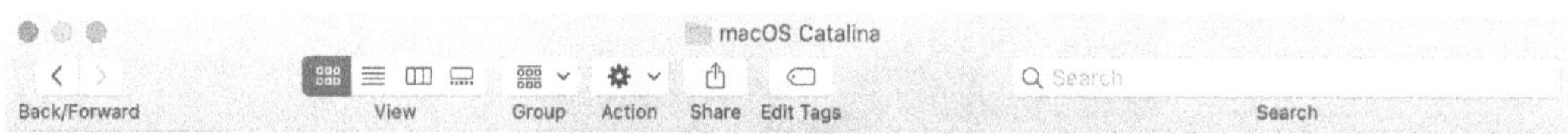

The next set of four **View** icons change how the contents of a folder are viewed – by **Icon**, by **List**, by **Column**, or by **Gallery View**.

The **Group** button offers a drop-down menu where you choose how to group files by name, kind, application, date last opened, date added, date modified, date created, size, or tag. The final option, none, leaves the folder unsorted.

The **Action** button provides a contextual drop-down menu that provides a set of tools based on whether an item is selected or not.

The **Share** button lets you share an item via Mail, Messages, Airdrop, or through third-party extensions. To configure the third-party extensions available in the **Share Menu**, click the Share button and select **More...** or open the **Extensions** preference pane in System Preferences. Select **Share Menu** in the sidebar if not already selected. Use the checkboxes to select which third-party extensions you wish to make available in Finder's Share drop-down menu.

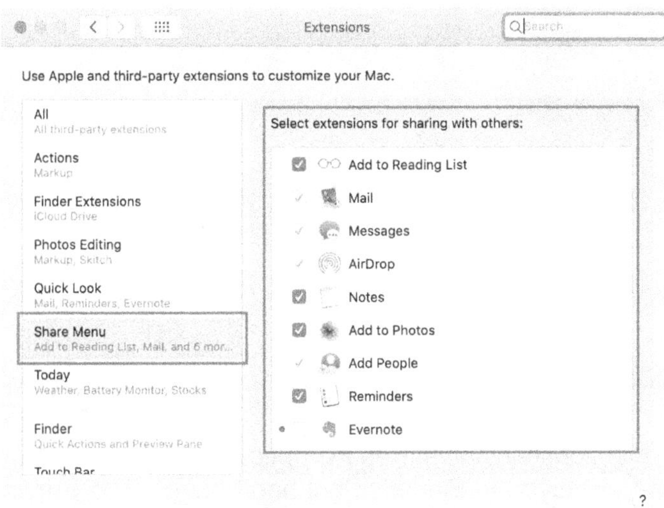

Back to the Finder toolbar, the **Edit Tags** tool allows you to add, change, and remove tags. When an untagged item is selected, this tool changes to the **Add Tags** tool, allowing you to add tags to the selected file. Finally, at the upper-right corner of the Finder window is a Spotlight search field.

macOS allows you to customize the Finder **Toolbar**, adding, removing, and rearranging tools as you see fit. Secondary click in an open area of the Toolbar to reveal a contextual menu. This menu allows you to choose how the tools appear. Tools can be displayed using both their **Icon and Text**, **Icon Only**, or **Text Only**. The current setting has a checkmark next to it. An option to completely hide the toolbar is also available.

The final option, **Customize Toolbar...** allows you to add, rearrange, and remove tools using the drop-down tools palette with the entire selection of available tools. You can also access this palette by selecting **Customize Toolbar...** from the **View** menu. Drag and drop the tools from the palette into the Toolbar. Rearrange as you see fit. You can choose how the tools will be displayed – **Icon and Text**, **Icon Only**, or **Text Only**. Click the **Done** button when finished.

The additional tools that are available include the **Path** tool, which displays the full path to the location shown in Finder's right-hand pane. You can also see the path by holding down the ⌘ (command) key while clicking on the title shown at the top of the toolbar.

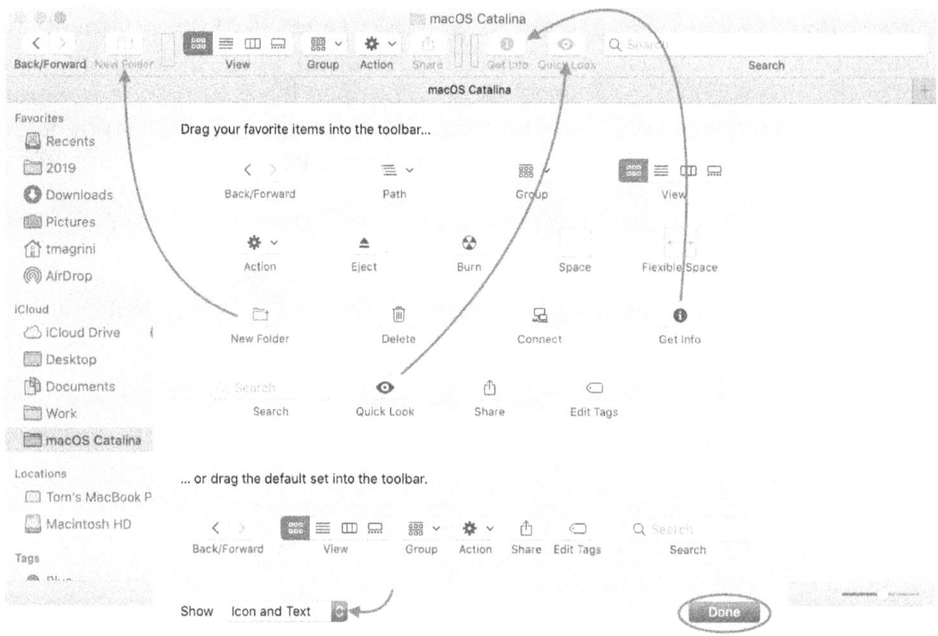

The **Eject** tool will eject optical media from the optical drive and will unmount any drive whose contents are displayed in Finder's right-hand pane. The **Burn** tool is used to burn files and folders to optical media.

The **Space** and **Flexible Space** tools are used to space out the tools in the toolbar by adding blank space between them.

The **New Folder** tool does what its name implies, creating a new folder in the current folder displayed in the right-hand pane.

The **Delete** tool sends the selected items to the Trash.

The **Connect** tool is used to connect to network servers and shared drives.

The **Get Info** tool opens the Get Info window, which displays information about the selected file such as its tags, kind, size, location, date created, date modified, its file extension, Spotlight comments, the default application which opens the file, and a file preview. The Get Info tool can be used on multiple files.

The **Quick Look** tool opens a preview of the selected file without launching the application in which it was created. Quick Look allows you to preview a file before deciding to open it. The Quick Look window provides an **Open with** button, allowing you to launch the application that created the file, a **Share** button, and if the application is Preview, **Rotate** and **Markup** tools. You also can open Quick Look by clicking on a file and pressing the spacebar.

A drop-down menu at the lower-left of the tools palette lets you select how the tools will be displayed using both their **Icon and Text**, **Icon Only**, or **Text Only**.

To add a tool to the Toolbar, drag it from the tools palette, and drop it onto the toolbar. Existing tools located on the Toolbar can be rearranged by dragging them. A tool is removed by dragging it off the Toolbar and back on to the tools palette. Click the **Done** button when finished customizing your toolbar.

Tools located on the Toolbar can be rearranged without having to use the drop-down tools palette. To move a tool, hold the ⌘ (command) key down while dragging the tool to its new location. You can also use the ⌘ (command) key to remove a tool. Hold down the ⌘ (command) key while dragging the tool from the Toolbar. The tool will disappear.

To revert to the default set of tools, drag the default set on to the Finder Toolbar and click **Done**.

Tag Files & Folders

Tagging files is a significant shift in the way you work with the file system. When using tags, files no longer need to be saved in a specific folder to create a relationship between them. Tags remove the need to have deeply nested folders within the file system to create relationships between different files. It doesn't matter where files are saved because Tags can be used to relate them to each other. The macOS Spotlight search feature allows you to immediately locate files based on their Tags regardless of where they reside in the file system.

Tagging files is a convenient way to organize related files, such as files from a project, without having to create a special folder or modify the locations of the files. You can customize the name to "Kitchen Remodel Project" or "Budget" in addition to by color.

There are several methods to tag an item in Finder. The first is to select the item, click the **Add Tags** tool in the toolbar, and select the appropriate tag. Another method is to select the file, secondary click on it, and add a Tag. Files can be tagged with one or more tags as needed. A third method is to select the file or files you want to Tag and select a Tag from the bottom of the Finder **File** menu. The fourth method is to select the files in Finder and click on the appropriate Tag in the Sidebar. The fifth method is to choose a Tag when saving a file for the first time.

To change or remove a tag from an item in Finder, select the file and click the **Edit Tags** tool in the Toolbar. Remove or modify any existing Tags. An alternate method is to secondary click on an item to remove or change any existing Tags using the contextual menu. A third method is to use **File > Tags...** to remove existing Tags.

To tag an open file, move the pointer to the right of the filename in the Title Bar, click on the drop-down arrow, and click on the Tags field. You can choose a tag from the list or create a new one. To change or remove a Tag from an open file, click on the arrow next to the file name in the title bar to reveal the drop-down menu. Remove or modify any existing Tags. This method does not work on all applications, most notably the Microsoft Office productivity suite.

Customize Tags

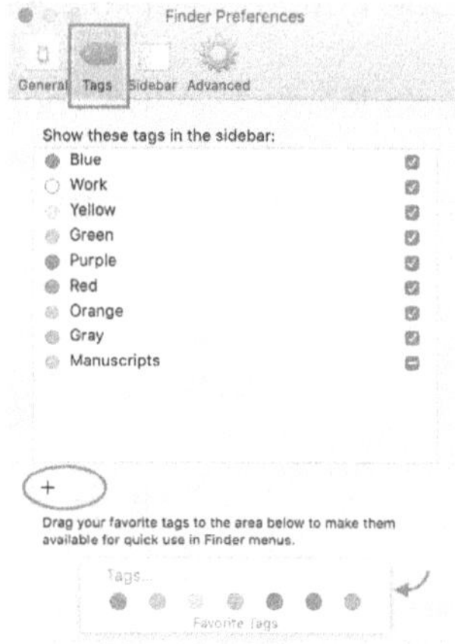

You can rename Tags, choose the tags you want in the Finder Sidebar, select your favorite tags in the Finder preference pane. Select **Preferences...** from the **Finder** menu. You can also access the preferences by entering **⌘,** (command+comma). Once the Finder preference pane appears, make sure **Tags** is selected from the set of four icons at the top of the pane.

To rename a tag, click on its name and rename it. The tag will appear under **Tags** in the Sidebar if its checkbox is checked. Drag the Tags to rearrange their order.

To add a new Tag, click the **+** button. To remove a Tag, highlight it and click the **–** button or secondary click on the Tag and choose **Delete**. You can also rename a tag by secondary clicking on it and choosing **Rename**.

To choose which Tags appear in the Finder Sidebar, check or uncheck the checkbox next to the Tag.

At the bottom of this pane are your **Favorite Tags**, which appear in Finder menus. To remove a Tag, drag it off the preference pane. To add a Tag, drag it from the list into the favorite **Tags...** box at the bottom.

A quicker way to create a Tag is to highlight an item and click the **Add Tags** button in the toolbar to reveal an option to enter the name of a new Tag. Begin typing in the field, and you will be given the option to create a new Tag. Press **return** when finished.

Search for Tags

All files associated with a Tag can be quickly retrieved using the Sidebar in Finder. However, there is no easy way to find files and folders tagged with multiple Tags in the Sidebar. The only method is to perform a tag search using Spotlight.

To search for a file that is tagged with both a blue and a purple tag, open Spotlight and enter the following search parameters.

```
tag:blue tag:purple
```

You can also search for tagged files by the Tag name. For example, if I rename the blue tag "macOS" and the purple tag "Apple." The following Spotlight search will return the same result as the search above.

```
tag:macOS tag:Apple
```

Create a Smart Folder

macOS offers several ways to create a Smart Folder. The first is to execute a search using Spotlight, selecting **Show all in Finder...** and then clicking **Save**. Other methods include selecting **File > Find**, using the **⌘F** (command+F) keyboard shortcut, or typing search criteria into the **Search** field of an open Finder window. Another method is to select **File > New Smart Folder** or use the shortcut **⌥⌘N** (option+command+N) in the Finder menu.

After selecting **Show all in Finder...**, you can save your search by clicking the **Save** button located in the upper-right of the Finder window below the Tabs. You are creating a **Smart Folder**, a dynamic list of items meeting your search criteria. By saving a search as a Smart Folder, you save time by not having to rebuild a search from scratch each time. When you click the **Save** button, a drop-down sheet will appear, allowing you to name the Smart Folder, save it, and display it in the Sidebar. I recommend saving frequently used searches in the Sidebar so you can access them quickly.

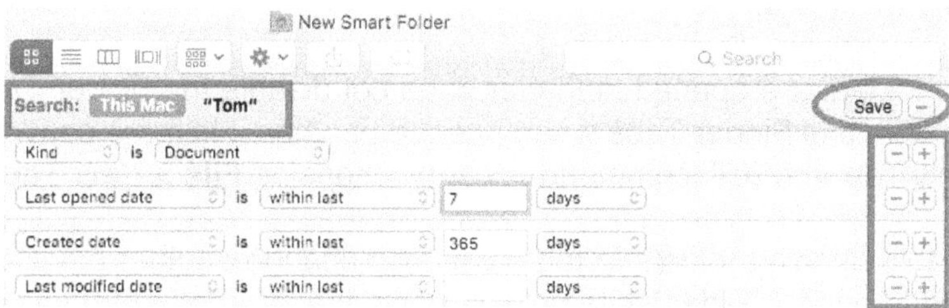

Smart Folders are dynamically updated and remain current as you add and delete items matching the search criteria. All items are conveniently displayed in a Smart Folder as if they were located in a single folder, regardless of where they reside in your file system. While the items only appear to be located in one folder, they remain safely tucked away in the folders in which you saved them.

To add additional search criteria, click the **+** button next to **Save**. You can choose the search scope with **This Mac** being the default. You also have the option of only searching within the current folder. That option is to the right of **This Mac**. Any search line can be removed by clicking the – button. Select **Other...** to reveal a list of over 100 attributes against which you can search.

Once you have perfected your search criteria, click the **Save** button to reveal a drop-down configuration sheet allowing you to name your Smart Folder, save it to a folder, and add it to the Finder Sidebar.

By default, all Smart Folders are saved to the **Saved Searches** folder. However, you can choose where to save your Smart Folder. The checkbox next to **Add to Sidebar** is checked by default. Uncheck it if you do not want your Smart Folder to appear in the Sidebar. Otherwise, your new Smart Folder will appear at the bottom of your list of Favorites.

Open a File & Close Finder

Holding down the ⌥ (option) key while double-clicking on a file or folder in a Finder window will open the file while simultaneously closing the Finder window. You can also accomplish the same thing with the shortcut **⌥⌘O** (option+command+O).

Disable Opening Folders in Tabs

By default, macOS opens all folders in a new tab. It is sometimes more convenient to have multiple windows open. If you prefer folders open in their own windows, you can disable this feature.

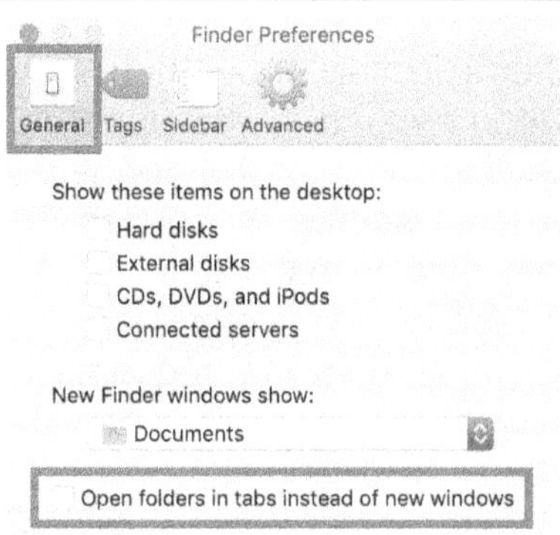

To disable opening folders in tabs, open the **Finder** preferences by entering **⌘,** (command+comma). Next, select **General** if not already highlighted. Uncheck the checkbox next to **Open folders in tabs instead of new windows**.

Changing how folders are opened in Finder does not disable the Finder Tabs feature. Therefore, you can use Finder Tabs when needed or when it is more convenient. You can open a new Tab with **⌘T** (command+T) or by choosing **File > New Tab**.

When you disable opening folders in tabs, you also change another macOS behavior. Double-clicking to open a folder while holding down the **⌘** (command) key now opens the folder in a new Finder window instead of a new tab.

Merge Multiple Finder Windows into Tabs

If you have multiple Finder windows open, you can merge them into one window with each Finder window becoming a Tab. To merge all windows, click on any Finder window then select **Window > Merge All Windows**.

Open a New Finder Window from a Tab

Any of the Tabs in a Finder window can be used to create a new Finder window. Secondary click on the tab you want to move to a new window and select **Move Tab to New Window**. Alternately, you can drag and drop a tab out of a Finder window onto the Desktop to make it open in a new Finder window.

The contextual menu revealed when secondary clicking on a Tab also allows you to create a **New Tab**, **Close Tab**, **Close Other Tabs**, **Move Tab to New Window**, or **Show All Tabs**.

Change the Icon Size, Spacing, Arrangement, & Sort

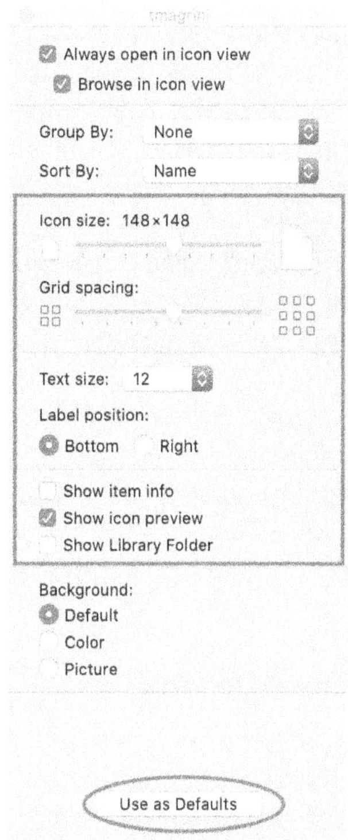

The default icon size in macOS is 64 x 64 pixels. While this is good for most applications, you may find it too small when trying to preview documents, pictures, or movies. macOS allows you to change the default icon size.

To change the default icon size, secondary click any open space in a Finder window to reveal a contextual menu. Choose **Show View Options**. You can also select **View > Show View Options** or enter **⌘J** (command+J). The Finder View Panel appears with the name of the folder located in the Title Bar at the top of the window. If the checkbox next to **Always open in icon view** is checked, this folder will always open in icon view.

The next section allows you to change the arrangement of the icons and how they are sorted. Use the drop-down menus to set your arrangement and sorting options.

In the next section, you can change the icon size using the slider. Icons can be made as small as 16 x 16 pixels or as large as 512 x 512 pixels. The macOS default is 64 x 64. The largest size is handy when sorting through a folder containing pictures or movies.

The next section allows you to change the text size for the label shown at the bottom of files and folders. The default text size is 12 points. Supported text sizes are 10, 11, 12, 13, 14, 15, and 16 points. The default label position is at the bottom of the files and folders. macOS lets you display the label at the bottom or to the right of an item.

The next section contains two checkboxes. The first, **Show item info**, will display the size of the file or the number of items a folder contains. The second checkbox, **Show icon preview**, is checked by default and will render a preview of the file content. If you uncheck it, macOS will display only default icons rather than rendering file content previews.

The next section allows you to change the background upon which icons are displayed. The default is white when in Light Mode and black in Dark Mode, but you have the choice of another color or a picture.

Clicking on the **Use as Defaults** button located at the bottom of the window makes your selections the default for the current folder and all of its sub-folders.

Show the User Library Folder

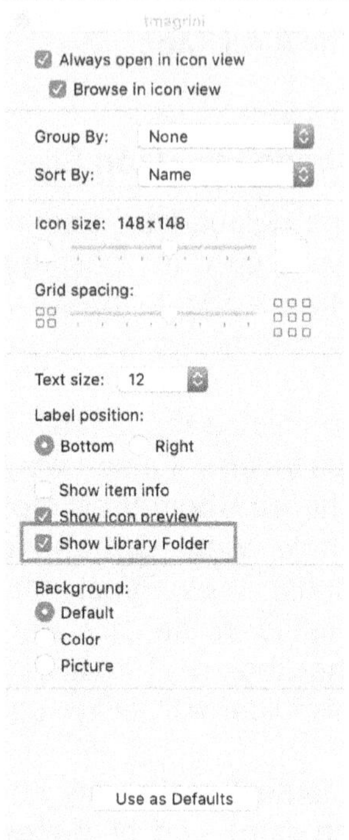

macOS allows you to toggle a switch to make the **Library** folder, which is usually hidden, visible. To make the **Library** folder visible, open **Finder** and navigate to your **Home** directory. Secondary click any open space in the Finder window showing your Home directory. Choose **Show View Options**. You can also select **Show View Options** from under Finder's **View** menu or enter **⌘J** (command+J). Check the checkbox next to **Show Library Folder**.

Once your Library folder is visible, you can use the keyboard shortcut **⇧⌘L** (shift+command+L) to go directly to it from any Finder window.

If you do not want to permanently make your Library folder visible and need only temporary access, hold down the ⌥ (option) key while selecting the **Go** menu. The **Library** folder will appear while you are holding down the ⌥ (option) key. Select **Go > Library**.

Show Hidden Files

macOS hides any file or folder when its name begins with a "." If you need to show hidden files, you can quickly see them with the keyboard shortcut **⇧⌘.** (shift+command+period). Hidden files and folders will now be visible in every Finder window. To revert to the macOS default, enter the keyboard shortcut **⇧⌘.** (shift+command+period) again to hide the files.

You can also enter the following commands in Terminal to show hidden files and folders.

```
defaults write com.apple.finder AppleShowAllFiles TRUE

killall Finder
```

To revert to the default where hidden files and folders remain invisible in Finder windows, enter the following commands in Terminal.

```
defaults write com.apple.finder AppleShowAllFiles FALSE

killall Finder
```

Change or Disable the Spring-Loading Delay

Try dragging a file or folder onto another folder, pausing for a moment without releasing your hold. Suddenly the folder will spring open to reveal its contents. What you have just experienced is a macOS feature called **Spring-loaded** folders. Once a Spring-loaded folder opens, you can repeat the same gesture to drill down through the directory structure until you reach your desired destination. The **Spring-loading delay**, the amount of time you must pause on a folder before it springs open, can be tweaked or disabled entirely.

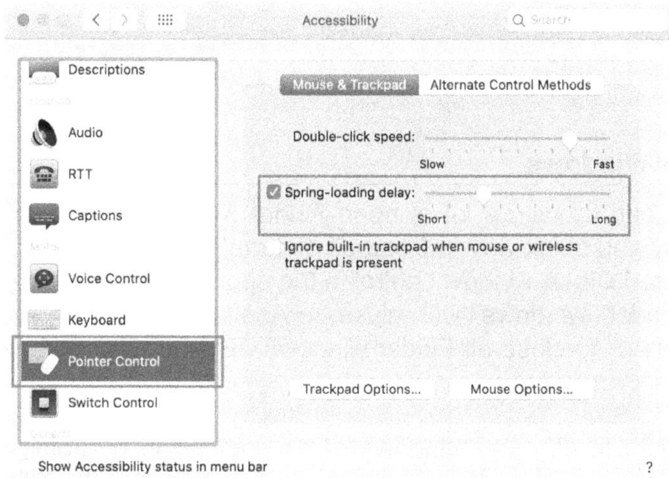

To adjust the Spring-loading delay, open the **Accessibility** preference pane, and select **Pointer Control** in the sidebar. Adjust the spring load **Delay** using the slider located next to **Spring-loading delay**.

If you want to disable the Spring-loading delay feature entirely, uncheck the checkbox next to **Spring-loading delay**.

The **Tab Bar** appears just below the Finder toolbar. Like macOS folders, Finder tabs are Spring-loaded. The tab will expand if you drag a file or folder and hover over it until the Spring-loading delay timer expires.

If you are in a hurry and don't want to wait for the Spring-load delay timer to expire, press the **spacebar** to bypass the delay and open a folder or tab immediately.

Select the Folder Displayed in New Windows and Tabs

macOS lets you select the folder when new **Finder** windows and tabs are opened. Launch the Finder preferences by selecting **Finder > Preferences...** or by entering **⌘,** (command+comma). Next, select the **General** tab. Use the drop-down menu under **New Finder windows show** to set your desired location. You can choose from your home directory, **Desktop**, **Documents**, **iCloud Drive**, or **Recents**. Selecting **Other...** opens a Finder window where you can choose another folder.

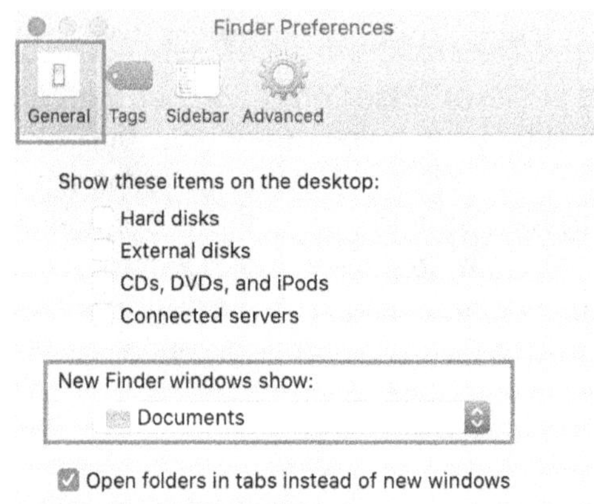

Close All Finder Windows

Sometimes you'll end up with a lot of open Finder windows. Wouldn't it be great if there was an easy and quick way to close all of them? Hold down the ⌥ (option) key while clicking the red **Close** window control in the upper left-hand corner of any Finder window. All Finder windows will close. Another option is to enter **⌥⌘W** (option+command+W) to close all Finder windows. By the way, these tricks work for any application.

You can also minimize all open windows of an application by holding down the ⌥ (option) key while clicking the yellow minimize window control in the Title Bar.

Show File Extensions

By default, macOS doesn't display file extensions, proving that learning the difference between those 3- and 4-letter extensions in Windows was a terrible waste of your time. For those of you switching from a Microsoft Windows PC to a Mac and are worried because you miss the comfort of seeing those 3 file extensions after every filename, macOS allows you to enable file extension display.

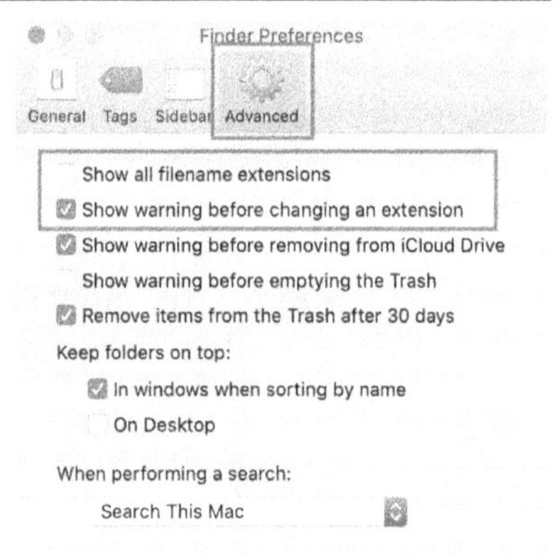

To have macOS show file extensions, open the Finder preferences, and select the **Advanced** tab. Check the checkbox next to **Show all filename extensions**.

Note that macOS will also warn you if you change a filename extension. You can disable this warning; however, I do not recommend it since changing a file extension could make a file unusable.

Backspace & Delete

The **delete** key on a Mac keyboard acts like the backspace key on a Windows PC. So how do you delete? On a Mac, the **delete** key works both ways – forward and backward. Hold down the **fn** key while pressing **delete** to have the key act like a delete key on a Windows PC does.

Delete a File Immediately

To delete a file immediately, highlight the file you want to delete in Finder and hold down the ⌥ (option) key while selecting **File > Delete Immediately...** or enter **⌥⌘delete** (option+command+delete). A dialog box will appear to confirm the deletion and warn that this action cannot be undone. Click the **Delete** button to delete the file immediately or **Cancel**.

Note that the Delete Immediately option will only appear in the **File** menu when you are holding down the ⌥ (option) key. When the ⌥ (option) key is held down, **Move to Trash** will change to **Delete Immediately**.

Change the Scroll Bar Behavior

In macOS, scroll bars only appear when you are scrolling. This is very different from Windows, where scroll bars are an ugly blight on the right and bottom edge of every window. If you are a former Windows user and miss your scroll bars, macOS can be configured to permanently tack those ugly scroll bars to the right and bottom edges of every macOS window.

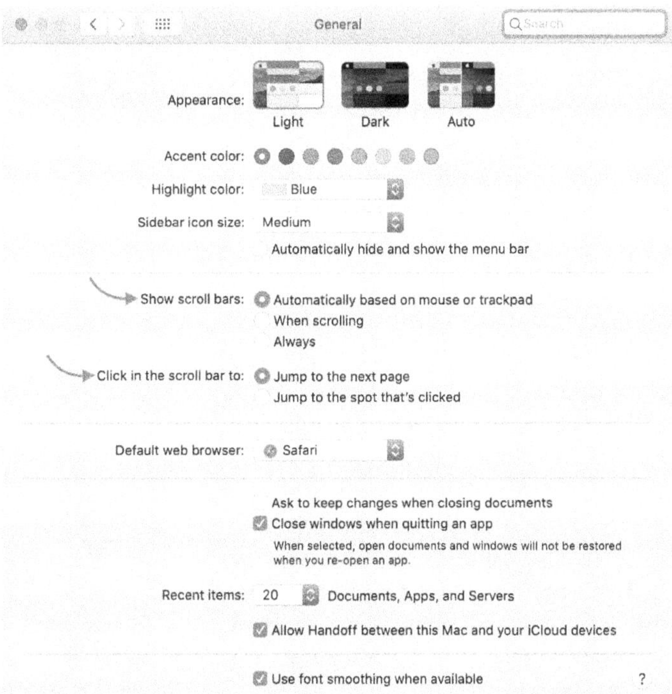

To change the behavior of the scroll bars, open the **General** preference pane in System Preferences. When set to **Automatically based on mouse or trackpad**, scrollbars will not appear unless the document requires scrollbars, and you have placed either one finger on the mouse or two fingers on a trackpad in preparation to scroll. This is the macOS default. If you like your scroll bars hidden until you are actually scrolling, choose the **When scrolling** option. The scrollbars disappear when you are finished scrolling. If you are a former Windows user suffering from scroll bar separation anxiety, select **Always**.

You have two options for clicking within a scroll bar. When **Jump to the next page** is selected, clicking within the scroll bar will page up or page down a single page at a time. When **Jump to the spot that's clicked** is selected, clicking within the scroll bar will take you to that spot in the document. For example, clicking ¼ of the way down the scroll bar will allow you to jump about a quarter way through your document. This feature is quite handy when you need to navigate quickly through a long document.

If you hold down the ⌥ (option) key while clicking within a scroll bar, macOS will temporarily toggle to the other option. For example, if you have configured macOS to **Jump to the next page**, holding down the ⌥ (option) key when clicking in the scroll bar will temporarily enable the **Jump to the spot that's clicked** option.

Change the Search Scope

When searching in Finder, macOS searches your entire Mac. You can change the search scope to limit it to the current folder or a previous search scope.

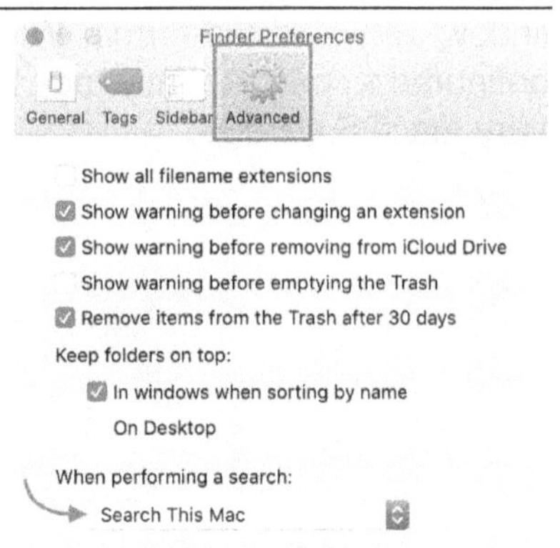

To change the search scope, open the Finder preferences by selecting **Finder > Preferences…** or by entering **⌘,** (command+comma). Select the **Advanced** tab. Use the drop-down list under **When performing a search** to select your desired scope.

Remove the Empty Trash Warning

Every time you empty the **Trash**, macOS asks you to confirm that you want to erase the items in the Trash. If you find this warning unnecessary, you can disable it.

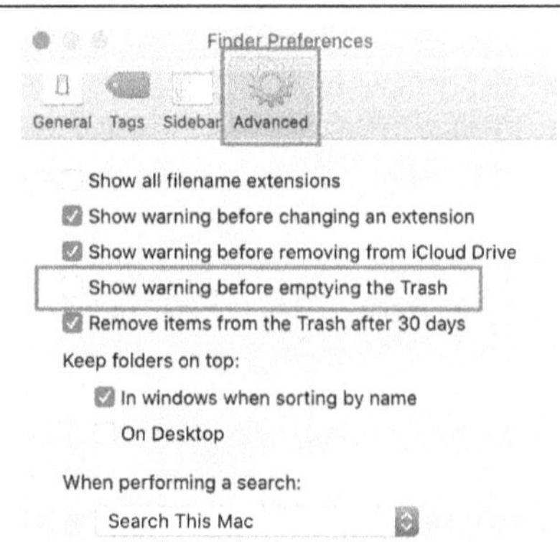

To tell macOS to stop confirming that you want to empty the Trash, open the Finder preferences by selecting **Finder > Preferences…** or by entering **⌘,** (command+comma). Next, select the **Advanced** tab. Uncheck the checkbox next to **Show warning before emptying the Trash**.

Remove the iCloud Drive Warning

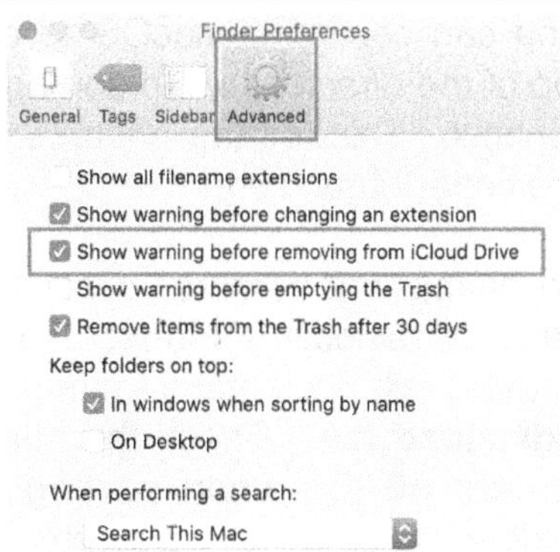

macOS will warn you when you remove a file from iCloud Drive. You'll see this warning if you move a file from iCloud Drive to the local storage on your Mac. If you feel this warning is unnecessary, you can disable it.

To disable this warning, open the Finder preference pane by selecting **Finder > Preferences...** or by entering **⌘,** (command+comma). Select the **Advanced** tab. Uncheck the checkbox next to **Show warning before removing from iCloud Drive**.

Remove Items in the Trash After 30 Days

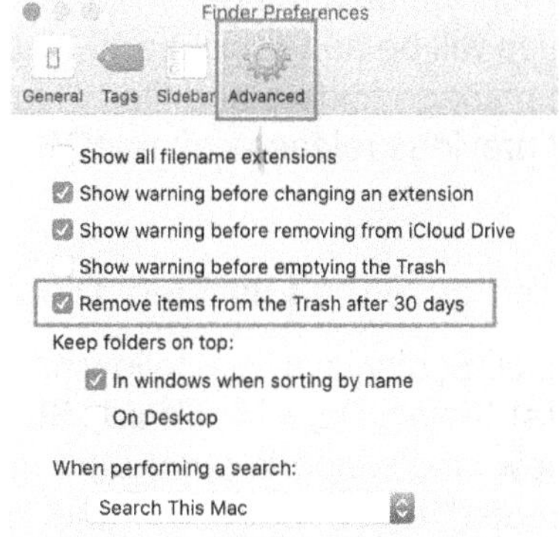

macOS can automatically delete items that have been in the Trash for 30 days. This is a handy feature that ensures old files you put in the Trash are not left hanging around indefinitely.

To enable this feature, open the Finder preference pane by selecting **Finder > Preferences...** or by entering **⌘,** (command+comma). Next, select the **Advanced** tab. Check the checkbox next to **Remove items from the Trash after 30 days**.

Quiet the Trash

macOS makes a sound that sounds like the crinkling of paper when emptying the **Trash**. This can be annoying if you're working in a quiet office environment or are listening to music. The sound of the trash emptying can disturb your concentration or the concentration of others.

To quiet the Trash when emptying, open Terminal and enter the following commands. This change takes effect immediately.

```
defaults write com.apple.finder FinderSounds -bool FALSE

killall Finder
```

Enter the following commands in Terminal to revert to the macOS default. This change takes effect immediately.

```
defaults delete com.apple.finder FinderSounds

killall Finder
```

Display Folders on Top

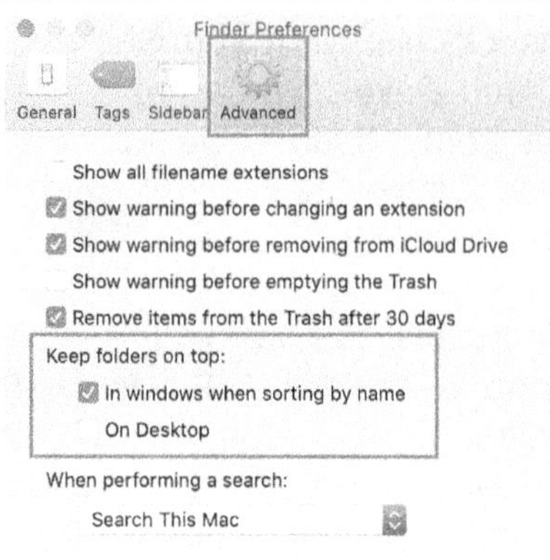

You can configure macOS to display folders at the top of the directory when sorting by name in a Finder window. This feature ensures that files and folders are better organized.

To enable this feature, open the Finder preference pane by selecting **Finder > Preferences...** or by entering **⌘,** (command+comma). Next, select the **Advanced** tab. Check the checkbox next to **Keep folders on top when sorting by name**. To keep folders on top of the Desktop, check the checkbox next to **On Desktop**. You can enable either or both options.

When enabled, Finder will sort folders by name, placing them all at the top of the list. Files will be sorted next and placed after the list of folders. I feel this is a far better way to manage folders and files. However, if you prefer the folder and file sorting behavior of previous releases of macOS, uncheck the checkbox.

Configure the List View Display

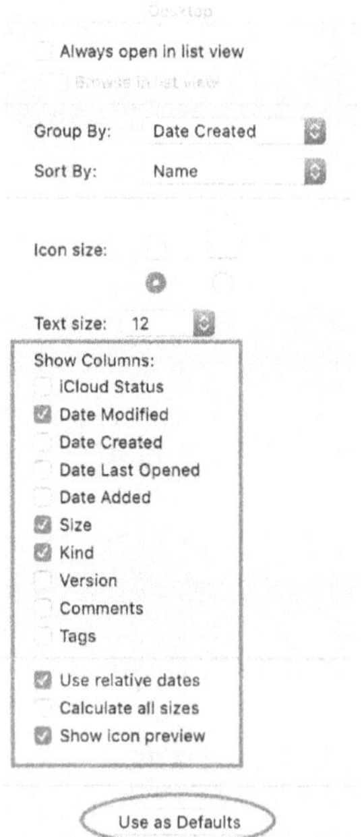

macOS displays the following three columns in the **Finder List View**: **Date Modified**, **Size**, and **Kind**. The Finder List View also supports other attributes such as iCloud status, date created, last opened, and added, size, kind, version, comments, and tags.

To change the columns shown in the Finder List View, open a Finder window and click the **List** View tool. Then enter **⌘J** (command+J) to display the View Options preference pane. Check the checkboxes next to the items you want to display. Be sure your Finder window is in List View. Otherwise, you will not see these options.

Click **Use as Defaults** to set your choices as the default when opening Finder windows. You can also configure Finder to **Always open in list view**, choose group and sort options, icon size, and text size.

Multiple Item Inspector

The Get Info feature provides information about a file. If you select multiple files and choose **File > Get Info** or enter **⌘i** (command+i), macOS will open a Get Info pane for each file. If you want to see the combined size of a group of files, you'll need to use the **Multiple Item Inspector**.

To launch the Multiple Item Inspector, hold down the ⌥ (option) key while selecting **File > Show Inspector** or use the keyboard shortcut **⌥⌘i** (option+command+i). Additional files can be added to an open Multiple Item Inspector window by holding down the **⌘** (command) key while clicking on them. The Multiple Item Inspector will dynamically update as new files are added.

Change the Title Bar Font Size

macOS allows you to change the size of the Title Bar font. To change the font size, enter the following commands in Terminal. The number equals the font size. In the example, the new font size is 14 points.

```
defaults write com.apple.finder NSTitleBarFontSize 14

killall Finder
```

To revert to the macOS default, enter the following commands.

```
defaults delete com.apple.finder NSTitleBarFontSize

killall Finder
```

Calculate Folder Sizes

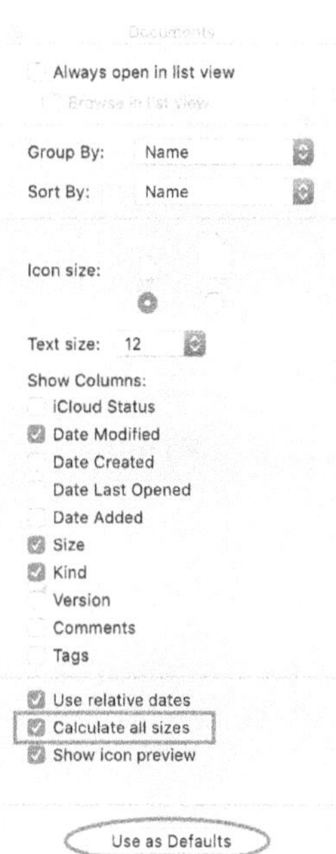

When you're viewing items in **List View**, you will notice that only files have an entry under the **Size** column. You will see a pair of dashes in the size column for folders as macOS does not calculate the size of folders.

If you would like to see the amount of disk space your folders are using, you need to tell macOS to **Calculate all sizes**. To enable this feature, select **View > Show View Options** from the Finder View menu or enter **⌘J** (command+J) to display the View Options preference pane. Check the checkbox next to **Calculate all sizes**.

This attribute is set on a per-folder basis. So if you would like to make this the default for all folders, click the **Use as Defaults** button.

Increase the Window Resize Area

Application windows can be resized by hovering your pointer over any of the window's borders until the resizing pointer, a double-headed black arrow, appears. Dragging the resizing pointer resizes the window. The area in which the pointer changes to the resizing pointer is quite small. It is sometimes difficult to get the pointer in the precise spot to make the resizing pointer appear.

This tweak increases the size of the area in which the pointer will change into the resizing pointer. Open Terminal and enter the following command. You will need to log out and log back in for the change to take effect.

```
defaults write -g AppleEdgeResizeExteriorSize 15
```

Feel free to try different numbers at the end of the command to make the area larger or smaller as you see fit.

To revert to the macOS default, enter the following command. You will need to log out and log back in for the change to take effect.

```
defaults delete -g AppleEdgeResizeExteriorSize
```

Add a Quit Command

Finder is the one application that you can't quit. The reason for this is that Finder is responsible for managing the macOS file system and must run all the time. If you check the **Finder** menu, you will not find a **Quit** command. That is because other than relaunching Finder through **Force Quit** or with a **killall Finder** command; Finder must run continuously.

Why would you want to add a Quit command to the Finder menu? Having a Quit command in the Finder menu is a quick and easy way to execute the **killall Finder** command to restart Finder.

Open Terminal and enter the following commands to add a Quit command to Finder.

```
defaults write com.apple.finder QuitMenuItem -bool TRUE
```

```
killall Finder
```

To revert to the macOS default and remove the Quit command from the Finder menu, enter the following commands.

```
defaults delete com.apple.finder QuitMenuItem
```

```
killall Finder
```

13

Window Snapping

There is only one feature I truly miss when switching between my Windows PC at work and my MacBook Pro at home – Microsoft's window snapping feature. Drag a window to the right edge of the screen, and it snaps to exactly half the size of your Desktop. Pick another window, and it snaps to the other half. This feature is excellent for comparing two documents side-by-side. While macOS supports Split View mode, it just isn't quite the same as the window snapping functionality of Windows.

Another feature I miss is the ability to maximize a window by dragging it to the top of the Desktop. I know I can maximize a window with the green Full-Screen button, but doing so hides the Menu Bar and the Dock. Hiding the Menu Bar can be problematic when using an app with lots of commands in the Menu Bar. Often it's more productive to not wait for the Menu Bar or the Dock to unhide when you need them.

Luckily there is a great, low-cost app in the Mac App Store that offers window snapping functionality, and like everything on a Mac, window snapping is more powerful and more fully-featured than Microsoft's implementation. Let's take a look.

Magnet

Magnet is simple, easy to use, elegant, and highly intuitive. It supports window snapping by dragging, keyboard shortcut, or through a drop-down menu from its Menu Extra. Magnet keeps your Desktop organized by letting you snap windows to use a quarter, third, half, two-thirds, or your entire Desktop. Neatly aligning your windows side-by-side eliminates having to switch apps constantly. I especially like the capability to maximize a window to full-screen without losing the Menu Bar and Dock. This is particularly important when you want to access the Application Menu without having to wait for it to unhide itself as it does in macOS Full-Screen mode.

If you are looking for Windows-like snapping features, Magnet delivers them in a powerful, customizable, and easy to use application. Because Magnet packs so many powerful features in a simple to use package, it is my recommended window snapping app for macOS. As I write this sentence, Magnet is the #1 rated app in the Mac App

Store productivity category with a rating of 4.9 stars and 41,000 reviews. Magnet is practically a steal at $1.99 and is available from the Mac App Store at https://apps.apple.com/us/app/magnet/id441258766?mt=12.

Set the Security & Privacy Settings

The first time you launch Magnet, you must authorize the application in the **Security & Privacy** preference pane in System Preferences. Click on the **Privacy** tab and select **Accessibility** from the sidebar. Unlock the pane by clicking on the lock at the lower-left and enter your credentials. Check the checkbox next to **Magnet** to authorize the application.

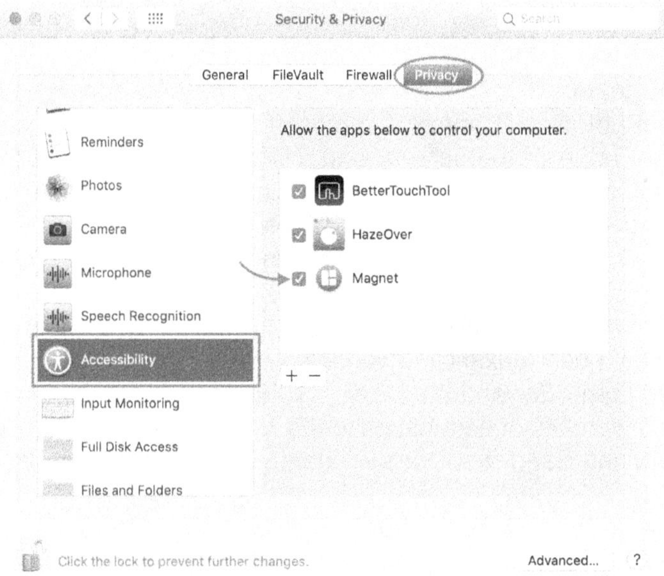

Launch Magnet at Start Up

To ensure you can always take advantage of Magnet's powerful window snapping capabilities, verify that Magnet is configured to launch when you start your Mac.

From the Magnet Menu Extra, select **Preferences...** to open Magnet's preference pane. By default, the checkbox next to **Launch at login** is checked. If you prefer to launch Magnet each time your Mac restarts, uncheck this checkbox.

The checkbox next to **Snap windows by dragging** is also checked. When unchecked, you have to use Magnet's keyboard shortcuts and Menu Extra to resize windows.

Unsnap to original size does what its name implies. When unsnapping a window, it returns to its original size before you resized it.

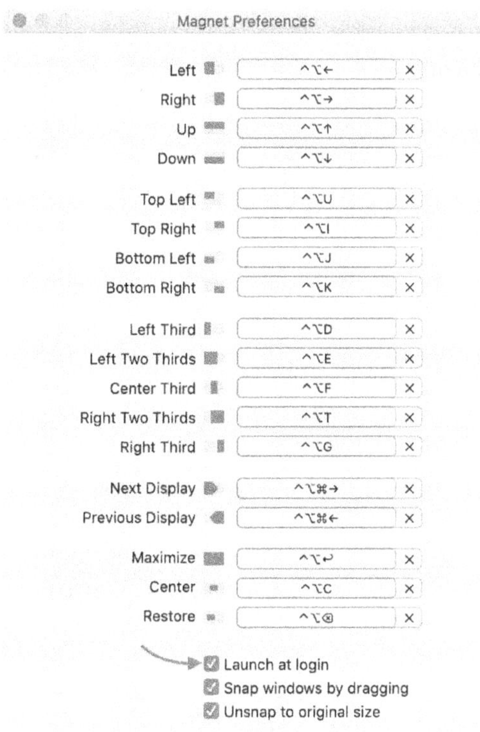

Sides do Halves

The simplest method of rearranging and resizing the windows on your Desktop is to drag them. Window snapping is accomplished by dragging a window to a location at the edge of your Desktop.

Let's say you want to compare two documents side-by-side. Drag one document to the left edge of your Desktop. The left half of your Desktop dims, previewing the result of the window snap. Release your hold on the window, and it resizes to the left half of your Desktop. Drag the other document to the right edge, and the right half of your Desktop dims. Release and the window, and it resizes to the right half of your Desktop. Simple!

Perhaps you'd prefer to compare the documents with one occupying the top half of your Desktop and the other the bottom half. To snap a window to the top half of your Desktop, drag it to the left or right side, just below either of the top corners. The top half of your Desktop dims to preview the snap. Release your hold on the window, and it resizes to the top half of your Desktop.

For the bottom half, drag the window to the left or right side, just above either of the bottom corners. The bottom half of your Desktop dims to preview the resize. Release your hold on the window, and it resizes to the bottom half of your Desktop.

You just learned the first rule of Magnet. Sides do halves.

If you prefer to use keyboard shortcuts, the default shortcut to snap a window to the left half of your Desktop is **^⌥left** (control+option+left arrow). To snap a window to the right half, use **^⌥right** (control+option+right arrow).

A window can be snapped to the top half of your Desktop with the keyboard shortcut **^⌥up** (control+option+up arrow). Use the keyboard shortcut **^⌥down** (control+option+down arrow) to snap to the lower half.

If you need another option, Magnet features a Menu Extra with a drop-down menu from which you can select **Left**, **Right**, **Up**, or **Down**.

Corners for Quarters

Dragging a window to any of the four Desktop corners snaps it to that corner and resizes it to a quarter of your Desktop.

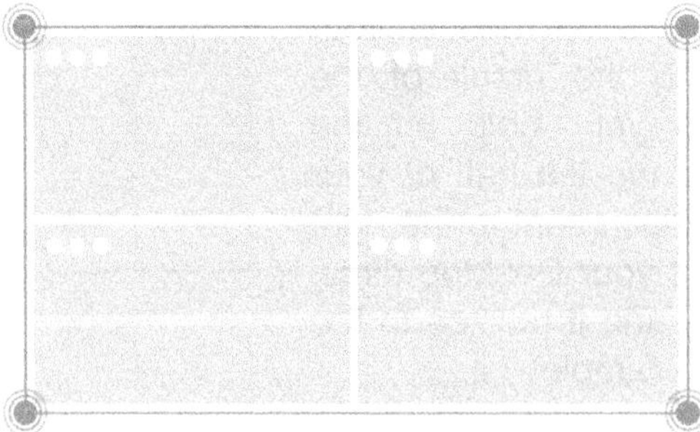

The second rule of Magnet is corners for quarters.

If you prefer to use keyboard shortcuts, the default shortcuts for the four corners of the Desktop – top left, top right, bottom left, or bottom right are **^⌥U** (control+option+U), **^⌥i** (control+option+i), **^⌥J** (control+option+J), and **^⌥K** (control+option+K), respectively.

From the Magnet Menu Extra, select **Top Left**, **Top Right**, **Bottom Left**, or **Bottom Right**.

Bottom makes Thirds

Drag a window to the bottom of your Desktop, and it snaps to the left, center, or right third. Move your pointer across the bottom edge of your Desktop without releasing your hold to preview your options. When you do so, you'll notice you have the option of resizing to a third or two-thirds of your Desktop.

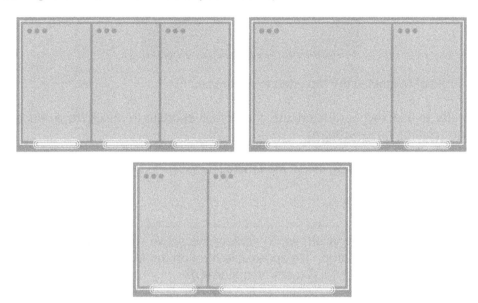

The third rule of Magnet is bottom makes thirds.

If you prefer to use keyboard shortcuts, the default shortcut to snap a window to the left third is **^⌥D** (control+option+D). Need the window bigger? The **^⌥E** (control+option+E) shortcut snaps a window to the left two-thirds of your Desktop. Use the keyboard shortcut **^⌥F** (control+option+F) to snap a window to the center third. The shortcuts for the right two-thirds and right third are **^⌥T** (control+option+T) and **^⌥G** (control+option+G), respectively.

From the Magnet Menu Extra, select Left Third, Left Two Thirds, Center Third, Right Two Thirds, or Right Third.

Top Edge to Maximize

Magnet supports a full-screen mode, called **Maximize**, which differs from the native macOS Full-Screen mode discussed in the Mission Control chapter. With Magnet, you can take a window to full-screen without hiding the Menu Bar and Dock, which is the default behavior when using the native macOS Full-Screen mode. This feature comes in handy when you're using an application that has many controls in the

Application Menu, and you don't want to wait for the Menu Bar to unhide in macOS Full-Screen mode. Similarly, Magnet's Maximize feature does not hide the Dock, allowing you to access it without waiting for it to unhide. To maximize a window, drag it to the top edge of your Desktop.

The final rule of Magnet is the top edge to maximize.

If you prefer to use keyboard shortcuts, the default shortcut to maximize a window is **^⌥return** (control+option+return).

From the Magnet Menu Extra, select **Maximize**.

Center a Window

Magnet features a **Center** option, which centers the active window, both horizontally and vertically, on your Desktop. It's accessible through the Magnet Menu Extra or by using the keyboard shortcut **^⌥C** (control+option+C).

Restore a Window

To restore a snapped window to its original size and location, drag it away from the edge of your Desktop, use the keyboard shortcut **^⌥delete** (control+option+delete), or select **Restore** from Magnet's Menu Extra.

Move a Window to Another Display

Magnet supports up to 6 external displays. You can use Magnet to move windows between displays.

The keyboard shortcut **^⌥⌘right** (control+option+command+right arrow) moves the active window to the next display.

Use the **^⌥⌘left** (control+option+command+left arrow) keyboard shortcut to move the window back to the previous display.

From the Magnet Menu Extra, select **Next Display** or **Previous Display**.

Ignore an Application

An **Ignore** option, accessible from Magnet's Menu Extra, lets you tell Magnet to ignore the currently active application. This option is handy if you are manipulating an application's windows and don't want Magnet's snapping features to engage.

Change the Default Keyboard Shortcuts

If you want to change any of the default keyboard shortcuts, select **Preferences**... from the Magnet Menu Extra to open the Magnet preference pane. Click on the **X** next to the keyboard shortcut you want to change or click on the keyboard shortcut itself to reveal **Type New Shortcut**. Enter your desired keyboard shortcut in this field. To return to the previous entry, click the circular restore button, which replaces the **X** shown to the right of the keyboard shortcut once you changed the default shortcut.

Disable Window Snapping by Dragging

Magnet lets you disable window snapping by dragging if you prefer to use only Magnet's keyboard shortcuts or its drop-down menu in the Magnet Menu Extra.

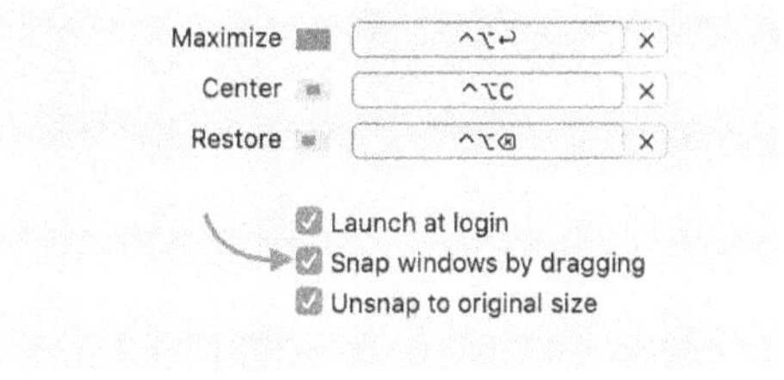

To disable windows snapping by dragging, launch the Magnet preference pane by selecting **Preferences...** from the Magnet Menu Extra. Uncheck the checkbox next to **Snap windows by dragging**.

Disable Unsnap to Original Size

When you drag a resized window away from the edge of your Desktop, Magnet restores it to its original size before you resized it. Sometimes you may want to disable this feature. For example, if you are rearranging windows on your Desktop, you may wish to keep them resized rather than have Magnet automatically return them to their original sizes.

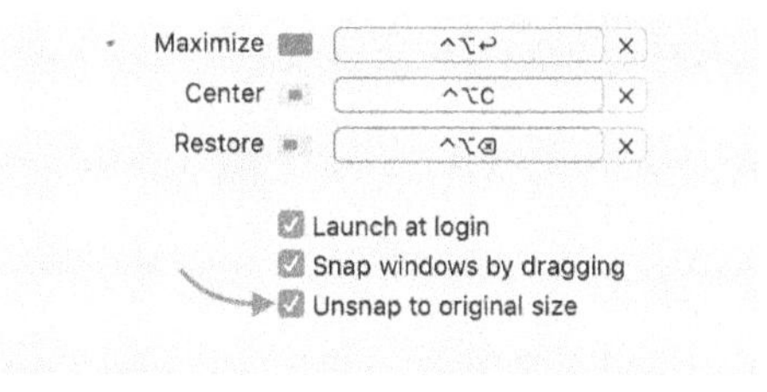

To disable this feature, launch the Magnet preference pane by selecting **Preferences...** from the Magnet Menu Extra. Uncheck the checkbox next to **Unsnap to Original Size**.

Use Magnet with a Vertical Screen

If you have your display set up vertically, which is great for editing documents using Microsoft Word or Apple Pages, Magnet easily adapts. Note the change in the snap areas when using a vertical screen, as shown in the image on the next page.

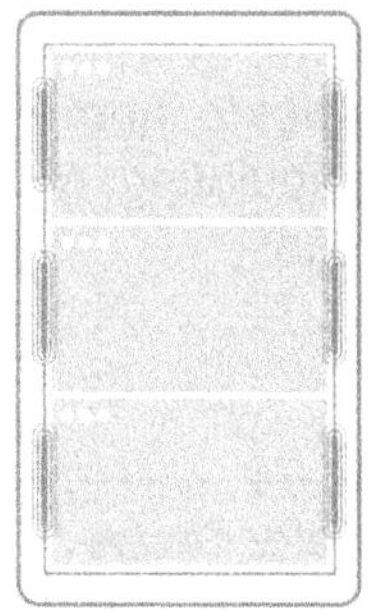    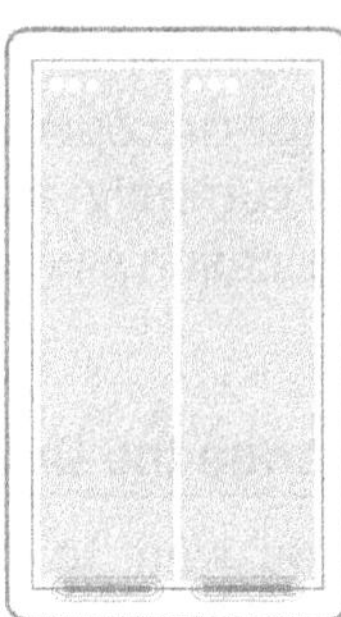

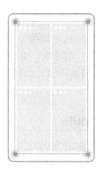

If your display is set up vertically, thirds use the sides, as shown in the first two images. Corners are still for quarters. Horizontal halves still use the sides. However, vertical halves now use the bottom.

14

Keyboard

In this chapter, we'll cover the keyboard. I know what you are thinking. "Why a chapter on the keyboard?" "Everyone knows how to use a keyboard." While I have covered various keyboard shortcuts throughout this book, I'll show you how to create custom keyboard shortcuts in this chapter. You can use keyboard shortcuts to speed up everyday tasks, to open applications, and execute commands within applications. If you are looking for a productivity boost, keyboard shortcuts are a very efficient method for you to do most things faster with a few keystrokes.

Disable the Caps Lock

Why should you disable the caps lock? Because things like thiS HAPPEN WHEN YOU ACCIDENTALLY HIT THE CAPS LOCK. If your Mac's caps lock is driving you nuts, macOS allows you to disable it.

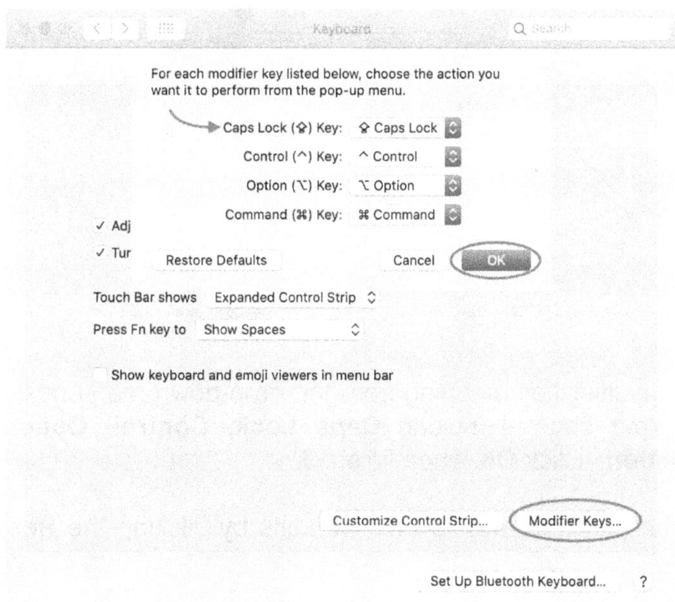

To disable the caps lock key, open the **Keyboard** preference pane, and select **Keyboard**. Next, click the **Modifier Keys...** button to reveal the Modifier Keys configuration sheet. Choose **No Action** from the drop-down list next to **Caps Lock**. If you want to enable the caps lock key later, you can do so by choosing **Caps Lock** from the drop-down list.

Change the Behavior of the Modifier Keys

macOS allows you to change the behavior of the modifier keys – **^ ⌘ ⌥ fn** – control, command, option, and function, respectively. Why would you want to change the behavior of the modifier keys? You may want to modify the layout if you are familiar with a keyboard layout that is different than the one on your Mac, like a Windows PC.

To change the mapping of the modifier keys, open the **Keyboard** preference pane from the System Preferences application. Click on the **Keyboard** tab. Next, click the **Modifier Keys...** button at the lower-right of the preference pane. A configuration sheet appears from under the title bar. If you have multiple keyboards, select the keyboard from the drop-down menu. You will not see this option if you do not have multiple keyboards connected to your Mac.

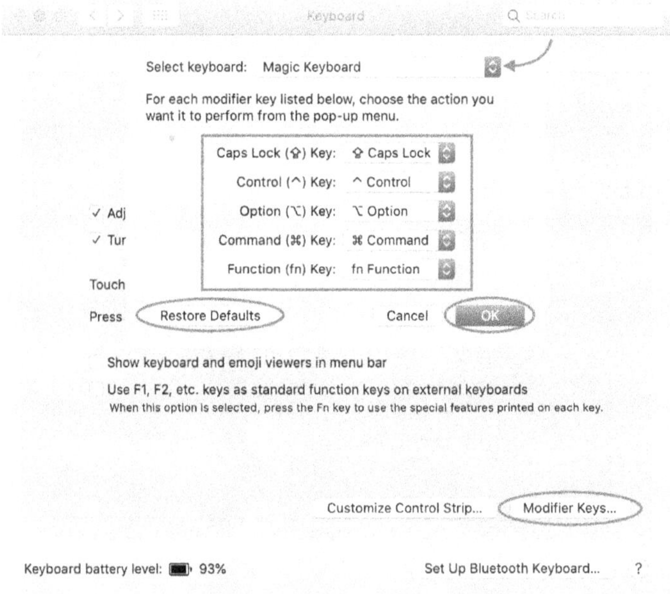

Choose the new modifier key mapping from the drop-down menu next to each of the modifier keys. Your choices include **Caps Lock**, **Control**, **Option**, **Command**, **Escape**, or **No Action**. Click **OK** when finished.

You can return the modifier keys to their defaults by clicking the **Restore Defaults** button.

Note that you can only change the behavior of the **fn** (function) key on keyboards that do not have a Touch Bar.

Turn Keyboard Backlight Off When Idle

One of the great features of a MacBook, MacBook Pro, and MacBook Air is that keyboard backlighting is standard on all models. Anyone who has fumbled around in dim light on a cheap Windows PC keyboard knows the value of keyboard backlighting. Keyboard backlighting is on by default.

If you would like to dim your keyboard lighting when your Mac has been idle for a while, open the **Keyboard** preference pane and select the **Keyboard** tab.

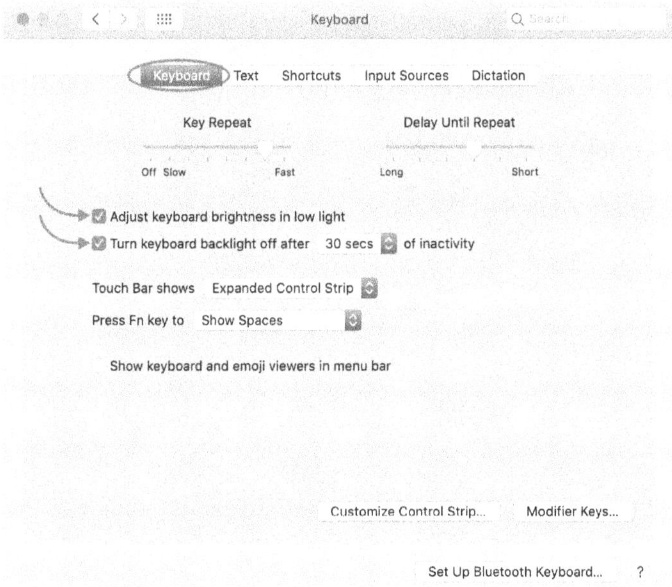

Check the checkbox next to **Turn keyboard backlight off after** and select **5**, **10**, **30 seconds**, or **1** or **5 minutes** from the drop-down menu.

Precisely Adjust the Keyboard Backlight

Sometimes it seems you never can get the keyboard backlight adjusted to your liking. One segment more is too much. One less is too little. Wouldn't it be awesome if you could adjust the keyboard backlight in smaller increments? macOS has a solution for you!

Hold down the ⇧⌥ (shift+option) keys while adjusting the keyboard backlight to adjust it in quarter-segment increments. This feature allows you to adjust the brightness in smaller, more granular increments. This trick also works when adjusting the display brightness and volume.

Make the Function Keys Act Like Function Keys

When you press an F (function) key, it executes the command associated with it (i.e., Mission Control, Launchpad, Play/Pause, Volume Up, Volume Down, Mute). On a Mac, you need to hold down the **fn** (function) key to use an **F** key as a standard **F** key, which is the opposite of how Windows PC keyboards work.

If you want to press **F12** and have it execute the keyboard shortcut configured in the **Keyboard** preference pane instead of increasing the volume, you have to hold down the **fn** (function) key while pressing **F12**. This is particularly confusing for former Windows PC users switching to a Mac. If you'd like the **F** keys to work as they do on a PC, macOS allows you to configure the **F** keys so that they act as standard function keys.

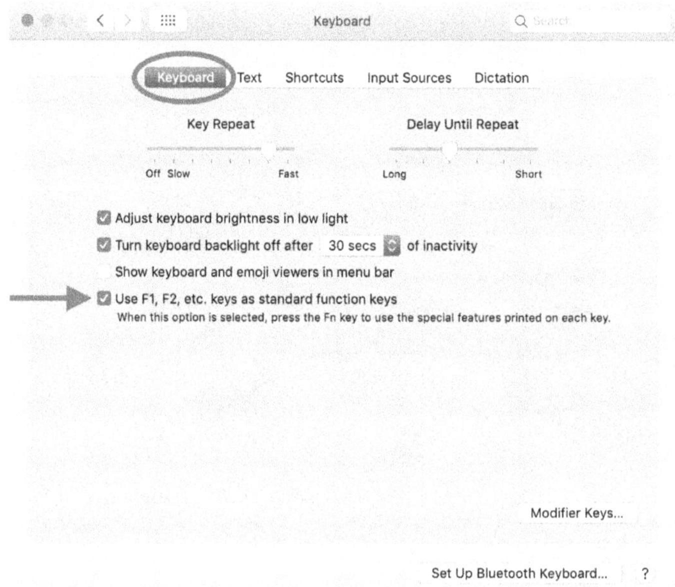

To make the **F** keys perform like function keys, open the **Keyboard** preference pane and select the **Keyboard** tab. Check the box next to **Use all F1, F2, etc. keys as standard function keys**.

How do you increase the volume and use the other special functions? Hold down the **fn** key while pressing an **F** key to use the special functions when the **F** keys are configured as standard function keys.

Note that you can only change the behavior of the **F** keys on keyboards that do not have a Touch Bar.

Show Keyboard and Character Viewer

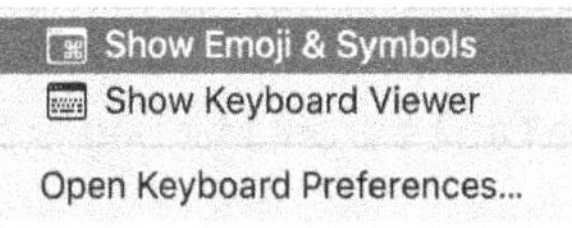

For quicker access to the **Keyboard Viewer** and the **Character Viewer**, you can add a drop-down menu in the Menu Bar. From the Keyboard preference pane, select **Keyboard**, then check the checkbox next to **Show keyboard and emoji viewer in menu bar**.

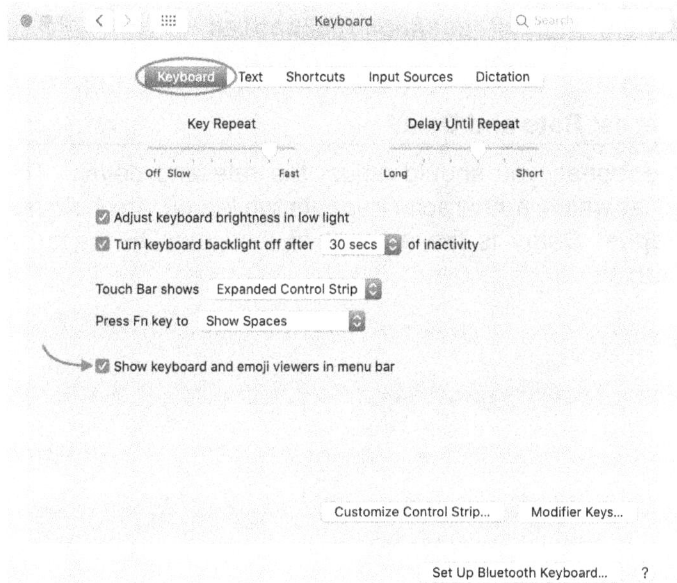

The Keyboard Viewer shows you where characters for other languages, symbols, and special characters are located on the keyboard.

The Character Viewer shows you a vast selection of emoji and symbols, including math and currency symbols, flags, bullets and stars, arrows, letter symbols, parentheses, pictographs, punctuation, and emoji.

Enable Key Repeat

By default, holding down a key in macOS does not activate key repeat as you might expect, particularly if you are used to Windows PCs. Instead, a contextual menu appears, which allows you to insert diacritic characters (i.e., accented and other non-English characters). Unless you often write in a foreign language, you may find this feature to be an annoyance. macOS allows you to make key repeat operate as you expect it to when holding down a key.

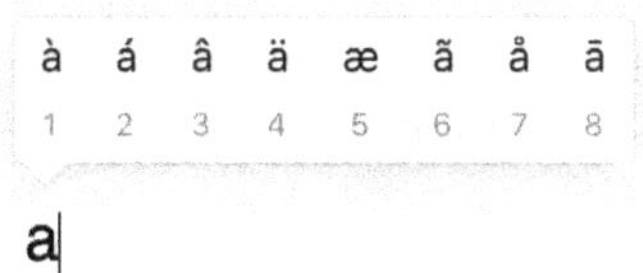

To enable key repeat, open Terminal and enter the following command. You need to log out and log back in for this change to take effect.

```
defaults write -g ApplePressAndHoldEnabled -bool FALSE
```

To revert to the macOS default, enter the following. You need to log out and log back in for the change to take effect.

```
defaults delete -g ApplePressAndHoldEnabled
```

Adjust the Key Repeat Rate and Delay

If you enabled key repeat, you should adjust the rate and delay. The **Key Repeat Rate** is the speed at which a character repeats while you are holding down its key. While the **Key Repeat Delay** is the amount of time macOS waits before it begins repeating the character.

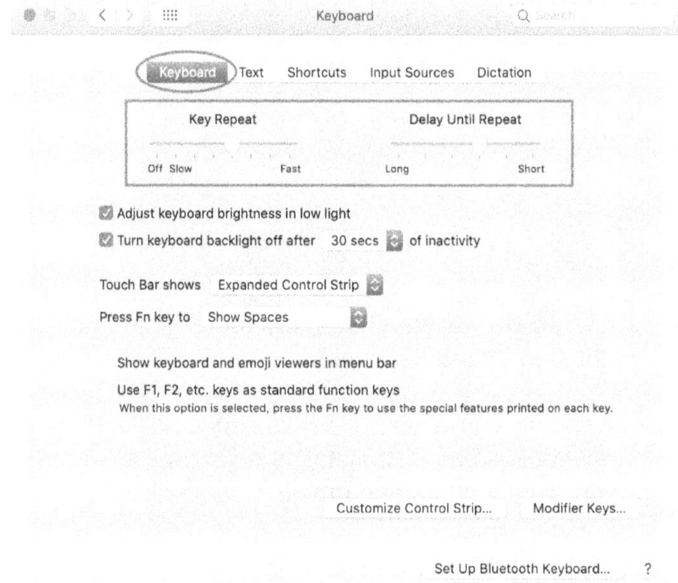

Open the **Keyboard** preference pane and select the **Keyboard** tab. To adjust the speed at which a character repeats while you are holding its key down, adjust the slider under **Key Repeat**. To adjust how long macOS waits until repeating a character, adjust the slider under **Delay Until Repeat**.

Create a Text Replacement

You can create text replacements in the **Text** tab in the **Keyboard** preference pane. The **Replace List** lets you create shortcut phrases or text for longer phrases. When you enter a text shortcut, macOS replaces it with the associated phrase listed in the Keyboard preference pane.

To create a text replacement, open the **Keyboard** preference pane and click the **Text** tab. Next, click the **+** at the bottom of the sidebar. Enter a text shortcut in the **Replace** column and the phrase you want to replace it with in the **With** column.

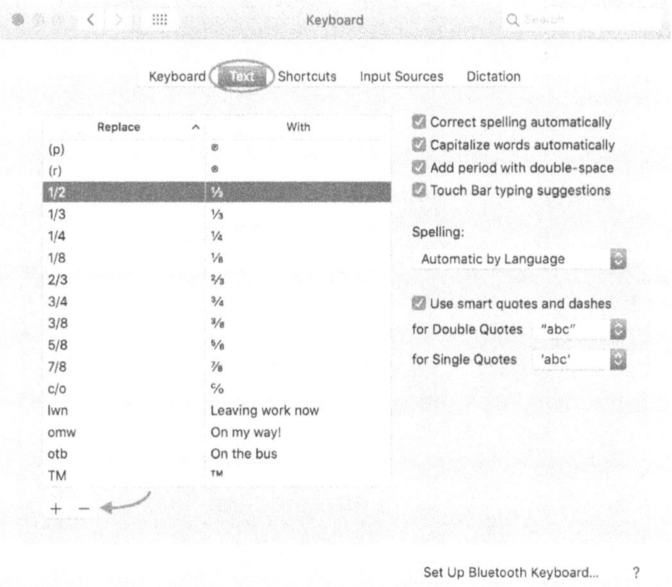

Text replacement works across Apple applications with iCloud keeping your replacements up to date across your Apple devices. Note that iCloud Drive must be enabled for this feature to work.

Take a Screenshot

You can take a screenshot of your entire Desktop, an area of your Desktop, a window, or the Touch Bar using a keyboard shortcut. To take a screenshot of your Desktop, enter **⇧⌘3** (shift+command+3). To capture a specific area of the Desktop or a window, enter **⇧⌘4** (shift+command+4) to bring up a set of crosshairs. Drag the crosshairs across the desired area and release your hold when done.

To take a screenshot of a window, press **⇧⌘4**, move the crosshairs over the window you want to take a screenshot of, press the **spacebar** to change the crosshairs to a camera, and click your mouse or trackpad. Your Mac will take a screenshot of the entire window. The window does not have to be the active window.

The **Screenshot Utility** is activated by pressing **⇧⌘5** (shift+command+5). It offers quick access to take a screenshot, record your screen, and several configuration options, including the save location and a timer.

The tools on the Screenshot Utility are separated into screenshot tools, screen recording tools, and options with a vertical separator between them. The tools are, from left to right, **Capture an Entire Screen**, **Capture Selected Window**, **Capture Selected Portion**, **Record Entire Screen**, **Record Selected Portion**, and **Options**. Once you have selected your choice, a **Capture** button appears at the right end of the Screenshot Utility next to **Options**. To close the Screenshot Utility, click the **X**.

Options allow you to change the save location of your screenshot and to set a timer for 5 or 10 seconds. Other options include **Show Floating Thumbnail**, **Remember Last Selection**, and **Show Mouse Pointer**.

If you own a MacBook Pro with a Touch Bar, you can take a screenshot of the Touch Bar by pressing **⇧⌘6** (shift+command+6).

Another feature that Catalina borrowed from the iPhone and iPad is the floating thumbnail found in the lower-right-hand corner of your Desktop. Swiping to the right saves your screenshot to your chosen save location. You can also do nothing, and your screenshot saves automatically. Clicking on the floating thumbnail opens your screenshot in the Markup app. You can also drag the floating thumbnail into a folder in Finder or into the Mail, Messages, Preview, or Photos apps. Screen recordings open in Quicktime Player.

Holding down the ^ (control) key while clicking on the floating thumbnail reveals a contextual menu with save and application options. You can choose to close or delete the screenshot or open the Markup app. You can also save the screenshot to the Desktop, Documents folder, or Clipboard, or open it in Mail, Messages, Preview or Photos. Screen recordings replace the Preview option with Quicktime Player.

Disable the Floating Thumbnail

The Floating Thumbnail was a new feature added in macOS Mojave, the release of macOS before Catalina. In releases before Mojave, screenshots were automatically saved to the Desktop folder. If you prefer that behavior, you can disable Floating Thumbnails.

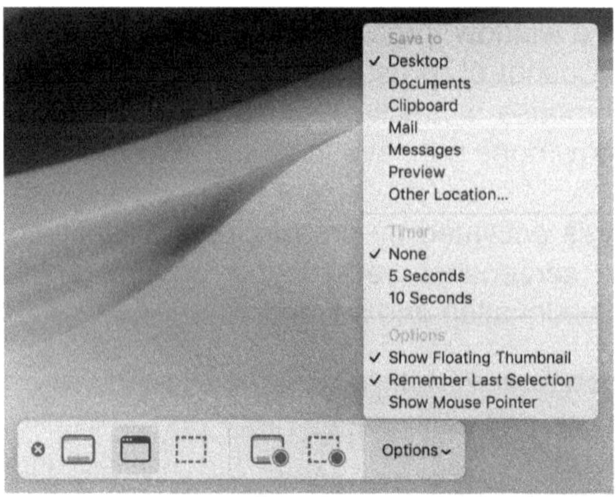

To disable floating thumbnail, open the Screenshot Utility by entering **⇧⌘5** (shift+command+5). Click **Options** at the end of the Screenshot Utility to reveal a contextual menu. Select **Show Floating Thumbnail** to remove the checkmark. Screenshots will be saved immediately to your chosen save location.

Change Screenshot Keyboard Shortcuts

macOS has predefined keyboard shortcuts to take screenshots, as shown in the table below.

⇧⌘3	Takes a screenshot of the Desktop and saves it to the Desktop or designated folder.
^⇧⌘3	Takes a screenshot of the Desktop and saves it to the Clipboard.
⇧⌘4	Takes a screenshot of a user-defined area and saves it to the Desktop or designated folder.
^⇧⌘4	Takes a screenshot of a user-defined area and saves it to the Clipboard.
⇧⌘4 + space	Takes a screenshot of a window and saves it to the Desktop or designated folder.
^⇧⌘4 + space	Takes a screenshot of a window and saves it to the Clipboard.
⇧⌘5	Launches the Screenshot Utility
⇧⌘6	Takes a screenshot of the Touch Bar and saves it to the Desktop or designated folder.
^⇧⌘6	Takes a screenshot of the Touch Bar and saves it to the Clipboard.

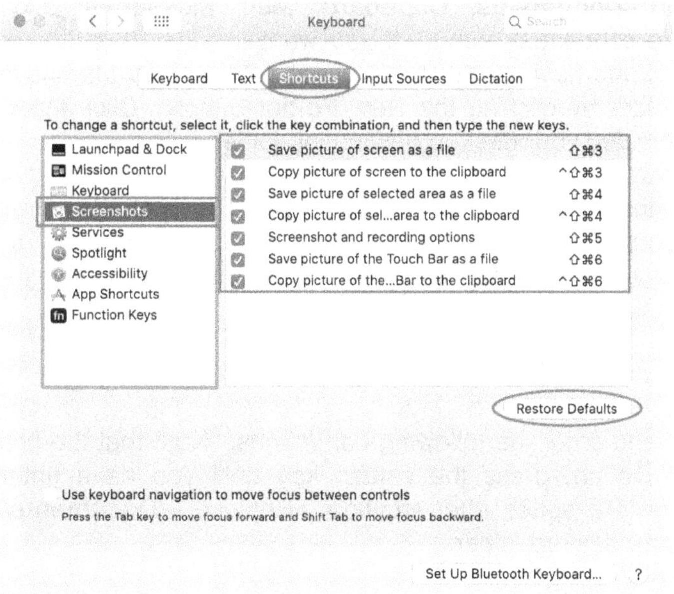

Note that **⇧⌘6** (shift+command+6) and **^⇧⌘6** (control+shift+command+6) only work if you have a MacBook Pro with a Touch Bar.

If you want to change the default screenshot keyboard shortcuts, you can redefine them in the **Keyboard** preference pane. You can also disable them if you do not need to take screenshots. Click the **Shortcuts** tab. Next, select **Screenshots** in the sidebar. The default shortcuts are listed in the right pane. Click on the existing shortcut to change it. Uncheck a shortcut if you want to disable it.

Click the **Restore Defaults** button to restore the default keyboard shortcuts.

Save Screenshots to the Clipboard

Saving screenshots to a file is handy if you need to annotate the screenshot. However, sometimes you need to copy the screenshot directly into a document. In that case, it is much easier to save a screenshot directly to the **Clipboard**. Add the **^** (control) key to the screenshot keyboard shortcut, and macOS saves your screenshot to the Clipboard. You can then paste the screenshot into your document by selecting **Edit > Paste** or entering **⌘V** (command+V).

Change the Screenshot Destination Folder

By default, macOS saves screenshots to the **Desktop** folder. If you take a lot of screenshots, your Desktop can quickly fill up with clutter. macOS lets you change the default destination folder to something other than the Desktop.

To change the destination folder for screenshots and screen recordings, open the Screenshot Utility by pressing **⇧⌘5** (shift+command+5). Click **Options** at the end of the Screenshot Utility to reveal a contextual menu. Click your desired destination folder. **Desktop**, **Documents**, **Clipboard**, **Mail**, **Messages**, and **Preview** are available from the contextual menu. If you want to save to a different folder, click **Other Location...** and navigate to your desired folder. You also have the option of creating a new folder by clicking the **New Folder** button. Click the **Choose** button once you have selected your desired destination folder.

You can also change the destination folder using Terminal. Determine where you want to save your screenshots. For this example, I created a folder called **Screenshots** in my **Documents** folder. The path I need to enter in the command to change the destination folder is:

```
~/Documents/Screenshots/
```

Launch Terminal and enter the following commands. Note that the first two lines are one command. Do not press the **return** key until you have entered the entire command. There is a space after location. Replace **~/Documents/Screenshots/** with the path to your desired folder.

```
defaults write com.apple.screencapture location
~/Documents/Screenshots/
```

```
killall SystemUIServer
```

Enter the following commands to revert to the macOS default of saving screenshots to the Desktop.

```
defaults write com.apple.screencapture location ~/Desktop/
```

```
killall SystemUIServer
```

Remove Shadows from Screenshots

macOS inserts a gray shadow around an image captured by a screenshot. If you want to remove this shadow, launch Terminal and enter the following commands.

```
defaults write com.apple.screencapture disable-shadow -bool TRUE
```

To revert to the macOS default, enter the following commands in Terminal.

```
defaults write com.apple.screencapture disable-shadow -bool FALSE
```

Set a Screenshot Timer

The Screen Utility allows you to set a timer for screenshots. Open the Screenshot Utility by pressing **⇧⌘5** (shift+command+5). Click **Options** at the end of the Screenshot Utility to reveal a contextual menu. Click either **5 seconds** or **10 seconds** to set your timer. Once you have set a timer, a capture button appears at the end of the Screenshot Utility with the timer you set. When you click the **Capture** button, the timer counts down until the screenshot is taken.

If you want to cancel the screenshot before the timer expires, move your pointer over the countdown timer and click **Cancel**. To remove the timer, open the Screenshot Utility, click **Options**, and select **None** under **Timer**.

Capture the Mouse Pointer

If you want the pointer to appear in your screenshot, open the Screenshot Utility by pressing **⇧⌘5** (shift+command+5). Click **Options** at the end of the Screenshot Utility to reveal a contextual menu. Click **Show Mouse Pointer**.

Change the Screenshot File Format

macOS saves screenshots in Portable Network Graphics (PNG) format, an open, extensible image format supporting lossless data compression. PNG was created as an improved, non-patented replacement for Graphic Interchange Format (GIF). macOS supports the ability to save screenshots in other graphics formats as well.

If you prefer to save your screenshots in **jpg** format, launch Terminal, and enter the following commands.

```
defaults write com.apple.screencapture type jpg

killall SystemUIServer
```

macOS also supports **tiff**, **PDF**, **bmp**, and **pict** formats.

To change the default file format for screenshots, replace **jpg** in the above command with your desired format.

To revert to the macOS default, enter the following commands in Terminal.

```
defaults write com.apple.screencapture type png

killall SystemUIServer
```

Custom Keyboard Shortcuts

Veteran Mac users know that keyboard shortcuts are a huge productivity booster, allowing you to perform routine and repetitive tasks more efficiently. Keyboard shortcuts are an alternative to executing a command through a drop-down menu using your mouse or trackpad. For example, you can quit a running application using the keyboard shortcut **⌘Q** (command+Q), which is much faster than using your mouse or trackpad to select **Quit** from the Application Menu.

I'm sure you noticed some drop-down menu items that you frequently use in various applications do not have a keyboard shortcut. This forces you to access the drop-down menu using your mouse or trackpad. If you find yourself using a particular command that does not have a keyboard shortcut, macOS allows you to create a custom keyboard shortcut.

Create a Custom Keyboard Shortcut

Let's walk through the creation of a custom keyboard shortcut for a specific application. First, open the **Keyboard** preference pane and click the **Shortcuts** tab. Next, click on **App Shortcuts** in the sidebar. The **Show Help menu** keyboard shortcut is listed under **All Applications** in the right-hand pane. Any existing application-specific keyboard shortcuts are listed in the right pane.

To create a new keyboard shortcut, click the **+** below the right pane. A configuration sheet appears from under the title bar. To create a keyboard shortcut that works in all applications, choose **All Applications** from the drop-down menu next to **Application**.

An **All Applications** keyboard shortcut works in any application that has the menu item as an option.

If you want to create a keyboard shortcut for a specific application, select the application from the drop-down menu next to **Application**. For this example, I am creating a keyboard shortcut for **Quicken**.

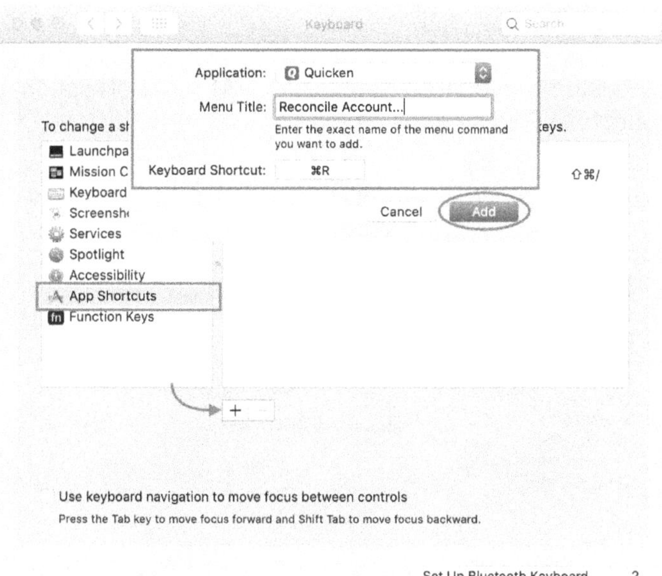

Next, enter the **Menu Title** exactly as it appears in the Application menu. I am creating a keyboard shortcut for the command to **Reconcile Account...**, which is located in the Accounts drop-down menu.

For submenus, you may have to enter the complete menu hierarchy. For example:

`Accounts->Reconcile Account…`

Note the **->** (hyphen+greater than sign) between the top menu item, **Accounts**, and the submenu item, **Reconcile Account...**. Be sure not to enter any spaces between the menu and submenu items.

Lastly, enter your desired keyboard shortcut in the field next to **Keyboard Shortcut**. In the example above, my new keyboard shortcut for the Reconcile Account command in Quicken is **⌘R** (command+R). Click the **Add** button when finished.

If the command has an ellipsis (three periods) appended to it, enter the three periods (...) or use the shortcut **⌥;** (option+;).

Sometimes a command is buried three or four levels in a menu hierarchy. In this case, the **->** (hyphen+greater than) is essential. For example, I often find an interesting article on the web that I want to share via a text. It would be cool if I had a keyboard shortcut so I could share the article more quickly.

In this case, the menu hierarchy is three levels, and I entered the following in the **Menu Title** field, separating each level with a **->** (hyphen+greater than). Be sure you do not enter any spaces between the menu and submenu items.

```
File->Share->Messages
```

Next, I entered my custom keyboard shortcut, **^⌥⌘M** (control+option+command+M), in the **Keyboard Shortcut** field as shown below.

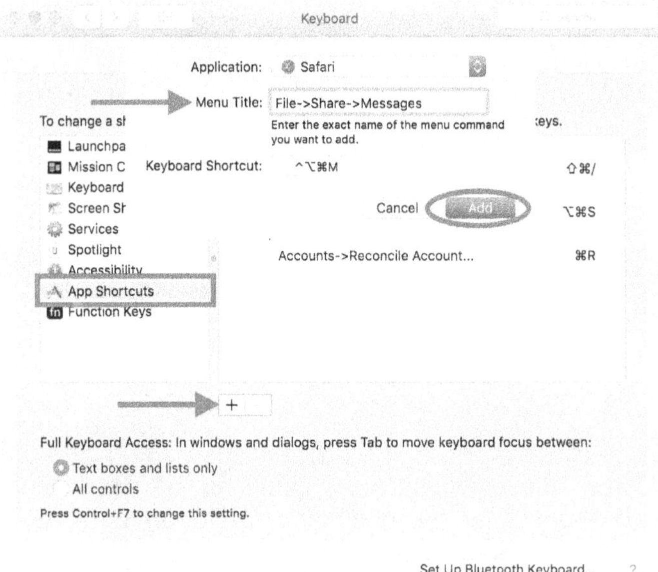

Reviewing the **File > Share** submenu in Safari shows my newly created keyboard shortcut to share via the Messages, **^⌥⌘M** (control+option+command+M). As you can see from the image below, I also created another keyboard shortcut to share using Evernote with the keyboard shortcut **^⌥⌘E** (control+option+command+E).

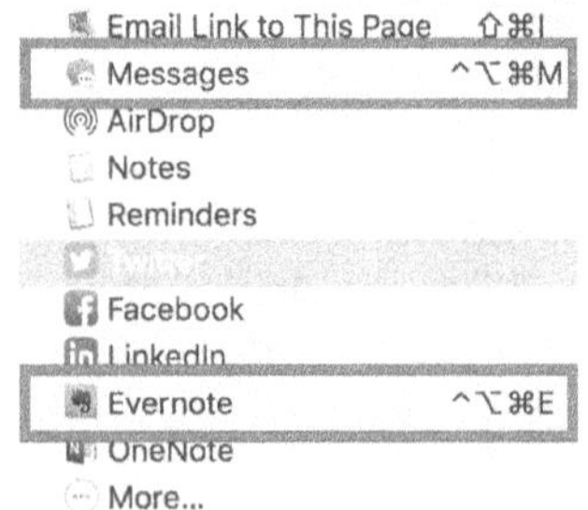

To remove a custom keyboard shortcut, click to highlight it and click the – button at the bottom of the right pane.

Launch Applications with Keyboard Shortcuts

HotKey is a nifty little utility by Peter Vorwieger that lets you define keyboard shortcuts to launch applications or open folders in Finder. The app features a Menu Extra that allows you to quickly launch an app or open a folder from its drop-down menu.

To configure your custom shortcuts in HotKey, open the HotKey preference pane by selecting **Preferences...** from the HotKey Menu Extra. Next, click the **+** button, which opens your Applications folder. Select the app and click the **Choose** button. To create a keyboard shortcut to open a folder, navigate to your desired folder using this Finder window, select the folder, and click **Choose**. Lastly, enter your new shortcut in the **Enter new Shortcut** field.

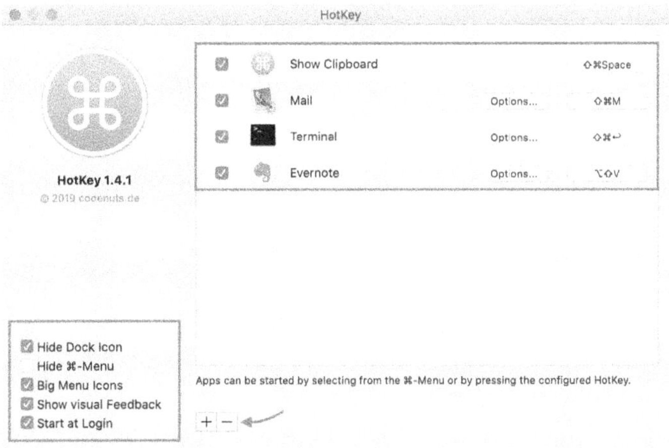

If you do not want to create a keyboard shortcut and want a convenient way to launch an application from the Menu Bar, you can leave the **Enter new Shortcut** field blank. You can launch the application or open the folder from the HotKey Menu Extra's drop-down menu.

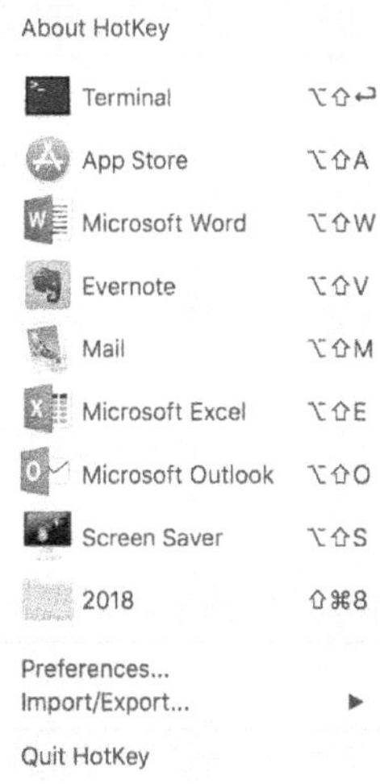

To remove a shortcut, click to highlight it and then click the – button.

Shortcuts are disabled by unchecking the checkbox next to them. Keyboard shortcuts that are unchecked are not shown in the HotKey drop-down menu.

HotKey comes with a pre-configured keyboard shortcut to **Show Clipboard**, which displays the contents of the clipboard on your Desktop when you enter **⇧⌘space** (shift+command+space). Press **⇧⌘space** again to dismiss the Clipboard. To disable this shortcut, uncheck the checkbox next to it. Note that HotKey will not allow you to remove the **Show Clipboard** keyboard shortcut.

Check the checkbox next to **Start at Login** to ensure HotKey is available every time you restart or log in to your Mac. The checkbox next to **Hide Dock Icon** does what you would expect it to do. When checked, the HotKey icon will not appear in the Dock. The checkbox next to **Big Menu Icons** toggles between small icons when unchecked and bigger icons when checked. Checking the checkbox next to **Hide ⌘-Menu** removes the Hot Key Menu Extra from your Menu Bar.

HotKey allows you to import and export your keyboard shortcuts if you want to share them or to make a backup. To export your keyboard shortcuts, select **Import/Export...** from the HotKey Menu Extra, then select **Import...** or **Export...** from the submenu.

HotKey App was available for free in the Mac App Store at the time of this writing at https://apps.apple.com/us/app/hotkey-app/id975890633?mt=12.

15

Touch Bar

Some MacBook Pro models feature a 2170 x 60-pixel touchscreen display called the **Touch Bar,** where the function keys are usually located. The Touch Bar is a dynamic input device with a strip of virtual keys that automatically change based on the active application. The far-right end features a Touch ID that allows you to unlock your MacBook Pro, unlock apps that require a password, or authorize Apple Pay. The **Control Strip**, which contains four controls, is located at the right quarter of the Touch Bar with the **esc** key located on the far left.

By default, the Control Strip contains four controls for brightness, volume, mute, and Siri, from left to right. Tapping the arrow located at the left end of the Control Strip reveals the full set of controls usually found on the top row of a physical keyboard – brightness, Mission Control, Launchpad, keyboard backlight, media playback, and the volume controls as shown below. When expanded, the Control Strip is called the **Expanded Control Strip**.

Holding down the **fn** key reveals the standard set of function keys, **F1** to **F12**.

The Touch Bar also serves as a virtual keyboard, offering quick access to standard tools and other functionality that you would usually access from the Application Menu. These tools are displayed between the **esc** key and the **Control Strip** in an area called **App Controls**. The tools available in App Controls change with the active application.

macOS lets you customize the controls that appear on the Touch Bar. You can change the controls shown in the Control Strip and Expanded Control Strip. Let's first start with Touch ID and Apple Pay and then move on to customization of the Touch Bar controls.

Setup Up Touch ID

Touch ID allows you to unlock and log into your Mac using your fingerprint rather than typing your password. You can also use Touch ID to make purchases from the iTunes Store, Mac App Store, Apple Books, and on websites that support Apple Pay. If you allow other members of your family to use your Mac, Touch ID supports multiple user accounts.

To set up Touch ID, open the **Touch ID** preference pane in System Preferences.

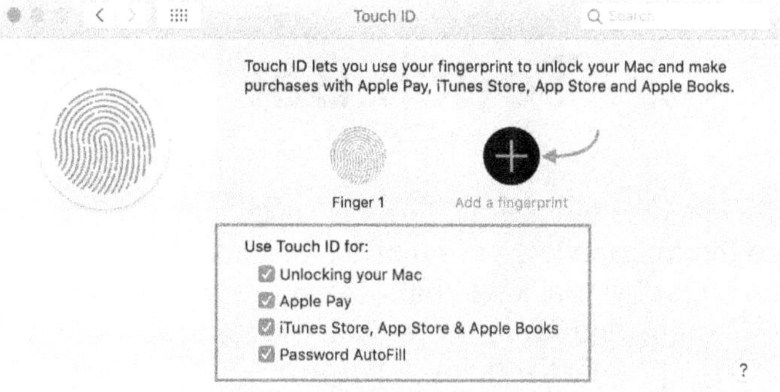

Next, click the **+** in the Touch ID preference pane to add your fingerprint. Place your finger on the Touch ID button and follow the instructions to lift and rest your finger to capture your fingerprint. Ensure that your finger is clean and dry for best results.

Repeat to add additional fingerprints. You can enter up to 3 fingerprints per user.

To delete a fingerprint, hover over an existing fingerprint with the pointer until an **X** button appears. Click the **X** button to delete it. You will be prompted to enter your password.

Ensure the 4 checkboxes under **Use Touch ID for** are checked so you can use Touch ID to unlock your Mac, pay using Apple Pay, make purchases from the iTunes Store, Mac App Store, Apple Books, and to enter a password when prompted.

Set up Apple Pay

If you did not set up Apple Pay when first setting up your MacBook Pro or if you need to make changes, open the **Wallet & Apple Pay** preference pane.

To add a new credit card to Apple Pay, click the **Details** tab. Next, click the **+** at the bottom of the sidebar. If you have multiple credit cards, select the default card from the drop-down menu next to **Default Card**.

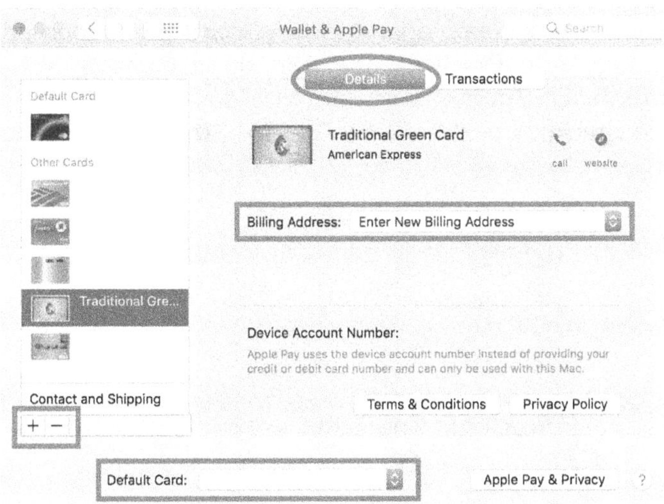

If you need to change your billing address, you can do so by selecting **Enter New Billing Address** from the drop-down menu next to **Billing Address**.

To delete an existing credit card, click the – button at the bottom of the sidebar.

Customize the Touch Bar

By default, the **Control Strip** is collapsed to the right side of the Touch Bar. If you tap the left expand arrow, the Control Strip is replaced by the **Expanded Control Strip**, as shown in the images below.

Touch Bar with the Control Strip:

Touch Bar, after tapping the left expand arrow to reveal the Expanded Control Strip:

macOS allows you to change what the Touch Bar displays, offering 5 different displays, which are configured in the Keyboard preference pane. You can configure your Touch Bar to display **App Controls**, the **Expanded Control Strip**, **F** keys, **Quick Actions**, or **Spaces**.

When configured for App Controls, the Touch Bar shows commonly used commands available in the active application. The Expanded Control Strip mirrors the macOS system tools located on the top row of keys on a MacBook Pro without a Touch Bar or when using an Apple Magic Keyboard. When set to **F1, F2, etc. Keys**, the Touch Bar displays the function keys. If you have created quick action workflows in Automator, the Touch Bar displays them when set to **Quick Actions**. Finally, the Touch Bar can be configured to show your Desktop Spaces.

To change the Touch Bar display, open the **Keyboard** preference pane. Click the **Keyboard** tab. Select **App Controls**, the **Expanded Control Strip**, **F1, F2, etc. Keys**, **Quick Actions**, or **Spaces** from the drop-down menu next to **Touch Bar shows**. Check the checkbox next to **Show Control Strip** to display the Control Strip.

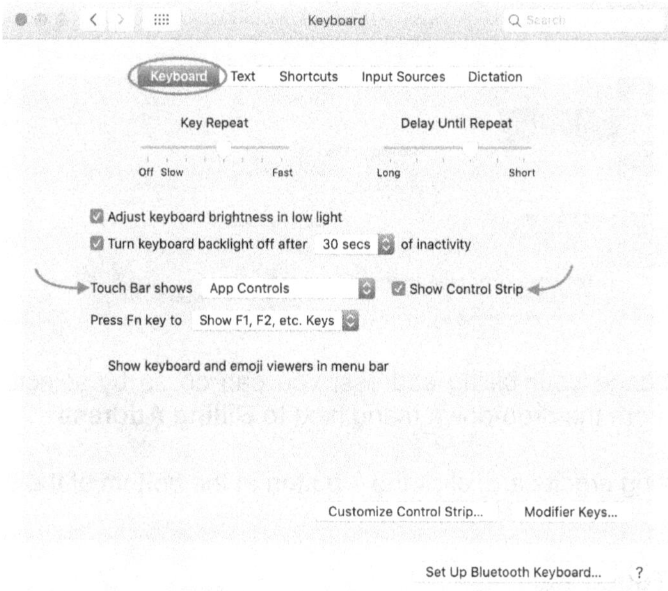

You can display the Control Strip with App Controls, Quick Actions, and Desktop Spaces. Each of these options can also be configured without the Control Strip. The Expanded Control Strip and F Keys options do not support the Control Strip. The following set of images depicts your Touch Bar configuration choices.

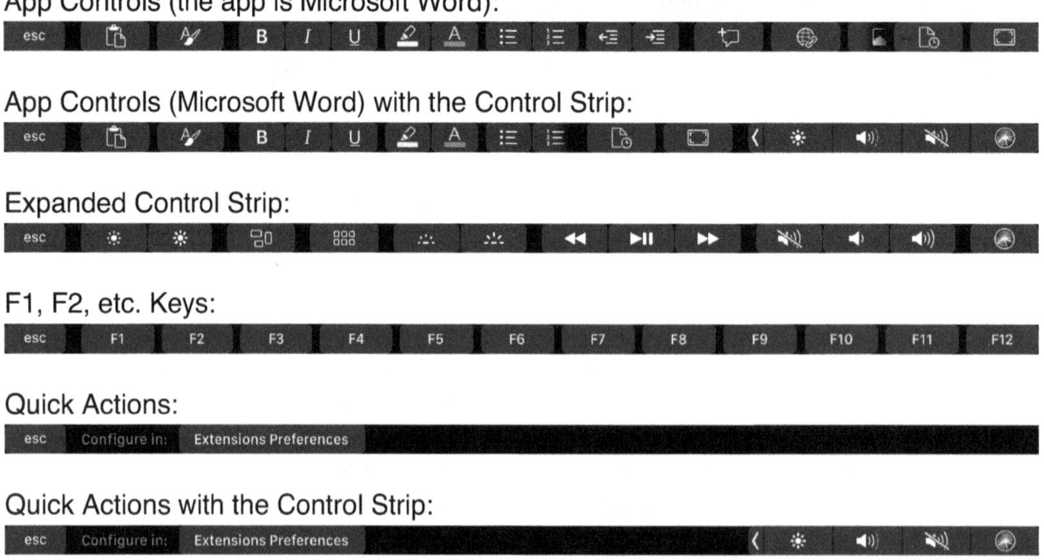

App Controls (the app is Microsoft Word):

App Controls (Microsoft Word) with the Control Strip:

Expanded Control Strip:

F1, F2, etc. Keys:

Quick Actions:

Quick Actions with the Control Strip:

Spaces:

Spaces with the Control Strip:

To return to the macOS default, select **App Controls** from the drop-down menu next to **Touch Bar shows** and check the checkbox next to **Show Control Strip**.

Configure the fn Key Toggle

By default, macOS toggles the Touch Bar display to show the F keys when you hold down the **fn** (function) key. This is similar to the behavior of a MacBook Pro without a Touch Bar or when using a physical keyboard like Apple's Magic Keyboard.

Once you have configured the main Touch Bar display, you can choose 1 of the 4 the remaining options to appear when you hold down the **fn** (function) key. Note that the Control Strip is only available on the main Touch Bar. You can choose from **App Controls**, the **Expanded Control Strip**, **F1, F2, etc. Keys**, **Quick Actions**, or **Spaces**. Note that you cannot configure the same display as the main Touch Bar.

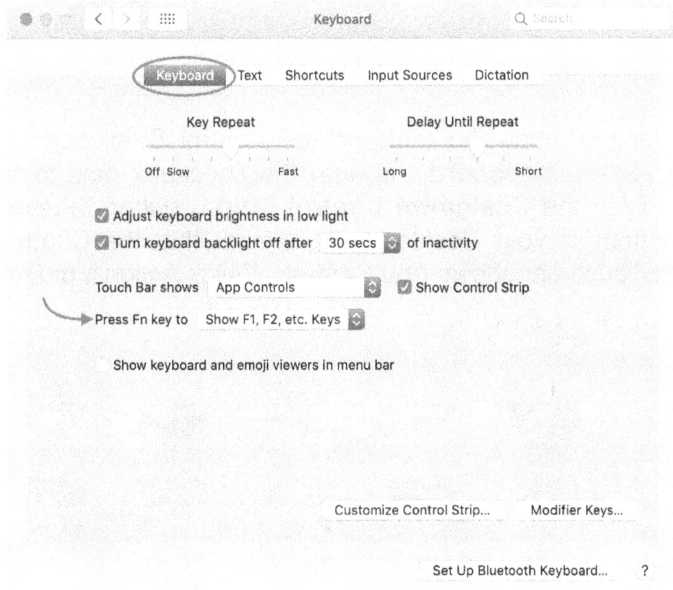

Open the **Keyboard** preference pane. Click **Keyboard** and select a display from the drop-down menu next to **Press Fn key to**.

Customize the Control Strip

By default, the Control Strip displays 4 tools – screen brightness, volume, mute, and Siri with an **esc** key at the far left, as shown in the image on the next page.

You don't have to settle for the default toolset. macOS lets you customize the Control Strip to meet your needs. Putting the tools you use most often at your fingertips increases your productivity.

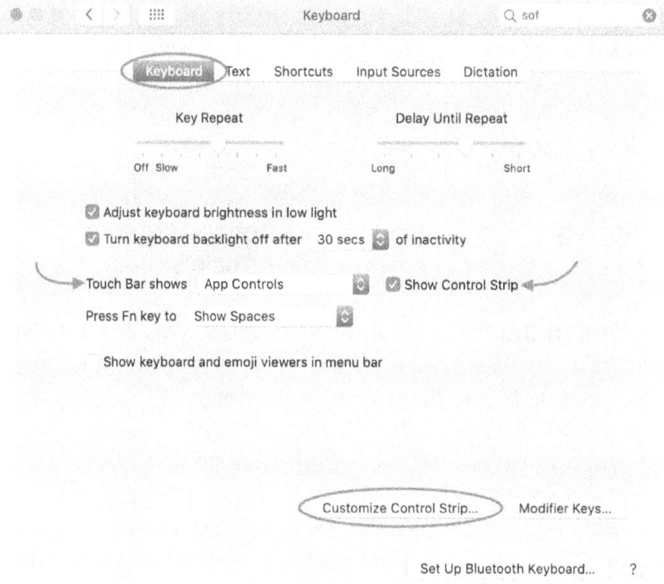

To add, remove, or rearrange the tools on the Control Strip, open the **Keyboard** preference pane. Select **Keyboard**. Ensure the checkbox next to **Show Control Strip** is checked. Click the **Customize Control Strip...** button to reveal a palette of 20 tools at the bottom of your Desktop. Remember that the Control Strip is only available when the Touch bar shows App Controls, Quick Actions, or Desktop Spaces.

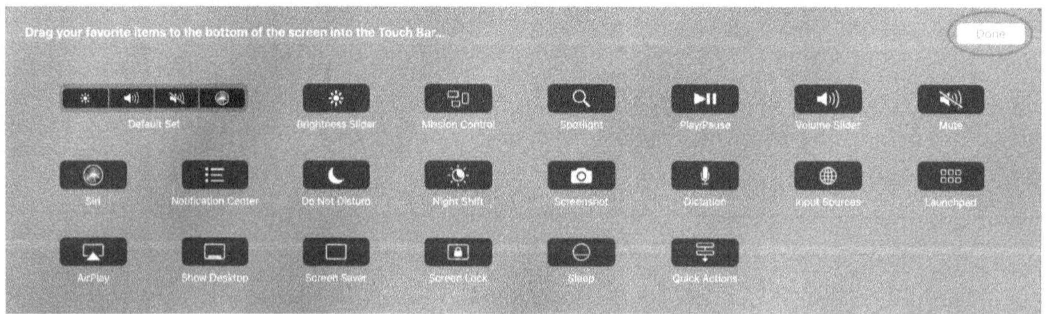

The icons on your Touch Bar jiggle similar to the way icons on an iPhone and iPad jiggle when editing. A **Done** button replaces the **esc** button at the far left of your Touch Bar.

The next part is going to seem a bit weird. To add a tool to the Control Strip, drag a tool from the palette to the Control Strip. This means you will drag the tool to the bottom of your screen and continue dragging until its icon appears on your Touch Bar. Once on the Touch Bar, the tool's icon is highlighted. Drag it left or right, and other icons move out of the way. When the tool is in your desired location, release your hold. If you are replacing an existing tool, position it over the icon you want to replace and release your hold.

Removing a tool from the Touch Bar is equally weird the first time you try it. Move your pointer to the bottom of your Desktop and continue until a tool on the Touch Bar is highlighted. Move left or right to highlight the desired tool. Drag the tool from the Touch Bar and on to the tools palette and release. You can also remove a tool by dragging it to the left end of the Touch Bar. A trash can and **Remove From Touch Bar** appears. Drag the tool into the trash can.

To rearrange the tools on your Touch Bar, move your pointer to the bottom of your Desktop and continue until a tool on the Touch Bar is highlighted. Move left or right until the icon you want to move is highlighted. Drag it to your desired location.

The Control Strip supports a maximum of 4 tools. macOS lets you choose less, supporting 1 to 4 tools. You can even have no tools in the Control Strip if desired, leaving more room for App Controls.

When finished, click the **Done** button on the tools palette or tap the blue **Done** button at the far left of your Touch Bar.

To revert to the default set of tools, drag the set of 4 tools called the **Default Set** to the Control Strip and click the **Done** button on the palette or Touch Bar.

Customize the Expanded Control Strip

The default set of tools on the Expanded Control Strip may look familiar if you have an Apple Magic Keyboard or have upgraded from a non-Touch Bar MacBook Pro. The toolset is the same set of tools in the same order on a keyboard with physical **F keys**.

You don't have to settle for the default set of tools. Similar to the Control Strip, macOS lets you customize the Expanded Control Strip. Placing your most frequently used tools on the Expanded Control Strip increases your productivity.

Another reason to customize the Expanded Control Strip is that two tools have trackpad gestures to invoke them – Mission Control and Launchpad. Besides, Siri is available in the Menu Bar, as a keyboard shortcut, and by saying, "Hey Siri." Replacing these tools frees up 3 spaces on your Touch Bar's Expanded Control Strip.

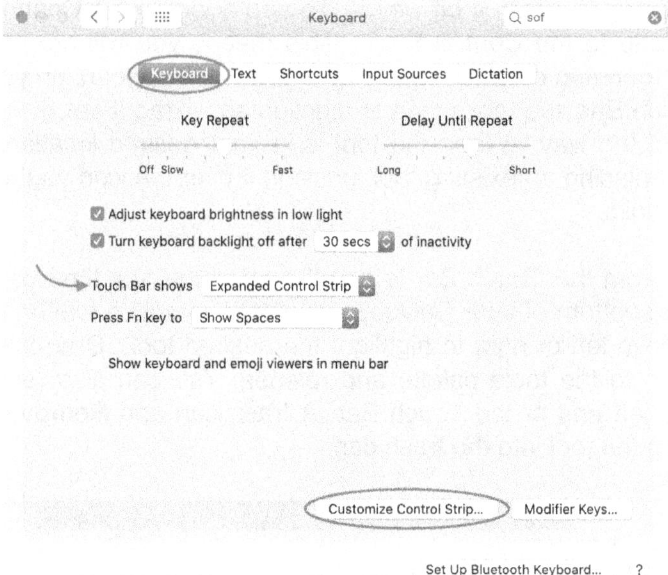

To add, remove, or rearrange the tools on your Expanded Control Strip, open the **Keyboard** preference pane. Select **Keyboard**. Ensure you have selected the Expanded Control Strip from the drop-down menu next to **Touch bar shows**. Click the **Customize Control Strip...** button to reveal a palette of 25 tools.

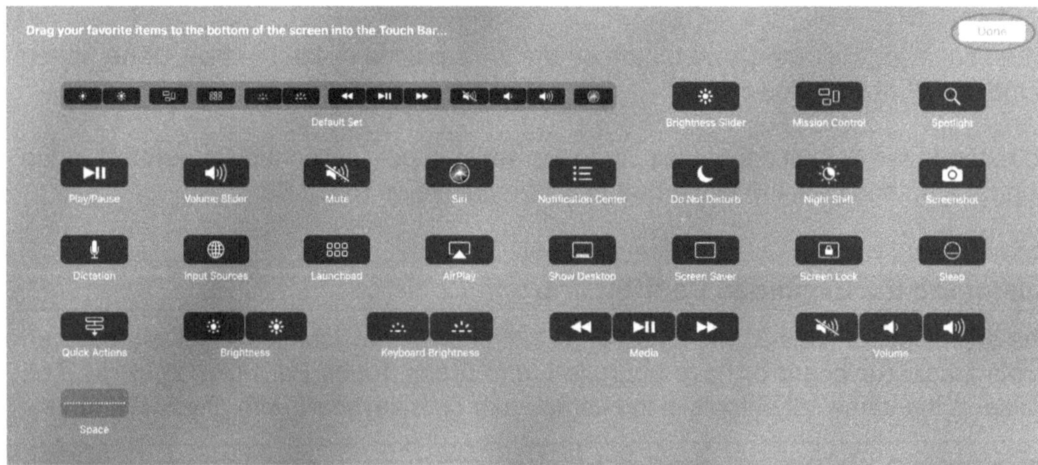

The icons on your Touch Bar jiggle similar to the way icons on an iPhone and iPad jiggle when editing. A **Done** button replaces the **esc** button at the far left.

To add a tool to the Expanded Control Strip, drag a tool from the palette to your Touch Bar. Once on the Touch Bar, the tool's icon is highlighted. Drag it left or right, and other icons move out of the way. When the tool is in your desired location, release your hold. If you are replacing an existing tool, position it over the tool you want to replace and release your hold.

To remove a tool from the Touch Bar, move your pointer to the bottom of your Desktop and continue until a tool on the Touch Bar is highlighted. Move left or right to highlight the desired tool. Drag the tool from the Touch Bar and on to the tools palette. You can also remove a tool by dragging it to the left end of the Touch Bar. A trash can and **Remove From Touch Bar** appears. Drag the tool into the trash can.

To rearrange the tools on your Touch Bar, move your pointer to the bottom of your Desktop and keep going until a tool on the Touch Bar is highlighted. Move left or right until the tool you want to move is highlighted. Drag the icon to your desired location.

The Expanded Control Strip has room for a maximum of 12 single button tools. Three tools support multiple controls – **Brightness**, **Keyboard Brightness**, **Media**, and **Volume**, each taking more room. macOS lets you place fewer tools on your Touch Bar, supporting 1 to 12 tools. You can even have no tools in the Expanded Control Strip if desired. However, that doesn't make much sense.

When finished, click the **Done** button on the tools palette or tap the blue **Done** button on your Touch Bar.

To revert to the default set of tools, drag the set of 7 tools called the **Default Set** to the Expanded Control Strip and click the **Done** button on the palette or Touch Bar.

Customize App Controls

If you configured your Touch Bar to show App Controls, you'd see a set of application-specific tools in the space between the **esc** key and the Control Strip if the application offers Touch Bar support. The App Controls area will be blank if an application doesn't support the Touch Bar.

While many applications populate the App Controls with a set of commonly used tools, most do not let you customize the tools on your Touch Bar. I'll show you how to create a custom App Controls Touch Bar to overcome this limitation later in this chapter. First, let's cover Safari and Mail, which allow you to customize their App Controls.

To check if an application lets you customize App Controls, check the application's **View** menu to see if it has a **Customize Touch Bar…** option. If this option is present, the app offers support to add, change, delete, and rearrange the tools in the App Controls. If this option is not present, the application does not allow you to customize the App Controls. If this option is grayed out, it is because you do not have the Touch Bar configured to show App Controls. Open the **Keyboard** preference pane and select the **Keyboard** tab. Choose **App Controls** from the drop-down menu next to **Touch Bar shows**. App Controls are available with or without the Control Strip.

Customize Safari App Controls

The default Safari App Controls are shown in the image below with the Control Strip in its usual spot on the right side of the Touch Bar. Note that I have customized my Control Strip with the Screen Lock and Launchpad replacing the Mute and Siri tools.

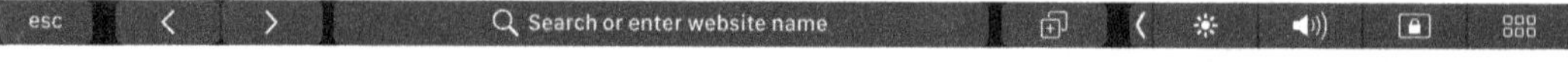

To customize the Safari tools on the Touch Bar, launch Safari and select **View > Customize Touch Bar...** to reveal the Safari tools palette.

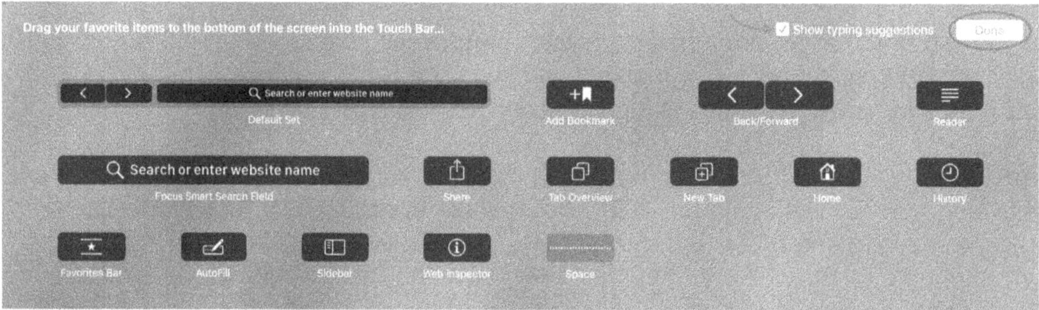

To add a tool, drag it from the Safari tools palette to the App Controls section of your Touch Bar. Once on the Touch Bar, the icon for the tool appears highlighted. Drag the icon left or right until it is in your desired location and release your hold. Note that you cannot drag an application tool to the Control Strip on the right of the Touch Bar.

To remove a tool from the Touch Bar, move your pointer to the bottom of your Desktop until a tool on the Touch Bar is highlighted. Move left or right until the tool you want to remove is highlighted. Drag the tool from the Touch Bar on to the Safari tools palette and release. You can also remove a tool by dragging it to the left end of the Touch Bar. A trash can and **Remove From Touch Bar** appears. Drag the tool into the trash can to remove it.

To rearrange the tools, move your pointer to the bottom of your Desktop and keep going until an icon on the Touch Bar is highlighted. Move left or right until the tool you want to move is highlighted. Drag the tool to your desired location and release.

To revert to the default Safari App Controls, drag and drop the **Default Set** from the Safari tools palette onto the Touch Bar.

If you check the checkbox next to **Show typing suggestions**, the Touch Bar suggests words you might want to use, saving time by letting you pick words with a tap on your Touch Bar.

Tap **Done** on the Touch Bar or click **Done** on the Safari tools palette when finished.

The image below shows my Touch Bar after I customized it with the tools I use most often. From left to right, the tools in my Safari App Controls are: Back/Forward, New Tab, Home, Reader, History, Tab Overview, and Share.

Customize Mail App Controls

To customize the Mail tools on the Touch Bar, launch Mail and select **View > Customize Touch Bar...** to reveal the Mail tools palette.

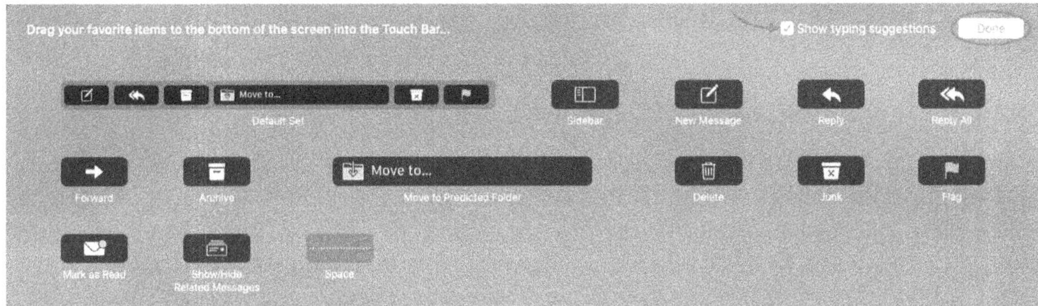

The default Mail App Controls are shown below.

Customizing your Mail App Controls is the same process as customizing the App Controls for Safari. To add a tool to the App Controls, drag it from the tools palette to the Touch Bar. Drag left or right until the tool is in your desired location then release your hold. Note that you cannot drag an application tool to the minimized Control Strip on the right of the Touch Bar.

To remove a tool from the Touch Bar, move your pointer to the bottom of your Desktop and keep going until a tool on the Touch Bar is highlighted. Move left or right until the tool you want to remove is highlighted. Drag the tool from the Touch Bar and on to the tools palette. You can also remove a tool by dragging it to the left end of the Touch Bar. A trash can and **Remove From Touch Bar** appears. Drag the tool into the trash can to remove it.

To rearrange the tools on your Touch Bar, move your pointer to the bottom of your Desktop until a tool on the Touch Bar is highlighted. Move left or right until the tool you want to move is highlighted. Drag the tool to your desired location.

To revert to the default Mail Touch Bar, drag and drop the **Default Set** from the Mail tools palette on to the Touch Bar.

If you check the checkbox next to **Show typing suggestions**, the Touch Bar suggests words you might want to use, saving time by letting you pick words with a tap on your Touch Bar.

Tap **Done** on the Touch Bar or click **Done** in the Mail tools palette when finished.

The image below shows my Touch Bar after customization with the tools I use most often. From left to right, the tools in my Mail App Controls are: New Message, Reply, Reply All, Forward, Flag, Sidebar, Junk, and Delete.

Configure the Touch Bar to Show F Keys

If you have an application that utilizes the **F** (function) keys, macOS lets you configure the Touch Bar to display the function keys when that application is active. This is a handy feature that eliminates the need to configure the Touch Bar to toggle **F** keys when you press the **fn** (function) key, allowing you to configure the Touch Bar to display another option when the **fn** (function) key is pressed.

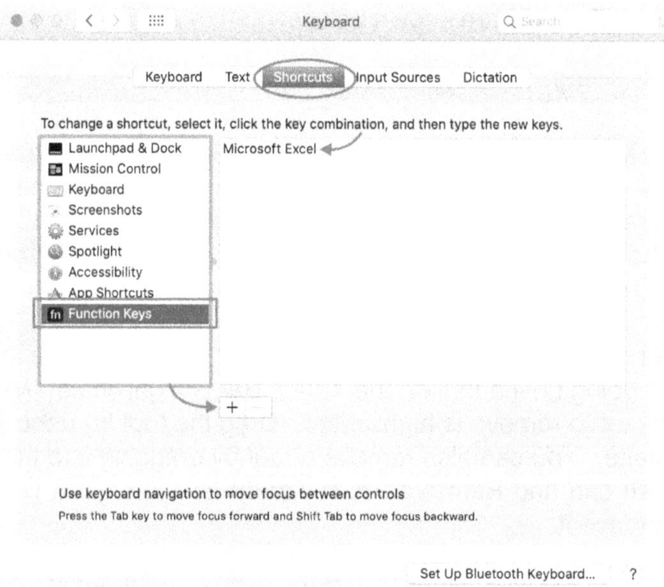

To configure the Touch Bar to show the function keys in a specific application, open the **Keyboard** preference pane. Click on the **Shortcuts** tab and select **Function Keys** from the sidebar. Click the **+** at the bottom of the right pane to open the Applications folder. Choose an app and click the **Add** button. The Touch Bar will always show the strip of function keys when your chosen application is active.

To delete an application, highlight it and click the – button at the bottom left of the right pane.

Enable Touch Bar Zoom

If you are having difficulties seeing the tools on the Touch Bar, you can enable Touch Bar zoom. This feature displays a larger version of the Touch Bar on your Desktop.

To enable Touch Bar Zoom, open the **Accessibility** preference pane in System Preferences. Scroll down and select to **Zoom** in the sidebar. Check the checkbox next to **Enable Touch Bar Zoom**.

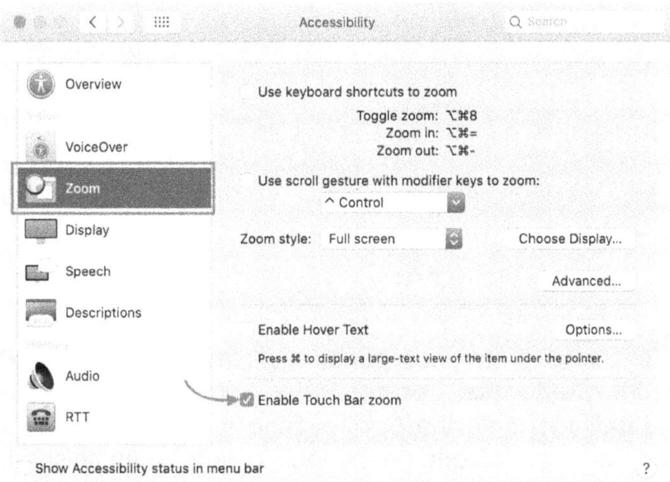

To zoom, place and hold a finger on the Touch Bar without tapping. A larger version of your Touch Bar with a circle target appears on your Desktop. Without leaving the Touch Bar, slide your finger left or right to highlight your desired button. When the circle changes color indicating the icon is selected, you can lift your finger off the Touch Bar to activate the tool.

The image above shows the Touch Bar on the Desktop with the target circle between the Volume controls and the Mute button.

Lock Your Mac with the Touch Bar

If you're tired of your roommates or kids posting stupid stuff on Twitter or Facebook when you leave the room with your Mac on, you can customize the Touch Bar to add a tool to lock your Mac.

Open the **Security & Privacy** preference pane. Click the **General** tab and check the checkbox next to **Require password**. Choose **immediately** from the drop-down menu. Enabling this feature will require you to enter your password when your Mac wakes from sleep or the screen saver.

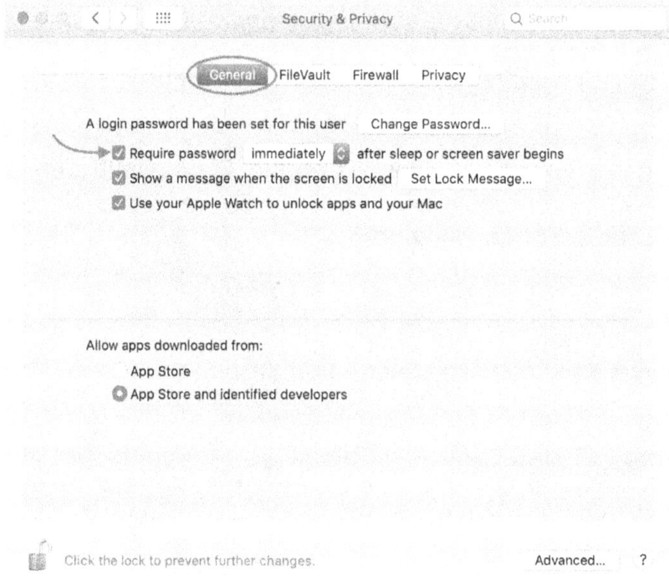

Next, open the **Keyboard** preference pane, click the **Keyboard** tab if not already highlighted. Click the **Customize Control Strip...** button to reveal the tools palette. Drag the **Screen Lock** tool onto the Control Strip or Expanded Control Strip. Tap **Done** on the Touch Bar or click **Done** on the tools palette when finished.

The Screen Lock tool is the second from the right in the image below.

Create a Custom Touch Bar

Now that you are familiar with the out-of-the-box macOS Touch Bar let's learn how to create a custom Touch Bar. We'll use an application I introduced in Chapter 2, **BetterTouchTool** by Andreas Hegenberg. BetterTouchTool lets you create a custom Touch Bar filled with buttons that execute over 200 predefined actions or keyboard shortcuts.

BetterTouchTool is available for $7.50 for a standard license or $21 for a lifetime license at the time of this writing. You can download a 45-day free trial of BetterTouch Tool from https://folivora.ai/.

In case you skipped the section on creating custom gestures in Chapter 2, I'll repeat the initial set up of BetterTouchTouch here. If you have already set up

BetterTouchTool, you can skip the next 2 sections and go directly to the section titled Configure Touch Bar Specific Settings.

Set the Security & Privacy Settings

The first time you launch BetterTouchTool, macOS will ask you to authorize it in the **Security & Privacy** preference pane of System Preferences.

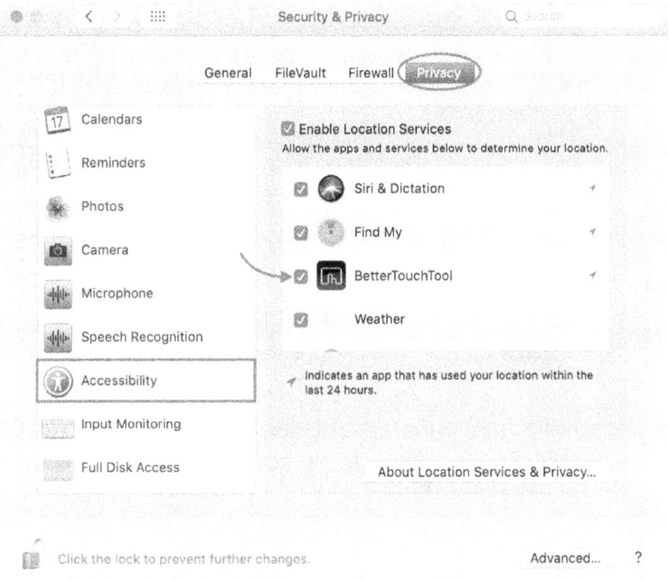

Click the **Privacy** tab and select **Accessibility** from the sidebar. If required, unlock the pane by clicking on the padlock in the lower-left corner and entering your password. Check the checkbox next to **BetterTouchTool** to authorize it. Relock the preference pane by clicking on the padlock or close the window.

Configure Basic and User Interface Settings

After downloading and installing BetterTouchTool, you'll notice a new Menu Extra in your Menu Bar. Click on this Menu Extra to reveal the drop-down menu and select **Configuration** to launch BetterTouchTool.

To access BetterTouchTool's preferences, click on the gear in the upper-right corner of the BetterTouchTool window, enter **⌘,** (command+comma), or select **BetterTouchTool > Preferences**. Next, select **Basic** under **Standard Settings** in the left sidebar.

There are a couple of settings that you should validate before creating your custom Touch Bar. Ensure the following items are checked: **Launch BetterTouchTool on startup** and **Enable automatic update checking**. Launching BetterTouchTool on startup ensures it runs each time you restart your Mac. Enabling automatic updates allows the app to automatically check for updates and ensures that you always have the latest version. **Allow crash log and anonymized usage data collection** is checked by default. This option helps the developer continually improve his app. I recommend you leave it checked.

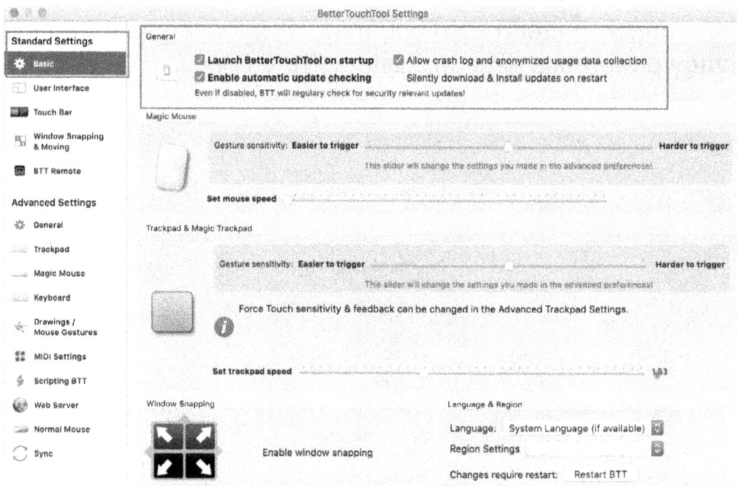

Next, select **User Interface** and validate that the checkbox next to **Show Menubar Icon** is checked. The Menu Bar icon is a convenient way to quickly configure BetterTouchTool, access documentation or go to the BetterTouchTool Community Forum.

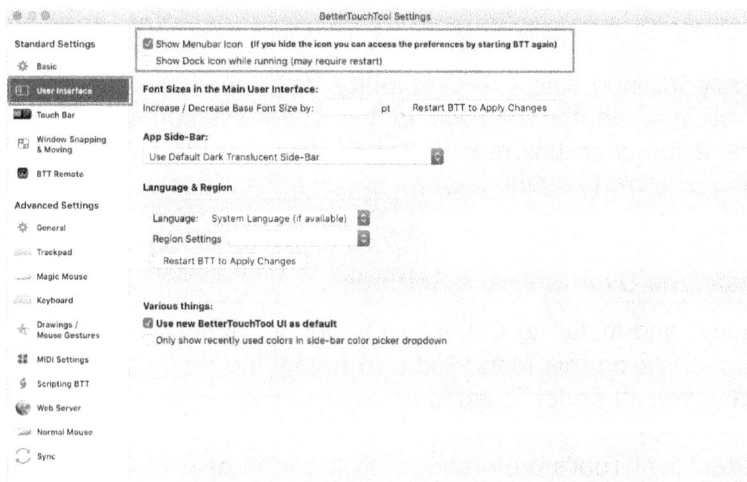

The BetterTouchTool icon does not appear in the Dock. If you want it in your Dock, check the checkbox next to **Show Dock Icon while running** and restart your Mac.

Configure Touch Bar Specific Settings

First, ensure that your Touch Bar is set to display the Control Strip. BetterTouchTool places an icon at the end of the Control Strip that you will use to access your custom Touch Bar. Review the Change the Touch Bar section in this chapter if you don't know how to configure your Touch Bar to show the Control Strip.

BetterTouchTool has additional configuration settings that are specific to the Touch Bar. Open the BetterTouchTool configuration pane by selecting **Configuration** from the BetterTouchTool Menu Extra in your Menu Bar.

Select **Touch Bar** from the drop-down menu at the top of the configuration pane. Next, click the **Touch Bar Settings** button next to the drop-down menu or click the gear icon in the upper-right corner to open the BetterTouchTool settings window.

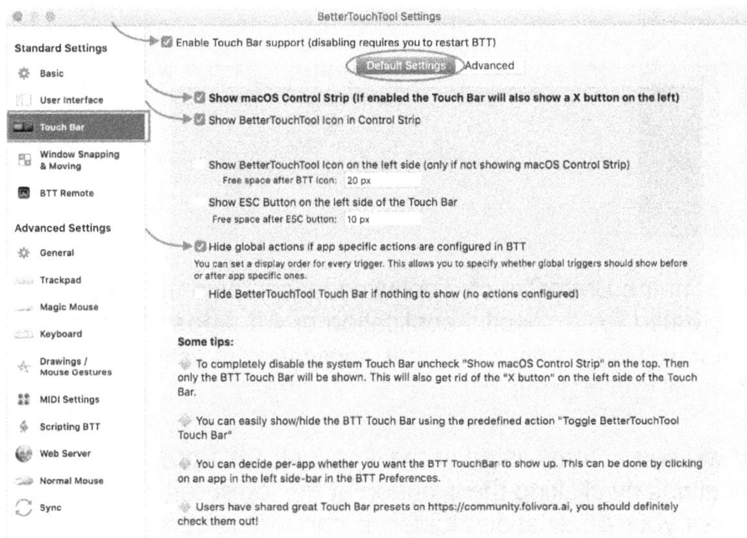

Touch Bar should be highlighted in the sidebar of the settings window, and the **Default Settings** tab highlighted. Ensure the checkboxes are checked, as shown in the image above.

You may have to restart BetterTouch for the BetterTouchTool icon to appear in your Touch Bar's Control Strip. You should see the BetterTouchTool icon at the end of your Control Strip once you have restarted BetterTouchTool.

Until you configure your first Touch Bar button, your Touch Bar will display a notice reminding you that you have not yet configured actions in BetterTouchTool.

Create a Custom Touch Bar Button

Let's create your first Touch Bar Button for your custom Touch Bar. First, select **Touch Bar** from the drop-down menu in the toolbar at the top of the BetterTouchTool configuration window. Creating a custom Touch Bar button consists of selecting whether it works in all apps or only in a specific app, defining the trigger, and assigning an action to the trigger.

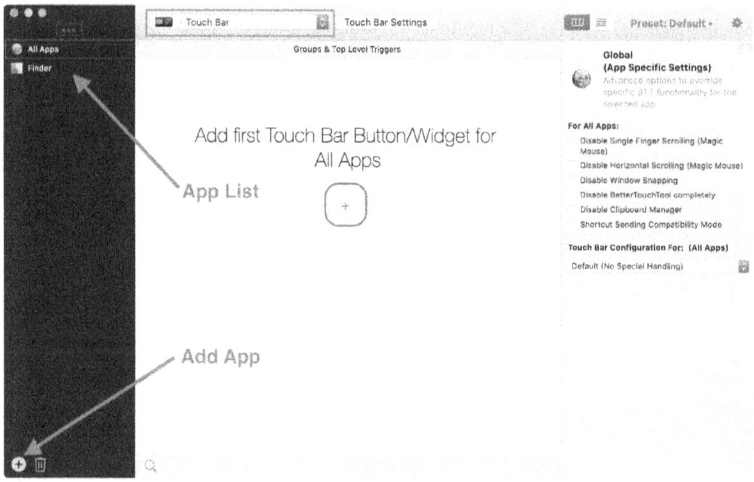

The black sidebar in the BetterTouch Tool window contains the **App List**. Touch Bar buttons can be created for a specific application or **All Apps**. A button created for a specific application will work only when that application is active. A button created for **All Apps** works in all applications.

By default, you will see 2 items listed in the App List, **All Apps**, and **Finder**. You can add other applications by clicking the **+** button at the lower-left corner of the window to select an app from your Applications folder or one that is currently running. You can also drag an application from your Application folder into the App List.

To create your first Touch Bar button, select All Apps or an application in the App List and click the large blue **+** button in the center of the BetterTouchTool window. For this example, I have selected All Apps. Clicking the blue **+** button reveals the **Trigger List**, where you will select your trigger. You can choose from **Normal Buttons & Groups**, **Touch Bar Widgets**, **Touch Bar Gestures**, and **BTT UI Separator**.

For our first button, I am going to create a button that opens Notification Center. After clicking the blue **+** button in the center of the BetterTouchTool window, select **Touch Bar button** under **Normal Buttons & Groups**.

Once you have selected a trigger, the next step is to configure it in the **Touch Bar Trigger Configuration** section. I named the button "Notification Center" in the text field under **Button Title**. Note that naming the button is required. BetterTouchTool will not display a nameless button on the Touch Bar.

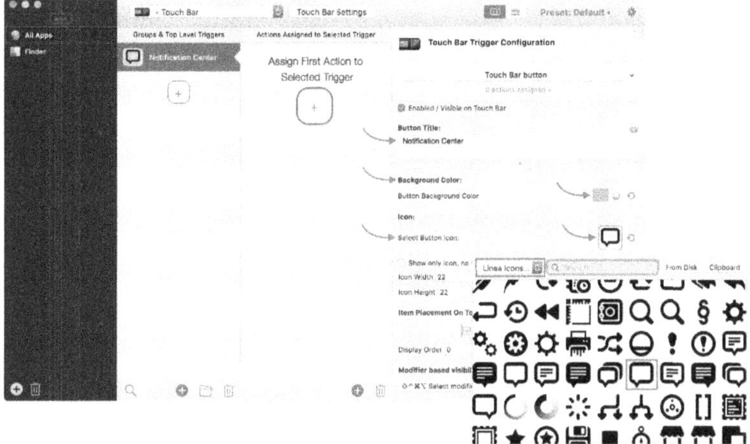

The default color for buttons is black, but you can change this by choosing a **Background Color** by clicking the black box to reveal a set of predefined colors or by choosing a color from the color wheel. I chose green. The final task is to select an icon. BetterTouchTool offers three sets of icons, which you can choose from using a drop-down menu.

Here is what our first button looks like on the Touch Bar:

The button title appears on your button by default. If you don't like it, you can remove the title by checking the checkbox next to **Show only icon, no text** to remove it.

Now we have to select an action for our button. Click the large blue button with the **+** under **Actions Assigned to Selected Trigger**. If you set up custom gestures, you'll recognize this configuration sheet. Type "Not" in the search field and select **Show Notification Center** from the list of search results.

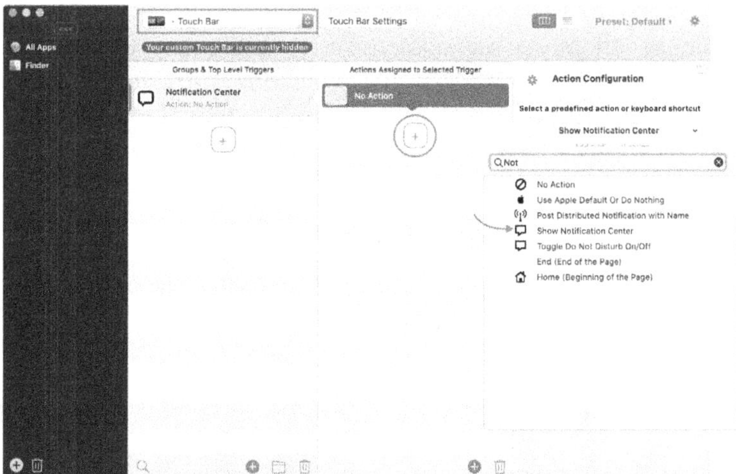

We have finished our first Touch Bar button. Give it a try. Tap the BetterTouchTool icon in your Control Strip to reveal your custom Touch Bar. Tap your newly created button and watch as Notification Center slides out from the right side of your Desktop.

That one Notification Center button looks rather lonely. Continue to add more buttons to fill out your custom Touch Bar using the same process we used to create the Notification Center button. Don't worry if you can't display all of the buttons you create. You can access any buttons hidden under your Control Strip by sliding your finger left along the Touch Bar.

Add a Touch Bar Widget

BetterTouchTool includes many handy widgets to display the weather, date and time, Dock, calendar, the song now playing, reminders, clipboard, and emoji. To add a widget to your custom Touch Bar, click the blue **+** button underneath the Notification Button we just created under **Groups & Top Level Triggers**. Select **Tough Bar Widgets** to display the list of available widgets. For this example, I'll select the **Weather Widget**.

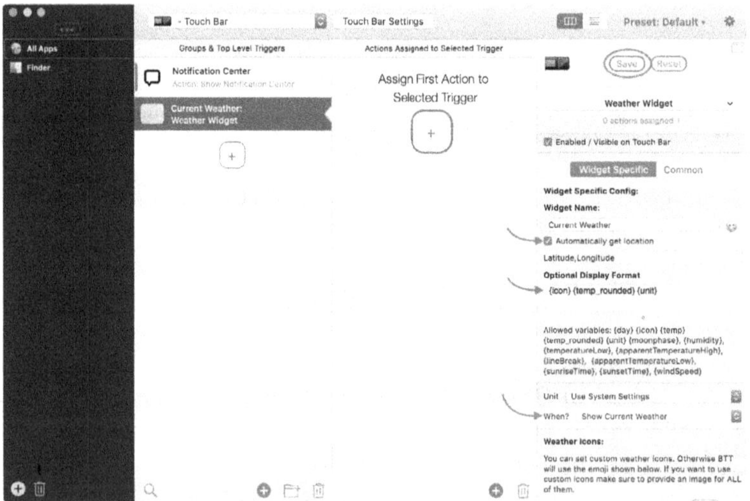

The Weather Widget offers a few customization options. First, it automatically determines your location by checking the checkbox next to **Automatically get location**. You can change the display format from the default by entering variables in the text field under **Optional Display Format**. Supported variables are listed below the text field. I selected {icon} {temp_rounded} {unit}. The widget also offers the choice of the current weather, today's weather forecast, or a forecast up to 7 days in the future. Click the **Save** button when finished.

Let's take a look at our Touch Bar with our Notification Center button and Weather Widget.

You can continue to add buttons and widgets to your custom Touch Bar until it is fully populated. Let's take a look at my custom Touch Bar.

From left to right, I have the following buttons and widgets on my custom Touch Bar – an application switcher, Notification Center, System Preferences, weather widget, date & time widget, battery widget, now playing widget, and a multiple action button we will learn about in the next section. But wait! It looks like there are more buttons under the Control Strip.

Sliding my finger to the left along the Touch Bar reveals additional buttons – Mission Control with Desktop Preview, new Desktop Space, hide all apps, and a button that puts my MacBook Pro to sleep.

Create a Multiple Action Button

BetterTouchTool doesn't limit your buttons to a single action. You can add additional actions to your button. A multiple action button is a perfect way to accomplish multiple actions with a single tap on your Touch Bar. The only limit to multiple action buttons is your imagination.

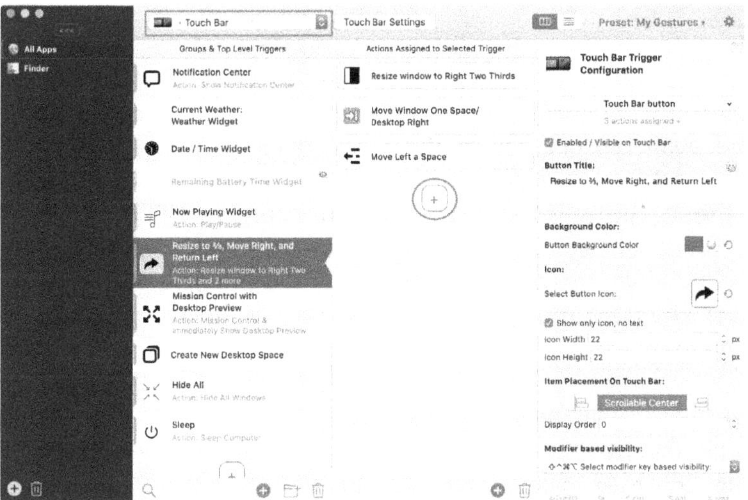

In the example above, I created a button that resizes the active window to the right 2/3 of my Desktop, moves the window to the next Desktop Space to the right, and then returns to the original Desktop Space by moving left one space.

To create a multiple action gesture, click the **+** button under the **Actions Assigned to Selected Trigger** pane for each additional action you want to add. Select your desired actions from the **Action Configuration** pane.

Control Touch Bar Button Visibility with Modifier Keys

A nifty feature of BetterTouchTool is that it supports modifier keys to control the visibility of buttons and widgets in your custom Touch Bar. This feature allows you to show certain buttons and widgets while pressing one or more of the modifier keys. This feature can be effectively used to create multiple custom Touch Bars accessible by first pressing the associated modifier key(s).

In the example below, I have configured the System Preferences button only to be visible while simultaneously pressing the ^ ⌥ (control and option) keys.

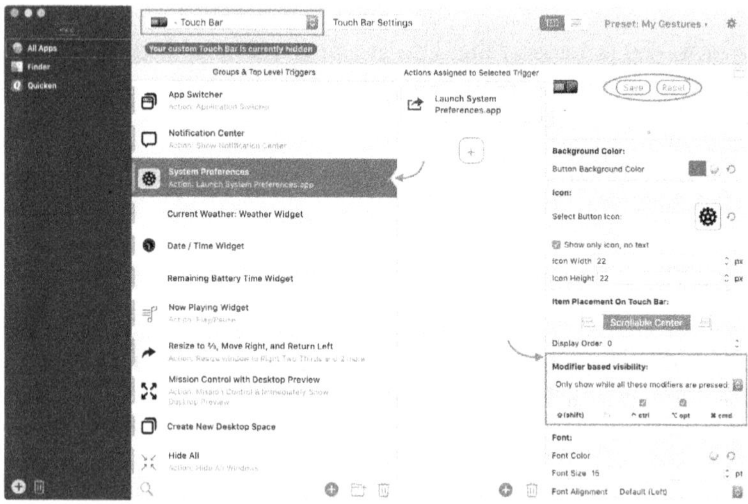

Modifier keys are added to a button or widget in the Touch Bar Trigger Configuration section by selecting a choice from the drop-down menu under **Modifier Based Visibility**. The available choices in the drop-down menu consist of: **Only show while all these modifiers are pressed**, **Show if some modifier keys are pressed, but NONE of these**, **Show if NO modify key is pressed OR if NONE of these are pressed**, and **Show always (don't care about modifiers at all)**. If you haven't configured modifier keys, the default is to display the button at all times regardless of whether modifier keys are pressed or not, essentially the last choice in the visibility drop-down menu.

Once you have made your selection from the drop-down menu, select the modifier key(s) you wish to use by checking the checkbox(es) above them. Supported modifier keys include the ⇧ ^ ⌥ ⌘ (shift, control, option, and command) keys. You can choose one or more modifier keys to control button and widget visibility.

Note that the **fn** (function) key is not supported because it is used to display the Touch Bar configured in the Keyboard preference pane.

Click the **Save** button to save your configuration or **Reset** to revert.

Create a Custom Touch Bar for an Application

If an application does not offer App Controls, you can use BetterTouchTool and the macOS keyboard shortcuts feature to fill this gap. Using an application's existing keyboard shortcuts and creating custom shortcuts for commands without one, you can configure BetterTouchTool to send a keyboard shortcut when you tap a button on your Touch Bar.

For this example, I'll create custom App Controls for Quicken, an app that doesn't offer Touch Bar App Controls. Using Quicken's Application menu, I note the keyboard shortcut for each of the commands I want to add to my App Controls. For the commands that don't have a keyboard shortcut, I'll create a custom keyboard shortcut using the Keyboard preference pane in System Preferences. If you are unsure how to create a custom keyboard shortcut, refer to the section titled "Create a Custom Keyboard Shortcut" in the last chapter.

Quicken provides keyboard shortcuts for the **Update** and **New Transaction** commands, which are ⇧⌘U (shift+command+U) and ⌘N (command+N), respectively. I created keyboard shortcuts in the Keyboard preference pane for the **Reconcile Account**, **Dividends** report, and **Save a Backup** commands, which did not have keyboard shortcuts, as shown in the image below.

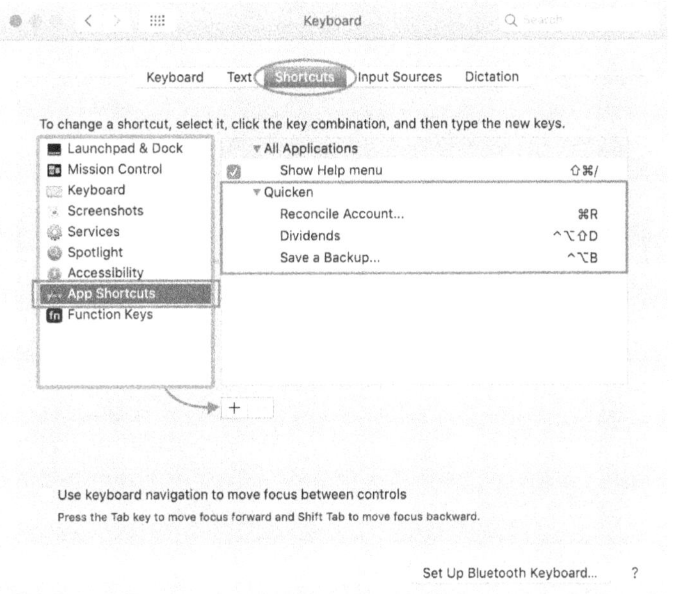

Once I created and successfully tested my custom keyboard shortcuts, I opened the BetterTouchTool configuration window to create my custom App Controls. First, I added Quicken to the app list (the black column on the left) by clicking the **+** button in the lower-left corner of the window. Since Quicken was already running, I chose **Select app from running apps** from the drop-down menu that appeared after I clicked the **+** button. I could have also chosen **Select app from file system**, which opens the Applications folder, and selected Quicken.

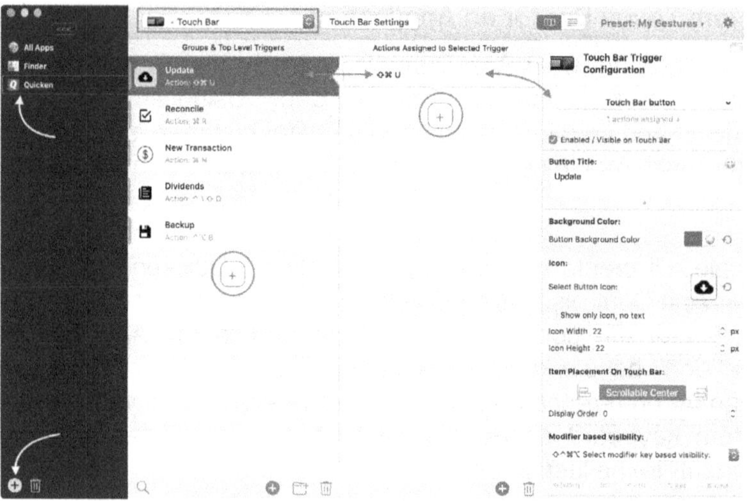

Ensuring Quicken was highlighted in the sidebar at the left, I clicked the blue **+** button under **Groups & Top Level Triggers** and selected **Touch Bar button** under **Normal Buttons & Groups**. After naming and selecting a color and icon, I clicked the blue **+** button under **Actions Assigned to Selected Trigger**. I entered the keyboard shortcut in the **Click to record shortcut** field under **Send Keyboard Shortcut**. I repeated this process for each button until I filled my App Controls Touch Bar.

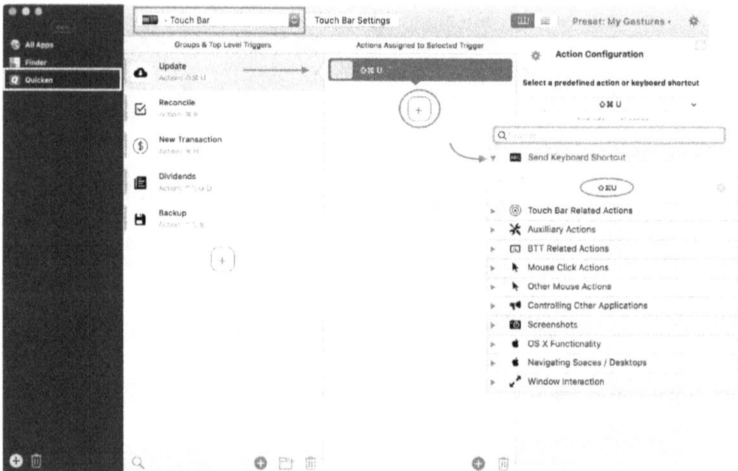

Here is my Quicken App Controls Touch Bar with the commands I use most often:

Rearrange your Custom Touch Bar Buttons & Widgets

The buttons on your custom Touch Bar are easily rearranged. To move a button or widget, open the BetterTouchTool configuration window from its Menu Extra. Click and drag a button or widget to a new location under the **Groups & Top Level**

Triggers column. A button or widget at the top of the list appears first, at the far left of your Touch Bar, with the remaining items appearing in order, top to bottom across your Touch Bar.

Modify a Custom Touch Bar Button or Widget

You can modify the appearance of a Touch Bar button or the action assigned to it in the BetterTouchTool configuration window.

To modify the button appearance, choose the app from the App List in the sidebar, then click on the button you want to modify in the **Groups & Top Level Triggers** column.

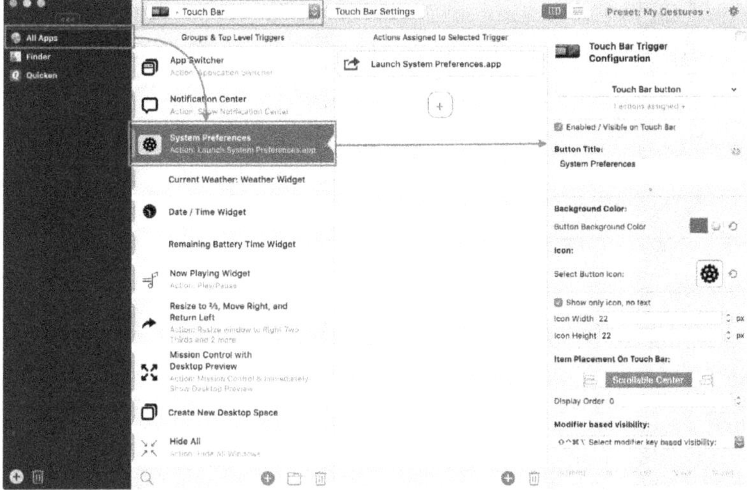

The button's appearance is modified in the **Touch Bar Trigger Configuration** panel. You can change button name, background color, icon, modifier key(s), size, and whether or not the button displays its title.

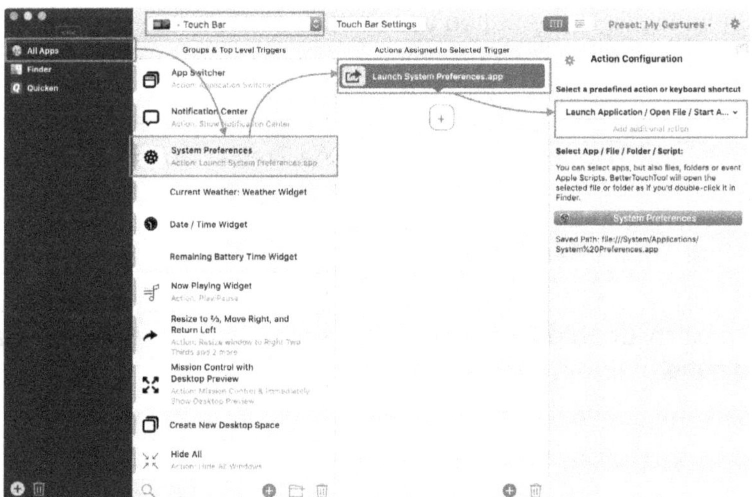

To modify the action assigned to a button, click on the button you want to change in the **Groups & Top Level Triggers** column to highlight it. Next, click the action under **Actions Assigned to Selected Trigger** in the middle panel of the BetterTouchTool configuration window. This reveals the **Action Configuration** panel, where you can change the assigned action or add another action.

Delete a Custom Touch Bar Button

BetterTouchTool offers three deletion options. You can delete the action associated with a button, you can delete the button (the trigger), or you can delete an application and its custom Touch Bar.

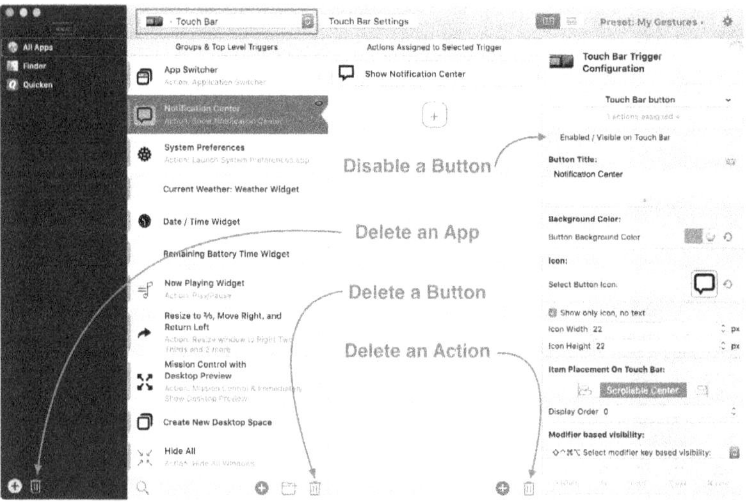

If you want to delete an application and its Touch Bar, highlight the application in the App List and click the Trash Can icon. Note that BetterTouchTool does not let you delete **All Apps** and **Finder** from the App List.

To delete a button, highlight the button you wish to delete in the **Groups & Top Level Triggers** list and click the Trash Can icon.

To delete an action associated with a button, highlight the action in the **Actions Assigned to Selected Trigger** list and click on the Trash Can icon.

Disable a Custom Touch Bar Button

If you prefer to disable a button rather than deleting it, you can do so by unchecking the checkbox next to **Enabled / Visible on Touch Bar** in the **Touch Bar Trigger Configuration** panel.

Import and Export your Touch Bar

If you want to share your Touch Bar with friends or want to create a backup, you can export your BetterTouchTool configuration to a file. BetterTouchTool's **Preset** feature lets you import and export your gestures.

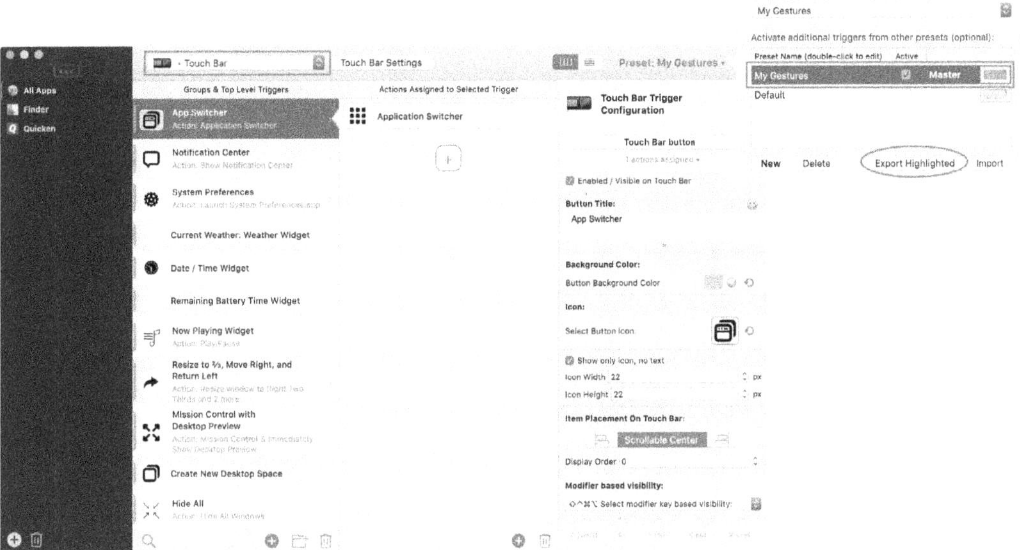

Click **Preset: My Gestures** in the upper-right corner of the BetterTouchTool configuration pane to reveal the Preset configuration sheet. Select the Preset Name from the list of presets and then click **Export Highlighted**. A save dialog opens. Click **Triggers & Settings**. Name your file, choose the save location, and press **Save**.

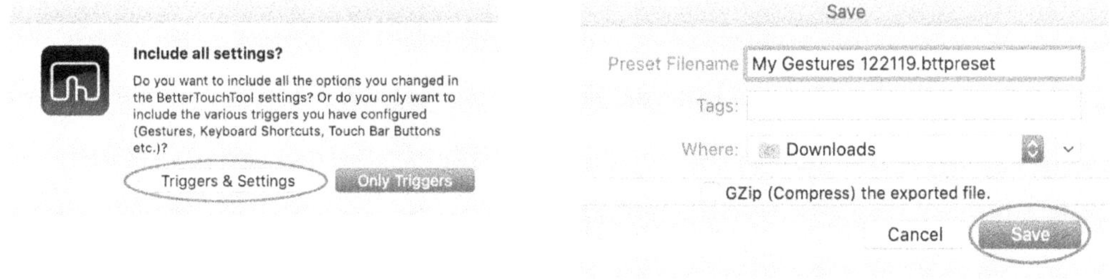

To import a preset file, click **Preset: My Gestures** and then click **Import** from the configuration sheet. Browse to the preset file, select it, and click **Open**.

16

Safari

For most users, **Safari** requires little customization and can be operated in an "out-of-the-box" mode. However, if you have made it this far, you and I both know that you are not like most users. There is much customization you can do to fine-tune Safari, change its appearance, and make it perform better.

Customize the Toolbar

The **Toolbar**, located at the top of the Safari window, offers tools to enhance your web browsing experience. You can customize the Toolbar, adding, removing, and rearranging the tools as you see fit. Secondary click in an open area of the Toolbar to reveal a contextual menu with a single option to **Customize Toolbar...**, which reveals a tools palette with the entire selection of available tools.

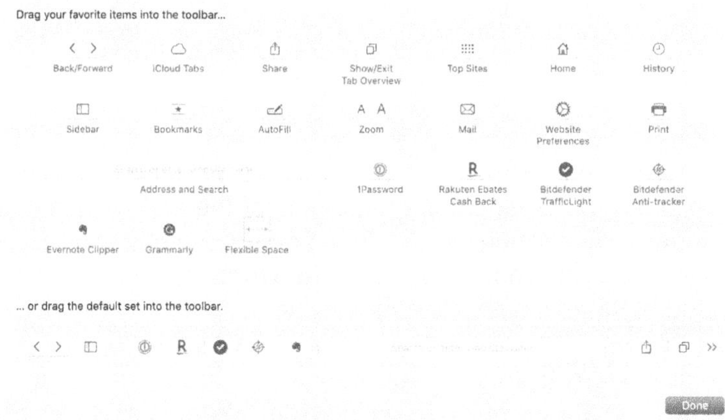

The tools palette allows you to add additional tools to the Toolbar by dragging and dropping them onto the Toolbar. Any extensions that offer a tool are shown on the tools palette. To add a tool to the Toolbar, drag and drop it. Existing tools located on the Toolbar can be rearranged by dragging them. A tool is removed by dragging it off the Toolbar and onto the drop-down tools palette.

Available tools include the **iCloud Tabs** tool, which displays the websites open in tabs on other devices associated with your iCloud account.

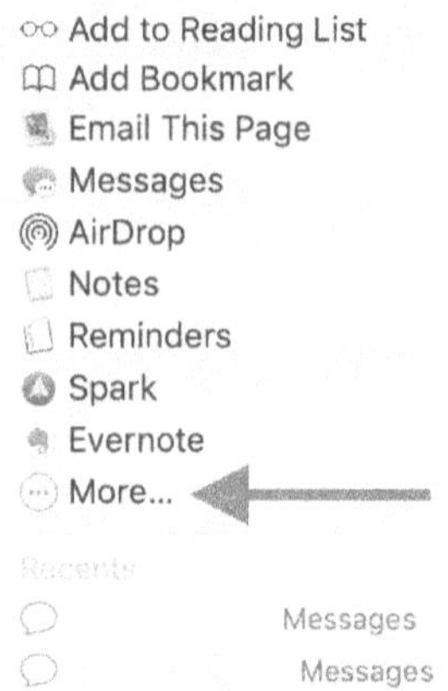

The **Share** button lets you share an item via Mail, Messages, Airdrop, or through third-party extensions. macOS lists your recent shares under **Recents**, allowing you to share an item quickly.

To configure the third-party extensions available in the **Share Menu**, click the Share button and select **More...** or by opening the **Extensions** preference pane from System Preferences. Select **Share Menu** in the sidebar if not already selected. Use the checkboxes to select which third-party extensions you wish to make available in the Share drop-down menu.

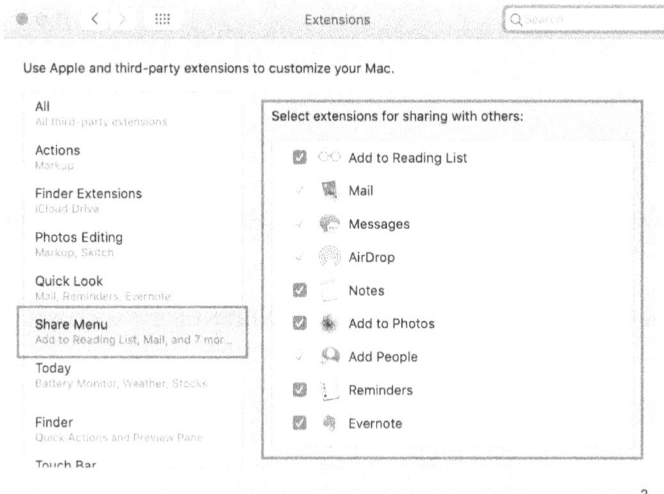

Back to the Safari toolbar, the **Show/Exit Tab Overview** button allows you to view all the pages open in Safari as tabs, small thumbnails of the web pages. This lets you quickly jump to a page by clicking on it. The **Top Sites** tool shows you your Top Sites, which are websites you frequently visit. The **Home** tool takes you to the Home page you configured in Safari's General preferences.

The **History** tool displays a history of web pages you have previously visited. The **Sidebar** tool toggles the Safari sidebar on and off. Safari's sidebar displays your bookmarks, reading list, and shared links. The **Bookmarks** tool toggles Safari's favorites bar on and off. The Favorites Bar conveniently lists the websites in your Favorites bookmark folder in a bar just below the Safari toolbar.

The **Autofill** tool tells Safari to automatically fill website forms with data such as your name, address, email, and phone number. The **Zoom** tool does what you would expect it to do – zooming in and out. The **Mail** tool lets you share a web page via Mail. The **Print** tool lets you print a web page.

The **Website Preferences** tool allows you to quickly configure various options for the website you are currently visiting. You can choose to display the Reader view, enable and disable content blockers, configure settings for page zoom, media autoplay, and pop-up windows, and control the camera, microphone, screen sharing, and whether you will allow the website to access your location information.

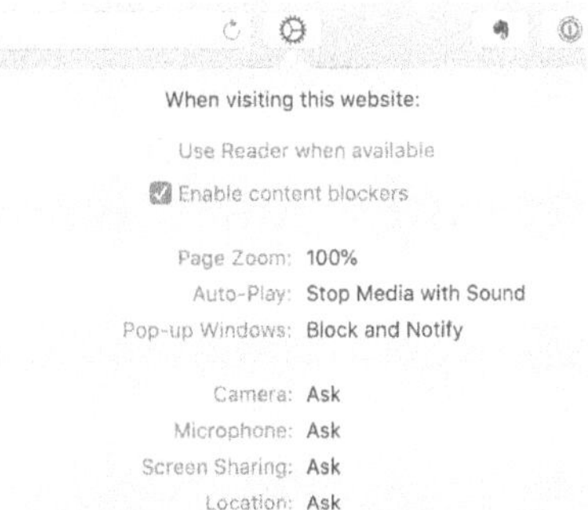

Any third-party tools that you have added are located to the right of the search bar. In the picture of the toolbar palette, you will see that I have added tools for 1Password, Rakuten Ebates, BitDefender, Evernote, and Grammarly. The **Flexible Space** tool is used to space out the tools in the toolbar by adding blank space between them. Click the **Done** button when finished customizing your Safari toolbar.

To revert to the default set of tools, drag the default toolset onto the toolbar and click **Done**.

Tools located on the Toolbar can be rearranged without having to use the tools palette. To move a tool, hold the ⌘ (command) key down while dragging the tool to its new location.

You can also use the ⌘ (command) key to remove a tool. Hold down the ⌘ (command) key while dragging the tool off the Toolbar.

Change the Default Browser

Safari is the default browser in macOS Catalina. The default browser is the browser that is launched when you click on a link in an email or another application. While it may seem odd, Apple allows you to choose another browser installed on your Mac as the default. If you want to change the **Default web browser**, open the **General** preference pane in the System Preferences application.

Note that you have to install other browsers first. Firefox, Chrome, and Opera are the usual suspects. Firefox is available at https://www.mozilla.org. Chrome can be downloaded at https://www.google.com/chrome/. Opera is available at https://www.opera.com. Once you have other browsers installed on your Mac, they will be listed in the drop-down menu next to **Default web browser**.

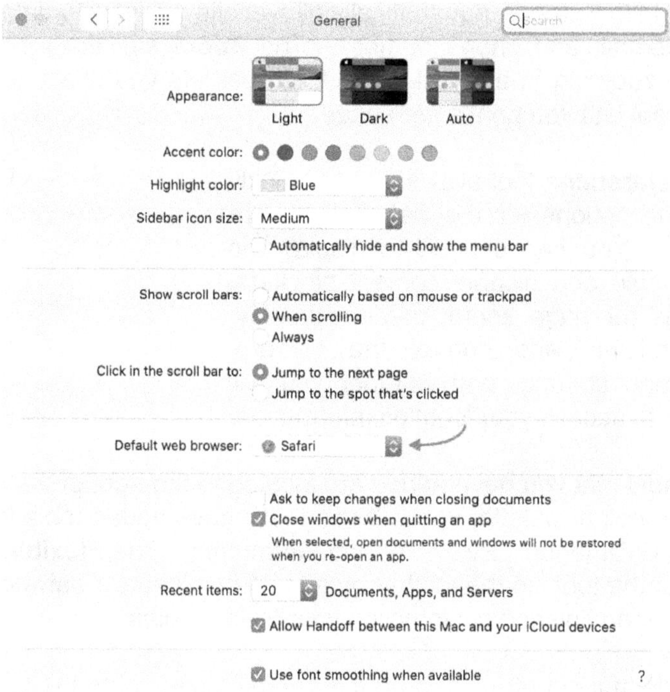

Configure Your Home Page

Your **Home Page** is the page your browser will navigate to when you click the **Home** button in Safari's toolbar.

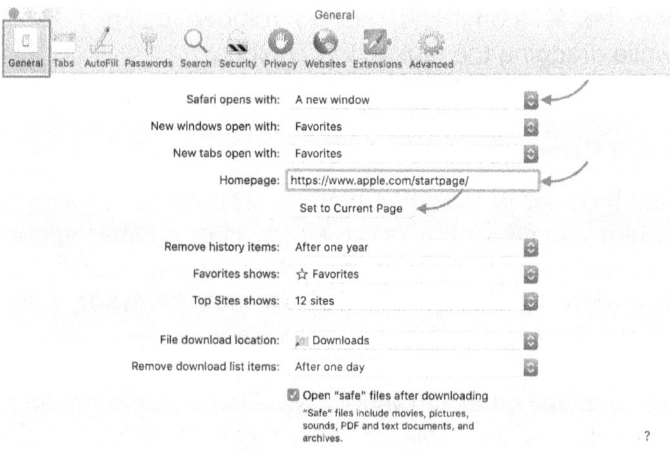

To configure your Home Page, browse to the site you want as your home page. Next, open the Safari preferences by choosing **Safari > Preferences...** or enter **⌘,** (command+,). Click the **General** icon at the top of the pane. Click **Set to Current Page** or type the URL of your desired Home Page in the field next to **Homepage**.

Choose How Safari Opens

You can configure how you want Safari to open from the General tab in the Safari preferences. Select **Safari > Preferences...** or enter **⌘,** (command+,) and select the **General** tab.

Look for **Safari opens with** at the top of the pane. You have the option to start Safari with **A new window**, **A new private window**, **All windows from last session**, or **All non-private windows from last session**. You can make your selection from the drop-down menu next to **Safari opens with**.

If you disabled the feature **Close windows when quitting an application** in the General preference pane in System Preferences, the drop-down menu will only offer to open Safari with **A new window** or **A new private window**. See the section "Stop Closed Windows from Reopening" in Chapter 19.

Choose How New Windows & Tabs Open

The drop-down menu next to **New windows open with** allows you to choose from **Favorites**, **Top Sites**, your **Homepage**, an **Empty Page**, the **Same Page** you most recently viewed, with **Tabs for Favorites**, or a set of tabs using a **Tabs folder**. The default is for Safari to open new windows with Favorites from your Favorites bookmarks folder.

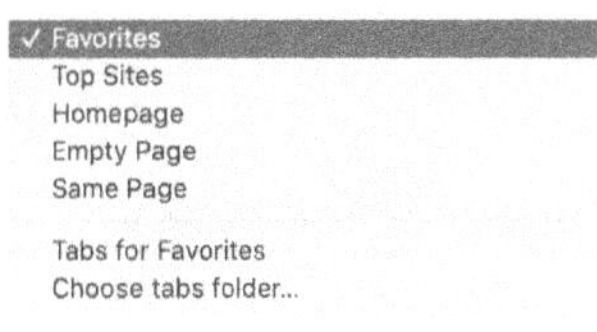

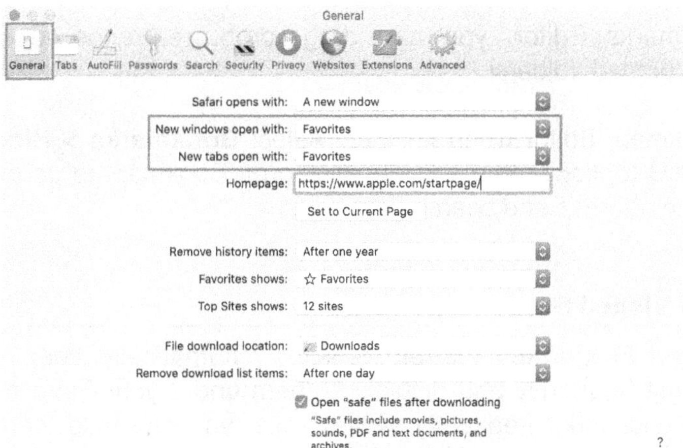

The drop-down menu next to **New tabs open with** allows you to choose from **Favorites**, **Top Sites**, your **Homepage**, an **Empty Page**, or the **Same Page** you most recently viewed. By default, Safari opens new windows and new tabs with your Favorites.

Add a Website to your Favorites

To add a website to your Favorites, click on the URL search bar to reveal your Favorites list. Drag and drop the website into your Favorites.

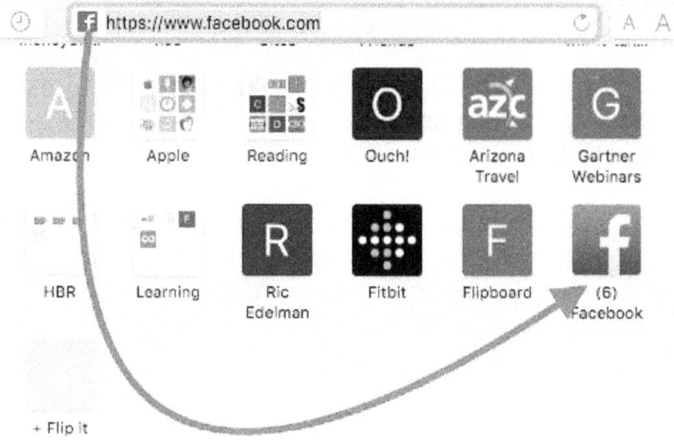

Manage Bookmarks

To manage your **Bookmarks**, select **Bookmarks > Edit Bookmarks** or enter **⌥⌘B** (option+command+B) to launch the Bookmarks Editor.

From the Bookmarks Editor, you can drag, drop, rearrange, delete, and add Bookmarks or Bookmark folders.

To hide the Bookmark Editor when finished, select **Bookmarks > Hide Bookmarks Editor**, enter **⌥⌘B** (option+command+B), click on a Bookmark to go to a website, or enter a URL in the address and search field.

Hide Frequently Visited Sites

Safari collects your **Frequently Visited** websites automatically, keeping track of the sites you visit most frequently and displaying them under your **Favorites**. If you do not want to see your most frequently visited sites, you can hide them by selecting **Bookmarks > Show Frequently Visited in Favorites**. When there is a checkmark next to this option in the drop-down menu, your Frequently Visited sites will be shown beneath your Favorites.

Show the Favorites Bar

Safari can display your Favorites when opening a new window or tab. If you want your Favorites available at all times, select **View > Show Favorites Bar** or enter **⇧⌘B** (shift+command+B). The Favorites Bar will appear directly below the Safari toolbar. Enter **⇧⌘B** (shift+command+B) to toggle the Favorites Bar off.

Select Your Favorites Source

Safari sources the websites for **Favorites** from the Favorites folder in your Bookmarks. You can change the default source for Favorites to any of your other Bookmark folders. This would come in handy if you configured Safari to display the Favorites Bar and want a Bookmarks folder to be used as your Favorites when opening a new window or tab.

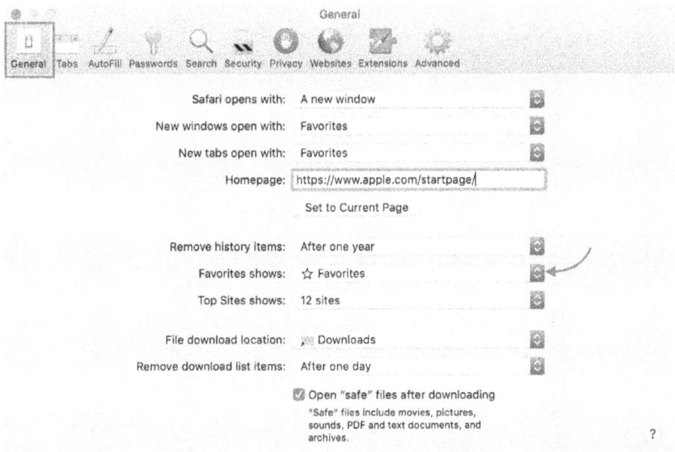

To change the folder used for Favorites, open the Safari preferences by choosing **Safari > Preferences...** or enter **⌘,** (command+,). Click on the **General** tab and select your desired folder using the drop-down menu next to **Favorites shows**.

Configure Top Sites

Top Sites is another method Safari uses to collect sites that you visit most often. You can configure Safari to keep 6, 12, or 24 sites in the Top Sites list.

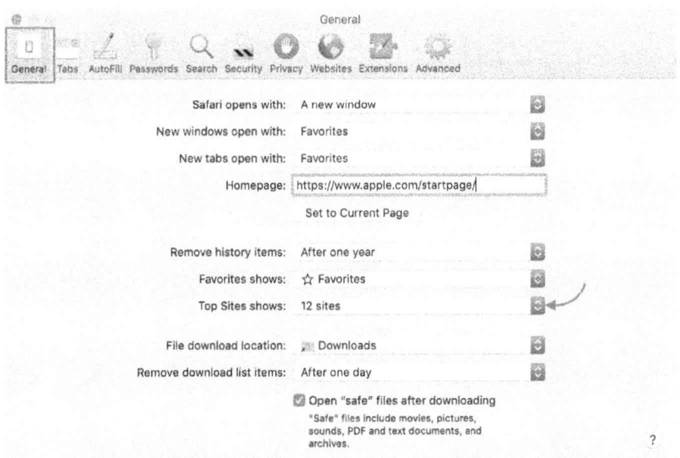

To configure the number of sites in the Top Sites list, open the Safari preferences by choosing **Safari > Preferences...** or enter **⌘,** (command+,). Click the **General** icon at the top of the pane and select 6, 12, or 24 sites in the drop-down list next to **Top Sites show**.

Add a Top Site

Adding a website to the **Top Sites** list is accomplished by dragging the website from the address and search field to the Top Sites tool on the Safari toolbar, as shown in the image below. Release your hold when the big green **+** appears.

Organize your Top Sites

To rearrange, organize, and delete your Top Sites, click on the **Top Sites** button from the Safari Favorites view.

Drag and drop the website thumbnails to rearrange them. To pin them permanently, click and hold until you see a blue stick pin appear in the upper-left corner of the thumbnail. Click on the stick pin to pin the website to your Top Sites list. Click the **X** to delete a site.

Remove Your Browsing History

Safari maintains a history of all websites you have visited. This is a handy feature if you want to return to a website but forgot to bookmark it.

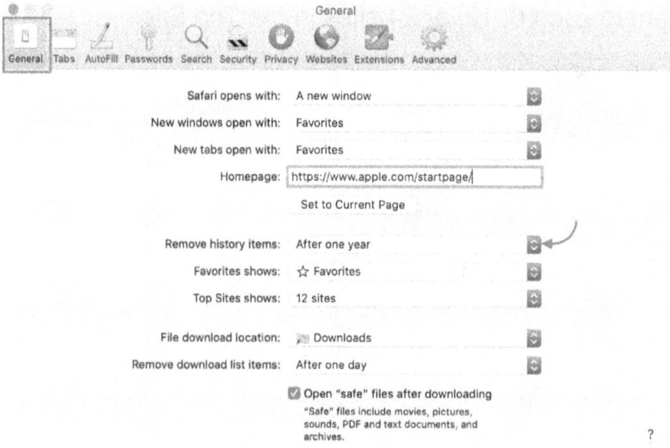

You can view your browsing history by date in Safari by selecting **History > Show History** or by entering **⌘Y** (command+Y). Select **History > Hide History** or enter **⌘Y** (command+Y) to hide your web browsing history. You can also search your web browsing history using Spotlight.

The length of time Safari keeps your history is configurable to one day, one week, two weeks, one month, one year, or manually. Make your selection from the drop-down list next to **Remove history items** in the **General** tab of the Safari preferences.

Choose Where to Save Downloads

Safari saves downloaded files to the **Downloads** folder by default. You can change this location to any folder by choosing **Other...** in the drop-down list next to **Save downloaded files to**. Navigate to your desired location and press the **Select** button. You can also configure Safari to ask you for the save location each time you download a file. Choose **Ask for each download** to select this option.

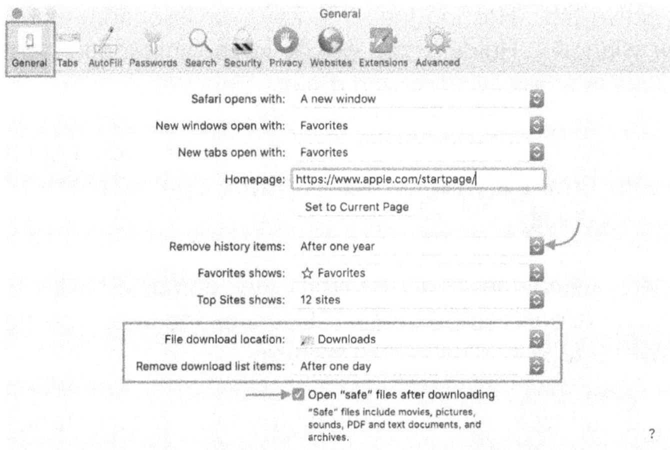

Safari maintains a list of all files downloaded. By default, this list is cleared after one day. You can configure Safari to remove this list **After one day**, **When Safari quits**, **Upon successful download**, or **Manually** in the drop-down list next to **Remove download list items**.

Safari automatically opens movies, pictures, sounds, PDF files, text documents, and archives upon downloading. You can change this behavior by unchecking the checkbox next to **Open "safe" files after downloading**.

Open Web Pages in New Windows

Safari opens new pages in tabs unless the page is designed for a specially formatted window. To configure how Safari opens new pages, open the Safari preferences by choosing **Safari > Preferences...** or enter **⌘,** (command+,). Click the **Tabs** icon at the top of the pane if it is not already selected.

Open pages in tabs instead of windows is set to **Automatically** by default. Two other configuration options are available – **Never** or **Always**. **Never** opens all pages in a new Safari window. If you choose **Always**, Safari creates a new tab even if a website requests a window of a particular size.

Holding down the ⌘ (command) key while clicking on a link opens a new tab. To turn this feature off, uncheck the checkbox next to **⌘-click opens a new link in a new tab**. Holding the ⇧⌘ keys (shift+command) when clicking on a link opens a new tab and makes it the active tab. Holding the ⇧⌥ keys (shift+option) while clicking a link opens it in a new window. Holding the ⇧⌥⌘ keys (shift+option+command) while clicking a link opens it in a new window and makes it active.

You can choose to make a new tab or new window active when it opens by checking the checkbox next to **When a new tab or window opens, make it active**. This feature is disabled by default.

You can switch tabs using the ⌘ (command) key combined with the numbers 1 through 9. This option is enabled by default. Uncheck the checkbox next to **Use ⌘-1 through ⌘-9 to switch tabs** to disable this feature.

You can configure Safari to show website icons on tabs, making it easy to see each website's logo when you are juggling multiple open tabs. Check the checkbox next to **Show website icons in tabs.**

Edit Autofill

Safari's **Autofill** feature automatically inserts data into online forms. The data includes your name, address, user name, password, credit card, or other information you previously entered into a web form. If you need to change this information because you moved, changed your login credentials, or received a new credit card, you can edit the information saved in Autofill from the Safari preference pane. Click the **Autofill** tab.

Safari will autofill information from your contacts card, which consists of your name, address, city, state, zip code, and phone number. This feature is handy when filling out shipping information when making an online purchase. To edit your contact information, click the **Edit** button next to **Using info from my Contacts card**.

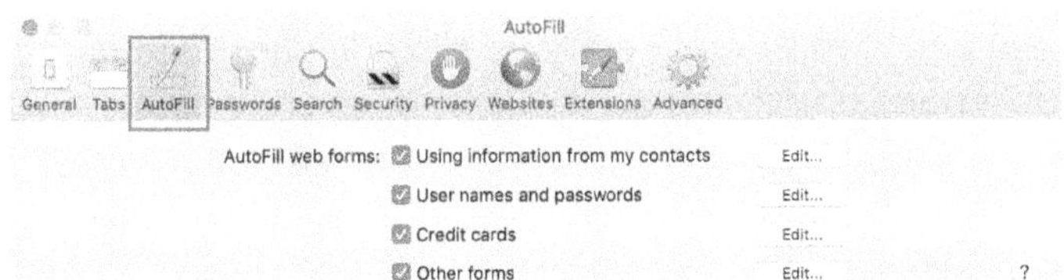

Safari securely saves your login credentials and automatically enters your user name and password when you revisit a website. To edit your login credentials, click the **Edit** button next to **User names and passwords**. Enter your password, and Safari switches to the **Password** tab where you can see the websites for which user names and passwords have or have not been stored. Double-click any item to edit your stored credentials or to **Remove** your credentials.

To add credentials for a website, click the **Add** button. Enter the URL, your user name, and password in the fields provided. You can also use the search field to find websites, user names, or passwords. To see the password for any site, double-click on the website name or highlight it with a single click and click the **Details....** button.

Safari securely saves your credit card number, expiration date, and cardholder name and automatically enters this information when needed to complete a purchase. To edit your credit card information, click the **Edit** button next to **Credit cards**. Enter your password and double-click on a stored credit card you want to edit. You can also **Add** new credit cards or **Remove** old ones. Click **Done** when finished.

The **Other forms** attribute allows Safari to save the information you entered on web forms and automatically enter the information when you revisit the web page. To view or edit, click the **Edit** button next to **Other forms**. Safari provides a list of all websites where you filled out a web form of some type. You can **Remove** any site or **Remove All**. Click **Done** when finished.

The information stored by Safari is available on your iPhone and iPad and other Macs using the same Apple ID. Information modified on any device is updated via iCloud.

View, Add, Edit, and Delete Passwords

Safari automatically stores your user name and password for websites that you visit and synchronizes them across all of your Apple devices. When you create a new account on a website, Safari offers the option to create and save a strong password for you. Safari automatically enters your user name and password, so there is no need to memorize passwords, and you can easily access your passwords through Safari's preference pane.

Safari's password feature allows you to implement a security best practice of creating a unique, strong password for every website you visit. Unfortunately, it is far too common for hackers to steal user name and password data. If you use the same password on every website, and it is stolen from one compromised website, hackers can use it to access other websites to steal your credit card data or money from your bank accounts. Using unique, strong passwords for every website ensures that your life won't be turned upside down if a data breach occurs at a website you frequent.

You can access your passwords from the Safari preference pane. Click **Passwords** at the top of the pane. You can also ask Siri by saying, "Show me my passwords," which takes you directly to the Password tab of the Safari preference pane. The pane displays a list of all websites where you saved user name and password data.

Ensure the checkbox next to **AutoFill user names and passwords** is checked to autofill your user name and password when visiting websites.

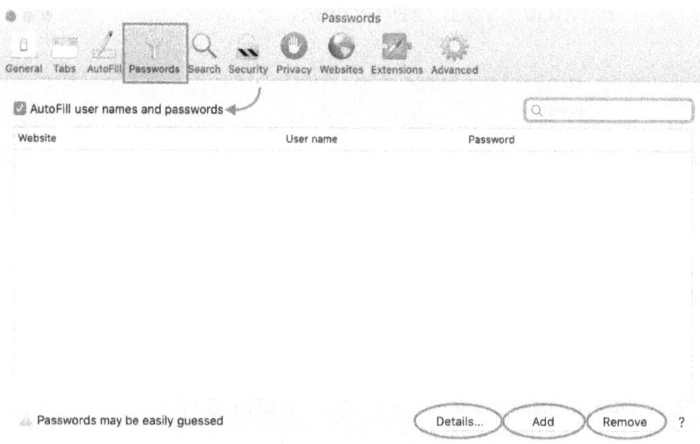

To view your user name and password for a website, click on the website in the list to highlight it and click the **Details...** button. You can add a user name and password by clicking the **Add** button to reveal a configuration sheet where you can enter the URL of the website and your user name and password. To delete a website and your credentials, click the website in the list to highlight it and click the **Remove** button.

A yellow triangle alerts you if a password is weak and easily guessed. Clicking on the triangle takes you to the website where you can change your password to a stronger one.

Help Defeat the Evil Empire

You can help defeat the Evil Empire's plans for galactic domination by configuring Safari to use a search engine other than Google. Google gathers a tremendous amount of your personal information, more than you realize, and most without your knowledge, to drive its advertising revenue. I bet you thought Google was a company that provides a free search engine. Nothing in this world is free. Google raked in $116.3 billion (yes, billion with a capital "B") in advertising revenue in 2018, making it the largest advertising company in the world. Google captured 38% of digital ad revenue in the United States and 32% of digital ad revenue worldwide according to data from Statista.com.

Google is the market leader in search with 62.5% of searches in the U.S. and 87.96% of searches worldwide done using Google's search engine. The Evil Empire tracks your searches, capturing detailed information on your search topics and which search results you clicked. Have you searched for information on a medical condition you'd like to keep private? Too late. The Evil Empire knows. Google states that its mission is "to organize the world's information and make it universally accessible and useful." That includes information that you may prefer to keep private.

It's no wonder the attorneys general of 48 states and the District of Columbia and Puerto Rico have joined an investigation into Google over possible antitrust violations due to its dominance in digital advertising and its use of consumer data. Leading Democratic presidential candidates are also calling for a breakup of Google, alleging it is a monopoly that hurts competition, invades privacy, and misuses consumer data.

If you prefer not to share information with Google, you can configure Safari to use a search engine that does not collect your personal information. Safari offers DuckDuckGo as an alternative search engine. Google's privacy policy, as of the writing of this book, is 8 pages long. DuckDuckGo's privacy policy is a mere 7 words, "We don't collect or share personal information." (https://duckduckgo.com/privacy). DuckDuckGo does not tailor search results to your previous Internet search history. Therefore you'll receive the same unfiltered results as any other DuckDuckGo user.

To configure Safari to use DuckDuckGo as its search engine, select **Safari > Preferences...** or by entering **⌘,** (command+comma). Click on **Search** and select **DuckDuckGo** using the drop-down menu next to **Search Engine.** Other options are Bing and Yahoo. However, both collect your personal data.

You can also switch to DuckDuckGo directly from the Safari search bar. Click the magnifying glass to reveal a drop-down list of search engines. Select DuckDuckGo or your desired search engine.

Configure Search Attributes

Checking the checkbox next to **Include search engine suggestions** in the Safari Search preferences allows Safari to query your chosen search engine for suggestions as you type your search terms. When the checkbox next to **Include Safari Suggestions** checked, Safari will suggest news, Wikipedia articles, music, weather, sports, stocks, and help from Apple as you type in Safari's Smart Search field.

Enable Quick Website Search lets Safari record information about your searches to speed up future searches. With this feature enabled, you can search within a website by entering the site's name, followed by the search term in Safari's search field. You can see and remove a site for which Safari recorded search information by clicking the **Manage Websites...** button. Click on any website to highlight it and click **Remove.** You have the option of removing all websites by clicking **Remove All**. Click **Done** when finished.

When **Preload Top Hit in the background** is enabled, Safari will begin to load the top search hit.

When the checkbox next to **Show favorites** is checked, Safari shows your favorite websites below the search field when you click in the Smart Search field when viewing a web page.

Block Fraudulent Websites

By default, Safari warns you if a website you are attempting to visit is suspected to be a fraudulent website running a phishing scam. Phishing is an attempt by cybercriminals to trick you into divulging personal information such as your user name, password, social security number, credit card number, banking, or other personal information.

Most phishing attempts start as a fake email that appears to be from a bank, credit card company, or major retailer, alerting you that you must take care of something immediately; otherwise, your account will be suspended or closed. The links in the email direct you to a fraudulent website that appears to be the real thing. If you enter your login credentials or other personal information, they will be captured by a cybercriminal, who will use your information to make fraudulent purchases, steal money from your accounts, or steal your identity.

Safari warns you if you visit a website that has been reported as fraudulent when the checkbox next to **Warn when visiting a fraudulent website** is checked. There is no reason to disable this security feature.

Prevent Website Tracking

Safari safeguards your privacy and can prevent advertisers from tracking your Internet travels. When you browse to a web page, your browser provides information to the website that can be used to identify you – your browser type (i.e., mobile or Desktop), operating system, browser plugins, previous webpage, Internet Service Provider, IP address, location, previous webpage's URL, download speed, CPU and GPU info, fonts, screen resolution, social media and websites you are logged into – all without your permission. All of this information taken together forms a digital fingerprint that can be used to identify you.

Apple's **Enhanced Tracking Prevention** fights fingerprinting by sharing only a simplified system profile. Safari also strips the tracking code from Twitter, Facebook, and other embedded social media content. Enhanced Tracking Prevention makes it more difficult for advertisers to gather data about your browsing habits to deliver targeted advertising to you. As you would expect advertisers are furious. Thank you, Apple!

With **Prevent cross-site tracking** enabled, website tracking data is periodically deleted, making it harder for an advertiser to track you across different websites.

By default, **Allow websites to check for Apple Pay and Apple Card** is enabled. This allows a website that uses Apple Pay to check if you have Apple Pay or and Apple Card.

Block Website Cookies

Safari allows you to block websites, third parties, and advertisers from storing cookies on your Mac. Cookies are small amounts of data that a website sends and stores on your Mac. Every time you go back to a website that sent Safari a cookie, Safari sends the cookie back. Cookies can be used to compile records of your browsing activity and can store passwords and credit card information and are, therefore, a privacy concern. Safari allows you to remove and block cookies that websites and third parties use to track you.

You have the option to **Block all cookies** in the **Privacy** tab in the Safari preference pane, which stops websites, third-party content providers, and advertisers from storing cookies on your Mac. However, doing so often prevents many websites from working. For example, your bank's website will not recognize you and may ask challenge questions to verify your identity or may not work at all.

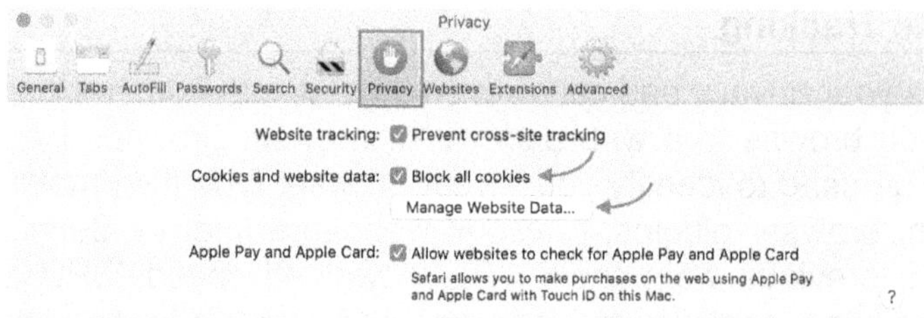

You probably already have cookies stored on your Mac. Safari lets you see which websites have stored cookies on your Mac and remove some or all of them. Click **Manage Website Data...** to see which websites have stored cookies on your Mac.

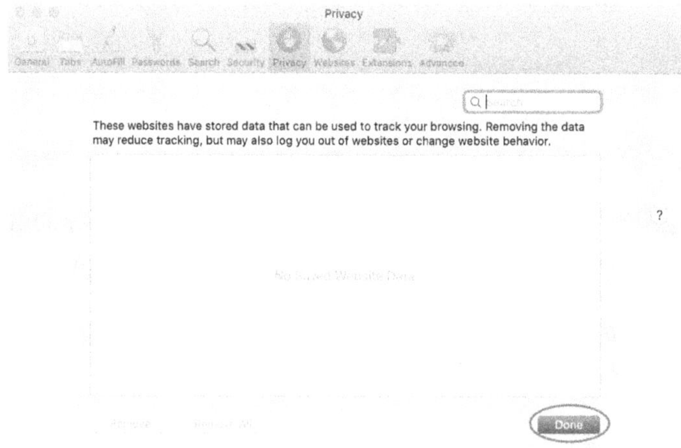

To remove individual website cookies, select the website and click **Remove**. You also have the option to **Remove All**. Click **Done** when finished. It is a good idea to delete cookies from your Mac periodically.

Configure Website Preferences

Safari allows you to customize settings to control how websites interact with Safari when you are browsing the web. From the Safari preference pane, you can customize settings to control pop-up windows, advertising, location tracking, content blocking, and which sites are allowed to download content to your Mac.

Many settings can be configured on-the-fly when you visit a website using **Website Preferences** tool in the Safari toolbar. To learn how to install the Website Preferences tool, see the section "Customize the Toolbar" at the beginning of this chapter.

Display Web Pages without Annoying Ads

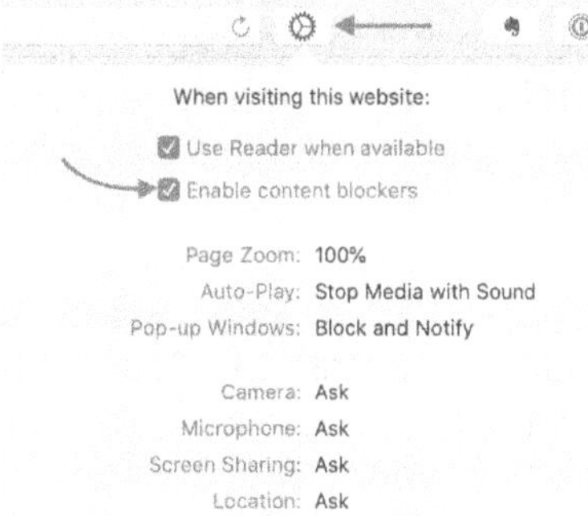

Nothing is more annoying than a web page filled with obnoxiously large amounts of advertising. Safari can be configured to default to **Safari Reader**, which removes the annoying advertising to display a clean, readable version of a website article.
To force a website to use Safari Reader, click the Website Preferences tool in the Safari toolbar and check the checkbox next to **Use Reader when available.** Once you have made your selection, click anywhere to make this dialog box disappear.

To configure websites to default to Safari Reader, open the Safari preference pane by selecting **Safari > Preferences...** or enter **⌘,** (command+,). Click on the **Websites** tab and then select **Reader** in the sidebar. The right pane populates with a list of websites and their Safari Reader configuration. Select **On** or **Off** in the drop-down menu to the right of each website. **On** configures the website to use the Safari Reader by default for all content.

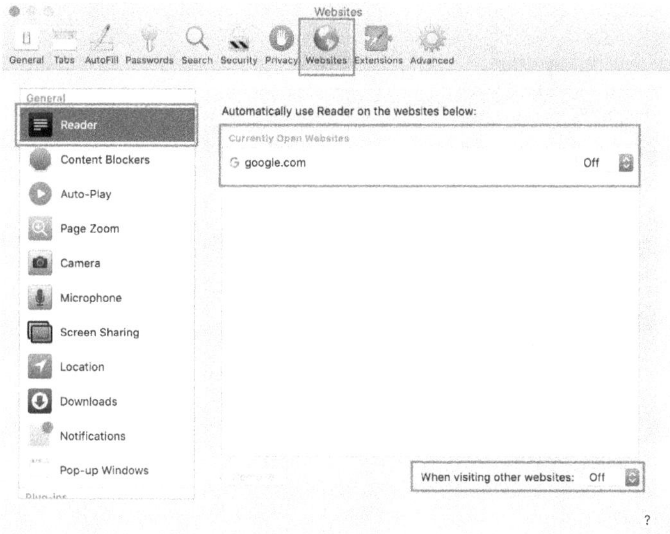

If you want to delete a website from the list, highlight it and click the **Remove** button. To configure Safari to always default to the Safari Reader view, select **On** from the drop-down list next to **When visiting other websites**. Website articles will use Safari Reader automatically, allowing you to enjoy ad-free web browsing.

Configure Content Blocking

Safari's content blocker blocks annoying advertisements and third-party tracking scripts to protect your privacy and enhance your web browsing experience.

To enable Content Blocking for any website, click on the Website Preferences tool in the Safari toolbar and check the checkbox next to **Enable content blockers.** Once you have made your selection, click anywhere to make this dialog box disappear.

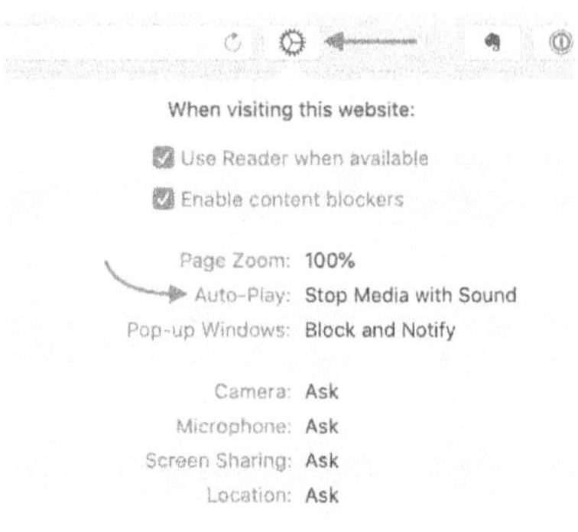

To ensure your content blocker is enabled for all websites, open the Safari preference pane by selecting **Safari > Preferences...** or enter **⌘,** (command+,). Click on the **Websites** tab and then select **Content Blockers** in the sidebar. The right pane populates with a list of websites and their content blocker setting.

To change a setting, select **On** or **Off** from the drop-down menu next to the website name. On blocks ads and other unwanted content from appearing on the website. Off allows ads and other unwanted content.

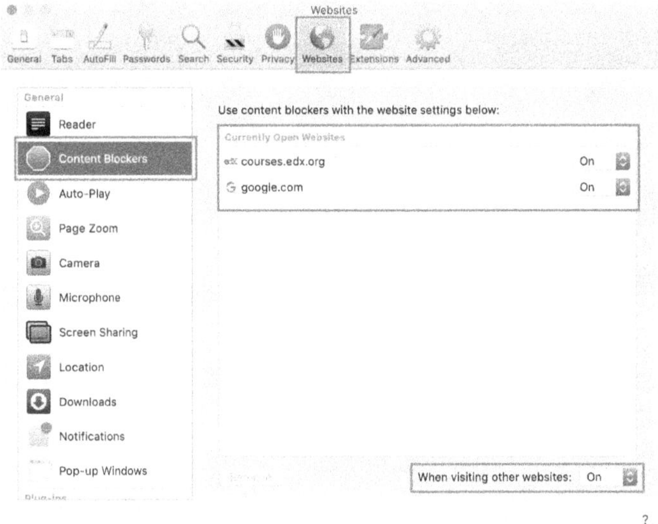

If you want to delete a website from the list, highlight it and click the **Remove** button.

To enable your content blocker for all websites, select **On** from the drop-down menu next to **When visiting other websites** in the lower-right corner.

Stop Auto-Play Videos

There is nothing worse than opening a bunch of tabs in Safari and then being assaulted by a cacophony of video blaring out of your speakers. You don't have to hunt down each one to kill or mute the annoyance because Safari lets you selectively block auto-play.

To configure auto-play settings for a website, click on the Website Preferences tool in the Safari toolbar, and select your desired setting next to **Auto-Play**. Options include **Allow All Auto-Play**, **Stop Media with Sound**, and **Never Auto-Play**. Once you have made your selection, click anywhere to make this dialog box disappear.

To review or change your Auto-Play settings, open the Safari preference pane by selecting **Safari > Preferences...** or enter **⌘,** (command+,). Click on the **Websites** tab and then select **Auto-Play** in the sidebar. The right pane populates with a list of websites and their corresponding auto-play settings.

To change any individual setting, use the drop-down menu to the right of the website name. You have the choice of **Allow All Auto-Play**, **Stop Media with Sound**, and **Never Auto-Play.**

If you want to delete a website from the list, highlight it and click the **Remove** button.

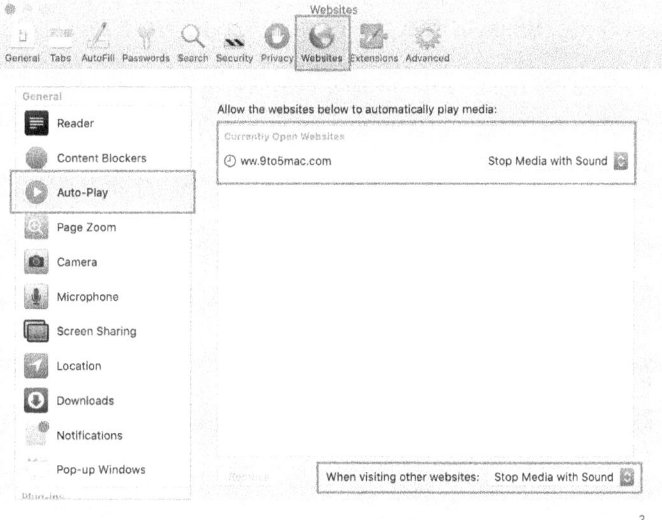

To block auto-play video for all websites, select **Never Auto-Play** from the drop-down menu next to **When visiting other websites** in the lower-right corner.

Configure Website Page Zoom

You can set the page zoom in Safari to make text and images appear larger (or smaller). Page zoom can be set individually by website, or you can set a default page zoom for all websites.

To set the page zoom for a website, click on the Website Preferences tool in the Safari toolbar, and choose your desired setting from the drop-down menu next to **Page Zoom**. You have the choice of 50%, 75%, 85%, 100%, 115%, 125%, 150%, 175%, 200%, 250%, and 300%. Once you have made your selection, click anywhere to make this dialog box disappear. Once you have made your selection, click anywhere to make this dialog box disappear.

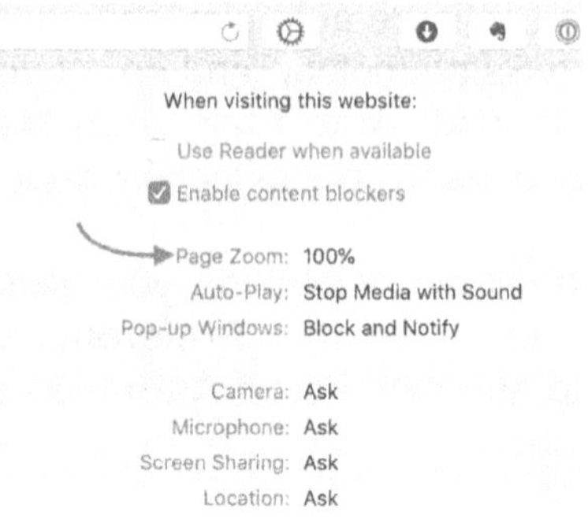

To review or change the page zoom for websites, open the Safari preference pane by selecting **Safari > Preferences...** or enter **⌘,** (command+,). Click on the **Websites** tab and then select **Page Zoom** in the sidebar. The right pane populates with a list of currently open websites and those for which you have configured a page zoom policy. To change any individual setting, use the drop-down menu to the right of the website name. You can choose from the following zoom options: 50%, 75%, 85%, 100%, 115%, 125%, 150%, 175%, 200%, 250%, and 300%.

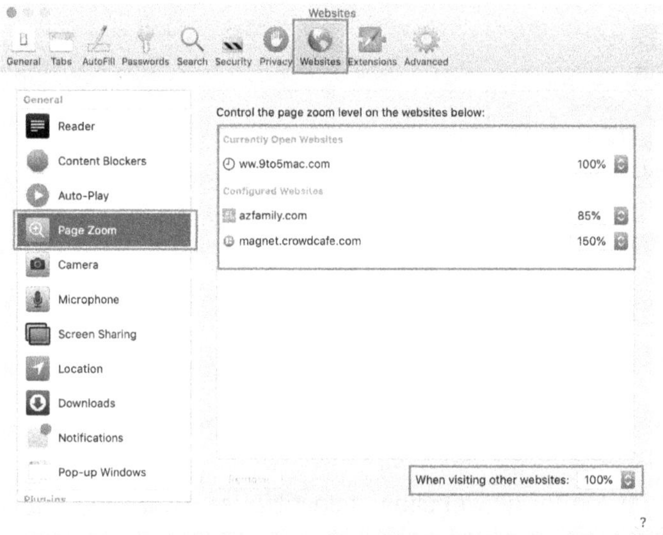

If you want to delete a website from the list, highlight it and click the **Remove** button.

To set the default page zoom for all websites, select your desired page zoom setting from the drop-down menu next to **When visiting other websites** in the lower-right corner.

Control Camera, Microphone, & Screen Sharing

Safari allows you to control access to your Mac's camera, microphone, and screen. To set these preferences for a website, click on the Website Preferences tool in the Safari toolbar, and choose your desired settings from the drop-down menus next to **Camera**, **Microphone**, and **Screen Sharing**. Available options for the camera and microphone are **Ask**, **Deny**, or **Allow**, while screen sharing options are **Ask** and **Deny**. Once you have made your selection, click anywhere to make the dialog box disappear.

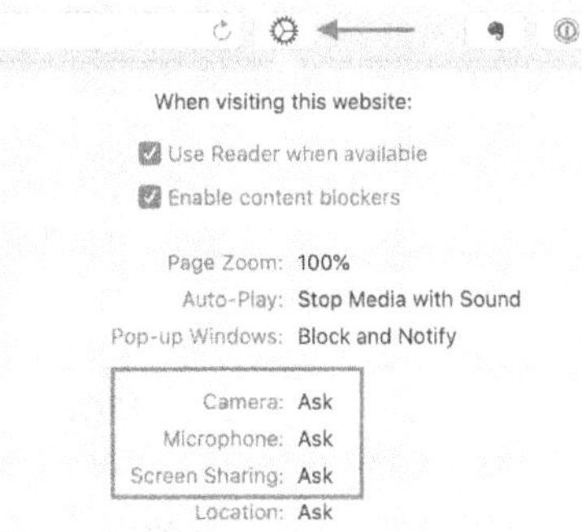

To review or change the camera, microphone, and screen sharing settings for websites, open the Safari preference pane by selecting **Safari > Preferences…** or enter **⌘,** (command+,). Click on the **Websites** tab and select **Camera**, **Microphone**, or **Screen Sharing** in the sidebar. The right pane populates with a list of websites and their settings. Use the drop-down menu to the right of the website and select **Ask**, **Deny**, or **Allow** for the camera and microphone settings. For screen sharing, your options are **Ask** or **Deny**.

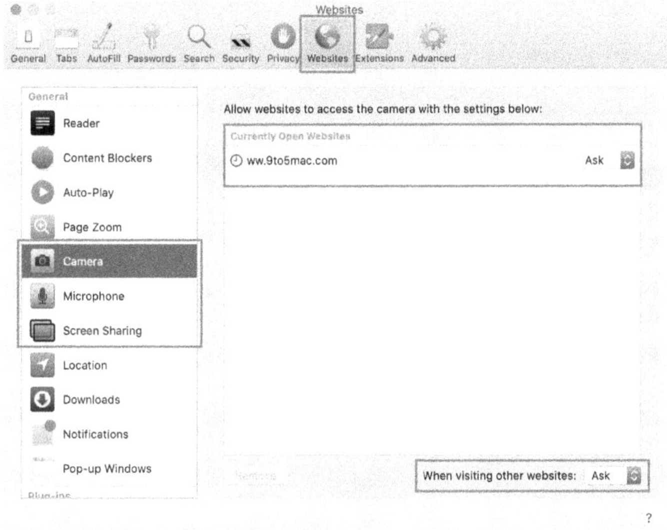

If you want to delete a website from the list, highlight it and click the **Remove** button.

To set the default camera, microphone, and screen sharing settings for websites, select your desired setting from the drop-down menu next to **When visiting other websites** in the lower-right corner of the preference pane.

Stop Websites from Snooping on Your Location

Websites can spy on your location. This can be quite handy if location information is necessary to deliver relevant content like the local weather, news, or nearby businesses. However, sometimes there is absolutely no reason for a particular website to know your location. Safari can be configured to ask your permission before providing your location information to a website asking for it.

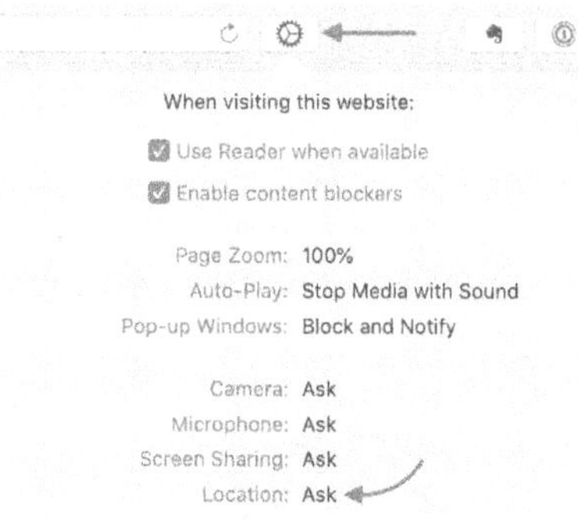

To stop a website from getting for your location data, click on the Website Preferences tool in the Safari toolbar and choose **Ask**, **Deny**, or **Allow** from the drop-down menu next to **Location**. The default is **Ask**. Once you have made your selection, click anywhere to make this dialog box disappear.

You can review and change your location settings in Safari preferences by selecting **Safari > Preferences...** or enter **⌘,** (command+,). Select **Websites** and click on **Location** in the sidebar. You will see a list of the websites for which you have configured a location policy in the right pane. A drop-down menu to the right of each website lets you select a location policy – **Ask**, **Allow**, or **Deny**. You can change the action for any website using this drop-down menu.

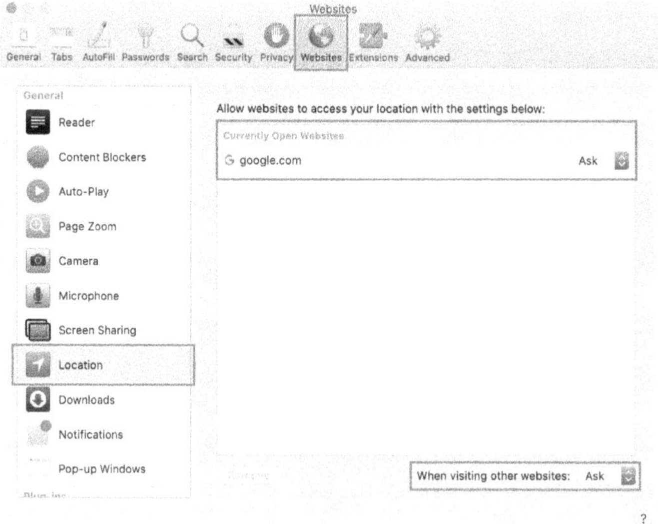

If you want to delete a website from the list, highlight it and click the **Remove** button.

Set the default policy for websites requesting your location data using the drop-down menu next to **When visiting other websites** in the lower-right corner. To stop all websites from snooping on your location, select **Deny** from the drop-down menu. You also have the option of **Ask** or **Allow**. When **Ask** is selected, Safari asks you if you want to provide your location each time a website requests your location.

Allow Downloads

Safari allows you to control which websites you will let download content to your Mac. The first time you download content from a website, macOS asks you if you want to allow downloads from the website. If you click allow, your content will be downloaded and your choice will become the default setting for that website.

You can review and change your download settings in Safari preferences by selecting **Safari > Preferences...** or enter **⌘,** (command+,). Select **Websites** and click on **Downloads** in the sidebar. You will see a list of the websites for which you have configured a download policy in the right pane. A drop-down menu to the right of each website lets you select a download policy – **Ask**, **Allow**, or **Deny**. You can change the download setting for any website using this drop-down menu.

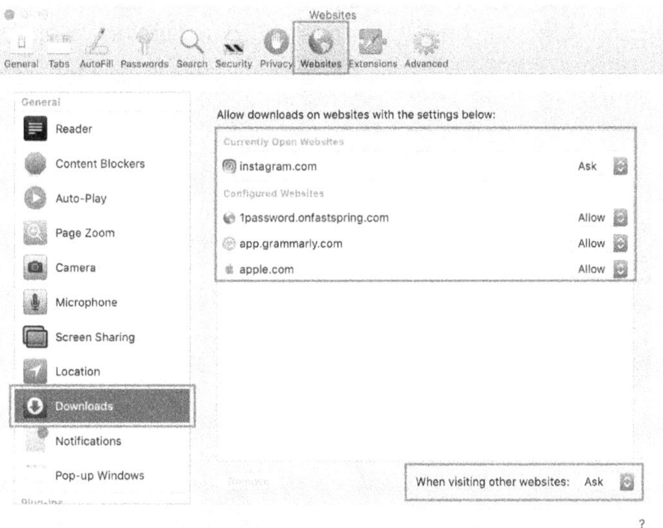

If you want to delete a website from the list, highlight it and click the **Remove** button.

Set the default policy for websites downloading content to your Mac using the drop-down menu next to **When visiting other websites** in the lower-right corner. Your options are **Ask**, **Deny**, or **Allow**. When **Ask** is selected, Safari asks you to allow downloading each time a website tries to download content to your Mac.

Configure Push Notifications

Websites utilizing Apple's push notification service can send notifications of breaking news, sports scores, a new post, or other info directly to your Desktop, even if Safari isn't running. By default, Safari notifications appear as a Banner on your Desktop and are saved to Notification Center. Clicking on them takes you to the website that pushed the notification to you.

If you remember from the Notifications Center chapter, a Banner appears in the upper-right corner of your Desktop and disappears automatically after a set amount of time. You can change how Safari notifies you, including disabling notifications entirely, from the **Notifications** preference pane in System Preferences. After opening the Notifications preference pane, click and highlight **Safari** in the left sidebar.

To disable Safari notifications entirely, toggle the switch next to **Allow notifications from Safari** to the off position. Once notifications are disabled, all configuration options in the Notification preference pane will be grayed out.

If you want to customize Safari notifications, ensure the switch next to **Allow notifications from Safari** is in the on position, as shown in the image below. The default alert style is Banners, which is highlighted in blue. You can change the style to an Alert by clicking on **Alerts**. An Alert stays on your Desktop until you respond or dismiss it. If you do not want Safari to send notifications to your Desktop, choose **None**. When configured to **None**, notifications no longer appear on your Desktop, but will be saved to Notification Center.

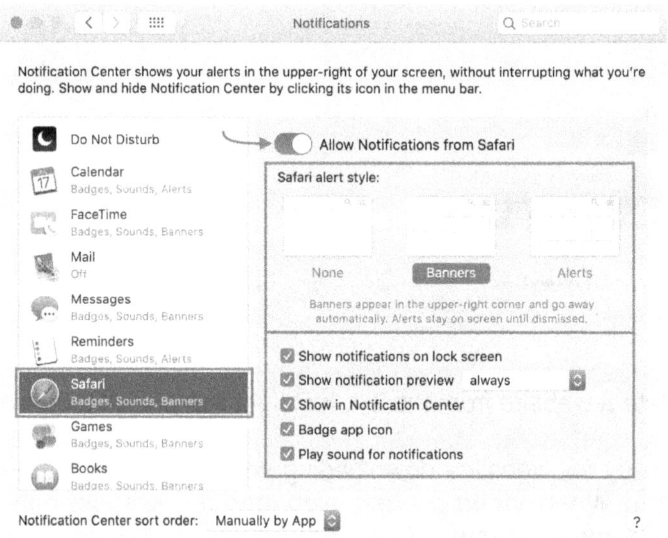

Once you have chosen your alert style, you can configure the various options shown below **Safari Alert Style**. The options are **Show notifications on lock screen**, **Show notification preview**, **Show in Notification Center**, **Badge app icon**, and **Play sound for notifications**. All of the checkboxes are checked by default.

Notifications received when your Mac was asleep appear on the login window when you wake your Mac. If you want to disable this feature, uncheck the checkbox next to **Show notifications on lock screen.** When you disable this feature, the drop-down menu next to **Show notification preview** disappears.

If you decide to keep **Show notifications on lock screen** enabled, you can choose when to show Mail notification previews from the drop-down menu next to **Show notification preview.** The default option is **always**, which displays notification previews on the login screen. The second option is **when unlocked**, which displays notification previews only when you are logged in to your Mac.

By default, the **Show in Notification Center** option is checked, which means Safari notifications will be saved in Notification Center. You have the option of disabling this feature by unchecking the checkbox. If you do so, you will only see Safari notifications on your Desktop and only if the alert style is set to **Banners** or **Alerts**.

The **Badge app icon** option displays the number of notifications in a red circular badge on the Safari icon in the **Dock**. Safari must be in the Dock for badges to appear. If you don't want the Safari app icon badged, uncheck this checkbox.

Safari notifications play a sound when they appear. If you prefer silent notifications, uncheck the checkbox next to **Play sound for notifications**.

Opt-In to Safari Notifications

Before a website can send you push notifications, you must choose to opt-in. If a website supports push notifications, you'll be asked if you would like to receive notifications when browsing to the website in Safari. Click **Allow** to opt-in or **Don't Allow** to opt-out. Don't worry. You can always change your mind later. If you no longer find notifications from a particular website useful, you can opt-out. Similarly, if you opted out, you can opt back in.

To change your Safari notification choice, launch **Safari** and open the Safari preference pane by selecting **Safari > Preferences...** or by entering **⌘,** (command+comma). Select **Websites**. The websites that have asked for permission to send push notifications are listed. Next to each website is a drop-down menu with two choices: **Allow** and **Deny** with the current status displayed. Use the drop-down menu to change your selection.

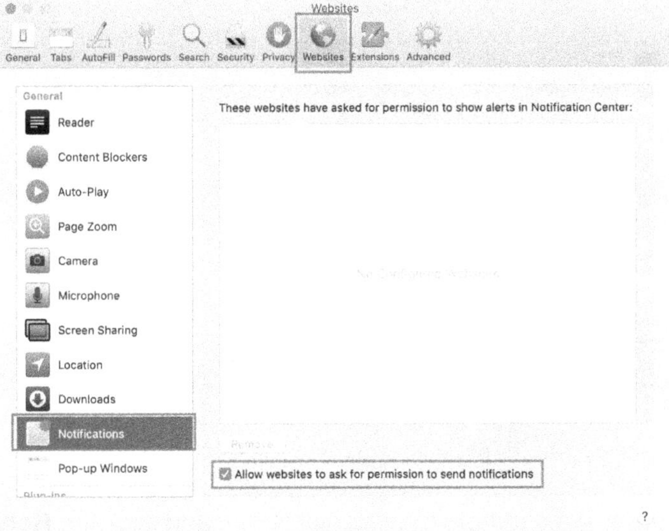

If you want to delete a website from the list, highlight it and click the **Remove** button. If you would prefer that websites not ask you to opt-in to their push notification service, uncheck the checkbox next to **Allow websites to ask for permission to send push**

notifications. Checking this checkbox stops websites from asking if you want to receive notifications from them.

Stop Annoying Pop-Up Windows

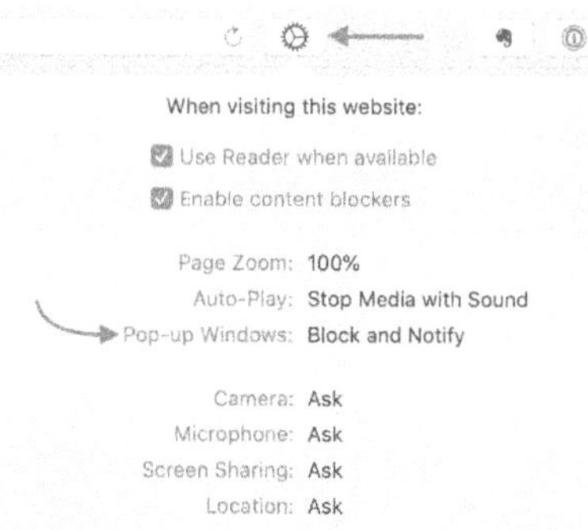

Safari blocks annoying pop-up windows and notifies you with a small pop-up window icon in Safari's address and search bar. However, some websites use pop-up windows to display essential content. Safari allows you to selectively block or allow pop-ups from specific websites.

To change the pop-up blocker configuration for a specific website, add the **Website Preferences** tool to your Safari toolbar. Click on the Website Preferences tool and choose **Allow**, **Deny**, or **Block and Notify** from the drop-down menu next to **Pop-up Windows**. The default is **Block and Notify**. Once you have made your selection, click anywhere to make this menu disappear.

You can also configure pop-up blocking from the Safari preference pane by clicking the **Websites** tab and selecting **Pop-up Windows** in the sidebar. You will see a list of currently open websites. Use the drop-down menu to the right of each website to choose **Block and Notify**, **Block**, or **Allow** pop-ups.

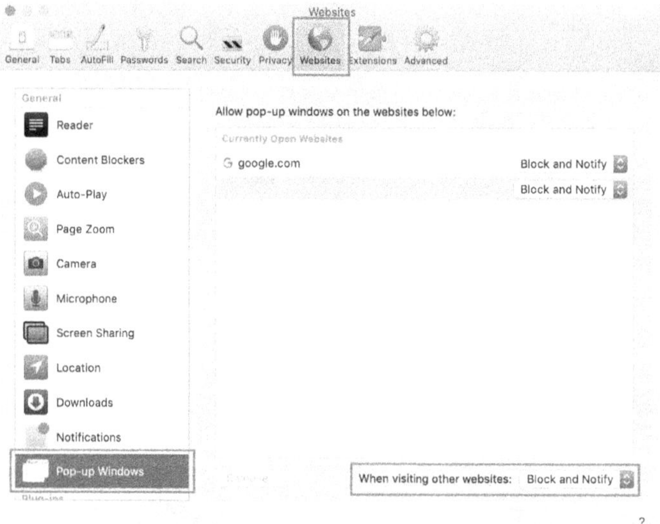

If you want to delete a website from the list, highlight it and click the **Remove** button.

You can change the default method for handling pop-up windows using the drop-down menu next to **When visiting other websites** in the lower-right corner.

Configure Policies for Internet Plug-Ins

You can control whether Safari will show plug-in content on websites. Plug-ins are used to show pictures, music, videos, animation, and other interactive features.

To see which plug-ins have been installed and which websites are using them, open the Safari preference pane. Select the **Websites** tab at the top of the pane. Next, scroll down to the **Plug-ins** in the sidebar and select a plug-in. The right pane populates with a list of websites for which you have configured a plug-in policy. To change any individual setting, use the drop-down menu to the right of the website name. You have the choice of **Ask**, **Off**, or **On**.

The **Ask** setting will configure Safari to ask you if the website can use the plug-in. When set to **Off**, Safari will display a placeholder instead of the plug-in content. Clicking on the placeholder allows the website to use the plug-in one time. The **On** setting lets the website always use the plug-in.

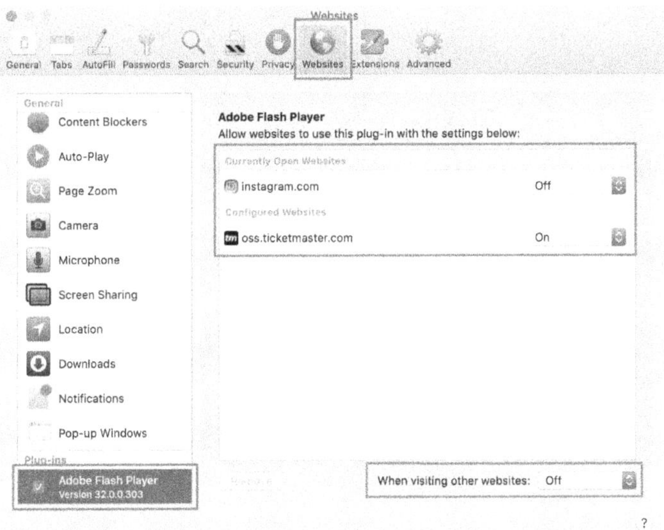

If you want to delete a website from the list, highlight it and click the **Remove** button.

To configure a global policy for an Internet plug-in, select **Ask**, **Off**, or **On** from the drop-down list next to **When visiting other websites** in the lower-right corner.

Manage Third-party Extensions

Extensions are small applications created by third-party developers to enhance your web browsing experience.

The **Extensions** tab in the Safari preference pane allows you to selectively enable or disable an extension, configure them if they have options, or uninstall them. This pane will be empty until you have installed your first Safari extension.

The Extensions in the sidebar shows the extensions that have been installed. You can select an extension to show any available options or to **uninstall** it. To disable an installed extension, uncheck its checkbox in the sidebar.

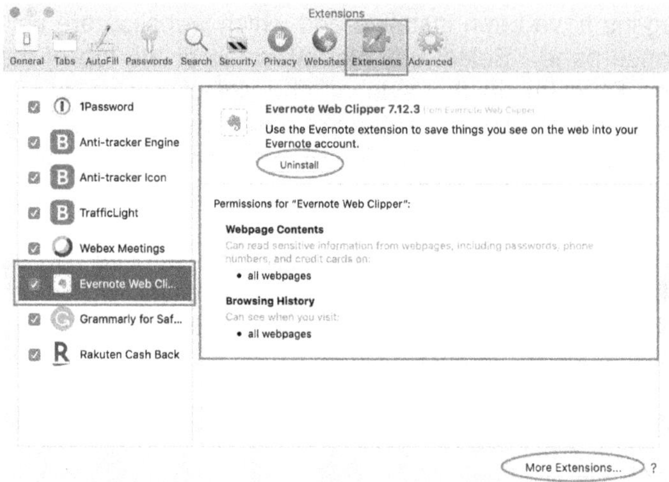

The **More Extensions...** button in the lower-right opens the Mac App Store, where you can find extensions to add new features to Safari. Extensions can be installed with one click, and there is no need to restart Safari.

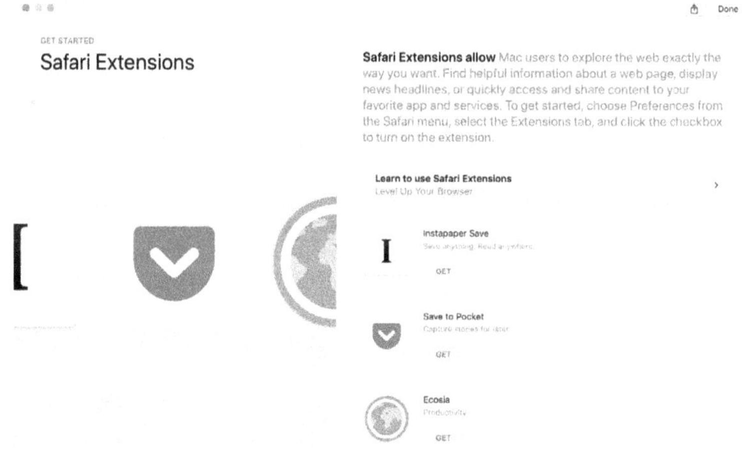

Display the Full URL

One of the features of Safari's streamlined design is that it does not show the full URL in its address and search field. Safari only displays the domain name, such as apple.com.

To configure Safari to always display the full URL, select **Safari > Preferences...** or by entering **⌘,** (command+,) to open the Safari preference pane. Click the **Advanced** tab at the top of the pane if it is not already selected. Check the box next to **Show full website address** next to **Smart Search Field**.

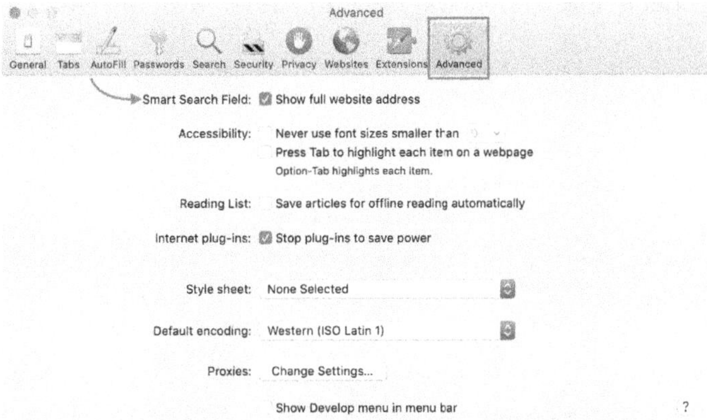

If you need to copy URL, clicking in the Safari Smart Search field reveals the entire URL, already highlighted to make it easier to copy.

Set a Minimum Font Size

Have trouble reading small text on some web pages? Safari lets you set the minimum font size.

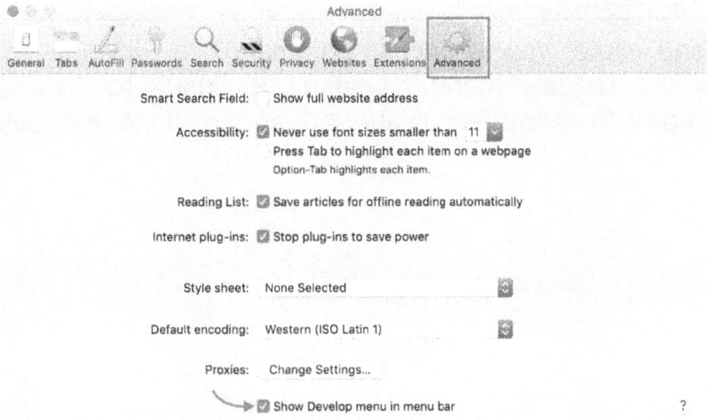

To set a minimum font size for text on web pages, check the checkbox next to **Never use font sizes smaller than** and select a font size from the drop-down menu. Your options are 9-, 10-, 11-, 12-, 14-, 18- and 24-point fonts. If you are unsure which font size you should choose, start with 11 or 12 points. Note that this feature will change the appearance of some web pages.

Save Articles for Offline Reading

If you want to save web pages in Safari's Reading List so you can read them when you are offline, check the checkbox next to **Save articles for offline reading automatically**.

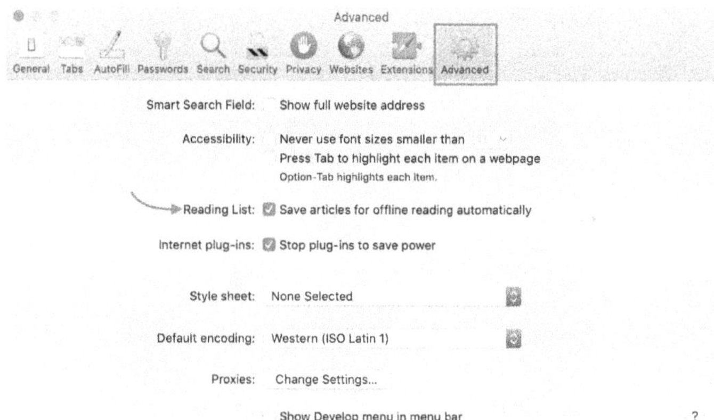

You can access your saved content from the Safari Reading List in the Sidebar. Enter **⇧⌘L** (shift+command+L) or select **View > Show Sidebar** to display the Sidebar. Click the icon that looks like a pair of reading glasses to see your reading list.

Show the Develop Menu

The **Develop Menu** allows you to access commands for developing websites with Safari. By default, the Develop Menu is hidden. To unhide the Develop menu, click **Show Develop menu in menu bar** in the **Advanced** tab of the Safari preference pane.

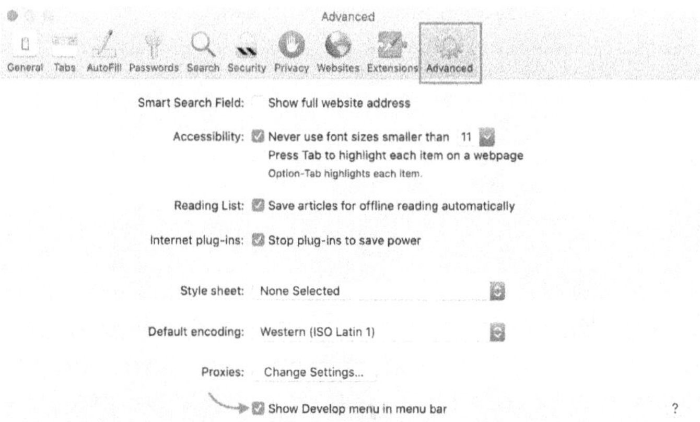

Pin a Web Site to the Tab Bar

The **Pinned Sites** feature allows you to pin your most frequently visited sites to the left side of the tab bar. Pinned sites refresh in the background, so they are always up to date. This feature is especially useful if you have a few websites that you like to visit throughout the day, like Facebook or a news site.

To pin a site to the Tab Bar, open the website in a Safari tab. Secondary click on the tab and select **Pin Tab** from the contextual menu. The pinned site moves to the left end of the Safari tab bar, joining your other pinned sites. Pinned sites can be rearranged by dragging them.

You can also pin a site by dragging the site's tab to the left and dropping it there. Once a site is pinned, you can quickly access it from any Safari window.

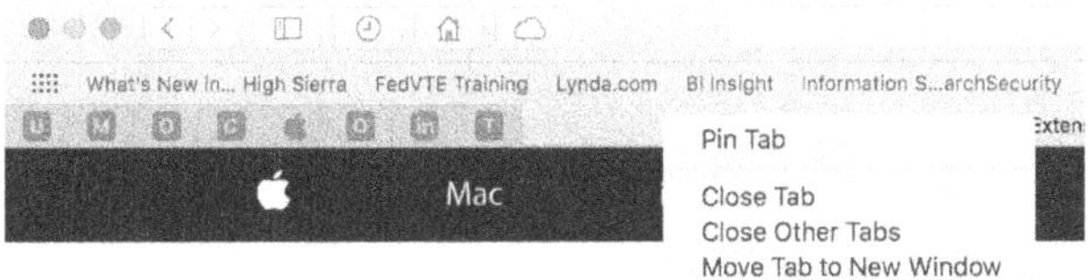

To unpin a site, secondary click on it and select **Unpin Tab**. The tab expands into a full-sized Safari tab. You can also drag the pinned tab to the right. To permanently close a pinned tab, select **Close Tab**.

Clear Web Browsing History

Safari offers the capability to delete your browsing history, cookies, and other website data. **Safari** makes this task much easier to accomplish. Also, you have control over the time period that you wish to delete.

To delete your web browsing history, cookies, and other website data, select **Clear History...** from the **Safari** menu. A dialog box appears, allowing you to choose to clear data from four different time periods: **the last hour**, **today**, **today, and yesterday**, or **all history**. Click the **Clear History** button to clear your web browsing history.

17

Mail

The default mail client in macOS is an application called **Mail**. Other than the configuration of mail accounts, Mail requires little customization and can be used "out-of-the-box." However, you can customize Mail to fine-tune it, change its appearance, and make it perform a little better to increase your productivity.

Change the Mail Application

Mail is the default mail client in macOS. The default mail client is the application that launches when you want to send an email from another application or web link. If you prefer to use another email client, Apple allows you to choose one.

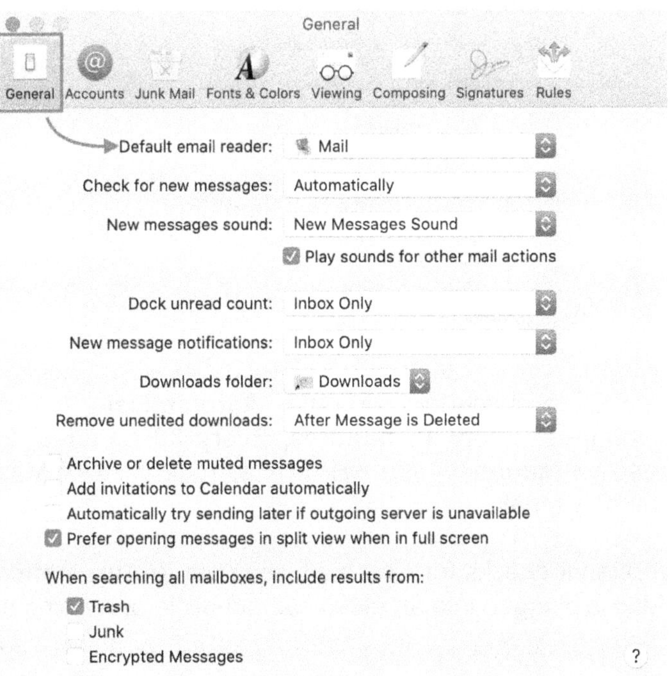

To change the default email client, open the Mail preference pane by choosing **Mail > Preferences...** or by entering **⌘,** (command+,). Click the **General** icon at the top of the pane if it is not already selected. Choose your desired mail client from the drop-down list next to **Default email reader**.

For email clients to populate the list, you first need to download and install an alternate mail client. Options include Spark by Readdle (my personal choice), Mail for Gmail, and Microsoft Outlook. If you don't see your mail client listed in the drop-down menu, choose **Select...** to open a Finder window to locate your email application.

Change How Frequently Mail Checks for New Email

To change the frequency with which **Mail** checks for new email, open the Mail preference pane by choosing **Mail > Preferences...** or enter **⌘,** (command+,). Click the **General** icon at the top of the pane if it is not already selected.

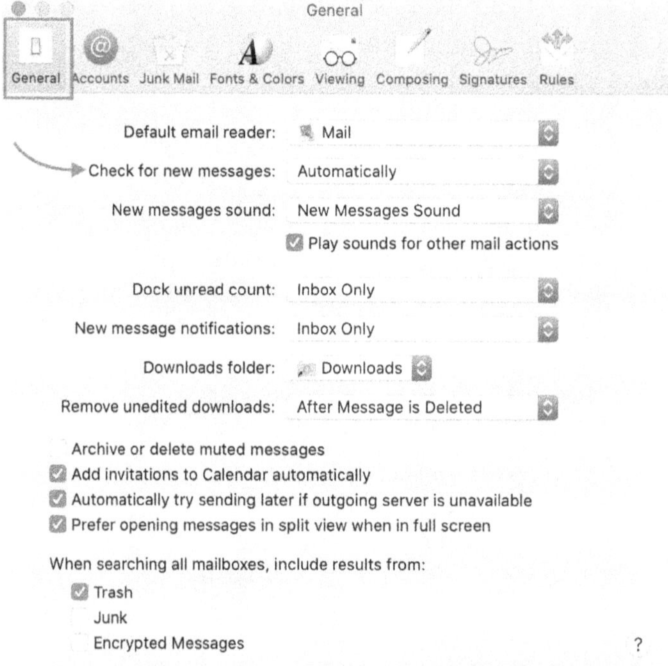

You can configure Mail to check for new email **Automatically** (the default), **Every minute**, **Every 5 minutes**, **Every 15 minutes**, **Every 30 minutes**, **Every hour**, or **Manually**. If you select **Manually**, you will have to click the **Get Mail** button in the Toolbar to check for new email.

Mail will vary how often it checks for new mail when set to **Automatically** depending on whether your Mac is plugged into an electrical recepticle or running on battery.

Change the New Mail Sound

You can select the sound when a new message arrives. Mail can also be configured to be silent. Use the drop-down list in the General tab in the Mail preference pane to select your new message sound.

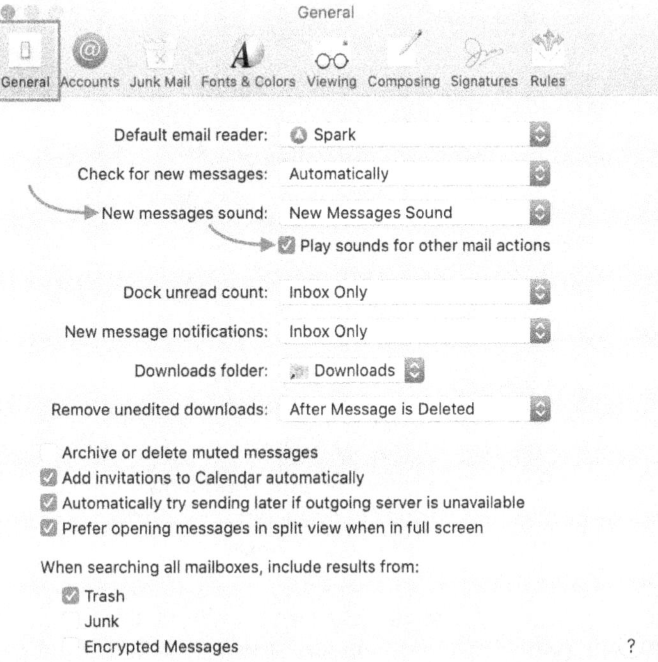

Uncheck the checkbox next to **Play sounds for other mail actions** if you want to disable sounds for other mail actions such as the sound when Mail sends an email.

Change Mail Notifications

When a new email arrives, macOS will display a notification on your Desktop. By default, the Mail notification style is a Banner. If you remember from the Notifications Center chapter, a Banner appears in the upper-right corner of your Desktop and disappears automatically after a set amount of time.

You can change how Mail notifies you, including disabling notifications entirely, from the **Notifications** preference pane in System Preferences. After opening the Notifications preference pane, click and highlight **Mail** in the sidebar.

To disable Mail notifications entirely, toggle the switch next to **Allow notifications from Mail** to the off position. Once notifications are disabled, all the configuration options in the Notification preference pane will be grayed out.

If you want to customize Mail notifications, ensure the switch next to **Allow notifications from Mail** is in the on position, as shown in the image on the next page.

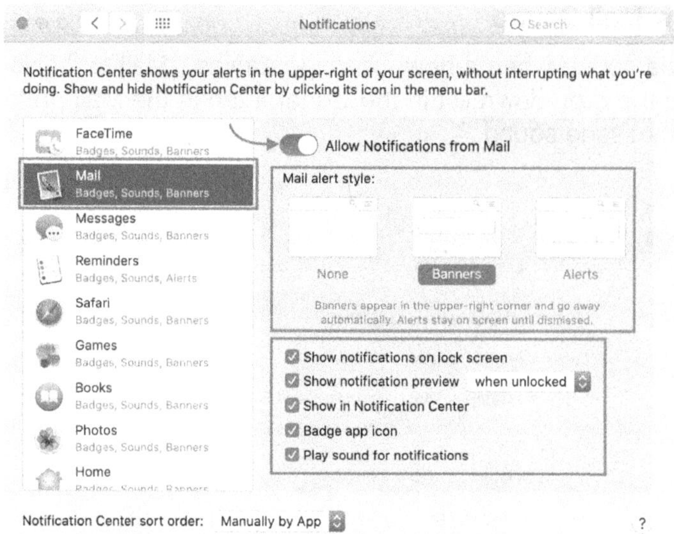

The default alert style is Banner, which is highlighted in blue. You can change the style to an Alert by clicking on **Alerts**. An Alert stays on your Desktop until you respond or dismiss it. If you do not want Mail to send notifications to your Desktop, choose **None**. When configured to **None**, Mail notifications will no longer appear on your Desktop, but will be saved to Notification Center.

Once you have chosen your alert style, you can configure the various options shown below the **Mail Alert Style**. The options are **Show notifications on lock screen**, **Show notification preview**, **Show in Notification Center**, **Badge app icon**, and **Play sound for notifications**. All of the checkboxes are checked by default.

Mail notifications received when your Mac was asleep will appear on the login window when you wake it. This creates a potential privacy issue. If you want to disable this feature, uncheck the checkbox next to **Show notifications on lock screen.** When you disable this feature, the drop-down menu next to **Show notification preview** disappears.

If you decide to keep **Show notifications on lock screen** enabled, you can choose when to show Mail notification previews from the drop-down menu next to **Show notification preview.** The default option is **always**, which displays Mail notification previews on the login screen. The second option is **when unlocked**, which displays previews only when you are logged in.

If the **Show in Notification Center** option is checked, Mail notifications are saved in Notification Center. You have the option of disabling this feature by unchecking the checkbox. If you do so, you will only see notifications on your Desktop and only if the alert style is set to **Banners** or **Alerts**.

The **Badge app icon** option displays the number of notifications in a red circular badge on the Mail icon in the **Dock**. Mail must be in the Dock for badges to appear. If you don't want the Mail icon badged, uncheck this checkbox.

Mail notifications play a sound when they appear. If you prefer silent notifications, uncheck the checkbox next to **Play sound for notifications**.

Change How the Mail Icon is Badged

If you configured Mail to display a badge showing the unread message count on its Dock icon, you can configure how Mail badges its icon.

Using the drop-down menu next to **Dock unread count**, you can choose to display the unread message count in your **Inbox Only**, across **All Mailboxes,** or unread messages received **Today**. Note that a badge appears on the Mail icon when the checkbox next to **Badge app icon** is checked in the Notifications preference pane in System Preferences.

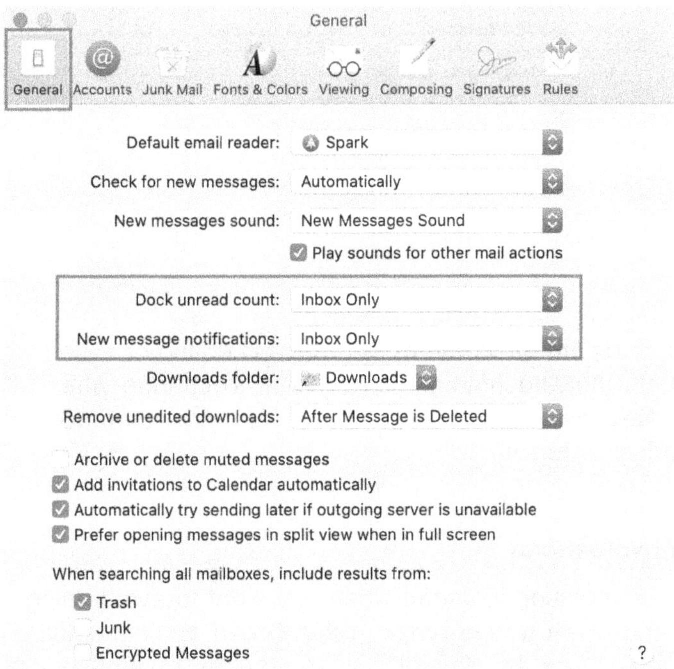

Choose When to be Notified

The **New message notifications** drop-down menu lets you select when you'd like Desktop notifications from Mail. You can configure Mail to notify you when a new email arrives in your **Inbox Only**, from someone in your **VIPs** list or **Contacts**, across **All Mailboxes,** or only when you receive a message **Today.** Note that you will only receive a Desktop notification when the Mail alert style is set to **Banners** or **Alerts** in the Notifications preference pane in System Preferences.

Choose Where to Save Attachments

By default, Mail saves attachments to the **Downloads** folder when you save an attachment. You can change this location to any folder by choosing **Other...** from the drop-down list next to **Downloads folder**. Navigate to your desired location and press the **Select** button.

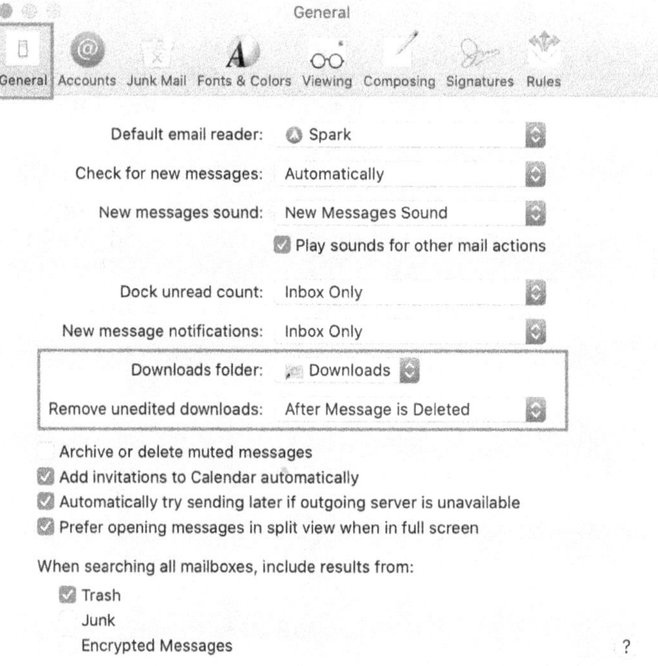

Mail is configured to delete attachments you haven't edited or saved when you delete the email containing the attachment. If you want to change when attachments are deleted, choose **Never** or **When Mail Quits** from the drop-down menu next to **Remove unedited downloads**.

Delete Muted Conversations

Muting an email conversation is useful when you want to avoid being distracted by a notification or sound when a new email in the thread arrives. Muted conversations remain in your Mail inbox by default. If you prefer to archive or delete muted conversations, check the checkbox next to **Archive or delete muted messages**.

Automatically Add Invitations to Calendar

Invitations you receive in email can be added to the **Calendar** application. To enable this feature, open the Mail preference pane and check the checkbox next to **Add invitations to calendar automatically**.

Send Later When the Mail Server is Unavailable

If your service provider's email server is unavailable, Mail saves outbound email messages in its Outbox until it can connect to the server at a later time. Uncheck the checkbox next **Automatically try sending later if outgoing server is unavailable** if you want Mail to open a dialog box showing other available email servers.

Open Messages in Split-View

Email messages open in Split-View mode when Mail is running in Full-Screen mode. If you do not like this behavior, you can disable it by unchecking the checkbox next to **Prefer opening messages in split view when in full-screen**.

Change the Mail Search Scope

When searching mailboxes, you can choose to include results from the Trash and Junk folders and Encrypted Messages. By default, Mail only searches inboxes and the Trash. Check the checkboxes under **When searching all mailboxes, include results from** to include messages in the **Junk** folder and **Encrypted Messages** in your searches.

Change Attachment Download Behavior

Mail automatically downloads attachments. If you prefer to download attachments manually, open the Mail preference pane and click the **Accounts** tab at the top of the pane. Next, select **Account Information**.

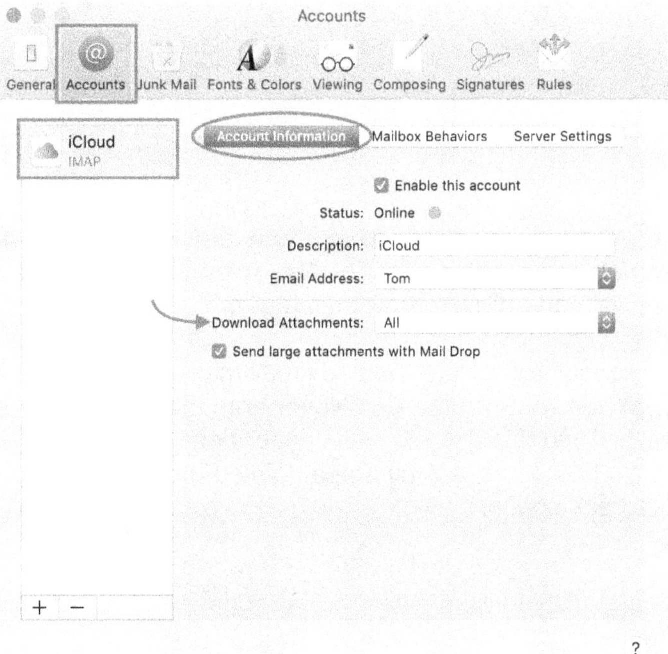

Downloading of attachments is configured on a per-mailbox basis. Select the mail account in the sidebar. Using the drop-down menu next to **Download Attachments:** select **All**, **Recent**, or **None**. Do the same for other email accounts, if desired.

Change Mailbox Behavior

To configure mailbox behaviors, open the Mail preference pane by choosing **Mail > Preferences...** or enter **⌘,** (command+,) and click **Accounts** at the top of the pane. Next, select **Mailbox Behaviors**. The majority of the configuration options should be left at their defaults with only two exceptions – the frequency that junk and deleted emails are erased.

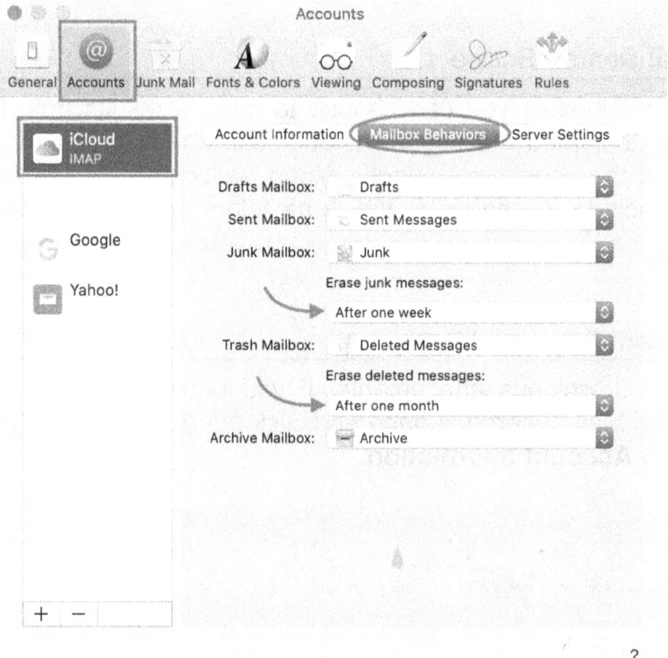

You can configure Mail to periodically delete junk email messages **After one day**, **After one month**, **When quitting Mail**, or **Never** by selecting your desired option from the drop-down list under **Erase junk messages**.

Similarly, Mail can periodically delete trashed email messages. Select **After one day**, **After one month**, **When quitting Mail**, or **Never** from the drop-down list under **Erase deleted messages**. If you'd like to keep all of your deleted emails, choose the **Never** option. However, it's best to have Mail erase deleted messages periodically to avoid needlessly using storage space.

Change the Mail Drop Threshold

When you try to send an email with an attachment larger than 20 MB, Mail automatically sends the attachment to your iCloud account. If the recipient is using the macOS Mail application, the large attachment is automatically downloaded and included in the email like any other attachment. For recipients using a different operating system or email client, a link is provided in the email along with the expiration date. An attachment expires after 30 days.

Some organizations have some pretty draconian limits on the size of attachments. I've seen some companies limit the size of email attachments to 10 MB, and even 5 MB. macOS allows you to change the default threshold for **Mail Drop** to a lower threshold. To change the default threshold for Mail Drop, launch Terminal and enter the following commands.

```
defaults write com.apple.mail minSizeKB 10000
```

The 10000 at the end of the command is the Mail Drop threshold in KB. Since 1 MB equals 1,000 KB, 10 MB equals 10,000 KB.

To revert to the macOS default, enter the following command in Terminal.

```
defaults delete com.apple.mail minSizeKB
```

Get Rid of Junk Mail

Junk mail is annoying and fills up your inbox. Mail has several configuration options to make junk mail less of an annoyance. Junk mail filtering is enabled by default, and junk email is moved to your Junk folder.

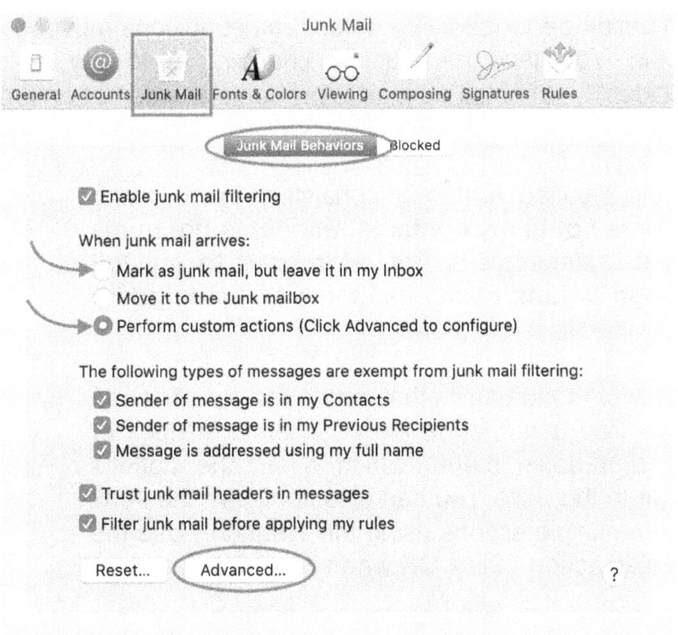

Mail offers an option where junk mail is marked as junk and left in your inbox. To select this option, click on the **Junk Mail** icon in the Mail preference pane and choose the radio button next to **Mark as junk mail, but leave it in my inbox**. You can mark any misidentified junk mail as **Not Junk**.

Mail also offers the option of configuring custom actions to identify and handle junk mail. To define custom actions, click the radio button next to **Perform custom actions (Click Advanced to configure)**. Next, click the **Advanced...** button at the bottom of the preference pane to reveal a drop-down configuration sheet.

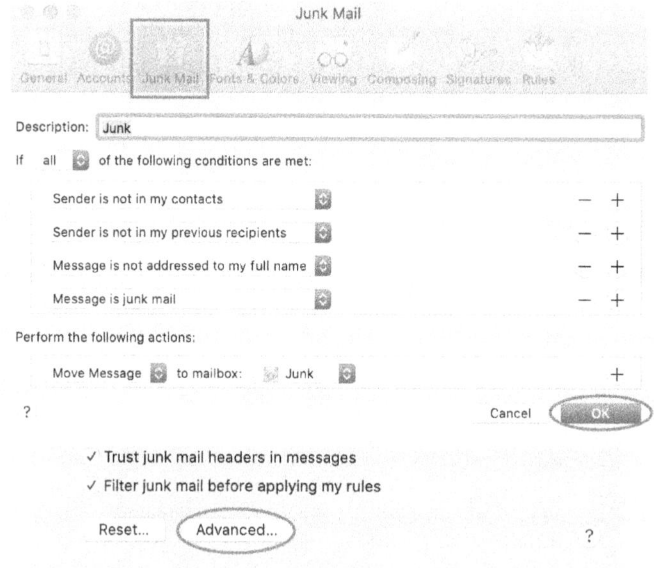

The configuration sheet allows you to configure the conditions necessary to identify junk mail and the action performed. By default, **all** conditions must be met to identify a message as junk. You have the option of changing **all** to **any**, which means any one condition will identify an email as junk. Any casts a wide net and may misidentify valid email as junk.

The default Mail rule is called **Junk**, and consists of the following conditions: **Sender is not in my contacts**, **Sender is not in my previous recipients**, **Message is not addressed to my full name**, and **Message is junk mail**. Use the **+** button to add a condition or the – button to remove one.

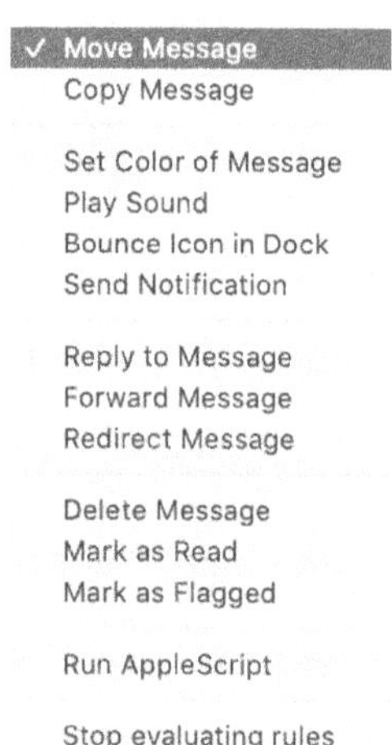

The default action is to move emails that match the conditions to the **Junk** mailbox. You can change the destination mailbox or action using the drop-down menu, which offers the options shown in the image to the right. You can also configure the Junk mail rule to perform multiple actions using the **+** button. Use the – button to remove an action. Click **OK** when finished.

Stop Squinting & Make Mail Fonts Bigger

Tired of squinting when trying to read email? There are two methods to increase the font size. You can temporarily increase the font size by using the **⌘+** (command +) keyboard shortcut. Conversely, the **⌘-** (command -) decreases the font size.

If you desire a more permanent fix, enter **⌘,** (command+,) to open the Mail preference pane. Click the **Fonts & Colors** icon at the top of the pane. You can change the **Message list font**, **Message font**, and the **Fixed-width font**. Click the **Select...** button to change the font and font size.

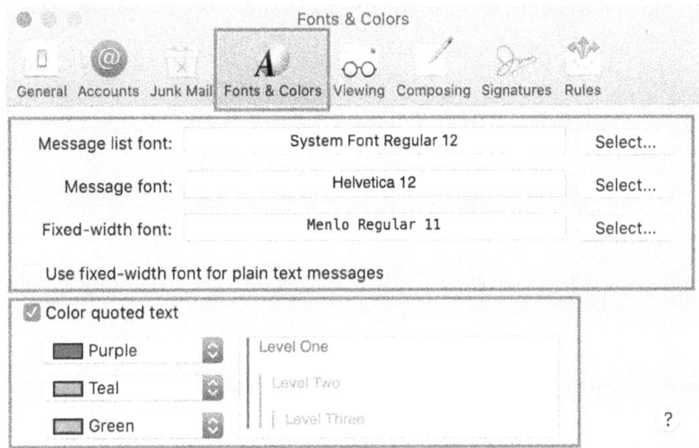

The **Message list font** is used for viewing the list of emails. The **Message font** is the font used for viewing and writing email. The fixed-width font is used for viewing and writing plain text email. Make sure you check the box next to **Use fixed-width font for plain text messages**. You also have the option to change the color of the quoted text when replying to messages. Select colors using the drop-down menus.

Configure Viewing Options

You can customize several viewing options in the Viewing tab of the Mail preference pane.

Mail can preview the first few lines of an email in the message list. This is a handy feature because you often can determine if you want to read, mute, or trash an email message based on the preview. Your options are to show 1, 2, 3, 4, or 5 lines. Select the number of preview lines using the drop-down list next to **List Preview**. To disable this feature, select **None** from the drop-down list.

Using the drop-down menu next to **Move discarded messages into**, you can choose whether to move an email to the Trash or Archive mailbox when you swipe left on an email in the message list.

By default, unread emails are bolded to help you differentiate them from emails you have already read. If you would like to disable this feature, uncheck the checkbox next to **Display unread messages with bold font**.

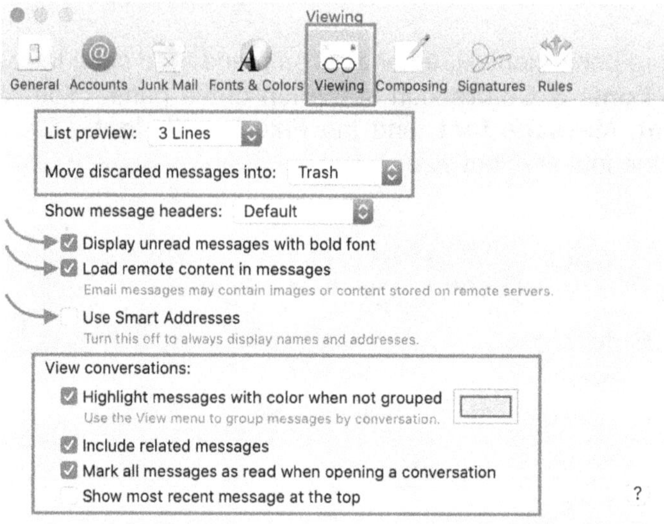

Loading of remote content, such as images, from a server is enabled by default. The downside is that information about your Mac can be revealed to the sender of the email. You can disable this feature by unchecking the checkbox next to **Load remote content in messages**. However, some emails will not display correctly as they require information from a server.

Mail will display a recipient's email address by default. When the Smart Address feature is enabled, Mail will only display the name. The recipient must be listed in the Contacts app, Previous Recipients List, or on a network server to display the Smart Address. To enable this feature check the box next to **Use Smart Addresses Preview** on the **Viewing** tab in the Mail preference pane.

The bottom section allows you to customize 4 conversation options. A conversation is a method of grouping email messages that are part of the same thread in the message list instead of listing each one individually. You can enable conversations by selecting **View > Organize by Conversation**. If you did not enable conversations, the **Highlight messages with color when not grouped** option will help you identify email messages that are part of a conversation.

When **Include related messages** is enabled, email messages located in other mailboxes will be included when you are viewing a conversation. When you open a conversation, all email messages in the conversation will be marked as read when the checkbox next to **Mark all messages as read when opening a conversation** is checked. You have the option of displaying the oldest or most recent email message in a conversation as the first email message in the preview area. To display the most recent email message, check the checkbox next to **Show most recent message at the top**.

Configure Composing Options

The **Composing** tab of the Mail preference pane is used to configure the options for messages that you create.

You can choose to compose your outgoing messages using **Rich Text** (the default) or **Plain Text** from the drop-down list next to **Message Format**.

Mail checks the spelling of your outgoing email as you type it. You have the option of having Mail check your spelling when you click send or never using the drop-down list next to **Check spelling**. You can also choose to have Mail copy or blind copy you by checking the box next to **Automatically** and selecting your choice from the drop-down menu.

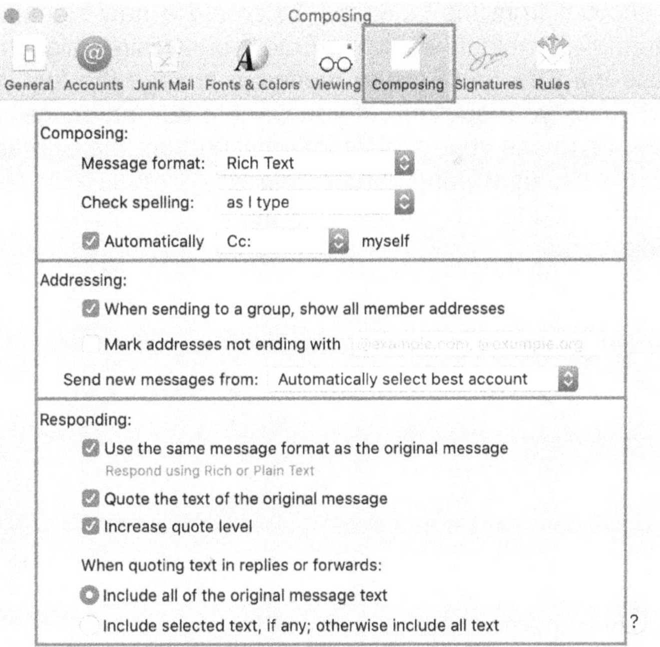

If you have multiple email accounts, Mail will select what it considers to be the best account to send from based on the currently selected mailbox, message, and the email address of the first recipient. If you want your mail to originate from a specific email account, select the account you want to use from the drop-down list next to **Send new messages from**.

The **Responding** section controls the behavior of messages when replying and forwarding email. You can choose to utilize the same message format as the original email by checking the box next to **Use the same message format as the original message**.

By default, Mail will quote the text of the original message when replying or forwarding an email, indenting all text included from the original email. Uncheck the boxes next to **Quote the text of the original message** and **Increase quote level** to disable these features.

Have you ever replied to an email and wondered why Mail truncated the original email? This odd behavior can be disabled. To include the entire original email in your reply, click the radio button next to **Include all of the original message text**.

Create a Signature

The **Signature** tab of the Mail preference pane allows you to create signatures for each of your email accounts. Mail automatically adds the signature to messages you create. You can have a unique signature for each mail account if you wish.

Select the email account from the sidebar. To create a new signature, click the **+** button at the bottom of the middle column. Enter your desired signature in the right pane. You can use the **Edit** and **Format** menus to change the font, layout, change text into links, and check your spelling. If you want to add an image, drag it into the right pane. If you want to use your contact information from the Contacts application, drag your vCard into the right pane. To delete a signature, first select the email account. Highlight the signature you want to delete and click the – button at the bottom of the middle column.

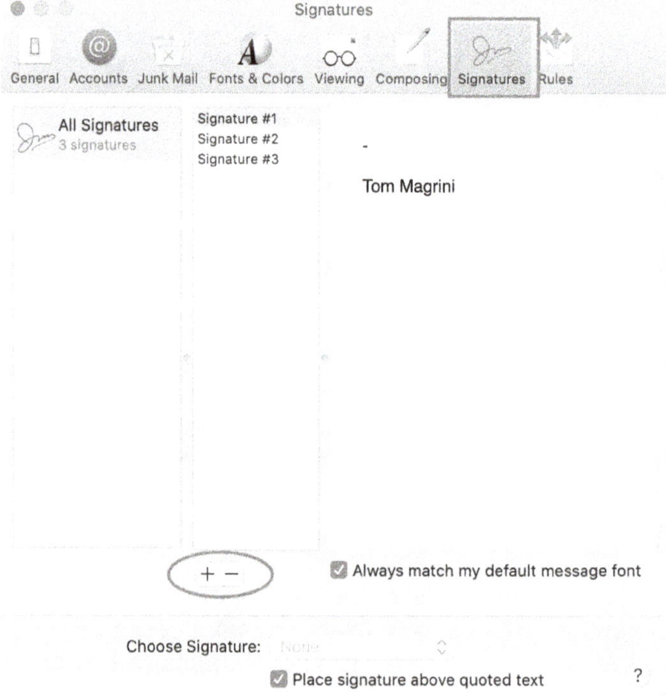

If you want your signature to use the message font you specified in the **Fonts & Colors** preferences, check the box next to **Always match my default message font**.

Create a VIP List

Not all email messages are created equal. You may want to highlight and prioritize messages received from certain people using Mail's VIP feature.

To add someone to the VIP list, first find an email message from them. Click the empty star next to their name in the email or secondary click on their name and select **Add to VIPs**. Once you have added your first person to the VIP list, a new VIP mailbox will appear in the Mail Sidebar and your Favorites Bar.

To remove someone from the VIP list, find an email from them and click on the star next to their name or secondary click on their name and select **Remove from VIPs**.

Manage Email Overload

The best way to manage email overload is the create rules so that Mail can automatically process and take action based on various mail attributes. You can use mail rules to organize your mail and highlight mail that is important, separating it from the noise. For example, you could create a mail rule for the email from your bank, move it to a special banking folder, play a sound, and bounce the Mail icon in the Dock to notify you. Mail supports 14 different pre-defined actions and 28 conditions, which you can combine to customize how you want your inbound email processed.

To create, modify, or delete mail rules, enter **⌘,** (command+,) to open the Mail preference pane. Click the **Rules** icon at the top of the pane selected. To modify, duplicate, or delete an existing rule, highlight it and click the **Edit**, **Duplicate**, or **Remove** button at the right. Click the **Add Rule** button to create a new mail rule.

Creating a new mail rule is easy. Rules have 2 components - **conditions** and **actions**. After clicking the **Add Rule** button, a configuration sheet will appear. To create a new rule, first name the rule in the **Description** field.

Next, choose whether **any** or **all** of the conditions have to be met to perform the selected actions. If you choose **any**, the action(s) will be performed if only one of the conditions is met. **All**, as the name implies, requires that all conditions be met to perform the action(s).

You can select from more than two dozen conditions from the drop-down list. To add multiple conditions, click the **+** button. Use the **–** button to remove a condition. Under **Perform the following actions**, select the action you want Mail to perform. To add multiple actions, click the **+** button. Use the **–** button to remove an action. Click **OK** when finished.

Create a Rule to Play a Sound

Not all email messages are created equal. You can configure Mail to play a sound and bounce the Mail icon in the Dock to notify you when mail arrives from someone in your VIP list.

Open the Mail preference pane. Select **Rules** and click on the **Add Rule** button. Enter a descriptive name in the **Description** field. In the conditions section, choose **Sender is VIP** from the drop-down menu. In the **Perform the following actions** section, choose **Play Sound** from the drop-down menu and choose whatever sound you like from the drop-down. Next, click the **+** button to create a new line. Select **Bounce Icon in Dock** from the drop-down menu. Click **OK** to finish and click **Apply** on the next dialog box.

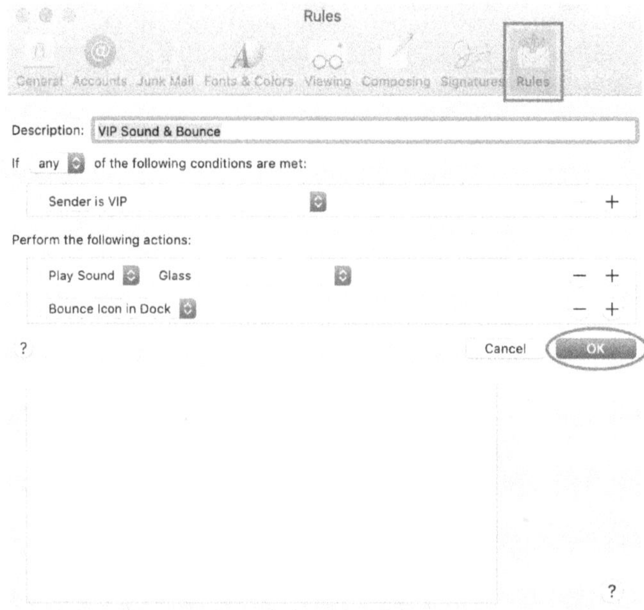

When you receive an email from someone in your VIP list, the Glass sound will play, and the Mail icon located in the Dock will bounce.

To remove a rule, open the Mail preference pane, select **Rules**, highlight the rule you want to remove and click the **Remove** button. Rules can also be disabled without deleting them. To do so, uncheck the checkbox next to the rules list to disable it. Check the checkbox to enable the associated rule.

Create an Auto-Response Rule

Mail lets you set up an email response that will be automatically sent upon receiving a new email. This is a handy feature to let those who sent you email know that you are out of the office, on vacation, in all-day meetings, or that your response will be delayed. When Mail receives a new email, it can immediately respond with a message of your choice.

To set up an automated response, enter **⌘,** (command+,) to open the Mail preference pane. Click the **Rules** icon at the top of the pane and click the **Add Rule** button to create a new mail rule.

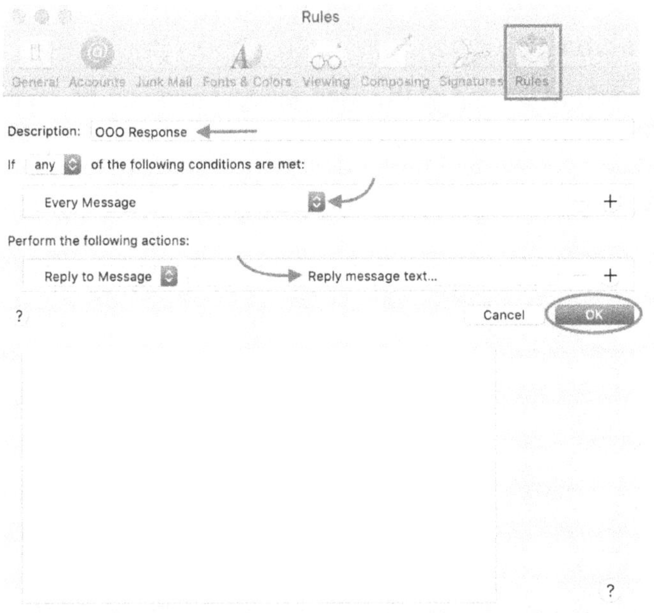

Next, name your rule in the **Description** field. Under **If any of the following conditions are met**, select **Every Message** from the drop-down menu. Then select **Reply to Message** in under **Perform the following actions**.

Click the **Reply message text...** button to reveal a configuration sheet and enter your desired response message.

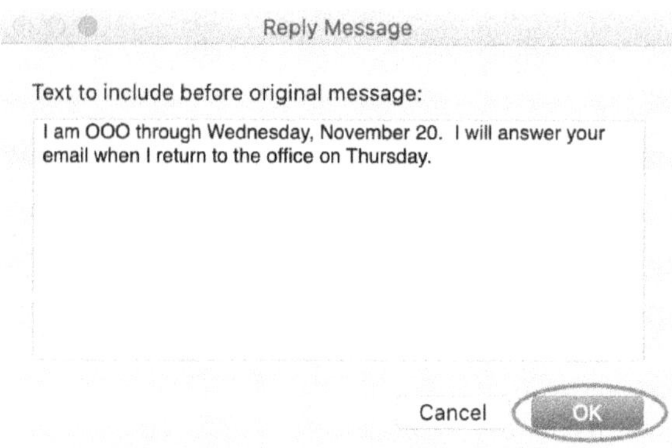

Click the **OK** button to save your message. Then click the **Apply** button to enable your new auto-response rule. If you want to check your rule, send an email to yourself. To disable your auto-response rule, uncheck the checkbox next to the name of your auto-response rule.

You can set up more complex rules so that Mail will respond only to specific senders, like your customers or clients, other employees in your company, family, or friends.

Customize the Toolbar

The **Toolbar** is located at the top of the Mail window and can be customized with the tools you use most often. You can add, remove, and rearrange tools as you see fit. Secondary click in an open area of the Toolbar to reveal a contextual menu and select **Customize Toolbar...** to reveal a tools palette with a selection of available tools.

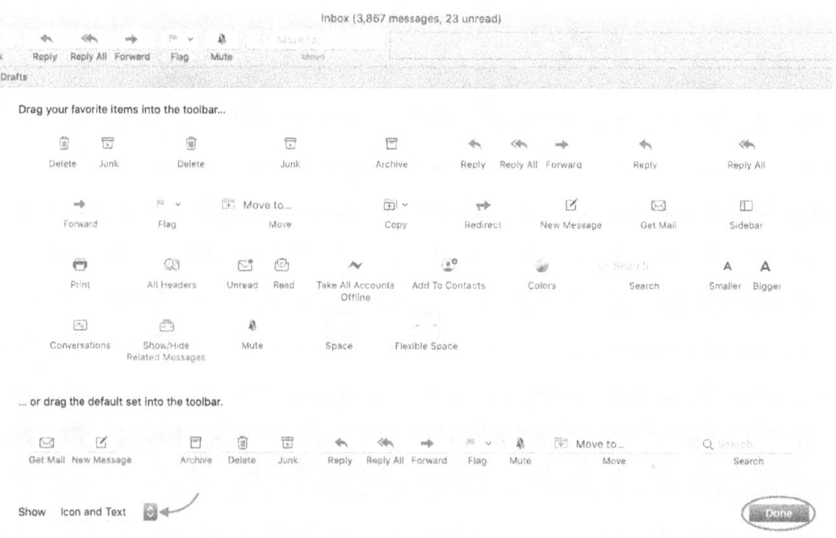

The tools palette allows you to add additional tools to the Toolbar by dragging and dropping them onto the Toolbar. Tools can be dragged off the Toolbar and dropped onto the palette to remove them.

To revert to the default set of tools, drag the default set onto the Mail toolbar to replace the existing toolset.

The Mail toolbar offers the option of displaying tool icons, text, or tool icons and text. Make your choice from the drop-down menu next to **Show** at the bottom of the tools palette.

Click **Done** when finished.

Any tool can be removed from the Toolbar at any time by holding down the ⌘ (command) key and dragging it off. Tools can be rearranged at any time by holding down the ⌘ (command) key and dragging them.

Customize the Favorites Bar

Directly below the Toolbar is the **Favorites Bar**, another customizable component of the Mail window. At the extreme left is the **Mailboxes** button, which you can use to toggle the **Sidebar** on and off. The space to the right of the Mailboxes button is completely customizable.

To customize your Mail **Favorites** bar, drag any item from the **Sidebar** on to the Favorites bar. You can drag individual mailboxes, section headings (i.e., **On My Mac**, **VIPs**, **Flagged**), a mail account, or a single flag. Practically anything in the Sidebar can be dragged to the Favorites bar. Clicking any item in the Favorites bar will change the Mail window to that view, and the button will turn a darker shade of grey to denote that it has been selected.

If an item has sub-items, a small triangular caret will appear to its right. In this case, the button will toggle the view on and off and display a drop-down menu. For example, clicking on **VIPs** in the image above will display all the messages from everyone you have designated as a VIP. If you click the caret to the right of the **VIPs** button, a drop-down list will appear, allowing you to select a specific VIP.

Drag any item to rearrange it. To remove an item from your Favorites bar, drag it off.

Use Natural Language Search

Like Spotlight, the **Mail** application supports natural language search capability. For example, if you are interested in seeing emails that have a photo attached, you can enter "emails with a photo attached" in the Mail search field.

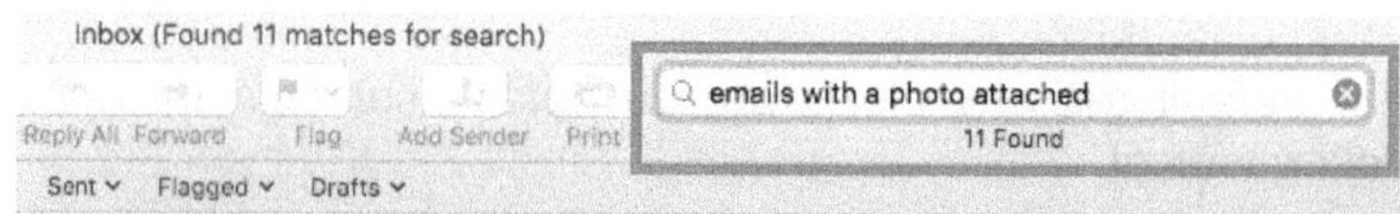

Override Dark Mode for Messages

If you prefer to read emails with a light background but want to use the macOS Dark Mode, you can configure Mail to use a light background when reading emails.

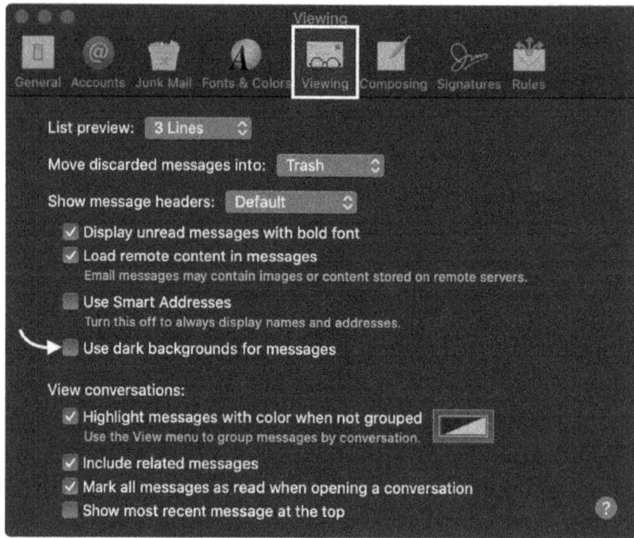

Open the Mail preference pane and select **Viewing**. Uncheck the checkbox next to **Use dark backgrounds for messages**. Note that you will not see this option if you have configured macOS to use Light Mode.

18

Security & Privacy

Switch to a Standard User Account

When you set up your Mac for the first time, you created a user account. By default, that account is an administrator account. The administrator account can change any setting on your Mac. Using your Mac for day-to-day work as an administrator poses a security risk. If your Mac becomes infected with malware while you are logged in as an administrator, the elevated privileges of the administrator account could allow malware easier access to system settings, applications, and other resources. Therefore, it is a safe computing best practice to perform day-to-day activities as a standard user and to reserve the administrator account for adjusting system settings and installing applications. If you are using your computer as a standard user and need to make a change that requires administrator access, you will be prompted for the administrator account credentials (user name and password).

If you have a brand new Mac and have just set it up, creating separate administrator and user accounts is a breeze. By default, Setup Assistant creates the default administrator account. You can use the **Users & Groups** preference pane in System Preferences to create a new standard account for your day-to-day computing activities. However, if you been using your Mac for a while, creating a new standard account won't work for you since all of your settings, applications, and data will only be accessible from your old administrator account. The solution to this dilemma is to create a new administrator account and then downgrade your existing account to a standard user.

To create a new administrator account, open the **Users & Groups** preference pane in the System Preferences application. Click the padlock in the lower-left corner if it is locked to make changes. Enter your password when prompted.

Click on the **+** at the bottom of the sidebar. A drop-down configuration sheet appears. Choose **Administrator** from the drop-down list next to **New Account**. Enter the **Full Name**, **Account Name**, **Password**, and click **Create User** to finish. Log out and log back in with your new administrator account to see if it works correctly and that you did not fat-finger the password.

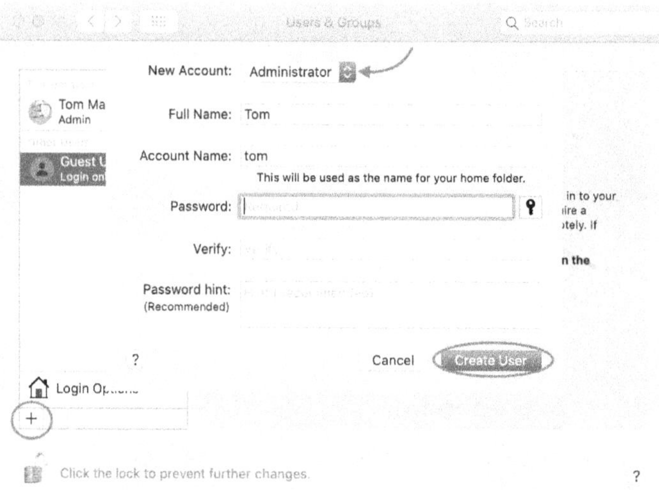

Using your new administrator account, launch the **Users & Groups** preference pane. Click the padlock in the lower-left corner to make changes if it is locked. Enter your password when prompted. Select your old administrator account, the one you want to downgrade to a standard user, from the sidebar. Uncheck the checkbox next to **Allow user to administer this computer**. Restart your Mac for the change to take effect.

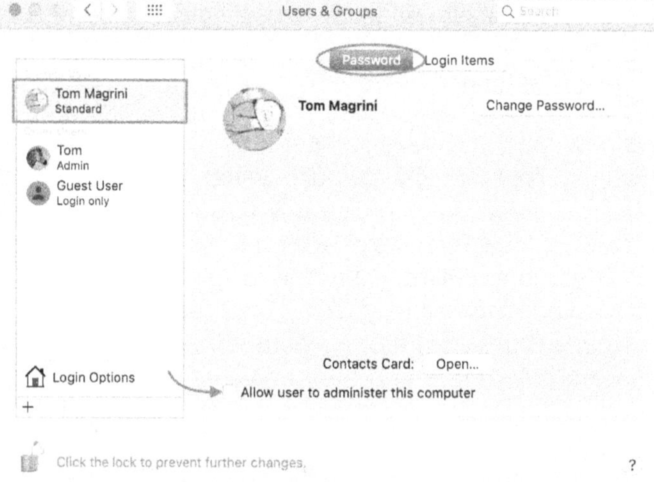

If you access financial sites like your bank, credit card, or broker, I suggest you create another standard user account to use exclusively for financial sites. Never browse the Internet or use email with your financial user account.

Require Administrator Access to Change Settings

It's a best practice to require administrator access to make changes to system settings in Systems Preferences, particularly if you have multiple people using your Mac. Even if you don't, you should do your day-to-day work as a standard user. Using an administrator account for day-to-day activities such as surfing the web or email poses a security risk. If your Mac becomes infected with malware while you are logged in as an administrator, the elevated privileges could allow malware easier access to system settings, applications, and other resources available only to the administrator.

To require system administrator access to change system-wide settings, launch the **Security & Privacy** preference pane. Click on **Advanced...** in the lower-right corner of any of the tabs.

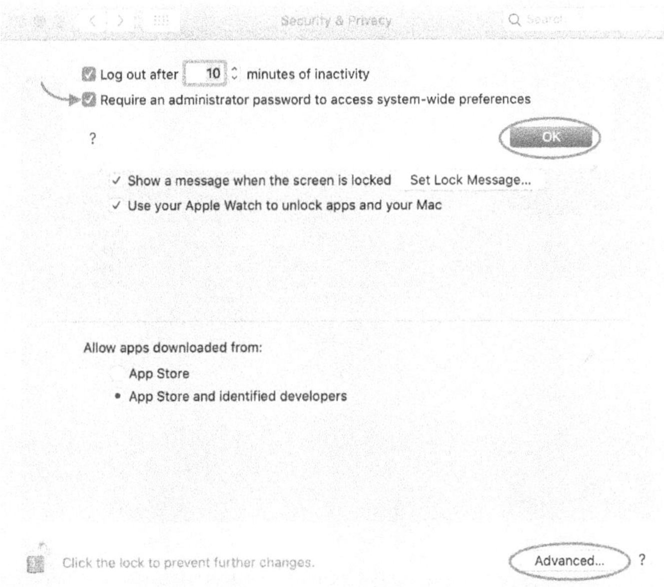

A drop-down configuration sheet appears. Check the checkbox next to **Require an administrator password to access system-wide preferences**. Click **OK** when finished. When this feature is enabled, a padlock will appear in the lower-left corner of each of the preference panes in System Preferences. You will have to click on the padlock and enter your system administrator credentials (user name and password) to unlock the padlock to make changes.

Allow Guests

The macOS guest user feature allows you to temporarily allow a guest to use your Mac without giving him or her access to your user account and without having to add them as a new user. A guest doesn't need a password, can't change macOS settings, and can't see your files. A guest can launch apps, and any files the guest creates are stored in a temporary folder, which is deleted when the guest logs out. Note that if you have FileVault disk encryption enabled, which I highly recommend, the guest user will only be able to use Safari and cannot create files. I show you how to enable FileVault disk encryption later in this chapter.

So what's the point of enabling the guest user? This account plays a role in the macOS **Find My** app, helping you locate your Mac if it is lost or stolen. You'll be able to locate your Mac using the Find My app if someone, including the criminal who stole it, logs in as a guest and uses Safari.

To verify that the Guest User is enabled, open the **Users & Groups** preference pane in the System Preferences application. Click the padlock in the lower-left corner if it is locked and enter your administrator credentials. Select **Guest User** from the sidebar. Verify that the checkbox next to **Allow guests to log in to this computer** is checked. Close the Users & Groups preference pane when finished.

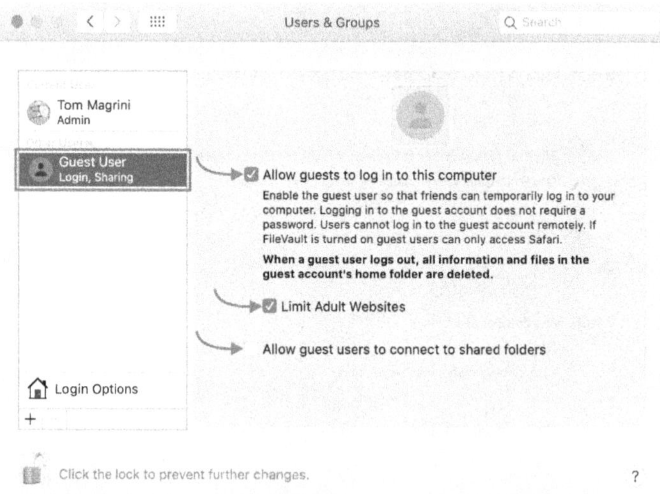

You can prevent guest users from surfing porn sites by checking the checkbox next to **Limit Adult Websites**.

Checking the checkbox next to **Allow guest users to connect to shared folders** lets a guest user access shared folders and files from another computer on your network.

Lock Your Mac

Locking your Mac helps protect your data and files from prying eyes and deters others from accessing your personal data. macOS lets you quickly lock your Mac. The first step is to ensure macOS is configured to require a password and that automatic login is disabled. Note that if you enabled FileVault disk encryption, macOS disables automatic login.

To configure your Mac to require a password, open the **Security & Privacy** preference pane in System Preferences and click the **General** tab. Click the padlock in the lower-left corner if it is locked and enter your administrator credentials.

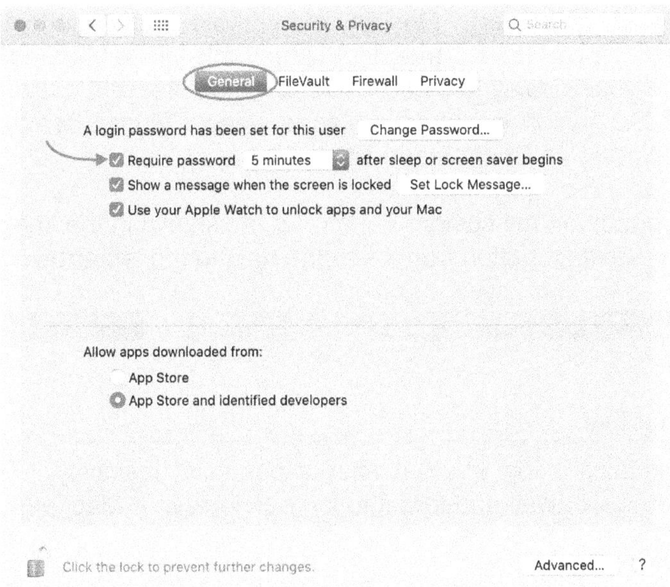

Check the **Require password** checkbox. macOS offers you the option of requiring a password **immediately** or after **5 seconds**, after **1**, **5**, or **15 minutes**, or after **1**, **4**, or **8 hours** after the display went to sleep or the screen saver began.

To lock your Mac immediately, use the keyboard shortcut **^⌘Q** (control+command+Q) or select ** > Lock Screen** from the Apple Menu. You can configure a Hot Corner to lock your Mac. You can also add a Screen Lock button to the Control Strip, as show in the image below. The Screen Lock button is the second from the right.

While locked, macOS continues running background processes and applications.

Put Your Mac to Sleep

Putting your Mac's display to sleep is an energy-saving feature that stops background processes and turns off your display. Putting your Mac to sleep is different from locking your Mac. When your Mac is sleeping, it cannot run background processes. Your Mac will go to sleep when the inactivity timer you set in the Energy Saver preference pane expires.

When asleep, your Mac will not lock until the **Require password** timer you set in the **Security & Privacy** preference pane expires. Note that the timer controls the length of time you (or someone else) will be able to access your Mac without entering a password. For example, if you set this timer to 5 minutes, your Mac will not require a password for 5 minutes after your Mac goes to sleep.

You can lock your Mac by putting its display to sleep using the keyboard shortcut ⇧^**power** (shift+control+power). On an older Mac, the shortcut is ⇧^**eject** (shift+control+eject). If you have a MacBook, MacBook Air, or MacBook Pro, you can close the lid to put your display to sleep. You can also create a custom gesture, Hot Corner, or Touch Bar button to put your Mac to sleep. Please see the chapters on Gestures, Desktop, Mission Control, and Touch Bar.

I created a sleep button on my custom Touch Bar, as shown in the image below. The Sleep button is the seventh button from the right, next to the left arrow.

Log Out when Inactive

macOS can automatically log you out after a period of inactivity. This is a great feature in case you walk away and forget to log out, lock your Mac, or put your display or Mac to sleep.

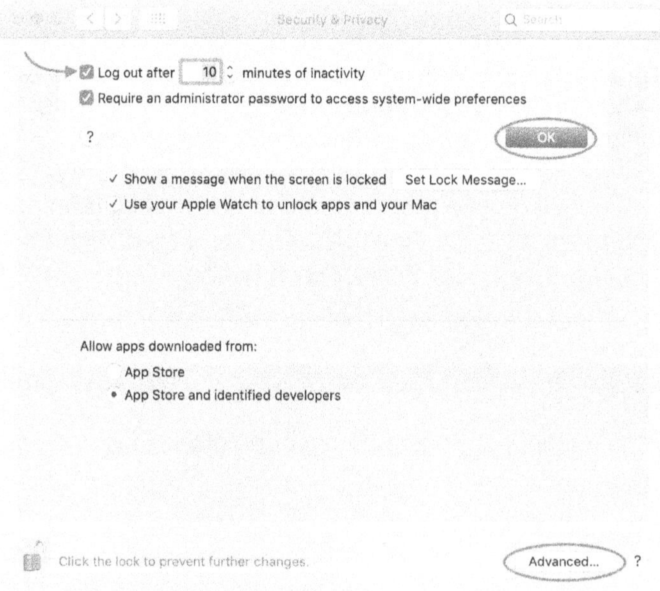

To set this inactivity timer, open the **Security & Privacy** preference pane in System Preferences. Unlock the preferences by clicking the padlock in the lower-left corner and entering your administrator credentials. Click the **Advanced...** button in the lower-right corner to reveal a drop-down configuration sheet. Check the checkbox next to **Log out after** and enter the number of minutes of inactivity. Click **OK** and close the preference pane when done.

Show a Message When Locked

macOS lets you configure your Mac to show a message when the screen is locked. It is an excellent idea to provide contact information on the lock screen in case you lose your Mac.

Open the **Security & Privacy** preference pane in System Preferences. Unlock the preferences by clicking the padlock in the lower-left corner and entering your administrator credentials. Click the **Advanced...** button in the lower-right corner to reveal a drop-down configuration sheet. Check the checkbox next to **Show a message when the screen is locked**. Click **OK** to close the configuration sheet.

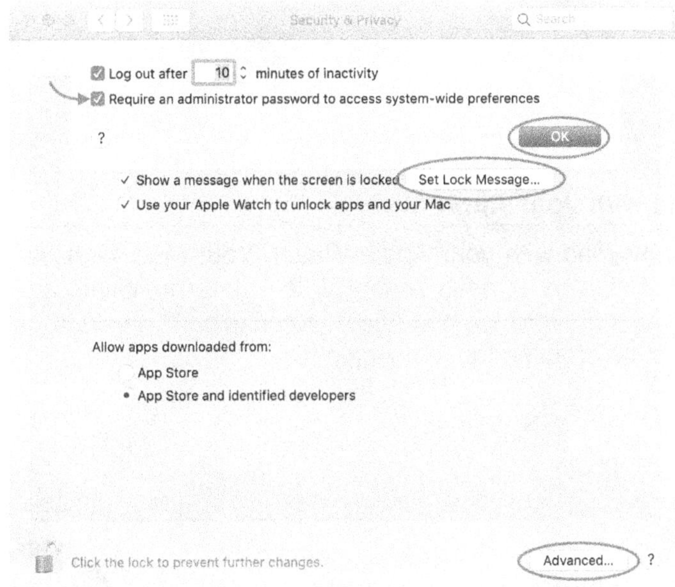

Next, click the **Set Lock Message...** button. Enter your message in the text box and click **OK**.

Disable Automatic Login

With automatic login enabled, anyone can access your Mac by restarting it. They will be automatically logged in with access to all of your files, Mail, Messages, and data. I highly recommend you disable this feature. Note that if you enabled FileVault disk encryption, macOS automatically disables automatic login.

To disable automatic login, open the **Users & Groups** preference pane in System Preferences. Unlock the preferences by clicking the padlock in the lower-left corner and entering your administrator credentials. Select **Off** from the drop-down menu next to **Automatic Login**. Once automatic login is disabled, your Mac will always ask for a user name and password when it starts.

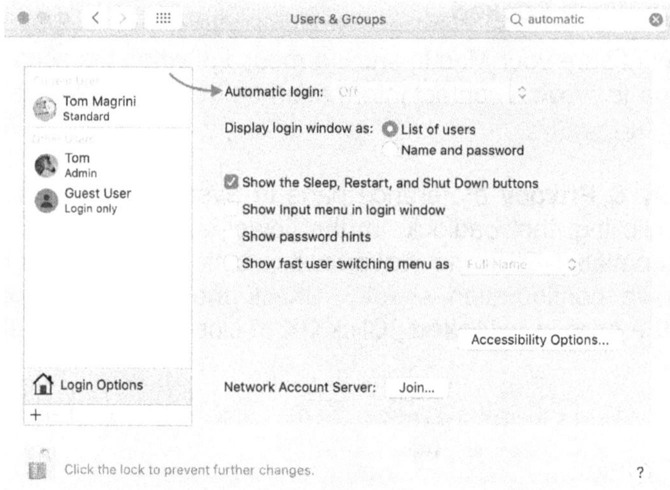

Unlock your Mac with your Apple Watch

You can unlock your Mac with your Apple Watch. Your Mac must be a mid-2013 or later model, your Watch must have watchOS 3 or later installed, and you must be signed into iCloud with the same Apple ID on both devices, and two-factor authentication must be enabled for your Apple ID.

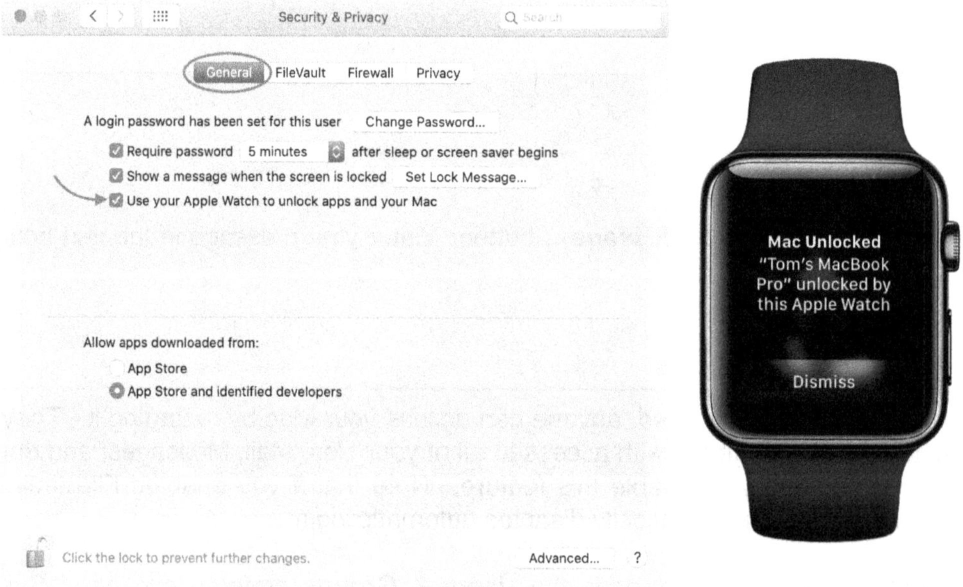

To enable Apple Watch Auto Unlock, launch the Security & Privacy preference pane and select the **General** tab. Unlock the preferences by clicking the padlock in the lower-left corner and enter your administrator credentials. Check the checkbox next to **Use your Apple Watch to unlock apps and your Mac**.

When you wake your Mac from sleep by touching the Trackpad or the keyboard while wearing your Apple Watch, your Mac will unlock, and a message will appear on your Apple Watch notifying you that it unlocked your Mac.

Encrypt Time Machine Backups

Hands down, Apple's **Time Machine** is the easiest backup application I have ever used. Its simple "set it and forget it" interface quietly backs up all of my critical data regularly without any intervention on my part. And the best part of Time Machine is how quickly and easily it can restore files or your entire Mac. Time Machine makes a copy of all of your files, including any data you would like to stay private. If you are concerned about unauthorized access, you should encrypt your Time Machine backup.

To encrypt your Time Machine backup, open the **Time Machine** preference pane in the System Preferences application. Unlock the preferences by clicking the padlock in the lower-left corner and entering your administrator credentials. Next, click **Add or Remove Backup Disk...** to reveal a drop-down configuration sheet that allows you to enable encryption on a new or existing Time Machine backup.

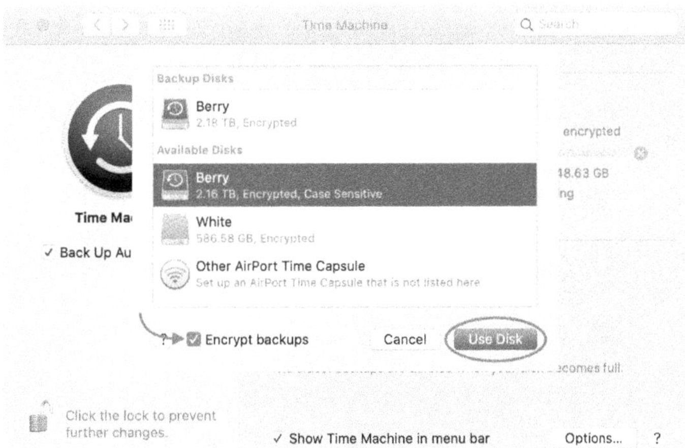

Select the disk drive you would like to encrypt under **Available Disks**. You can select a new drive for your Time Machine backup or select an existing one. Check the checkbox next to **Encrypt backups** to enable encryption. Click the **Use Disk** button. Enter a backup password and hint on the next configuration sheet. Click **Encrypt Disk** when finished.

Make Gatekeeper Less Restrictive

Apple's App Store is the safest and most reliable place to download and install applications because Apple reviews each application before it's accepted, checking for malicious or junk software. If an application is later found to be malicious, Apple will remove it.

Gatekeeper makes your macOS computing experience safer by stopping applications that are not digitally signed with an Apple Developer ID from being installed. Gatekeeper protects your Mac from malicious software by ensuring it is from a trusted source, an Apple Developer, and verifying the application hasn't been tampered with. Gatekeeper will block the installation of any application that is not signed by a valid Apple Developer ID.

Gatekeeper allows you to download applications from the App Store and Apple Developers. You also have the option of making Gatekeeper more or less restrictive. Open the **Security & Privacy** preference pane in System Preferences. Click **General**. Ensure the padlock in the lower-left corner is unlocked. If not, click it and enter your administrator credentials when prompted.

You have two available options: **App Store** and **App Store and identified developers**. The most secure setting, **Mac App Store**, effectively means you cannot install applications unless they have been downloaded from Apple's Mac App Store. The less restrictive setting, **Mac App Store and identified developers**, ensures that Gatekeeper checks that the application you downloaded is signed with a valid Apple Developer ID.

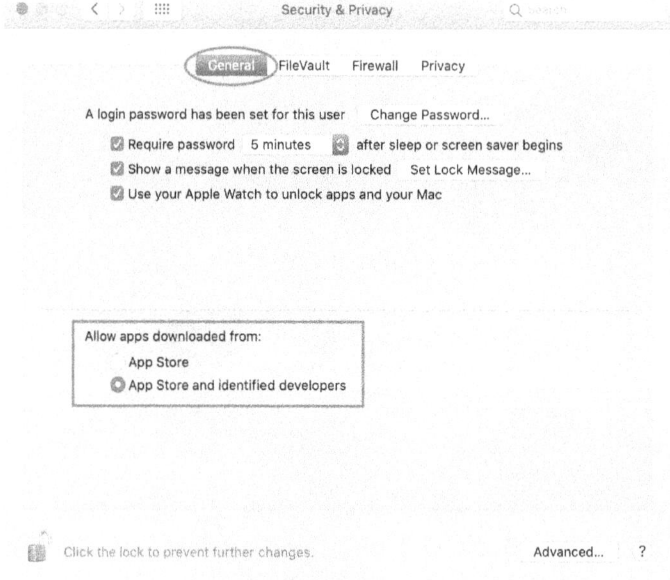

If you want to install unsigned software, macOS allows you to perform a manual override of Gatekeeper on a case-by-case basis. However, I recommend you only install applications that I have introduced in this book or those that have been reviewed by a reputable publication. If you try to install an unsigned application, Gatekeeper blocks it from being installed and display a warning dialog box. Clicking **OK** only acknowledges the warning.

To install an unsigned application after a Gatekeeper warning, you need to unblock the installation by opening the **Security & Privacy** preference pane in the System

Preferences application. You will see a message at the bottom of the **General** tab telling you why Gatekeeper blocked the install. If you want to continue the installation, click the **Open Anyway** and macOS will install the application.

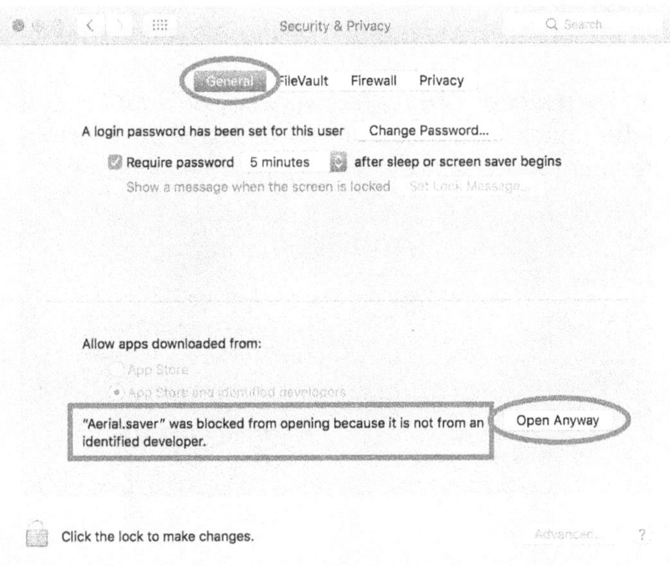

Encrypt Your Drive with FileVault

Encrypting your Mac's disk protects your data in case your Mac is ever stolen. Encryption, combined with the other security customizations covered in this chapter, makes it more difficult for a thief to access your data. macOS' **FileVault** will encrypt your entire drive.

Before enabling FileVault, there are a few things you need to consider. If you are in the habit of forgetting your password and lose your backup recovery key, your data is unrecoverable. This means your data is gone for good. FileVault's encryption is so strong, it's virtually impossible to break it to access your data. You can set up FileVault to use your iCloud password, so some risk is mitigated, but this will not help you if you forget your iCloud password.

Note that FileVault could degrade the performance of some older Macs with slower hard disk drives. You'll notice the performance degradation when opening large files. If your Mac has a Solid State Drive (SSD), you will see no performance degradation.

If you want a truly secure system, FileVault is the way to go for the maximum level of security. To encrypt your entire drive with FileVault, open the **Security & Privacy** preference pane in the System Preferences application. Click **FileVault**. Ensure the padlock in the lower-left corner is unlocked. If not, click it and enter your administrator credentials when prompted.

Click the **Turn On FileVault...** button. You'll be asked if you want to use your iCloud account to unlock your encrypted disk and reset your password if you forget it or use a recovery key instead of your iCloud account. If you choose the recovery code, you'll be presented with your 20-digit recovery code. Make a copy of this code and store it in a safe place, not on the Mac you are encrypting. If you lose both your password and the recovery key, you will not be able to access any of the data on your disk drive. It is a terrible idea to keep a copy of your recovery key on your Mac. If you forget your password, you will be unable to access any of the data on your Mac, including the recovery key. Store your recovery key in a safe, external location.

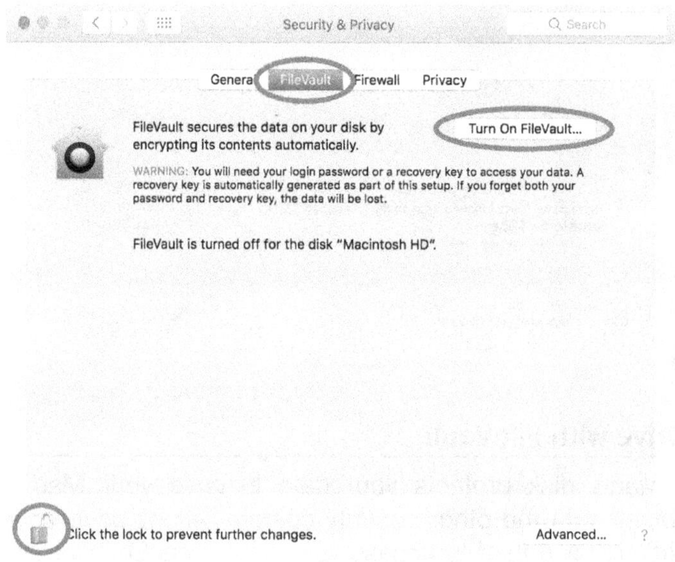

If there is more than one user account configured on your Mac, you'll be asked to identify the users who are allowed to unlock the encrypted drive. Each user is required to enter his or her password to unlock FileVault. Click the **Continue** button to continue. You will be asked to click **Restart** in the next dialog box to begin the encryption process. This is your last opportunity to change your mind. If you've changed your mind, press the **Cancel** button.

Stay Safe & Secure with VPN

If you have a MacBook, MacBook Pro, or MacBook Air, you probably use public Wi-Fi available at Starbucks, hotels, airports, and other businesses. Public Wi-Fi is horribly insecure. It doesn't matter if the service is free or if you have to pay a fee. When using public Wi-Fi, your traffic is sent in the clear, allowing anyone to capture the data you send and receive. Sometimes bad guys will camp out in public places and set up their laptops to mimic a legitimate public Wi-Fi service with a tantalizing name such as FREE Airport Wi-Fi. All they have to do is wait for victims to connect, capture private data, and use it to steal a victim's identity, drain bank accounts, or hack into their computer.

A Virtual Private Network (VPN) protects your data by encrypting it while it travels over public Wi-Fi and the Internet. With identity theft dramatically on the rise, it is just plain reckless to use public Wi-Fi without a personal VPN. There are other reasons why you need a personal VPN account. A VPN makes you anonymous by hiding your Mac's actual IP address, replacing it with the IP address of the VPN service. This makes it more difficult for your Internet Service Provider, employer, the government, or others to track your online activity. If you are traveling in a foreign country, you may lose access to Netflix or to social media sites that the local government censors. A personal VPN allows you to access services the government considers objectionable or are unavailable in foreign countries. If you want to protect your privacy and security when online, you should use a personal VPN service.

If your company provides a VPN for business use, don't use it for personal use. Company VPNs are monitored for misuse. Do you really want your employer knowing your personal browsing habits? I think not. That's another reason why you should sign up for a personal VPN service. There are lots of choices available for fees ranging from free to $20 a month. Why not choose one of the free VPN services? The free services are more restrictive regarding maximum bandwidth, the ability to stream video, and are funded by annoying advertising. If you can live with these inconveniences, choose a free VPN service, otherwise better services are available for a nominal monthly or yearly fee.

The VPN service I highly recommend is **NordVPN**, available at https://nordvpn.com/ and the Mac App Store. NordVPN is a five-star *PCMag.com* Editor's Choice and Best of Year 2017. It features 5,468 servers in 59 countries at the time of this writing. NordVPN has a no logs policy, so you don't have to worry about your privacy. NordVPN states, "We don't track, collect, or share your private data." "It's none of our business." NordVPN also has 24x7 customer service. Six devices can be connected simultaneously, so you can use NordVPN on your Mac, iPad, and iPhone at the same time. Unlike many VPN providers, NordVPN offers unlimited bandwidth.

NordVPN offers four plans. A monthly plan costs $11.95 a month, but you can save money by signing up for a one-, two-, or three-year plan. A one-year plan is $6.99 a month, and a 2-year plan is $4.99 a month. The best value is the 3-year plan at $3.49

a month. All plans come with a 30-day money-back guarantee, and you can cancel at any time if you are not satisfied.

NordVPN performs well using the Ookla speed test available at http://www.speedtest.net/. A nice feature is that I can use the same account on my Mac, iPhone, and iPad. NordVPN even supports Windows PCs if you occasionally cross over to the dark side.

Enable Find My Mac

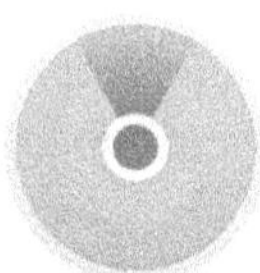

If your Mac is ever lost or stolen, you can use the **Find My** app on your iPhone or iPad to locate it in the Maps app, play a sound, lock it, or erase it to keep your data safe. To use this feature, the **Find My** app must be enabled in the **iCloud** preference pane before your Mac is lost. You cannot enable Find My Mac after the fact.

To enable Find My Mac, open the **Apple ID** preference pane in System Preferences. Click **iCloud** in the sidebar and scroll until you see **Find My Mac** in the right pane under **Apps on this Mac using iCloud**. Ensure the checkbox next to **Find My Mac** is checked.

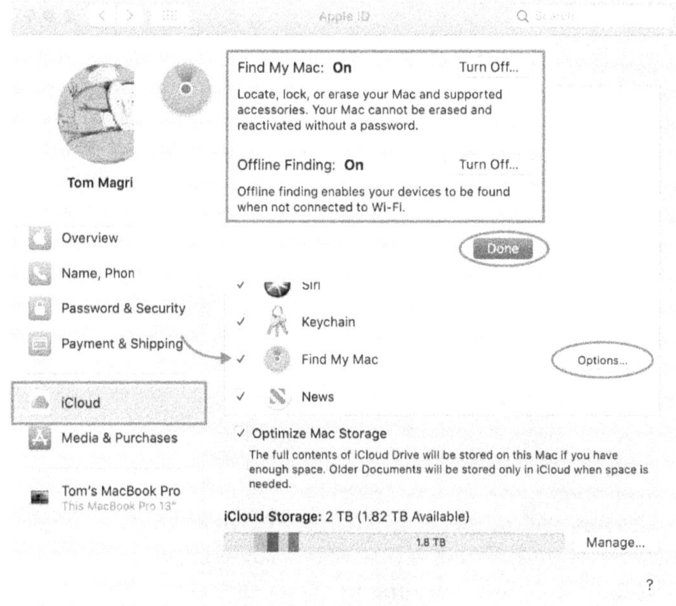

Next, click the **Options...** button to reveal a drop-down configuration sheet. Ensure that **Find My Mac** and **Offline Finding** are both turned on.

If your Mac is lost or stolen, you can use the **Find My** app on your iPhone, iPad, or another Mac to locate it on a map, play a sound, lock it with a 6-digit passcode, or erase it to protect your data. If you do not have another Apple device handy, you can log into your iCloud account with your Apple ID and use the **Find My iPhone** app to locate, lock, or erase your Mac.

If your Mac is lost or stolen, Apple recommends that you change your Apple ID password as well as passwords for email, banking, and social media sites to prevent someone from accessing your data or using these services. You should also change the passwords on merchant sites, like Amazon.com, where your credit card info is stored. You should also report your lost or stolen Mac and its serial number to local law enforcement.

Remotely Lock or Erase your Lost Mac with your iPhone or iPad

If your Mac is ever lost or stolen, you can use the **Find My** app on your iPhone or iPad to remotely lock or erase your Mac to prevent others from accessing your data.

Launch the Find My app on your iPhone or iPad. The Find My app displays your Apple devices on a map and provide a list of your **Devices**. Tap your lost Mac in the device list to see its location on the map, the address of its location, and to get directions or play a sound to help you find it. If your Mac is currently offline, enable a notification by switching the switch next to **Notify When Found** to the on position. Swipe up on the device panel to access the additional options shown in the images below.

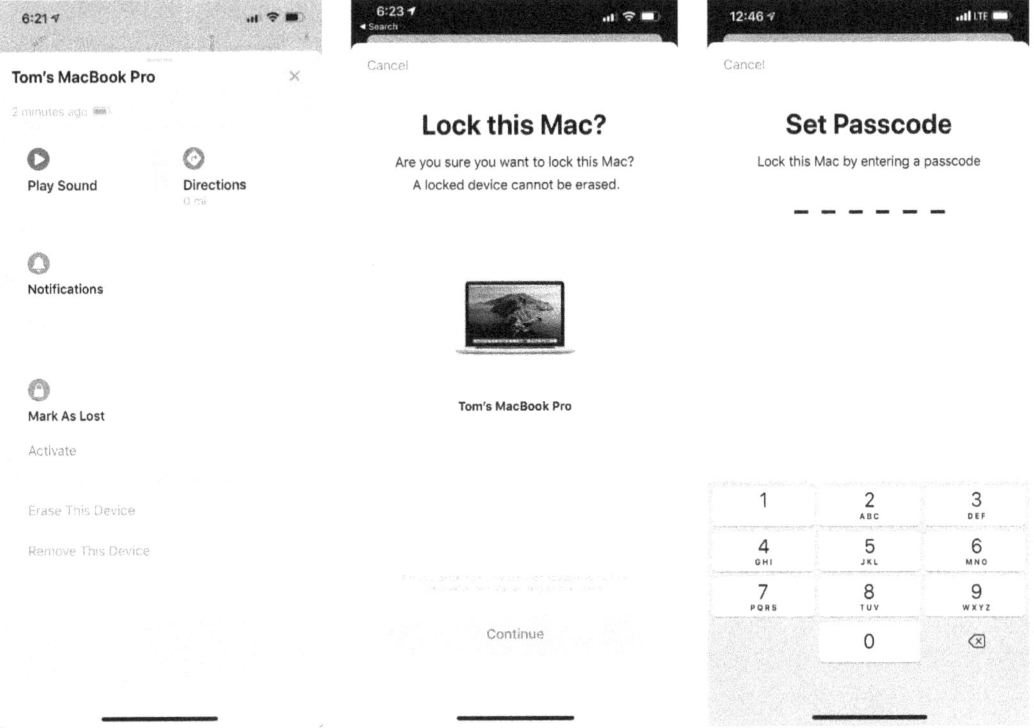

6:23
Search
Cancel
Erase Mac?
All content and settings will be erased when this Mac connects to the Internet. An erased Mac cannot be located or tracked any longer.
Tom's MacBook Pro
Continue

To lock your Mac and protect your data, tap **Activate** under **Mark as Lost**. You will be asked to confirm that you want to lock your Mac. Tap **Continue** or **Cancel**. If you tap **Continue**, you will be asked to set a 6-digit passcode. This passcode is required to unlock your Mac, so do not lose it. After you have found your Mac or it is returned to you, you can unlock it with this passcode.

If your Mac is not currently online, it will be locked the next time it comes online.

You can also display a message on your lost Mac's display with your contact info in case it is found.

To erase your Mac, tap **Erase This Device** and **Continue** on the next screen. This will remotely erase all personal data from your Mac. Click **Cancel** to cancel.

If you erased your Mac and it is later found and returned to you, you will have to restore your data. Therefore, it's a good idea to keep a current Time Machine backup or enable iCloud Desktop and Documents. Of course, you need to do these things before your Mac is lost or stolen. See the chapter on the Menu Bar to learn how to back up your data to Time Machine. To learn how to enable iCloud Desktop and Documents, see the chapter on Finder.

Remotely Lock or Erase your Lost Mac with iCloud

If you do not have your iPhone or iPad handy, you can log into your iCloud account at www.icloud.com using your Apple ID and password to locate, lock, or erase your lost or stolen Mac. Launch the **Find My iPhone** app from iCloud. Select your Mac from the drop-down menu under **All Devices** at the top of the window. If your Mac is online, its location is displayed on the map. A window at the upper-left of the page allows you to play a sound, lock, or erase your lost Mac.

If you have simply misplaced your Mac, **Play Sound** will tell your Mac to loudly play a sound even if the sound is muted.

You can lock your Mac by selecting the **Lock** option. A window appears to confirm that you want to lock your Mac. Select **Lock** or **Cancel**. Create a 6-digit passcode in the next window and confirm it. This passcode is required to unlock your Mac, so do not lose it. After you have found your Mac or it is returned to you, you will need this passcode to unlock it. If your Mac is not currently online, it will be locked the next time it comes online.

You can also display a message on your lost Mac's display with your contact info in case it is found.

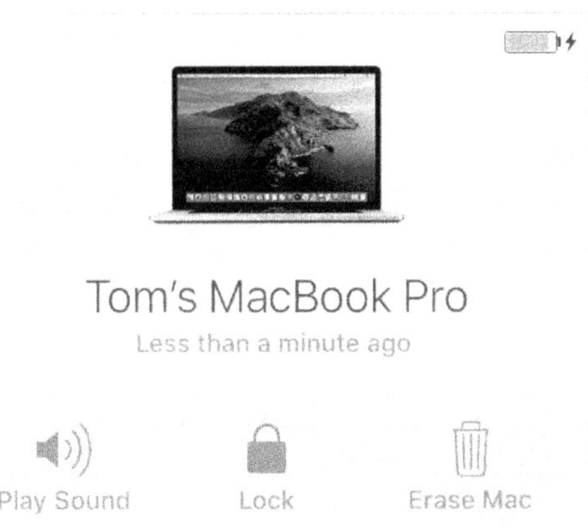

The last option is **Erase Mac**. A window appears to confirm your desire to erase your Mac and stating that all content and settings will be erased. Select **Erase** or **Cancel**. Your Mac will be wiped to protect your data.

If your erased your Mac and it is later found and returned to you, you will have to restore your data. Therefore, it's a good idea to keep a current Time Machine backup or enable iCloud Desktop and Documents. Of course, you need to do these things before your Mac is lost or stolen. See the chapter on the Menu Bar to learn how to back up your data to Time Machine. To learn how to enable iCloud Desktop and Documents, see the chapter on Finder.

Create Strong Passwords with 1Password

1Password is a third-party, best-in-class application that allows you to create unique, strong passwords for every website or application you use. Passwords can be synchronized across your Apple devices using iCloud. 1Password can even log you into a website with a single click. 1Password has won many awards, including "Best Rated Password Manager" by Trustpilot, "Best Password Manager" by *Wired*, "Top Pick for Password Managers" by Wirecutter, a Webby Award for "Best Services and Utilities App," and "Highest Rated Password Manager" by Crowd..

With 1Password you can easily implement a security best practice of creating a unique, strong password for every website or application you use. 1Password creates strong passwords for you with its Password Generator. Using unique, strong passwords ensures that your life won't be turned upside down if a data breach occurs at a website you frequent.

You'll never forget a password again, and your passwords are synchronized across your devices, even if you have crossed over to the dark side, and they are Android or Microsoft devices. Your passwords are encrypted with 256-bit AES encryption and secured behind a single Master Password – the only password you have to remember. Companion applications for your iPhone and iPad are available and automatically synchronize your passwords and other secure data using iCloud. 1Password supports both Touch ID and facial recognition.

1Password can log you into your favorite websites with a single click. A Menu Extra and keyboard shortcut ensure that your passwords are always available. 1Password protects more than just passwords. You can store your credit cards, bank account numbers, and create secure notes. 1Password's Security Audit feature finds duplicate passwords, weak passwords, and old passwords.

Monthly and annual subscriptions are available for $3.99 a month or $35.99 a year. A family subscription is available for $6.99 a month or $59.99 a year. 1Password is available at:
https://apps.apple.com/us/app/1password-password-manager/id568903335.

Enable the Firewall

The macOS firewall blocks unwanted, incoming connections to your Mac. However, like previous releases of macOS, it is disabled by default in macOS Catalina.

macOS allows signed software to receive incoming connections. This means that any apps you installed from the Mac App Store and signed apps allowed by Gatekeeper to receive incoming connections.

The macOS firewall is designed to block unwanted incoming network connections. The firewall provides another layer of protection against malware. If your Mac is already infected with malware, the firewall won't help as the macOS firewall, like other operating system firewalls, will not protect you from malware making an outbound connection.

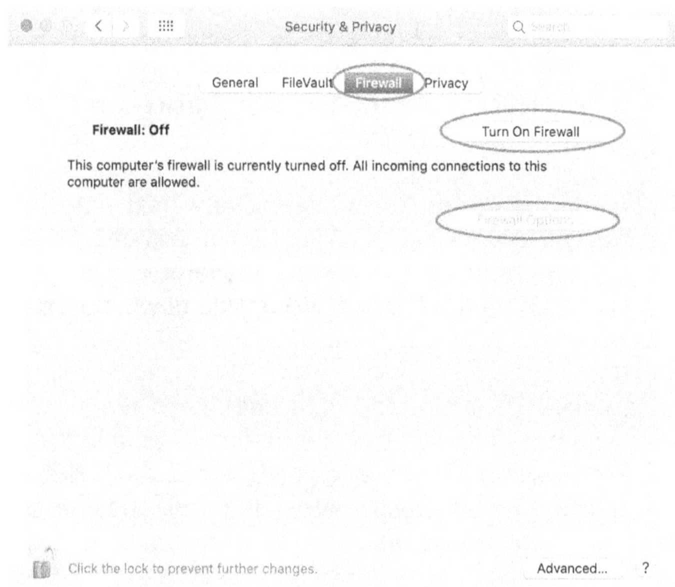

To enable the macOS firewall, open the **Security & Privacy** preference pane, and click the **Firewall** tab. Next, click the **Turn On Firewall** button. Once the firewall is enabled, the **Firewall Options...** button becomes available. Click on it to reveal a firewall configuration sheet.

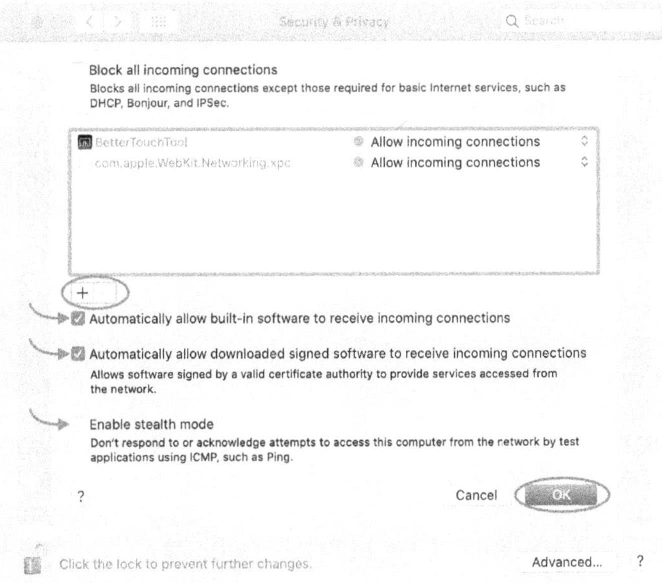

The checkbox next to **Block all incoming connections** should be left unchecked. Checking it will configure the firewall to block sharing services, including file, screen, and music sharing. When checked, only basic services required for Internet connectivity are allowed.

The checkboxes next to **Automatically allow built-in software to receive incoming connections** and **Automatically allowed downloaded signed software to receive incoming connections** should be checked. This allows apps you downloaded from the Mac App Store and from Apple developers to receive incoming connections.

Checking the checkbox next to **Enable stealth mode** prevents your Mac from replying to pings and probes from other computers.

To add an app or service, click the **+** button, which opens your Applications folder where you can select the application you want to receive incoming connections. Note that you do not have to add apps that you downloaded from the Mac App Store as they are already exempted. Nor do you need to add applications that are signed by a valid identified Apple developer.

Click the – button to remove an application from the list of exempted applications.

Set Up Parental Controls with Screen Time

A significant change to parental controls arrived in macOS Catalina with **Screen Time**. Screen Time first launched on iPhones and iPads in 2018. Screen Time records the amount of time spent using apps, social networking, web surfing, and gaming. You can use Screen Time to limit device and app usage and to block apps and websites. Screen Time can be configured from any Apple device and applied across all devices signed in with the same Apple ID. A common use of Screen Time is to enforce parental controls over a child's screen time, web, and app usage. Those upgrading from an earlier version of macOS are probably familiar with the parental controls in the Users & Groups preference pane. In macOS Catalina, parental controls are configured in the new Screen Time preference pane in System Preferences.

The Internet is a dangerous place, and protecting your kids can be a parent's full-time job. macOS makes protecting your kids a little easier by letting you control the apps your children use, which websites they visit, and how much time they spend online.

To enforce parental controls, you must first create a dedicated account for each of your children in the Users & Groups preference pane. Be sure to create these accounts as standard users and not administrators. Separate accounts ensure any restrictions you configure do not affect your application usage and web browsing.

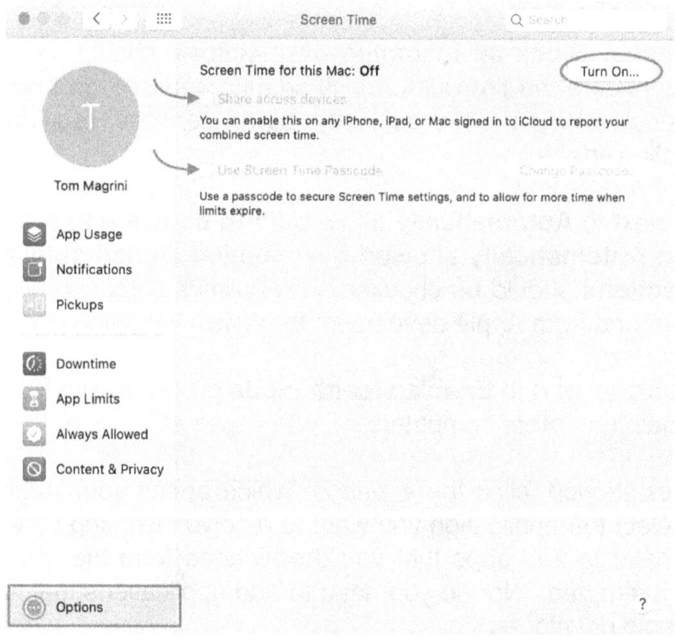

The next step is to open the Screen Time preference pane from System Preferences and enable it. From the Screen Time preference pane, select your child's account in the upper-left corner of the pane. Next, click **Options** in the lower-left corner and click the **Turn On...** button.

Screen Time can enforce the same parental controls across all devices signed in with the same Apple ID. Check the checkbox next to **Share across devices** to enable.

You should next set a 4-digit passcode by checking the checkbox next to **Use Screen Time Passcode** and entering a 4-digit passcode. Setting a passcode prevents your child from making changes to the Screen Time restrictions you set. macOS will ask for your passcode twice. You'll be asked to enter your Apple ID and password on the **Screen Time Passcode Recovery** sheet. While you can skip this step, I highly recommend you don't. If you ever lose your passcode, you can recover it using your Apple ID and password. If you need to change your passcode, you can do so by clicking the **Change Passcode...** button, entering your old passcode and your new passcode.

Schedule Downtime

Downtime is time away from screens and devices. To enable Downtime, click **Downtime** in the sidebar and click the **Turn on...** button. Enter start and end times next to the **Every Day** radio button. Click the radio button next to **Custom** to configure a different schedule for each day of the week. Uncheck the checkbox next to any day that you do not want to restrict your child's screen time.

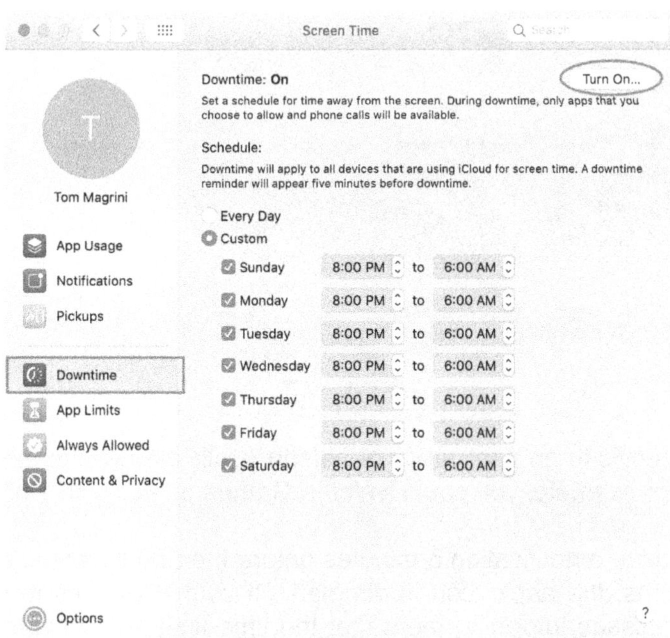

Your child will receive a downtime notification 5 minutes before downtime starts. If your child tries to use their device during downtime, they will see a message informing them that it's their scheduled downtime. Your child has the option to send a request to you for more time.

Set App Limits

App Limits allows you to control the amount of time your child can spend each day using specific apps, categories of applications, and websites. Categories include Games, Social Networking, Entertainment, Creativity, Productivity, Education, Reading & Reference, Health & Fitness, Other, and Websites.

To enable App Limits, click **App Limits** in the sidebar and click the **Turn on...** button.

Once you have enabled App Limits, click the **+** button to add an application or category. Use the checkboxes to select an application or category from the list on the configuration sheet. Next, configure a time limit in the **Time** section. You can choose to set a daily limit **Every Day** or create a weekly schedule by selecting the radio button next to **Custom**, which lets you set limits for each day of the week.

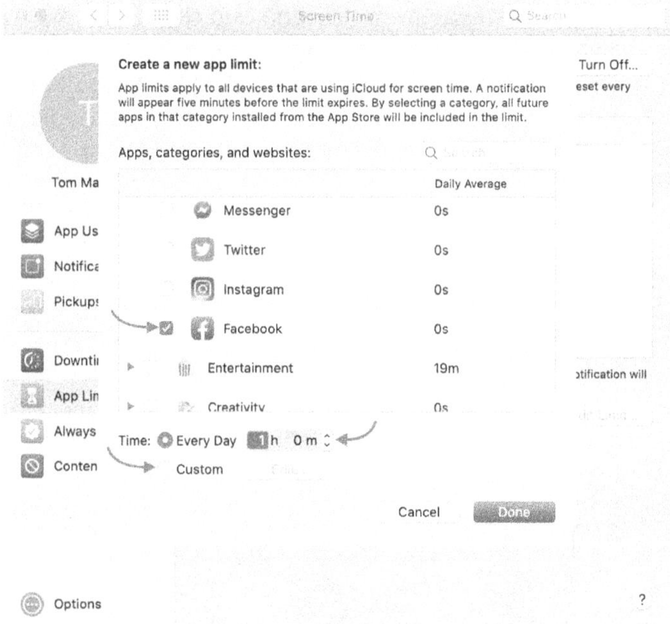

Time limits are specific to an application or category, allowing you to set different time limits for each. For example, you could limit the **Games** category to 1 hour per day.

Your child will receive a notification 5 minutes before the app limit time expires. Once the app limit expires, the app's icon is dimmed. If your child tries to open the app, they will see a message informing them that the time limit has been reached for the day. Your child has the option to send a request to you for more time.

Always Allow Apps

As its name suggests, **Always Allowed** is a list of applications that you let your child use at all times and without time limits. Always allowed apps are allowed even during downtime. Phone, Messages, FaceTime, and Maps are always allowed by default; however, you can change them here.

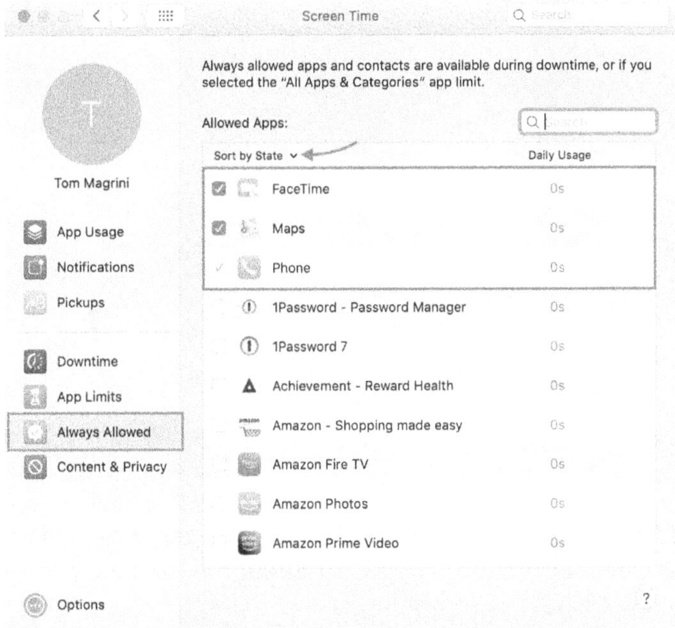

To add an app to the always allowed list, check its checkbox. To remove an app from the always allowed list, uncheck its checkbox. Apps can be sorted by **Daily Usage**, **Name**, or **State** (allowed or not).

Configure Content & Privacy

Now that we have configured applications and time limits, it's time to restrict explicit content, downloads, and purchases and configure privacy settings. macOS allows you to configure granular content settings. For example, you can block adult websites, songs with explicit lyrics, and restrict movies and television by age rating.

Select **Content & Privacy** from the sidebar and click the **Turn On...** button. There are four categories of settings: **Content**, **Stores**, **Apps**, and **Other**.

Content allows you to restrict websites that your child can access. You have the choice of **Unrestricted Access**, **Limit Adult Websites**, or **Allowed Websites Only**. Select your desired choice using the radio buttons under **Web Content**.

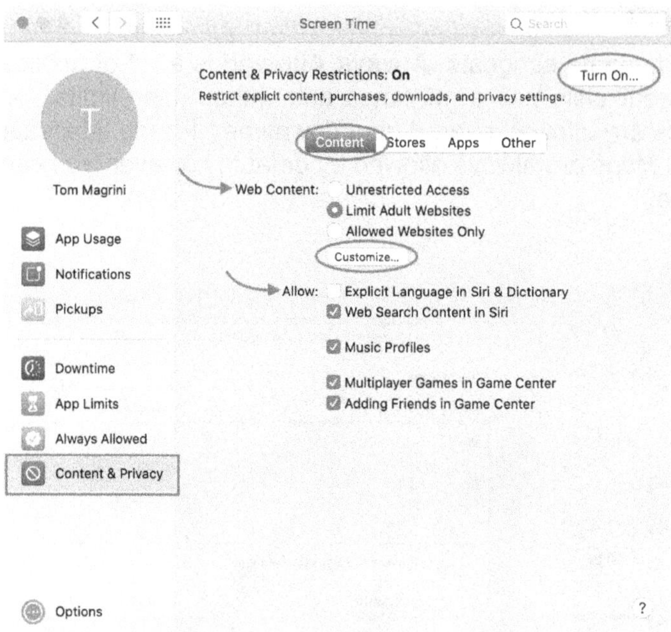

Selecting **Allowed Websites Only**, the most restrictive setting, allows you to configure a list of websites that you will your child to access. Click the **Customize...** button to open a pre-populated configuration sheet with a list of child-appropriate websites selected by Apple. You can add to this list by clicking the **+** button and entering a website on the next configuration sheet. Websites can be removed by highlighting them and clicking the – button.

The next section allows you to configure restrictions on explicit language, web search content, music profiles, and Game Center.

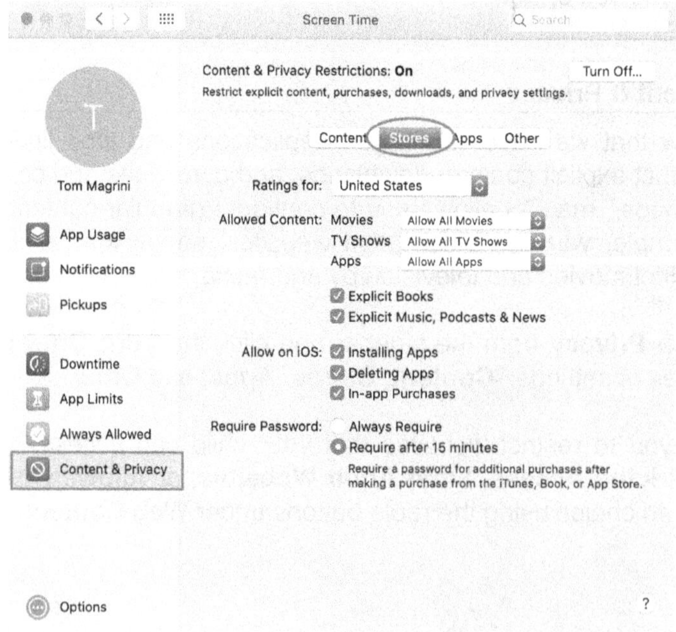

The **Allowed Content** section in the **Stores** tab allows you the set age-appropriate restrictions for movies, TV shows, and applications by age rating. You can also restrict explicit content in books, music, podcasts, and news.

The **Allow on iOS** section allows you to stop your child from installing or deleting apps and from making in-app purchases on their iOS device.

Require Password settings allow you to always require your Apple ID and password when making purchases. A second option allows you to not require your password for subsequent purchases made within 15 minutes of the first purchase where you entered your password.

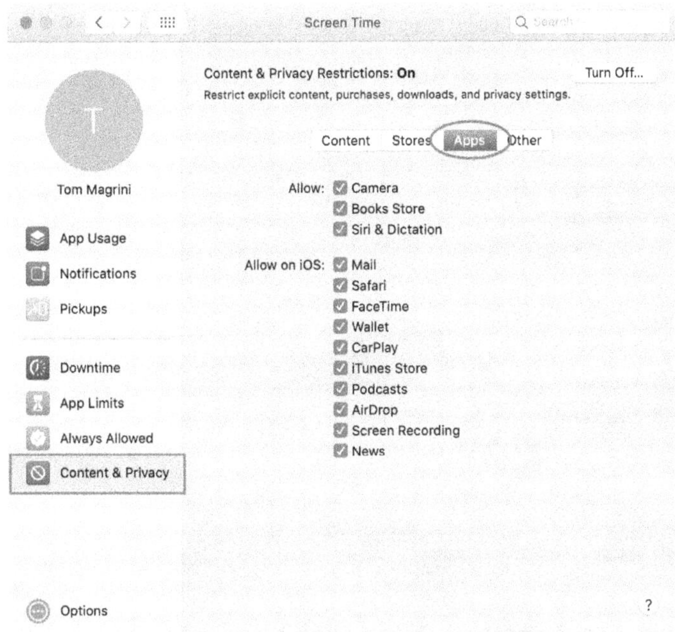

The **Apps** tab offers control over applications on macOS and on iOS. Uncheck the checkbox next to an app to stop your child from accessing it.

The **Other** tab allows you to restrict your child from making changes to the passcode, account, cellular data, do not disturb while driving, TV provider, and background apps on their iOS device.

Clicking the **Open Privacy Settings...** button opens the Privacy tab of the Security & Privacy preference pane, which offers more granular control over macOS privacy settings.

View the App Usage Report

Screen Time reports provide insight into daily and weekly device and app usage. To view an App Usage report, open the **Screen Time** preference pane in System Preferences. Click **App Usage** in the sidebar.

Screen Time displays app usage by week and day, defaulting to **Today** when opened. You can navigate to a specific day using the left and right arrows in the upper-right corner or by clicking on a day in the bar chart.

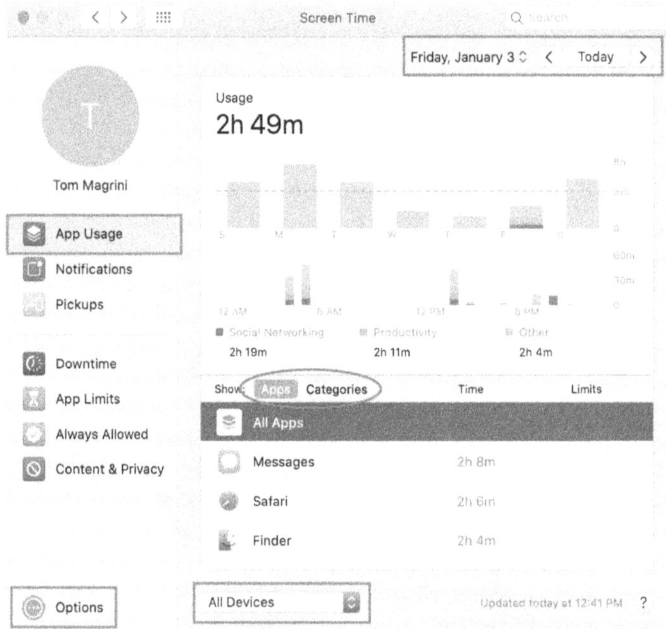

You can switch between **Apps** and **Categories** by clicking the buttons at the bottom of the chart. Categories are **Productivity**, **Social Networking**, **Entertainment**, **Education**, **Reading & Reference**, and **Other**. Usage time is listed for each category and reflected in the chart. When set to **Apps**, you can scroll through the apps to see usage time for each. Website usage is displayed at the bottom of the list by website.

Screen Time reports on the combined usage for an Apple ID across all Apple devices with **All Devices** being the default. If you want to see usage on a specific device, select it from the drop-down menu.

There is a caveat regarding the usage time of an application. If an application is open on your Mac but is not active and is hidden behind other windows, the usage timer will incorrectly report that the app was in use. Accurate reporting of app usage is only possible if you close each app before launching a new one. If you are using the Screen Time report to check how long your child was using a particular app, Screen Time may inaccurately show that your child used that app longer than he or she actually used it. In other words, I wouldn't ground my child based solely on an App Usage report.

View the Notifications Report

The **Notifications Report** provides insight into the volume of notifications you receive from each application. I find this report useful as it allows me to understand which applications are sending the most notifications and tune them accordingly to reduce the "noise."

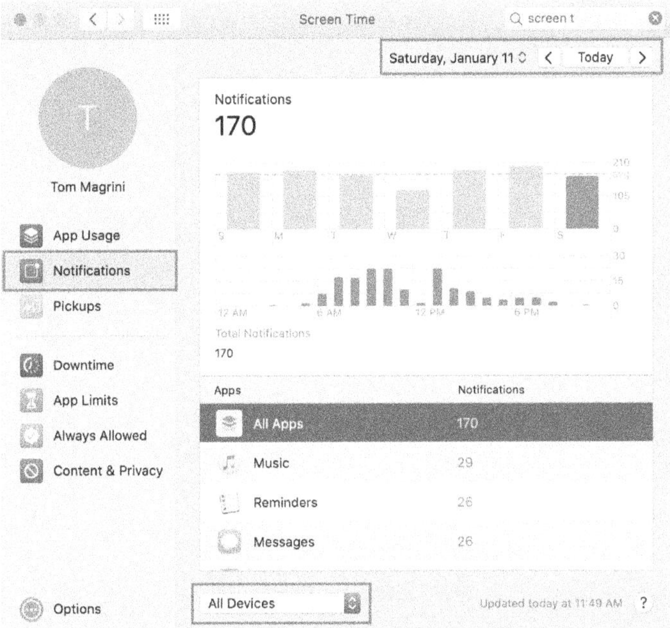

To view the Notifications report, open the **Screen Time** preference pane and click **Notifications** in the sidebar.

Similar to the App Usage report, the Notifications report defaults to **Today** when opened. The Notification report shows you the number of notifications you received each day and week. You can navigate to a specific day using the left and right arrows in the upper-right corner or by clicking on a day in the bar chart.

The bottom section of the chart displays the number of notifications sorted by highest to lowest number by application. Scroll to see more apps.

Notifications are reported across all Apple devices where you are signed in with the same Apple ID. **All Devices** is the default. If you want to see notifications on a specific device, select it from the drop-down menu.

View the Pickups Report

The Pickups report shows you how many times you picked up your mobile device(s). A pickup is logged each time you interact with your phone or tablet. Details show you when and how often you picked up your mobile device(s). For example, if you unlock your iPhone or iPad or use a "Hey Siri" command, it is counted as a pickup.

To view the Pickups report, open the **Screen Time** preference pane and click **Pickups** in the sidebar.

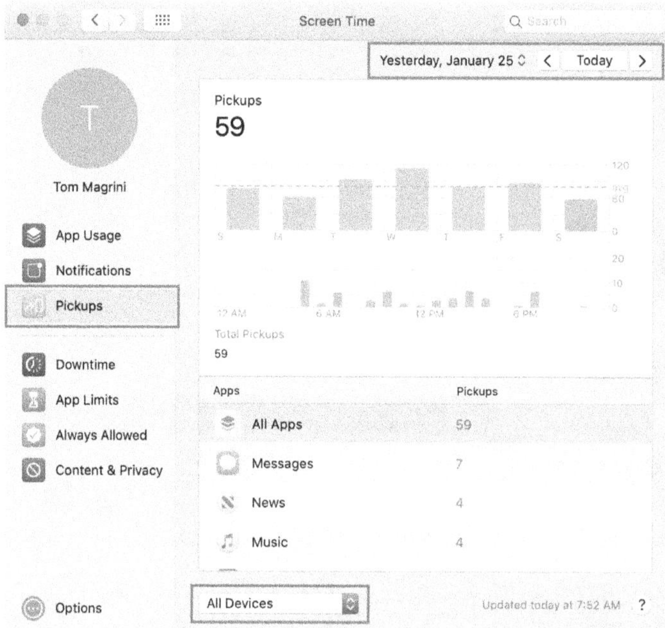

Similar to the App Usage and Notifications reports, the Pickups report defaults to **Today** when opened. You can navigate to a specific day using the left and right arrows in the upper-right corner or by clicking on a day in the bar chart.

The bottom section of the chart displays the number of pickups sorted from highest to lowest number by application. Scroll to see more apps.

Pickups are reported across all Apple devices where you are signed in with the same Apple ID with **All Devices** as the default. If you want to see Pickups on a specific device, select it from the drop-down menu.

Restricting Explicit Content in Music

If you are worried about the content your child is listening to in the **Music** app, you can restrict explicit content in the Music preferences. Launch Music and open its preferences by selecting **Music > Preferences...** or by entering **⌘,** (command+,). Click the **Restrictions** tab and unlock the padlock using your administrator credentials.

In the **Disable** section, you can restrict access to Music profiles, Apple Music, the iTunes Store, and Shared Libraries. Check the checkbox next to any item you want to restrict your child's access.

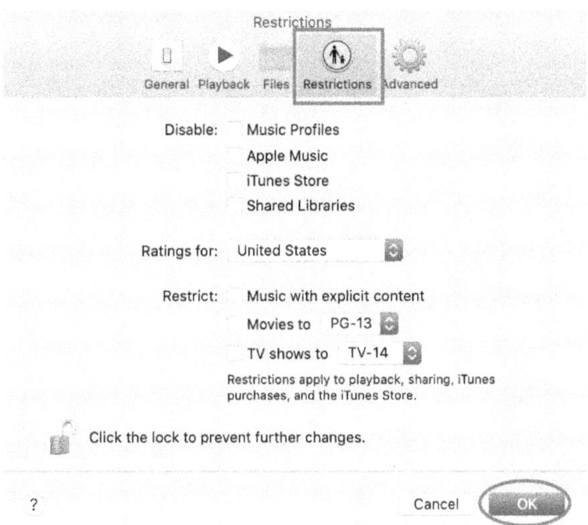

macOS automatically selects ratings by country. In the **Restrict** section, you can block music with explicit content and limit movies and TV shows by age-appropriate ratings. Click the **OK** button when finished.

19

A Bunch of Tricks, Tweaks, & Hacks

Create a Bootable macOS USB Flash Drive Installer

If you own multiple Macs that you want to upgrade to Catalina, you are facing a lot of downloading from the App Store. Another option is to create a bootable USB flash drive installer. A bootable USB installer also comes in handy when you want to do a clean install of macOS. You'll need a copy of the macOS Catalina installer and a USB flash drive with at least 16 GB capacity. Be sure there is nothing important on the USB drive, as it will be erased as part of the creation of the installer.

Creating a bootable USB flash drive installer is a multi-step process.

1. Download macOS Catalina from the **Mac App Store**.
2. While Catalina is downloading, connect your USB flash drive to your Mac and launch **Disk Utility**.
3. Select your USB drive in the left-hand pane. Erase the USB drive. Disk Utility will pick the name **Untitled**. Don't bother naming it as it will be renamed automatically as part of creating the USB installer.
4. When macOS Catalina finishes downloading, you will see the window below, which asks you to click continue to start the installation of macOS Catalina. **STOP HERE!** Exit the installation by quitting.

macOS Catalina
To set up the installation of macOS Catalina, click Continue.
Continue

5. Open Terminal and enter the following command. All four lines are a single command. **Do not** press the **return** key until you have entered the entire command. Because this command uses **sudo**, you will need to enter your root password when prompted. Don't worry if nothing appears in Terminal as you type your password. This is a security feature.

```
sudo /Applications/Install\ macOS\
Catalina.app/Contents/Resources/createinstallmedia --volume
/Volumes/Untitled
```

6. Terminal will ask to erase your USB drive. Enter **Y** and press **return**.

```
Erasing Disk: 0%... 10%... 20%... 30%...100%...
Copying installer files to disk...
Copy complete.
Making disk bootable...
Copying boot files...
Copy complete.
Done.
```

7. You can quit Terminal when it is done creating the installer disk. Open Finder and check the Devices in the Sidebar. You should see a device called **Install macOS Catalina**.
8. You are now finished with the creation of your macOS Catalina USB flash drive installer.

To use your flash drive to install Catalina, insert your USB drive into your Mac and hold down the ⌥ (option) key while restarting. The startup disk menu will appear once your Mac has rebooted. Select your USB installer drive to continue booting your Mac directly into the macOS Catalina installer. Follow the on-screen instructions. It should take about 45 minutes to an hour to complete the installation.

Tweak Background Updates

macOS automatically downloads and installs macOS and app updates in the background. If you would like to review the updates macOS plans to make to your Mac before they are installed, macOS offers several configuration options. Open the **Software Update** preference pane to configure background updates. Software Update will check for a macOS update when you launch it.

To ensure that your Mac always runs the current version of macOS, ensure the checkbox next to **Automatically keep my Mac up to date** is checked. When checked, your Mac automatically checks the App Store for updates. If you uncheck this checkbox, macOS will no longer check or notify you of the availability of updates. You will have to check the App Store for updates manually.

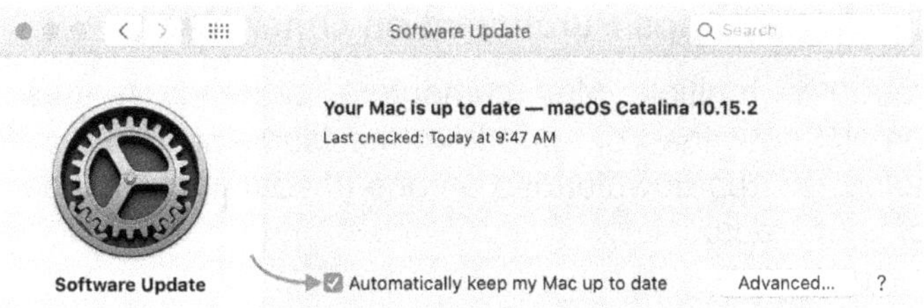

When automatic updates are enabled, you can control how updates are downloaded and installed by clicking the **Advanced...** button. Check the checkbox next to **Check for updates** to have your Mac check for updates automatically. Uncheck the checkbox to disable this feature.

Your Mac downloads updates without asking you if the checkbox next to **Download new updates when available** is checked. Uncheck this checkbox to disable this feature.

When the checkbox next to **Install macOS** updates is checked, your Mac installs macOS updates automatically, ensuring your Mac is always running the latest version of macOS. Uncheck this checkbox to disable this feature.

If you would like macOS to install updates for apps you purchased from the Mac App Store, check the checkbox next to **Install app updates from the App Store**. macOS automatically updates applications without asking for permission. Uncheck this checkbox to disable downloading of application updates.

Check the checkbox next to **Install system data files and security updates** to have macOS install system files and security updates automatically. Uncheck this checkbox to disable this feature.

At a minimum, you should check the checkboxes next to **Check for updates**, **Download new updates when available**, and **Install system data files and security updates** to ensure you receive the latest updates automatically.

When Software Update is configured to download and install app updates, you can see which apps were updated by launching the App Store app and clicking **Updates**. Disabling any of the automatic installation options requires you to open the App Store app to review the list of updates and manually choose which ones to update.

Automatically Download Apps Purchased on Other Macs

If you own multiple Mac computers, a handy feature is to turn on automatic download of apps from the Mac App Store. With this feature enabled, an app downloaded on one of your Macs will be downloaded to all of your Macs.

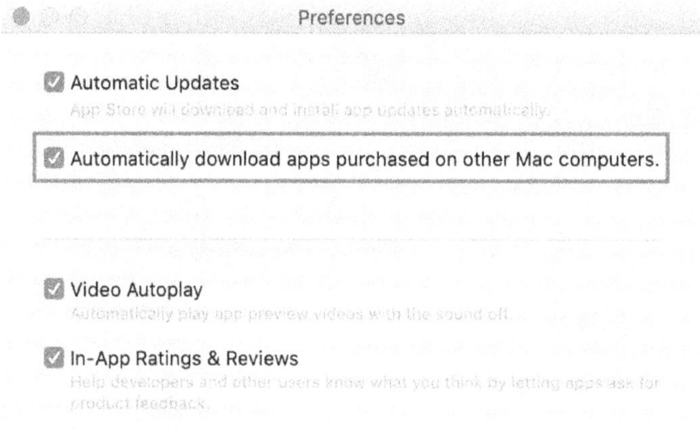

To enable automatic download, open the Mac App Store application and enter **⌘,** (command+,) to launch the App Store preference pane. Check the checkbox next to **Automatically download apps purchased on other Mac computers**.

Find a Lost Pointer

Have you ever lost the pointer? Sometimes it's difficult to find the pointer on the Desktop, particularly when it's hidden in the Desktop background. How do you find it? Most people either shake the mouse or shake a finger back and forth rapidly, hoping they will be able to see the pointer as it moves. Apple added a neat little feature that capitalizes on this behavior by making the pointer grow progressively larger as you move your finger back and forth on the trackpad or shake your mouse.

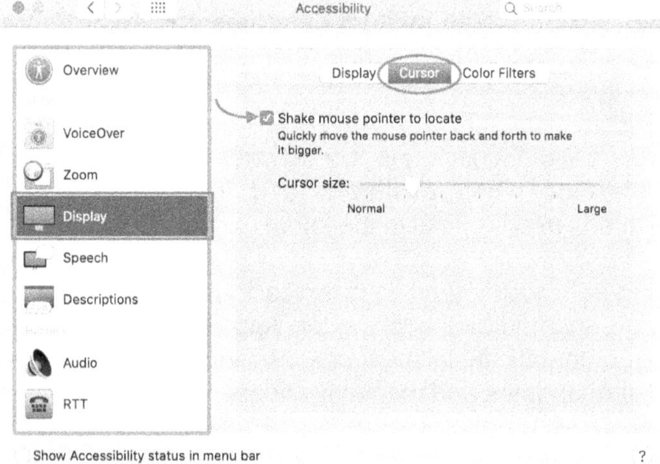

To enable shake to locate, launch the **Accessibility** preference pane and select **Display** from the sidebar. Next, click the **Cursor** tab. Check the checkbox next to **Shake mouse pointer to locate**.

Change the Pointer Size

While you can use the **Shake mouse pointer to locate** feature to find a lost pointer, maybe the default macOS pointer is a little bit too small for you, especially if you're using a larger monitor. For example, the pointer is sized perfectly for my 13-inch Retina MacBook Pro. But when I connect my MacBook to my 27-inch monitor, the pointer is so small I often have trouble finding it. macOS allows you to change the size of the pointer from the default size to gigantic.

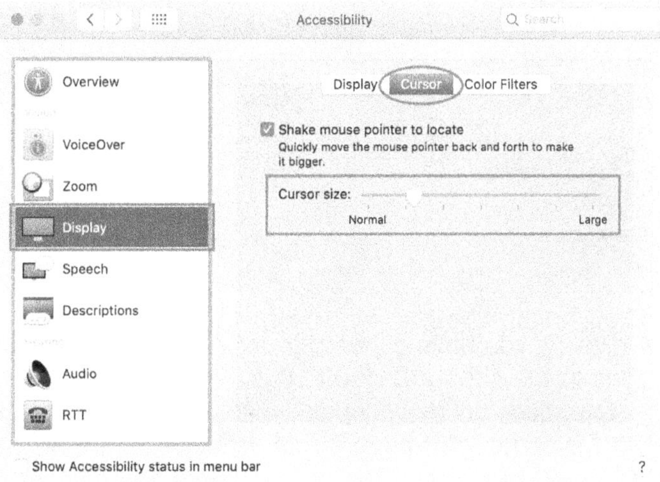

To change the pointer size, open the **Accessibility** preference pane and select **Display** in the sidebar. Slide the **Cursor Size** slider until your pointer is at the desired size.

Even a small change makes a big difference when using a large monitor. Note that changing the pointer size also changes the cursor size in word processing applications and the crosshairs used to take screenshots.

Adjust Retina Display Resolution

Mac laptops and Desktop computers with Retina displays can adjust the display resolution to provide larger, more easily readable text or more usable screen real estate. For example, my 13-inch Retina MacBook Pro has a native resolution of 2560 x 1600 pixels at 227 pixels per inch (ppi). Although its native resolution is 2560 x 1600 pixels, the default resolution is set to appear like 1280 x 800 pixels.

To change the display resolution, launch the **Displays** preference pane from the System Preferences application. Click on **Display** and select the **Scaled** radio button. As you hover your pointer over the available options, from **Larger Text** to **More Space**, the example display on the left side of the pane previews the resolution. When the **Default** resolution is selected, your Retina display looks like a 1280 x 800-pixel display.

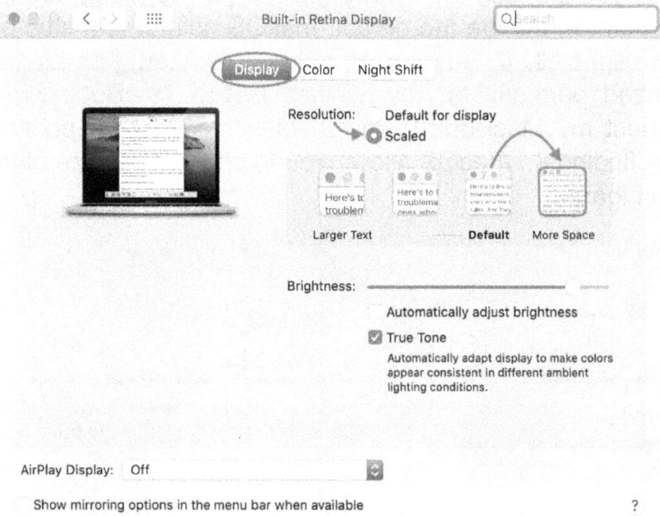

Depending on your display, you have either four or five options. For most, the default setting or the next one to the right of **Default** is usually the best option. If you prefer more screen real estate, click on **More Space**, which provides more usable screen real estate, but at the expense of readability as windows and fonts appear smaller. The **Larger Text** setting makes everything appear bigger and easier to read, but with the loss of screen real estate. The following two images compare the **Default** and **More Space** settings, respectively.

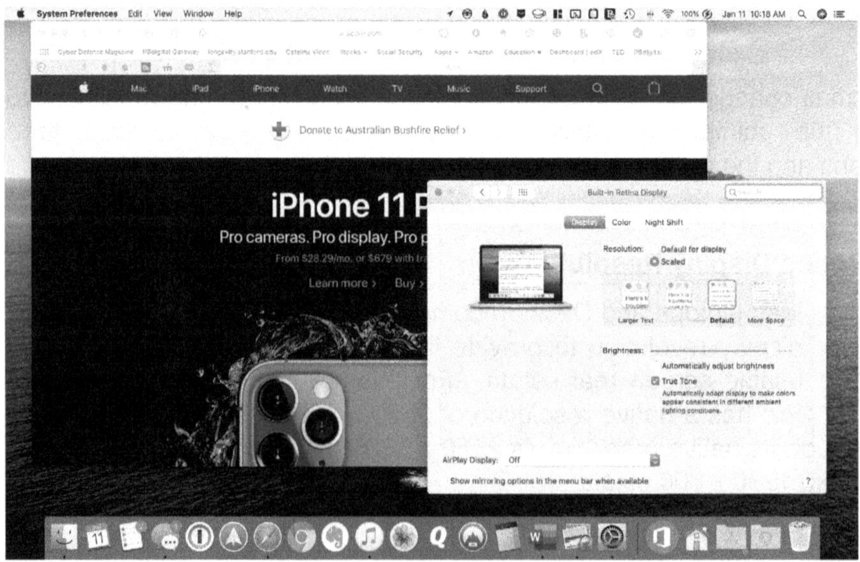

If you have multiple displays, changing the resolution of the built-in display has no impact on external displays. You will need to separately configure your external displays in the Displays preference pane, choosing a separate resolution for each. Or you can let macOS choose a resolution that works best for both displays, which is the **Default for display** setting.

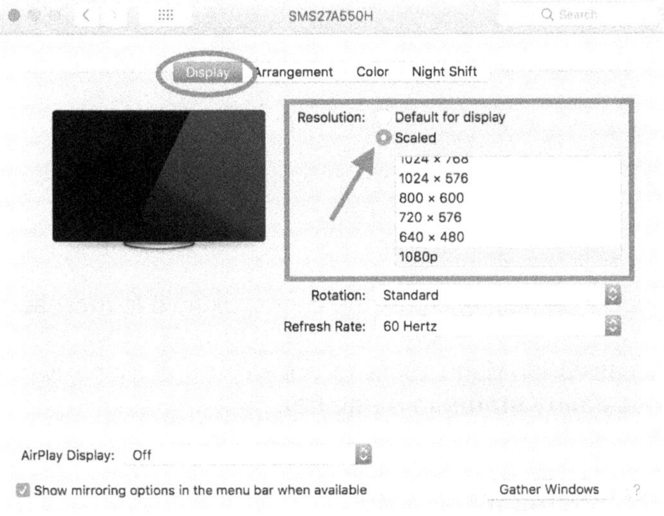

To configure the resolution of an external display, launch the Displays preference pane and select **Display**. A version of the Display preference pane appears on each of your displays. If you would prefer to see them all on one display, click the **Gather Windows** button in the lower-right corner.

External displays always run at native resolution unless you have specified a scaled resolution. To set a scaled resolution for an external display, select the **Scaled** radio button, and choose a resolution from the list. If you hold down the ⌥ (option) key while clicking the **Select** button, you will have more resolution choices, as shown in the image on the previous page.

Increase Contrast

You can significantly improve the readability of the system font, windows, and menus by reducing transparency and increasing the contrast. This setting increases the contrast of on-screen items such as borders around buttons and darkens the text and other interface elements without changing the contrast of the screen itself.

To increase contrast, open the **Accessibility** preference pane. Select **Display** from the sidebar. Check the checkbox next to **Increase contrast** and drag the slider next to **Display contrast** to increase or decrease the display contrast. Changes take effect immediately.

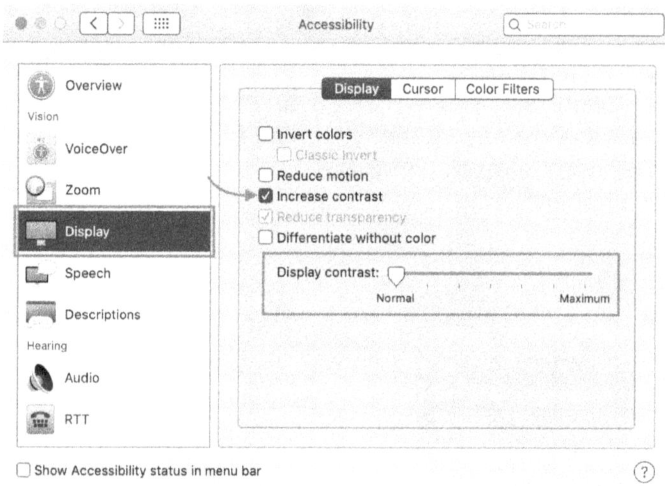

To revert to the macOS default, uncheck the checkbox next to **Increase contrast**.

If you want the Accessibility Menu Extra to appear in the Menu Bar, check the box next to **Show Accessibility status in menu bar**.

Change the Font Smoothing Strength

If you have an older, non-retina Mac, you may find that the macOS system font appears a little blurry and is harder to read compared to older versions of macOS. Turning off LCD font smoothing in the **General** preference pane in System Preferences is not a good option as doing so makes the system font appear jagged and thinner. However, manually tweaking font smoothing can make subtle improvements in its appearance on your non-retina Mac.

To change the strength of font smoothing, launch the **Terminal** application, and enter the following commands. Note that the command is a single line. Do not press **return** until you have entered the complete command. Log out and log in for this change to take effect.

```
defaults -currentHost write -globalDomain AppleFontSmoothing -int
2
```

When you use this command to change the font smoothing value, a – will appear next to **Use LCD font smoothing when available** in the **General** preference pane.

To revert to the macOS default font smoothing strength, enter the following commands. Note that the command is a single line. Do not press **return** until you have entered the complete command. Log out and log in for this change to take effect.

```
defaults -currentHost write -globalDomain AppleFontSmoothing -int
3
```

Changing the integer to 0 has the same effect as disabling LCD font smoothing in the General preference pane. Another valid entry is the integer 1. However, the difference between 1 and 2 is so subtle that it is almost impossible to discern.

Precisely Adjust the Volume

Sometimes it seems you never can get the volume adjusted to your liking. One segment more is too much. One less is too little. Wouldn't it be awesome if you could adjust the volume in smaller increments? macOS has a solution for you!

Hold down the ⇧⌥ (shift+option) keys to adjust the volume in quarter-segment increments, allowing you to precisely adjust the volume. This trick also works when adjusting the display brightness and the keyboard backlight.

Temporarily Quiet the Volume Adjustment

macOS makes an annoying popping sound each time you press the **F11** or **F12** key to decrease or increase the volume. If you're working in a quiet office environment, the incessant popping can disturb your concentration or the concentration of others. It is also annoying and loud when listening to music using earbuds.

To temporarily quiet the popping sound when adjusting the volume, hold down the ⇧ (shift) key while pressing **F11** or **F12**. Unfortunately, this trick doesn't work when adjusting the volume in quarter segment increments. To turn off this annoying, loud popping sound, check out the next tweak.

Permanently Quiet the Volume Adjustment

macOS allows you to permanently disable the annoying popping sound it makes when adjusting the volume. This is a blessing to anyone who routinely uses earbuds or headphones. Also, your office mates will appreciate not being disturbed by your Mac's popping sounds.

To permanently turn off the annoying popping sound, open the **Sound** preference pane in System Preferences. Next, click **Sound Effects**. Uncheck the checkbox next to **Play feedback when volume is changed**.

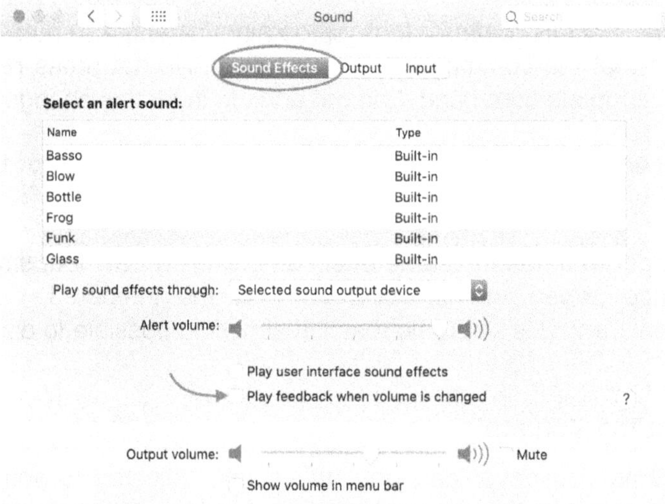

Disable User Interface Sounds

Your Mac plays various sound effects for actions like dragging and dropping an item to the trash. If you want to disable these sound effects, open the **Sounds** preference pane and uncheck the checkbox next to **Play user interface sound effects**.

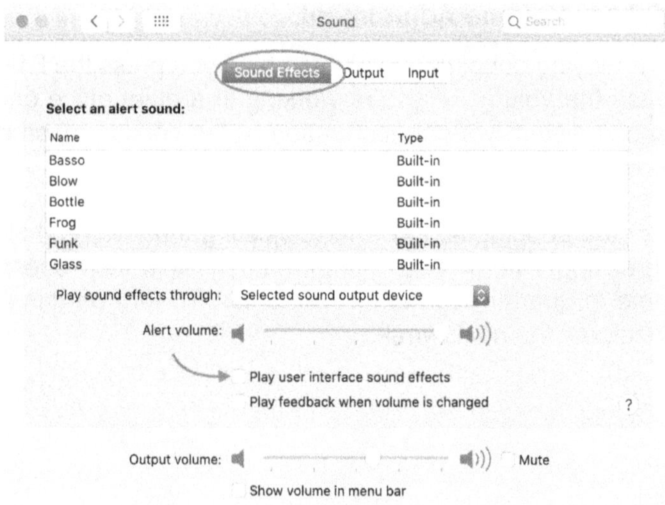

Make Help Center Behave

The macOS **Help Center** has a rather obnoxious habit. It refuses to act like other windows by stubbornly refusing to go to the background when it is not the active window. Help Center stays on top of all other windows, whether it is active or not. This tweak changes this rather obnoxious behavior and forces Help Center to act like all other macOS windows.

First, close the Help Center window if open. Enter the following command in Terminal. This change takes effect immediately.

```
defaults write com.apple.helpviewer DevMode -bool TRUE
```

The next time you open Help Center, you'll notice its more polite behavior. It no longer blocks other windows when it is not the active window.

To revert to the Help Center's default behavior, enter the following command in Terminal.

```
defaults delete com.apple.helpviewer DevMode
```

Save Changes Automatically When Closing Documents

macOS asks you if you want to save any unsaved changes when you close a document. You can turn off this behavior and have macOS automatically save unsaved changes to your documents when you close them.

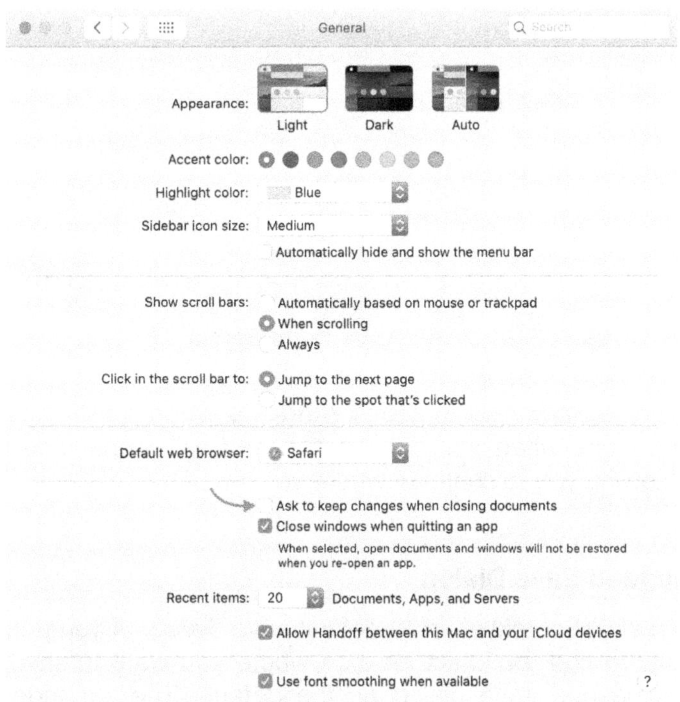

To enable automatic save of documents when closing them, open the **General** preference pane and uncheck the checkbox next to **Ask to keep changes when closing documents**.

Stop Closed Windows from Reopening

A handy feature of macOS is that it can reopen windows that were open the last time you quit an application. This a useful feature if you're working on a document and want it opened each time you launch the app. However, this feature can be annoying if you want to start fresh each time you launch an application but have to close the old windows first.

Open the **General** preference pane. Check the box next to **Close windows when quitting an application**. When this feature is enabled, open windows will close when you quit an app and will not automatically reopen the next time you launch the app.

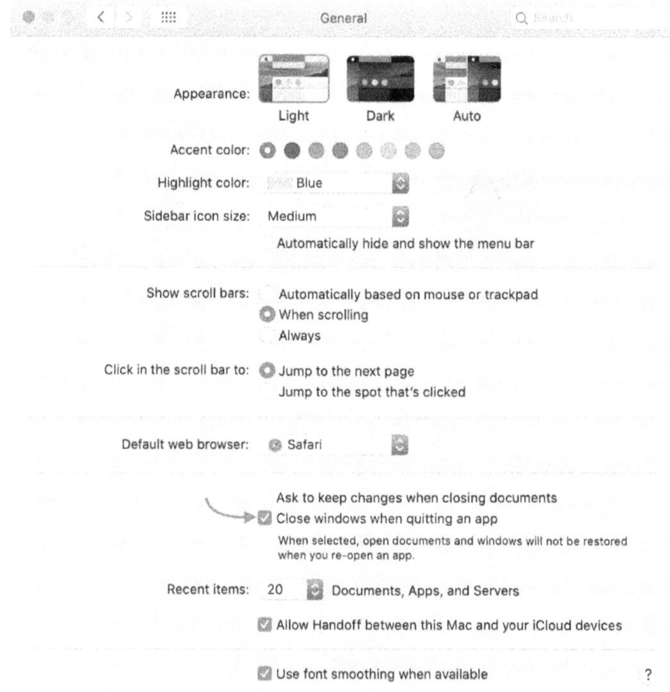

If you uncheck the checkbox next to **Close windows when quitting an application**, open windows will close when you quit an app and will reopen the next time you launch the app, allowing you to continue where you left off.

Enable the Expanded Save Dialog

macOS offers a small list of folders in its default save dialog. If you prefer to navigate the folder hierarchy to find the exact location where you want to save your file, you can enable the expanded save dialog as the default. The expanded save dialog displays the Finder Sidebar and allows you to navigate to your chosen destination folder. To switch between the minimalist and expanded views, click the little triangle at the end of the **Save As** field.

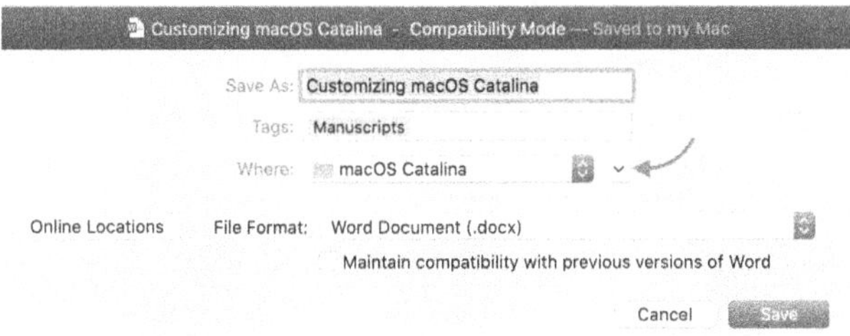

Multiple Libraries in Photos

Photos stores all of your photos in a single photo library. If you have a large volume of photos, management of them becomes increasingly difficult as the photo library grows in size over the years. Creating photo libraries offers an option for better management than utilizing a single, gigantic Photos library.

To create a new photo library, quit Photos if it is currently open. Hold down the ⌥ (option) key while launching Photos. A dialog box appears and asks you which photo library you want Photos to open.

Click the **Create New...** button and enter a name for the new photo library when prompted. If you want to save your new photo library in a location other than the **Pictures** folder, select a new location from the drop-down list next to **Where**. Click the **Save** button when finished, and Photos will open your new library. To create additional Photos libraries, simply lather, rinse, and repeat.

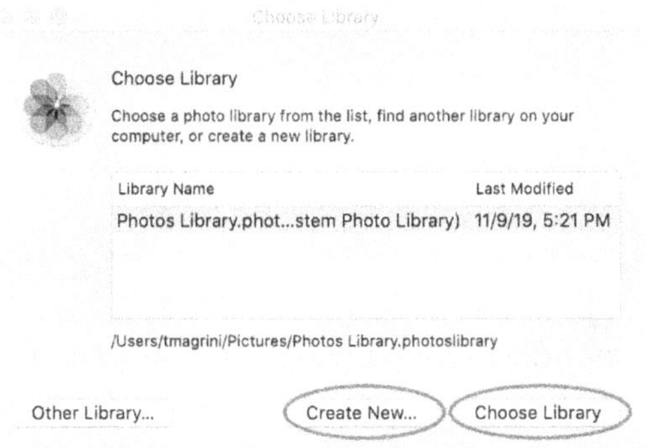

Note that once you have multiple photo libraries, Photos will consider the last one you opened as the default. That means the library you last used will open automatically when you launch Photos. If you want to open another photo library, you will need to hold down the ⌥ (option) key while launching Photos. A dialog box will appear asking you which photo library you want Photos to use. Select the appropriate library and click **Choose Library**.

Synchronize External Calendar Sources

The **Calendar** application can synchronize calendars between email services and Facebook. It only takes a couple of steps to configure Calendar to synchronize with an external source. Launch the Calendar application.

Select **Calendar > Add Account...** to reveal a configuration sheet. Click the radio button next to the desired source and enter your login credentials when prompted.

To change how often Calendar synchronizes with external sources, select **Calendar > Preferences...** or enter **⌘,** (command+,) to launch the Calendar preference pane. Select **Accounts** at the top of the pane.

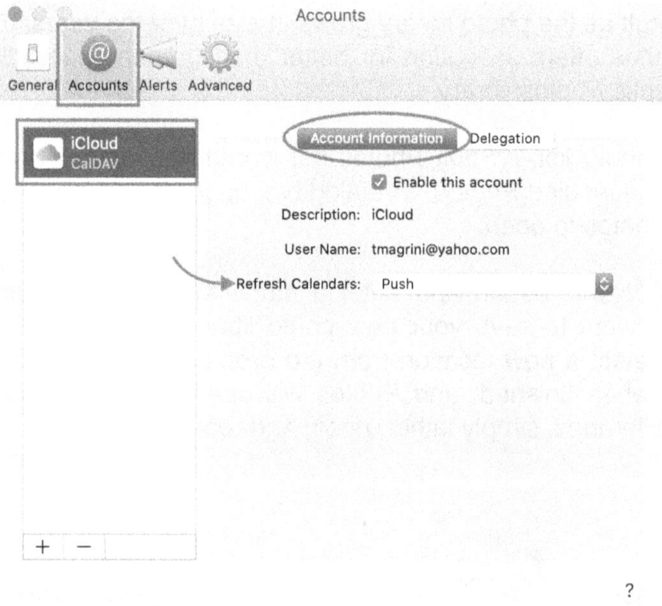

Select the account in the sidebar. You have the choice of synchronizing every 1, 5, 15, or 30 minutes, every hour, or manually. For iCloud, you have the additional choice of **Push**, which updates your calendar immediately after a change is made. Close the Calendar preference pane when finished.

Subscribe to a Calendar Feed

iCalendar, often referred to simply as iCal, is a standard Internet calendar format that allows you to share calendars. Apple's **Calendar** application utilizes the iCal format. By default, Calendar does not have holidays preloaded. You have to subscribe to an iCal feed to add holidays to your calendar. You can subscribe to Apple's U.S. Holidays calendar at webcal://files.apple.com/calendars/US32Holidays.ics.

Many calendars are available on the Internet for holidays in other countries. You can subscribe to sports schedules, religious holidays, and academic schedules, to name a few examples. All you need is a calendar download link. You can subscribe to almost any iCal calendar you stumble upon on the Internet.

There are two methods to add an iCal file to the Calendar, subscribing or importing. A website must allow you to access the iCal file directly to subscribe to a calendar. The URL will begin with **webcal://** for you to subscribe. Some websites have a **Subscribe** button to make subscribing quick and easy. After clicking subscribe, a dialog box appears with the URL of the calendar feed populated in the **Calendar URL** field. Click **Subscribe**.

If the website doesn't provide a subscribe button and only allows downloading of the .ics file, secondary click on the download link and select **Copy Link**. Next, launch the Calendar application if it is not already open. Choose **File > New Calendar Subscription** or enter **⌥⌘S** (option+command+S). Paste the URL to the calendar file you just copied into the dialog box and click **Subscribe**. Next, you'll be presented with a dialog box to configure options such as event color, alerts, attachments, and how often to automatically refresh the calendar. If you plan to synchronize this calendar with your iPhone, iPad, or other Macs, select **iCloud** as the location.

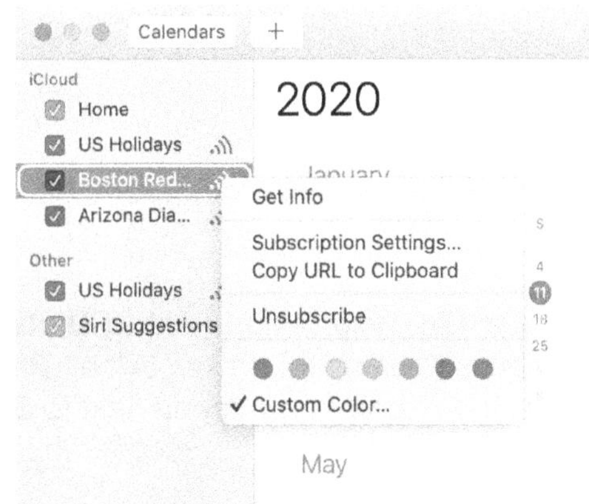

Another method is to import a calendar by downloading the .ics file. I do not recommend this method. Subscribing is the preferable option as calendars to which you are subscribed are automatically updated and easily removed.

To change subscription settings, color, or to remove a calendar to which you are subscribed, click the **Calendar** button at the top of the Calendar window to reveal the sidebar. All calendars to which you are subscribed are listed. A subscription is denoted by an icon that looks like a Wi-Fi icon. Secondary click on a calendar to access subscription settings, change the color, or **Delete** the subscription using this contextual menu.

Talk to Your Mac with Dictation

Dictation is one of my favorite macOS features. Dictation is extremely useful, allowing you to quickly turn your thoughts into large blocks of text, whether you're writing a term paper, a report, an email, posting to Facebook, or tweeting your followers.

Dictation is system-wide. You can dictate in any application anywhere text can be entered. This includes not only the usual suspects like Microsoft Office, Apple Pages, and Mail, but other time savers like the address bar in Safari, the search box in Google.com or at Amazon.com, or in a web form. macOS lets you dictate text anywhere you can type it.

To turn Dictation on, open the **Keyboard** preference pane in System Preferences. Click on the **Dictation** tab.

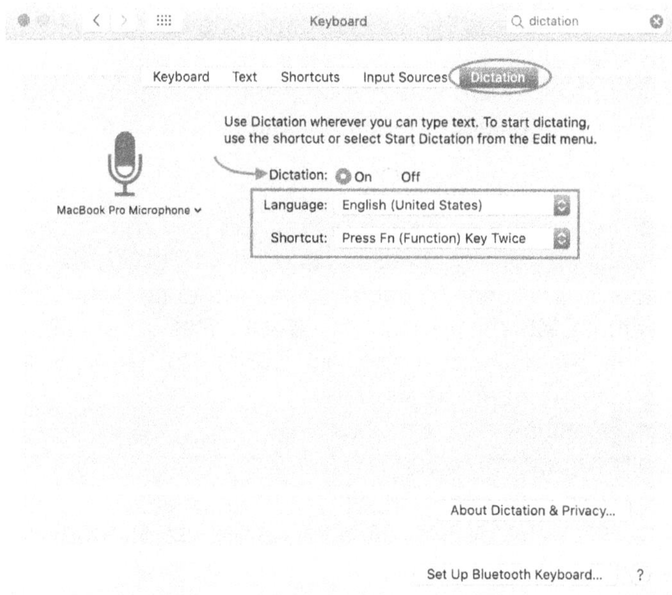

Click the **On** radio button next to **Dictation** to enable. The default shortcut to start dictation is to press the **fn** key twice. Press the **fn** key once to finish. You can change this using the drop-down menu next to **Shortcut**.

Hit the **fn** key twice to start dictating (unless you changed the keyboard shortcut in the Dictation & Speech preference pane). Your Mac will beep, and the Dictation icon will appear to let you know macOS is ready to listen.

It's cool to see your text appear as you speak. You can edit your text live without having to stop dictating. Move your pointer or highlight the text you want to correct and dictate your corrections or use the keyboard. Press the **fn** key again to finish dictating.

Tell Your Mac to Talk to You

macOS includes several voices for text to speech applications, such as reading an iBook. The default voice is a male voice named Alex. macOS allows you to change the voice, download new voices, and change the rate of speech in the **Accessibility** preference pane.

To change the voice macOS uses for text to speech, open the **Accessibility** preference pane. Select **Speech** in the sidebar at the left.

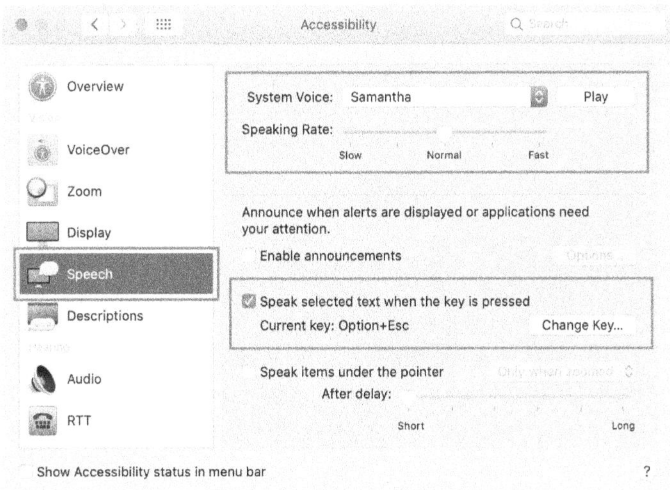

Use the drop-down menu next to **System Voice** to change the voice or select **Customize...** to download other voices. For iPhone and iPad users who like Siri's voice, choose **Customize...** from the drop-down menu and download Samantha's voice. Change the **Speaking Rate** using the slider. You can hear a sample by pressing the **Play** button.

The voice you selected is used when your Mac reads to you. If you check the box next to **Speak selected text when the key is pressed**, you will be able to highlight any text and have it read to you by pressing **⌥esc** (option+escape), which is the default. You can change this keyboard shortcut by clicking the **Change Key...** button.

Change Your Profile Picture

It's easy to change your profile picture, and you can use any picture for your profile. Apple provides a set of default pictures you can use. If you don't like the defaults, you can choose a picture from iCloud, Photos, a folder on your Mac, or you can take a picture using your Mac's camera.

Open the **Users & Groups** preference pane. Click the **Password** tab. Click on your user name in the left sidebar. You'll see your current profile picture in the right-hand pane. Hover your pointer over the existing picture until **edit** appears. Click **edit**. Select your desired profile picture from the selections in the left sidebar. Use the slider to size your picture. Click **Save** when done.

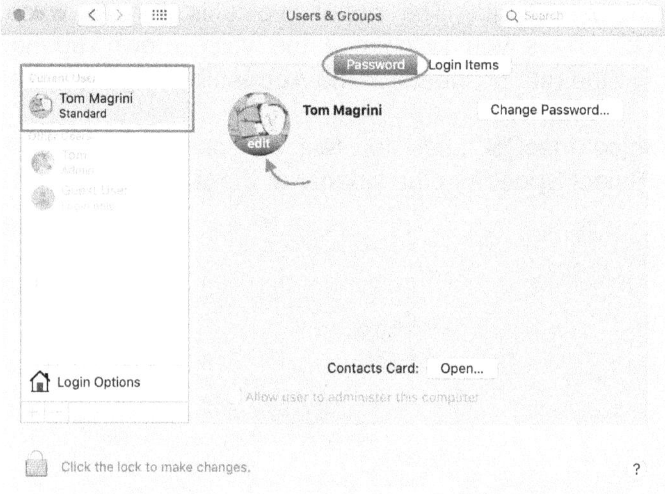

To use a picture located in a folder on your Mac, open Finder, locate your desired picture, and drag it onto your current profile picture in the **Users & Groups** preference pane. When you see a large green **+**, release your hold.

Enable Sticky Keys

If you have trouble holding down two or more modifier keys simultaneously, the **Sticky Keys** feature allows modifier keys to be set without having to press all of them concurrently. The following modifier keys can be enabled as sticky: **⇧ ^ ⌥ ⌘ fn** (shift, control, option, command, function). When the Sticky Keys feature is enabled, pressing a modifier key will stick it. The "stuck" key will be displayed in the upper-right of the screen to let you know it was pressed. To "unstick" the key, press it again.

To enable Sticky Keys, open the **Accessibility** preference pane in the System Preferences application. Select **Keyboard** in the sidebar and check the box next to **Enable Sticky Keys**.

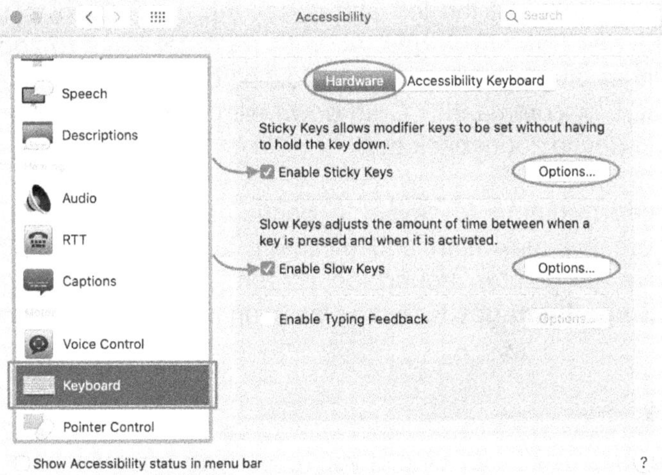

Click the **Options...** button to configure sound and display options. By default, macOS will beep and display the key in the top right of the screen when a modifier key is stuck. You can select where you want the sticky keys to display with choices of the upper-right (the default), upper left, bottom right, or bottom left of the display.

macOS allows you to configure the amount of time you have to hold down a sticky key, called the **Acceptance Delay**, before it is accepted. To enable this feature, click the checkbox next to **Enable Slow Keys** in the Accessibility preference pane. Click **Options** to reveal a slider that allows you to adjust the Acceptance Delay.

Zoom the Entire Display

macOS allows you to zoom the display using a keyboard shortcut or scroll gesture. To enable the display zoom feature, open the **Accessibility** preference pane in the System Preferences application.

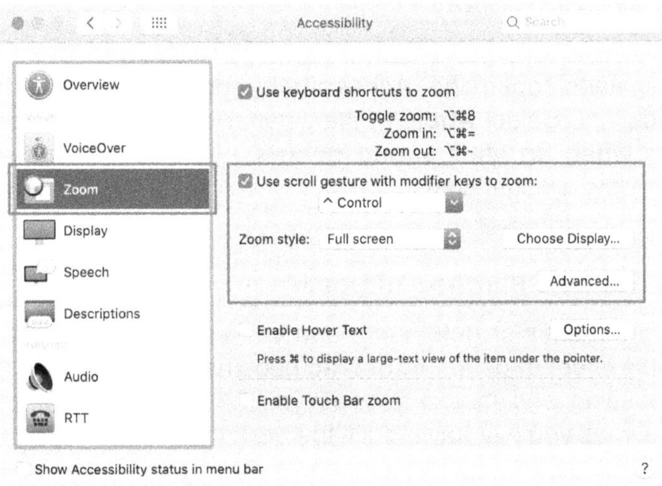

Select **Zoom** in the sidebar at the left and check the boxes next to **Use keyboard shortcuts to zoom** and **Use scroll gesture with modifier keys to zoom**. The scroll gesture is a two-finger drag up to zoom while holding down the chosen modifier key, ^ ⌥ ⌘ (control, option, or command). Drag down with two fingers while holding down the chosen modifier key to zoom back out.

Click the **Advanced...** button to reveal a configuration sheet, offering additional settings to configure the maximum and minimum zoom and to control the screen image as you move the pointer around the screen. Ensure you have checked the checkbox next to **Smooth images** to avoid pixelation as the images become larger.

Set Visual Alerts

Sometimes you have to quiet your Mac. If you're working in a quiet office environment, the cool alert sound you found may not be appreciated by your office mates. However, you still want to be alerted when a new message or email arrives. Instead of using an audible alert, macOS can flash the screen to alert you.

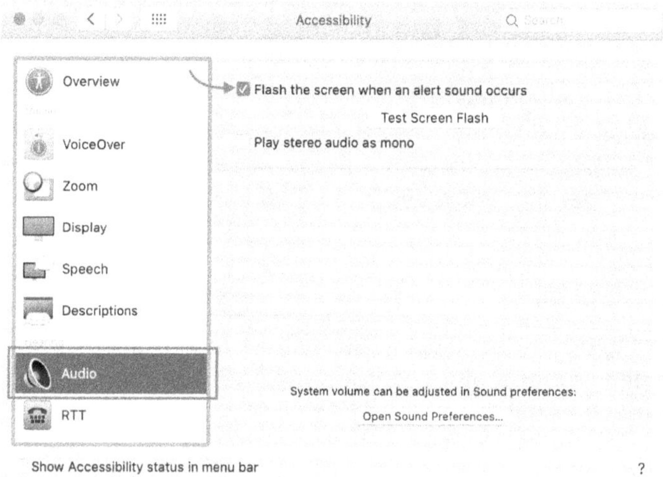

To turn on visual alerts, open the **Accessibility** preference pane in the System Preferences application. Select **Audio** in the sidebar and check the checkbox next to **Flash the screen when an alert sound occurs**. You can click the **Test Screen Flash** button to preview a visual alert.

Kill the Spinning Rainbow Pinwheel of Death

Occasionally Finder crashes or gets hung, and you are forced to experience Apple's spinning rainbow pinwheel of death. Your Mac becomes unresponsive as the rainbow pinwheel defiantly spins and mocks you as you twiddle your thumbs and hope it disappears. Sometimes you just have to kill the darn thing.

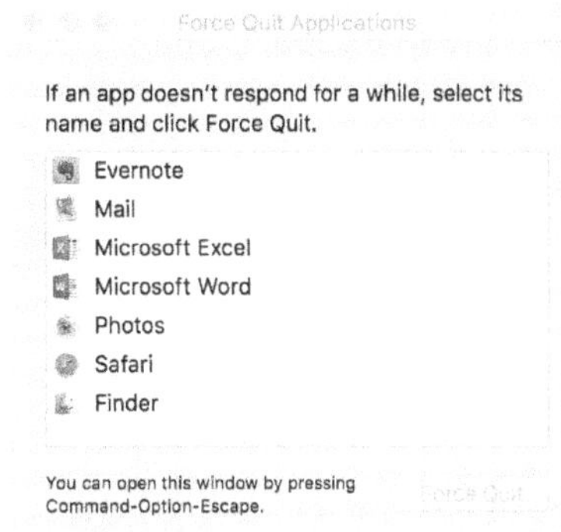

To kill the pinwheel, relaunch Finder by holding down the ⌥ (option) key and secondary clicking on the Finder icon in the Dock. Choose the option to **Relaunch** Finder. Sometimes Finder becomes so hosed that you have to switch to another Desktop Space for this command work.

An alternate method is to select ** > Force Quit...** and choose Finder from the list of applications. Click the **Relaunch** button to kill the spinning pinwheel. You can also display the Force Quit dialog by entering **⌥⌘esc** (option+command+escape).

Uninstall Unwanted Apps

In macOS, you can uninstall an application by dragging it from the **Applications** folder to the Trash. You also can uninstall apps in Launchpad by clicking and holding until the apps begin to shake, and an **X** appears in the upper-left corner of the app's icon. Clicking the **X** deletes the app. Compared the process to uninstall an application on a Windows PC, this almost sounds too good to be true. And it is. Applications distribute many files throughout your system. Often applications leave their detritus scattered across your hard drive or SSD after they are deleted using the above two methods.

AppCleaner is a small application that will thoroughly uninstall unwanted apps, hunting down their associated files, and safely deleting the detritus. To delete an app with AppCleaner, launch AppCleaner and then drag the unwanted app from the Applications folder and drop it into the AppCleaner window. AppCleaner finds all files associated with the unwanted app. Delete the app by clicking AppCleaner's **Delete** button.

AppCleaner is free to download from the following website:
http://www.freemacsoft.net/appcleaner/

Restore a Previous Version of a Document

Many applications automatically save versions of documents as you are working on them. This safety feature lets you restore a previous version of a document if needed. macOS allows you to browse through various document versions and restore an older version. Versions are typically saved every hour, and when you open, save, duplicate, rename, or revert to an earlier version of the document. If you are actively making changes to your document, macOS saves more frequently.

To restore a previous version of a document, open the document if it is not already open. Select **File > Revert To > Browse All Versions...** to see which versions are available. Browse through the available versions and click the **Restore** button to restore the previous version you selected. You also have the option to revert to the last saved version, which is timestamped by macOS, by selecting **File > Revert To > Previous Save**.

This feature may not be available in third-party applications, most notably the Microsoft Office 2016 productivity suite.

Enable the Hidden macOS Power Chime

When you connect your iPhone or iPad to their chargers, they emit a chime to let you know they are connected to power. By default, your Mac does not sound a power chime when you connect it to power. This hidden tweak configures macOS to sound a chime when you connect your Mac to AC power.

To enable the hidden power chime, first disconnect your Mac's power connector. Launch Terminal and enter the following commands.

```
defaults write com.apple.PowerChime ChimeOnAllHardware -bool TRUE

open /System/Library/CoreServices/PowerChime.app
```

Now reattach the power connector, and your Mac will emit an iPhone-like chime to indicate it is connected to power. Be sure the sound is not muted and is turned up so you can hear the chime.

To disable the hidden power chime, enter the following commands in Terminal.

```
defaults write com.apple.PowerChime ChimeOnAllHardware -bool FALSE

killall PowerChime
```

Restart or Shut Down Immediately without Confirmation

When restarting or shutting down, a dialog box appears confirming whether you want to restart or shutdown. The advantage of this dialog box is that it gives you 60 seconds to **Cancel** in case you change your mind. Clicking the **Restart** or **Shutdown** button causes your Mac to restart or shut down before the 60-second timer expires.

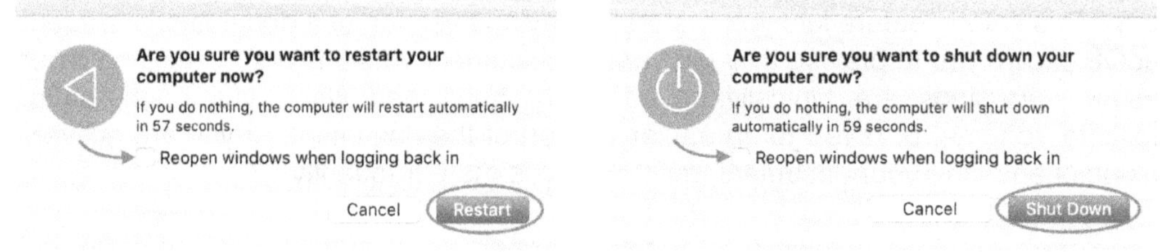

If you want to reopen the windows you currently have open, check the checkbox next to **Reopen windows when logging back in**. Otherwise, click the **Restart** or **Shut Down** button.

If you want to skip this dialog box and restart or shutdown immediately, hold down the ⌥ (option) key while selecting **> Restart** or **> Shut Down**. Your Mac will skip the dialog box and restart or shut down immediately.

About the Author

Tom Magrini has written eleven books about computers and technology. He has authored eight editions of the best-selling *Customizing macOS* series. This series helps Mac users completely customize their macOS user experience with hundreds of tweaks, hacks, secret commands, and hidden features. Tom is also the author of three editions of *Cut the Cord: How to Watch TV without Paying a Cable or Satellite TV Bill.* *Cut the Cord* shows readers how to save money by ditching expensive cable and satellite TV for streaming video over the Internet.

During the day, Tom is an information technology professional with over 35 years of experience as a network engineer, network architect, IT manager, and IT director. He has worked with Macs since 1984 and still fondly remembers his first Apple Macintosh computer with its 8 MHz Motorola 68000 processor, 9-inch 512 x 342-pixel black-and-white screen, 128 kB of RAM, and built-in 400 kB 3½-inch floppy drive. Tom has worked with NeXT computers and the NeXTStep operating system, the forerunner to Apple's macOS. And yes, he has even crossed over to the dark side and has worked extensively with Windows PCs.

During the week, Tom is a busy IT director, leading a team of IT professionals who maintain two data centers and the data network, telephony, Wi-Fi, Office 365 messaging, server, storage, operating systems, fiber optic cable infrastructure, and a public safety radio system for a large municipality. Tom has also taught programming, operating systems, Cisco Networking Academy, and wireless technology courses as a Computer Information Systems professor at two colleges. He has worked for numerous technology companies, including SynOptics Communications, Bay Networks, FORE Systems, 3Com, and Cisco Systems. Tom is also a certified ITIL® Expert, holds a GIAC Security Leadership Certification (GSLC), and has achieved eleven Cisco networking certifications.

When Tom isn't working on his MacBook Pro or hanging out with his family and dogs, he enjoys reading, writing, movies, and the beautiful Arizona weather with its 300+ days of sunshine.

Books by Tom Magrini

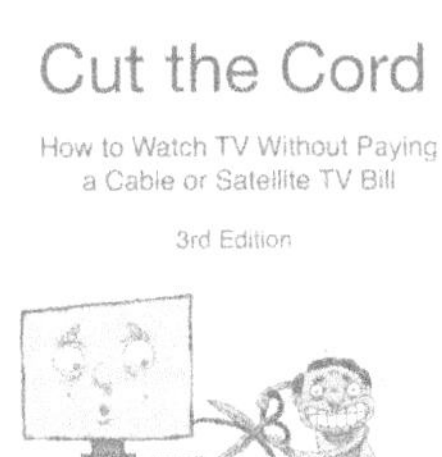

Cut the Cord
How to Watch TV Without Paying a Cable or Satellite TV Bill
3rd Edition

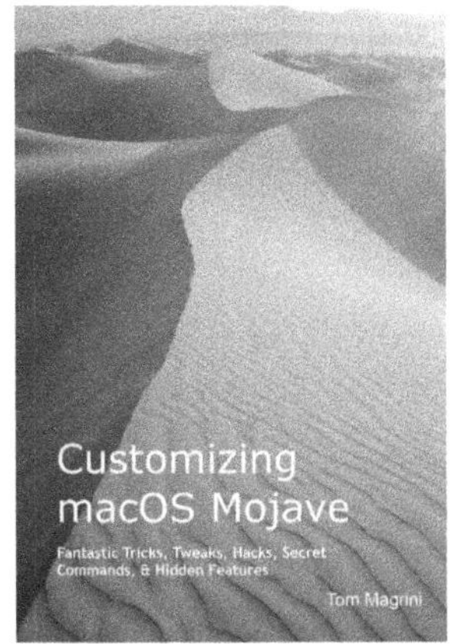

Cut the Cord
How to Cut Your Cable or Satellite TV Cord & Save Big Bucks
2nd Edition
Tom Magrini
Updated for 2018

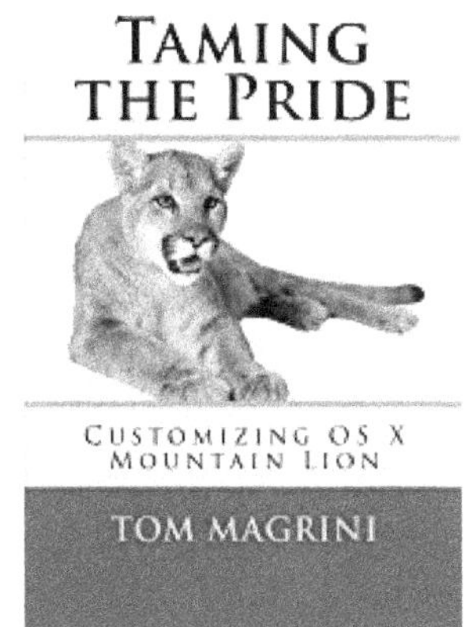

www.ingramcontent.com/pod-product-compliance
Lightning Source LLC
Chambersburg PA
CBHW081505050326
40690CB00015B/2928

* 9 7 8 1 6 9 1 8 4 7 5 4 9 *